MW00851082

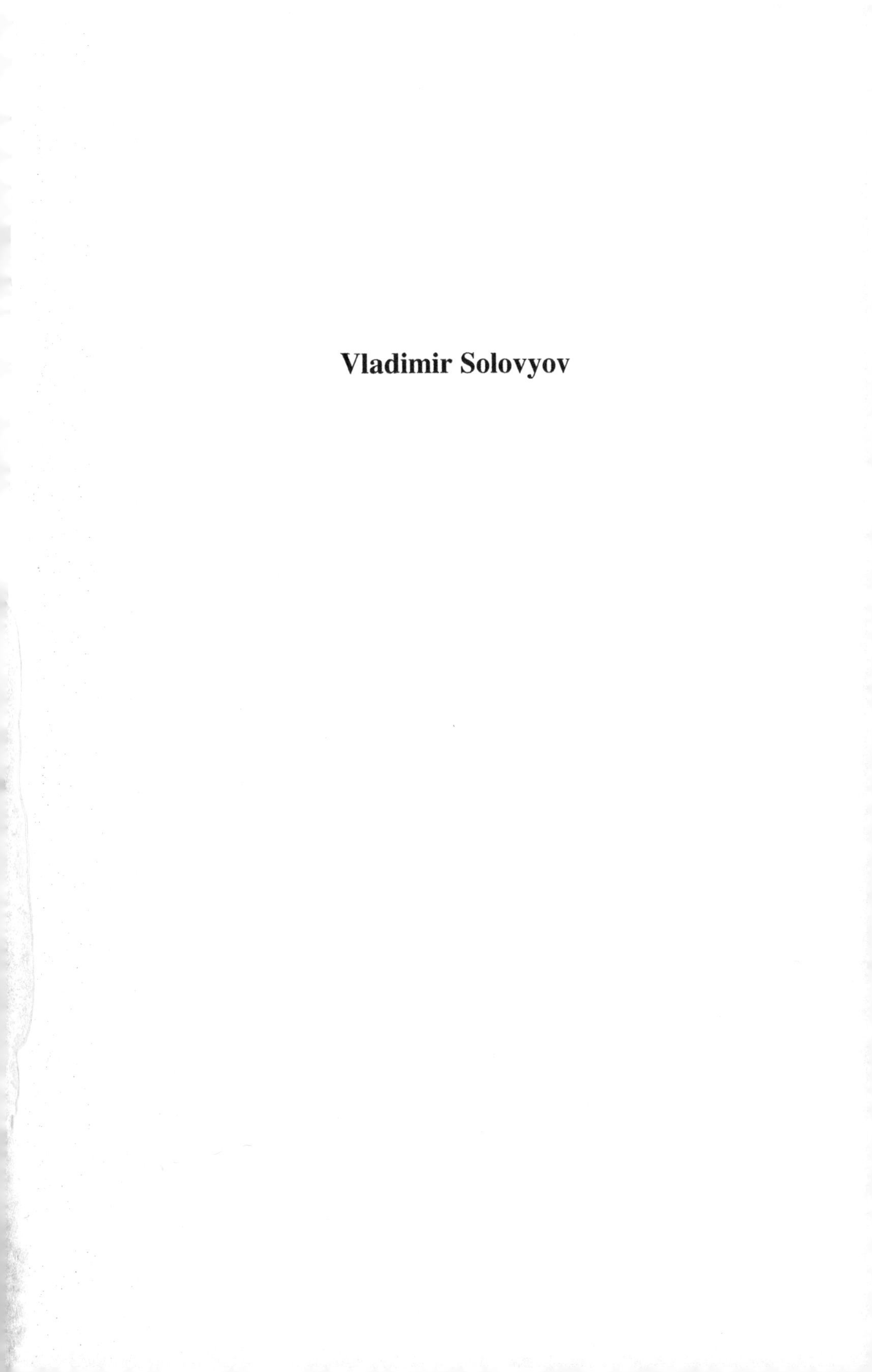

Vladimir Solovyov

SERGEY M. SOLOVYOV

Vladimir Solovyov

His Life & Creative Evolution

Translated by Aleksey Gibson
Preface by Jonathan Sutton

Angelico Press

Sergey M. Solovyov

This Angelico Press edition, excepting the Translator's Note and Preface by Jonathan Sutton, is a reprint of the edition published by Eastern Christian Publications in 2000.

For information, address:
Angelico Press, Ltd.
169 Monitor St.
Brooklyn, NY 11222
www.angelicopress.com

ppr 979-8-89280-020-4
cloth 979-8-89280-021-1

Cover design
by Michael Schrauzer

Table of Contents

Part Two: Rome

Part Three: Twilight

Translator's Note

Having worked on this translation and its publication for many years, I am pleased that Angelico Press is adding this edition to its collection of Russian Philosophy, and hope it will reach a new and wider audience of people interested in the life and work of Vladimir Solovyov.

Well before Irène Posnoff—the indomitable founder and editor of the press La vie avec Dieu—handed me a copy of the first Russian edition of *Vladimir Solovyov: His Life & Creative Evolution* (Brussels, 1977) with the suggestion that I translate it, I had been familiar with Solovyov's legendary stature among Russian religious thinkers and his legacy in various translations. In my parents' library I had delved into *Russia and the Universal Church* (1948), S. L. Frank's *A Solovyov Anthology* (1950), *Les fondements spirituels de la vie* (1948) as well as two fine editions from Vienna, *Die Erzhälung vom Antichrist* (1947) and *Die Sinn der Liebe* (1948). In many ways, this piecemeal introduction to Solovyov inspired me to pursue my studies in Russian and, by the time I completed my first degree at the School of Slavonic & East European Studies in London, I felt more or less competent to accept the invitation to translate Sergey Solovyov's biography of his uncle Vladimir. Youthful enthusiasm soon ran into the complexities of Solovyov's thought, and I realized that my lack of the training in Classical, Patristic, and German philosophy would make this a long-term project. Fortunately, I found in Jonathan Sutton's *The Religious Philosophy of Vladimir Solovyov: Towards a Reassessment* (1988) the key to translating many of the concepts that eluded me in English as well appropriate renderings for the titles of Solovyov's main works. For his help I am still extremely grateful.

The final impetus to publish the first edition in 2000 came from my meeting with Igor Vishnevetsky, a specialist in the life and work of Sergey Solovyov. Professor Vishnevetsky had befriended Sergey Solovyov's daughter Natalia in Moscow, and he kindly shared with me the corrections she had made to the Brussels edition. He then agreed to write the introductory essay about Sergey Solovyov that covers the decade in Sergey's life (1913–1923) when he worked in increasingly harrowing conditions to complete his *magnum opus*. This essay is complemented by Father Michael Meerson's remarkable account of the fate of the original manuscript in Russia and his role in bringing it to light.

I dedicate this Angelico Press edition to the memory of Elisabeth Stenbock-Fermor (1900–2001); a great teacher, scholar, and friend who ever admonished me "Do not neglect the Solovyov!"

Aleksey Gibson
September 2023
Washington, DC

Preface to the Angelico Press edition (2024)

I welcome, very warmly, the new availability of Aleksey Gibson's English translation of Sergei Solovyov's biography of his uncle, the philosopher Vladimir Solovyov. Sergei Solovyov's account of the life and ideas of this key figure in nineteenth-century Russian culture still holds its rightful place among the most accomplished and revealing works about him, alongside the accounts offered, in the 1930's, by Konstantin Mochulsky and Dmitry Strémooukhoff.

It is no accident that Sergei Solovyov included the words "creative evolution" in the very title of his study. They bring to mind, very tellingly, the sheer vitality of Vladimir Solovyov's life's work, the burst of new and fresh thinking onto the intellectual landscape as he found it at the beginning of his twenties. It has become a commonplace to refer to Vladimir Solovyov as "the father of Russian philosophy." But this hardly conveys the very scale of his impact. In November 1874, he defended his Master's thesis, *The Crisis of Western Philosophy: Against the Positivists*—which defence itself came close to being a *succès de scandale*—an emergence on his scene like that of Solovyov's compatriot Igor Stravinsky and the "sound world" which he created in the twentieth century.

It is undoubtedly the case that today's reader of Sergei Solovyov's book will approach it against a very different backdrop from that which existed in 1977, when the original Russian-language version was published in the West, in Brussels, by *Foyer Oriental Chrétien*. We owe an enormous debt of gratitude to Fr Michael Meerson for successfully getting the full Russian text out of the Soviet Union in the first place, and making known the manuscript's then already five-decade survival in an archival holding in Moscow.

Since the 1970's Vladimir Solovyov and his ideas have attracted increasing—and various kinds of—attention in academic and also Church circles. His works caught the eye of twentieth-century ecumenists who saw him as an "ecumenist *avant la lettre*," and now, topically, Solovyov also figures as a very early ecologist. As the Swiss scholar Manon de Courten showed in compelling detail in her study of 2004, the philosopher proved to be a committed activist in drawing attention to—and ever returning to—the concerning theme of the far-advanced damage (specifically desertification) done in late nineteenth-century Russia by unenlightened agricultural practices. This active concern on Solovyov's part coincided in time with John Ruskin's generally better-known expressions of alarm and urgency regarding pollution. The ecological "axis" in Solovyov's thought—made explicit by him in the first half of the 1880's and framed in the explicitly Biblical terms of our stewardship of, and responsibility for, the Earth and its natural resources—while at least touched upon in my own work, was brought out very fully in the late Oliver Smith's book of 2010, *Vladimir Soloviev and the Spiritualization of Matter.*

The great scope for applying Solovyov's ideas creatively to twentieth- and twenty-first-century concerns became further evident when the distinguished Dutch philosopher Evert van der Zweerde, based at Radboud University in Nijmegen, conceived and headed a Dutch-funded research project, between 1998 and 2002, under the heading "Vladimir Solovyov and the Values of Civil Society." That project opened with a large international conference on Solovyov in September 1998 and included, in late 1999, a two-day workshop, for invited Solovyov specialists, on *Justification of the Good*, Solovyov's major work on moral philosophy. Overall, the project yielded three successfully researched and completed doctoral theses, those of T. Kochetkova, M. de Courten, and P. Schrooyen, and one Master's thesis, that of V. Smerdov. These young scholars came from Ukraine, Switzerland, the Netherlands, and Russia respectively.

The interdisciplinary nature of the project was firmly reflected in the central participation of Nijmegen-based Professor Machiel Karskens, specialising in political thought, and of Dr Frances Nethercott (School of History, St Andrews University), a leading—maybe *the* leading—British specialist on Russian intellectual history, especially that of the nineteenth century.

The 1998 conference in Nijmegen and the subsequent publication of a large collection of papers delivered there form a notable milestone in the growing field of Solovyov studies. A no less notable milestone was the well-attended international conference convened in Kraków in June 2019 by Sister Teresa Obolevitch, a professor at the John Paul II University there. Professor Obolevitch has made a remarkable contribution to research and teaching on philosophy in Russia over two decades.

All the above-mentioned scholarly activity testifies strongly to the continuing vitality of Vladimir Solovyov's ideas and to their capacity *still* to attract and engage our minds, even to generate controversy within new parameters and twenty-first-century contexts. In 1996, in Oxford, I gave a paper (further worked on for the Nijmegen conference of 1998) in which I suggested that Vladimir Solovyov had the rare quality of being both a reconciler *and* a polemicist. This dual aspect of his response to other minds and situations perhaps accounts for the richness of present-day reflection on his philosophy.

In order to place Sergei Solovyov's biography of the philosopher in its right context and make that context sufficiently appreciated, I need to mention just two more aspects of the recent and present-day terrain in which new readers pick up a copy of, and embark on reading, Aleksey Gibson's translation of Sergei Solovyov's book. One of these is the proliferation of books on philosophy and theology issued by just two publishers in those fields: the Kyiv-based *Dukh i litera (Дух і літера)*, affiliated with the Kyiv-Mohyla Academy and headed by the indefatigable Dr Konstantin Sigov, and the publishing wing of Moscow's Biblical-Theological Institute, headed by Dr Alexei Bodrov. With all the unpredictability, recurring paper shortages, and other vicissitudes of publishing during the earliest years of the post-Soviet era, these two publishing houses have, between them, succeeded in bringing out more than four hundred titles.

The other key factor is the growth, since the 1960's, of the comparative study of religions and, in particular, the enormous growth of scholarly concern with, and research into, mysticism as such, its nature, and its different manifestations within particular Christian denominations, in non-Christian faiths, and among a plethora of non-aligned "seekers" and secularly raised "pilgrims," both young and not so young.

In considering Vladimir Solovyov, it is immensely beneficial and rewarding to move *beyond* broad generalities. An excellent example of a sound approach can be seen in the following short—and historically detailed—reflection offered by the late Fr Boris Bobrinskoy, who was Dean of the Orthodox *Institut St Serge* in Paris between 1993 and 2005. Speaking at one of the autumn conferences on Orthodox spirituality at the Monastery of Bose near Turin at the end of the 1990's, Fr Boris affirmed the following:

> Orthodox Christian theology *came of age* in the twentieth century. It was a whole succession of lay philosophers and theologians in the nineteenth century—figures such as Ivan Kireyevsky, Alexei Khomyakov and Vladimir Solovyov—who paved the way for that "coming of age." It was they who *created a language* in which people within the Church *could* reflect in new ways and also talk coherently about problems affecting the contemporary world. And, what did *that*, in turn, do? That equipped and strengthened the Church on the very eve of the incoming Age of Martyrdom which it was to experience under Soviet rule.

The creation, by Solovyov among others, of a new language for coherent reflection is presented as a providential preparation for the historically specific age of martyrdom that was to come to believers with the imposition of Bolshevik rule.

Wholly in keeping with the spirit and scope of Vladimir Solovyov's broad-ranging, even encyclopedic, thought, I need, in these few pages, not only to focus on the enduring topicality of some of the problems which preoccupied him in his day, but also to direct the reader's attention, at least briefly, to the philosopher's gaze on the past and future.

Plato held a singularly important place in Solovyov's thought and was the subject of an important essay that contains some autobiographical traces, *The Drama of Plato's Life,* published in 1898, just two years before the philosopher's death at the age of forty-seven. A very illuminating observation was made by Professor Janko Lavrin in his preface to Richard Gill's English translation of *The Drama of Plato's Life*, which came out in 1935: "In trying to explain the character and even the sequence of Plato's works by means of the inner drama of Plato's disappointment, he [Solovyov] incidentally clarified and overcame his own pessimistic leanings."

In the opening decade of the twenty-first century, two scholars came forward with analyses of Solovyov's very personal as well as scholarly "engagement" with Plato, one in English and one in Russian: Frances Nethercott in 2000 and Anatoliy Tikholaz in 2003.

The forward-looking dimension of Solovyov's thinking found sustained expression in the philosopher's reflections on the nature of prophecy and the role of the prophet. This was most prominent in his large but uncompleted work of 1885–1887, *The History and Future of Theocracy.* However, public perceptions of Solovyov himself as some kind of prophet in the landscape of late imperial Russia caused him considerable discomfort, and even anguish. Some, in the public arena, alleged that he was a self-proclaimed prophet, one who more or less arrogantly assumed the right and the moral authority to speak out independently on controversial issues in society at large from *outside* the established frameworks of State and Church.

Wearing the mantle of public "prophet" could prove a quite onerous—or, at the very least, ambivalent—experience, as Solovyov's more famous elder contemporaries Dostoevsky and Tolstoy could each attest on the basis of their own experience. Likewise with Solovyov, but from a much earlier age. The series of lectures by which he is probably best known among today's readers, *Lectures on Godmanhood (Чтения о богочеловечестве)*, attracted crowds which filled the lecture hall to overflowing, and pretty well all the existing eyewitness accounts highlight the young lecturer's own charisma and his sense of self-assurance as he spoke.

For all the advantages to be had from a position where he could speak relatively freely, because he operated *outside* institutional structures, Vladimir Solovyov found it irksome to be referred to as a "prophet." Two lines in his poem "A Modest Prophecy" make this very clear:

> I have been elevated among the prophets by enemies:
> They have given me this title in mockery.

Aspects of prophecy and the prophet's role were taken up by Marina Kostalevsky in her book of 1997 comparing Vladimir Solovyov with Fyodor Dostoevsky. They were also considered by Pamela Davidson (a professor at the School of Slavonic and East European Studies, University College London) in a paper which she gave in St Petersburg in May 1999 at a conference on Solovyov's own engagement with Jewish culture, convened by that city's Free Jewish University, a paper that was published as a journal article in October of the following year. Prophecy has run as a thread through Professor Davidson's subsequent work.

Oliver Smith was working on his major study of Solovyov's thought (published in 2010), and, as his work on the philosopher progressed, he became increasingly absorbed in the whole phenomenon of, and in Biblical reflection upon, prophecy. It happened that he had secured a major grant to research the subject full-time in Germany, starting in the academic year 2013–2014. A fatal climbing accident on 6 April 2013 cruelly ruled out his pursuit of that research.

Ernest Radlov, editor of the nine-volume and then co-editor [with Sergei Solovyov] of the ten-volume editions of Solovyov's *Collected Works,* held that Vladimir Sergeyevich was a moral philosopher above all else. That is a very sound interpretation of his life's work. I believe that the most fitting way for me to end my Preface would be to cite one of Iris Murdoch's lectures on moral philosophy. It appears as the second of three lectures published in her book *The Sovereignty of Good* (1970). I value it for her emphasis on the immensely close connection between experience, vision, and action. Of all things, that three-way connection distinguished the life and work of the religious philosopher Vladimir Sergeyevich Solovyov. Iris Murdoch affirms this: "Freedom is not, strictly, the exercise of the will, but, rather, the experience of accurate vision which, when this becomes appropriate, occasions action."

Dr Jonathan Sutton
(Leeds, England)

Sergey Solovyov as a Historian of Philosophy and Culture

Sergey Mikhailovich Solovyov (1885-1942) was a typical product and – to a certain extent – a victim of his own family.

He achieved significant results as a Symbolist poet and published five collections of respectable verse (together with a long narrative poem about his travels to Italy) before turning thirty-one. Although inferior in artistic strength to his relative Aleksandr Blok and to his close friend Andrey Bely, Sergey Solovyov was able to articulate a distinctive poetic voice of his own. He belonged to the same company of eccentric and somehow tragic figures of the Russian "Silver Age" such as the suicidal poet Count Vassily Komarovsky and the visionary composer Aleksey Stanchinsky. Like Komarovsky and Stanchinsky, Solovyov was not immune to the luring voice of non-existence, which eventually destroyed these two brilliant men. Solovyov's early well-controlled unromantic poems and his overtly dogmatic defense of a "realistic" Symbolism bear a convincing testimony to the inner conflict with which he lived. In 1921, upon receiving the news of Blok's death, he wrote to his friend Bely: "[W]e attempted to struggle with an outside beast without understanding [...] that all those threatening 'beasts' from the outside were only the projections of our inner passions."[1] These daemonic "projections" closely watched Solovyov throughout his Symbolist years; in 1911, the young poet attempted to take his own life by throwing himself out of a window. The attempted suicide was caused by his tormenting love affair with an aspiring actress (later known for her portrayal of Lenin's mother); by his increasing spiritual turmoil; and–above all–by

---

[1]RGALI (Moscow, Russia), 53-1-274. 1.

the acute aestheticism of his youthful worldview. Fortunately, Sergey Solovyov survived, but this incident cast a long shadow over his life.

The young Sergey was perceived by his family and friends as a philosopher and a future heir to his uncle Vladimir. Indeed, he studied at the Philosophy Department of Moscow University, before eventually turning to the Classical languages.

Sergey Solovyov's greatest accomplishment, however, was in the field of academic research. He confessed in his unpublished *Memoirs* that reading a novel usually resulted in a headache, but two hours of philological study made him relaxed and happy. Still in his teens, Sergey Solovyov diligently corrected proofs of the multi-volume *History of Russia* by his grandfather Sergey Mikhailovich Solovyov and helped his father, Mikhail Solovyov, edit the posthumous collected works of his uncle Vladimir. The pinnacle of those studies is the present monograph on Vladimir Solovyov, commissioned in the early 1920s by the publishing house *Kolos* as a commemoration of the twenty-fifth anniversary of the philosopher's death.

Sergey Solovyov, the future biographer of his famous uncle, was born into the family of Vladimir Solovyov's younger brother Mikhail (1862-1903) and the painter Olga Kovalenskaya (1855-1903). Since his very first years, he had been exposed to the exhilarating atmosphere that reigned among the members of the Solovyov clan. Vladimir Solovyov (1853-1900) was a frequent guest at his brother's apartment in Denezhny Lane (in Moscow). In his *Memoirs,* Sergey Solovyov recollected those visits as the happiest and most mischievous events of his childhood. An unbeatable conversationalist and a prankster, his uncle Vladimir presented the most congenial and charming combination of the mundane and the lofty, a truly Solovyovian way of transforming the ordinary into the exceptional.

> [U]ncle Volodya was of course better than anybody else. Sometimes he dined with us, and we had red wine and fish with capers and olives. Against my father's will, Uncle Volodya poured with generosity

> the forbidden beverage of Bacchus into my glass. When Uncle Volodya dined with us, all rules were forgotten, everything was allowed, and everybody was happy. I asked Uncle Volodya about everything that I was interested in, or could not understand. And he provided me with clear and concise answers. For example, I asked him: "What is the family crest?"
> "Well, answered Uncle Volodya, when the Russians were illiterate, they drew a thing instead of writing their family names. For example the Lopatins used to draw a shovel [*lopata*] on their house."

A curious document of the Soviet era, the medical files of the Kashchenko Hospital, where Sergey Solovyov was treated after a psychic breakdown following his arrest, testify that at the age of thirteen (!) he used to have "serious argument[s]" with his uncle over the "Gnostic origin of Sophia the Wise [sic!]."[2] This record is proven to be accurate: after the death of Sergey Solovyov's elder daughter, Natalia Sergeevna, I was entrusted – according to her wishes – with sorting her family papers. One of my findings was a notebook that contained a definition of Divine Sophia, in Vladimir Solovyov's own hand, dated 1898 (clearly, a response to the inquisitive thirteen-year-old Sergey) and later incorporated into the preface to his collected *Poems* (1900):

> The more perfect and closer to us the revelation of true Beauty (which clothes the Deity and leads us with all His strength away from suffering and death), the finer the line that separates this Beauty from her simulacrum: that false and powerless beauty, which only perpetuates the domain of mortal sufferings [and death]. The Woman clothed in the Sun is already in labor: she must reveal the Truth, bear the Word; but

[2]"Delo o bol'nom Solov'eve Sergee Mikhailoviche." #3557. *Moskovskaia bol'nitsa im. Kashchenko* (June 9, 1936 - July 18, 1941). #42713. *Kazanskaia psikhiatricheskaia bol'nitsa*. (August 3/2, 1941 - March 2, 1942): 25, reverse side.

> the ancient serpent gathers all his last forces against her; he wants to drown her in poisonous streams of pleasant-looking lies and verisimilar deceptions. All this has been foretold, the end is foretold too: when all her false likenesses evaporate as the sea foam which gave birth to Aphrodite Pandemos, Eternal Beauty will bear fruit, and from her will come forth the salvation of the world.[3]

By the age of fifteen Sergey's liberal and vaguely religious worldview was already in place, and he discussed it extensively in correspondence with his schoolmate Boris Bugaev (who had not yet taken the pen name of Andrey Bely). Such subjects as modernism, Christianity, and projects for Russia's future were at the center of their intellectual arguments, in which Bely appeared to be a "Slavophile" and conservative,[4] while Sergey Solovyov defended the "Westernist cause."

Solovyov was still in high school when he lost his parents. Soon after the death of Uncle Vladimir his father Mikhail became incurably ill. Everybody knew that the end was nearing, and upon hearing the news of his father's death, Sergey's mother shot herself. A striking record of this extraordinary event–tainted with high mystical pathos–is preserved in Bely's letter of 19 March 1903 to his confidant Emil Medtner: "Those days were joyous. The sky was close. I was happy over the grave of [the] Solovyov[s]. St. Seraphim passed somewhere not far from me."[5] Bryusov had noted in his diary that Seryozha Solovyov was unusually "solemn" at the funeral of his parents. One may trace Solovyov's strangely unchurched attitude towards suicide back to the events of March 1903.

---

[3] Cf. Vladimir Solov'ev, preface to the third edition of *Stikhotvoreniia Vladimira Solov'eva* (Moscow, 1922 [7th edition]), xiii.

[4] A position which Bely followed–in a curious way–with his support of the Revolution of 1917-1918. He perceived the Revolution as a revelation of Russia's "inner self."

[5] Manuscript Collection of Russian Public Library. 167-1-11.

Чем совершеннее и ближе откровение настоящей красоты, одевающей божество и Его силою ведущей нас к избавлению от страдания и смерти, тем тоньше черта, отделяющая ее от лживого подобия — от той обманчивой и бессильной красоты, которая только увековечивает царство страданий и смерти. Жена, облеченная в солнце, уже мучается родами: она должна явить истину, родить слово, и вот древний змий собирает против нее свои последние силы и хочет потопить ее в ядовитых потоках благовидной лжи, правдоподобных обманов. Все это предсказано, и предсказан конец: в конце Вечная красота будет плодотворна, и из нее выйдет спасение мира, когда обманчивые подобия ее исчезнут, как та морская пена, что родила простонародную Афродиту. В. Соловьев.

Part of Vladimir Solovyov's definition of Divine Wisdom in his own hand, 1898 (see pages xxi–xxii).

After his attempted suicide in 1911, Sergey Solovyov spent considerable time in several medical institutions. Upon his release in 1912, he graduated successfully from Moscow University, and married Tatyana Turgeneva, the younger sister of Bely's companion Asya Turgeneva. The newly wed couple went to Italy for their honeymoon; also, this was a time when Solovyov faced the Christian faith, and Catholicism in particular, as an alternative to the spiritual turmoil in which he had already been living for a few years.

He started working on Vladimir Solovyov's literary biography immediately after his return from Italy. The first draft was completed in June 1913. It contained a study of Vladimir Solovyov's poetry with regard to the idea of the Universal Church, which Sergey Solovyov defined as a pre-verbal experience of Divine Wisdom and transfigured Nature. He presented this draft, "The Idea of the Church in the Poetry of Vladimir Solovyov," at meetings of the Moscow and St. Petersburg Religious Philosophical Societies. The full text appeared in the 1916 collection of Solovyov's *Theological and Critical Sketches*. [6] Only the initial eight chapters of the essay are of an independent value; Solovyov reworked the remaining part into a lengthier and a much more balanced study.

As compared to the final, monograph version, "The Idea of the Church in the Poetry of Vladimir Solovyov" seems to be quite timid in terms of the personal recollections and biographical details that make the later book so engaging. But Sergey Solovyov's distinctive point of view is already in place: "If we wish to find the element that unifies all [Vladimir] Solovyov's activities, we seek for it in vain in his philosophy, or poetry. For many years he abandoned both philosophy and poetry. [...] Philosophy for him was the cognition of supreme wisdom, *Sophia* [...] The same feminine hypostasis of Divinity reveals herself in human history as the Church. Also, she was the poet's Muse, his 'eternal companion'."[7] Although one could find this characteristic a bit simplistic, a more friendly reading might admit that Sergey Solovyov makes a bold move and places a key notion of

---

[6]Solov'ev, Sergei. *Bogoslovskie i kriticheskie ocherki* (Moscow: I. I. Kushnerev & Co., 1916), 143-172.
[7]Ibid., 146.

his uncle's philosophical and poetic system outside the domain of systematic idealism. He links Sophia-Wisdom and God's "feminine hypostasis" to the Bergsonian intuitive and ever-changing cognition of an unfolding lifestream. But the dualistic metaphysics of the intelligible (or constructed) and the innate (or intuitive) does not provide a satisfying answer to a most obvious question: *If Sophia-Wisdom (also hypostasized as the Muse and the Church) is philosophically r e a l , how can she elude the constructed system that stems from the intuitive experience of her presence?*

The new draft of the same study, entitled – humbly – "A Biography of Vladimir Sergeevich Solovyov," was completed on 28 July 1914 (of the Gregorian calendar) and published as the editor's preface to the sixth edition of Vladimir Solovyov's collected *Poems*.[8] A remarkable number of otherwise overlooked facts from numerous sources distinguish this version from the initial essay. "A Biography of Vladimir Sergeevich Solovyov" exemplified a further advance in the historization and contextualization of Vladimir Solovyov. For the first time Sergey Solovyov dared discuss the complexities of his uncle's evolution, including the "fateful collapse of his ecclesiastic idea"[9] and his conflict with the Russian modernists.[10] Furthermore, some statements read like a premonition of Sergey Solovyov's own future: "In the ages of the Ecumenical Councils," he wrote about his uncle's alleged Catholicism, "only Rome [...] was indeed a stone and a pillar of the Orthodox faith, which had been persecuted in the Eastern Church."[11]

In the year that the "Biography of Vladimir Sergeevich Solovyov" was published Sergey Solovyov was ordained deacon and soon became a priest without a parish: much to the surprise of his old Symbolist friends. He enrolled as a student in the Holy Trinity Theological Academy in Sergiev Posad and worked on a thesis devoted to the Gospel theology of St. John (which he completed in 1918, shortly before the Academy was closed).

---

[8]Solov'ev, Sergei, "Biografiia Vladimira Sergeevicha Solov'eva," in Vladimir Solov'ev, *Stikhotvoreniia*, 6th ed. (Moscow: 1915), 1-57.
[9]Ibid., 31.
[10]Ibid., 42-43.
[11]Ibid., 13.

Another remarkable event of those years was his trip to Galicia in 1915. Occupied by the Russian army during the initial phase of World War I, Galicia became a playground of rival political and religious forces. The Russian imperial government introduced a policy of instant "Easternization" in this most western enclave of Ukrainian culture. Those, who like Greek Catholic Metropolitan Andrej Szeptyckyj, strongly opposed the new regime, were imprisoned without a trial on the charges of complicity in anti-Russian conspiracy. (Metropolitan Andrej was not a Russian citizen and therefore charges against him were legally dubious). It is worth mentioning that the ecumenical program of Vladimir Solovyov exerted a considerable influence over Metropolitan Andrej (who happened to know the philosopher personally) and over many other prominent Greek Catholics. Sergey Solovyov wrote from Lwów: "The Greek Catholic monks all knew about Uncle Volodya, and one of them, a young pink-faced Ukrainian, said to me about him: 'If there would be more people like him, it might be good to live in this world'."[12] Sergey Solovyov's openly pro-Catholic views forced him to give detailed explanations to some of his friends. Solovyov maintained that there was no conflict between his Philocatholicism and a truly Orthodox understanding of the doctrine of Christianity. On August 25, 1915 he wrote to Sergey Mansurov: "Bishop Fyodor, the Rector of the Academy, told me that Western theology is rooted in *will,* while Eastern theology is rooted in the *mind*. But the fruit of will is *faith,* while the fruit of mind is *knowledge*. And faith is before knowledge, although the former can't replace the latter."[13] This distinction between the Western *will* and the Eastern *mind* refers to the well-known Catholic concept of *potencies of soul,* which are: will, mind, and memory. With will placed before mind, it was memory that

[12]A letter of February 9, 1915, currently in my possession.

[13]Private collection, Moscow (original in Russian). I am indebted to Countess Antonina Komarovskaya for allowing me to copy this text and to use it in print. The following is the information about Sergey Solovyov's addressee with which she provided me. Sergey Pavlovich Mansurov (1890-1929) was born in Constantinople in the family of the secretary of the Russian Embassy. He graduated from the Department of History and Philology at Moscow University where the poet Boris Pasternak and the linguist Prince Nikolay Trubetskoy, the future Eurasianist, were his classmates. In 1926 he was ordained priest.

increasingly drew Solovyov's attention in the decade that followed. He relied heavily on the virtues of his own durational memory in attaining the successful completion of the task of his life: a definitive biography of Vladimir Solovyov which would facilitate the dialogue between Western and Eastern traditions. Along with his detailed, although unfinished, *Memoirs,* he was aiming at presenting his own family history as a history of the path by which Russian culture should arrive at enlightened universalism. In that sense, he extended the framework of Vladimir Solovyov's philosophy of history. However egocentric it may seem, this great project was born out of the wish to comprehend one's own place in the unfolding of history.

Under the distinct influence of Bely (who was back from Switzerland and finished with his apprenticeship in Anthroposophy), Sergey Solovyov hailed the Revolution of 1917 as a celebration of a cosmic Easter of "ecclesiastical love and peace"[14] and a promise for the much cherished unification of East and West. He actively supported the Russian Catholic Church, legalized by the Provisional Government, and participated in ecumenical meetings that took place in St. Petersburg. But this freedom of faith would not last long.

In 1918, with the Communists firmly in power in Central Russia, the new religious policy largely resembled the notorious imperial persecution of all "un-Russian" denominations. Chapter three of a secret instruction on the implementation of the Decree on the Separation of Church and State outlawed all "religious organizations" that happened to have headquarters outside Russia. Furthermore, the Russian Orthodox Church, which gained new strength from the Council of 1917-1918, was facing both inner and outside challenges. Moreover, the beginning of the 1920s was not a good time for Sergey Solovyov's personal life: by 1922 he was separated from his wife. During this difficult period of family crisis, sometime in 1920, he formally joined the outlawed Russian Catholic Church for the first time. By 1921, however, he was an Orthodox priest again. In 1923 he returned to Catholicism and confessed to his elder daughter Natalia that he regarded this return as "a form of [civil] suicide, since suicide is prohibited by our Church."

---

[14]Rev. Sergei Solov'ev,*Vopros o soedinenii tserkvei v sviazi s padeniem russkogo samoderzhaviia*. (Moscow: Moskovskaia prosvetitel'naia komissiia, 1917), 16.

By that time Solovyov happened to meet a person who – somewhat miraculously – convinced him that a larger biography of his uncle was still a publishable project.

Ferapont Ivanovich Sedenko (1886-1938) was a bibliographer and an editor of the Leningrad publishing cooperative *Kolos*. [15] He also published essays under the pen name of Vityazev. It was due to his active involvement that Solovyov's memoirs about Blok (written immediately after Blok's death in 1921) and some of Blok's letters to Solovyov came out in 1925.[16] Two other major projects facilitated by Vityazev were Solovyov's new biography of Vladimir Solovyov (1922-1923) and a critical edition of the correspondence between Sergey Solovyov's mother and her cousin Aleksandra Kublitskaya Piottukh, the mother of Aleksandr Blok (1927).[17] In surviving prefaces to both texts, Solovyov emphasized Vityazev's role in the completion of the projects. It is quite possible that Sergey Solovyov's unfinished *Memoirs,* on which he worked in the early 1920s and continuously revised later (the last surviving typescript is dated 1936), were also written for *Kolos*. As compared to the two previous versions of his uncle's biography, this book is narrated in an almost impersonal and low-key tone. But the feeling of a detailed and cozy narrative is a mere illusion. Every page in the biography testifies to the necessity of applying lofty existential criteria to the philosopher's quest for a "holistic, synthesizing system of knowledge." For Sergey Solovyov, this system was valid only in connection with the human side of Vladimir Solovyov. "To me is dear the man full of goodness," he wrote in the conclusion of the book, "whose malicious and evil tongue was torn out by a Seraph and replaced by the wise sting of the serpent. With the poison of its dialectics, this sting mortally wounded the opponents of truth, who

---

[15]Meaning "ear of wheat" in Russian.

[16] Sergei Solov'ev, "Vospominnaiia ob Aleksandre Bloke" in *Pis'ma Aleksandra Bloka,* comp. and ed. S. M. Solov'ev, G. I. Chulkov, A. D. Skaldin, V. N. Kniazhnin (Leningard: Kolos, 1925), 9-45.

[17] Solovyov's foreword and the letters – copied by Dmitri Pines, who also assisted Bely's widow with the poet's bibliography and sorting out of the poet's archive, – are stored in RGALI. Most of the originals were lost during the terror of the 1930s; I have in my possession only a few original letters which were handed to me by Natalia Solovyova.

failed to see the flaming ember of love, with which the same Seraph had replaced the prophet's fleshly and trembling heart."

Alas, Sergey Solovyov's memoir about Blok was the only text that Vityazev was able to drag through the Soviet censorship; by then, Father Sergey was under the scrutiny of the authorities. Eventually, *Kolos* was closed and any hopes for publication waned. Vityazev perished in The Great Terror.

But this was only half of the story.

After the completion of his *opus magnum,* Sergey Solovyov devoted all of his time to the heroic profession of a Russian Catholic priest and to literary translations (which paid his and his daughters' bills). Occasionally, he composed a poem or two, but after 1922 any publication of his own work was simply impossible. He remained very active socially, lecturing on theological subjects and the Catholic cause, shocking his old literary friends (who were mildly in favor of Orthodoxy at best, but often simply atheists) with his Catholic priesthood, and continued his solitary crusade for the unification of Eastern and Western Churches. At that time the Russian Orthodox Church was split by the Renovators' schism (supported by the atheist government); while many Church hierarchs were either in prison (some, like Patriarch Tikhon, were under house arrest), or had been executed. Anyone who failed to side with the oppressed Orthodox clergy was viewed by most believers as a defector. When the casuistic Soviet prosecution charged several prominent Catholics in 1923 with state treason, it – in a way – echoed a very mixed public attitude towards the Roman Church. Sergey Solovyov, however, had his own lifelong aura of an eccentric, which successfully protected him until the end of the 1920s, when he remained the only Russian Catholic priest in Moscow, with a small but a devoted parish of approximately thirty people.[18] Everybody who met him at that time remembered Father Sergey Solovyov as a true "confessor," *"vir Catholicissimus"* [19] who had no fears or illusions about the future. His elder daughter Natalia, who in time became the closest person to him in the world,

---

[18]Diaconus Basilius, *Leonidas Fiodoroff: de vita et operibus enarratio* (in Russian) (Romae: Tipografia poliglotta Vaticana, 1966), 612.
[19]Idem.

also recollected that most of his time at home was spent in passionate prayer.

When on the night of 15/16 February 1931 Father Sergey Solovyov was arrested in his Moscow apartment, the Soviet political police seized only the mediumistic writings of Vladimir Solovyov and his French manuscript *Sophie* (which is how those papers ended up in RGALI, which for half a century was under the direct control of the Ministry of the Interior). Anticipating his arrest, Solovyov took care of his most important papers: he "lent" a manuscript of his *Memoirs* to a childhood friend, the writer Natalia Venkstern. The manuscript of *Vladimir Solovyov: His Life and Creative Evolution,* however, was in Vityazev's hands. It was not uncommon in the 1930s to think that a deposit in a state archive would prevent the political police from further interest in one's papers. Vityazev negotiated the conditions of depository purchase with Vladimir Bonch-Bruevich and his assistants, who were busy collecting rare materials for the newly organized State Literary Museum in Moscow. A curious note about the bargaining between Vityazev and the state archivists reads: "Solovyov S. M. – 'Vladimir Solovyov: His life and Creative Evolution.' A manuscript. 450 p. At about 20 printers sheets. (Not published). From F. I. Vityazev. Our price is ~~1600~~ 1000 rubles. Give him 800."[20] Vityazev agreed to the deal. The manuscript was purchased by the Museum and in 1941 transferred to the Central (currently, Russian) State Archives for Literature and Arts (RGALI). This is how Sergey Solovyov's masterpiece survived its author's arrest and Vityazev's execution.

As for Sergey Solovyov himself, his arrest and subsequent pre-trial detention led to a total psychic collapse. His initial sentence of four years of exile in Kazakhstan had been reduced – after a petition filed with the Political Red Cross by a group of friends and endorsed by the then omnipotent Maksim Gorky – to temporary confinement in a "specialized" mental hospital near the capital. After spending a total of a year and a half in prison, Sergey Solovyov returned home. He continued to live in his Moscow apartment having been haunted by an acute sense of guilt and the inability to reconcile himself with what happened to him and to his parish. He refused to read and write; he never looked in the mirror or allowed anybody to

[20]Private collection (original in Russian).

take his picture; moreover, he refused to pray.[21] The prosecutors tried to convince him of the "subversive character" of Catholic activities in Russia, which Solovyov with his enlightened patriotism was unable to comprehend. All his parishioners (with an exception of a government informer who named them) ended up in jail. As a priest, he considered himself responsible for this. Much worse, the Catholic hierarchs in Moscow, who were – like Msgr. Neveu – foreign nationals, refused to offer any substantial support to a strange Russian priest who had caused them so much trouble.[22] Sergey Solovyov lived through the 1930s in a whirlwind of sickness, apocalyptic visions, and still very bright recollections of his own past. Contrary to what one may read in some sources, his daughters Natalia and Olga stayed with him from the time of his release from prison and took great care of their ailing father.[23] Fully aware of who Sergey Solovyov was, Natalia Sergeevna started to bring order to his very rich literary archive: she copied his poems, *Memoirs* and managed to put most of his manuscripts into the hands of trustworthy people. By the end of the 1930s Solovyov spent long periods in the Kashchenko Mental Hospital: he had been diagnosed with an incurable psychic disorder. One may, however, question whether he was really sick. If the entire country went mad, could a former Symbolist poet who was haunted by the visions of the dead and executed be indeed a madman?

When war with Germany broke out, the Kashchenko Hospital was evacuated to Kazan, the capital of the Tatar Republic, where Sergey Solovyov died on 2 March 1942 of heart failure.[24]

---

[21]These and other facts are borrowed from Natalia S. Solovyova's unpublished memoir "Pamiat' ob otse" (dated: Moscow, August 1994), which she wrote at my request. For the published account cf.: Solov'eva, Nataliia. "Otsom zaveshchannoe," *Nashe nasledie* 27 (1993): 60-65.

[22]Natalia Solovyova recollected her only visit to Msgr. Neveu, when upon learning of Rev. Sergey's arrest he offered her a good dinner: "The only thing I can help you with." It certainly was beyond young Natalia's understanding what a respected French citizen could be afraid of in 1931.

[23]Olga later thought of herself as a Russian Catholic, while Natalia was quite happy with her very liberal Orthodoxy.

[24]E. L. Feinberg. "Poslednie dni Sergeia Mikhailovicha Solov'eva," an unpublished manuscript. The prominent Russian physicist Evgeny Feinberg was the brother of Natalia Solovyova's second husband, literary scholar Ilya Feinberg; Evgeny took care of the dying Solovyov and organized his funeral.

As a strange relic of a distant past, Solovyov's monograph remained in almost complete oblivion until the early 1970s, totally plunged into the Bergsonian lifestream of history (or what one may identify with it). Even the inquisitive editor of Vladimir Solovyov's *Collected Poems and Verse Plays* (Moscow, 1974), Professor Zara Mintz, never read it through. It took a young Moscow historian to bring it to press in 1977. (For the extraordinary story of the book's first publication written by this former Moscow historian, Father Michael Axionov Meerson, see the Appendix.)

As for my part, I promised Natalia Sergeevna Solovyova to bring her father's masterpiece back to Russia. For the 1997 Moscow edition I used the Brussels version but corrected it against the RGALI manuscript. I tried to be as faithful to the original text as possible. The final, authoritative version of the book was the result of this diligent preparation.

The present translation prepared by Aleksey Gibson is based on the corrected 1977 version. His excellent translation is fully faithful to the original and is a result of meticulous but rewarding work. One may only rejoice at the thought that Sergey Solovyov will eventually be speaking to the largest Christian audience in the world in a language that we all share.

Igor G. Vishnevetsky
November 1998

The History of the First Publications of Two Manuscripts:

La Sophie
by Vladimir Solovyov

and

Vladimir Solovyov: His Life and Creative Evolution
by His Nephew Sergey Solovyov

In 1967, Evgeny Rashkovsky, a member of our unofficial seminar on Russian religious philosophy in Moscow, told me that he had found in Vladimir Solovyov's archive at TsGALI (now RGALI) two unpublished works: the dialogue *La Sophie* by Vladimir Solovyov, and Sergey Solovyov's biography of his famous uncle. At that time, I was working on my master's thesis at the Department of History at Moscow University under the direction of Prof. Sergey Sergeevich Dmitriev. The topic of my research was the history of the publishing house *Put'* (1911-1917), an offshoot of the Moscow Vladimir Solovyov Society, that published the writings of Berdyaev, Bulgakov, Florensky, Evgeny Trubetskoy, et al.[25]

Dmitriev was a very helpful and protective academic adviser. He not only accepted my proposal and promoted its cause at the department but also guided my research to conform to the acceptable vein of a mere "history of a Russian publishing institution." This guidance prevented me from provoking the requisite Soviet ideological criticism against the participants of *Put'*, the so-called "Vekhovtsy"

[25]In 1989 Evgeny Gollerbakh, a Russian scholar from Leningrad, visited me in New York and asked for my guidance on his project for writing a history of the *Put'* publishing house. I told him about all the archive materials that I used for my study and gave him the necessary bibliography and some suggestions. Two years later he brought me the draft of his study, which I read with satisfaction and interest as he had given a fuller historical account of the publishing activities of *Put'* than what I had managed to do in my master's thesis. He eventually published this very useful study under the title "Religiozno-filosofskoe izdatel'stvo *Put'* (1910-1919),"*Voprosy Filosofii* 2 (1994): 123-165; 4 (1994): 129-163.

and "God-seekers", accused by Lenin as the worst enemies of the state and expelled from the Soviet Union in 1922. Dmitriev also provided me with all the necessary academic recommendations for obtaining official access (*dopusk,* in Russian) to the archives closed to the general public and to the Special Stock (the so-called *Spetskhran*) in the Lenin Library, where, among other books, both Western theological and Russian émigré literature was kept for use by special permission only.

In 1965-72, I was also running a small underground religious press which, among other things, reprinted and published the works of Russian religious thinkers, of whom Vladimir Solovyov was obviously a major representative. The press also published the writings of Father Alexander Men', who was himself a follower and admirer of Solovyov's.[26]

At one of the meetings of our small editorial board, which included Father Men', Evgeny Barabanov, and myself, I proposed to obtain from TsGALI a manuscript entitled *Vladimir Solovyov: His Life and Creative Evolution* for the purposes of publication. The archive's policy, however, did not allow copying manuscripts in their entirety; only a few pages were allowed to be copied after vexing paperwork. Eventually I devised a technique that was certainly illegal. Hiding some pages of the manuscript under my jacket, I would leave for lunch, while keeping all the checked-out papers on my desk. I would then take a taxicab and rush home, where whatever primitive photo equipment I had was ready for copying. After copying these pages, I would rush, in the same manner, back to TsGALI, to put the pages back into the manuscripts and return them.

In this manner I copied *Vladimir Solovyov: His Life and Creative Evolution* by Sergey Solovyov, Vladimir Solovyov's *La Sophie*, his unpublished article on the Russian Schism, and the correspondence of Sergey Bulgakov with Glinka-Volzhsky.

Publishing these materials in samizdat, however, turned out to be riskier than I had thought. My underground publications were

[26]On Men's series of books as an historical unfolding of Solovyov's philosophy of religion, see my article "The Life and Work of Father Men'" in *Seeking God: The Recovery of Religious Identity in Orthodox Russia, Ukraine, and Georgia*, ed. Stephen K. Batalden, (DeKalb: Northern Illinois University Press, 1993).

being rapidly disseminated in Moscow, Leningrad, and other cities, and some copies were seized by KGB officers during various people's house searches. Apparently the KGB in Moscow started searching for my press, as strange looking persons began to watch my apartment and my telephone got tapped. A reader working in Soviet archives always had to check the material out by leaving his/her signature, and only two people kept signing for Vladimir Solovyov's archive at that time–Rashkovsky and myself. Under these circumstances, a publication of Solovyov's *Life* would have made Rashkovsky look suspicious to the Soviets, and it most certainly would have lead KGB agents directly to me as an underground publisher. In 1972 a dissident leader Viktor Krasin was arrested. Among other things, he was charged with possessing and disseminating a whole library of "anti-Soviet" books, which he did, for the purpose of educating the Soviet dissident movement. I provided him with quite a few of these books, either published in the West or by my underground press. After I learned that Krasin, heavily pressured by the KGB, had given in and begun providing evidence against his fellow dissidents,[27] I decided to emigrate. I left Russia in December 1972 and settled in France, where I worked for the YMCA-Press in Paris and the Foyer Oriental Chrétien in Brussels. The Foyer eagerly published Sergey Solovyov's *Vladimir Solovyov: His Life and Creative Evolution* in 1977, and in its preface referred to the "Providence that in mysterious ways preserved the manuscript for publication." My own introduction, entitled "Solovyov in Our Days," was discreetly sandwiched between the introductions by Krasnov-Levitin and Anthony Wenger who wrote about the life of Sergey Solovyov. As far as Vladimir Solovyov's *La Sophie* was concerned, I gave the manuscript to Fr. François Rouleau who published it in the collection of Solovyov's French writings: Vladimir Soloviev, *La Sophie et les autres ècrits français* (Lausanne: L'Age d'Homme, 1978).

Although I was out of danger and could have edited these publications under my own name, I preferred to stay out of sight in order to avoid jeopardizing the careers of my friends–the Rashkovskys (Maria Rashkovskaya, Evgeny Rashkovsky's wife, was a staff worker

---

[27]See Victor Krasin, "How I Was Broken By the K.G.B.," *The New York Times Magazine,* March 18, 1984.

at TsGALI) and, especially, Sergey Dmitriev, who was in even greater a danger in his capacity as my academic adviser, i.e., the person who had provided me with the pass (the *dopusk*). I felt extremely grateful to him and dreaded ruining his academic career.

I am very glad that Prof. Igor Vishnevetsky has now prepared the new scholarly and complete publication of *Vladimir Solovyov: His Life and Creative Evolution* for the Russian reader. (His version is certainly more complete because, in my hasty copying, I missed one page from the manuscript.) I am also very glad that this book is now being made available in an English translation.

Very Rev. Michael A. Meerson

Author's Foreword

This book took me less than a year to write; however, having completed it, I can say in the words of Pushkin, "The longed for moment has arrived, my labor of many years is finished." From adolescence I have gathered material for the life of Vladimir Solovyov, but my first biography of him proved to be too condensed to satisfy its readers.[1] Now when Sergey Lukyanov came to my assistance with his *Material for the Biography of Solovyov*, which illuminated the period of Solovyov's life that was least familiar to me (his youth), I realized I could no longer postpone this work. If I can convey to my readers only a fraction of the spiritual pleasure that I experienced during this year in resurrecting the image of a deceased loved one, I will have fulfilled my task.

Beginning in the fourth year of *gymnasium*, when I first read *The National Question in Russia*, Solovyov exerted a great influence on the development of my personal worldview. Afterwards, there was a great deal in Solovyov that was foreign to me, and my views underwent a certain evolution. I would not, for example, reprint my article "The Ideal of the Church in the Poetry of V. Solovyov" and my first biography, without certain minor changes. Borrowing the expression of Lev Lopatin, I have had to work out my personal worldview as much under the influence of Solovyov as in a stubborn, agonizing struggle with it. The blatant contradictions between the ideas of Solovyov in the various periods of his creativity (the decades of the 1870s, 1880s, and 1890s), have made the division of his followers into several mutually disagreeing camps inevitable. Before one can reconcile these contradictions and understand the basic idea that runs through the entire life of Solovyov, it is necessary to accept them objectively and not ignore them.

---

[1] For details of Sergey Solovyov's earlier biographifies of Vladimir Solovyov see Igor Vishnevetsky's introduction to the present translation, "Sergey Solovyov as a Historian of Philosophy and Culture."

I would like to express my deep gratitude to Sergey Lukyanov and Ernst Radlov,[2] whose tireless labor considerably mitigated the writing of this biography, and to the publishing house Kolos in the persons of F. I. Vityazev and V. P. Brovkin who have fulfilled my desire of providing the Russian public with a complete biography of Solovyov.

Not being a specialist in philosophy, I have considered it too daring to comment on questions that are "purely philosophical." In these matters I have deferred to the opinions of those more knowledgeable and abstained from personal conclusions. This side of Solovyov has already been investigated on numerous occasions by Evgeny Trubetskoy, Lev Lopatin, Ernst Radlov, and Vladimir Ern. I have examined Solovyov more as a person, theologian, poet, and publicist.

My next work with regard to the legacy of Solovyov will be the publication of a translation of his work in French *Sophie*, or *Les principes de la religion universelle*, written in 1876 in Cairo and Sorrento, as well as the publication of a collection of his poetry and several articles about church questions that were written in Vienna and Zagreb in 1886.

Sergey M. Solovyov
28 August 1923

[2] Ernst Lvovich Radlov was a professor of philosophy and a close friend of Solovyov's. With Sergey Solovyov he coedited the complete works of Vladimir Solovyov and added a biographical sketch of his own to this edition.

Introduction

Soon twenty-five years will have passed since the death of Vladimir Solovyov and there is still an imperative need for his complete biography. It has already been remarked on numerous occasions that the story of Solovyov's life holds as much interest as his work. Merezhkovsky was correct in saying that unlike Tolstoy, who revealed himself in his writings, Solovyov always carefully concealed himself from the public. All the same, one cannot help asking whether it is a good idea to lift the veil that Solovyov threw over his intimate life and whether we have the right to recreate his inner state of mind on the basis of material that he never intended for publication.

But such is the fate of a great man: his personal life, sooner or later, becomes common property. I have approached my work with the hope that a detailed biography of Solovyov will shed light on a number of aspects of his life and career that have hitherto not been illuminated. In the course of his short and tempestuous life Solovyov underwent not one but several spiritual crises. Although we shall discover contradictions when we trace, step by step, the path of his development, we shall still attain, in the end, a single, comprehensive vision of the world. We shall see, for example, that in the 1890s Solovyov will repeat word for word what he had asserted in the 1870s. The ideal of an organic synthesis, of a positive All-Unity [*vseedinstvo*] was Solovyov's fundamental idea. He could never adhere to one of "two hostile camps": neither to secular culture nor to clerical asceticism; neither to the Westernizers nor to the Slavophiles; neither to the representatives of free mysticism nor to the holders of ecclesiastical authority. In the meantime, his desire for action, for influence on society, for the implementation of his ideals, forced him to conclude temporary truces with one or another camp, and even, as he himself expressed it, to "carry on diplomacy."

Naturally, following Solovyov's death a bitter dispute arose over his legacy and, as the poet Andrey Bely says, "a variety of ignorant castes ranked him among their own." Those castes, which during the philosopher's life cried with one voice, "you are not one of ours!" now with no less bitterness began to cry, "he is one of ours and only ours!" And yet again, Christ's words about the nation that stoned its prophets, only to erect monuments to them, are justified.

Solovyov's life can be divided into three periods. The first is purely speculative and Slavophile, and involves the struggle with materialism and positivism; the second is ecclesiastical and journalistic and is marked by the struggle with nationalism; the third is synthetic and entails a return to philosophy, the pursuit of poetry and criticism, and a struggle with Nietzsche and Tolstoy. This period begins with *The Justification of the Good* and ends with *Three Conversations* and the poem "Three Meetings."

This tripartite division of Solovyov's life finds an analogy in the life of the founder of Western theology, St. Augustine, whose fundamental ideas, as Ernst Radlov has shown, were so akin to those of Solovyov's. With Augustine, the first period was also purely speculative; when, armed with Platonism, he waged polemics with the mystical naturalism of the Manicheans. The second period formed the groundwork for his dogma about the Church and coincided with the struggle against the Donatists. The third period was devoted to moral and mystical pursuits, and included the teaching about grace and his struggle with Pelagius. Solovyov was particularly fond of tripartite divisions and we shall be faithful to his spirit, dividing our work into three sections that correspond to the three stages of his development. The first part comes to an end at the beginning of the 1880s, while the third takes shape at the beginning of the 1890s. Our task has been made considerably easier by the previous work of Solovyov's friends and admirers. Immediately after his death, Vasily Velichko published *Vladimir Solovyov: His Life and Works*, which contains some interesting material. The friends of Solovyov, Ernst Radlov and Sergey Lukyanov then undertook an enormous and selfless task: Radlov collected and published three volumes of Solovyov's letters (the fourth volume is ready for printing), while Lukyanov published three volumes of material for the biography of Solovyov. In his work Lukyanov examines in detail the philosopher's life till the end of the 1870s. In passing, he also includes valuable material for the study of that era, in particular, for that of the history of the Moscow Religious Academy. In reconstructing the youth of Solovyov, the biographer can only follow Lukyanov obediently, taking as an example his strictly scientific method and objectivity, which is suffused with a feeling of sincere love for his hero. Later we will have to strike out on an independent course. If in the beginning we find ourselves in the splendid terrain shaped by the patient hand of Lukyanov, with the 1880s we must hack a road for ourselves through dark thickets. However, the closer we approach the present, the easier becomes the biographer's task: for the 1890s we have at our disposal the rich material of our own memories.

Mention must also be made of two prominent biographical studies of Solovyov, Evgeny Trubetskoy's *The Worldview of Vladimir Solovyov* (Moscow, 1913) and Michel d'Herbigny's *Un Newman russe* (1911).[3] Compared to the work of Lukyanov these two books can hardly be called objective. Trubetskoy's book is written in a polemical mode. Throughout the entire two volumes Trubetskoy carries on a persistent quarrel with Solovyov and accepts precious little of what was characteristic of his latter years (i.e. his theoretical philosophy, aesthetics, poetry, and *Three Conversations*). The life of Solovyov is portrayed by Trubetskoy as a series of delusions: his philosophy of the first and middle period is related entirely to Schelling, his schemes for a theocracy are described as a "temptation," and his theory of love is depicted as a rosy romance. There is not a great deal of biographical information in Trubetskoy's book, but there is some that is extremely valuable. The small book by the French theologian d'Herbigny is very elegantly written; it is inspired and imbued with a feeling of deep respect.

Some of the other articles about Solovyov, such as the splendid article by Lopatin, will be mentioned in the appropriate chapters of this book.

In that part of Russian society that is interested in philosophical and religious questions, one can sense, of late, a coolness toward Solovyov. The negative attitudes of Rozanov and Merezhkovsky to Solovyov on the one hand, and of the specialists in philosophy on the other, cannot but exert their influence. While there is interest in the personality of Solovyov, his eccentricities, his jokes, and his occult studies; his fundamental works, such as *A Critique of*

---

[3] Michel d'Herbigny's book was translated into English by Anna M. Buchanan as *Vladimir Soloviev: A Russian Newman* (London: R. & T. Wasbourne, 1918).

Abstract Principles, *The History and Future of Theocracy*, and *The Justification of the Good*, are either respected more than they are read or are dismissed as the ponderous constructions of an obsolete scholasticism. One can often hear, as well, scornful opinions of Solovyov from the representatives of so-called neo-Orthodoxy, a movement closely tied to the old Slavophilism. Considering as decisive Solovyov's own view of his vocation and his work, we have always held to the opinion that the romantic and occult episodes of his life have no interest for us. It is impossible to affirm, like Merezhkovsky, that the real and "interesting" Solovyov was only a mute prophet and that his major works were only a mask destined for the public. By nature Solovyov was, above all, a philosopher, and his "serpentine" dialectic was as rooted in the inner sanctum of his soul, as his "dovelike" poetry. The construction of an all-embracing, synthetic system of knowledge remained forever his basic aspiration. It is likewise impossible to ignore his sustained career as a publicist. He considered it his sacred duty and his personal "penance," to "sweep out the litter" of Russian social life, and his fascination with the gentle beauty of Lake Saima did not deafen in his soul a prayer to the God of justice: "So that the surge of violence / Will break on the stones of Finland."

Solovyov strove not to expose his personality, but to "till the soil" and build in stone. Believing love to be the creative and organizing principle of life, he sought the realization of this love through philosophical synthesis and social justice. The synthesis of the spiritual and the material, of East and West, of Russia and Europe, of Orthodoxy and Catholicism, – this is what is most characteristic about Solovyov.

During his middle years, Solovyov found himself sharply at odds with the Russian government and Russian society. Two of his major works, *The History and Future of Theocracy* and *Russia and the Universal Church* could only be published abroad; the first appeared in Paris, the second in Zagreb. Having become, in his own lifetime, not only a Russian but also a European writer, Solovyov remains as such now, and his popularity continues to grow in Germany and France. I believe that the publication of the complete biography of Solovyov is a timely event, all the more so as several writings of an intimate nature, which had long been concealed, have come to light in circumstances beyond my control and evoked rumors offensive to the memory of the deceased philosopher. My task is to give a just hearing to this material. Although the ties of blood could be an obstacle to an objective biography, Solovyov's commandment "keep yourself from idols" is too memorable for me. Above all, I feel certain that, having depicted my uncle as he was, without any false idealization, I can only heighten his authority and charm.

Сѣмя жены сотретъ главу змія. (Бытія III)

Сотворилъ Мнѣ величіе Сильный и свято имя Его (Еван. Луки I).

И явилось на небѣ великое знаменіе: жена, облеченная въ солнце, подъ ногами ея луна, на главѣ ея вѣнецъ изъ двѣнадцати звѣздъ (Апокал. XII).

Одно, навѣки одно. Пускай въ ускорившемся храмѣ
Во мракѣ адскій блескъ и громъ среди темницъ;
Пусть пало все кругомъ, — одно не брошено храма
И лишь недвижима съ разрушенной стѣны

В. Соловьевъ

Scriptural epigraph and first stanza of Vladimir Solovyov's poem "The Sign," in his own hand, 1898 (see page 477).

Part One

Sophia

Not believing the deceitful world,
Under the coarse bark of matter,
I touched the imperishable purple
And recognized the radiance of divinity.

Three Meetings

Part 1 - Chapter 1

Solovyov's Origins and Family

> The natural bond with past generations, or the family religion of the past, has an absolute meaning; it is an expression of perfect good.
>
> *Justification of the Good* (part III, ch. 19, 2)

Purely Slavic blood flowed in the veins of Vladimir Solovyov. Though he belonged to the clergy on his father's side, his distant paternal ancestors came from the Great Russian peasantry.[1] On his mother's side he was descended from a Ukrainian family, with a touch of Polish blood. His grandfather Mikhail Vasilevich Solovyov was an archpriest and religious teacher at the Moscow Commercial College. He was an enlightened clergyman of the epoch of Metropolitan Filaret[*] and had absorbed some of the Latin culture that flourished at the beginning of the nineteenth century. I have kept his Latin Bible with the inscription "*ex libris Michael Soloviovus.*" Intellectual gifts, however, were not the principal attributes of Father Mikhail, but rather his kind and pure heart which left an impression even on his features; he had gentle, clear blue eyes, a large, fairly fleshy pointed nose, and a downy white beard. When Vladimir

---

[*] Filaret (Drozdov [1781-1867]), metropolitan of Moscow (1825-1867). Having received a Westernized education that combined neo-Scholasticism with Protestant Biblical theology and pietism, Filaret began his career in the Church as rector of the St. Petersburg Religious Academy (1812) where he attempted to restore – with some success–more authentic Orthodox teachings and spirituality to the Russian Church of his day. As the highly influential metropolitan of Moscow, Filaret was chosen by Alexander II to draft the Proclamation of the Emancipation of the serfs in 1861. Although supportive of the imperial system and close, at times, to the court, Filaret zealously defended the prerogatives of the Church and its hierarchy.

Solovyov described the appearance of the Elder Ioann in "A Short Story about Antichrist" he must have had this grandfather in mind: "He was a very aged, but hale old man, with yellowish, even greenish, white hair and beard. He was tall and lean, with full, slightly rosy cheeks, lively flashing eyes, and a touching, good-natured expression on his face and in his speech."[2] In the story "Resurrection" by another grandson, Vsevolod Sergeevich, Father Mikhail is also undoubtedly portrayed. If Vladimir Solovyov was especially proud of his clerical origins and showed them off (*The Justification of the Good* is dedicated to his priest grandfather), then Vsevolod Solovyov was somewhat ashamed of this background and tried to conceal it. In "Resurrection" he portrays his grandfather without mentioning that he was in holy orders, so that the behavior of the fictional grandfather is not always comprehensible. For example, Vsevolod recounts that, although the grandfather would never pass judgment on anyone, if someone related a sordid incident in front of him he would sigh, "sins! sins!" and would run off to pray. (It is characteristic that during the speech of the Antichrist at the ecumenical council the Elder Ioann also sighs loudly.) In any case, such behavior is not entirely usual for an ordinary, lay grandfather...

Mikhail Vasilevich was very affectionate and good with children, for whose amusement he would act like a bear. A resemblance to this grandfather was seen most distinctly in two representatives of the family; in my father, Mikhail Sergeevich, and in his sister Maria (Bezobrazova). According to Vasily Velickho, who quotes Sofia Martynova as his source, when Vladimir Solovyov was eight years old, his grandfather took him to the sanctuary of the church and, making the child kneel by the altar, prayed fervently and consecrated him to the service of God. Mikhail Vasilevich spent his entire life at the Moscow Commercial College (where his son the historian was born), but in 1860, feeling his strength decline, he left this position and was transferred to the parish of the Holy Protection in Levshino. Here he felt homesick for the Commercial College and was often to be seen in the courtyard of his new church looking silently and sadly in the direction of Ostozhenko. Moving elderly people from familiar places can be dangerous, and Father Mikhail did not serve for long at the church of the Protection. He died on 30 October 1861 when his grandson Vladimir was eight.

Vladimir Solovyov's grandmother Elena Ivanova Shatova came from a family of civil servants and was of an entirely different mold. Possessing a sharp sarcastic mind and a great practical sense, she held the gentle Mikhail Vasilevich firmly in her grasp. After his death she moved in with her son the historian, whom, according to Vsevolod Solovyov, she greatly respected and whom she even somewhat feared. Vsevolod told me that when he was flogged with birch rods in his childhood, Elena Ivanovna would vouch for this ceremony, which his gentle mother could not bear. She was godmother to the young Vladimir; she loved him very much and slept in the same room with him. Coming from a civil service background, she was not overly fond of the clergy and, as her son expressed it, "represented the principle of progress in the family."

In his autobiographical *Notes for My Children* Sergey Mikhailovich relates:

> At the time of my adolescence, certain priests' families began to feel dissatisfied with their position and aspired to find a way out of it, to revitalize themselves, to stir themselves. Our family belonged to this number. In our household the principle of progress was represented primarily by my mother. While the relatives of my father were priests, deacons, and sacristans who remained in the villages, the relatives of my mother were, for the most part, lay people. As a result, most of their friends also belonged to the laity. There were even some clergymen whom my mother greatly disliked; by their habits and behavior these men had not distinguished themselves favorably from their secular acquaintances.
>
> This opposition to the clergy, which, of course, my mother tried to promote on every suitable occasion, left a strong impression on me. It inspired in me an aversion to a religious vocation and the desire to escape one as soon as possible and to enter a secular college. My sisters were sent to a boarding school, which was then a very rare event among clerical families, but it would have been even more

> strange to send me to seminary, especially, as in my mother's words, such places were a synonym for every kind of nastiness. My father wavered and delayed, but it became impossible to delay any longer... Finally, he decided to give up on a religious vocation and to send me to a *gymnasium*.[3]

Sergey Mikhailovich's sister Elizaveta died in her youth, and he became estranged from his other one, Agnia.[4] Evidently, not without the influence of his mother, Sergey Mikhailovich felt an aversion from an early age to a religious education and to the religious life, which was subsequently reflected in his evaluation of the reforms of Peter the Great. As often happens, the son took more after his mother than his father. In Elena Ivanovna's family, however, there was one important ecclesiastical figure. Vladimir Solovyov writes in his autobiography: "One should note among my father's relatives on his mother's side her uncle Avraamy (archbishop first of Astrakhan, then of Yaroslavl). As a child, my father was taken to see him at the monastery of Tolgsk, near Yaroslavl."[5] In his *Notes* Sergey Mikhailovich calls this relative simply Avraam, not Avraamy. A large portrait of this Avraam, wearing his bishop's robe and holding a crozier, always hung in the dining room at my grandmother's.

The piety and gentleness of Mikhail Vasilevich, the common sense of Elena Ivanovna, and the iron will and intellectual strength of Sergey Mikhailovich betray few of the inclinations of the enigmatic Volodya. Everything that was mystical, poetic, and demonic he inherited from his mother's side, which was descended "from an ancient and unusually talented Little Russian family. One branch of this family (in the provinces of Poltava and Kharkov) suffered a mysteriously tragic fate; to the other belonged the famous Ukrainian philosopher Grigory Skovoroda."[6*] In his autobiography Vladimir Solovyov writes, "The Ukrainian Socrates, Skovoroda, was her (that is, my mother's) great-uncle (or great granduncle)." Vladimir Solovyov inherited a great deal from this "mysteriously tragic fate" and from the wandering sage Skovoroda. About his

* Grigory Savvich Skovoroda (1722-1794), itinerant Ukrainian philosopher and poet.

grandfather on his mother's side he writes, "My maternal grandfather and godfather, Vladimir Pavlovich Romanov, became involved in the Decembrist conspiracy on account of his acquaintance with Bestuzhev* and Ryleev† and spent nine months in the Peter and Paul Fortress. As a result of the trial he was demoted to the lower ranks. Later, however, he was promoted (in the Black Sea fleet), sailed around the globe, fought in the Crimean War and died a rear-admiral." To this we can add that in 1828 Vladimir Pavlovich sailed with the fleet at Anapa and Varna and was wounded in the head by a bullet. Having spent twelve years in retirement, he was called to serve again and took part in the siege of Sebastopol where he displayed heroic courage and was struck in the leg by fragments of a bomb. He retired from active duty in 1861. Vladimir Solovyov was named in his honor and made his godson. Legends about the great deeds of his grandfather at sea probably encouraged in the boy a youthful heroism and a certain militarism, to which he always remained loyal. At the end of this life, for example, he portrayed the aged general in *Three Conversations* with sympathy and addressed himself to Wilhelm II in this fashion:

> Heir of sword-bearing armies!
> You are loyal to the standard of the cross,
> *The fire of Christ is in your steel.*

The legacy of the rear admiral manifests itself more distinctly in his great-grandsons. The sons of Vsevolod Sergeevich broke with the intellectual and literary traditions of the family and became naval officers.

Vladimir Solovyov's maternal grandmother was Ekaterina Fedorovna Brzhesskaya. The Brzhesskys, or as Velichko spells it, *Bzhesskys*, were Russified Poles, landowners in the Kharkov and Kherson provinces. Fet‡ was acquainted with the Brzhesskys from

* Aleksandr Bestuzhev (1797-1837), romantic writer, poet, critic, and translator as well as Decembrist.
† Kondraty Ryleev (1795-1826), romantic poet and Decembrist.
‡ Afanasy Afanasievich Fet (1820-1892), lyric poet and friend of Solovyov's. His poetry, which spans the Russian Golden and Silver Ages, was influenced by the work of Schopenhauer and had a particular appeal for Solovyov.

his youth; he knew Ekaterina Fyodorovna, and dedicated several poems to Aleksandra Lvovna Brzhesskaya. "According to the opinions of those who remembered her personally," Lukyanov says of Ekaterina Fedorovna, "she was an energetic, enterprising person, not without a strong sense of family 'honor,' but also loving."[7] Her brother Aleksey Fyodorovich Brzhessky had literary interests and published his poems in the journals of the 1840s and 1850s.

Poliksena Vladimirovna (Vladimir Solovyov's mother) had three brothers: Vladimir, Vadim, and Pavel. Vladimir was close to the Solovyov family. He died young and his daughter Katya was brought up in the household of her aunt. This is the same Katya Romanova who became Vladimir Solovyov's first love. Uncle Vadim was apparently a great dandy and "gentleman," and a person of dubious morals.[8] He dabbled in literature and made friends early on with his nephew Vsevolod, exerting, it would seem, a not very good influence on him. It was through Uncle Vadim that the seigniorial pretensions and habits of Old Russia entered the austere household of the Solovyovs. Not without the influence of Vadim did Vsevolod turn out to be, alone of all the family, a man of the world, early breaking with his professorial origins. Subsequently, the uncle and nephew quarreled decisively, but of this we shall speak later.

Let us now turn to the parents of Vladimir Solovyov. The historian Sergey Mikhailovich Solovyov was thirty-two and a half years old when his second son, Vladimir, was born. He was already a full professor and had published several volumes of his *History of Russia*. Because of his great influence on Vladimir we must pause for a moment to consider the characteristic traits of Sergey Mikhailovich. This is all the more necessary, as Russian society has not always portrayed him accurately. Sergey Mikhailovich was an original hardheaded Russian, combining in his personality the most contradictory attributes. Born prematurely, by his own efforts he turned himself from a weak, nervous, and sensitive child into a man of iron will and a tireless worker. Beneath his icy crust and his proud exterior, and in his mechanically ordered life, there was hidden the fire of his wrath and a gentle poetic heart. The memoirs of Sergey Mikhailovich strike many readers as oppressive, thanks to the harsh judgments he passed on his contemporaries. One should remember, however, that Sergey Mikhailovich had to fight stubbornly at every stage of his career. First of all, he was an outsider, a parvenu in the noble milieu where the authority of Karamzin* still reigned, and it was especially this authority which he challenged with his *History of Russia*. It is worth noting that when Sergey Mikhailovich was invited to give lessons in Russian history to the Tsarevich Alexander, Prince Vyazemsky–an admirer of Karamzin–protested against this; and Stroganov, Solovyov's patron, summoned him and anxiously asked "'You are not going to say anything against Karamzin, are you?'" "I then became angry," writes Sergey Mikhailovich, "and said that he had nothing to worry about as I had neither the motivation nor the time to bother the Heir to the throne with criticism of *The History of the Russian State*."[9] But there was also a more important reason for Sergey Mikhailovich's alienation from the prevailing trends in society. By virtue of his moral and social ideals, which he had formed on his own, he could not join either one or the other of the dominant parties: He always swam against the current. A Russian patriot and a confirmed Westernist, the founder of the critical method in Russian history (he is known as the Russian Thucydides) and a firmly believing Orthodox, a liberal who hated Nicholas I and despised Metropolitan Filaret, and a gloomy pessimist and conservative in the era of the Great Reforms, Sergey Mikhailovich never had any bearings outside himself, outside his own conscience and faith. This position of a lonely, indefatigable fighter turned him into a somewhat sullen and difficult man. He could be strange. His bursts of anger would break like storms and everything would shake and tremble around him. After such fits, however, Sergey Mikhailovich would literally fall ill and suffer an attack of bile. Having decided to write, at all costs, the *History of Russia* and to erect for himself a "monument not made by human hands," he arranged his life in a mechanically regulated fashion and produced a volume a year. He always rose at seven o'clock and immediately set to work. Later he would go to the university or the archives. He never went to bed later than eleven. After evening tea he dedicated an hour to looking over proofs or light reading, which

---

* Nikolay Karamzin (1766-1826), writer of the Sentimental school and reformer of the Russian literary language; after 1803 author of the conservative, twelve-volume *History of the Russian State*.

consisted primarily of books about geography. In summer he worked without a break and rose at six. Notwithstanding, his family was large (there were twelve children, of whom four died in childhood) and the first years of his married life were spent in difficult material conditions. His wife, Poliksena Vladimirovna, made it the goal of her life to preserve her husband's peace and the children were raised in a pious fear of their father. Not only was it impossible to speak to Sergey Mikhailovich during the course of his working day but even to catch his eye when he passed through the room. No guests were permitted for evening tea, with the exception of Fridays when friends of the professor would gather. Curiously, despite the harsh order imposed by Sergey Mikhailovich, his children adored him. To the end of their lives both Vladimir and Mikhail maintained a reverentially tender attitude towards their father, which is best described by the Roman concept of *pietas*. This feeling for his father undoubtedly exerted an influence on the world-view of Vladimir Solovyov, for whom the ideas of "fatherhood" and the "universal father" played such an important role. For his children, their father was the embodiment of higher justice. My aunt Maria Sergeevna told me that once as a child they promised to take her to the theater, but at the last minute they changed their minds and decided to stay home. The girl fell into complete despair and decided to resort to an insanely daring measure. She rushed to her father with the cry "They promised to take me to the theater and now they won't!" To everyone's surprise Sergey Mikhailovich raised his wrathful voice, "What? They promised to take you and will not? Take her!" *Roma locuta, causa finita est*. But Maria Sergeevna also told me of another incident. At the time of the Turkish war, she and a friend Katya Lopatina decided to run away to Herzegovina to play the part of Joan of Arc. The plan was revealed and the flight was not successful. When Sergey Mikhailovich saw the runaway returning he cried: "Take her away from here! I am going to kill her!" And it was only in the evening that he talked gently with the girl, finding in her act of folly the inherited traits of some grandmother.

Sergey Mikhailovich was a fairly rare person, but he was also typically Russian, combining a deep faith with a passion for science and civilization. In this respect, along with his self-sufficient and independent character, he reminds one very much of

Lomonosov.[*] Like Lomonosov, in contrast to many Orthodox people, he would "not agree to play the fool before the Lord God." He could not tolerate two things: folly and cunning, considering one and the other to be signs of spiritual weakness. He despised Suvorov for such folly. Considering activity and struggle to be the foundations of life, he had an aversion to the East and was a confirmed European. "For the man of the East," Sergey Mikhailovich would say, "the typical garment is the long robe, a symbol of inactivity and softness. For the European the ideal garment is the tail-coat which leaves all parts of the body free for movement." He himself recognized that there was a certain *hastiness* in his character, which was mistaken for punctuality; he was always the first to arrive anywhere. When his health broke down and he began to suffer from heart and liver disease, he was worried most lest he not be able to complete the *History of Russia,* and refused to go for a cure until his work was done.

Despite this regimented way of life, reminiscent of a German scholar, Sergey Mikhailovich was not at all a prosaic man. He deeply appreciated not only poetry but also music, to which his son Vladimir was thoroughly indifferent. Every Saturday evening he steadfastly attended the Italian opera and every Sunday morning went to the Divine Liturgy. For him Italian opera replaced Vespers... When his daughter Masha, who possessed a splendid voice, sang in the evenings he would listen and say, "I hope you will become a singer; our family must be descended from some kind of nightingale."[†] He loved Pushkin exceptionally, as both poet and historian, and considered his *History of the Pugachov Revolt* to be the foundation of modern Russian history, as opposed to the unscientific history of Karamzin. He held that Lomonosov was a great scholar, but a poor poet. Not long before his death, Sergey Mikhailovich was walking in the country with the same daughter Masha. It was a quiet evening; Sergey Mikhailovich grew pensive and recited the concluding words of Goethe's poem "Auf allen

---

[*] Mikhailo Lomonosov (1711-1765), man of science and letters with universal interests.

[†] In Russian *solovei* means nightingale.

Gipfeln ist Ruh"* in Lermontov's translation, changing one of the words:

> The road raises no dust,
> The leaves do not stir . . .
> Wait a little, Seryozha,
> And you too will rest.

In the course of this narrative we will return more than once to Sergey Mikhailovich.

Marriage to such a great man as Sergey Mikhailovich, who exerted pressure on everything around him, completely stifled the individuality of his wife, Poliksena Vladimirovna. She was literally overwhelmed by his twelve children and his twenty-eight volumes of history. It was not, however, by chance that she was the mother of Vladimir Solovyov. As the years went by his resemblance to his mother grew more pronounced. In her youth Poliksena Vladimirovna was a beauty of the oriental type; she possessed large black eyes, a narrow and stately forehead, and an aquiline nose. "In childhood I was a great dreamer," my grandmother admitted to me. "I would pass by an aspen tree and be afraid of seeing Judas." But children put an end to her fantasies. How could there be time to daydream when one infant had measles and another whooping cough, and when they were playing tricks again on Sergey Mikhailovich at the university, and when Samarin† was berating the latest volume of the *History*? A sense of the fantastic, however, did manifest itself in Poliksena Vladimirovna until the end of her days in a certain continual anxiety, fastidiousness, and sense of foreboding. Sergey Mikhailovich loved to tease her about this trait, calling it her "*Khersonstvo*,"[10] that is, the legacy of her Ukrainian family, "one branch of which had suffered a mysteriously tragic fate." Vladimir Solovyov himself, although he was a favorite son, was not adverse to teasing his *maman* and her melancholy. "Why do you write in such a sad tone? Do you have any particular grievances?"[11] This teasing sometimes went beyond the limits of filial piety as he replaced "*Mammá*" with "*Mammán*" (with the associations of

---

* The correct title of Goethe's poem is "Über allen Gipfeln."

† Yury Samarin (1819-1876), important Slavophile thinker.

"mammoth"), the "Great Martyr Mammas", and finally "two-legged *maman*." Among her sons, Vsevolod had a particularly warm and tender feeling for his mother. As he was the firstborn he remembered his mother while she was still young and not overburdened with children and tomes of history. Traits of the youthful Poliksena can be found in the mother of André, the hero of Vsevolod Solovyov's novel *The Enchantment*.

In a touching poem Vsevolod also recalled how as a sick child he drew close to his mother while she read aloud "Ruslan and Lyudmilla":

I remember how behind the window the blizzard
moaned and whined,
And the snowflakes filled up the panes,
But in our room, warmed by a cheerful fire
The antique lamp turned to gold the icon frames.

I remember how I pressed close to you, a sick child.
On my burning forehead you placed your hand
And recited, leaning over me, a wonderful tale,
Which carried me far away from myself
Into its fabulous world.

I remember how the enormous moon rose in the sky,
How it flooded with silver the palace and
gardens of Chernomor,
How the nightingale began to sing in the bushes,
Arguing with the magical sounds of an unseen choir.

Some kind of marvelous charms descended on us.
I drifted far into the gardens of Chernomor.
But this world blended mysteriously with our room
And the moon shone on me with the comforting rays
of your eyes –
And in the melody of the poem flowed your voice.

Vladimir Sergeevich also wrote in his autobiography, "My mother taught me how to read and write, as well as sacred history. She read to me the poetry of Zhukovsky, Pushkin, and Lermontov, and a collection of edifying stories under the title *The School of Piety*." Poliksena Vladimirovna read and reread during her whole life her husband's *History of Russia*. The facts and personalities of Russian history were something familiar and immediate to her. Like Sergey Mikhailovich, she especially loved Vladimir Monomakh[*] and Peter the Great. She despised the Tsarevich Aleksey and hated Empress Anna Ivanovna[†] as though she were a disagreeable lady with whom she was personally acquainted. In her old age Poliksena Vladimirovna developed certain eccentricities and became upset by trifles. When I would dine at her house in St. Petersburg it would happen that if a certain dish did not turn out well my grandmother would silently push aside spoons, forks, and salt-cellars and the terrible words would resound, "For shame!" In general she was a gentle, loving, and self-sacrificing woman, hiding in herself many undeveloped resources. Among her children she especially loved Vsevolod, although she had to conceal this feeling timidly as his father got on poorly with his firstborn and as his brothers did not love him. After him she loved Mikhail and, most of all, her youngest daughter Poliksena. After her husband's death in 1879, Poliksena Vladimirovna lived with her unmarried daughters Nadezhda and Poliksena in Moscow in the large Likhutin house on Zubovsky square. Vladimir Solovyov kept a study in her flat, in which he would stay when he was in Moscow. (During the 1880s he had still not entirely abandoned Moscow for St. Petersburg and divided his time between the two capitals.) When her favorite daughter Poliksena moved to St. Petersburg in 1896, Poliksena Vladimirovna followed her, while Nadezhda remained in Moscow living with their old governess Anna Kuzminichna. In contrast to her sister Poliksena, Nadezhda was an incorrigible Muscovite and, having spent a week in St. Petersburg as a guest, declared she could no longer live "without the Church of the Dormition at Mogiltsy." In the summer Poliksena Vladimirovna often lived with her eldest daughter Vera

[*] Great Prince of Kiev (1053-1125).
[†] Empress of Russia (1730-1740).

Popova in dachas around Moscow, in Udelnaya, Mukhino, and Pokrovskoe-Streshnevo. Poliksena Vladimirovna died in June 1909. Her coffin was taken to Moscow and buried in the cemetery of the Novodevichy monastery between the graves of her husband and her son Vladimir.

The children of Poliksena Vladimirovna were born in this order: Vsevolod–1 January 1849; Vera–18 January 1850; Nadezhda–5 June 1851; Vladimir–16 January 1853; Lyubov–20 September 1857; Mikhail–16 April 1862; Maria–9 October 1863; and Poliksena–20 March 1867. Between Vladimir and Lyubov there were two more girls, Lyubov and Olga, who died in infancy. Between Lyubov and Mikhail was the elder Sergey, a gifted and charming child who died at age seven from scarlet fever. Between Maria and Poliksena was the younger Sergey who also died in infancy.

The eldest son, Vsevolod, whose historical novels have won for him a considerable reputation among Russian readers, did not resemble his brothers. He was not loved by his family, and it seems to me that they were not entirely just towards his unusual and sadly complicated life. He grew up spoiled by his mother who was still young and comparatively free from other concerns. As we have already mentioned, he fell under the influence of his uncle Vadim Vladimirovich. He was not gifted enough for intellectual pursuits and tried to become a man of the world. He dressed elegantly, wore scent, and wrote poetry. Of all the Solovyovs, he more than the rest, gave the impression of being a Russian nobleman, and even a Polish magnate; just as, of all the children, only his appearance spoke of their Polish ancestry. He was short, and his sickly, pale blue, bulging eyes looked glassy; at an early date he began to hide them behind a pair of dark blue pince-nez. He was always clean-shaven and combed his hair into a topknot. Beneath his very straight and handsome nose he maintained a small, dark, well-groomed mustache. In his later years he grew extremely stout, which was especially unattractive considering his shortness. In his youth, however, judging from his portraits, he was very handsome and looked like a "gentleman." As a young man he wrote a great deal of poetry, of which comparatively little appeared in his collected works. According to these poems one can say that he possessed an indisputable poetic talent, which he did not know how to develop. Like his brothers, he especially admired Fet, and in his verse one can hear echoes of Fet's musicality. Having completed his studies at Moscow University in the faculty of jurisprudence, Vsevolod Solovyov, as a lonely young man without a penny to his name (his father had strictly informed him that he must now support himself), set off for St. Petersburg to begin his career. He lodged in furnished rooms which belonged to a Russified Dutch family, the Lamperts. The landlord's eldest daughter Olga Iosifovna captivated Vsevolod Sergeevich and he married her. Soon after, he discovered his vocation as a historical novelist. The enormous success that these novels (in particular the series about the Gorbatov family) enjoyed with a large, and especially provincial, audience had a pernicious effect on his talent. He began to write quickly, between other pursuits, without polishing his style. Nevertheless, his novel *The Enchantment*, into which he put considerable effort, is very interesting and shows that Vsevolod Sergeevich was capable of producing more than he actually did. His other novels, *The Magi* and *The Great Rosicrucian,* testify to his serious involvement in occult sciences, and after his death he left behind a rich library of mystical literature. Vsevolod Sergeevich was extremely close to Dostoevsky, and it seems he had more in common with the author of *The Brothers Karamazov* than did his brother Vladimir, who in his *Three Speeches in Memory of Dostoevsky* spoke about everything but Dostoevsky himself, using the name of the great writer to advance his own ideas, which were at times not only foreign, but openly hostile, to the creator of "The Legend of the Grand Inquisitor."

Vsevolod Sergeevich's life was marred by domestic catastrophe. Having married Olga Lampert, he took in his wife's younger sister Adèle. Vsevolod and his wife were not very happy with each other, and gradually a mutual love developed between him and his sister-in-law. The affair ended with his divorce from Olga and marriage to Adèle. In his second wife Vsevolod found his ideal and loving companion for life. From her he had three children, the sons Boris and Yury, and a daughter to whom he gave his favorite name Zina (as he did to the heroine of *The Enchantment*). Vsevolod's son from his first marriage, Sergey, found himself in a tragic position between his father and mother. He grew up a handsome, brilliant, and talented boy, but his nerves were highly strung. He died soon after his father's death, leaving a wife and daughter. Vsevolod Sergeevich's first marriage had already provoked the indignation of his father, and his judgment in the matter had become law for the family. Although the father was no longer alive at the time of Vsevolod's divorce and remarriage to his sister-in-law, one can imagine how these events were met with in the family. Vladimir Sergeevich made a point of maintaining relations with Olga Iosifovna, having broken every tie with his brother. "I have seen Olga and Seryozha twice, they are doing well," he wrote to his mother on 27 January 1886.[12] "I see her (Olga) often enough. For the time being she is all right. She brought Seryozha with her, whom I like more than before, although he is completely unmanageable. He must certainly be sent to *gymnasium*."[13]

At this point a new catastrophe befell Vsevolod Sergeevich. Living in Paris and restoring his shattered nerves, he fell into the company of Elena Petrovna Blavatskaya.* Sensing in him a mystically gifted nature inclined to spiritualism, Blavatskaya paid court to Vsevolod, and he temporarily came under her sway. She even began to prepare him for a trip to India, but he soon broke his ties with the Theosophical Society. After the death of Blavatskaya he wrote a book called *The Contemporary Priestess of Isis,* in which he exposed the fraudulent aspects of Theosophy. As a result of his misadventures, Vsevolod was utterly repudiated by his brothers and sisters. Only his mother and elder sister, Vera, the friend of his childhood, did not break with him.

A bitter hostility existed from an early age between Vsevolod and Vladimir. While still almost boys they had locked horns, having both fallen in love with their cousin Katya Romanova. (In Chapter Three we will mention in more detail the history of this relationship.) To a certain extent the relations between the brothers recall those between Dmitry and Ivan Karamazov. Although Vsevolod resembled Dmitry still less than Vladimir resembled Ivan, it is quite likely that Dostoevsky wrote *The Brothers Karamazov* under the influence of his acquaintance with the Solovyov brothers. This is all the more possible, as the third brother Mikhail (about

---

* Known to the English-speaking world as Mme Blavatsky (1831-1891).

whom Dostoevsky could have heard from both brothers), undoubtedly possessed some of the traits of Alyosha Karamazov, playing in his family the role of universal peacemaker and comforter. In particular, Vsevolod could have told something about his younger brother to Dostoevsky, to whom he was close, as the full break between Vsevolod and Mikhail occurred significantly later. However much the brothers had quarreled, their relations were not broken until Vsevolod Sergeevich published his father's autobiographical notes in *Russkii vestnik*.[14]

At that time, for reasons of censorship, these memoirs could not be published in their entirety. In his version of them, however, Vsevolod Sergeevich distorted his father's image beyond all recognition, discarding all the progressive, liberal passages, in favor of the conservative. The younger brothers Vladimir and Mikhail considered this a sacrilege, an outrage against their father's memory, and published a shrill protest in *Vestnik Evropy* with their signatures attached.[15] What else could be done? The distorted memoirs were in print and the liberal Sergey Mikhailovich had been converted by his *Kammerjunker* son into a conservative. As the complete text of the *Notes for My Children* could not be published, Vladimir Solovyov published an article in *Vestnik Evropy* entitled "S. M. Solovyov" with quotations from the *Notes* that revealed, on the one hand, the secret of the Solovyov family's clerical origins (concealed by Vsevolod), and on the other, the harsh opinions of the historian about Metropolitan Filaret. Relations between the brothers were sundered at this point and not renewed before their deaths. The sisters took the side of the younger brothers, while their mother and Vera Sergeevna tried to stay neutral. They had to maintain relations with Vsevolod on the sly because the brothers and sisters regarded every sign of sympathy for Vsevolod as complicity in his crime. To make matters worse, everyone involved had an irascible and stubborn personality...

For all his difficult inner experiences, in terms of material conditions Vsevolod lived incomparably better than his brothers. In St. Petersburg he had a splendidly furnished apartment, with "the finest study", as they said, in the city. The cleanliness and comfort of the apartment, with its mirrors, old paintings, and modern bathroom, can be explained by the fact that his wife was Dutch and that her brother Oscar was married to an Englishwoman. Vsevolod Sergeevich compensated for the unsympathetic attitude of society and literary circles by enjoying the fame of being an all-Russian writer and the favor he enjoyed in ruling spheres. In contrast to his father and brothers, Vsevolod was a monarchist without reservations and an Orthodox follower of Father Ioann of Kronshtadt,* who baptized his children. He treated his brother Vladimir with disdain and maligned him by saying, "he hoped to become a Roman cardinal." But the death of Vsevolod was unexpected and strange. He survived his brother Vladimir by only three years and died on 20 October 1903, in the same year as his brother Mikhail, who survived him by a few months. In the autumn of 1903 Vsevolod had come to Moscow on business, despite being thoroughly ill. His condition became acute and he was forced to go to hospital. His wife and children came from St. Petersburg to visit for a few days and then returned home. Meanwhile, his illness took a rapid turn for the worse and he died in the hospital in the arms of his favorite sister Vera, who looked after him unselfishly to his last day. His nephew Sergey Nilovich Popov (Vera's son) also visited him. He was a young man of great kindness who was especially fond of his uncle Mikhail, but who also managed to be on good terms with all his uncles; with Vladimir he drank, with Vsevolod he dined, and with Mikhail he went to the races. He acted as a nurse to his dying uncles Mikhail and Vsevolod and received their last breaths. Vsevolod died quietly. Speaking with his sister about his unsuccessful life he remarked, "My whole life I have played Don Quixote."

Of course, in the dispute among the brothers, truth was not on the side of Vsevolod. But I cannot help thinking that, over the years, the feeling of a bitter injury grew inside Vsevolod, with the awareness that his brothers and sisters passed him by without considering his dark fate. In one of his unpublished poems he himself speaks of this destiny:

> I did not expect, nor seek, either strife or victories,
> I did not prepare my soul for storms or passions,
> In an incomprehensible foreboding of grief and disaster

---

* Father Ioann Sergiev of Kronshtadt (1830-1908), influential pastor, preacher, and miracle-worker. Later canonized by the Russian Orthodox Church.

I pined throughout my youth over my lot.

But if I could have discerned more clearly
The approaching gloom of *my strange fate*
It would have been better to die in the days of my youth,
It would have been better to depart from passions
and struggle.

I would not have languished for heavenly rays
For shining crests of mysterious mountains,
And in the madness of the heart, praying only to dreams,
I would not have understood the filth and shame of life.

And perhaps, I would have carried with me forever
The radiant star of the eternal spirit,
And that star would now be burning brightly
In that kingdom of light, the path to which I
will not find.

The consciousness that "the radiant star of the eternal spirit" is hiding in his soul, that this star is darkened by the filth and shame of passions, that he has lost his way to the heavenly homeland, for which he madly pines, is found throughout all Vsevolod Solovyov's poetry.

Yes, I fear that to the summons of the weary soul,
Laden with earthly cares,
No one will come to the sacred door
Nor will let me enter the brilliant chamber.

Yes, I fear that at the wonderful feast
I will enter, as the slave of life who has
Partaken of the evil of the day,
And the golden shades will flee from me in terror.

This conception of his soul, as a celestial ray of light trapped in the mire of the material world, drew Vsevolod Sergeevich to Buddhism. He studied a great deal of Indian philosophy and wrote a poem entitled "Buddha." In his novel *The Exile* the hero discovers for himself that the only escape from the tragic conflict of life is to abandon his entire past and to leave for India. Subsequently, this interest in the wisdom of Hinduism yielded more and more to a simple, heartfelt faith. In his novel *The Great Rosicrucian* the simple, humble village priest Father Nikolay is juxtaposed to the magician and occultist Prince Zakharev-Ovinov. After reading the novel Father Ioann of Kronshtadt declared, "Oh, Vsevolod Sergeevich! What a seer of the heart you are!"

Vsevolod was cut from an entirely different cloth than his father and brothers and, perhaps, only he accepted Russian Orthodoxy in its oriental guise with its "Tsar-Batyushka," its total passivity, humility, awareness of the fundamental corruption of human nature and the impotence of the individual before fate, and its hope for divine mercy. He did not love Peter the Great, the favorite hero of his father and brother; instead, his ideal was Tsar Aleksey Mikhailovich "the Most Serene."* From a letter of Aleksey Mikhailovich to Ordin-Nashchokin he borrowed the expression "evil whirlwinds" for the title of one of his novels. All the titles of his novels about contemporary life were characteristic of him: *The Enchantment*, *Evil Whirlwinds*, and *The Flowers of the Abyss* (this last one was never completed). The eerie, mysterious music of fate resonates throughout those works of Vsevolod Solovyov where he has discarded the sugary-smooth style of the patriotic novels ("But if I could have discerned more clearly the approaching gloom of my strange fate..."). "Some kind of evil whirlwinds have driven me my entire life," says Anikeev, the hero of *Evil Whirlwinds*. The author could have said the same thing about himself. He was a product entirely of the Romanov side of the family with its "enigmatically tragic fate."

Vsevolod Solovyov could have become a great and serious writer, had he understood better the nature of his talent and not been tempted by the cheap laurels, with which the readers of *Niva* crowned him. His favorite authors were Dostoevsky and Dickens, and he dreamed of becoming a Russian Dickens or Walter Scott. His dreams were not justified and he is almost forgotten by the Russian public. The wreath on his coffin with the inscription "To a Great Russian Writer" seemed an irony of fate. In society Vsevolod

---

* Father of Peter the Great, reigned from 1645 to 1676.

Sergeevich created a charming impression with his vitality and wit, although he did inspire a violent antipathy in many people. Even people who were hostile to him, however, delighted in his manner of reciting poetry. I have a charming childhood memory of meeting him in Moscow in September 1896. I was playing with the neighborhood children in the courtyard next door when my nanny ran in crying excitedly, "Uncle Vsevolod has arrived!" Along the way she told me with the same delight, "a fat man walks in and immediately embraces papa... Well, I think this is the St. Petersburg brother." Heavy and perfumed, Vsevolod Sergeevich sat next to my father, who was twice as thin as he. They were carrying on a lively conversation, complete with romantic memories, witticisms, and terrifying stories. Vsevolod was very much afraid of dead bodies, and when he came with his young son from St. Petersburg to view the coffin of his father, he immediately fainted upon entering the room. This trait prevented him from becoming a physician, to which he aspired in his youth. Upon his first entry into an anatomical theater he lost consciousness. This whole atmosphere of the romantic and the terrible, together with his many gifts and the splendid dinners with liqueurs that he would give at the Bolshoy Moskovsky, drew me at the age of ten to my stout St. Petersburg uncle. Of an evening I would enter the dark drawing room and if it smelled of scent, it meant that Vsevolod Sergeevich *had passed* through the room, and in fact, he would be sitting in my father's study, and my grandmother would delight in the spectacle of the brief reconciliation between the brothers. I listened with rapture to the terrible story of how Uncle Vsevolod once saw a deceased friend on a bench in the garden, then cried out and ran away. "Gray cat," Uncle Vsevolod turned to me, "now I will tell you how they used to beat me, it will be useful for you to hear this." Vsevolod's crime consisted in his stealing some kind of flagon from his mother's dressing table. The crime was revealed. "They decided to have me flogged. For this they always summoned my grandmother Elena Ivanovna. A certain part of my clothing is removed. Mama looks away in order not to see the torments of her son..." At this point the story was interrupted by the woeful cry of my grandmother, "Oh, Vsevolod! What are you telling!" followed by universal laughter.

Vera Sergeevna was a year younger than Vsevolod, and they grew up together. Vera resembled her father physically and, to some extent, mentally. She was fair, with large blue eyes, and bright golden curly hair. Of all the sisters, optimism, a steady character, and domesticity distinguished her. Like her father she was, above all, a person of duty. Strict with herself, she was also often strict with others. This severity, however, was mitigated by a great and active sense of charity. She married a professor of Russian history Nil Aleksandrovich Popov who came from a simple priest's family and was a typical representative of his class. He was a person of exceptional gentleness, good humor, and a positive cast of mind. Nil Aleksandrovich was many years older than his wife and their marriage was based, apparently, not on romantic passion but on feelings of respect and duty; it was completely happy. The large apartment of the Popovs in the building of the archives of the Ministry of Justice at Deviche Pole (Nil Aleksandrovich was director of the archives), created an impression of happy domestic coziness. The Popovs had one son and three daughters. The eldest daughter, Poliksena, dedicated herself to teaching, and to this day she is head of a *gymnasium* at Znamenka. Their son, Sergey Nilovich, became interested in literature in his youth. His first efforts in verse and prose were greeted sympathetically by his uncles Vsevolod and Mikhail, and he published a collection of stories *From the Kingdom of Idleness*, in which there is a great deal of humor and a feeling for nature.

Nil Aleksandrovich's death in 1891 weighed heavily on Vera Sergeevna. She became morose and, not confining herself to the upbringing of her children, devoted herself to philanthropy and the care of the sick, working in a hospital as a nurse. At the same time she strictly honored the memory of her departed relatives, tending their graves at the Novodevichy monastery and holding requiem services for them on the appointed days. Always in black, sad and severe, she seemed to reign in the vicinity of Deviche Pole, dividing her time between the hospital and the monastery. Her life was like the application of Kant's categorical imperative. Not long before her death she said to me, "I always do what seems to me particularly difficult and unpleasant."

On account of the similarity of their ages and inner qualities, Vladimir was drawn to his sister Nadezhda, who was two years his senior. She was a tall, beautiful, and proud girl. More than anything she valued wit; she loved the theater and a busy social life. With time she developed serious hysterical tendencies and often cried. Never marrying, she attached herself entirely to her old governess, Anna Kuzminichna, with whom she lived until the old woman's death. The other part of her self she gave to her brother Vladimir, who became her domestic idol. She was deeper and more refined than her elder sister, but her character was uneven, passionate and difficult.

The third daughter, Lyubov, was profoundly unhappy. Like Vsevolod, she was not loved by the family. Sergey Mikhailovich could not forgive her coarse tone and her attitude to her mother. Chivalrously devoted to his wife, Sergey Mikhailovich would not tolerate his children speaking disrespectfully to Poliksena Vladimirovna. If this occurred at dinner, without speaking, Sergey Mikhailovich would strike the table a few times with his heavy thumb and they would sit panic-stricken. The distinguishing feature of Lyubov's personality was a certain romanticism that in her later years turned into hypochondria. She married a Doctor D. V. Stepanov, but he soon died, leaving her with a son, Yury. The boy grew up chubby and flourishing, but he died suddenly as well. Lyubov was left entirely alone. She had no idea of how to keep track of her finances and, having quickly spent all of her father's inheritance, she became heavily dependent on her relatives. Her brother Vladimir helped her especially diligently, although he was as poor as a church mouse.[16] Lyubov also suffered from an unhealthy obesity and immobility. In early childhood I told my relatives, "I saw God in a dream. He looked like Aunt Lyuba and wore a green hat and played the violin." Evidently the concepts of the *immense* and the *infinite* had merged with my impression of Aunt Lyuba. It was extremely difficult to find a topic of conversation with Lyubov Sergeevna. I once exerted myself an entire evening and could force out of myself only one sentence, "Which do you prefer, tea or coffee?" Lyubov Sergeevna died alone in a hospital and good people, strangers, buried her.

The third brother, Mikhail, was my own father, therefore my judgments could be suspected of bias. But almost everyone who knew him recognized him to be an utterly exceptional man. For all his intellectual inclinations and his acute artistic taste, he was somewhat suppressed by his father and brother, and devoted his whole life to them. In childhood he felt a sense of reverence and adoration for Vladimir. When he had grown up a little he became his brother's first and almost only friend, and shared all of his ideas. "They're all swine but you," Vladimir Solovyov wrote in one of his letters to him.[17] Mikhail was a very proper, capable family man. "My dear Misha, my shaggy German [*nemchura mokhnataia*]," Vladimir addresses him.[18] After an intense period of mysticism in his youth, Mikhail Sergeevich showed more and more an inclination towards purely intellectual pursuits. Being officially only a teacher of geography at the Fourth Moscow *gymnasium*, he almost never left his study, reading in different languages and taking notes. In the summer he spent his time exclusively on gardening. In the 1880s, together with his brother, he devoted himself ardently to the idea of the reunion of the Churches. At this time he translated from Greek *The Didache of the Twelve Apostles*. Most of all he read in French; becoming carried away by Lammenais, he prepared to write a long study about him. Other French writers, such as Renan, Taine, Flaubert, and Zola had their influence on him. At the end of his life he was deeply involved in Scriptural criticism and subscribed to the new literature on the subject. He possessed a thorough knowledge of Hebrew and collaborated with Vladimir Solovyov in translating the dialogues of Plato. According to Fyodor Korsh and the reviewer of *Russkie vedemosti*, his translations were more successful than those of his brother. It turned out that he had a subtler knowledge of Greek and paid more attention to the artistic qualities of the finished product. He redid his translation of the *Apology of Socrates* three times.

From childhood Mikhail Sergeevich suffered from poor health. He developed a kidney disease at an early date, to which were added, at the end of his life, diseases of the liver and heart. Despite such infirmity, he was an unusually strong, sober and quiet man. Aside from spiritual strength he also possessed considerable physical strength, which he maintained by working constantly in the fresh air with a spade. He was a genuine gardener and subscribed to Immer's seed catalogue. Around the house he planted rare varieties of flowers and trees and laid out beds and paths. For his and his wife's family Mikhail Sergeevich, like his father, possessed an infallible moral authority. Family disorder and dissension deprived him of much time and energy as everyone turned to him as an intermediary. His mind was analytical, accurate, somewhat sarcastic and inclined to skepticism. His aesthetic interests held an important place in his life; he understood not only poetry but also painting and music. It seems that of all the sons he recalled his father the most. Like Sergey Mikhailovich, he could burst into such a fit of rage that everyone around him quaked. In appearance, however, he took after his priest grandfather. (In contrast to his father, his features were prominent and sharp.) With time, as a result of his continual reading of French literature, his face also began to resemble that of a medieval French knight: his pointed nose, clear blue eyes, and golden pointed beard were suited to the lace collar of a Guise. Vladimir Solovyov often turned to his younger brother for advice, and my father told me that Vladimir concealed from him his excessively harsh reaction to Strakhov, evidently fearing lest Misha exert his cooling influence on his polemical ardor. In a worldly sense, if Vladimir was foolishly extravagant, then Mikhail was sensibly generous. He hated stinginess, loved to dine in a good restaurant, and helped the poor continually. Like Vladimir he had for the destitute, in the words of Velichko, some kind of "mystical passion." When he was living in the country the poor would gather from the whole region and guard him on all his journeys. If a peasant's house burned down or if a cow died they would immediately set off "to Mikhail Serge'ich." But most of all, he loved the blind, and when the "Song of Lazarus" could be heard at the window he would go into ecstasy and distribute not coins but banknotes. Both brothers vividly expressed traits of St. Francis of Assisi, and Vladimir persuaded his brother to write a life of the "Seraphic Father" for the Pavlenko biographical series. Mikhail Sergeevich died at age forty-one in 1903. He is buried at the Novodevichy monastery among my mother's Kovalensky relatives, not far from the grave of his priest grandfather.

The youngest daughters, Maria and Poliksena, were Mikhail's friends. Maria resembled her younger brother a great deal. She had the same narrow face and blue eyes, but she also had something "Egyptian" about her. When Vladimir Solovyov, following his return from Egypt, caught sight of Maria lying on a sofa propping up her cheeks with both hands, he cried out, "What's this! What's this! It's Egyptian!" Afterwards he would call his sister either "Maria the Egyptian," or the "daughter of the pharaohs," or simply "the Egyptian." The younger sisters were more talented than the older ones. Maria had a fantastic and agitated soul. She sang splendidly and often passed into ecstasy. She married a specialist in Byzantine history Pavel Bezobrazov and had three daughters. Because of her inner nature, however, she was not suited to normal family life. She adored her husband and was prepared to make any sacrifice for the sake of her children, but something drew her away from earth. For a long time she lived in Paris with her cousin Ekaterina Selevina (née Romanova). She loved everything French and, unique among her sisters, shared her brother's attachment to Catholicism. Maria Sergeevna was extremely humble. Misfortunes befell her almost her entire life: poverty, the illnesses of her husband and children, degradations of all sorts. Her ecstatic nature and her mysticism, however, never failed her. She once glimpsed, beyond the gray sky of Vasilevsky Island, the radiance of paradise. She died in 1918 while taking her children, after her husband's death, away from starving St. Petersburg. On the train she caught typhus and died in the station at Kharkov, but for her, all earthly life was a station.

The youngest daughter, Poliksena, famous in literature under the name "Allegro," lives to this day. If there is a rule *de mortuis aut bene aut nihil*, then undoubtedly *de vivis nihil*. Therefore we shall be brief. Poliksena was richly endowed from childhood. She was interested in painting, singing, and poetry, and it is in the last that she has found her final vocation. She was much younger than Vladimir, but eventually their difference in age evened out. In St. Petersburg they drew much closer to each other; although moving in the circle of *Vestnik Evropy*, Vladimir Sergeevich thoroughly disapproved of his younger sister's enthusiasm for the current trends, the Merezhkovskys, and the circle of *Mir iskusstva*. Over the years her resemblance to her father and brother has grown considerably. In many essential ways she recalls Vladimir Solovyov more than any other member of the family: her dominant masculine character, her laughter, wit, and puns, and primarily, the belief, which permeates all her work, that "everything which revolves disappears in darkness" and that "only the sun of love remains motionless." When Poliksena Sergeevna gave an address on "the meaning of love" according to Vladimir Solovyov at the session of the St. Petersburg Religious-Philosophical Society dedicated to the tenth anniversary of Solovyov's death, many of the audience were stunned. In setting forth the ideas of her brother, Poliksena Sergeevna had only expounded her own sacred credo.

An introduction to the family in which Vladimir Solovyov grew up would not be complete without a mention of Anna Kuzminichna Kolerova, who, having entered the Solovyov household as a young woman to be governess to the Solovyov children, ended up becoming a member of the family for the rest of her life. A poor orphan, the daughter of a priest, she received her education in Odessa at school run by the Vorobyov sisters, who had a great influence on her. Vladimir Solovyov called her the "Prophetess Anna" because of her ability to have prophetic dreams. In general she was very *terre-à-terre*, but her attachment to the family was deep. Despite a certain querulousness, she was good-natured. Over the years Vladimir eventually forgave her limited worldview, her exclusive interest in the careers of her charges, and her not entirely delicate handling of his affairs of the heart; in short, everything about her which combined the psychology of a priest's daughter, a school-girl, and an old maid. Leaving aside elevated matters, Vladimir Solovyov could play checkers with the old lady for hours.

Such were the circumstances in which this strange and lonely boy, sunk in a world of mystical reveries, would grow up. Let us now turn to a description of his childhood.

Endnotes for Part 1 Chapter 1

---

1. See Vasilii Velichko, *Vladimir Solov'ev: zhizn' i tvoreniia*, (St. Petersburg, 1902): "His paternal ancestors in the fifth and sixth degrees were peasants" (21).
2. *Sobranie sochinenii Vladimira Solov'eva*, eds. Ernst Radlov and Sergei Solov'ev, 2nd ed., vols 1-10. (St. Petersburg: Prosveshchenie, 1911-1914), vol. 10, 208-209; afterwards, *SS*.
3. *Zapiski S. M. Solov'eva*.
4. Sergei M. Luk'ianov, *Materialy k biografii Solov'eva* , vols. 1-3. (Petrograd, 1916-1921), vol. 1, 7.
5. I have kept the autobiography of Vladimir Solovyov in its fragmentary, manuscript form. Several passages are completely illegible. Words are often not written out and occasionally, in place of a word, there is only an initial.
6. Velichko.
7. Luk'ianov, vol. 1, 10. While Lukyanov writes "Bzhesskaia," Fet and Solovyov wrote "Brzhesskaia."
8. *Pis'ma Vladimira Solov'eva*, ed. Ernst Radlov, vols. 1-4. (St. Petersburg, 1908-1923), vol. 3, 103; afterwards, *P*.
9. *Zapiski S. M. Solov'eva*, 146.
10. Luk'ianov, vol. 1, 17.
11. *P*, vol. 2, 9.
12. Ibid., 46.
13. Ibid., 47.
14. Russkii vestnik (Feb. 1896).
15. Vestnik Evropy (April 1896): 889.
16. *P*, vol. 2, "I hope that Lyuba is doing all right" (50).
17. *P*, vol. 4, 115.
18. Ibid.,

Part 1 - Chapter 2

Childhood and School Years

> A strange child I was then,
> Strange dreams had I.
> *V. Solovyov*

At the beginning of his *Notes for My Children* Sergey Solovyov states: "On the fifth of May 1820 at eleven o'clock in the evening, on the eve of Ascension, a son, Sergey, was born to the priest of the Moscow Commercial College; *a weak, sickly, prematurely born baby*, he did not open his eyes for an entire week and did not cry." Like his father, Vladimir Solovyov was born prematurely. "I was born a seven-month-old baby and was not strong enough at my birth to cry, but only let my mouth gape open without a sound, like a newborn sparrow."[1]

Vladimir Solovyov was born on 16 January 1853, the day of the Veneration of the Chains of the Apostle Peter. On account of the infant's weakness, the christening was postponed to 8 March when it was held at the Church of the Resurrection at Ostozhenko. The godparents were his grandfather Vladimir Pavlovich Romanov and his grandmother Elena Ivanovna Solovyova.

Velichko remarks about the childhood of Vladimir that he especially loved everything that conveyed the national spirit; he knew a multitude of folk songs and was literally in love with the coachman, a strapping fellow with a large beard who embodied the strength of the simple Russian people. He did not need or seek friends among children of his own age, having spiritually outgrown them early on, but he related to everything around him with such an extraordinary sensitivity and impressionability that he gave personal names even to inanimate objects. For example, he called his favorite book satchel Grisha and his pencil, which he usually carried on a long string over his shoulder like a sword, or around his neck, Andryushka. This childish trait later became the basis for one of his fundamental philosophical ideas and therefore deserves special attention. It is difficult to determine exactly when he began to acquire, or more correctly, to absorb greedily, the rudiments of the liberal arts; in any event, this happened at a very early age. Between the ages of six and seven he loved to pretend that he was a Spaniard and would throw the flaps of his coat over his shoulders like a real hidalgo and would tell his little sister Nadezhda, who was close to him in age and mentality, various improvised novellas in the spirit of medieval Castile.[2]

Aside from his mother and the governess Anna Kuzminichna, there was also a nanny, Anna, who came from the serfs belonging to Poliksena Solovyova to look after Vladimir and Nadezhda.[3] Until the end of her life, Anna would visit her former charges.

In his autobiography Vladimir Solovyov comments:

> Although he was not directly involved in our upbringing, our father exerted the most beneficial influence on us. Aside from the significance he held in the family as a man of moral authority wholly dedicated to intellectual labor and the life of the mind, he knew, without interfering in our lives as children, how to exercise the best influence on us at the most important moments of our, or at least of my, inner development. Thus, when as a child, I was possessed by such an extreme religious mania that I had decided not only to become a monk, but, in view of the possibility of the imminent arrival of the Antichrist, had begun to subject myself to every kind of self-torture in order to become accustomed to torments for the sake of the faith, my father, himself a deeply religious man but devoid of eccentricity, gave me on my name's day, along with the lives of the saints, Dr. Petiskus's *Olympus* which was amply illustrated with pictures of the Greek gods and goddesses. These bright pictures immediately captured my imagination and *broadened and mitigated my religiosity*.

With regard to the ascetic self-tortures of the boy Volodya, Velichko remarks, "He began to test and harden his will for the glory of God. In winter he purposefully removed his blanket and froze, and when his mother came to cover him, thinking that the blanket had slipped off in his sleep, the child asked that he not be prevented from doing what he thought necessary."[4]

The episode with the *Olympus* of Dr. Petiskus is utterly characteristic of both father and son. The bright images of the Olympians indeed *broadened* and *mitigated* the boy's religiosity. In his article of 1896 "S. M. Solov'ev," Vladimir Solovyov says about his father, "The breadth of his intellectual vision, which enlightened and humanized his patriotic feelings, exercised the same positive influence on his religious feelings. The profound heartfelt faith of the author of the *Notes* was perfectly free from that *tension* which a superficial view takes for strength."[5]

Throughout his life Solovyov felt the softening and broadening effect of the beauty of antiquity as an antidote to ascetic intensity and eccentricity. In 1882 in the poem "Three Heroic Feats" ["Tri podviga"] he recollects Pygmalion and Galatea, Perseus and Andromeda, Orpheus and Eurydice. At Easter in 1887 he declared, "My friend, then, as now, Adonis rose from the grave;" and at the end of his life, when passing Troy, he greeted the shade of Homer:

> Something here has been orphaned,
> Someone's lamp has gone out,
> Someone's joy has flown away,
> Someone sang – and fell silent.

For his recalling Adonis during the services of Holy Week and his address to his "dear friend," Solovyov was "very much in trouble" in the eyes of another not so much "dear" as severe friend, the old lady Anna Fyodorovna Aksakova, to whom he had to justify himself with great care. He wrote to her that he was thinking not of the Greek Adonis but of the Syriac *Adone* or *Adonae*, who had nothing to do with Aphrodite and whose name, being a true prefigurement of Christ, was the same as the Hebrew word for God *Adonai*. In the end, however, he could not resist aiming a barb against the asceticism of the Holy Fathers, "I must say about the Fathers of the Church, that their inability to appreciate beauty (either in the form of mythological representations or in the form of interesting ladies) is a type of one-sidedness that I do not envy in the least. With them Christianity finds itself in its most strained and exclusive state, it is not free; this is not the highest form of Christianity."[6] Evidently, Solovyov never forgot that along with the lives of the saints his father had given him Dr. Petiskus's *Olympus*...

While encouraging the aesthetic inclinations of his son, Sergey Mikhailovich also cultivated in him a love for natural science:

> Thanks to my father, children's books on natural sciences also formed an important element in my early reading and were not without influence on my further mental growth. I especially remember one little book with the title *The Cosmos* (not, of course, Humboldt's) with little colored pictures of various antediluvian animals. Even to the present day an understanding of the cosmogonic process is associated in my imagination with the notion of some kinds of earthly monsters.
>
> The social milieu of our family was extremely brilliant with respect to education and it undoubtedly exerted an indirect sway over my inner development. Among the closest friends of my father's who gathered once a week at our home were the most famous scholars and literary men of Moscow of that time.

In the autobiographical poem "Three Meetings" ["Tri svidaniia"], written between 26 and 29 September 1898, Solovyov recalls, "Thirty-six years have passed, / Since the childish soul unexpectedly felt / The pain of love with the anxiety of troubled dreams." His first passion was for Yulinka Sveshnikova, with whom he played on the Tversky boulevard. "In his ninth year," Velichko relates, "he knew his first love, childish but extremely ardent. He was captivated by the pretty Yulinka Sveshnikova who was his age, and the innocent courting began when, from among the entire crowd of children on the Tversky boulevard, he chose her alone to play and run with. . . . Yulinka soon preferred another to him. Noticing this he became passionately indignant and came to blows with his happy rival and on the next day he entered the following lines in his child's diary, "'I did not sleep all night; I got up late and pulled on my socks with difficulty.'"[7]

This little childish drama with its moments of passion that included a rival and a duel resulted in the "first meeting" with the mysterious heavenly friend. On the feast of the Ascension she appeared to him in church during the hymn of the Cherubim with a "radiant smile," "holding in her hand a flower from otherworldy lands." The flood of passions dried without a trace in the boy's soul; he became "blind to the things of the earth."

A duel, a duel! Liturgy on Ascension Day.
The soul rages in a flood of passionate torments.
Set aside... all earthly... cares...–
The singing poured forth, stood still, and died away.

The altar is revealed... But where is the priest, the
deacon?
And where the crowd of worshippers?
The flood of passions suddenly dried without a trace.
Azure around me, azure in my soul.

Penetrated by golden azure,
Holding in your hand a flower from otherworldly
lands,
You stood with a radiant smile,
Nodded to me and disappeared in mist.

The mysterious figure had already long before stared "on misty nights" into the window of the room where Volodya and his grandmother Elena Ivanovna slept.

Near, far, not here and not there,
In the kingdom of mystical reveries,
In the world invisible to mortal eyes,
Where there is neither laughter nor tears,

There, goddess, I first glimpsed you
On a misty night.

A strange child I was then,
Strange dreams had I.

In a strange form you appeared,
Your voice sounded vaguely,
And for a long time I took you
To be the troubled creation of a child's dream.

Thus the early childhood of Vladimir Solovyov passed in a large family under the benevolent aegis of his father and mother in reading *The School of Piety*, *The Lives of the Saints*, *Olympus*, and *The Cosmos*; first in fear of the Antichrist and in ascetic self-denial, then in paying court on the Tversky boulevard and in secret dreams about a heavenly friend. However, the age of reason soon arrived. If until recently Sergey Mikhailovich had had to moderate his son's ascetic impulses by distracting him from the Antichrist with pictures of the Olympians, then he soon had to wage an entirely different struggle with him: Volodya had become a complete nihilist. Developing, as always, his ideas to the end and not being satisfied with theory, he put his new beliefs into practice.

In August 1864 Vladimir Solovyov entered the third class at the first Moscow *gymnasium*; he was then eleven years and seven months old. The *gymnasium* was located by the Prechistensky gate on the Volkhonka. The parallel classes of the first *gymnasium*, which were originally housed in the same building, were reorganized within a year as the fifth *gymnasium*. Mikhail Malinovsky remained the director of both *gymnasia* until 1870. Accepted as pupil of the first *gymnasium*, Solovyov later transferred to the fifth where he completed his secondary education.[8]

In general, Vladimir was a successful student and received a 5 in all subjects, except for physics, mathematics, and cosmography, which did not come easily to him.[*] In one of his journals Malinovsky made the remark, "Pay attention to algebra." The passing grades in mathematics are explained, evidently, by the well-known leniency of the director and teachers to the son of the rector of the university and by his brilliant success in other subjects. In the yearly reports the final

---

[*] In Russia exams are graded on a scale of 1 to 5.

grade in math usually appears as a 3 or a 4, and only on the final certificate is there a 5 in all subjects. In this regard Aleksandr Shvarts, who was also a student at the first *gymnasium*, commented to Lukyanov, "I am sorry to say that, knowing my former director Malinovsky, I very much suspect that the sudden rise in the grades depended not so much on the achievements of Vladimir Sergeevich as on the diligence of Mikhail Afanasevich [Malinovsky]."[9]

The staff of the fifth gymnasium consisted of the following:

The Inspector D. F. Miller	Geography
The Priest I. F. Kasitsyn	Religion
A. L. Linberg	Geography
K. M. Tomson	German
D. F. Nazarov	Mathematics and Natural Science
V. P. Basov	Latin
E. V. Belyavsky	Russian
K. I. Zhinzifov	Greek
F. E. Budde	History
B. I. Dobromyslov	Latin

The caliber of the instructors was fairly high; in particular, the teacher of Russian, Belyavsky, was especially likable. "Being a deeply religious man and an advocate of implementing Russian national principles, he treated with harsh disdain those who manipulated these principles for the purpose of promoting obscurantism and the enslavement of the living forces of society and who aggravated the religious and national tensions of our fatherland."[10]

The students also loved the teacher of Greek, Zhinzifov, a Bulgarian national poet, who wrote under the pseudonym "Rayko." He was ardently devoted to Russia and saw in her the salvation of his homeland. In addition, he had a weakness for wine. After the final examinations he invited his students to his home and treated them to so much champagne that many of them had to spend the night.

The instructor of Latin, Basov, was an authority in his field and a strict teacher; he was generous with 1s. Basov was also the translator of Madvig's Latin grammar. The "good Greek" and "terrifying Latinist" was a general phenomenon in Russian *gymnasia* during the second half of the nineteenth century. The mathematician Nazarov was a thoroughly knowledgeable and interesting teacher; he treated Vladimir with special attention seeing that he had such difficulty with math. Budde, the good-natured German, was, however, a rather ineffective history teacher. The students made a laughingstock of him for his inability to express himself in Russian. "A translation of Weber served as a textbook of general history; stuffed with facts and dates it was hardly intelligible to those using it and difficult to assimilate. When the textbooks of Dmitry Ilovaysky appeared, the students breathed more freely and were taught Russian history according to them."[11]

The director behaved as an important dignitary; he would make his appearance at the gymnasium with the ribbon of an order around his neck, wearing a white tie, and holding a top hat in his hand. The students were rather afraid of him and did not like him to enter a classroom; but to the "rector's son" he showed great respect. On the occasion of Solovyov's defense of his master's thesis, Malinovsky sent this letter to his father:

> Dear Sir!
>
> It befell me yesterday to spend three and a half hours under the influence of a strong and pleasant charm such as I have not experienced in a long time and for which I was indebted on that day to the undoubtedly brilliant triumph of word and thought which I heard and saw coming from the unprecedentedly young candidate who with his talent utterly captivated the attention of several hundred listeners of diverse caliber and who won without exception the deepest sympathy of all the numerous solid representatives of the true intelligentsia of this capital city who had attended the defense.... The young magician who so wonderfully took possession of not only the sincere but also respectful sympathy of every one of us yesterday was, of course, as you realized from the first, Vladimir Solovyov, the former

> Volodya Solovyov of the fifth gymnasium on whom I once placed a gold medal.

Further on, Malinovsky congratulates the father on having "such a treasure as your Vladimir Sergeevich," and on his "significant triumph, a certain precedent for a long and gloriously fruitful scholarly career, inherited and happily continued by him from his father, famous in the world of learning and in the nation."[12]

Among Solovyov's friends at the *gymnasium* were a number of people who later made names for themselves: the famous historian Nikolay Kareev;[*] the younger son of the novelist Aleksey Pisemsky, Nikolay (his elder brother was a classmate of Vsevolod Solovyov's); and Prince Dmitry Tsertelev who later became a close friend of Vladimir. "I was in the same *gymnasium* with Solovyov," Tsertelev recalls in his memoirs, "and I still remember his thin, pale figure in the sixth year during breaks; but as he was a year ahead of me we were not acquainted and met only later when I was already in my first year at university. I remember that evening well. Several students from various departments had gathered at P. A. Zilov's and among them were Solovyov and Pisemsky."[13]

As a schoolboy Vladimir began to display a sense of mischief. "At *gymnasium*, he greatly developed as a person," Velichko declares, "he became cheerful, witty, sociable, and even mischievous. For a year and a half he even felt, one might say, a surge of adolescent militarism; he would rush to the windows if troops were passing by, attended parades and maneuvers, and ardently maintained the importance of bravery as the principal masculine virtue."[14] At the age of twelve or thirteen he "demonstrated with animation the great danger that China would represent in the future for Russia and all Europe."[15] Thus, all the germs of the future were already present in the boy; the fear of Antichrist, the idea of the yellow peril, the militarism of *Three Conversations*, and the certitude that "the sword and the cross are one."

---

[*] Nikolay Kareev (1851-1931), historian of the French Revolution

Vladimir was loved by his schoolmates and he himself behaved toward them as a loyal and courageous knight, as the following story of the teacher of Russian, Belyavsky testifies:

> The director was angry for some reason with the top student of one of the older classes and ordered him to wipe his name off the so-called golden board. After this was done, it appeared at the following lesson that all the names on the golden board, which at that time included seven, had been removed. An investigation began that led nowhere. Then the director, knowing that the students hid nothing from me and in view of a serious breakdown of order, asked me to find out who had done this. I was afraid to take on such a delicate commission; if the students would not tell me, then something of a shadow would fall between us and, meanwhile, if a bad student had done it, serious trouble could threaten him. I entered the classroom and looked at the board on which were only traces of the smeared yellow chalk. After seeing this, I asked, trying to remain calm, "Who did this?" Immediately, a tall handsome young man stood up and answered with long gravely lowered eyelashes, "I did it." This student was Vladimir Sergeevich Solovyov, who was the second student in the class, the first being Nikolay Kareev. "Why did you do this?" "If Kareev is removed from the board then we did not wish to remain on it." This was stated in such a way that I did not find it possible to show that I thought he had acted badly and I decided to report how the matter stood to the director. His situation was very difficult, he told me, as he would have to report this act of Solovyov's to his father, who was then rector of the university. I stated that according to my opinion as this deed confined itself solely to the breakdown of school discipline it should be punished only by the school and not be brought to the attention of his parents. How this matter ended, I do not know.[16]

Vladimir undoubtedly did not take part in sordid adventures, if there were such, among the *gymnasium* students. His inclination to romantic enthusiasms served him as a natural defense against the failings of youth. His friends teased him though on account of some girl named L–vich. It appears, however, that he did not have any conscious religious or moral restraints from the age of twelve, having undergone a severe religious crisis, with which we must become acquainted in detail. In his autobiography Solovyov explains:

> My independent mental development began at age thirteen with the onset of religious skepticism. The progression of my thoughts in this direction was perfectly logical and in four years I experienced one after the other all the phases of the negative development of European thought over the past four centuries. Passing from iconoclasm and doubt about the necessity of external religious practice, I advanced toward rationalism and disbelief in miracles and the divinity of Christ. I became a deist, then a pantheist, then an atheist and a materialist. I settled on each of these stages with enthusiasm and fanaticism. Thus, at the period of my Protestantism I did not confine myself to indifference to church services, about which I had previously been passionate, but surrendered myself to practical iconoclasm and threw out of the window onto a rubbish heap several icons that were in my room. When I hit upon the fact that there was no God and that there was only matter, I preached this new faith to one of my friends[17] with such fervor that instead of offering any objection he remarked, "I am amazed at only one thing, why you do not pray to this matter of yours?" My father, seeing clearly what was going on inside me restrained himself from direct counteraction, but indirectly tried to show me that he regarded my unbelief as an illness that saddened him greatly, but from which he was certain I would have to recover in the end. This attitude on the part of a man of intellectual and moral authority was, of course, the best; in any case it produced more of an effect on my stubborn and self-assured mind than direct arguments, against which I would always find something to object. My only recourse, then as now, was to convince myself that I was more intelligent, more

developed, and more perceptive than my father, which, of course, I could not do with complete confidence and an untroubled conscience. Therefore, I tried very hard not to raise this question which remained in the depths of my soul in the form of some kind of uneasiness that grew stronger when I noticed the signs of my father's hidden grief. My unbelief arose on its own, in opposition not only to the family milieu but also to many of my close friends with whom I argued constantly. Later, however, in the higher classes of the *gymnasium* my negative way of thinking was nourished by reading and conversation with two or three friends of a nihilist orientation. I found confirmation of my ideas in certain books, most all in the enormous eighteen volumes of the Belgian Professor Laurent, *Etudes sur l'histoire de l'humanité*, especially in the volume entitled *La philosophie du XVIIIe siècle et le christianisme*.* These books could be found in my father's study; I read them quietly away from him, mainly in the summer at the dacha when he would go to Moscow to work in the archives. Renan's *Vie de Jésus* disappointed me, partly, probably, because I had passionately wanted to read it and partly, perhaps, thanks to the lack of any real seriousness in this author's entire worldview with respect to religious subjects. My father, knowing with what difficulty and with what amount of money I acquired Renan's work, shrugged his shoulders and said, "Some guide you've found. You would have done better to read Salvador,† if you want something heavy in that field. Not only are Renan's ideas false, but so are his quotations."

An even less favorable impression was made on me by our native nihilists, among whom my older friend adored Pisarev‡ in particular.

I entered university with a completely determined and negative attitude toward religion along with the need for a new, positive intellectual sustenance. In the natural science, to

* François Laurent (1810-1887), jurist and historian at the University of Ghent.
† Joseph Salvador (1796-1873), French Jewish historian.
‡ Dmitry Pisarev (1840-1868), journalist, critic, and materialist philosopher.

> which I thought I would devote myself, the specific details did not interest me, but only the philosophical aspect. I therefore studied only two sciences, plant morphology and comparative anatomy. Having sought philosophy in science, I naturally turned to philosophy itself. My interest in it was stimulated, but not satisfied, by the famous work of Lewes.* After him I read Kuno Fischer,† the *Ethics* of Spinoza, the *Logic* of Hegel, and the main works of Feuerbach. Materialism, which I had reached through my own efforts earlier, now took on a refined idealistic character under the influence of Spinozism and Hegelianism.

Solovyov's nihilist phase lasted from age twelve to sixteen, that is from 1865 to 1869. During this period he let his hair grow. Although his long hair later made him look like a monk or a prophet, it first appeared as an expression of nihilism after the fashion of the '60s when long hair was considered a sign of freethinking. One cannot help wondering how Malinovsky, the director of exalted rank, reconciled himself to Vladimir's nihilism and long hair. It was probably possible for him to ignore the convictions of the rector's son, while in matters of hair and dress the *gymnasium* students of those years enjoyed great freedom. "As the form of dress for the students of the *gymnasium* and *progymnasium* at that time they introduced single-breasted caftans of dark green cloth with black buttons and a turnup collar with loops of blue cloth. The *gymnasium* students contrived, however, to remove these distinguishing loops and would then appear in public as 'civilians.' They wore this bluntly altered cut at home and when visiting."[18] When Anatoly Korsh met Solovyov at the home of his classmate Pisemsky, Solovyov was in "civilian" clothes and looked like a dandy; he was wearing "a fashionable cravat of the period with wide embroidered ends."[19] In general, the atmosphere at the *gymnasium* in the '60s was friendly, if one considers the degree of familiarity that existed between the teachers and pupils. Within a few years all this would change with the reforms of Dmitry Tolstoy who instituted a reign of bureaucratic conformism:

---

* George Henry Lewes (1817-1878), English philosopher and critic.

† Kuno Fischer (1824-1907), Silesian philosopher.

uniforms, knapsacks, smoothly shaved heads. My father, who graduated from the first *gymnasium*, hated it with all his might and told me how he envied the students of the Polivanov *gymnasium* their ordinary clothes, black jackets, and soft caps... If he were with someone in a cab passing the first *gymnasium* he would ask ostentatiously, "What building is this?"

Lopatin attests to the extremes of Solovyov's atheism. "I never met later such a passionately convinced materialist. He was a typical nihilist of the '60s."[20] To his friends, such as Lopatin, who was two years younger, Solovyov seemed to be a "Satan," a dangerous tempter.

> Solovyov shook my naive childish faith to its foundations when I was, at most, twelve years old, and since then I have had to construct, prematurely and tortuously, my own worldview in a constant struggle with him. This struggle lost its edge around the time of my fifteenth birthday when we agreed on philosophical idealism.... Only when I turned seventeen did I truly become of the same mind as Solovyov. At that point he had already passed through his enthusiasm for Schopenhauer and, after that, for Hartmann,* and had firmly settled on the speculative truth of Christianity. He was now ahead of me as a defender of true religious beliefs.[21]

The following story by Lopatin shows how Solovyov, not being satisfied by theory, would put his convictions into practice. "I remember how walking in Pokrovskoe-Glebovo we once wandered into a cemetery and Solovyov, in a fit of violent freethinking, knocked over the cross on a grave and began to jump on it, to the great embarrassment, and even fright, of my brother and me. A local peasant caught sight of this and ran up to us swearing with the most foul language. It was a good thing that the matter ended only with this!"[22]

Solovyov also managed to disturb another devout friend, Nikolay Kareev, by declaring that he did not believe in relics.[23]

---

* Eduard von Hartmann (1842-1906) attempted a synthesis of speculative idealism and the natural sciences.

Velichko informs us that Vladimir commented to his father concerning Laurent's work, "Christianity is pretty well taken care of here," to which Sergey Mikhailovich replied with a line from *Domostroi*,* "You deserve a good box on the ears for that."[24] Kareev, however, expresses doubt about the plausibility of this story,[25] and it seems to me as well that such a conversation was not possible between father and son. In his autobiography Solovyov states, first of all, that his father refrained from direct arguments, and secondly, that he read Laurent on the sly from his father when he was away from the dacha in Moscow. Besides, however quick-tempered Sergey Mikhailovich might have been, the phrase, "You deserve a box on the ears for that," was decidedly not in keeping with the general spirit of his pedagogy. He was "saddened" by his son's atheism and knew very well that this sorrow would act on the boy's feelings better than the measures recommended by *Domostroi*.

Solovyov studied at the *gymnasium* from 1864 to 1869 and entered university at age sixteen. His rapid familiarity with all the phases of European thought over the last four centuries coincided exactly with these years at the *gymnasium*. By his own account, from age twelve Vladimir experienced in succession: Protestantism, "iconoclasm," deism, pantheism, and materialism. By age fourteen he had moved on to pure materialism and atheism. At sixteen Spinoza fell into his hands, which was for him like St. Augustine's discovery of Plato, the threshold of a positive religious worldview. As a student, Solovyov was still very far from Christianity, and even farther from the definite ecclesiastical position that he reached in the '80s. One cannot help asking at this point, if Solovyov experienced, by his own admission, pantheism before materialism, how was it possible that the pantheism of Spinoza became a way out of materialism for him? If his autobiography was not at our disposal, his evolution would seem to have been as follows: at age twelve his child's faith yielded to iconoclasm and the denial of relics and all church ritual, after which he became a materialist until his discovery at sixteen of Spinoza, that is, of pantheism. In his autobiography, however, Solovyov indicates

---

* Literally *Household Management*. A popular work of Old Russia that prescribed all aspects of social behavior according to religious authority and traditional family obligations.

that in the course of four years he experienced both deism and pantheism before materialism. Two solutions to this question are possible. Either Solovyov went through deism and pantheism quickly and superficially before his materialist phase at fourteen, after which he arrived consciously at pantheism under the influence of Spinoza, or else, in composing his autobiography he somewhat schematized his adolescent evolution by attributing to himself the progression of European thought in the same sequence and logic. In any case, Solovyov did not pass directly from atheism to the Christian faith, and from age sixteen he underwent a complicated philosophical evolution that led from Spinoza and Hegel,–by way of Kant, –to Schopenhauer and Schelling.

A description of Solovyov's adolescence would not be complete without mention of his relations with the Lopatin family, which was extremely close to the Solovyov household. Mikhail Nikolaevich Lopatin was a friend of Sergey Mikhailovich and a man of moderately liberal tendencies who worked in various judicial departments in Moscow.[26]

Lopatin's wife, Ekaterina Lvovna, née Chebysheva, was the sister of the famous mathematician Pafnuty Chebyshev. The Lopatins lived in a house of their own in the Gagarinsky lane; it was comfortable and old-fashioned with an entresol and a deep, shady garden. The Lopatins' elder sons, Nikolay and Lev, were about the same age as Vladimir Solovyov, while their younger son Vladimir was the same age as Mikhail Solovyov and his close friend. Nikolay possessed an expansive Russian nature and was known for his physical strength and dexterity, and his splendid renditions of Russian songs. Lev was a quiet, self-contained boy who was inclined to philosophy. In a letter to Stasyulevich, Solovyov related some of his adventures with the Lopatin brothers around the village of Pokrovskoe-Glebovo:

> The author of the book under discussion (L. M. Lopatin) and his elder brothers were the first friends of my childhood, adolescence, and youth. It was especially during this middle period that we became very close to one another, sharing our common perils and successes. We were students in different

schools[27] but we spent our summers together in the village of Pokrovskoe-Glebovo-Streshnevo near Moscow, where our parents had their dachas for many years. At that time our main objective consisted in inspiring terror in the inhabitants of Pokrovskoe, in particular those of the female sex. Thus, for example, when the residents of the dachas were bathing in the Khimki stream that flowed a verst from the village we would rush up to the bathers and would cry with our voices disguised: "Fire! Fire! Pokrovskoe is on fire!" and they would have to throw on whatever was at hand while we would leap into the bushes, delighting in our triumph. We also invented and skillfully spread rumors about ghostly apparitions which we then acted ourselves. The eldest Lopatin (not the philosopher) was distinguished among us by his physical strength and dexterity, and was also a great master of producing wild and terrifying sounds. He seated me on his shoulders while the other brother covered us with a white sheet. This figure of unusual shape and size then suddenly emerged out of the cemetery next to the park on a moonlit night when the public, composed especially of ladies, was walking in the park. It first moved slowly into the distance and then rushed at a full gallop into the very midst of the strollers, emitting inhuman shrieks. For the other classes of the local population we arranged the arrival of the Antichrist. As a result the peasants dragged us by our collars to our parents more than once, and the Pokrovskoe priest, no stranger to literature, bestowed on us the name the "Robber Brothers" that stuck with us. The three actresses who lived in Pokrovskoe, Mesdames Sobeshchanskaya, Voronova, and Schubert, became the special object of my persecutions and arranged to have me flogged, but to my greatest sorrow this intention was not carried out for some reason. Sometimes, however, our pursuits took on a more scientific character. Thus, we became interested in observing the history of the development of amphibia, for which we released into a basin that we specially built a multitude of tadpoles which, however, soon died on account of the discomfort of the

> premises without attaining the higher stages of development. Moreover, we had had the sense to construct our zoological station just under the windows of my father's study, who declared that we ourselves formed an object worthy of zoological observations, for which, however, he had no time. We then turned to the practical study of geography; my special task was to investigate the currents of streams and rivulets, and the depths of ponds and marshes, while the active role of my friends consisted for the most part in turning to strangers for help in rescuing me from dangerous situations.[28]

The friendship between Lev Lopatin and Solovyov lasted to the end of his life. We have already seen how in adolescence "Levushka" was troubled by his older friend's atheist fanaticism and that he had to work out his views in conflict with Solovyov. They agreed at one point on "philosophical idealism," but not for long. First of all, in the realm of pure philosophy they were drawn together mostly by a negative attitude, a common hostility to positivism and materialism. In this respect Solovyov's *Critique of Abstract Principles* corresponds to several ideas in the critical chapters of Lopatin's *The Positive Tasks of Philosophy*, but differs from it in the method of proofs. In terms of personal doctrine, the philosopher-friends diverged quite markedly from each other. Whereas Solovyov derived his philosophy from Spinoza, Hegel, and Schelling, and always inclined toward natural philosophy; Lopatin was close to Cartesianism. In the '90s polemics flared up between the two friends on the matters of free will, the concept of substance, and phenomenalism, which we will discuss later. Furthermore, Solovyov did not remain attached to the position of "philosophical idealism," and in the '80s he would adopt a purely ecclesiastical worldview with a strong Catholic tendency. Lopatin did not regard with sympathy his friend's new faith, to which Solovyov surrendered himself with all the consistency and stubbornness with which he had clung to his "faith in matter" at fourteen. Lopatin also differed from Solovyov on account of the latter's "radicalism": to the end of his life Solovyov continued to evolve, while Lopatin, having created his system early in life, settled down and firmly held to his positions once they were formed. This difference, however, did not prevent Lopatin from providing a splendid description of Solovyov's philosophy and from recognizing his childhood friend to be "the most original philosopher in all Europe in the last twenty-five years."[29]

A shared love of the fantastic and terrible made the two friends especially close. Lopatin was famous in Moscow for his talent for telling frightening stories. Solovyov dedicated his eerie poem "The Sorcerer-Stone" to him. Throughout his life Lopatin was deeply involved in hypnotism and spiritism. Although Solovyov was an enthusiast in his youth for table turning, he subsequently spoke harshly about such pursuits. He liked Ivan Aksakov's saying that spiritism was a "revelation from the back door." "My friend Lopatin," he writes to Strakhov,* "is seriously involved in hypnotism thinking that he can prove by this means the existence of the divinity and the immortality of the soul. I tried to prove to him that this is none other than the worst form of sodomy."[30]

Solovyov loved to tease his friend good-naturedly. He addressed one letter to him first as: "To Tigris Mikhailovich Lopatin", then: "To *Euphrates* Mikhailovich," and finally, having crossed out "Tigris" and "Euphrates," he wrote: "To Lev." [i. e. "To Leo"]. Usually he called him "Levon" as did the rest of his circle of friends from the Polivanov *gymnasium*. Solovyov once played on him the following trick; he composed a poem that was supposedly by Lev Mikhailovich, forged his signature, and inserted the piece of paper in a book that Lev had lent him. Solovyov returned the book to Lopatin in company and made a gloomy face saying worriedly, "I advise you to be more careful, you forgot a highly dangerous document in your book." As Lev Mikhailovich become upset Solovyov pulled out the piece of paper and read the poem in which each stanza began with the words, "Ah, madam, madam, madam!" "Ah, madam, madam, madam! / For you I will give all … / If you are Eve, and I am Adam…" etc. Lev Mikhailovich soon calmed down. When Solovyov censures Puskhkin for his epigrams the parable about the mote and

---

* Nikolay Strakhov (1828-1896), critic, essayist, and philosopher. Of a Hegelian orientation, Strakhov maintained a holistic philosophy and an "organic" view of Russian history; he was close to both Dostoevsky and Tolstoy.

the log inevitably comes to mind. For the sake of a witticism Solovyov spared neither his father nor mother…

Turning to the university years of Solovyov, we bid farewell to Pokrovskoe-Glebovo where the boy Volodya received his first impressions of nature, where he first learned to love the Sovereign-Earth. Abandoning Pokrovskoe, Sergey Mikhailovich began to spend his summers at a dacha at Neskuchny Sad, where Vladimir Solovyov dated his first poetical efforts. Till the end of his life, however, Solovyov retained a fondness for Pokrovskoe and loved to make his way there on foot from Moscow jumping over fences and recalling episodes of the "Robber Brothers." Pokrovskoe is now a station on the Moscow-Vindavsk railway line; when the train stops at "Pokrovskoe-Streshnevo" the splendid melancholy landscape spreads beyond the window. Pokrovskoe is all overgrown with pensive weeping willows drooping their branches over the ponds that are drying up and gradually turning into marshes.

One more childhood memory is connected with Pokrovskoe. Two years before his death, in an attempt to reanimate the ideals of social justice, Solovyov made some sympathetic notes about Chernyshevsky.* He characterized him as person without "any kind of pose, tension, or tragic self-pity; there was nothing personal or evil about him, only an extreme simplicity and dignity;" and concluded, "Above the ruin of a mercilessly broken existence there arises the quiet, sad, and noble image of a wise and just man."

The spark of sympathy toward Chernyshevsky was struck in Solovyov during the summer of 1864 before he entered the *gymnasium*.

> One summer evening stands out clearly among my adolescent memories. We lived not far from Moscow in a dacha in the village of Pokrovskoe-Glebovo. My father, who did not work any less in the summer than in the winter, would

---

* Nikolay Chernyshevsky (1828-1889), radical journalist, critic, thinker, revolutionary, and author of the famous novel *What is to Be Done?*(1863). Arrested in 1862 for his participation in student and peasant disturbances, Chernyshevsky was sentenced in 1864 to seven years of hard labor in Siberia and twelve years of exile in the Arctic.

devote only Sunday to his children and acquaintances who would come from Moscow and the area around it for the whole day. The evening I am recalling, however, was not on a Sunday; after dinner Evgeny Fyodorovich Korsh* and Nikolay Khristoforovich Ketcher† arrived unexpectedly. Because of my age I was not in a position to appreciate Korsh as I should have, with his great erudition and fine wit that made an even stronger impression (on adults) on account of his habitual stutter. All the same, I loved Ketcher from early childhood with his (then) close-cropped hair, his immense straw hat, and his very wide, but too short, sailcloth trousers, which he would apparently also wear in winter, and for the fierce good-natured expression on his face, and, finally, his loud cheerful voice and unceremonious jokes with everybody that were accompanied by a loud laugh: *Dulce ridentem Lalagen amabam / Dulce loquentem.*‡

The guests had something to tell my father and they were getting ready to join him on his customary evening walk. I asked to go with them, and my father, after a moment's hesitation, agreed. But my hopes for the entertaining conversation of Ketcher were not realized. He was gloomy and did not laugh at all. It turned out that he and Korsh had come to convey the news, which they had only just received from St. Petersburg, of the verdict that had been passed by the special Senate court which sentenced the famous writer Chernyshevsky, who was accused of a political crime, to hard labor in Siberia. Both guests looked despondent, but my father, agitated and with his face flushed, spoke in a strained indignant whisper that from time to time turned into a shriek.[31]

We cannot help observing that the quotation from Horace is inserted here inappropriately; did Ketcher's laugh really recall the

* Evgeny Korsh (1810-1897), liberal journalist and editor.
† Nikolay Ketcher (1809-1886), physician and man of letters.
‡ "I loved Lalaga sweetly laughing / Sweetly murmuring."

"sweet laughter" of smooth-tongued Lalaga? Fet, however, did not address these lines to Solovyov in vain:

> Let that time not be forgotten and let
> Those days return to us
> When with your lips
> Catullus recited to me.

Endnotes for Part 1 Chapter 2

[1]. *P,* vol. 1, 150.

[2]. Velichko, 9-11.

[3]. Luk'ianov, vol.1, 38.

[4]. Velichko, 11.

[5]. *SS*, vol. 7, 355.

[6]. The letters to Anna Aksakova have not yet been published.

[7]. Velichko, 12.

[8]. Information about the student years of Vladimir Solovyov is taken from Lukyanov's *Materialy*, vol. 1, 63-91.

[9]. Luk'ianov, vol. 1, 64-5.

[10]. Ibid., 73.

[11]. Ibid., 71.

[12]. Velichko, 23-25.

[13]. D. N. Tsertelev, "Iz vospominanii o Vl. Solov'eve," *S.-Peterburgskie vedemosti* 211 (1910).

[14]. Velichko, 14.

[15]. L. M. Lopatin, "Vl. Solov'ev i kniaz' E. N. Trubetskoi," *VFP* (Sept.-Oct. 1913): 356.

[16]. Luk'ianov, vol. 1, 121.

[17]. This friend was probably Lopatin.

[18]. Luk'ianov, vol. 1, 124.

[19]. Ibid., 124.

[20]. L. M. Lopatin, *Filosofskie kharakteristiki i rechi*, 123.

[21]. L. M. Lopatin, "V.S. Solov'ev i E. N. Trubetskoi," *VFP*, 11 (1913): 345-46.

[22]. Lopatin, "V.S. Solov'ev i E. N. Trubetskoi," 356, note.

[23]. Luk'ianov, vol. 1, 112.

[24]. Velichko, 15, 16.

[25]. Luk'ianov, vol. 1, 110.

[26]. Ibid., 105.

[27]. Lopatin was in the Polivanov *gymnasium*, while Solovyov was in the fifth.

[28]. "M. M. Stasiulevich i ego sovremenniki v ikh perepiske," ed. M. K. Lemke, vol. 5, 370-72.

[29]. Lopatin, "Filosofskie kharakteristiki i rechi," 120.

[30]. *P*, vol. 1, 50.

[31]. *SS*, vol. 12, 338.

.

Part 1 - Chapter 3

University – Katya Romanova

Oh, if in exchange for the bitter suffering,
To which a fatal will has condemned me,
I could give you golden days and years,
Together with the most beautiful flowers,
So that in a new world of light and freedom
You could rest from the malice of life!

V. Solovyov

Vladimir Solovyov entered Moscow University in the autumn of 1869 and spent exactly four years there. His life as a student did not flow smoothly, however, and it is no easy task to reconstruct now his meandering between the department of physics and mathematics and the department of history and philology. Solovyov entered university at sixteen when he had only just begun to abandon his adolescent materialism under the influence of Spinoza. As his main interest was, of course, philosophy (which at that time was taught by Pamfil Yurkevich),* he first enrolled, in accordance with his historian-father's wishes, in the department of history and philology. During the first year, however, he transferred to the department of physics and mathematics; evidently his long-standing interest in natural philosophy compelled him to pursue science in earnest: "I entered the University with a completely determined and negative attitude toward religion along with the need for a new, positive intellectual sustenance. In the natural sciences, to which I thought I would devote myself, the specific details did not interest me, but only general conclusions and the philosophical aspect. I therefore studied seriously only two sciences, plant morphology and comparative anatomy."

---

* Pamfil Yurkevich (1827-1874), while professor of philosophy at the University of Moscow opposed the influence of materialism.

The professor of botany Nikolay Kaufman wrote about Solovyov after his exams, "The examination I gave the son of Sergey Mikhailovich was a real feast of the soul. I was delighted by his answers and his brilliant, unexpected generalizations. At that time there was no doubt in my mind about his genius, which was subsequently recognized."[1] According to Nikolay Kareev, the unfavorable impression left by the study of Greek under professor Felkol appears to have precipitated Solovyov's withdrawal from the philological department.[2] Besides botany and comparative anatomy, however, physics and mathematics were also taught in the same department, subjects that had always been a stumbling block for Solovyov. "As far as I can recall," Kareev notes, "even in the first year Solovyov encountered some kind of trouble in analytical geometry, from which Prof. Zinger would cut students mercilessly."[3] Difficulties of a similar kind repeated themselves and resulted in Solovyov's failing the exams and withdrawing from the science courses.

In his "Curriculum vitae" Solovyov states, "In 1872 I left the department of physics and mathematics and enrolled in the department of philology and history (at the same university) as an auditor."[4]

Solovyov did not make it to the fourth year in physics and mathematics, but spent two years in one of the lower courses. Velichko reports that the failed examination occurred between the second and third years, which suggests that Solovyov repeated the second year. Lukyanov, however, considers that in spite of his poor grades he could have advanced to the third year if he had received a 2 (and not a 1 or a 0) and cites Lopatin's testimony that Solovyov spent two years in the third-year course, without taking the sessional exams in 1872. His failure in physics could not have taken place at this time, however, as it was taken only in the first two years. As far as my own recollections are concerned, I remember some of Solovyov's remarks about his unsuccessful exams that my father passed on to me. On one occasion he stamped his foot and repeated only the words, "Let us take a plate," a phrase he evidently learned in a physics class. Another time, Solovyov tried to convince an examiner that the differences in the structures of the reproductive organs of men and women corresponded to their mental differences. The examiner interrupted him somberly, "You will spare me this philosophy and draw the fallopian tubes instead," which Solovyov could not do… The problem on this occasion was obviously one of anatomy, not physics.

Solovyov's decision to study in the physics and mathematics department and take courses in the sciences did not happen, of course, by accident. Natural science exerted a great influence on him, and he always kept a certain attachment to the theory of Darwin, defending him against the attacks of Strakhov and Danilevsky.* He also made use of the idea of natural selection in his article "About Beauty in Nature" and *The Meaning of Love*. In his article of 1899 "The Idea of the Superman" Solovyov states:

> I in no way regret that at one time the greatest objects of my love were palaeosauri and mastodons. Although "philanthropy for small beasts," to use an expression of one of Dostoevsky's heroes, compels me to feel even now certain pangs of conscience for those leeches that I dissected with a razor in order to obtain a "cross-section," (especially as this was a pointless act of evil), and just as my efforts in histology were more fatal for the government-issued microscopes than they were edifying for me, I remember only with gratitude, having repented of the unjust destruction of these younger kin, my past enthusiasm. I know that it was useful for me, and I think it was also necessary and useful for all of Russian society in its younger generations, to pass through the cult of natural science after the abstractions of Hegelianism.[5]

Thus, even in his student years Solovyov felt "philanthropy for small beasts" and an aversion toward vivisection. In a letter to his cousin Katya he speaks with indignation about those who "cut up unfortunate animals."[6]

---

* Nikolay Danilevsky (1822-1885), natural scientist and theoretician of a pan-Slavism. Danilevsky believed it was Russia's destiny to assert its specific "Slavic historico-cultural type." He also envisaged the creation of a new pan-Slavic empire based in Constantinople. His *Russia and Europe* was first published in 1869 and went into three editions by the time of his death.

Solovyov was, of course, a poor natural scientist. In the third year of his studies in the department of physics and mathematics (1871-1872), after repeated failures with microscopes, plates, and test tubes, he began to feel disgusted with science. "Do not study anything too assiduously," he writes to Katya on 12 October 1871, "and for God's sake not the natural sciences. By itself this knowledge is perfectly empty and illusory. Only *human* nature and life are worthy of study in themselves, and one can get to know them best of all in works of true poetry; therefore I advise you to read the great poets as much as possible."[7] He writes even more harshly on 26 March 1872, not long, evidently, before the third-year exams that he did not take:

> I am of the opinion that *to study* the vain illusions of external phenomena is still more stupid than *to live* by vain illusions. But the main point is that this "science" cannot attain its goal. People look into microscopes, cut up unfortunate animals, boil some kind of rubbish in chemical retorts and imagine that they are studying nature! One should inscribe on the foreheads of these asses:
>
> Nature does not allow the veil
> To be removed from her body,
> And you cannot force out with machines
> That which your spirit cannot divine.
> Instead of living nature, they embrace her dead skeletons.[8]

Of course, in such a mood it was difficult to devote himself to exams. In general, Solovyov's ties with the university were weak. Afterwards, having entered the Religious Academy as an auditor, he commented to Katya, "In any event, the Academy does not present such absolute emptiness as the University."[9] In the '90s when the chair of philosophy at Moscow University was occupied by Solovyov's younger friend Lev Lopatin and his disciple Sergey Trubetskoy, Solovyov himself was only a *privatdocent* in retirement. During the time he was enrolled, Lukyanov maintains, "Solovyov had little sympathy for 'university affairs.'" While he was a student he kept strictly to himself and was involved in non-university life as much as, if not more than, in university life. According to Kareev's apt expression, "Solovyov did not exist as a student and had no friends at the university. Among university people he was considered to be some kind of eccentric dissident, even at the time when he should have been occupying a position in the ranks of the professors first of Moscow, then of St. Petersburg."[10]

Solovyov attended with interest the lectures given by Sergey Usov and Nikolay Bugaev, professors with aspirations toward philosophy. All the same, Lukyanov claimed accurately enough, "There was not one professor at Moscow University about whom we could say that he was an immediate influence or an overwhelming inspiration to Solovyov; neither can we acknowledge the right of any of his classmates to the title of intimate or like-minded friend."[11] The only exception was Yurkevich, in whom Solovyov found a genuine teacher, a sympathetic mentor, and a guide to whom he was indebted as much for his help in university matters as in philosophy.

On 18 April 1873 Solovyov submitted two petitions, the first, for withdrawal from the student body; the second, for permission to be admitted to the examinations for the degree of *kandidat* in the department of history and philology. In accordance with the petition, Solovyov was withdrawn from the university and accepted in the capacity of a former student and a private individual for the exams. (Solovyov was never an "auditor" as he claimed in his "Curriculum vitae.") On 7 June, seven weeks after submitting the petition, Solovyov successfully passed the exams in history and philology and was awarded the degree of *kandidat*. He received a 5 in all subjects, except for Greek and ancient history, in which he received a 4. Lukyanov suggests that the professors did not make the same strict demands on him as they did on the full-time students of the department. "Considering that Solovyov took his exams as a private individual, and in view of his exceptional aptitude," affirms Vladimir Gérié, "I did not demand a special knowledge of history from him on his exam, as I would have of a student of our department. I knew that even as a *gymnasium* student he had read all the volumes of his father's history that had been published up till then, and he had a phenomenal memory."[12]

From everything that has been mentioned we can conclude that during the academic year 1872-1873 Solovyov was registered in the department of mathematics and physics, but that instead of studying the sciences he was preparing for his *kandidat* exams in the humanities. After all, he would not have been capable of taking them without any kind of preparation or of preparing for them only in the few weeks between the petition of April 18 and the beginning of the exams! In his "native" department of philosophy everything went smoothly, but his four-year sojourn in the natural sciences was strewn with thorns and his love of philosophy must have been great in order for him to master analytical geometry and physics. But the department of philology also left a painful memory. In the spring of 1873, at the time of his *kandidat* exams, Solovyov used to study with some friends in the apartment of a student by the name of V. A. Andreev. A professor of Roman law, Nikita Krylov, once dropped in on Andreev's father, who owned a tea and wine shop on the Tversky boulevard. Having become tipsy and being unaware of the presence of Solovyov among the students, he began to make crude jokes about his father on account of the abundance of his children. "Vladimir Solovyov had a complete fit," Kareev related, "they somehow managed to calm him down and I took him home."[13]

Solovyov's student years coincided with a period of intense and rapid philosophical evolution. Around 1872, when he turned nineteen, Solovyov had already formulated in two remarkable letters to Katya Romanova (nos. 11 and 18) the attitude to Christianity that we find in his mature works. Acknowledging Christianity to be unconditional truth, he aspired to elevate faith "to a new level of rational consciousness"[14] and to replace faith based on hearing with the faith of reason, as the Samaritans said in the Gospel, "'It is no longer because of your words that we believe, for we have heard for ourselves, and we know that this is indeed the Savior of the world, the Christ.'"[15] In other words, he wished to reconcile evangelical faith with modern philosophy. In the interval between 1869 and 1872, however, between Spinoza and Christianity, Solovyov experienced a strong enthusiasm for Schopenhauer, whose philosophy dictated many lines of his letters to Katya Romanova, whom he was trying to convert to the path of self-denial and renunciation of life. Lopatin describes Solovyov's philosophic evolution in this way:

> Thanks to Spinoza, God, although in a very abstract and naturalistic form, returned to Solovyov's worldview for the first time. Later, he enthusiastically read Feuerbach who, though also greatly influenced by materialism in the last phase of his philosophical career, never became a dogmatic materialist and generally did not go beyond an undefined and very capricious advocacy of sensualism in his theoretical views and the cult of humanity in his practical conclusions. At the same time, Solovyov was becoming seriously acquainted with the works of J. S. Mill and was struck by his refined and original skepticism that equally condemned both materialism and spiritualism while insisting as much on the absolute inscrutability of the existence of spirit as on the existence of matter... Finally, the ideas of Kant and, in particular, of Schopenhauer provoked a deeper revolution in Solovyov. Schopenhauer captivated him completely as no other philosopher ever had or would. There was a period in Solovyov's life, albeit a short one, when he accepted all of Schopenhauer, with all his general views and private opinions, with his limitless pessimism and his misty hopes for redemption from the sufferings of the world through submersion in Nirvana.[16]

Aside from the German philosophers, some of his Russian teachers could have influenced him as well; most of all, Pamfil Yurkevich and perhaps the professor of church history Aleksey Ivantsov-Platonov.[*]

In 1874 Solovyov wrote the article "About the Philosophical Works of P. D. Yurkevich" and before his death commemorated him in "Three Character Sketches: Troitsky,[†] Grot,[‡] Yurkevich."

---

[*] Aleksey Ivantsov-Platonov (1835-1894), leading church historian of this period.

[†] Matvey Troitsky (1835-1899), representative of English positivism and inveterate opponent of metaphysics and German idealism.

[‡] Nikolay Grot (1852-1899), professor of philosophy at Moscow University, president of the Moscow Psychological Society, and founder in 1889 of the journal *Problems of Philosophy and Psychology* . Initially a positivist, under the influence

Influenced partly by the Slavophiles and partly by the Bible, Yurkevich believed "the heart to be the focus of spiritual life." Contrary to the rationalism of German systems, his philosophy was a synthesis of biblical concepts and Platonism, which was in complete harmony with the theology of the Orthodox East. According to Yurkevich whereas reason, or the head, is not a generative force but an illuminating and governing one, the spiritual life arises and is born in the heart. "The soul exists not only as light but also as a being illuminated by it. Spiritual life is born before this light of reason in obscurity and darkness, that is, in the depths inaccessible to our sight.... The human mind is the summit and not the root of man's spiritual life."[17] He did, however, warn against the extremes of mysticism that can sweep aside the rational principle. "The mind, as the ancients said, is the governing or ruling part of the soul, and mysticism which immerses itself in the immediate impulses of the heart without transforming them into abstract, stable, and firm ideas or principles of the mind, is contrary to the properties of the human spirit."[18]

Was it not in the spirit of Yurkevich that Solovyov expressed himself in an unpublished letter of 1892 to Sofya Martynova:

> What is it that will live after our death and which must form the object of all our concerns during life? That which we now call our *heart*, that is, our inner self, which will be clothed with the appropriate imperishable body at the resurrection of the flesh.... Try then to perfect in you that which loves and which hates, that which is tranquil and which is anxious, which rejoices and grieves, i.e. your heart or the inner self (that which thinks and reasons *through* your mind).

To the memory of his other teacher, Aleksey Mikhailovich Ivantsov-Platonov, Solovyov dedicated a heartfelt obituary:

---

of Plato, Bruno, Kant, and Schopenhauer, Grot later developed a philosophy that was to reconcile metaphysics with the modern discipline of psychology.

> At a certain stage of spiritual development sincere faith excludes fanaticism which is either a sign of spiritual immaturity or else the "leprosy of hypocrisy." For those like the late Father Ivantsov who believe inwardly in Christianity, it cannot be turned into some kind of system of external obligations that can be implemented and supported by force, making of the religion of love a pretext or justification of every evil. A personal gentleness of character and a good nature combined with firmness of conviction and a deep religiousness naturally fostered in the late A. M. Ivantsov that true tolerance which permits, without waiving the absolute rectitude of one's faith, the recognition of the relative rights of another's opinion. Although partly attached to the Slavophile circle, A. M. Ivantsov preserved the independence of his religious thought.[19]

From another portrait by S. Kedrov we can seen that Solovyov was not being tendentious in his obituary nor was he imposing his own ideals onto Ivantsov. "In the personal life and career of Ivantsov-Platonov the ideals of Metropolitan Platon about honorable service to science and Christian humanism could not have been better embodied.... [He] regarded the reforming movement from the point of view of his ideas about Christian justice and love.... Sympathizing with the Slavophiles on certain matters, Ivantsov-Platonov regarded them critically on others. 'Our love for our country,' he said, 'must not be free of self-deception; we must not dream so much about our national virtues, deliberating exaggerating them, adorning our country with nonexistent perfections, and chauvinistically extolling it at the expense of all other nations.'"[20]

It is understandable that this teacher of Christian humanism, who united the strength of a scholarly mind with the warmth of an evangelical faith, played a large role in the life of Solovyov. His relations with Ivantsov-Platonov were ruined, however, in 1883 when he published his first work about the union of Churches, *The Great Controversy and Christian Politics*, which provoked the wrath of Ivantsov-Platonov. Solovyov responded to him in a gentle and respectful tone and maintained contact with him until 1888 when a final catastrophe took place. On 27 November 1887 Solovyov wrote to Anna Aksakova in an unpublished letter, "Si c'est notre ami Ivantsov, qui vous a parlé de ma mauvaise humeur, je n'y compris rien: la seule fois qu'il m'a vu, j'etais au contraire trés gai." In another letter to Aksakova of 2 March 1888 Solovyov already refers to Ivantsov as his "former friend." "My former friend Ivantsov has published a little book in which he refutes simultaneously Catholicism and all the Protestant sects. In the present conditions of our press to polemicize against Catholicism in Russia means an attack on an opponent who is bound; this is simply a *dishonorable act*, after which I no longer wish to see Ivantsov. I am very indulgent toward personal weaknesses and vices, and if this respectable archpriest stole or broke the seventh commandment it would in no way disturb our friendship. But in questions of social morality I am obliged to be intolerant." Evidently, Solovyov's obituary about Ivantsov was an act of reconciliation. "Pure good will was undoubtedly the predominant motive in the life and career of A. M. Ivantsov.... Everything passes, only love remains. Eternal memory to the deceased servant of Love."[21]

During the obscure period of transition that starts at the beginning of the '70s, having abandoned his previous materialism, but without finding a positive religious alternative, Solovyov began to enthuse over spiritism and discovered that he was a very powerful medium. It was his acquaintance with the Lapshin family in St. Petersburg that influenced him in this regard. Ivan Osipovich Lapshin devoted himself to oriental studies while his English wife Susanna (née Droin) possessed a fine education and a musical talent.[22] Solovyov taught her Latin and Greek and initiated her into the study of Spinoza and Plato; he also corresponded with her in French. All the "mystics" of the period gathered at the Lapshins, the spiritualists Anna Aksakova and Varvara I. Pribytkova (whom Vsevolod Solovyov loved very much, calling her "Varvarishche-Chudishche"), and the philosopher and "pan-psychist" Aleksey Kozlov. According to the memoirs of Susanna Lapshina, Solovyov was interested in spiritualism most of all between 1872 and 1873; later on he avoided participating in seances and cooled toward spiritism, deeming its doctrines irreligious.[23] Velichko reports that, "having become acquainted with the Lapshins, Solovyov became a medium for automatic writing."[24] Solovyov's manuscripts from almost all periods of his life are covered with mediumistic writings, which we will consider later. Even at this time "strange people" in Moscow had begun to gather around Solovyov, mystics who wavered between Orthodoxy, spiritualism, and . . . drinking bouts. They saw in the young philosopher a "superhuman being." "Do they really think," Solovyov once said to my father, "that I don't have it in me to found some sect?" Afterwards, in the '90s when he had renounced his earlier large-scale practical endeavors in favor of philosophy and journalism, certain people referred to Solovyov with biting irony as a "failed messiah." In general, this milieu with its strange enthusiasts recalled that of Nikolay Stavrogin in Dostoevsky's *The Devils* and there was more than one Shatov who was prepared to exclaim with bitterness, "You used to mean so much to me in my life, Vladimir Sergeevich!" Solovyov commemorated more than one of these old friends in his poem "Metempsychosis" written "during an attack of cholera" in 1892.

They arrived from afar
Two old friends.
One drinks like a sponge,
The other is insane,
But both remembered
A past friendship.[25]

Nomina sunt odiosa: I can only say that these loyal friends were laid to rest long ago; they belonged neither to the intellectual nor literary worlds and their names are extinguished.

While the young Vladimir was learning from Yurkevich that the heart is the source of spiritual life, he was in fact already leading an intense emotional life. His letters to his cousin Katya remain for us a precious testament to the flowering of his heart in these years and the struggle between his emotional impulses and the commands of the superior part of his soul which was trying to restrain them through reason. Let us now consider this youthful romance of Solovyov, that is, if the word romance can be applied to his stubborn summons to his "dear Katya" to take the path of "self-denial of the will."

Ekaterina Vladimirovna Romanova, the daughter of Poliksena Solovyova's brother Vladimir, was born on 19 April 1855 in the province of Kherson and was thus two years younger than her cousin Vladimir. Katya's mother, Aleksandra Stanislavovna Vishnevskaya was the daughter of a Catholic father and an Orthodox mother. Having divorced her first husband when Katya was four, she married Konstantin Shevyakov and died when Katya was around seventeen. Katya's father also entered into a second marriage, but died of tuberculosis when his daughter was not yet twelve.[26] In this way Katya fell from her family nest at an early age; first the divorce of her parents, then the death of her father and finally, that of her mother. Her cousin's lines can be applied to the girl: "Oh, poor child, between two hostile camps / You have no refuge." Still during the lifetime of her father, who had settled down with his new family, Katya Romanova moved into the home of the Solovyovs in Moscow with her grandmother Ekaterina Fyodorovna (née Brzhesskaya) and her younger sister Poliksena. This would have happened when Vladimir was twelve, Katya nine, and Poliksena seven. Poliksena soon left the scene, dying in adolescence of tuberculosis. In his novel *The Enchantment*, Vsevolod Solovyov describes the appearance of the girl Zina in the family of the hero. It would be a mistake to identify Zina with Katya, but Vsevolod undoubtedly incorporated certain features of his cousin in his work, though in more lurid shades. Her early sufferings, the loss of her parental home, her irregular nomadic life, followed by life in the household of the famous, terrible uncle Sergey Mikhailovich who was foreign in blood and spirit and who looked askance at this creature of Kherson, her early head-turning success in society, the attention and poems of her cousin Vsevolod, the dubious "fatherly" caresses of her bachelor uncle Vadim, and finally, the deep and selfless love of the ascetic Vladimir; all this fostered in Katya's soul a sense of tragedy and conflict. She was very beautiful, with dark enigmatic eyes and black hair. In his story "At the Dawn of Misty Youth" Vladimir Solovyov describes her as "a gentle semi-ethereal girl … in a pale blue dress with a braid tossed carelessly over her back."[27] Portraits did not do her justice; looking at her photographs it is difficult to understand the charm that she spread around her. Her beauty was, in fact, terrible and destructive, and she was often the victim of her own charm. She subsequently married a man she did not love, yielding to the entreaties of his mother. Having been rejected once by her, her suitor (named Selevin) tried to shoot himself, but having missed, stubbornly tried a second time. He attended the wedding ceremony still not completely healed from his wound and was scarcely able to stand on his feet. After their marriage he proved to be unbearable and cruel, and Ekaterina was soon forced to leave him. She was left with three children: a daughter Ksenia, a son Vladimir, and a younger daughter Anna. The latter, whom her mother called "Nyusia," died of tuberculosis as a girl, like her aunt Poliksena. Vladimir became a sailor and Ksenia, who inherited her mother's beauty and talents, and her father's fair hair and eyes, settled in the south of France and Switzerland, and married a certain Polisadov, an artist who converted to Catholicism in Paris and entered the Dominican Order.

Having lived with the Solovyovs from the age of nine, Katya left Moscow at twelve and began her life of wandering in the south of Russia. In 1871 she settled with her grandmother Ekaterina Fyodorovna on the estate of Fyodorovka in the Aleksandrinsky district of Kherson province. Accustomed from childhood to traveling and living in the country, Katya was to be a nomad for the rest of her life. Having raised her children on estates in the provinces of Volynia and Kharkov, she later lived with her daughter in Paris and Switzerland, visiting Moscow and St. Petersburg from time to time. In this respect she very much recalled her cousin Vladimir. After their initial childhood intimacy, which occurred when Vladimir was between the ages of twelve and fifteen (that is, when Katya was between nine and twelve), their relations were interrupted for a few years. In the summer of 1871, however, when he was suffering from overwork and nervous tension, Vladimir went to stay with his grandmother at Fyodorovka for a month's rest. In order to restore her pale and wasted grandson Ekaterina Fyodorovna earnestly treated him with camphor. Aside from his grandmother, Vladimir found at Fyodorovka his young second cousin or "aunt" Vera Mikhailovna Petkovich and his cousin Katya. With Katya, who was then sixteen, he formed a platonic friendship, but it was his attractive "aunt" who captivated him. Apparently it is this aunt who appears under the name Liza in the story of 1892 "At the Dawn of Misty Youth." In it the narrator relates how a year before a journey to Kharkov (which took place in the spring of 1872) he had "on one fine summer evening, initiated his cousins into the mysteries of transcendental idealism." In these recollections Liza is described as "blue-eyed but passionate" yet a few lines later becomes "a green-eyed blonde."

> Strolling with her in the allées of the deserted country park I explained to her, not without animation, though becoming confused in my speech, that space, time, and causality are only subjective forms of our knowledge and that the entire world in its forms of existence is only a conception of ours, that is, it does not exist at all in essence. When I arrived at this conclusion my interlocutress, who had been watching me seriously the whole time with her large greenish eyes, smiled and remarked with obvious slyness:
>
> "But how is it that yesterday you talked only about the last judgment?"
>
> "About what last judgment?"
>
> "Well, whatever you called it; that it is necessary to destroy everything. If, according to you, the world does not exist, why do you want to destroy it so much?"
>
> This contradiction confused me only for a moment.
>
> "But when a terrible dream or nightmare is oppressing you, don't you want to save yourself from it?" I replied triumphantly.
>
> Suddenly, without any apparent reason she broke into a ringing laugh. "What is it" I asked with displeasure.
>
> "Imagine," she said, laughing and squeezing my hand, "imagine this, I dreamt last night that my James (this is what they called her setter) was not a dog at all, but the commander of a Belorussian Hussar regiment and all our officers had to salute him, but instead of addressing him as Your High-Born Honor [*Vashe Vysokoblagorodie*] they were obliged to say Your Flea-Born Honor [*Vashe Vysokoblokhorodie*]."

> She concluded this unexpected communication with an equally unexpected kiss and then suddenly ran off, shouting to me from afar:
>
> "Let's pick berries in the strawberry beds. I've noticed that many of them are already ripe."
>
> I went to pick strawberries, although the categorical imperative, which common people call conscience, hinted to me clearly that this was not, on my part, the self-denial of the will but the complete opposite, the self-assertion of the will.[28]

Apparently, Liza-Vera, the cheerful coquettish girl with green eyes and a sharp sarcastic mind, attracted the young metaphysician especially by her difference from him, by her naturalness and physicality; but in her green eyes which he first described as pale blue, then green (they were evidently a kind of sea-green), his imagination perhaps discerned the first ray of those eyes about which he would write many years later, "I see your emerald eyes, / The bright countenance rises before me."[29]

Ekaterina Selevina (Katya) told me that in relation to Vera Mikhailovna, Solovyov conducted himself with the madness of young Werther, roaming through fields at night, and so on; but this passion was transient. On 21 December 1871 Solovyov wrote to Katya, "You are very much mistaken if you think that I am entirely immersed in my *folly*, as you utterly correctly call my ridiculous romance; this folly of mine has long since ceased to be a disturbance, and it has now almost completely passed. Indeed, only sometimes does the recollection of it return on sleepless nights."[30] On 7 March 1872, upon hearing the news of Vera Mikhailovna's marriage, Solovyov speaks of her with a hint of indifferent disdain, "Why do you pity Vera? I, on the contrary, hope that she will turn out to be an excellent woman a 'faithful spouse and a virtuous mother;' indeed they say that before her marriage E. was as unsteady and changeable as she. Vera's principal shortcoming was her pretentiousness, the desire to seem that which she could not be, but now, when her position is completely defined, she has nothing to pretend about, and this desire must disappear."[31]

A more serious and intellectual relationship formed between Vladimir and Katya in the summer of 1871. For a certain time she was sick with a fever and he diverted her by reading Heine. From that summer a frequent correspondence arose between them. Apparently Katya's life was not easy and Vladimir tried to cultivate in her his own ascetic and pessimistic worldview. "Perhaps it is even good that this external life is turning out so depressingly for you; the wise saying 'the worse, the better' is fully applicable to this life. Joy and pleasure are dangerous because they are illusory, but misfortune and grief appear as the only salvation. It will soon be two thousand years since people have known this, but meanwhile they do not cease to pursue happiness like small children. Let us not, my dear, be like little children in this regard."[32]

Evidently Solovyov's religious crisis occurred between 1871 and 1872. In the summer of 1871 he still presented himself to Liza solely as the interpreter of Schopenhauer alone, whose entire philosophy, according to Lopatin, he had wholeheartedly accepted. In 1872, however, Christian convictions make their appearance in Solovyov's letters, the asceticism of Schopenhauer forming only a preliminary stage for the asceticism of the Gospel. "True life is in us," he wrote to Katya on 27 January 1872, "but it is suppressed, distorted by our narrow personality, by our egoism. One must discover this true life, as it is in itself, in its purity, and the means by which it can be attained. All of this was revealed to humanity long ago by *true* Christianity, but in the course of its history Christianity itself has experienced the influence of this false life, of that evil which it should have destroyed; this lie has so darkened, so obscured Christianity that at present it is as difficult to understand the truth in Christianity as it is to reach this truth directly on one's own."[33]

In the spring of 1872 Solovyov was again planning to go to Kharkov and Fyodorovka for a meeting with Katya. On 7 March he wrote, "I hope to see you before Holy Week in Kharkov, from where I will go to Fyodorovka for ten days to breath some fresh air; the beginning of spring in Moscow is unbearable for me."[34] In "At the Dawn of Misty Youth" Solovyov recalls this journey:

> I was nineteen at the time; it was the end of May. I had only just passed the university entrance exams and was on my way from Moscow to Kharkov where I was to make an

> extremely important declaration of love to a cousin of mine, for whom I had already felt a tender and utterly sublime love for three or four months. For her sake I decided to make a very large detour, as the real goal of my trip was the Kirghiz steppes where I intended to restore my health, which had been ruined by the excessive reading of German books, with a koumiss cure.[35]

One must, of course, exercise great caution when citing this story as an autobiographical document. It was written in 1892 when Solovyov found himself in an exceptional, erotically tense mood, or to use his own phrase about Plato, when he was "dragged down by erotic slime."[36] On this occasion he treats the sublimely ascetic mood of his youth with too much irony and depicts his relations with Katya with tendentious distortion. However naive it may have been to drag a seventeen-year-old girl onto the path of "self-denial of the will," Solovyov's feelings for her, as his letters show, were very deep and not only comic. The story contains many autobiographical inaccuracies as well. The meeting with Olga-Katya in Kharkov in the spring of 1872 is described as the dénouement and end of a deep passion and the last attempt to convert young women to the path of self-denial... In reality, the whole long and torturous romance with Katya was still to come. Furthermore, the episode of the "fall" with Julie is probably pure invention, though on the basis of this story Archbishop Antony (Khrapovitsky)* in his article "The False Prophet" hastened to deny the widespread opinion about Solovyov's virginity as a young man. If indeed there were "falls" in his life, they occurred significantly later. Of course, in this instance, Solovyov himself was guilty of providing material for the conclusions of Archbishop Antony as the story is written autobiographically and lacks artistic objectivity. The meeting in Kharkov with Olga-Katya, however, probably does reflect accurately what had happened:

---

* The future metropolitan of Kiev and head of the Russian Orthodox Church in Exile, Antony Khrapovitsky (1864-1934) was an arch-conservative opponent of Solovyov and his work.

I went to see Olga. Of course, our meeting did not happen as I had imagined. It began with my not finding her at home, which somehow did not enter into my plans. Leaving a note, I went on my way. Thus, when I came by a second time she was already warned of my presence; there were no grounds for a fainting fit or other extraordinary scenes. She had just returned from a walk in the countryside. I noticed a great change in her; she did not at all resemble that gentle semi-ethereal girl who had remained in my memory ever since our last meeting in the country when, after bathing, she left the changing-room in a pale blue cotton dress with a dark braid thrown carelessly over her back. She was now a completely mature, elegant young woman with carefree manners. She looked at me daringly and intensely with her dark eyes which were slightly reddened from the sun and wind; there was something independent and decisive about her.

After the usual cursory questions about relatives, one's health and the like, I got down to business. She had written that she loved me; I was now to explain my own view of our relations. I spoke briefly and unconvincingly. I myself felt that I was repeating some kind of lesson learned by heart; each word rang in my ears as something strange and utterly unappealing. To tell the truth, these words of mine were completely wooden.

She listened to me with a thoughtful expression, leaning on a table. When I had finished my speech with the inevitable invitation to join me on the path of the self-denial of the will, she looked for a long time into the distance with motionless eyes and then suddenly lowering her hand she raised her head. Gazing at me intently she said with a calm and firm voice:

"I do not want to deceive you. I am mistaken in my feelings. You are too intelligent and ideal for me and I do not love you sufficiently to share your views and tie my life to yours forever. You have rejected every pleasure while I live only for pleasures. I will always love you as a relative. Let's be friends."

> I hasten to note that this was my last attempt at converting young women to the path of self-denial of the will. I left Kharkov that very evening... [37]

In fact, Solovyov did not leave that evening for Moscow. On 21 May he wrote to Ivan Lapshin from Kharkov, "I reached Kharkov safely and even happily, but I am now in a proper state of depression that is reinforced by the thought of the long journey to come and the two-month stay in the company of livestock [i.e., the koumiss cure]. Such despondency overtook me yesterday that I almost decided to return to Moscow or to the Kherson countryside where my cousin lives, but today reason prevailed and tomorrow I will make my way to Saratov where I hope to find a letter from you with news from the world of the spirits."[38]

On the basis of this correspondence it is difficult to say exactly when Solovyov's friendly and didactic attitude toward Katya became romantic and when the discussion of marriage arose between them. After the meeting in Kharkov in the spring of 1872 a temporary discord evidently occurred between the young people. Otherwise, how can one explain that on 31 December 1872 Solovyov was "saddened" by Katya's refusal to marry Prince Dadiani and "decisively and insistently" advised her to accept the offer.

> Your refusal of Prince Dadiani saddened me greatly. Of course I cannot judge this matter at 1,000 versts, not knowing anything well enough; but it seems to me that it would have been better for you to have accepted his offer. If he is a good man then on account of his wealth and position you could accomplish a great deal of good through him or with him, which you could not do on your own. In any case, the reasons you give for your refusal are very poor: "I don't love him enough," etc. I am very sorry that you believe the vile fable that has been concocted by the vile scribblers of the vile novels in our vile century; the fable about some kind of special supernatural love that is meant to unite two hearts for mutual happiness, without which one cannot be permitted to marry legitimately; whereas, on the contrary, genuine

> marriage must not be a means to pleasure or happiness, but must be an act of heroism and self-sacrifice. And so you supposedly do not like family life; but must you do only that which you like doing or which you love?[39]

Having been convinced that Katya did not wish to join him on the path of renunciation, Solovyov abandoned the thought of marriage. His letters to Katya adopted a severely moralizing, even coarse, character. He bitterly criticized her plans to devote herself to popular education, finding fault with her absentmindedness and her manner of expressing herself. "You argue strangely about proprieties and their violation.... Still more unpleasant for me was the hostile and nearly ferocious tone with which you speak about your relatives. If you possess little love and meekness (which, however, I do not believe), then it is very sad and nothing to be proud of."[40]

Katya, however, maintained a deep feeling for Solovyov and did not reconcile herself to his rejection. Around the summer of 1873 talk of marriage between Vladimir and his cousin surfaced in the Solovyov home and his parents began to take precautionary measures. Sergey Mikhailovich was distraught and decided to forbid the marriage. In 1873 Vladimir wrote to Katya:

> Personal and family relations must always occupy *second* place in my existence. This is only what I wanted to say when I wrote to you that I cannot give myself to you *entirely*...
>
> You know, my dear, that our relationship depends not on us or on our love. You know what kind of obstacles will not permit our union (although it is somewhat difficult for me to write directly about this, I must add that I have in mind uniquely that union which is sanctified by law and the Church: there can be no talk of any other kind of relation between us). To remove these impediments is very difficult, but possible. In any case, it is necessary to use every means. For the present, I propose the following: we will wait three years, in the course of which you will devote yourself to your inner development, and I will work on laying the foundation

for the future realization of my principal mission; I will also try to attain a definite social position that I could offer you.[41]

But already in a letter of 25 July the passionate words are expressed, "there [in St. Petersburg] I have need of nothing and no one aside from my Katya.... My joy, my dear, in these moments of mental exhaustion and despair only your love can sustain and encourage me: remind me of it more often, I beg you. I still do not completely believe in it, forgive me. Yours forever, Vl. Solovyov."[42] The separation from Katya was for him "four months of anguish."[43]

Vladimir now regarded a new proposal made to Katya entirely differently from the one made by Prince Dadiani. "What you write to me, dear Katya, about the proposal made to you was very unpleasant for me, not only on account of my senseless, nasty jealousy, as a result of which there is a clawing at my heart every time someone else even merely pronounces your name, and not only because a proposal was made to you, but even more because it is very, very painful to step over others and, dreaming about the salvation of humanity, to become, by some kind of wicked irony, the involuntary cause of the unhappiness of another."[44]

Jealousy added fuel to this fire as the "gentlemen" Vsevolod and Uncle Vadim appeared on the scene. In society gossip and scandal began to be spread about Katya.

"What kind of impossible nonsense have I not heard about you from various parties. I have been amazed at the inventiveness of the human imagination. I did not believe any of it for a moment."[45]

"Suffering as I constantly do from my own trustfulness, I have far too many reasons for warning you: do not put your trust in people in general, and St. Petersburg gentlemen in particular."[46] "Thus, be careful, it is much more important for you than for me. You will believe me, my life, that it is only with the greatest repugnance, only out of extreme necessity, that I touch this filth; I cannot be indifferent when they fling this filth *at you*."[47]

In the autumn of 1873 Solovyov was enrolled in the Moscow Religious Academy and settled at Sergiev Posad. In solitude, surrounded by the Greek Fathers of the Church and German philosophers, his love for Katya flared up.

"Your letter, which I have just received, has inspired in me such extraordinary joy that I began to converse loudly with the German philosophers and Greek theologians who in a touching union fill my abode. They have never seen me in such unseemly delight and one weighty Father of the Church even fell off the table in indignation."[48]

Finally, on 8 October Solovyov already addressed Katya as his fiancée. "It was only toward morning that I dozed off a bit and saw you almost as if in reality. I have a feeling of Katzenjammer. If my serenity is at all dear to you, if you love me not only in words, write to me a few lines, even if once a week. Farewell my treasure, I embrace you with all the strength of my imagination; will the time come when, finally, I can embrace you for real, my joy, my torment!"[49] While Katya was living in St. Petersburg, Solovyov sought from the beginning of the summer a pretext to go see her. On 25 July he wrote:

> I was completely ready to leave for St. Petersburg; they asked, why are you going there *now*? On this and that business. But in St. Petersburg you can't get any business done in the *summer*, you won't find any of the people you need to see as everyone leaves town. But I have to do research in the Public Library. It would be much more convenient to work there in the winter and you won't find anyone in the library now either. What then? My only choice was either to admit that I was going to St. Petersburg only to see you and that there I have need of nothing and no one aside from my Katya, (but to tell the truth directly would be an irreparable stupidity), or have to agree with the sound arguments of my parents and accept the offer of papá to accompany him to St. Petersburg on Sunday the first of December at eight o'clock in the evening. I agreed to this and, it seems, acted prudently."[50]

Apparently, Sergey Mikhailovich did not follow through on his plan to go to St. Petersburg on 1 December, for it is precisely on this day that Vladimir wrote to his mother from there. From the lines "show this letter to papá" and "ask papá about Pamfil Danilovich's health" it is obvious that his father remained in Moscow. As he had been living since the autumn at Sergiev Posad, Vladimir had evidently emancipated himself sufficiently from his family to travel to St. Petersburg without inventing further pretexts. An unpublished letter to his mother documents the unexpected catastrophe of his marital hopes:

> I did not reply to your letter until now, dear maman, because I could not say anything definite about what is worrying you. Now I have the pleasure of being able to set your mind completely at rest. That which you so fear (why, I don't know) and which I desired and considered almost certain (although not as soon as you apparently believed) has proved to be, by virtue of circumstances beyond my control, perfectly *impossible*. It goes without saying that this can in no way alter my feelings for Katya; please take this into account and if you wish to speak of her to me, then speak of her as you did at Neskuchny after your return from St. Petersburg: at that time your opinion of her was impartial and showed that sympathy which you must have for her, which was not the case in your last letter. I will leave St. Petersburg as soon as possible; unfortunately, I can't do without it, which is the fault of Peter the Great, not Katya. I will probably be in Moscow at the end of the month. In all respects I feel well; in any case, I will not lose my mind and I will not die earlier than in nine years, I vouch for this and sign my name to it.... Please ask papá about Pamfil Danilovich's health. Show this letter to papá (and never speak about any of these circumstances to anyone).

What happened? From the Solovyovs' old servant Marya Pavlovna Zagrebinaya (a very kind old woman who lived with Poliksena Vladimirovna to the end of her life and is very accurately portrayed in Zinaida Hippius' story "Twilight of the Spirit") I learned the following: On a frosty winter night the engaged couple were heading somewhere in a sleigh. On the way Katya wanted to drop in for a moment at a house where there was a large and lively social gathering. She asked Vladimir to wait for her in the sleigh. One hour passed, then another. Vladimir stared at the brilliantly illuminated windows of the house and began to freeze. Finally he ordered the coachman to turn back.

Life had had the last say in the affair and Sergey Mikhailovich could finally rest assured. Vladimir renounced his dreams of marriage but remained a faithful knight of his former fiancée and did not allow even his mother to speak ill of her in his presence. He returned to his cell at Sergiev Posad where the "weighty Father of the Church" could lie calmly on the table without being disturbed by the joyous outbursts of the young theologian. In Katya's last action we recognize the character of Zina who appeared to Vsevolod as an "enchantment." Vladimir was not entirely just to his novelist-brother: as the hero of *The Enchantment*, André, experiences the same sufferings. If Vladimir saved Katya from certain "gentlemen," then André, likewise, tries in vain to rescue Zina from the social quagmire in which she is surrounded by various "Kokós" and "Vovós"... The elder brother was a Don Quixote as well.

Writing in 1892, Vladimir Solovyov was indeed unjust toward his youthful passion. Katya was the godmother of his worldview that was coming into being; he confided in her his secret thoughts:

> As regards my opinion about the ability of woman to understand higher truth, then without doubt she is fully capable, otherwise she would not be human. But the point is that because of her passive nature *she cannot discover* this truth *on her own*, but must receive it from a man. This is a fact: not one religious or philosophical doctrine was founded by a woman, but teachings that have *already been established* are accepted and spread primarily by women. I believe that during the impending revolution in the consciousness of the human race women will play an important role.[51]

At this time Solovyov was feverishly working out the fundamentals of a new universal religion and was expecting the imminent triumph of goodness, truth, and justice over the world of falsehood and evil. The "last sigh of his sick soul" was that "at the universal feast of the rebirth" his companion "would appear more pure and radiant than all." "The glorious and painful times are drawing near and it will be well for him who can await them with hope and not with fear."[52] "Without this task, without this great mission I would have nothing to live for; without it I would also not dare to love you. I would have no kind of right to you, if I was not thoroughly certain that I could give you what others cannot. You have seen, and always will be able to see, a multitude of people at your feet who possess all the external advantages over me. In the meantime, for the present, I am nothing…"[53]

To no one else did he confide his secret dreams and plans, neither to papá, nor to Pamfil Danilovich, nor to Lev Lopatin, but only to the light-headed and restless Katya who left him to freeze in a sleigh on a December night in St. Petersburg. In her restless, loving, suffering, and false soul, he also encountered for the first time that soul of the world which, though possessed by the forces of chaos, strives toward light and freedom in the love for the One God; that soul about which he spoke in 1895 during a moonlit night in a Finnish pine forest, "I see the goddess, the universal soul, yearning for the One God."[54]

Of course, this love for Katya, which smoldered for so long and was immersed in philosophy and moralizing, was not the true love that unites two souls for earthly and eternal life. After all, Solovyov himself, having just recently discovered Pisarev and then Schopenhauer, considered the idea of a "special supernatural love that is intended to unite two hearts for mutual happiness" to be "the vile fable that has been concocted by the vile scribblers of the vile novels in our vile century" and insisted that Katya marry the wealthy Prince Dadiani, whom she did not love, in order to do good with the help of his capital. At that time he believed marriage to be *only* an act of heroism and self-sacrifice, and from this act of heroism Katya prudently slipped away, leaving her fiancé in the frost. Real love, uniting two souls for eternal life still lay in Solovyov's distant future.

Endnotes for Part 1 Chapter 3

[1]. Luk'ianov, vol. 1, 138.

[2]. Ibid., 132.

[3]. Ibid., 209.

[4]. *P*, vol. 2, 337.

[5]. *SS*, vol. 9, 265.

[6]. *P*, vol. 3, 64.

[7]. Ibid., 57.

[8]. Ibid., 64-65.

[9]. *P*, vol. 3, 105.

[10]. Luk'ianov, vol. 1, 175.

[11]. Ibid., 183.

[12]. Ibid., 147.

[13]. Ibid., 264.

[14]. *Istoriia i budushchnost' teokratii*, *SS*, vol. 4, 243.

[15]. *P*, vol. 3, 75.

[16]. Lopatin, "Filosofskie kharakteristiki i rechi," 124-25.

[17]. *SS*, vol. 1, 181.

[18]. Ibid., 186.

[19]. *SS*, vol. 9, 414.

[20]. *U Troitsy v Akademii (1814-1914 gg.)* S. Kedrov, "Studenty-platoniki v Akademii," 202-232.

[21]. *SS*, vol. 9, 415.

[22]. Luk'ianov, vol. 1, 251.

[23]. Ibid., 252.

[24]. Velichko, 19.

[25]. *P*, vol. 1, 234; *SS*, vol. 12, 111.

[26]. Luk'ianov, vol. 1, 265-310.

[27]. *P*, vol. 3 (1911), 297; *SS*, vol. 12, 301.

[28]. *SS*, vol. 12, 292.

[29]. *Stikh.* (7th Ed.), 117; *SS*, vol. 12, 16.
[30]. *P*, vol. 3, 58.
[31]. Ibid., 62-63.
[32]. Ibid., 58.
[33]. Ibid., 60-61.
[34]. Ibid., 62.
[35]. *SS*, vol. 12, 289.
[36]. *SS*, vol. 9, 224.
[37]. *SS*, vol. 12, 301-302; see also S. M. Luk'ianov, "Inosheskii roman V.S. Solov'eva v dvoinom osveshchinii," Pg. 1914.
[38]. *P*, vol. 1, 157.
[39]. *P,* vol. 3, 75-76.
[40]. Ibid., 75-76.
[41]. *P*, vol. 3, 82-83; see also letter no. 14, 81.
[42]. Ibid., 84-85.
[43]. Ibid. 86.
[44]. Ibid., 93.
[45]. Ibid., 92.
[46]. Ibid., 95.
[47]. Ibid., 96.
[48]. Ibid., 100.
[49]. Ibid., 103.
[50]. Ibid., 84.
[51]. Ibid., 97.
[52]. Ibid., 98.
[53]. Ibid., 106.
[54]. Velichko, 54.

Part 1 - Chapter 4

The Religious Academy – Solovyov as Docent and Master

Long had I rested on placid laurels,
On a delightful couch without thorns or burrs,
When suddenly out of the Sarmatian steppes
There appeared a new enemy, the brave Solovyov.
This villain had only just been born,
But had already managed to shake the root of evil,
Aiming at me the arrow of intellect and the javelin of faith,
He endeavors to wipe my throne off the face of the earth.

Satan's speech from the play
Solovyov in the Thebaid
by Fyodor L. Sollogub

Having passed his university exams in the spring of 1873, Solovyov went to stay with his friend Nikolay Kareev in the village of Oksovo in Smolensk province. On 19 June he wrote to his mother, "I had a very safe and pleasant journey from Vyazma to Kareev's village (twelve hours). The province of Smolensk seems nicer than I had anticipated: large dense forests with picturesque clearings, streams and rivers, which I crossed at fords and so on. The place where I am now staying is not so bad either; the Dnepr is a verst away. In spite of the foul weather I feel well enough, which is what I wish for you as well."[1]

In the autumn Solovyov took up residence at Sergiev Posad, having been enrolled as an auditor at the Moscow Religious Academy "through a personal letter of Metropolitan Innokenty to the rector."[2] His father, however, did not look favorably upon his son's entering the academy; we have already noted how negatively he viewed the clerical profession from which he had escaped. In general, he could hardly have been pleased with his son's behavior. On the one hand there were the awkward years at the university when he wavered between two departments, and on the other, the "*Khersonstvo*"–the romance with his cousin Katya and the plans for marriage, and now finally, the enrollment at the Religious Academy and rumors about embracing the monastic life. On this point Sergey Mikhailovich, who understood his son well, could be tranquil. On 2 August 1873 Vladimir wrote to Katya, "You are probably aware that I will be residing at the Religious Academy for almost a year for my theological studies. They imagine that I am capable of becoming a monk and that I am even contemplating becoming a bishop. Let them think what they want –I won't try to talk them out of it, but you can see that this would not suit my goals in the least. At one time monasticism served its lofty purpose, but now the time has come to go out into the world in order to transform it, not to run away from it."[3] Subsequently, Solovyov somewhat changed his views about monasticism. In 1886 he wrote, again from Sergiev Posad, to Canon , "The Archimandrite and monks are after me, hoping that I will become a monk, but I will think a great deal before making a decision about this."[4] Apparently, in the '80s Solovyov considered the monastic life again, and it was only his trip to Valaam in 1891 and the unfavorable impression made by the monks there that compelled him to reject, once and for all, the angelic habit as his way to salvation.[5]

However much the temperaments of father and son diverged, they undoubtedly remained on excellent terms. In raising his children Sergey Mikhailovich adhered to the principles of humanism and allowed his sons complete freedom, limiting himself to mild criticism and sarcasm. What could one do if such an inveterate Muscovite had produced a "Pecheneg" for a son! Besides, Sergey Mikhailovich was, in fact, far from what he appeared to be to outsiders. Many of his son's experiences were familiar and comprehensible to him. In his youth Sergey Mikhailovich had dreamed of creating a synthetic philosophy of Christianity that would reconcile faith and reason. He had also been at one time an ardent Slavophile and asked Konstantin Aksakov* to be godfather to his eldest daughter, Vera. Watching his son rush into Slavophile circles, even into the enemy camp of the

* Konstantin Aksakov (1817-1860), ardent Slavophile, erstwhile follower of Hegel and later advocate of the common people versus the Westernized aristocracy and intelligentsia of Russia.

extreme right led by Katkov* and Lyubimov, he probably remembered his own youth and consoled himself with the thought that it would all come out in the wash.

Vladimir lived like a hermit at Sergiev Posad with German philosophers and Greek theologians "filling his abode in touching union."[6] Archbishop Nikolay (Ziorov) recalls:

> In appearance he was tall and very lean with long hair falling to his shoulders. He was stoop-shouldered, sullen, pensive, taciturn. I remember how he entered our auditorium for the first time... Wearing a fur coat, high warm boots, and a beaver hat with a scarf around his neck, he went up to the window and stood by it without acknowledging anyone... He drummed his fingers on the window pane, then turned around and left the way he came in... After this episode, I saw him only when he would be walking by with Aleksandr Khitrov, another first-year student at the Religious Academy, or when he was on his way from the Academy to the old hotel where he had moved and would live for a time. He did not become close to other students. How he made friends with Khitrov, I do not know, but I heard that "vodka" had something to do with it. I was told subsequently that Khitrov took to drink and died in Moscow at the Khitrov market.[7]

Professor Mitrofan Muretov has also left a vivid portrait of Solovyov in those years:

> He had a small, and as far as I can recall, round head; his hair was long and black like a horse's tail or mane. His face was small and round like a young woman's, with a bluish cast; his eyes were large and very dark with strikingly drawn brows, but they were lifeless and expressionless as though somehow stationary and directed unblinkingly somewhere far off. His neck was dry, thin, long, and pale. His back looked the same

* Mikhail Katkov (1818-1887), at first a moderate Slavophile and then after the Polish uprising of 1863 a staunch conservative. In 1856 Katkov founded *Russkii vestnik,* one of the most influential journals of the period.

> way and was covered by a long, narrow, and already threadbare coat-jacket of dark fabric. His long and narrow hands, with their deathly pale, frail, slender fingers were, for the most part, thrust into his coat pockets or used to push back his hair. For some reason I want to call such fingers medieval; they were probably well suited to the violin or cello. He wore narrow, threadbare, black trousers with somewhat frayed hems over his long legs, and high boots with heels that were worn down on the inside. Something tall, slender, dark, retiring, and perhaps enigmatic; such was the impression Vladimir S. Solovyov left on me.[8]

Although Solovyov remained sullen and aloof at the academy, he felt more at home there than at the university. He wrote to Katya:

> I now find myself in an original enough situation. My arrival has created at the academy almost the same impression as that of the sham inspector in that famous town "from which even if you gallop for three years you won't reach another country." The professors here imagine that I have come with the exclusive goal of disturbing their peace with my criticism. Everyone is amiable to me in the extreme, like the chief of police with Khlestakov.* In gratitude, I leave them in peace as much as possible (at least those lectures that I have attended until now are decent enough). But they rate themselves and their profession very poorly and can in no way believe that an outsider, a nobleman and a graduate of the university, can entertain the fantasy of studying theological subjects; in fact I am the first such case, so they assume I have some kind of practical goals in view. In any event, the academy does not present such absolute emptiness as the university. The students, for all their coarseness, seem to be sensible people; besides, they are cheerful in a good-natured way and great masters of drinking, in general they are good sorts. I won't however, be able to make friends with them, there won't be time.[9]

* Reference to the hero of Nikolay Gogol's play *The Inspector General* (1836).

It seems that the influence of the academy on Solovyov was more profound than one would gather from this letter. In those years it still preserved the spirit of Metropolitan Platon.* Its magnificent library with the works of Aristotle in every edition, in addition to the writings of Boehme and Swedenborg, probably had a great deal to offer the young philosopher. It is also possible that Solovyov's particular interest in Sophia was awakened at the academy. Pavel Florensky,† a professor at the Religious Academy wrote to Lukyanov:

> Vladimir Solovyov was close to Dimitry Golubinsky, the son of the famous archpriest and philosopher Fyodor Golubinsky,‡ who, as it turns out, profoundly cherished the idea of *Sophia*, which he passed on to Bukharev. Dimitry Golubinsky, who revered the memory and intellectual legacy of his father, probably communicated it to Solovyov as well. Apparently, Solovyov took this idea directly with him from the academy, as afterwards he devoted himself especially to searching for literature on that subject (i. e. his trips abroad). It seems to me that Solovyov entered the academy simply for theology and church history, but then, having come across the idea of Sophia, which was already rooted in his soul, he abandoned the academy and theology in general, and devoted himself to Sophia in a special way. This is, of course, my own conjecture.[10]

As confirmation of Florensky's conjecture I can mention that when I read the copy of Boehme's *Christosophia* in the academy's library I noticed that the notes in blue pencil in the margins greatly recalled the handwriting of Solovyov, who, alas, did not stand on ceremony with the books of the academy and covered them with

---

* Platon (religious name of Nikolay Gorodensky [1803-1891]) was successively metropolitan of Riga, Kherson, and Kiev (1882). He was known for his ecumenical interests and was favorably disposed to the Church of Rome as a "sister church".

† Pavel Florensky (1882-1943), scholar, priest, and religious philosopher greatly influenced by Solovyov.

‡ Fyodor Golubinsky (1797-1854), promoter of idealist thought at the Moscow Religious Academy.

pencil marks, especially in the '80s when he was refuting the current polemics against Catholicism, which, as Father N. A. Kolesov has testified, were so hateful to him.[11] The traditions of Fyodor Golubinsky, who was strongly influenced by scholastic philosophy and wrote in Latin, were still alive at the academy. One should also recall that "at the time when essays on philosophy and discussion about the meaning and significance of Kant were common at the Moscow Religious Academy, *Vestnik Evropy*, the journal published by Moscow University, referred to Kant, Fichte, and Schelling as madmen and to their work as 'German nonsense.' The young students were amazed at the ignorance and absurdity of the university journal's opinions."[12]

A number of professors at the academy exerted an influence on Solovyov's developing worldview, most of all, Aleksandr Gorsky,* whose lectures he attended diligently. "... Gorsky's presence is markedly reflected in Solovyov's theological ideas," notes Muretov. "Such, for example, was his explanation of the exaltation of the Mother of God far above the angelic orders by the fact that the angelic nature, although in itself higher than human nature, is lower or more restricted in relation to the Godmanhood. Thus, the humanity of the Mother of God, which has been made divine, places her closer to the Godmanhood of the Savior who sits at the right hand of the Father and makes her more honorable than the cherubim and seraphim. The limits of the angelic nature are explained, according to Gorsky, by Genesis 6:2 and the attraction felt by evil spirits to the flesh not only of humans but also of swine and even to the empty and waterless places of the earth."[13]

In the autumn of 1873 Solovyov composed at Sergiev Posad his first published work. "I am writing the history of religious consciousness in the ancient world (the beginning has already been published in the journal). The purpose of the work is to provide an explanation of ancient religions, which is necessary, because without it a full understanding of world history, in general, and Christianity, in particular, is not possible."[14] This effort was limited to the first chapter, which Solovyov called in a letter to Katya the "small beginning of my beginning."[15] Solovyov returned to the history of

---

* Aleksandr Gorsky (1812-1875), scholar and rector of the academy from 1864.

religious consciousness in the ancient world in the first chapters of *The Great Controversy and Christian Politics* (1883) and in the article "Primitive Paganism: Its Living and Dead Remains" (1890). The "small beginning of my beginning" appeared in *Pravoslavnoe obozrenie* in the November 1873 issue under the title "The Mythological Process in Ancient Paganism." Based on my father's remarks, I considered this to have been his *kandidat* thesis, but according to Lukyanov, who cites a letter of Solovyov to Lopatin, the opening chapters or synopsis of *The Crisis of Western Philosophy* were written for his *kandidat* degree. In "The Mythological Process" Solovyov generally follows the work of Schelling and Khomyakov, while taking into consideration the research of Max Müller, Adalbert Khan, Bienfait, Karl Ritter, Pavel M. Leontev, Kreutzer, Bubsen, and others. According to Solovyov, the mythological process can be divided into three episodes:

> a) The spiritual divinity, already defined as a material principle, still preserves its preeminence and unity in spite of the multiplicity of forms in which it appears such as the gods of the sky: the uranic period;
> b) The spiritual divinity which has submitted to the law of external appearances becomes capable of suffering in the form of a sun god or demi-god, a heroic mediator between heaven and earth: the solar period;
> c) The spiritual god who has fully merged with material nature descends completely to earth appearing exclusively in organic earthly life: the phallic period.[16]

In a review of 1890 of Sergey Trubetskoy's book *Metaphysics in Ancient Greece*, Solovyov remarks about his own early efforts, "Without taking responsibility now for all the particulars in the exposition of this youthful work, I still consider its main idea to be sound."[17]

Vladimir Ern voiced the opinion that Solovyov's first work was "The Vital Meaning of Christianity" (a philosophical commentary on the doctrine of the Logos according to St. John the Theologian).[18] Although this article was published in the January

1883 issue of *Pravoslavnoe obozrenie* with the date of 16 January 1872, we concur with Lukyanov that this date is a misprint for 1882.[19] The theme of the article and its manner of exposition do not belong to the beginning of the '70s when Solovyov had only just freed himself from Schopenhauer and was still a long way from St. John the Theologian.

At Sergiev Posad Solovyov also wrote the first chapters of his master's thesis, *The Crisis of Western Philosophy*, which were published in 1874 in the January and March issues of *Pravoslavnoe obozrenie*. "I continue to study the Germans and I am writing an article (also for the journal) about the contemporary crisis of western philosophy which will then become part of my master's thesis; I have already written a synopsis of it."[20] (This synopsis was probably submitted as part of the *kandidat* exams as well.)

The publication of these three articles ("The Mythological Process" and the two chapters of *The Crisis of Western Philosophy*) provided Yurkevich with the grounds for proposing on 18 March 1874 to the department of history and philosophy that Solovyov be granted a leave of absence and permission to travel abroad. In his proposal he refers to still another work by Solovyov, his translation of Kant's *Prolegomena to Any Future Metaphysics*. "Mr. Solovyov has supplied this translation with notes," Yurkevich remarks, "that relate to the general method of science. I have personally found this philosophic work to be the most convincing proof of the brilliant and, in view of the times, rare preparedness of Solovyov for the interpretation and study of philosophy."[21] This youthful translation of the *Prolegomena* was published significantly later in 1889 in *Trudy moskovskogo psikhologicheskogo obshchestva*. Within seven weeks an affirmative response was given to Yurkevich's recommendation by the department of history and philology, and Solovyov began to prepare for the defense of his master's thesis.

In the summer of 1874, while staying at Neskuchny, he tried his hand at writing poetry for the first time. During this summer he wrote "To Prometheus" and translated a distich of Plato, "You, my radiant star, are gazing at the stars" (using four lines to translate the two lines of the original Greek). He also translated Heine's "Night Voyage." As far as the poem "To Prometheus" is concerned, later on in his life it would hardly have been possible for Solovyov to affix his name to such lines as, "When your soul shall see in one world falsehood with truth, good with evil," and "that only in the delusion of childish opinion do falsehood and evil live." He never published this poem.

On 20 July Solovyov wrote to Prince Dmitry Tsertelev, "At present I have begun to devote myself to poetry, and for now it seems fairly successful. I will read to you when we meet." The publication of *The Crisis of Western Philosophy* formed the basis of the correspondence between Solovyov and Tsertelev. Having taken an interest in his work, Tsertelev wrote to Solovyov voicing his objections, which the latter answered in a lengthy letter. Thus arose their lifelong friendship. The two men had both been students at the fifth gymnasium (although in different classes) and at Moscow University, but they became friends only in 1874. The first letters use the polite form of address, but as of 18 April 1875 Solovyov adopted the familiar form.

Like Solovyov, Prince Tsertelev was a philosopher-poet. In Leipzig he received a doctorate in philosophy for his work on the gnoseology of Schopenhauer, *Schopenhauers Erkenntnis-Theorie* (Leipzig, 1879)[22] and published a Russian book called *The Philosophy of Schopenhauer*. His poetry betrays the strong influence of his uncle Aleksey Tolstoy and, in general, suffers from an excess of philosophizing; throughout an entire volume he expounds the philosophies of Schopenhauer and Buddhism and retells various Hindu legends. Without a doubt Prince Tsertelev was a poet and several of his poems are genuinely splendid, for example:

> Pursuing truth in the chaos of thoughts and doubts,
> And tearing the elegant covering off life,
>
> You called the whole abyss of appearances a lie and a shadow.
> Madman, you forgot that you yourself are only a shadow of this shadow,
> In its succession of eternally glittering dreams.[23]

Tsertelev translated a great deal of Heine and later published his translations of *Manfred*, *Macbeth* and the first part of *Faust*. He eventually turned away from Schopenhauer and in latter years he inclined toward Leibniz in philosophical matters. His friendship with Solovyov was very warm and deep, as we can judge from Solovyov's poem "To a Friend from Youth": "That which we then / Did not finish saying / Eternity has recorded / on dark tablets."[24] Later their paths diverged; Tsertelev joined the camp of the conservatives, while Solovyov found himself in the circle of Stasyulevich* and *Vestnik Evropy*. But this difference apparently never ruined their relationship and Solovyov was a guest on many occasions at Tsertelev's estate, Lipyaga, in the Spassky district of Tambov province. Among other things, Prince Tsertelev was known for his extraordinary absentmindedness. In his comedy *I Said that He does not Know How to Eat*, Solovyov portrays his friend in the part of Prince Rasteryaev, who throws his galoshes at the feet of a society lady and then exclaims, striking his forehead, "What awful absentmindedness! Imagine, I was utterly certain that this was a box of sweets that I brought you!"[25]

Upon the death of Solovyov, Tsertelev composed these cordial lines:

> The bygone years rise before me like a dream,
> At this moment I bid farewell to you forever,
> But that which was sounds like a question without an answer,
> And passes by like a shadow, slipping away without a trace.

Solovyov's first letter to Tsertelev, dated 19 June 1871, was a reply to his objections to the opening chapters of *The Crisis of Western Philosophy*. In a long unpublished letter of 20 June (covering eight pages), Solovyov continued his argument and concluded by saying, "At present I have begun to devote myself to poetry, and for now it seems fairly successful. I will read to you when we meet." On 13 September he wrote, "I don't have a single proper poem in a

---

* Mikhail Stasyulevich (1826-1911), historian, journalist, social activist. As leading editor of Russia's only major liberal journal, *Vestnik Evropy (The Herald of Europe)*, Stasyulevich often found himself in opposition to both the extreme left and extreme right.

finished from; I will devote myself to *Hamlet* to relax after my return from St. Petersburg."[26] It is not known whether Solovyov translated even part of *Hamlet* as no traces of it can be found among his manuscripts. In the same letter he adds, "The conversation about Lermontov, as you guessed, was resumed at the Sollogubs'. Undoubtedly, Lermontov has the advantage of reflection and a negative attitude toward every day reality, although I agree with Sollogub that in the artistic realm Pushkin is higher ... I thoroughly agree with your observation concerning 'das Ewig-Weiblich,' although on the other hand, I must acknowledge the sad truth that this '*ewig-Weibliche*,' in spite of its obvious groundlessness, by some kind of fatal necessity *zieht uns an* with an irresistible force." Characteristically, Solovyov's attitude to the "eternal feminine" was, at this time, still negative (both friends inclined to Buddhism) and although he states "das Ewig-Weibliche zieht uns an" with an irresistible force, he forgot that, according to Goethe, "das Ewig-Weibliche zieht uns *hinan*," that is, "upwards."

With Count Fyodor Lvovich Sollogub, whom he called in his memoirs "the most original and attractive man of all the people I have ever known,"[27] Solovyov formed a close friendship. He was a worldly and very witty man with a fine artistic taste; he drew well and wrote poetry, mostly humorous, in the style of Kozma Prutkov. (We will discuss his play *Solovyov in the Thebaid* in the following chapter.) Solovyov loved to rest from his labors while dining at Sollogub's hospitable and brilliant home, which was animated by the beauty and elegance of its hostess, Natalya Mikhailovna Sollogub (née Bodet). Natalya Mikhailovna was known for her exceptional command of French language and literature, and in 1887 Solovyov went to see her at Rozhdestvino, near Serpukhov, in order to rework the French of *La Russie et l'Eglise Universelle*.[28] Talk of any romantic relationship between Solovyov and Countess Sollogub is out of the question, although in the '70s she was not above flirting with him in a gentle urbane fashion, calling him "*bel hermite*" and gave him her photograph with the inscription "in memory of a year." The aged Fet was not indifferent to her beauty and sang her praises:

O Berenika! In my heart I sense
The absent splendor and power of your beauty,
And I recall the golden scattering of
Your divine tresses.

By the autumn of 1874 Solovyov's thesis was ready, and he set off for St. Petersburg in order to defend it after taking his master's exams. His brave and blithe mood matched the polemical theme of his thesis in which he declared war on the positivists. He was sure of his powers and this certainty was brilliantly justified. In an elatedly humorous tone he informed his parents of his arrival in St. Petersburg, "In the year 7382 from the creation of the world, in the year 1874 from the Incarnation of God the Word, on the 25th day of September, at half-past eleven a.m. we arrived safely and triumphantly in the imperial city of St. Petersburg, illuminated by the bright northern radiance of the sun, in which we cannot help seeing the special action of Divine Providence."[29]

Solovyov took his master's exams in the following order: history and philosophy (12 October); logic, metaphysics, and psychology (26 October); ethics and ancient languages (9 November). The thesis was presented at a session of the department faculty on 16 November and the defense was scheduled for the twenty-fourth; Professor Mikhail Vladislavlev was appointed the official opponent.[30] As Solovyov's first philosophical work presents such great interest and contains so many positions that are characteristic of all his later philosophy, we must dwell momentarily on its contents. The title of the thesis appeared on the cover as *The Crisis of Western Philosophy* with the next line reading *Against the Positivists*. This gave Lesevich* grounds for accusing Solovyov of incorrect terminology as the word *crisis* cannot be used with the preposition *against*. In response, Solovyov declared, "Since the word *crisis* can never be used with *against*, then the line 'against the positivists' obviously refers not to *crisis* but to the whole title, signifying that this work called *The Crisis of Western Philosophy* is directed against the positivists, as for example, *De civitate Dei contra paganos* or *De Spiritu Sancto contra*

* Vladimir Lesevich (1837-1905), philosopher of critical positivism.

Eunomium, and so forth. In such cases, as these examples show, a punctuation mark is not required."[31]

"At the basis of this work," Solovyov begins his thesis, "lay the conviction that philosophy, in the sense of abstract, *exclusively* theoretical knowledge, has come to the end of its development and belongs irrevocably to the world of the past."[32] This conviction differed from positivism by referring not only to metaphysical but also empirical philosophy. Moreover, in contrast to the positivists, Solovyov described this completed philosophical development as something useful and promising of results.

As a speculative form of knowledge, philosophy has always been a matter of *individual reasoning*. In the Middle Ages individual reasoning was in opposition to tradition, authority, and the faith of the masses; in modern times it is in opposition to the reality of nature, to physical appearance. If in medieval philosophy the struggle was between individual reason and authority, then in modernity the struggle is between this same reason and nature, between spirit and matter. According to Solovyov, the struggle of speculative reason with authority began in the ninth century with John Scotus Eriugena who declared both "the absolute sovereignty of reason and the impotence of every authority before it."[33] He then depicts the development of scholastic thought in three phases; 1) Christian doctrine, confirmed by the Catholic Church as divine revelation, is absolute *truth*; but my personal thinking *does not conform* to this doctrine, my reason does not agree with it. Ergo, my thinking is mistaken and my reason is in error. Postulate: reason must be subordinated to authority and renounce independent thinking. 2) But if my thinking is rational then it cannot contradict *truth*; thus, if the doctrine of the Church is true, it must be in agreement with my rational thinking... Postulate: the contradictions between reason and authority must be removed, they must be *reconciled*. 3) But this reconciliation proves to be, in fact, an acknowledgment of the exclusive rights of reason, and the apparent condition: *recta ratio verae auctoritati non obsistit* actually grants to reason an absolute significance. Indeed, reason does not contradict *true* authority; but what kind of authority is true? That which does not contradict reason: *vera auctoritas rectae rationi non obsistit* . . . Thus, reason alone is true and authority loses any kind of meaning; if it is in agreement with reason then it is obviously not *necessary*, if it contradicts reason then it is *false*.[34]

Solovyov then turns to modern philosophy and demonstrates the development of rationalism by means of this syllogism:

1. (The major of dogmatism): That which truly exists is known by a priori knowledge.
2. (The minor of Kant): But in a priori knowledge only the forms of our thinking are known.
3. (The conclusion of Hegel): Ergo, the forms of our knowledge are that which truly exists.

Or:

1. We conceive that which exists [*My myslim sushchee*].
2. But we conceive only concepts [*My myslim tol'ko poniatie*].
3. Ergo, that which is, is a concept [*Ergo, sushchee est' poniatie*].

The development of empiricism can be represented by this syllogism:

1. (The major of Bacon): That which truly exists is known in our actual experience.
2. (The minor of Locke and others): But in our actual experience only various empirical conditions of consciousness are known.
3. (The conclusion of Mill): Ergo, the various empirical conditions of consciousness are that which truly is.[35]

Deeming the development of abstract western philosophy finished and believing its cardinal error to be the hypostasizing of abstract concepts, Solovyov, by way of Hartmann's *Philosophy of the Unconscious* addresses finally the philosophy of a totally unified and concrete spirit [*vseedinii i konkretnii dukh*]. He values Hartmann for his effort to establish and introduce into philosophy the concept of a primordial spiritual principle which embraces everything that exists and is independent of our consciousness.[36] Solovyov sums up the general results of western philosophy in three theses:

1. *In logic* or the theory of knowledge: *the recognition of the one-sidedness* and *therefore falsity* of both orientations of philosophical knowledge in the West; namely, the purely rationalistic orientation which provides only *possible* knowledge and the *purely empirical* which does not provide knowledge of any kind nor, by the same token, *any confirmation of a true philosophical method.*

2. *In metaphysics: the recognition of the quality of the total absolute principle of the concrete totally unified spirit*, instead of the previous abstract essences and hypostases.

3. *In ethics*: the recognition *that the final goal and highest good are attained only by the totality of beings by means of the necessary and absolutely expedient transformation of the world's evolution, the end of which is the destruction of the exclusive self-assertion of individual beings in their material difference and their restoration as kingdoms of spirits which have been embraced by the universality of the spirit of the absolute.*

At this point it appears that these final, inevitable stages of *Western* philosophical development affirm in the form of *rational knowledge those very* truths which were established in the form of *faith* and *spiritual vision* by the great theological teachings of the *East* (which belong partly to the ancient East, but more particularly to the Christian East). In this way, the most recent philosophy tries to unite the *plenitude of the spiritual contemplations of the East* with the logical perfection of *Western form*. Relying, on the one hand, on the data of *positive science*, this *philosophy* offers, on the other, assistance to *religion*. The realization of this *universal synthesis* of science, philosophy, and religion (the first and still far from perfected principles of which form the "philosophy of the *superconscious*") must become the *highest* goal and the final result of intellectual evolution. The accomplishment of this goal will be the *restoration of the perfect unity of the intellectual world* in fulfillment of the commandment of the wisdom of antiquity... This is followed by a quotation from Heraclitus which we cite from a Russian translation, "Bind together: the whole and non-whole, the united and the myriad, the melodic and the unmelodic; out of all create the one, and out of the one, all."[37] From his youth Heraclitus was one of Solovyov's favorite philosophers. Later he would quote him in *The Meaning of Love*, "Eros and Hades are one"; and at the end of his life he accused Lopatin of attempting "*to dam the entire flow of Heraclitus*" with his theory of dynamic substances.

> And with every year, gaining in motion,
> The river of time flows more swiftly,
> And, sensing from afar both the sea and freedom,
> I calmly say: *panta rhei*![38]

Thus, the point of departure for Solovyov was the same as for his contemporary Nietzsche: they both began with Schopenhauer and Heraclitus, but having embarked from the same shore they sailed in exactly opposite directions.

Borrowing from the reminiscences of Pyotr Morozov, who was a student at the University of St. Petersburg, Lukyanov describes Solovyov's defense, which was held on the 24th of "an overcast November day."[39] "There appeared before us a well proportioned youth with an icon-like face framed by long black hair parted down the middle. His face showed the faint signs of a beard and his deep eyes had some kind of special and, as it seemed to us, strange look that was focused somewhere above the heads of the audience. It was as though the short introductory speech he read were written on the opposite wall."[40] This speech did not take more than a quarter of an hour, after which the dean of the faculty, Izmail Sreznevsky, gave a very cordial welcoming speech to the representative "of the young generation of scholars." He was followed by the official opponent, Professor Mikhail Vladislavlev, who, though adopting a moderate line of attack, managed to strike a few sensitive blows against the candidate. As became clear later, Vladislavlev's attitude toward Solovyov was restrained and not completely sympathetic. "Solovyov replied very briefly to all his objections in a reserved and apparently shy manner, while continuing, as before, to look not at the audience but somewhere above their heads, into the distance..." When the unofficial opponents, the representatives of positivism, Mr. Lesevich and Mr. de Roberti,* appeared, however, Solovyov suddenly came to life and began to speak harshly, ridiculing his opposition. In a feuilleton "About the Disputation of Mr. V. Solovyov" that appeared on 24 November in *Birzhevye vedemosti*, Nikolay Mikhailovsky† portrayed Solovyov's behavior in a very distorted manner. Foaming at the mouth, Mikhailovsky compared the defense to a bullfight, "If the opponents, especially Mr. Vladislavlev, allowed themselves to throw more or less pointed banderillas at the candidate, the latter bore these minor irritations with the meekness of a young man who has passionately devoted himself from an early age to the torments of philosophical thought. In his debate with Mr. de Roberti he behaved entirely differently."[41] Mikhailovsky was disturbed by the fact that Solovyov, "this young person who has flown at such an early age from the transitory earth to the eternal sky of philosophy... has learned so well how to vary his attitude to his audience." According to Mikhailovsky, Solovyov took his leave while the audience was applauding not him, but his opponents. The pamphlet concludes in a style that has already become a perfect parody of the lawyer in *Brothers Karamazov*: "O laborers of learning, great and small, famous and not famous, how I pity you! Piling stone upon stone in building your edifice, you finally achieve a spacious and productive result... When, suddenly, –bang! Vladimir Solovyov, without refuting you, without even trying to refute you, without even knowing you, with one successful parry of the banderilla thrust at him attracts to his side the sympathy of society!... 'Rus, Rus! Whither are you rushing?' asked Gogol many years ago. What do you think, gentlemen, whither indeed is she rushing?"

In two articles "The Philosophical Disputation of 24 November" (*Grazhdanin*, 2 December) and "Further about Solovyov's Defense" (*Moskovskie vedemosti*, 9 December) Nikolay Strakhov treated Solovyov extremely sympathetically and energetically defended him from the slander of Mikhailovsky and company. "First of all, they accused him of ignorance and inveterate falsehood... Secondly, they accused him of rudeness. Ignoring all the

* Evgeny de Roberti (1843-1915), representative of the "philosophy of sociology" in Russia.

† Nikolay Mikhailovsky (1842-1904), leading populist critic and editor.

harshness of Mr. de Roberti's remarks, they began to publish and repeat that it was only Mr. Solovyov who was abrupt, that he was flattering and humble in his debates with the official opponents, but with outsiders was rude and arrogant, that he was, in short, crafty and calculating... the pamphleteers were thrilled and became inexhaustible on this theme, the one that is most dear to them."[42]

After Professor Mikhail Karinsky (a master of theology) voiced his objections, "there finally appeared," according to Morozov, "our friend Idelson, who nervously and hastily tried to sort out his copious notes in the fading winter day; in any case, hardly anyone heard him."[43]

On the whole, Solovyov's defense was a triumph, and the degree of master of theology was conferred on him to the accompaniment of the audience's friendly applause. The clamor created by this debate took a long time to die down in the press as indicated by the pamphlet of Mikhailovsky and the articles of Strakhov. The most enthusiastic response of all came from Aleksey Suvorin who wrote a feuilleton on 1 December for *Sankt-Peterburgskie vedemosti* under the name "The Unknown" that concluded with the words, "May God grant you all the best, Vladimir Sergeevich."[44] Konstantin Bestuzhev-Ryumin declared , "Russia can be congratulated on having a man of genius."[45]

It is worth noting that Strakhov's attitude to Solovyov, even at the beginning, was not as favorable as one might think from reading his newspaper articles. In a letter to Lev Tolstoy one can already detect the sour notes of mistrust that foretell the coming polemics of *The National Question in Russia*. Tolstoy disliked Solovyov on every possible count, finding him "cerebral." From the tone of his letter it would appear that Strakhov was justifying himself to Tolstoy for his laudatory articles. "I wrote two (articles) about Solovyov... they are rather dry and light. I share your opinion of Solovyov; although he has renounced Hegel openly, he secretly admires him. All his criticism of Schopenhauer is based on this. But matters get still worse. Rejoicing that he has discovered metaphysical *essence*, Solovyov is already prepared to see it everywhere, face to face, and is inclined to believe in *spiritism*. Besides all this, he is terribly sickly, as though emaciated; one fears that he won't end well. But the more I read of his little book, the more talented it seems to me. What mastery of language! What logic and force!"[46]

Strakhov was not the only one to be struck by the candidate's emaciated appearance. His former gymnasium director Malinovsky noticed that his pupil was wasting away and wrote to his father expressing the wish that "his health, obviously exhausted by the enormous amount of work, would begin to match his success quickly and completely… May the Lord help him to deal victoriously with his ailments as well and triumph over his proclivity to illness, as he annihilated and triumphed over the stratagems of the infuriated homespun positivists, materialists, nihilists, and so on, in the persons of those who opposed him: the ungifted and equally insolent doctor of mathematics R. and the talented but wayward Volfzon and Lesevich and their company, who in their fury began to gnash their teeth. He thoroughly defeated these gentlemen, routing at the same time those who rendered him the full tribute of justice, his serious opponents, Mr. Vladislavlev, Mr. Karinsky, and partly Mr. Sreznevsky."[47]

"To the East! Away from rotten Europe!" thus Suvorin understood Solovyov's message. But already in his first work one can find the embryo of Solovyov's future westernism. He does not simply reject the West, nor does he attack the development of western thought from John Eriugena to Hartmann but, rather, finds it necessary to unite the mystical revelations and theological doctrines of the East with the logical form of western philosophy. Solovyov recognized and accepted the great achievements of western civilization. He summons us not to the East but to a new future that belongs neither to the East nor the West but is a synthesis of one and the other. In an unpublished work written in French in 1876 he felt to be while in Egypt "entre l'Orient pétrifié et l'Occident qui se décompose." Subsequently, Solovyov became more convinced of the petrifaction of the East and strongly modified his opinion concerning the disintegration of the West; placing a high value on European civilization he even, as Anatoly Koni somewhat inaccurately claimed, "identified it with Christianity."

On 4 October, during his stay in St. Petersburg, his teacher Yurkevich died. Solovyov had already written to Tsertelev on 13 September, "Since Yurkevich is not in a state to give lectures, he has asked me to take over for the second half of the year, which means I must hurry up with my master's thesis."[48] During the first days of December, with the feeling of a victory gained, Solovyov returned to Moscow in order to take Yurkevich's place and to give his lectures "in his spirit and orientation."[49] At a session of the department of history and philology of the University of Moscow on 9 December 1874 three candidates were presented for the vacant chair of the late Yurkevich: Ivantsov-Platonov proposed Mikhail Karinsky, a master of theology; Tikhonravov proposed Matvey Troitsky, a professor of the University of Warsaw; and Vladimir Gérié proposed Vladimir Solovyov. We must make special mention of Gérié's attention to the young Solovyov. We have already seen how this stern professor, the terror of the university, had been indulgent to Solovyov at the time of his *kandidat* exams; now he was nominating him, the neophyte master for the chair of philosophy in preference to Professor Troitsky, a doctor of philosophy and an experienced professor. Furthermore, he arranged for Solovyov to teach his own courses and "so as not to embarrass him" attended his lectures only once.[50] Till the end of his life Gérié was a loyal friend of Solovyov. When his coffin was being lowered into the grave, Vladimir Ivanovich appeared by its side and uttered a few words whose warmth and sincerity were worth more than the emotional and bombastic speeches of Gartung, Speransky, and others. "You always brought with you joy and hope, Vladimir Sergeevich," Gérié began ...

Karinsky's candidacy was rejected as he was a theologian, not a philosopher; this left Troitsky and Solovyov. The dean, Nikolay Popov, raised the possibility of appointing two instructors of philosophy, rather than one, a proposal that met with the unanimous approval of the faculty. During their next meeting on 12 December, the members of the department put the candidates' names to the vote: Troitsky received four electoral votes and eight non-electoral, while Solovyov received eight electoral and three non-electoral (which probably included Tikhonravov's and Storozhenko's).

In his "personal memorandum" Ivantsov-Platonov insisted on the impossibility of simultaneously teaching two opposing schools of philosophy in the same university: the metaphysics of Solovyov and the empiricism of Troitsky. "One," Ivantsov-Platonov states, "is primarily an admirer of philosophical idealism and the strictly syllogistic method of thought; the other regards any kind of idealism extremely unsympathetically. Recognizing the inductive method as the *only organ* of knowledge about matter and spirit, he considers the syllogistic method absolutely insupportable. One regards the post-Kantian period of German philosophy with special love and respect, although without distinguishing its various shortcomings and exaggerations; while according to the other, 'all of this philosophy is a lie squared and cubed, spreading in all directions and completely masking reality: idealism transformed into patent nonsense and idealism leading to nausea'."[51]

Evidently, having tolerated the failure of Karinsky's application, Ivantsov wanted, at least, to prevent the appointment of Troitsky. Fyodor Korsh, Karl Gerts, and Aleksandr Duvernois agreed with Ivantsov. The mathematician Nikolay Bugaev took the role of mediator at the general session of the university council. Holding in high esteem both Solovyov and Troitsky he referred in his memorandum, first of all, to the practice of German universities where the presence of two professors of different schools is considered perfectly possible and even stimulating, and secondly, tried to demonstrate with wit that Solovyov and Troitsky had much in common and did not exclude but rather complemented one another. Disagreeing with Ivantsov, Bugaev maintained that Troitsky did not entirely reject the *syllogism* and all *formal* logic, just as Solovyov did not reject the *inductive* method. If Troitsky had a negative regard for German post-Kantian philosophy, then Solovyov, as well, "in characterizing all western philosophy according to two tendencies (rationalism and empiricism) has labeled rationalism empty and empiricism meaningless..."[52] On this point Bugaev failed to notice that in calling empiricism meaningless, Solovyov was attacking not German philosophy but namely that school of English thought to which Troitsky belonged...

At the session of the university council held on 19 December where the *pros* and *contras* for Troitsky were heard (Tikhonravov, Storozhenko, and Bugaev voted *pro*; Ivantsov, *contra*), a decision was made "to request from the rector of the University of Warsaw information concerning any impediments to the transfer of the permanent Professor Troitsky from that university to a position at this one."[53] In the meantime, in expectation of Troitsky's arrival, Solovyov took Yurkevich's chair on his own. On 8 January 1875 he wrote to Tsertelev, "In the summer I am going to London for a year and a half, leaving the chair to my newly elected colleague Troitsky, about whom it seems, you have heard."[54]

On 27 January Solovyov delivered his introductory lecture at Moscow University under the title "Metaphysics and Positive Science."[55] But what course did he actually teach during the spring semester of 1875? In a letter of 8 January to Tsertelev he remarks, "I will give a historical introduction to metaphysics;" but in his first lecture he announced that the subject of the course would be "an investigation of the latest German metaphysics."[56] (In his "curriculum vitae" of 1890 he called this course "a history of the most recent philosophy."[57]) In any case, the course given by Solovyov in 1875 was not very long as Shrovetide fell in February and Holy Week began in April.[58] We share Lukyanov's opinion that, for the most part, Solovyov gleaned the contents for his lectures from his thesis, adapted "to the level of his students' understanding, or even not adapted."[59] His students, as Leonid Belsky has related, found his lectures very difficult.

Parallel to the courses he taught at the university, Solovyov also taught the history of Greek philosophy one hour a week at Gérié's lectures for women. "Solovyov explained the dialogues of Plato," Gérié recalls, "reading extracts from them in translation. I cannot say what charmed the audience more, the ancient Greek sage or his young interpreter; I rather think the latter... In order not to embarrass him I was present at only one of his lectures and do not remember exactly what he spoke of then. But I remember well the charming impression he made with his elegant figure, handsome face and pale complexion, along with his dark half-closed eyes that gazed into the distance and his slightly trembling voice. He was a real prophet of Plato."[60] Elizaveta Polivanova recalled him in a similar fashion. "He lectured to us primarily about Plato and his worldview and analyzed a number of his dialogues. The lectures grew more and more interesting and were often enthralling; for example, there was one about the dialogue of Phaedrus where the conversation is about the cold-blooded orator and the orator who possesses pathos, which the lecturer himself did in the highest degree. The fascination of Vladimir Solovyov's lectures was rendered still more effective by his magnificent diction and his remarkably beautiful voice which I can still remember."[61] Polivanova has also left us the physical description of Solovyov that she jotted down in her notebook at the time. "Solovyov has remarkably beautiful blue-gray eyes, thick dark eyebrows, a handsome forehead and nose, and thick, dark, rather long and somewhat wavy hair; his mouth is not especially beautiful, mostly on account of the rather bright color of his lips against his dull pale face; but his face itself is splendid and has an unusually inspired expression as though it were not of this world; it seems to me that such were the faces of the early Christian martyrs. Solovyov's entire aspect is also suffused with an expression of extreme goodness. To look at, he is very thin and frail."[62] From Polivanova's memoirs we learn that Solovyov began to give his lectures at the women's courses before those at the university and that the first was on 14 January. This lesson was devoted to the definition of the fundamental property of human nature. Disagreeing with the Aristotelian definition of man as a *social animal* (as sociability is characteristic of other animals), Solovyov defined man as a laughing animal. "All animals accept exclusively the circumstances of their physical nature provided to them by their sensations; these circumstances have for them the meaning of absolute reality; therefore animals do not laugh. The realm of human knowledge and will extends infinitely beyond all physical phenomena and representations. Man has the ability to rise higher than any physical phenomenon or object and can regard them critically. Man examines a fact and if this fact does not correspond to his ideal concepts, he laughs. In this very characteristic particularity lies the root of poetry and metaphysics. Since poetry and metaphysics are characteristic only of man, he can be defined as a poeticizing and metaphysicizing animal. Poetry is not at all a reproduction of reality, it is a mockery of it."[63]

From such statements we can see that the young Solovyov was still far from his future idea about *spiritual corporeality* and had a very limited appreciation of art. The poetry of Goethe and Pushkin is by no means a "mockery of reality" but the acceptance and intensification of it, until it takes on the significance of a spiritual symbol. The highest form of poetry does not remove us from empirical reality, but reveals the laws of the spiritual world within it. Solovyov's preference in the '70s for Lermontov over Pushkin was typical, especially in view of the former's "negative attitude toward factual reality;" at this time Solovyov was a romantic and was far closer to Hoffmann than to Goethe. As we have seen from the descriptions of Muretov and others, there was something spectral, disembodied about even Solovyov's entire appearance as though he were some kind of "phantom." At that time he considered the task of philosophy and theurgy to be the dematerialization of the material world, the restoration of the realm of pure spirits. This view would subsequently undergo a great evolution. Although in one of his more mature and polished works, *The History of Theocracy*, he defines the material world wholly in the spirit of Plato as "the realm of rioting shadows,"[64] and although he returned at the end of his life to the study of Plato, feeling an invincible desire to immerse himself anew and more profoundly than before in this eternally fresh stream of philosophic thought that was the first to recognize itself,[65] his work *The Drama of Plato's Life*, however, appears to be something of a judgment on Plato and, partly, on himself. To the end, Solovyov preserved the distinction that separates Plato from Christianity, abstract idealism from the religion of the divine incarnation. Plato's efforts to construct, by means of the idea of Eros, a bridge between the intelligible world and the material remained in Solovyov's eyes only an experiment that ended in a wreck.

Of course, Solovyov never completely overcame his romanticism and in the last period of his life he took romantic irony to unbelievable heights. This side of him blinded him to many spiritual and aesthetic phenomena. For example, he was not capable of appreciating the realism of Lev Tolstoy and the entire world of visual art was closed to him. A place like Hapsal meant more to him than all of Italy, from Venice to Rome. But genius is inevitably one-sided; after all, Goethe was excluded from realms where Solovyov was at home. Among his female students, as well, Solovyov encountered the fierce opposition of materialists and positivists. One of them, according to Elizaveta Polivanova, drew a caricature of Solovyov portraying him as extraordinarily tall and uttering these remarks, "What kind of nonsense these gentlemen talk! It's disgusting even to listen to it. As if there were something that really exists! Everything in the world is but a phantasmagoria. And the world itself is a phantom, –I myself am a phantom, and so are all of us!"[66]

In 1875 Solovyov had to defend his thesis from the attacks of Lesevich and Kavelin.* In the January issue of *Otechestvennye zapiski* Lesevich published the article "How Dissertations Sometimes Get Written: Vl. Solovyov's 'The Crisis of Western Philosophy: Against the Positivists'." The title alone indicates that Lesevich's tone was not the most pleasant. Solovyov, who was always known for his polemical fervor and his fondness for the "games of Ares," did not remain in his debt and repaid him with the highly caustic article "A Strange Misunderstanding" which appeared in the February issue of Katkov's *Russkii vestnik*. At the conclusion of his article Solovyov explained away his opponent's criticism by suggesting that "Lesevich understood absolutely nothing about the work he reviewed. In such cases there remains for me only to give him one good piece of advice, to fulfill the intention he expressed at my defense to flee as far as possible not only from me but from any kind of philosophy."[67]

Matters stood entirely differently with Kavelin, who published a brochure at the beginning of 1875 with the title "A Priori Philosophy or Positive Science?: Concerning the thesis of Mr. V. Solovyov." In the June issue of *Russkii vestnik* Solovyov replied to Kavelin with his unpolemical article "About the Reality of the External World and the Foundation of Metaphysical Knowledge." "The criticism of Mr. Kavelin," he states at the beginning, "is perfectly free from a polemical character and in no way requires of me the petty and mean task of self-defense."[68]

According to Tsertelev, after defending his thesis, Solovyov "immediately became a celebrity in Moscow. Editors sought his collaboration, ladies invited him to tea on impulse, and his literary rivals tried to fling mud at him."[69] To this time dates Solovyov's meeting with Ivan and Anna Aksakov that took place at the home of the Sollogubs "opposite the church of St. Nicholas at Tolmachi, near

* Konstantin Kavelin (1818-1885), social thinker who attempted to reconcile positivism with moral idealism.

Ordynka." "We dined today with *the greats*: Uncle Yusha* and Anna Fyodorovna Aksakova would like to see me; they are presently downstairs with grandmother and will come up, but not together so as not to frighten me at once... Anna Fyodorovna's desire 'to have a look' at me is explained by a certain noise that reached Moscow from St. Petersburg where I spent several months before beginning my career with my master's defense at the university."[70]

At this time Solovyov had not yet abandoned his studies in spiritism, as a letter of Strakhov's to Tolstoy testifies, "Rejoicing that he has discovered metaphysical *essence*, Solovyov is already prepared to see it everywhere, face to face, and is inclined to believe in *spiritism*."[71] In fact, for Solovyov, who aspired to the reconciliation of faith and reason, to the union of ancient mystical revelations with the findings of contemporary science, spiritualist phenomena were valuable facts, empirically obtained evidence of the reality of the world of the spirits. Solovyov wrote to Tsertelev on 8 January 1875, "I am more and more convinced of the importance and even necessity of spiritualist phenomena for the creation of a modern metaphysics, but in the meantime I do not intend to profess this openly as it would serve no purpose and give me a bad reputation." On 18 April he wrote again to Tsertelev, "Have you seen the article by Vagner in the last issue of *Vestnik Evropy?* It's extremely curious. The obvious unsatisfactoriness of that explanation which Vagner provides for phenomena, whose objective reality he absolutely admits, testifies especially strongly in favor of spiritism."[72]

Although the spiritualists, particularly Lapshin and Aleksandr Orfano, attempted in every possible way to lure Solovyov into their camp, he was already at this time treating spiritualism with great caution and mistrust. A letter of Orfano to Lapshin written in Moscow on 9 March 1875 typifies Solovyov's attitude in this regard. Having indicated that Solovyov had returned from St. Petersburg with considerably less *prejudice* against spiritism than before, Orfano remarks, "Imagine my amazement when he told me that two days ago, having returned from a soirée where a seance was held, he wanted to verify for himself the movements and raps that he had seen and heard, and that to his great astonishment within a few minutes after sitting

---

* Yury Samarin.

down at his night table the same spirit began to whirl around and answer his questions with knocks, claiming that it was Yurkevich. Since then he has continued to experiment with spiritism and if he is not yet entirely convinced, then he is very near to being so. You can imagine what changes these facts must have on his convictions; this belief, which he had found absurd, has turned into an objective truth."[73]

From this letter it is clear that Solovyov had held a *prejudiced* view of spiritualism and thought it to be *absurd*. We subscribe, as well, to Lukyanov's opinion that "all things considered, Solovyov never became completely immersed in the troubled waters of spiritism."[74] Evidently, during his stay in St. Petersburg the influence of the Lapshins, his brother Vsevolod, and others dispersed some of his biases against spiritism, but it was the apparition of his beloved Yurkevich that definitely enticed him into communicating with the shades of the departed. We will provide a detailed treatment of Solovyov's further experiments in spiritualism in the following chapter, but we should note, in the meantime, that toward the '80s his attitude to it became completely negative. In a letter of 1883 to the populist teacher Vasily Fyodorov, Solovyov remarked, "For a certain time I was seriously interested in spiritism and had the occasion to be convinced of the reality of many of its phenomena, but I consider the practical pursuit of this subject to be very harmful, both morally and physically."[75] And in 1887 he stated in a letter to Strakhov, "I absolutely agree with and approve the main thesis of your introduction, namely that one cannot attain religious truth by means of spiritualism."[76] During these years Solovyov was not known for his religious observance, but even then he attached great importance to the sacrament of the Eucharist and went so far as to propose the idea that "man possesses a special, sidereal body that is naturally subject to atrophy if he does not partake of the sacred mysteries for a long time."[77] The sidereal body is a term borrowed from Paracelsus and means the same as the "astral body" in contemporary spiritualism.

Such was Solovyov's life in 1875; he rested from his intense labors of the previous years and enjoyed their fruits, and for a short while he played the teacher, not the student. The "vengeance of his enemies" only kindled his polemical ardor, while the "slander of friends" still slept in the mists of the future. A new and great work was being formed in his mind, but for this he would need to do research in the British Museum, and he eagerly prepared for the trip abroad. His love for Katya had become a thing of the past. Surrounded by the "games of Ares" and sometimes by the "games of Bacchus," his dreams still remained indifferent to the "games of Cyprus," but in the spring of 1875 he underwent a strong, tempestuous, and tragic infatuation that passed as quickly as it had exploded.

Among Solovyov's students at the course organized by Gérié were two young women, Zinaida Sokolova and Elizaveta Mikhailovna Polivanova (no relation to the famous pedagogue Lev Polivanov). Solovyov was quite friendly with Sokolova's brother Aleksandr and was often a guest at their home. On one occasion Sokolova conveyed to Elizaveta Polivanova that Solovyov would like to make her acquaintance. Their first meeting took place on Prechistensky boulevard on 4 May. Within a few days Solovyov began to visit the Polivanovs and became friends with Elizaveta's parents and her brothers, especially the youngest, Seryozha. The family spent their summers at Dubrovitsy in the Podolsk district on the banks of the Pakhra. Sometime in 1875 Solovyov paid a visit to the Polivanovs there and his intimacy with Liza grew.

"It is no wonder that our place was to his liking, " wrote Elizaveta Polivanova in her memoirs, "the locality of Dubrovitsy is enchanting, with a great many walks, each one nicer than the other. Our life was carefree and varied, but its principal charm derived from the absence of every form of conventionality in addition to the unusual cordiality of my parents and the great kindness with which they treated everyone around them." The summer guests included three aunts and a multitude of cousins and friends so that from thirty to forty people would sit down to table. River excursions, horseback riding, and carriage drives were arranged; in bad weather billiards and the piano offered diversion.[78]

The young philosopher plunged into this noisy, happy atmosphere during the height of May and spent a great deal of time with Liza.

"He spoke about his extensive plans for the future. At that time he fervently believed in himself, in his vocation to carry out a revolution in the realm of human thought. He aspired to reconcile faith and reason, religion and science, to discover hitherto unknown paths for human consciousness. When he spoke of this future he would become entirely transformed. His gray-blue eyes would somehow darken and shine, looking not in front of him but somewhere into the distance ahead of him, and it seemed that he was already seeing before him a picture of this wonderful future."[79]

On the first of June Solovyov proposed marriage to Elizaveta Mikhailovna. "On the first of June, on Pentecost Sunday itself," recalls Polivanova, "we were together at the Liturgy. Escaping from the unbearable closeness, we made our way to the choir and then went out onto the roof of the church, from which a magnificent view, which I had promised to show him long before, opens out over the environs of Dubrovitsy."

> I sat on the threshold of the door while Vladimir Sergeevich stood three steps away from me at the very edge of the roof, resting his foot on the low balustrade. It was cool and a very fresh breeze was blowing. Fearing lest he catch cold I suggested that we return to the choir loft.
>
> "No, no!" said Vladimir Sergeevich.
>
> And suddenly, unexpectedly, unpredictably, he told me that he loved me and asked me to be his wife.
>
> Strange as it might seem, for the entire duration of our acquaintance no thought of love had entered my mind. I was startled, stunned. I lost my head.
>
> I saw before me his pale agitated face, his eyes that were fixed on me with an expression of anxious expectation. At the same time, I myself was seized by the fear that he might fall off the roof at any moment …
>
> I muttered something; what I do not know.
>
> He insisted on a categorical answer.
>
> I answered *yes*, and in this lies my deepest guilt before him. But at that moment I was not thinking about this, I do not even know if I was thinking about anything at all.

People started leaving the church, and we went down.[80]

The contented Solovyov left for Moscow for two days and when he returned to Dubrovitsy, Elizaveta Mikhailovna was compelled to tell him that she did not love him with real love and that she could not marry him. This explanation cost her a great deal and she cried…

Solovyov found the strength to comfort her and decided to remain at Dubrovitsy until the day after the next. It appeared that the former friendship between the young people had been restored, but on the following day, when they were sitting on a hillock,

> Solovyov fell silent for a moment and then suddenly prostrated himself on the earth and uttered a groan.
>
> "And to think, how happy we could have been!"
>
> Tears reached my throat, and then an uncontrollable flood poured from my eyes.
>
> "You see," I could scarcely mutter, "a return to our simple earlier friendship is impossible…"
>
> "Impossible…" he responded like an echo.
>
> Solovyov said that he was going somewhere far away, probably abroad. His parting words were, "If you come to love me, write and I will come, whenever it might be. Otherwise, we will not see each other, unless my feeling disappears…"[81]

On his departure Solovyov left two poems with Elizaveta Mikhailovna. One of them, "To Prometheus," we have already mentioned, the other was published for the first time in Polivanova's memoirs and betrays the influence of Plato.

In this earthly life we are shadows, shadows…
Life being a play of shadows,
A succession of distant reflections
Of eternally radiant days.

But the shadows and their former features
Have already begun to merge.
No longer will you recognize

Your former lucid dreams.

The gray twilight before dawn
Has clothed the entire earth;
A trembling of greeting has already
Possessed the prophetic heart.

The prophetic voice does not deceive.
Believe, the shadow passes –
Grieve not; soon will arise
The new, eternal day.

The poem "What fate has declared, I will not reject" ["Chto rokom suzhdeno, togo ne otrazhu ia"] bears the date: June 1875-1877. In the sixth and seventh editions of Solovyov's poetry I ascribed it to his romance with his cousin Katya as it is written in her album in his hand. Following the publication of Polivanova's memoirs, however, I decided in favor of Lukyanov's suggestion the "this poem was inspired by his feelings for E. M. Polivanova."[82] The date of 1877 applies equally to Polivanova as during the years 1877-1878 Solovyov found himself again at Dubrovitsy where he wrote the poems "In the former years of love's adversity" ["V bylye gody liubvi nevzgody"] and "What good are love and caresses to you" ["Zachem tebe liubov' i laski"] which already refer undoubtedly to Elizaveta. As for the content of the poem, it very much reflects Solovyov's mood following her refusal to marry him. The awareness that "he must travel the earthly path, homesick for the radiant sky of the native land," the "farewell, then!" addressed to the beloved girl, the desire to give her, at the price of his bitter suffering, golden days and years and all the best flowers so that she could rest from the malice of life in a new world of light and freedom; all this speaks of Polivanova and recalls the lines "Grieve not; soon will arise / The new, eternal day," in the poem "In this earthly dream we are shadows, shadows..."

Meeting Katya Romanova in St. Petersburg at the end of the '70s when their romantic relationship had already been relegated to the past, he could easily have written in her album a poem inspired by the love for another woman. The references to "the malice of life" and "the painful visions of confused dreams" also belong to Polivanova, for she too had suffered deeply in the spring of 1875. For understandable reasons, she omitted from her memoirs a very important fact; at this time she was in love with a man who had married another woman. She saw in Solovyov a friend and comforter, but not a lover; and suddenly, she had to inflict a cruel blow against this friend! Elizaveta Polivanova was in no way a flirt; she was more intellectual and refined that Katya, and Solovyov had found in her a soul that eagerly welcomed his ideas.

As it turned out, the blow was not so cruel. On 27 July Solovyov wrote to Tsertelev from Warsaw, "I feel exceedingly well (in terms of my morale`) and am considering in detail the plan of my work."[83] Solovyov's translation of Heine that he made at Dubrovitsy in June obviously expresses his own mood at this period in his life.

If you are deceived in love,
Fall in love again soon,
But even better, take your staff
And set out to wander.

You will see mountains and seas, –
And a new way of life,
And the noisy wave will extinguish
The fire of your love.

You will hear the mighty cry of the eagle
High in the heavens
And you will forget your
Childish sorrows.[84]

Solovyov was soon sent by the University of Moscow to England primarily to study manuscripts of Hindu, Gnostic, and medieval philosophy at the British Museum.[85] His official letter of certification was issued on 18 June 1875, and on the twenty-first he left Moscow. According to Heine's directions, having been deceived in love, he took his staff and set out to travel. As regards the second piece of advice, "fall in love again soon," then Solovyov, if indeed he followed it, did so in an unprecedented form. Rejected by an earthly love, he was to meet "an eternal friend" in the reading-room of the British Museum and in the Egyptian desert.

Endnotes for Part 1 Chapter 4

1. *P,* vol. 2, 1.
2. Luk'ianov, vol. 1, 315.
3. *P*, vol. 3, 89.
4. *P,* vol. 1, 171.
5. *P*, vol. 4, 122; and letter to his brother Mikhail, *Bogoslovksii vestnik* 38 (1915).
6. *P*, vol. 3, 100.
7. Luk'ianov, vol. 1, 326.
8. Ibid., 327.
9. *P*, vol. 3, 105.
10. Luk'ianov, vol. 1, 344, note 662.
11. The Priest N. A. Kolesov, "My Acquaintance with V. S. Solovyov," *Chteniia v obshchestve liubitelei dukhovnogo prosveshcheniia* (October 1910).
12. "Pamiati pochivshikh nastavnikov," (Sergiev Posad, 1914), article by S. Glagolev, "Protoierei F. A. Golubinskii."
13. Luk'ianov, vol. 1, 355, note 640.
14. *P,* vol. 3, 105-06.
15. Ibid., 102.
16. *SS*, vol. 1, 25-26.
17. *SS*, vol. 4, 305.
18. *Sbornik pervyi o Vlad. Solov'eve* (Moscow: Put', 1911), 209.
19. Luk'ianov, vol. 1, 354, note 683.
20. *P*, vol. 3, 106.
21. Luk'ianov, vol. 1, 351.
22. Ibid., 109.
23. D. N. Tsertelev, *Stikhotvoreniia* (St. Petersburg, 1883), 61.
24. *Stikh*. 3rd. edition, 102.
25. *SS*, vol. 12, 224.
26. *P*, vol. 2, 224.
27. *P*, vol. 3, 275; *SS*, vol. 12, 482.
28. *P*, vol. 4, 113.
29. *P*, vol. 2, 2.
30. Luk'ianov, vol. 1, 397-98.
31. *SS*, vol. 1, 210.
32. Ibid., 27.
33. Ibid., 30.

34. Ibid., 29-30.
35. Ibid., 133-35.
36. Ibid., 142.
37. *Geraklit Efesskii*, translated by V. Nilender, 7.
38. *P*, vol. 3, 213.
39. Luk'ianov, vol. 2, 29.
40. Ibid., 30.
41. Luk'ianov, vol. 1, 424.
42. Ibid., 433.
43. Ibid., vol. 2, 32.
44. Ibid., vol. 1, 421.
45. Ibid., 416.
46. Correspondence of Lev N. Tolstoy with Nikolay N. Strakhov, letter of 1 January 1875.
47. Luk'ianov, vol. 1, 80.
48. *P*, vol. 2, 224.
49. Ibid., 225.
50. Luk'ianov, vol. 2,140.
51. Ibid., 65.
52. Ibid., 71-85.
53. Ibid., 70.
54. *P*, vol. 2, 225.
55. *SS*, vol. 1, 197.
56. Ibid., 205.
57. *P*, vol. 2, 337.
58. Luk'ianov, vol. 2, 109.
59. Ibid., 92.
60. Ibid., 140.
61. Luk'ianov, vol. 3, 48.
62. Ibid., 45.
63. Idem.
64. *SS*, vol. 4, 622.
65. *SS*, vol. 12; *Tvoreniia Platona*, vol. 1, v.
66. Luk'ianov, vol. 3, 48.
67. *SS*, vol. 1, 215.
68. Ibid., 216.
69. D. N. Tsertelev, "Iz vospominanii o Vl. Solov'eve," *Sankt-Peterburgskie vedemosti* 211 (1910).
70. *P*, vol. 3; *SS*, vol. 12, 482.
71. Luk'ianov, vol. 1, 435.

---

72. *P*, vol. 2, 226.
73. Luk'ianov, vol. 2, 94-95.
74. Ibid., 95.
75. *P*, vol. 3, 5.
76. *P*, vol. 1, 31.
77. Luk'ianov, vol. 2, 142.
78. Luk'ianov, vol. 3, 52-53.
79. Ibid., 55.
80. Ibid., 56-57.
81. Ibid., 58.
82. Luk'ianov, vol. 3, 75, note 1288.
83. *P*, vol. 2, 227.
84. Ibid., 84.
85. Luk'ianov, vol. 3, 64.

Part 1 - Chapter 5

First Travel Abroad

He beheld a vision
Unattainable to the mind,
And deeply the impression
Engraved itself in his heart.

Pushkin

At first Solovyov considered spending some time in Berlin mainly in order to meet Hartmann. But already on 27 June he wrote to Tsertelev from Warsaw, "I have spent a few extra days in Warsaw so I will not be able to stay in Berlin; besides, Hartmann is probably not there now. I will meet him on the way back... I feel exceedingly well (in terms of my morale) and am contemplating the plan of my work in detail. For the time being it is turning out smoothly and orderly, even symmetrically, on the lines of a Kantian-Hegelian trichotomy. It is only unpleasant to have to read so much rubbish."[1]

Solovyov was dreaming neither of Berlin, nor "Paris, the center of the world," nor "the Spanish realm," nor "the bright splendor of the multi-colored orient," but rather, the British Museum and made the journey from Warsaw to London in forty-eight hours. The crossing from Ostend to Dover took seven hours; there was a storm and he was constantly seasick.[2]

Even in the solitude of London "various people turned up," "two or three British cranks and two or three docents from Moscow." In London Solovyov met, first of all, Ivan Yanzhul, whose reminiscences of his stay there in 1875 were published in the third volume of Lukyanov's *Materials for the Biography of Vladimir Solovyov*. Before his departure from Moscow, Yanzhul visited Sergey Mikhailovich who took him aside for a confidential chat. "'I am told that you are on your way to London, where my son Volodya will soon be. Do you know him?' I replied that I had seen him only once. 'He is a good boy,'"–the esteemed historian remarked, – 'but he still doesn't know how to get on in the world, he spends too much because of his lack of experience; they'll rob him. If you would be so kind, if you do meet him, and that is very likely, if you care to, could you look after some of his affairs and help him, in view of his inexperience. I will be much obliged to you, and I will be more at ease knowing that he will be near a man who will be well disposed to him in case of need.'"[3]

The Yanzhuls conscientiously fulfilled Sergey Mikhailovich's commission and moved him from an expensive hotel, which he had described to his mother as "a small, cheap hotel," to the furnished rooms of a Mrs. Siggers where they themselves were staying.

"I see our docent I. I. Yanzhul almost every day," Solovyov wrote to his mother on 17/29 July. "He and his wife are very useful to me, especially in practical matters."[4]

Yanzhul's recollections of Vladimir Solovyov betray a rather critical tone. "His master's thesis, *Against Positivism*, sickened me, first of all, because I myself was something of a positivist at the time, but mainly because it was said openly in Moscow that Vl. S. was a friend of *Lyubimov* and *Leontev*, the overt enemies of his honored and respected parent, and that he was not ashamed of being in those places where they publicly slandered him (that is, his father). How much this was true, I, of course, do not know, but there is no doubt that later, when I first met him abroad, Vladimir Solovyov did not conceal his intimacy with the circle of *Moskovskie vedemosti*, which was very repellent to me, and once, on some occasion that I do not recall, he naively recommended to me the patronage of Lyubimov!!! Thus, with regard to the personality and merit of the young Solovyov, I had arguments both for and against him; an attitude that was quite removed from the idolization of all his qualities that arose during the last years of his life in the circle of *Vestnik Evropy*, to which I also, perhaps, adhered in view of the enormous changes that clearly took place in the development of his entire moral outlook."[5]

Yanzhul's wife, the famous Ekaterina,* had a gentler view of Solovyov, but even so, it went no further than a sentiment of compassionate sympathy. "This Solovyov is a strange man," she wrote to her parents on 6/18 July 1875. "He is a very frail, sickly man

* Ekaterina Yanzhul was a well known pedagogue.

with a mind that developed at an unusually early age and is devoured by skepticism and seeks salvation in mystical beliefs in spirits. Personally, he inspires my sympathy and pity; people assume he will go insane because he has done too much mental work for his years. When I first saw him I was struck by his gloomy, ascetic appearance."[6]

The kind-hearted Ekaterina Yanzhul worried especially about Solovyov's diet. "The self-absorbed Vladimir Solovyov literally forgot to eat," Ivan Yanzhul recalled, "and when my wife, who took him into her care, would often ask, 'Have you eaten today, Vladimir Sergeevich?' He would answer, "No, I forgot, and, it seems, I forgot to eat yesterday as well.'"[7] Even at that time Solovyov felt an aversion to meat and as he could not bear English cooking, he would lunch on fish and vegetables served in Italian tavernas, and in the evening Ekaterina Yanzhul "fed him on fish jelly." But to make up for it, he drank with pleasure English stout, beer, and cider, "made from fermented apples."[8]

Solovyov was treated more warmly by "a young scholar from Kharkov, M. M. Kovalevsky, an *excellent man of girth*."[9] "From the very first he attracted my sympathy," Maksim Kovalevsky* says about Solovyov, "– it is ridiculous to admit –on account of his handsomeness and his prophetic look. I have never seen more beautiful and pensive eyes. His face was inscribed with the triumph of the intellect over the animal. I soon had new grounds for loving Solovyov: the simplicity and equanimity of his comportment, combined with an unusual impracticality, a great mental vivacity, and a continual inner turbulence."[10]

Relations between Yanzhul and Solovyov did not progress smoothly and on one occasion they even erupted into a public scandal. On 15 July, his name day, Solovyov treated his Russian friends to champagne at Bodiaga, a Spanish tavern on Oxford Street. Yanzhul

---

* Maksim Kovalevsky (1851-1916), a sociologist, spent much of his life abroad. After studying in Berlin, Paris, and London, he returned to Russia to teach at Moscow University but was deprived of his professorship in 1887 for his political views and went into exile until 1905. Although a follower of Marx and Engels, in practice Kovalevsky was a moderate liberal and believed Russian tsarism could be transformed into a constitutional monarchy.

and Kovalevsky describe the scene that ensued somewhat differently. We will begin with Yanzhul's version: "The conversation turned to Belinsky;* Vl. Solovyov declared, 'What about Belinsky? What did he do?... I have already accomplished far more than he and I hope to surpass him during my lifetime and achieve much more.'... Although a great deal had already been drunk, and perhaps because of that, I could not restrain myself, listening to such self-adulation, and remarked to Solovyov that it 'was shameful to speak about oneself in such a way, that it would be better to wait until other people would recognize him as his equal!'–when suddenly, to my great distress, – this was happening in a public place crowded with people,–Vladimir Solovyov burst into sobs at my remark with tears pouring from his eyes. I quickly begged his pardon."[11]

According to Kovalevsky, Yanzhul was the first to offend Solovyov by remarking, "'You do think a lot of yourself, Vladimir Sergeevich! You consider yourself to be a second Belinsky!'–to which Solovyov replied, 'Belinsky was not an independent thinker, but I am.' I had to take my friends home quickly," Kovalevsky recounts, "I put Solovyov to bed with my own hands. On the following day he returned to our society again on the same footing and there was no mention of the previous day's quarrel."[12] Evidently, the main culprit in the altercation was neither Solovyov nor Yanzhul, but the sherry.

At first Solovyov was very pleased with the city. "I have settled fairly well in London," he wrote to his mother. "I spend most of my time in the library, I have been out of the city once and have been a few times in the parks. Here, a park means a large field in the middle of the city, much larger than Deviche Pole (and there are several such places); across the field are scattered clumps of trees and flowerbeds. These parks are the reason why London is known for its pure air and is the healthiest city in the world... I think I will spend all of my time in London and visit Paris and Switzerland on the way back."[13]

Aside from Yanzhul and Kovalevsky, of the Russians in London, Solovyov met Professor Kapustin from Moscow, about whom he wrote on 31 July/12 August, "Kapustin, whom I met before

---

* Vissarion Belinsky (1811-1848), influential literary critic of the period 1830–1848.

his departure, will probably be arriving soon in Moscow."[14] He also attended the salon of Olga Alekseevna Novikova (née Kireeva)* where there gathered various leading members of the Church of England who were interested in the idea of rapprochement between the Orthodox and Anglican Churches.[15] He also became acquainted with Nikolay Orlov, "a deacon at the Russian church here;" (Orlov was also a master of theology and a professor of Russian language and literature at King's College in London). By "two or three British cranks" Solovyov was referring to William Rolstan,† "an Englishman studying Russia,"[16] and the famous zoologist Alfred Russel Wallace,‡ who was devoted to spiritualism. "Of the English, I have become acquainted with the celebrated zoologist Wallace, which will provide me with the pleasure of staying sometimes in the real countryside–he lives about 40 versts from London."[17]

Let us now cast aside all these externals of Solovyov's life in London in order to dwell on the main reason for his coming here; on what transformed his London sojourn into "a blessed half year."

> Will I forget you, blessed half year?
> Neither phantoms of passing beauty,
> Nor the life of mortals, nor passions, nor nature,
> None but you possess my soul.
>
> Let human myriad's dash about
> Under the din of fire-breathing machines,
> Let the soulless piles be built, –
> Holy silence, I am here alone.
> . . . .

* Olga Novikova was the sister of Solovyov's friend Aleksandr Kireev and a woman of letters.

† William Rolstan (1829-1889), English writer, took an interest in Russian folk songs and tales.

‡ Alfred Russel Wallace (1823-1913), author of studies on natural selection and Darwin.

Most of the time I am alone in the reading-room;
And whether you believe this or not –God knows
That mysterious forces chose for me
Everything that I could read about her.

But when sinful caprices inspired me
To take a book "of quite another kind"–
I found here such stories
That made me go home in shame.[18]

Ivan Yanzhul left the following description of Solovyov's studies in the British Museum:

> As I sometimes kept an eye on him in the museum while he was working I noticed that he would spend whole hours in my vicinity bent over some sort of book about Kabbalah that contained curious and strange drawings and symbols, thoroughly absorbed and oblivious of what was going on around him. A concentrated, sorrowful expression as though of some kind of inner struggle was reflected in his face almost constantly. He sat close enough to me so that I had the opportunity to witness this scene many times. When I addressed him such questions as, "Well, Vladimir Sergeevich, what have you been thinking about?"–or,– "How can that book, which you have been reading for so long, be interesting to you? Why don't you exchange it?" etc., I would receive such replies as, "Me? Nothing in particular... Yes, it's extremely interesting; one line of this book contains more intellect than all the learning of Europe. I am very satisfied and happy that I found this edition."[19]

To the time of Solovyov's first journey abroad dates his heavily bound album that I have titled in my first biography of Solovyov, which is appended to the sixth and seventh editions of his poetry, "Album I." This contains the prayer to Most Holy Sophia that Solovyov either found in Gnostic or Kabbalistic texts, or composed himself on the basis of these sources.

Prayer for the Revelation of the Great Mystery

In the name of the Father and the Son and the Holy Spirit

Ain – Soph, Jah, Soph-Jah

With the ineffable, terrible, and omnipotent name I invoke the gods, demons, humans, and all living things. Gather together the rays of your power and block the source of your desire and be the participants of my prayer. May we be able to perceive the pure depth of Zion, may we find the priceless pearl of Ophir and may the roses be joined with the lilies in the valley of Sharon.

Most holy divine Sophia, essential image of beauty and the sweetness of the supersubstantial God, the radiant body of eternity, the soul of the worlds and only sovereign of all souls, by the ineffable and beneficial descent of your first son and beloved Jesus Christ, I pray to you: descend into the spiritual dungeon, flood our darkness with your radiance, melt the fetters of our spirit with the fire of your love, grant us light and freedom, appear to us in a visible and substantial form, incarnate yourself in us and in the world, restoring the plenitude of the ages, and may the abyss be sealed in its boundary, and may God become all in all.[20]

The pages of this album are covered in mediumistic writing. At this time Solovyov was convinced that by means of automatic writing he was receiving revelations from heavenly spirits and from Sophia herself. For the most part, these revelations are in French and are signed in French as *Sophie* or partially in Greek as *Soφia* [sic]. All of Solovyov's manuscripts are covered with similar messages from the spiritual realm. Sometimes a phrase in one of his articles is interrupted, scribbles appear, followed by a few legible words, then everything drowns again in scribbles after which the article continues. In later years, these entries have a less mediumistic character. They are written freely without scribbles in the sweeping hand of Solovyov, somewhat in imitation of Sofia Khitrovo's English handwriting. In the '80s these writings become more infrequent, and in the '90s they almost disappear. I cite some of the entries that date, apparently, to his time in London:

> I approve of Swedenborg's opinion about the nothingness *mentis humanae, quoad est in suo proprio*. You must allow yourself to be absolutely controlled by the higher influence. We will communicate to you by means of letters everything that you must do with regard to your future enlightenment by the spiritual world. I have touched the edge of the angelic robe.

This is followed by further scribbles and the signature *Sophie*.

> Sophie. Mange un peu plus aujourd'hui. Je ne veux pas, que tu t'épuises. Mon chéri, nous voulons te préparer pour la grande mission, que tu dois remplir. Médite toujours sur les principes. Ne donne pas un accès aux pensées de désespoir, mais chasses aussi l'orgueil et l'ambition.
>
> This is what you must know concerning the heavenly and divine modus of minerals: gold, mercury, copper, silver, iron, tin, and lead. Seven spirits: the first is Lucifer (*Saturnus*–lead); the second, Michael (*Jupiter*–tin); the third, Uriel (*Mars*–iron); the fourth, Gabriel (*Luna*–silver); the fifth, Anaiel (*Venus*–copper); the sixth, Raphael (*Mercurius*–mercury); the seventh, Shamail (*sol*–gold).
>
> 7 spirits, 7 primordial elements, 7 planets, 7 metals, 7 churches.

This is accompanied by a diagram:

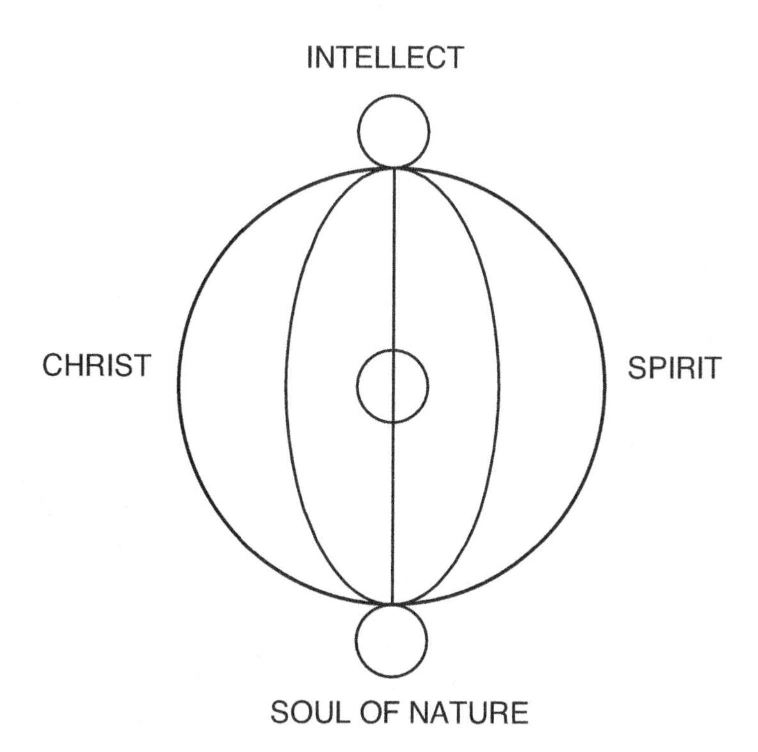

The restoration of Christ as an individual man = the union of the divine logos with the individual soul of Jesus.[21]

On the same sheet of paper can be seen fragments of that work which Solovyov described in his letter of 27 June to Tsertelev: "it is turning out smoothly and orderly, even symmetrically on the lines of a Kantian-Hegelian trichotomy."[22] One such fragment reads:

> The world process is absolutely necessary and expedient. Chance and arbitrariness are only present in human ignorance. Hitherto (until me) theosophical systems, which possessed spiritual foundations, did not have a true idea of the world process: either they ignored it completely (neo-Platonism, Swedenborg), or admitted the element of chance

and arbitrariness (the Fall), Kabbalah, Boehme; both one and the other accepted, as a result, devils and eternal hell.

Alternately, philosophical systems that had a real understanding of the world process as necessary without any kind of arbitrariness, were devoid of spiritual foundations. Therefore, the process appeared to be either purely ideal or even abstractly logical (Hegel) or purely natural (evolutionary materialism); some united idealism with naturalism (the natural philosophy of Schelling, the system of Hartmann), but, as a result of the absence of spiritual foundations even these latter, comparatively perfect systems, could not define the true goal and meaning of the process; for this goal... is the spiritual divinity of the world.

In his last system Schelling combines a logical understanding of the process with a certain notion, even if highly incomplete and rather confused, about spiritual principles; therefore, with him the goal, as well, of the process does attain a fairly satisfactory definition. Thus he maintains, along with a recognition of a concrete spiritual world, as do Boehme and Swedenborg–an absence of devils and hell. For this reason, Schelling is a true precursor of the universal religion. The teachings of Boehme and Swedenborg are a complete and superior theosophical expression of the old Christianity. The positive philosophy of Schelling is the first embryo, weak and imperfect, of the new Christianity or the universal religion of the eternal Testament.

Kabbalah and neo-Platonism
Boehme and Swedenborg
Schelling and I

The Law
Neo-Platonism–Kabbalah–the Old Testament
The Gospel
Boehme–Swedenborg–the New Testament
Freedom
Schelling–I–the Eternal Testament.

Thus passed Solovyov's life in the "holy silence of the British Museum."

> And once here–it was toward autumn,
> I said to her: O, blossom of divinity!
> You are here; I feel it, why have you not revealed
> Yourself to my gaze since my childhood?
>
> And I had only to think this word
> When suddenly all around me is filled with a golden azure,
> And before me she shines anew, –
> Her face alone, –it alone.

In spite of the apparition of "the face" of his mysterious friend, Solovyov's mood in London began to deteriorate gradually. At first, the city had pleased him so much that he planned to spend an entire year there.[23] He also intended to travel in October to Newcastle and in January to Bristol "without any particular goal."[24] But apparently his health was growing worse. A friend of Elizaveta Polivanova wrote to her, "I have received very sad news about our Vladimir Solovyov: in England he has begun to pursue spiritism and his health has worsened. I am told he is eating little meat and that he hopes to give it up on principle. I am deeply sorry for him. He is indeed a rare scholar and a splendid person."[25]

Aside from the comforting influences of Sophia, Solovyov undoubtedly had, as well, some disturbing and terrifying mystical experiences. "Half-jokingly, half-seriously," Maksim Kovalevsky recalls, "Solovyov told me that at night an evil spirit named Peter persecuted him, predicting his imminent death."[26] Following the arrival in London of Aleksandr Aksakov, Solovyov began to attend spiritualist séances, but his impression of English spiritism was mostly negative. "English spiritism left on me exactly the same impression that French spiritism did on you," he wrote to Tsertelev, "charlatans on the one hand, blind believers on the other, and a small kernel of real magic, which in such a milieu it is almost impossible to recognize. I attended a séance at the home of the famous Williams and found that his conjurer is more impudent than skillful. He produced 'Egyptian darkness,' but no other marvels. When a little bell that was flying in the dark landed on my head I seized, along with it, a muscular arm whose owner did not declare himself to be a spirit."[27]

About this séance Maksim Kovalevsky had this to say: "He (Solovyov) convinced Yanzhul and me to go with him to a spiritualist séance at the Metaphysical Society which was located, at that time, almost opposite the British Museum on Great Russell Street. The tickets had been purchased in advance for five shillings apiece. We were seated in a circle; the lamps were extinguished. Every few seconds the sounds of a harp could be heard. Suddenly, Solovyov took the hand of the person sitting next to him, the Russian correspondent of *Golos*, and then seized the hand of the man holding the harp. The latter began to struggle and slightly grazed the head of the Russian correspondent with the harp. Everyone was reduced to a state of confusion and the lights were turned on again. They severely reprimanded us and threatened to throw us out if we repeated such behavior."[28]

Writing to Tsertelev from Paris on 2 November, Solovyov summed up his impressions of spiritism in London: "The local spiritism (and consequently spiritism in general, for London is its center) is something very pitiful. I saw the celebrated mediums, I saw the celebrated spiritualists, and I don't know who is the worst of them. Among the spiritualists the most outstanding is Wallace. A rival of Darwin, he is in many regards a respectable man, but in terms of spiritism he has become the humble pupil of Allan Kardec (with whom now, thanks to a translation, the English have become acquainted, proving that they were Kardecists in everything but name); moreover, having become a spiritualist, this remarkable explorer considers it his duty to believe blindly every medium. As far as the later are concerned, indisputably the best of them, Jim and Kate Fox (now Mrs. Jenkin), were the founders of modern spiritism. I met them both. They are ill and do not practice. Jim says, 'quand j'étais medium.' With regard to those who are currently active, one is better off 'respecting them in silence,' to borrow the words of a bishop."[29]

Toward the end of September, Solovyov began to feel homesick; his hopes for a warm winter in London were not justified and he stocked up on warm clothing.[30] Unexpectedly, on 26 October he wrote to his mother laconically, "It would be completely useless to send me a fur coat, as it is colder here indoors than outside. Winter has not yet begun, but I have already caught a serious cold. Fortunately, my studies require that I spend a few months in Egypt, for which I am departing the day after tomorrow."[31]

Solovyov could not disclose to anyone the reason for his unforeseen departure from London:

> I said to her, you have revealed your face,
> But I must see the rest of you.
> What you did not begrudge a child,
> Do not refuse a youth.
>
> "Go to Egypt!"–The voice resounded inwardly.
> To Paris then! – And so the steamer bore me south.
> Intuition did not even struggle with reason:
> Like an idiot, reason fell silent.

In his letter to his mother of 17/26 October Solovyov reported that he was setting off for Egypt, "the day after tomorrow." Thus, we can assume he left "the misty shore of Albion" on 28 October. If on his way to England, he had been seasick while passing through the Pas de Calais, on this occasion he could repeat the lines of Boratynsky, "Seasickness has gently spared me, / The billows spray me with the foam of health." "During the two-hour crossing from Dover to Calais I did not feel the slightest sign of seasickness in spite of the strong rolling of the ship. This is very comforting, as I will have to spend 72 hours on the sea.... Paris put me in an excellent mood; I feel completely healthy, in London I was beginning to fall ill."[32]

The mood of Solovyov's letter was indeed extremely cheerful. On 6 November he wrote to his mother from Parma, "The further south I travel the more healthy I feel. I passed through France and northern Italy without stopping.... Thanks to the pince-nez I bought in Paris, I could see all the places through which I traveled; I saw the Alps, I saw Lombardy, however, until now I have not found anything striking. I like the Russian countryside more than the Italian. It's nice here only because it's still as warm and green as it is at home in August; in the outskirts of Milan I saw haymaking and in Chambéry the dahlias and asters in full bloom."[33]

According to Lukyanov's calculation, Solovyov spent twelve days in Paris. At first, he considered travelling through Greece, "I will write to you, probably from Athens, where the steamer will be moored for awhile."[34] But on 12 November Solovyov informed his mother from Cairo, "I boarded a steamer at Brindisi, which, after three days, without landing anywhere else, deposited me yesterday morning in Alexandria."[35] In "Three Meetings" Solovyov described his trip thus:

> To Lyon, Turin, Piacenza, and Ancona,
> To Fermo, Bari, Brindisi, and hence
> The British steamer already rushes me away
> On the trembling blue lap of the sea.

"The trip through Italy," Solovyov wrote to his mother, "was extremely pleasant, as well as, especially, the voyage across the Mediterranean for the whole time it was clear and warm as though it were July; the sea was completely blue, the nights moonlit. I didn't suffer from seasickness or any other illness; on the contrary, since Paris I feel better than usual."[36]

On the morning of 11 November Solovyov arrived in Alexandria. Having made a tour of the city in a few hours, he continued on his way and arrived the same evening in Cairo where the hotel Abbat, "the best in the whole world, comfortable, and modest" offered him "credit and shelter."

During the days following his arrival in Egypt, Solovyov climbed the pyramid at Cheops, explored the underground tombs and Joseph's well, swam in the Nile, and "saw the real sphinx."[37] The Sphinx "sends its sincere greetings to mama whom she considers for some reason to be kin."[38] Evidently, Solovyov saw a resemblance to the Sphinx not only in the features of his sister Masha, but also in those of Poliksena Vladimirovna.... In Cairo Solovyov visited the minister of foreign affairs, "a clever Armenian." He did not see the Russian consul general, Leks, as he was in Alexandria. He made especially close friends with the famous General Fadeev, who was staying in the same hotel. "I often see General Fadeev–a Russian bear, who, however, is far from stupid."[39] Solovyov dedicated a few stanzas of "Three Meetings" to him.

The occupant of number ten amused everyone–
He recalled the old days in the Caucasus...
It's no sin to name him–he died long ago, –
And I have nothing bad to say about him.

This was the famous Rostislav Fadeev,
He was a warrior in retirement and commanded a pen.
Capable of summoning a cocotte or a local council–
A host of resources were concealed in him.

Solovyov's letters to his mother serve as an extended commentary to a line in the poem, "Coins rattled around in my pocket." "Life is rather more expensive here than in London."[40] "If a dispatch of money cannot be expedited from the ministry, then I will ask papá to send 200 rubles as soon as possible."[41] I received the money (960 francs), but I had trouble changing the promissory note. After settling my debts and paying for my rooms (where I moved from the hotel) one month in advance, I am left with 40 rubles."[42]

Solovyov must have concealed from both his father and mother his main reason for staying in Cairo. "I will remain here until I have learned Arabic, i. e. probably 4 or 5 months. Then, perhaps, I will return directly to Russia, for there is definitely nothing for me to do in Western Europe," he wrote to his mother.[43] With his father he shared his thoughts about local politics, "In the meantime, aside from the stupid war with the Abyssinians, there is nothing," he wrote on 10 December. "Tell papá that there shouldn't be an Eastern problem until 1877, and if there should be one, it will be the messiest; in any case all the Europeans, aside from the English, are safe."[44] "I can report to you *la nouvelle du jour*: the English financial commission, which arrived in order to seize Egypt has received absolutely nothing from the Khedive and has set out for Upper Egypt, having nothing better to, and will then return home. The English consul must have announced that all this was only a misunderstanding."[45]

Having settled into the comfortable hotel Abbat, Solovyov "awaited the secret meeting."

And here once during a quiet hour of the night,
Like the cool breath of a breeze:
"I am in the desert–follow me there."

We can ascertain the date of Solovyov's trip into the desert on the basis of letters to his mother. On 25 November in a letter marked "Masr-el Caero," he informed her, "I have abandoned the splendid local sites for the desert. When you receive this I will be in the Thebaid, 200 versts from here, in a wild and uncivilized place, to where and from where there is no mail, and from where it is impossible to reach any other realm unless you go on foot. I will stay there about a month."[46]

Already on 27 November Solovyov wrote to his mother, "My trip to the Thebaid, about which I wrote in my last letter, proved impossible. Having traveled about twenty versts from Cairo, I was practically killed by Bedouins who mistook me at night for a demon. I had to spend the night on the bare earth, etc., as a result of which I retraced my steps."[47] On 31 December he wrote, "The incident with the Arabs amused me more than it frightened me. I will tell you about it when we meet."[48]

Evidently, the third meeting with the eternal friend took place between 25 and 27 November 1875, as Solovyov spent the night in the desert either between the twenty-fifth and twenty-sixth, or between the twenty-sixth and the twenty-seventh. At that time Solovyov recorded his vision in a short poem, "All in azure today my empress appeared before me" ["Vsia v lazuri segodnia iavilas' predo monoiu tsaritsa moia"] dated "1875, Cairo." But in 1898 he would portray it in detail in "Three Meetings;" let us attend to it.

Having described how, after his encounter with the Bedouins, he had spent the night on the bare earth at a temperature of 0 degrees, listening to the howling of the jackals, Solovyov continues:

And long I lay in a terrible drowsiness,
And suddenly there was a breath, "Sleep, my poor friend!"–
And I fell asleep; when I completely awoke, –
The earth and the circle of the sky were scented with roses.

And in the purple of the heavenly brilliance
With eyes full of an azure fire
You gazed at me like the first radiance
Of the universal day of creation.

What is, what was, what will come in the ages–
One motionless gaze here encompassed it all...
Before me shine blue seas and rivers,
And a distant forest and the heights of snowy mountains.

I witnessed it all, and all was as one, –
As one image of womanly beauty...
The immeasurable was enclosed in its boundary, –
Before me, in me–You alone.

. . . .

A single moment only! The vision withdrew–
And the sphere of the sun rose above the horizon.
In the desert–silence. The soul prayed,
And the blessed ringing did not cease within.

At dinner at the Abbat Solovyov "related the facts, while concealing the vision." But for all his secretiveness, he was not spared the witticisms of the general and paid heed to his warning:

"And if you would find it insulting
To be taken for a madman or simply a fool–
Do not talk any further about
This shameful incident in front of anyone."

There also remains to consider the lone testimony of Vera Pypina-Lyatskaya, the daughter of Aleksandr Pypin.* "He (that is, Solovyov) began to talk of his trip to Egypt in a simple, friendly way... He recalled in great detail how he had visited there various ascetics who have retreated from human society and settled in huts in deserted places, and how he wanted to experience for himself their mystical ecstasies. He wanted to see the famous light of Tabor, which he did."[49]

* Aleksandr Pypin (1833-1904) was a well known historian of Russian literature and thought.

It is difficult to say when Solovyov could have visited the hermits of the Thebaid and immersed himself in the contemplation of the light of Tabor. It could not have been, of course, during the night when he slept on the ground, listening to the howling of the jackals; on this occasion there was no question of either caves or anchorites of any kind. We know that Solovyov had intended to settle in the Thebaid about 200 versts from Cairo in a "wild, uncivilized place," where, perhaps, he hoped to find remnants of the ancient Thebaid desert community. But we also know that this trip never took place, and, having gone twenty versts from the city, Solovyov returned with "traces of a rosy smile" on his soul and holes in his boots. Can we trust the testimony of Pypina-Lyatskaya? Solovyov's friend Count Fyodor Sollogub depicted his trip into the desert in his comedy *Solovyov in the Thebaid*. In the play there are no references to any meetings with the mysterious friend nor to any sort of Gnostic mysticism; however, for all the humor of the play one can discern a profound and true idea. Solovyov is portrayed as a young warrior and ascetic who terrified Satan from his first appearance on earth.

> This villain had only just been born,
> But had already managed to shake the root of evil,
> Aiming at me the arrow of intellect and the javelin of faith,
> He endeavored to wipe my throne off the face of the earth.
>
> With a daring stride he makes his way across the desert
> And enters the Thebaid like a modern pilgrim,
> To temper himself for the struggle with prayer and fasting.
> But he will receive his final blow from my hands.[50]

Like a modern Oedipus, Solovyov enters into single combat with the Sphinx, which appears as a ludicrous and ignorant instrument of an evil force. At first, he disgraces Satan with the strength of his intellect and dialectical reasoning, then triumphs over the temptations of the seven deadly sins, like St. Anthony of Egypt who overcame the charms of the queen of Sheba. It is obvious that Solovyov's stay in Egypt had a vivifying effect on him. Like Basil the Great, who withdrew into the caves of Egypt after acquiring the pagan wisdom of Athens, after months in the British Museum studying of

Gnostic literature, Solovyov felt compelled to experience that desert where at one time Moses had seen the burning bush on Mt. Horeb and where later Paul of Thebes and St. Anthony the Great established the foundations of Christian monastic life. In 1891, comparing his fate with that of Moses, Solovyov recalled the land of the pharaohs:

> And dimly can I see the palaces,
> Where I studied under the priest of the sun,
> And the painted gods,
> And the pale-blue gilded Nile.[51]

At the end of January 1876, Solovyov's life in Cairo was enlivened by the arrival of his friend Dmitry Tsertelev whose uncle, Count Aleksey Tolstoy, had died at Krasny Rog on 28 September 1875 in his presence. Profoundly shaken by the death of his favorite uncle, Tsertelev decided to travel. He greeted the New Year in Athens and planned to go on to Italy, but at Solovyov's invitation, he made his way first to Cairo. "You must certainly come to Cairo," Solovyov wrote to him on 20 January 1876. "I am staying here until March. This trip will divert you. This country is extremely unusual and the climate is superior, not to speak of the pleasure you will give me. If, however, there is no way you can come, then I will try to go to Athens or Italy in February, if you will be there. But I hope that you will come here, and then at the beginning of spring we can go together to Italy or Paris. It's completely out of the question that you should be on your own now."[52]

"In Cairo I found that Solovyov was no longer staying at the Abbat," Tsertelev recalled. "He had moved into rooms in the home of the family of a photographer by the name of Désiré, but it turned out that in the same house there was a room free on a floor below, which I rented[53]... The door from my room opened directly onto a roof, where Solovyov and I sat in the evenings."[54]

Solovyov evoked these nights on the photographer's roof in 1897:

> Do you remember
> Those nights long ago, –
> When the dawn would meet us
> From the East with silence.

With brief hints,
Revealing the depth of life,
The fateful mystery
Would silently rise.

That which we then
Did not finish saying,
Eternity has recorded
On dark tablets.[55]

With Tsertelev, Solovyov wrote a short dialogue "Evenings in Cairo." At that time Solovyov was attracted to this genre, not without, of course, the influence of Plato whom he had studied assiduously while giving his lectures on ancient philosophy at Gérié's courses.

At the end of his life, having returned to Plato, Solovyov wrote his famous *Three Conversations*. In "Evenings in Cairo,"[56] as in *Three Conversations*, one of the characters is a lady or rather two ladies, the first and the second). The subject of the dialogue is spiritualism: the doctor, the representative of positivism (who, according to Princess Ekaterina Tserteleva, is Dr. Vladimir Popov who was in Cairo at that time) depicts spiritualist phenomena as a pack of stupid tricks, absurdities, and nonsense. The ladies passionately defend spiritualism; a séance is arranged, the spirit of Socrates appears and carries on an argument with the doctor in the manner of the Socratic dialogues: "'Do I have to repeat to you what I told my pupils before my death so that they would not confuse Socrates with that body from which his dose of hemlock was liberating him?'"

While he was still in Cairo, Solovyov began that work which he described in his letter to Tsertelev of 27 June, "For the time being it is turning out smoothly and orderly, even symmetrically, on the lines of a Kantian-Hegelian trichotomy."[57] Solovyov had sketched out some parts in London, and in Cairo he wrote the first chapter. What kind of work is this?

First of all, we must consider why Solovyov wanted to write something in a foreign language and publish it abroad. From London he had written to his father, "I will try to return to Russia by July, if only I can manage to finish the piece that I am now working on, which must be published in English and for which I have already found a suitable translator."[58] On 1/13 May he wrote again to his father, "In Paris I will be working on the publication of my book *Principles de la religion universelle*, which is small in size but great in significance; I have asked the abbé Guettée* to correct the French in which it is written. Among other things, he takes on this sort of work (he corrected the book by the minister Tolstoy about Catholicism) and was recommended to me in this regard by the priest in Nice."[59]

Perhaps Solovyov desired that a work which expounded the principles of a new universal religion should be published in an international language like English or French, or perhaps he foresaw the impossibility of publishing it in Russia on account of the censorship. The title, *Les principes de la religion universelle*, did not occur to Solovyov immediately; in a letter to his mother of 4 March he describes his composition as "a certain work of a mystical theosopho-philosopho-theurgo-political content in the form of a dialogue."[60]

I have in my possession the manuscript of this work in French dated "Cairo and Sorrento 1876" and titled *Sophie*. It consists of three chapters in dialogue and three chapters written as articles. Its outline, which is in Russian, was probably conceived while he was still in London:

> Foreword:
> Ch. 1. About the three types of philosophy in general.
> Ch. 2. The metaphysical character of man and the general possibility of metaphysics.
> Ch. 3. About positive metaphysics in particular. Its formal principles. Its relation to the other two types of philosophy, to religion, to positive science, to art, and to life.

* René François Guettée (1816-1892) was notable as a French Catholic priest who was received into the Russian Orthodox Church. During the publication of his *Histoire de l'Eglise en France* (1847-1857) Guettée was accused of Gallican tendencies by Catholic authorities and in 1857 was deprived of his faculties. Having made contact with Orthodox circles, Guettée joined the Russian Church and received a doctorate in theology from the Moscow Religious Academy for his work *The Schismatic Papacy*. He and Solovyov would later engage in polemics about the relationship between the Catholic and Orthodox Churches.

Exposition of principles.
Ch. 4. Anthropological foundations of positive metaphysics.
Ch. 5. Theological principles.
Ch. 6. Cosmogonic and soteriological principles.
Ch. 7 Eschatological principles.

The following diagram appears at this point:

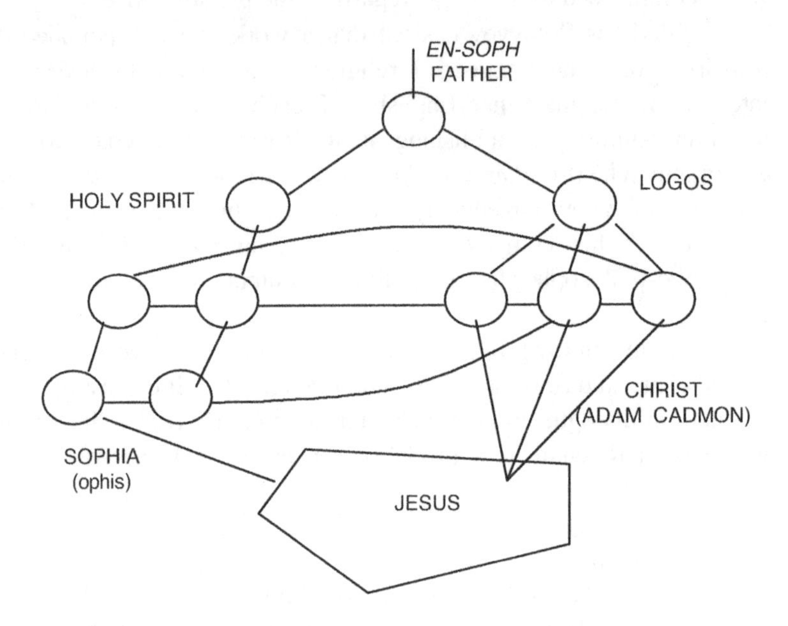

Sophie is structured as a dialogue between the philosopher and Sophia. Aside from the influence of Plato, there is present here something of the dialogues between the poet and the Muse in *Les Nuits* of de Musset.[61] In the beginning the character of a dialogue is strictly maintained, the speeches of the philosopher are noticeably distinct from those of Sophia. Gradually, however, the conversational element grows dim and gives way to a monologue. Finally, Solovyov abandons the original form and adopts the style of a philosophical dissertation. In general, the work is written very carelessly; the abundance of ideas breaches every genre and by the end it dissolves into autographic writing.

Under the general title, *Sophie*, is found the following heading:

Première triade.
Les premiers principes. (Le Caire. Février 1876). Premier dialogue. Le principe absolu comme unité (principe du monisme).

In Cairo Solovyov probably also wrote the second dialogue. "Le principe absolu comme dualité (principe du dualisme)." The third dialogue which, like the preceding, is called the "second dialogue" is dated "Sorrento Mars 1876." It treats the philosophy of the cosmic and historical process. The most artistically polished of the dialogues is the first, short one that begins:

> *Sophie*. Entre l'Orient pétrifié et l'Occident, qui se décompose, pourquoi cherches-tu le vivant parmi les morts?
> *Le philosophe*. Un rêve vague m'a mené aux bords du Nil. Ici, dans le berceau de l'histoire je croyais trouver quelque fil, qui à travers les ruines et les tombeaux du présent rattacherait la vie primitive de l'humanité à la vie nouvelle, que j'attends.

Sophia comes to the aid of the young philosopher and wants to reveal to him the mystery of the new universal religion. The philosopher asks her, is this religion Christianity in its perfected state or is it something different?

"What do you call Christianity?" asks Sophia. "Is it the papacy, which instead of purifying itself from the blood and filth with which it has covered itself in the course of centuries, sanctifies and approves of them, declaring itself infallible? Is it Protestantism, divided and impotent, which wants to believe, yet believes no longer? Is it the blind ignorance, the routine of the masses, for whom religion is only an old habit from which they are beginning to free themselves? Is it the mercenary hypocrisy of the priests and the powerful of the world? Know that the universal religion will come to destroy all this forever."

"I am not confusing," the philosopher replies, "the condition of the Christian world in a given epoch with Christianity itself. I mean living Christianity, not its tomb. I am asking if the universal religion is the religion of Christ and the Apostles, the religion that established a new world, that inspired the saints and martyrs?"

> *Sophia*. I will respond to your question with a comparison: the universal religion is the fruit of a great tree whose roots are formed by primitive Christianity and the religion of the Middle Ages. Contemporary Catholicism and Protestantism are its dried up and barren branches that it is time to cut off. If you call the whole tree Christianity, then the universal religion is, without doubt, only the final fruit of Christianity, Christianity in its perfection. But if you give this name only to the roots and trunk then the universal religion is not Christianity. You must know further that those same roots have also produced other shoots; ignorant people (*les ignorants*) seeing these plants, so different in form and size, have thought that they are of a different origin. But when the time comes for the harvest of the fruits, their mistake will become obvious, as the whole world will see that all these trees bear the same fruits and are therefore of the same origin.

The philosopher expresses the fear lest the term "the universal religion" give rise to a false interpretation:

> *The Philosopher*. There are people who believe themselves called to universalize Christianity. The device that they use for this is the most simple and easy kind. They remove from Christianity everything that is positive and characteristic in it and, in such a way, they obtain something that is neither Christianity, nor Islam, nor Buddhism; and this nothing they call the universal religion, the religion of Humanity and still other splendid names. I fear that at first sight they will mistake the true universal religion for this kind of naive

invention. I also know Jews and Muslims who treat the Torah and Islam in this manner. I think the same phenomenon can be found among Brahmins and Buddhists. All these fine people, without knowing each other have arrived at results that resemble each other as one zero does another; and they believe themselves to be great thinkers and heroes of humanity. There are also others who go even further; they remove from their universal religion not only the tenants of positive religion but religious principles in general: God, the soul, and all superhuman reality.

Sophia. I do not know these people. With regard to the misunderstanding about which you speak, I anticipated it with the comparison I just made. In order to obtain the fruits one does not cut down the tree on which they grow.

The Philosopher. The quasi-universal religion of these fine people resembles a tall and barren tree trunk that can give neither fruit nor shade.

Sophia. But the true universal religion is a tree with countless branches, laden with fruit and spreading its shade over all the earth and the worlds to come. It is not the product of abstraction or generalization, it is a real and free synthesis of all religions, which does not remove from them anything positive but rather supplies them with that which they do not possess. The only thing that it destroys is their narrowness, their exclusiveness, their mutual denial, their egoism, and their hatred.

Further on, Sophie arrives at a definition of "the absolute principle of all things." The philosopher puts forward the gnoseological doubt of the possibility of knowledge of the absolute principle, "'Can you prove to me that the absolute principle (*le principe absolu*) of all things is accessible to our knowledge?'"

"'O poor children," exclaims Sophia, "always mistaking words for ideas and ideas for reality! It's a question of words! Do you not know that knowledge, and I am speaking about knowledge of real entities and not about logical or mathematical abstractions, do you not know that knowledge is relative by its own nature? One knows something only in relation to one thing or another, one knows only more or less. Do you know me, the one who is speaking with you?'"

The Philosopher. How could I not know you!

Sophia. You know me undoubtedly as a phenomenon, that is, to the extent that I exist for you, or in my external appearance. You cannot know me as I am in fact, that is, my intimate thoughts and feelings such as they are within me and for me. You know them only when they reveal themselves outwardly in the expression of my eyes, in my words and gestures. They are only external phenomena, but meanwhile...

The Philosopher. But meanwhile, when I look into the deep azure of your eyes, when I hear the music of your voice, are these only external phenomena of sight and hearing that I perceive? My God! I know your thoughts and your feelings, and through your thoughts and feelings I know your inner being.

Sophia. And in such a way all beings know each other. Through external phenomena are known internal phenomena, and through these being (*l'être*) is known, that which a philosopher has termed the intelligible character (*le caractère intelligible*).

The Philosopher. And so, the philosophical distinction between being-in-itself and appearance is false?

Sophia. It is not their distinction that is false but their arbitrary division. Ignorance confuses being-in-itself with appearance. Abstract philosophy divides them absolutely. You must take the royal way; between confusion and abstract separation is the via media: distinction and correspondence. Appearance is not being-in-itself, but it finds itself in a definite relationship with it, it corresponds to it.

Thus, if it is impossible to know the absolute principle in itself, relative knowledge of it in its manifestations is possible. Having received an answer to the objection raised by skepticism, the philosopher turns to the objection of an opposite character, having in mind, evidently, Hegel.

The Philosopher. But what will you say about those philosophers who directly oppose the skeptics by maintaining that in knowing the manifestations of being in their general forms, we know, absolutely and directly, being-in-itself and that, therefore, being does not distinguish itself from such knowledge?

Sophia. A similar theory proposes that being, in manifesting itself, that is, in acting, is transformed without a trace into its action, and ceases to be itself, losing its own individual existence. Inasmuch as an action presupposes an agent, if the agent ceases to be, every action also ceases: nothing cannot be productive!

Finally, Sophia arrives at a definition of the absolute principle of things; it is not being (*l'être*) itself.[62]

We must say that the absolute principle is not being, that is, it cannot be either the direct object of our external feelings or the direct subject of our inner consciousness. That it is not to be identified with being is evident from still another point of view. It is the principle of every being; if it were itself being, being would prove to be outside every being, which is absurd. Thus, it is clear that the principle of being cannot be defined as being.

The Philosopher. Then must I define it as non-being?

Sophia. You could do this with impunity, and by so doing you would only be following the example of many great theologians, and even Orthodox theologians, who, without in any way being misguided, called God a *non-being*. But in order not to confuse timid minds, it is better to refrain from this term, since by *non-being* the ordinary mind always envisages a deficiency or the absence of being. And it is also evident that, in this sense, non-being cannot be the predicate of the absolute principle. We saw that in manifesting itself, that is, by coming into being (in realizing itself), it does not exhaust itself by its manifestation... If you define deprivation or deficiency as impotence (*impuissance*), the opposite will be power, or the positive possibility, force. In this way the absolute principle, not being as such, is the force of being, which is obvious, since it manifests itself, that is, produces being. And since, in manifesting itself, it cannot exhaust itself or pass without trace into its manifestation, it always remains as the *force*[63] of being, so that this is its permanent and individual attribute. And since he who possess power surpasses the one over whom he holds it, we must say that the absolute principle surpasses being, that is, it holds sway over it, that it is *Superens-hyperasios*. It is analytically clear that the absolute principle in itself is unitary and simple, since plurality presupposes relativity. This unity and absolute simplicity is the first definition of the absolute principle, by which it was known to the East, and since the religious man always desires to become like his God, and in this way to unite himself with Him, the constant aspiration of the eastern religions has been to make man remove himself from any plurality, from every form, and hence from every being. But the absolute principle is the principle of every being; unity is the principle of all plurality, simplicity is the principle of the complex, purity from all forms produces them. It is *hen kai pan*[*] [one and all]. Thus, those who want to know it only as *hen* [the one], only in its unity, will know it only halfway, and their religion, theoretically as well as practically, will remain imperfect and powerless. Such is the general character of the East. The Western tendency, on the contrary, is to sacrifice the absolute and substantial unity for the plurality of forms and individual characters, so that they cannot even conceive of unity other than as a purely external order; such is the character of their Church, their state, and their society. The universal religion is called to unite these two tendencies in their truth, to know and to realize the true *hen kai pan*.

In the second dialogue, "Le principe absolu comme dualité," Solovyov addresses the realization of unity and simplicity in itself,

---

[*] Written in Latin letters in Solovyov's manuscript.

which in the hierarchy of essences surpasses all predicates and the being of the absolute principle. At this point Solovyov outlines his philosophy of the Trinity, combining Kabbalistic and theosophical elements with the Trinitarian teachings of Augustine that he later developed in *Philosophical Principles of Integral Knowledge, Lectures about Godmanhood,* and the third part of *La Russie et l'Eglise universelle*. Already in the *Lectures about Godmanhood* the Kabbalistic elements subsided in favor of a theological conception, and in *La Russie et l'Eglise universelle*, Solovyov tried to reconcile his Trinitarian teaching with Catholic doctrine, introducing the idea of the *filioque* as a necessary part of it. Later on, we shall see what Solovyov kept from *Sophie* till the end of his life, and what he discarded as youthful delusion. In the meantime, let us note that Solovyov always upheld apophatic theology, and at the end of his life in the article "The Concept of God," which was meant to defend Spinoza from Vvedensky,[†] he vindicated the "superpersonality" of God. His polemic with Lopatin also dates from this time as well as the denial of "dynamic substances," with which his friend from his youth wanted "to dam up all the flow of Heraclitus."

In the first dialogue, the absolute principle or God is defined as non-being or the potentiality (*puissance*) of being. In the second dialogue Sophia defines matter and potentiality in the same way. In response to the philosopher's questioning the possibility of giving the same definition to contrary principles, Sophia declares:

> Contemplate both the similarity and the difference. The absolute principle and the universal matter are distinct from being in equal degrees; the attributes of being are foreign to them in equal measure. They are also both not to be identified with non-being, they are not nothing, they are the potentiality (*puissance*) of being. But the absolute principle is a positive potentiality (*puissance positive*), the freedom of being (*la liberté de l'être*); the material principle, being the necessary aspiration, or gravitation toward being, is its negative potentiality; it is only privation, the *absence* of being (*la privation, le manque de l'être*).

[†] Aleksandr Vvedensky (1856-1925), neo-Kantian, idealist philosopher.

His stubbornly held view of the Divinity as the potentiality of being, the denial of a personal God, and the declaration of his "superpersonality" show that Solovyov always maintained the opinions of Plato and Spinoza, which placed him in opposition as much to the Cartesian views of Lopatin as to Aristotelian theology, for which the Divinity is considered to be an *actus purus*.

In the second dialogue we find those Kantian-Hegelian trichotomies about which Solovyov wrote to Tsertelev.[64] On the margins is drawn a diagram that will be reproduced almost literally in *Philosophical Principles*:

En-Soph	*Logos*	*Sophia*
spirit	will	good
intellect	knowledge	truth
soul	feeling	beauty

Let us compare this diagram with the trichotomies of *Philosophical Principles*:

1.	2.	3.
Being as such	*Essence*	*Being*
(God)	(content or idea)	(the means or mode of being, nature)
1. Spirit	Good	Will
2. Intellect	Truth	Representation
3. Soul	Beauty	Feeling

The difference in the latter is that the theosophical terms are replaced by philosophical ones: instead of *En-Soph* we have Being as such (God); place of Sophia, Essence (content or idea), and instead of Logos, Being (the means or mode of being, nature). In the third group "knowledge" is replaced by "representation."

The divine nature is revealed in the tri-unity of Soul, Intellect (*Intellecte*), and Spirit (*Esprit*). The function of the Soul is love; the function of Intellect, thought; the function of Spirit, happiness (*la béatitude*), freedom, repose. The correlative nature of these states is obvious; man thinks in order to be happy; he is happy while loving and thinking. In general, love is the principle or cause, thought is the means, and happiness or repose is the end and goal. Man is the most perfect of organic forms, uniting in himself universality (*l'universalité*) with individuality.

"We must say," concludes Sophia, "that absolute being in its concrete manifestations is a great man, a man who is at the same time absolutely universal and absolutely individual. Just as the three Hypostases are perfectly individual, the great man also contains in himself three persons: the spiritual (*spirituel*), the intellectual (*intellectuel ou rationnel*), and the emotional (*animique*). The sexual character of the spiritual person is feminine, while that of the rational person, which is the spouse of the soul, is masculine; the Spirit is beyond these distinctions." Later we shall see that this "most perfect of organic forms," this "great man" is identified by Solovyov with the historic personality of the Godman Christ.

Such are the first two chapters of the "mystical-theosopho-philosopho-theurgo-political" treatise. Of course, these are only rough drafts, that primordial chaos out of which will subsequently appear his strict and polished schemes. For students of Solovyov it is especially interesting to witness the birth of his worldview, to perceive the embryos of the future in these vague and formless lumps.

On 4 March Solovyov wrote to his mother from Cairo, "I have not found sufficient nourishment for myself in Egypt, which is why I am leaving in eight days for Italy with Kalachov (the son of the director of the archives) who has been staying here the whole time. Tsertelev is leaving even earlier."[65]

On 20 March he informed his mother from Sorrento, "Having left the land of Egypt on 12 March, after a favorable sailing I arrived in Naples on the 16th, where I spent two days and telegraphed you about sending money. I left for Sorrento together with Kalachov... Sorrento, as you probably know, is a small coastal town in sight of Naples and Vesuvius, and is distinguished in every possible way for its natural beauties, which I have, however, not yet managed to enjoy by virtue of the ceaseless rain and stormy winds that are typical of this month. I am staying in a fairly inexpensive hotel right on the sea and I am thinking of remaining here till the end of April, which is the best month in Italy."[66]

It is possible that this "inexpensive hotel right on the sea" is the old hotel Cocumella where Pavel Bakunin (brother of the famous Mikhail) later stayed, as well as Mikhail Sergeevich Solovyov. A description of this hotel and garden, at exactly the same time of year as Vladimir Solovyov's stay, can be found in Hippolyte Taine's *Voyage en Italie*:

> I spent an hour in the garden of the hotel: this is a terrace on the shore of the sea on a small hillside. Such a sight offers a feeling of complete happiness. Around the house is a garden that is entirely green and planted with lemon and orange trees, which are laden with fruit like the apple trees in Normandy. The fruits simply fall to the earth at the foot of the tree. Other shrubs and plants of pale or bluish green color cover the expanse of the cliff. On the bare branches of the peach trees pink flowers, tender and delicate, are beginning to show. The floor is paved with shiny bluish paving stones and the terrace curves around the sea whose wondrous azure fills the entire space.[67]

In this hotel, a former Jesuit monastery, Solovyov wrote the remarkable third chapter of *Sophie*, "The Cosmic and Historical Process."

Initiated into the mysteries of the three Divine worlds, the philosopher asks Sophia whence derived the world in which we live, move and have our being. If everything in these three worlds is unitary and spiritual, then in this "fourth" world the contrary principles reign: plurality, division, hatred, coarse materialism.

"This is not a fourth world," replies Sophia, "this is only the third world, the world of souls and bodies, in a state of separation from the first two."

The origins of this world of enmity and division are explained by the Fall of the Soul. The Soul is situated between two forces: the Divine force of the Intellect and the ideal world that governs it, and the anti-divine, demonic force of natural or external Intellect, the analytical and negative force which it [the Soul] governs. In itself the Soul is feminine, and its happiness and power is subordinate to the masculine active force of the Divine Intellect. Releasing within itself blind desire and asserting its selfhood, the Soul passes from a state of passivity and potentiality into an active state and becomes Spirit, but this is now the spirit of evil; it is no longer Soul but *spiritus*, the spirit of darkness and evil. "The soul is Satan, which in this case is wisdom." In its fall the Soul "begets" Satan, the blind cosmic Spirit, and the Demiurge, the rational force, which is, however, negative and external, the principle of form, of order, and relations that are strictly external. The cosmic process thus commences: *bellum omnia contra omnia*. In the struggle with the Demiurge, the cosmic spirit, Satan, produces *time*, change, motion, the destruction of order. The Demiurge in its struggle with Satan produces *space*, order, repose (*stasis*), the static principle. The struggle of Satan and the Demiurge results in the cosmogony, and the Soul, in a state of ruin and suffering, takes on the appearance of matter or the substratum of the process. In his struggle with the Demiurge, Satan concentrates himself, condenses himself, and produces the weight and inertia of matter. The realm of the Demiurge is ether or weightless fluid, the forms of which are warmth, light, and electricity. These phenomena are only a modification of ether in its relations to matter; such, likewise, are mechanical movement, sound, and chemistry. Rarefaction and lightness are the typical traits of ether, just as condensation and weight are typical of matter. In the same way, the visible world represents a material nucleus, surrounded by a thin and ethereal atmosphere. The center is occupied by a cosmic fire that is cold and dark, the home of Saturn (*domus Saturni*). With its aerial army the Demiurge penetrates into every place of the nucleus of the cosmic spirit bringing universal enmity and division. This blind enemy is cast out of the center and is shattered into pieces from which arise the multitude of stars and planets. The Demiurge directs its main efforts against the Sun; it surrounds it with an ethereal atmosphere and attempts to penetrate its center. The spirit of the cosmos resists it and makes every effort to break through the ether. The struggle would be endless if the Demiurge did not resort to military cleverness. In several places it retreated, and the masses of material atoms, meeting with no opposition, tore away from the Sun and scattered themselves throughout space, forming the solar system. Sunspots are the remnants of the fissures created by the atoms when they fell away. The weakened Sun cannot oppose the Demiurge and has become its throne; it no longer has a material nucleus and is entirely permeated with ether. The earth became the most differentiated and organic of planets and the most capable of accepting the influence of the Soul. Of the other planets, Saturn is the least subject to the influence of the Demiurge; this is the planet of the chaotic Spirit of Satan.

The Soul of the world, located on earth, possesses it and produces the living soul, organism in its true sense. Solovyov accepts Darwin's theory, within its legitimate limits, that explains the origin of species by natural selection and the struggle for survival. It should not be forgotten that the basis for creation is chaos; order and law are only on the surface. Finally, the cosmic (telluric) process advances to the formation of the most perfect of organisms, the human, in its two aspects, the male and the female. The male organism bears the stamp of the Demiurge, while the female is more or less free of it. The goal of the cosmic process is the realization of the Soul and God in the Soul, the creation of an individual human organism. The goal of the historical process is the creation of a perfect social organism. History is also a struggle between Satan and the Demiurge, in other words, eternal enmity and war. Satan wants to place as great a number of people under his command as possible and to create the appearance of unity. The egotistical will is Satan's home in man; reason and justice are the domain of the Demiurge. The first God whom humanity worships is the Spirit of the cosmos, that chaotic desire that lies at the foundation of the world. The dominion of Satan contends with the Demiurge; mythology is a product of the struggle of the Demiurge with the spirit of chaos in the human consciousness. The mythological process follows the cosmic process and contains three periods: 1) the Uranic or astral, 2) the Solar, and 3) the telluric or organic.[68] This process concludes with the liberation of the Soul and the appearance of conscioiusness (*la conscience*). The Spirit of the cosmos and the Demiurge do not lose their power completely, but this power is no longer blind; it is subordinated to consciousness. At this point the historical process begins; its cast of characters are the Hindus, the Greeks (later replaced by the Romans), and the Jews. With the Hindus, the soul, just liberated from the dominion of the cosmic powers, is intoxicated by its freedom and the consciousness of its unity with the Divinity. It dreams, and in its dreams all the higher creations of humanity are found in embryo: philosophy, poetry, magic. But this is all in a confused form; as in a dream everything is confused, everything is one, and everything is nothing. Buddhism declared the last word of Hindu consciousness: everything that exists and that does not exist is in equal degree an illusion, a dream.

With the Greeks and Romans the soul liberates itself not only from the cosmic forces but also from itself, and it begins to receive influences from its divine spouse, the eternal Logos, which are beauty and intellect, art, philosophy, and in the case of the Romans, moral order. But with the Greeks, and still more with the Romans, the inspiration of the Logos is distorted by its ape, the Demiurge. Therefore, Greek philosophy ended in sophistry in the first instance, and in skepticism in the second. At the same time, Greek art represents the beauty of the external features of the body more often than inner beauty, the beauty of expression. Likewise, the moral order of the Romans created an external structure based on force. Besides, the Greeks and Romans apprehended the Logos only ideally, that is, as an idea, but the Soul is greater than an idea and that which apprehends it only as idea, in the end, loses its power over it. The Soul is personality, the "I" (ego), and a strong personality, even without any kind of ideas, is already something. Since for the Greeks and Romans personality was poorly developed, when they lost their ideas they had nothing left. In order to save humanity there was need for a nation that was ultra-individualistic and even egotistical; this nation was the Jews.

In Judaism the soul begins to apprehend the inspiration of the divine Spirit, the first hypostasis, while still preserving the imprint of the first natural hypostasis, the Spirit of chaos or Satan. The goal of the world process is the production of the perfect social organism, the Church. The first of the incorporeal souls, which surrenders itself entirely to the Logos in love (*en devenant amoureuse*), unites itself with it and becomes its individual human soul. When the ideal union of humanity with the Logos demonstrated its lack of solvency in Greek and Roman culture, on the one hand, and when, on the other, the religious and national egoism of the Jews was transformed into universalism, at the moment when in both the East and West man found the world to be an empty place and was grasping at suicide as the only defense against despair and anguish, the divine Logos, in union with a human soul, was born in Judaea. Since at the birth of our Savior a form was already provided by the divine Logos, there was no need for a father. The parthenogenesis found among many species of animals, bees for example, proves that the union of two sexes is not, in general, absolutely necessary for the reproduction of animal organisms. There is no absolute difference between human and animal organisms; thus, the physical possibility of the parthenogenetic birth of our Savior cannot be disputed.

Following his death, resurrection, and ascension, our Savior became the sole head of the Church, visible and invisible, which comprises one single living organism. From this time the definitive influence of the invisible world on the visible has begun. But before it reaches its goal, the Church must still endure the great struggle with the forces of this age, which although overthrown are not annihilated, having only changed the sphere of their activity. Before the appearance of Christ they acted on mankind mainly in the external forces of nature. After the arrival of Christianity, external nature lost its power over man. Nature had become for man something outwardly objective and material; it became materialized, that is, it was subordinated to man and could consequently no longer restrict him. In order for the forces of this age to have some kind of influence over man they had to act in a new sphere. This was possible for them, as humanity could not, naturally, be suddenly regenerated in its entirety. Primitive Christianity was not an absolute religion and had its limits, which were theoretical and practical. At first, Christianity, having only conquered the Spirit of chaos (Satan), could not be impartial to the just vanquished enemy. Constituting the result of this struggle, it had to preserve the traces of the struggle and hatred, especially among the minds that were more practical than contemplative, among people of will and not of intellect. These could not see in Satan the instrument of Divinity; they saw in him only the enemy, hence their dualism, the separation of the Kingdom of God from the Kingdom of Satan, the division of people into the elect and the damned, the doctrine of hell and eternal torments; all of these are absurdities and horrors that came to an end with the collapse of historic Christianity.

To this theoretical dualism was united a practical dualism; Christ originally appeared as the principle of the other world, having nothing in common with the things of the earthly world (God and Caesar). This was, of course, a temporary situation, because the Church gradually began to permeate the state, becoming its spirit, and completely mastering the hearts, thoughts, and life of its people. As long as the state was pagan, only strife was possible between it and the Church. The Demiurge (who took Satan's place in the world following his confinement in the abyss after the arrival of Christ), seeing that the Church was growing only more splendid from the persecutions, resorted to other methods. Through the intermediary of the Emperor, who found himself entirely under its influence (Constantine), it effected an external, feigned, that is, imaginary, submission of the state to the Church, while in no way changing the pagan and demiurgic principle of the state, neither transforming nor Christianizing it. The empire of Constantine did not differ in any substantial way from that of Diocletian. The Church accepted the compromise and constituted something of a social hermaphrodite under the name of the Byzantine Empire (*Bas-Empire*).

Matters were different in the West where the Church had to deal not with an organized state, but with the chaotic forces of the barbarians. It preserved its authority and subdued the barbarians, but it did not have the power to effect their rebirth. The conversion of the barbarians was only on an individual basis; the masses remained in paganism and created in feudalism a force hostile to the papacy. In its struggle with the empire and feudalism, the Church lost its purely spiritual and peaceful character and turned itself into the military monarchy of the popes. In earthly spheres earthly powers naturally win. Having triumphed over the empire, the papacy was defeated by the feudal kings. Toward the end of the Middle Ages, the Demiurge enjoyed a double success, in the victory of the monarchy over the papacy and in the transformation of the Church (itself) into a worldly power. Later on, reason, which had been suppressed by ecclesiastical authority, rebelled and wrecked the Church, but as the Church was the sole representative of Christianity, the rejection of the Church appeared as the rejection of Christianity itself, which now advanced with rapid stride: Episcopalian Protestantism, Presbyterianism, Unitarianism or Socinianism, deism, atheism (or materialism). In the practical realm, the progress of the Demiurge was the following: royal absolutism, parliamentarianism, republicanism, socialism, and anarchism. Now that all the external or demiurgic forces of life have collapsed, the Soul must find within itself the principles of a new life. It must return to itself, withdraw its forces from the external and concentrate itself, potentialize itself. This return of the Soul begins in the realm of theory, hence the development of contemporary speculative philosophy, which aspires to the creation of an inner world. Being the philosophy of the subjective soul, the soul in itself, contemporary philosophy thus distinguishes itself from ancient philosophy, that is, the philosophy of the objective logos. Contemporary poetry is also a manifestation of the soul by virtue of its subjective character. Individual contemporary philosophers also express the thoughts of the soul. That which it thinks, it communicates to people who are capable of understanding and expressing well its revelations. This theoretical incarnation of Sophia–the development of contemporary philosophy–can be found in the work of Jakob Boehme, Swedenborg, and Schelling. The real incarnation of Sophia is the universal religion.

Since 1878 a new, third era has begun. In the first period, before the birth of Christ, humanity was influenced by souls that were still incorporeal, that were naive and not tried by experience, genii (naivety is the characteristic trait of genius). In the second period the influence of the dead reigned (that is, from the birth of Christ to the end of the nineteenth century); hence its conscious, reflective, and experimental character. In the third period, beginning in the years 1878–1886, the division between the dead and the living ceases; the two worlds are united. When unseen humanity becomes more numerous than visible humanity, it will inundate the latter.

The shorter third chapter "La morale et la politique" follows the second dialogue. The dynamic form that was gradually disappearing in the second dialogue is completely eradicated here.

The morality of the universal religion derives from the concept of love. "The universal religion–the religion of the soul, the special function of the Soul–is love; the morality of this religion can have no other principle apart from love." In this instance love means the erotic, which Solovyov always considered to be the highest and most perfect form of love, citing the marital symbols of the "Song of Songs" and the Revelation of John.

Love has three stages. Natural love, which is sexual in its origin, can be extended to other relationships, even if they derive from sexual relations. After this comes intellectual love, by which we love that which we do not know directly, or rather, those objects that are not directly accessible to our feelings. It can also be expanded more or less. Such is patriotism, love for humanity, and finally love for God as the basic principle of all things of the substance of the universe. The *Amor Dei intellectualis* of Spinoza is the last stage of this kind of love.

Natural love possesses a spontaneous force but lacks universality; intellectual love comprises universality but lacks spontaneity. The third stage, which is a synthesis of the two preceding, unites the spontaneous force of natural love with the universality of intellectual love; this is absolute love. In order to obtain this character it must possess as its object an individual being, accessible to feelings but which also represents the universal principle or embodies it.

Every being finds itself in a loving relationship to two beings: to one more perfect than itself, which it loves with an "ascending" love, and to one less perfect, which it loves with a "descending" love. But since quantity finds itself in an inverse relationship to perfection and since the perfect being is unique, then the objects of "descending" love are always more numerous than the objects of "ascending" love. The sole object of the latter is Sophia. She finds herself in direct relations with the elect of humanity (who are necessarily men, as she is a woman), who love her with an ascending love and are loved by her with a descending love. These in turn find themselves in a direct relationship with a large quantity of individuals (necessarily women), by whom they are loved with an ascending love and whom they love with a descending love; these in turn are the objects of the ascending love of the majority of men, etc.

Among the elect of the first rank is the one who finds himself in the most intimate relations with Sophia and is the *great high priest of humanity*. The second rank, which consists of women, forms the first council. Then follows the third rank (the second rank of men) which provides priests of the second rank or metropolitans of the universal church. The third rank (of men) are archbishops; the fourth–bishops; the fifth–deans; the sixth–priests in the proper sense; the seventh–deacons; the eighth–believers; the ninth–catechumens; the tenth–neophytes.

The second form of division is into farmers, craftsmen (*démiurges, artisans*), and priests.[69]

The third division applies to the parts of the globe. Humanity is separated into seven large areas: Africa, the Orient, Central Asia (*la haute Asie*), India, the West, America, and Russia. These large landmasses are broken up into smaller units: parishes (*paroisses*), quarters (*quartiers*), houses, yards, and families. In this way the family is only the lowest rung of the social ladder and persons of the higher ranks cannot have families in the proper sense...

On the margins of the second page of the manuscript of the first dialogue there is an outline of such a program for the universal church:

1 pope.
7 patriarchs.[70]
46 metropolitans.
722 archbishops.
7,000 bishops.
70,000 deans.
700,000 priests.
700,000 candidates for the priesthood.

Immediately next to this there is a translation of the concluding lines of the second part of Goethe's *Faust*:

Everything that passes
Is only a likeness.
The unattainable has been made real
And the unutterable

Has been realized here.
The Eternal Feminine
Draws us all.[71]

The outline then continues:

4 classes:

1. Priests — The living law.
2. Craftsmen } workers, active in regard to external nature,
3. Farmers } passive in society.
4. Women — not workers, passive in regard to external nature, active in society

Legislators, producers, manageresses.

Following this we have the dialogues reworked in the form of articles: "Des trois phases du principe absolu et des trois hypostases divines." Then the three chapters: "I. Du besoin métaphysique de l'homme. II. De la possibilité de la connaissance métaphysique. III. De la realité de connaissance métaphysique."

As mentioned before, these articles are interrupted by automatic writing, such as, for example, "Think about me. I will be born in April 1878. Sofia." "Osborne. I will reveal the great mystery. People can rule over the forces of nature, if they completely renounce all earthly goals. You see clearly, oh my friend, everything that is necessary for this. You must try to overcome the Demiurge in yourself in order to master his powers outside you."

Such is this work of a "mystical-philosopho-theurgo-political content." As the first draft of Solovyov's future system, *Sophie* contains certain positions that he would try to vindicate for the rest of his life; here *in nuce* is all of the future Solovyov. First of all, we see the aspiration to reconcile the mystical revelations of the ancient religions and Christianity with the findings of modern philosophy and the natural sciences. Regarding mechanical movements, sound, and chemical reactions as modifications of ether, Solovyov cites the scientific theory of the unity of physical forces. As an explanation of the cosmogonic process he accepts Darwin's theory within certain limits, and with regard to Christ's immaculate conception from Mary, he refers to the phenomenon of parthenogenesis among bees. In philosophy the predominant influences are Spinoza and Schelling; in theology, a tendency toward the apophatic theology of the East. The explanation of the cosmic process as a result of the fall of the Soul of the world (the Gnostic Sophia Akhamot) and her alienation from the heavenly bridegroom, the divine intellect, and her conversion into the active and spiritual power of evil, chaos lying at the foundation of the universe; the belief in the liberation of the suffering Soul of the world and her return to the heavenly bridegroom – all this will appear in a purified and improved form in the third part of *La Russie et l'Eglise universelle*. The extremely inconsistent and inaccurate terminology of *Sophie*[72] is replaced by intelligible diagrams. Solovyov will make no further reference to the Demiurge and the system presented in *Lectures on Godmanhood*, *The History of Theocracy*, and *La Russie* will gradually become more Christian; the Gnostic and Kabbalistic terminology will be replaced by a theological one. In *La Russie*, Solovyov will already demonstrate a definite aspiration toward reconciling his cosmogonic system with Catholic orthodoxy. His views on primitive Christianity and Catholicism will also change abruptly in the '80s. Among the lasting elements of Solovyov's worldview that are typical of *Sophie* are the negative attitude to Hindu consciousness, the superiority of Greek religion and philosophy over Hinduism, and in turn, the depreciation of Hellenism in the light of Judaism. Only the Jewish soul accepted from the first the direct influences of the divine Logos; only it had a strong consciousness of personality, of the ego, and therefore only one individual Jewish soul, having loved the divine Logos, could enter into a hypostatic union with it and form the unique personality of the Godman. In the '80s Solovyov's philosophy of Christian history underwent a considerable evolution. His low estimate of Byzantium remained unchanged, but Constantine, who appears in *Sophie* as only the instrument of evil, of the Demiurge, is praised by Solovyov in *The History of Theocracy* as "the Caesar equal to the apostles."[73] If on the first page of *Sophie* we find harsh judgement passed on the papacy, which instead of purifying itself of centuries of blood and filth, has declared itself infallible, then in *La Russie et l'Eglise universelle*, Solovyov substantiates the dogma of papal infallibility. The future of humanity is already depicted in *Sophie* as the "universal church" headed by *a single high priest* to whom is now given the name "pope." In the '80s the universal church is characterized by Solovyov as a theocracy, and the universal high priest, who in his youthful dreams was the first beloved of Sophia, now appears as the actual Roman Pope Leo XIII.

Solovyov soon rejected the idea of publishing *Sophie*, a decision that was undoubtedly dictated by wisdom. The publication of such a work would have completely convinced such people as Yanzhul and General Fadeev of Solovyov's insanity and he "would be mistaken for a madman or simply a fool." He would have fallen from the heights to which he had raised himself with *The Crisis of Western Philosophy* and would have evoked the deserved laughter of the man of politics and the deep sigh of the serious mystic. Solovyov's abiding desire was always to implement his schemes in the actual politics of the present day and to squeeze the historical process into "Hegelian trichotomies." In these instances, insights of genius sometimes become mixed with childishly helpless illusions. During his first trip to Egypt, Solovyov displayed his interest in politics when he wrote to his father that "there shouldn't be an Eastern problem until 1877, and if there should be one it will be the messiest."[74] We have seen that Solovyov identified the 1878 with certain mystical hopes, that in that year a new, third era would begin with the re-birth of Sophia in the consciousness of humanity. From this year on Solovyov expected great political events and he was not mistaken. But what can one say about that political and social system which he proposed in *Sophie* with the division of all humanity into classes according to the degree of "being in love" with Sophia? Obviously, Solovyov himself saw that all this was nonsense, and having crammed all of his politics into a few pages, gave up writing any further.

The composition of *Sophie* was also halted by an unexpected disaster. Solovyov injured himself on the way back from Mt. Vesuvius and took to bed. He reported about his fall on Vesuvius in letters of 20 April to his brother Mikhail and to his friend Tsertelev, and in an undated "encyclical" to his sisters. From the content of the latter, it appears that it was written later than the letters to his brother and friend, not long before his departure from Italy.

In his letter to Mikhail he explained: "Two weeks ago, on my way back from Vesuvius I fell from my horse, injuring my knee and smashing both arms. I lay in bed for four days without moving and now I can hardly walk."[75]

To Tsertelev he wrote, "I can write to you only a few words: my arm hurts. Returning from Vesuvius, I managed to cripple myself, and perhaps I shall be a cripple the rest of my life. I am in a sorry state and have no plans of any sort."[76] In his memoirs Tsertelev provides the reason for the fall at Vesusvius. "A group of boys crowded around him begging. Solovyov distributed among them his small change, but as they continued to press around him, he threw them his money-bag as proof that he had nothing more; when this did not help, he thought he could save himself by flight."[77]

After his accident Solovyov spent a week in bed in Naples where he was "attended by a good German doctor, and then in Sorrento by two Russians."[78] Two ladies also extended him sympathy, Mme Auer and Mlle Train,[79] who "plucked the lint off him."[80] Nadezhda Evgenevna Auer, whom Solovyov would meet again in Finland in the '90s and to whom he dedicated a few poems, was the wife of the famous violinist Auer. In Sorrento Solovyov experienced a fleeting romantic attraction toward her. Mme Auer had recently married and was missing very much her husband who was in St. Petersburg. On one occasion, having recovered from his wounds, Solovyov asked her to spend the evening with him. She agreed on condition that Solovyov allow her to hear her husband's voice or the sound of his violin; like many people she believed in Solovyov's magical gifts. When they were alone, Solovyov gave her such a look that she became frightened. The lamp was extinguished and in the air could be distinctly heard the sound of a distant violin. The lamp then lit itself again and Solovyov, tortured by the tension, fell on his knees before Nadezhda Evgenevna and sobbed...

Solovyov was "thoroughly sick" of Italy;[81] the "virtuous ladies" had departed, the wound had healed, and on 27 April he informed Tsertelev, "in a few days I am leaving for Paris."[82]

Solovyov arrived in Paris on 13 May, "after many misfortunes and vexations."[83] On the way he stopped at Nice where he wrote the poem, "The Song of the Ophites."

We will marry the white lily with the rose,
With the scarlet rose.

The poem was inspired by ideas in Gnostic literature. In the rough draft a variant reads:

We will find the radiant *Pleroma*.[84]

It is at this point that the theme of the "white lily" appears in Solovyov's work.[85] In "Album I" Sophia informs him, "the white lily will blossom in March."

From Cairo Solovyov wrote to his mother, "I am leaving for Paris where, for the purification of my conscience, I will do a bit of studying in the Bibliothèque Nationale, and after spending a few days in London, I will return to Moscow in July via Kiev."[86]

From Paris he wrote to his father, "I will spend about six weeks in Paris and after collecting my books in London I will return to Moscow via Ostend and Berlin in time for your name day.[87] In Paris I will be working on the publication of my book *Principes de la religion universelle*, which is small in size but great in significance; I have asked the abbé Guettée to correct the French in which it is written. Among other things, he does this sort of work (he corrected the book by the minister Tolstoy about Catholicism) and was recommended to me in this regard by the priest in Nice."[88] A few days latter on 28 May he wrote, "With regard to my work, I need to publish it as it will be the basis for all my future studies and I can do nothing without citing it."[89] By the tone of this letter we can conclude that Sergey Mikhailovich was somewhat troubled by his son's behavior. The publication in Paris of *Les principes de la religion universelle* hardly pleased him and his return to Russia through Kiev probably inspired fresh suspicions with regard to his cousin Katya... "As far as I can remember I never planned on going there," Vladimir said in his defense, forgetting that on 4 March he had written to his mother, "I will return to Moscow in July via Kiev."

On 16 May he wrote the poem in hexameters, "Vis eius integra, si versa fuerit in terram." The title of the poem is taken from the *Fabula smaragdina*, which Solovyov translated as, "His force is whole when he returns to the earth."[90]

Solovyov's impressions of Paris were negative. "I have not been to see anyone anywhere (today I was only at the Russian church). I study at home and tomorrow I must obtain a pass in order to do research in the Bibliothèque Nationale; the accursed French have played nothing but tricks on me up until now. I do not know of a baser nation (I am speaking of the male sex), they are worse even than the English and the Ethiopians of Egypt."[91] Solovyov did not go to the theater once and of the famous people, he only visited Renan who produced on him the impression of being "a most raucous chatterbox."[92] In a letter to Ivan Yanzhul of 27 May he describes Renan as, "a most vacuous chatterer with bad manners."[93] My father told me that when Vladimir Solovyov went to see Renan he found a venerable epicurean surrounded by lady admirers and that upon meeting the Russian guest he exclaimed majestically, "Jeune homme, les idées, c'est la principale chose."

"In Paris I felt such a general sense of depression descend on me that at the first opportunity I dropped all of my activities and studies and headed for Moscow without looking back," Solovyov writes to Tsertelev from Neskuchny already on 19 June 1876.[94] From the line "I returned from abroad two weeks ago" we can conclude that Solovyov returned to Russia around 5 June, without, evidently, stopping in London.

But what was the fate of *Les principes de la religion universelle*?

"I did not publish my work in French for various reasons, " Solovyov wrote to Tsertelev, "but once I have significantly expanded it and provided it with the appropriate number of Greek, Latin, and German quotations, I will publish it in Russian as my doctoral dissertation because I have neither the ability nor desire to write a special work for this purpose."[95]

Thus, Solovyov was hoping to receive a doctoral degree for *Sophie*! At that time he had very little understanding of the state of affairs both of the people around him and of Professor Vladislavlev. The matter of his doctoral degree dragged on for many years and Solovyov had to abandon the idea of presenting his *Philosophical Principles of Integral Knowledge* as a dissertation; this work remained unfinished and Solovyov began to write the more academic *Critique of Abstract Principles*.

Nikolay Strakhov wrote to Lev Tolstoy on 12 September 1876 from St. Petersburg, "It gave me great pleasure to see Vladimir Solovyov. His health is considerably stronger, he does not eat meat and does not drink wine. Perhaps he will improve, I desire this very much. 'With whom did you become acquainted? To whom did you listen?' – 'With no one and to no one.' – 'What were you doing?' 'I was writing my book *The Principles of Positive Metaphysics*, and even in Paris I did not go to a single theater. I did meet, however, Renan, whom I did not like as a person, and Wallace, whom I found limited. The spiritualists are such rubbish that I couldn't bear them; I am completely cured (that is, of spiritism); but then I can please you by telling you that Wallace said Darwin has become something of a spiritualist: his wife turned out to be a medium (as did Butlerov's).' Vl. Solovyov has already completed a book; it will be 400 pages long, he is ready to publish it and he will come to St. Petersburg before Christmas for his doctor's degree."[96]

Thus ended Solovyov's strange intellectual mission. Having traveled all over Europe, he almost failed to notice it. Only the British Museum and the Egyptian desert left on him an indelible impression. He returned to Russia a confirmed Slavophile. The East had petrified and the West was decomposing. "I won't travel anymore," he wrote to his father from Paris, "either to the cemeteries of the East or to the latrine of the West, but since many knowledgeable people have predicted for me a life of wandering I will simply wander in the outskirts of Moscow."[97]

In fact, Solovyov lived in Russia without a break for ten years, that is, until 1886. However, the predictions of the knowledgeable people were correct because beginning in 1886 Solovyov traveled abroad on five occasions to the following destinations; Zagreb, Paris, Scotland and France, Egypt, and Cannes, not counting his stays in Finland.

Although Solovyov considered the East "petrified" and compared it to a cemetery, dubbing it "a heap of old rubbish and fresh s...,"[98] it was, all the same, closer to him at that time than the West. He even thought of a journey to India where mysterious voices were summoning him. "I will set out for Egypt and perhaps India."[99] And in his program for a division of humanity into seven parts "the West" (that is, Europe) represents only one part alongside Africa, the Orient, Central Asia, India, and America. Solovyov's blindness toward Italy is surprising. "I saw the Alps, I saw Lombardy, however, until now I have seen nothing striking. I prefer the Russian countryside to the Italian."[100] "I was pretty bored with Italy,"[101] and finally, in a letter to Yanzhul he calls Italy "the most vulgar country in the world."[102] Neither the natural beauty, nor art, nor churches of Italy produced any kind of impression on Solovyov. This betrays his complete indifference to the objective and his extreme subjective lyricism. The favorite country of Goethe, Gogol, and Boratynsky appeared to him to be the "most vulgar." Italy evoked almost the same reaction from his friend Fet:

> Italia! You have lied to the heart.
> How long have I cherished you in my dreams,
> But the soul does not find you kindred,
> And your air did not strike me as my own.

And in his letter to Turgenev:

Everywhere, gentle and silent,
Stands before you the olive tree
Or the umbrella of a young pine,
But the eternally iridescent dreams
Will carry you under the shade of the birch,
To the streams of your native land.

For Solovyov in 1876 the future of humanity lay in the revelations of the latest German metaphysics and in the hidden powers of Slavdom. He would soon pronounce his credo in the public lectures "Three Forces" and would be hailed by the old Slavophiles headed by "Uncle Yusha" Samarin as their best hope.

We have seen that during his trip abroad Solovyov's poetry blossomed for the first time. The poem written in London, "Although we are chained by invisible shackles forever... [Khot' my navek nezrimymi tsepiami...]" still produces the impression of versified rationalism; the Egyptian poems "To my empress belongs a lofty palace [U tsaritsy moei est' vysokii dvorets]" and "Song of the Ophites" are already full of music and images. The poem "Near and far, not here and not there [Blizko, daleko, ne zdes', I ne tam],"[103] probably dates to 1876 as well. We can assume this on the basis of a list of titles of projected poems that is found on the same page of the manuscript: 1) To Saturn, 2) To the Uranian Sophia, 3) *Hen kai pan*, 4) To Prometheus Bound, 5) "The image of this world passes", 6) "To Russia," 7) "Stars", 8) "The New May" (*1 May 1876*), 9) "Phantoms." The choice of themes, as well as the date "1 May 1876," indicate 1876. Having surveyed the personal notes of Solovyov that belong to the period of his first trip abroad, we come away with the impression that during the years 1875–76 he was seized by some kind of mystical whirlwind. Having absorbed by the age of twenty-three German philosophy, theology, and Kabbalah, and having enjoyed a brilliant victory at his master's defense, as well as a meeting with Sophia in the Egyptian desert, he felt himself to have been placed at some lofty height. Most likely, there arose before him the temptation of imagining himself to be a "superman," that high priest of the universal Church, the first elect of Sophia, whom he described in Sorrento. Even at this stage, Solovyov possessed in the feeling of humility the antidote to the temptations of superhuman pride. In the same "Album I" we find the poem:

> When in my barren field
> I sowed the seed of truth,
> It arose, and hastily
> I gathered the first harvest.
> I was not the one who cultivated or cherished it,
> Who watered it with rain,
> Who fanned it with cool breezes,
> Or warmed it with clear sunlight.
> Oh no! With thorn and thistles
> I trampled the heavenly sowing,
> With the weeds of worldly aspirations
> I choked and smothered it.[104]

The mystical storms soon died down. Toward the beginning of the '80s Solovyov passed from subjective ecstasies to the objective principle of ecclesiality [*tserkovnost'*]. The chimeras of his youth began to appear to him as childishness... But we will not run ahead.

Endnotes for Part 1 Chapter 5

1. *P*, vol. 2, 227. In this edition of the letters there is an obvious misprint of 27 July instead of June.
2. *P*, vol. 2, 3.
3. Luk'ianov, vol. 3, 95-96.
4. *P*, vol. 2, 5.
5. Luk'ianov, vol. 3, 96.
6. Ibid., 124-25.
7. Ibid., 126.
8. *P*, vol. 2,6.
9. Ibid., 5.
10. Luk'ianov, vol. 3, 136.
11. Ibid., 132-33.
12. Ibid., 138.
13. *P*, vol. 2, 5-6.
14. Ibid., 7.
15. Luk'ianov, vol. 3, 139.
16. *P*, vol. 2, 5.
17. Ibid., 11.
18. "Three Meetings," *SS*, vol. 12, 80.
19. Luk'ianov, vol. 3, 126.
20. *Stikh*., 7th ed., 330-31; *SS* vol. 12, 148.
21. At this time Solovyov wrote the words Sophia and Logos mixing Russian and Greek letters. Sophia is always written with a capital S [C in Russian] and a Greek φ, while Logos is always written with a lower case λ.
22. *P*, vol. 2, 227.
23. Ibid., 4.
24. Ibid., 11,12.
25. Luk'ianov, vol. 3, 63.
26. Ibid., 137.
27. *P*, vol. 2, 228.
28. Luk'ianov, vol. 3, 136.
29. *P*, vol. 2, 11.
30. Ibid., 11, 12.
31. Ibid., 13.
32. Ibid., 13.
33. Ibid., 13.
34. Ibid., 14.
35. Ibid., 14.

36. Ibid., 14.
37. Ibid., 16.
38. Ibid., 17.
39. Ibid., 17.
40. Ibid., 16.
41. Ibid., 19.
42. Ibid., 21.
43. Ibid., 16.
44. Ibid., 16.
45. Ibid., 21.
46. Ibid., 18.
47. Ibid., 19.
48. Ibid., 21.
49. V. Pypina-Liatskaia, "V. S. Solov'ev: Stranichka iz vospominanii." Golos minuvshego (Dec. 1914).
50. Luk'ianov, vol. 3, 284.
51. *Stikh.*, 7th ed., 101.
52. *P*, vol. 2, 230.
53. Solovyov had informed his mother about moving from the hotel on 31 December (*P*, vol. 2, 21).
54. Luk'ianov, vol. 3, 256.
55. *Stikh.*, 7th ed.; SS, vol. 12, 65.
56. "Evenings in Cairo" was published in Luk'ianov's Materialy, vol. 3. 248-255.
57. *P*, vol. 2, 277.
58. Ibid., 11.
59. Ibid., 27.
60. Ibid., 23.
61. Solovyov especially valued *Les Nuits* of de Musset as well as his *Le Souvenir*.
62. In this work Solovyov constantly uses the term *l'être*. In Russian one has to translate this word in various ways: either by the word "essence" ["*sushchestvo*"], or "entity" ["*sushchnost*"], or "being" ["*bytie*"].
63. *Puissance* means both might and possibility. Here it evidently means the "potentiality" of being.
64. *P.*, vol. 2, 227.
65. Ibid., 23.
66. Ibid., 24.
67. Hippolyte Taine, *Puteshestvie po Italii*, Russian trans. by P. P. Pertsov, vol. 1, 36.

68. Solovyov repeats here the outline of his first work *The Mythological Process in Antiquity*.
69. In the entire structure of this *aristocratic commune* one can see the influence of Plato's *Republic*.
70. Evidently for each part of the globe.
71. In the last two lines Solovyov repeats the mistake that we have already noted in his letter to Tsertelev of 13 October 1874 (P, vol. 2, 224). Solovyov replaces the concept of the preposition *hinan* [upwards] with that of *an* [on]. According to Goethe the Eternal Feminine draws us *upwards* ("carries us higher" in Fet's translation). According to Solovyov, it draws us on to *itself*.
72. For example, Satan is called sometimes "the spirit of the cosmos" or "the spirit of chaos," even though the concepts of cosmos and chaos are opposed to each other.
73. *SS*, vol. 4, 622.
74. *P*, vol. 2, 20.
75. Luk'ianov, vol. 3, 323.
76. *P*, vol. 2, 231.
77. Luk'ianov, vol. 3, 325.
78. *P*, vol. 2, 232.
79. Ibid., 28.
80. Ibid., 26.
81. Ibid., 26.
82. Ibid., 232.
83. Ibid., 27.
84. *Stikh*., 7th ed., 301; *SS*, vol. 12, 149.
85. The "Prayer for the Revelation of the Great Mystery" already speaks of the union "of the roses with the lilies in the valley of Sharon."
86. *P*, vol. 2, 27.
87. Sergey Mikhailovich celebrated his name day on 5 July.
88. *P*, vol. 2, 27.
89. Ibid., 28.
90. *Stikh*., 7th ed., 67 and 301.
91. *P*, vol. 2, 28.
92. Ibid., 233.
93. *P*, vol. 4, 147.
94. *P*, vol. 2, 233.
95. Idem.
96. Luk'ianov, vol. 3, 358.
97. *P*, vol. 2, 28.

98. Luk'ianov, vol. 3, 348.
99. *P*, vol. 2, 229.
100. Ibid., 15.
101. Ibid., 96.
102. *P*, vol. 4, 147.
103. *Stikh.*, 7th ed., 213 and 355.
104. *SS*, vol. 12, 89.

Part 1 - Chapter 6

The Philosophical Principles of Integral Knowledge
Lectures on Godmanhood
The White Lily – Death of Sergey Solovyov

> We will marry the white lily with the rose,
> With the scarlet rose.
>
> *V. Solovyov*

After his return from abroad in the autumn term of 1876, Solovyov lectured in logic and the history of ancient philosophy at the University of Moscow. In a letter to Tsertelev dated, apparently mistakenly, 1878 (it was obviously written in the autumn of 1876), Solovyov reports, "It's already been awhile since I started lecturing at the University and, to my surprise, the students are very satisfied and even prefer me to Troitsky."[1]

At this time Solovyov was working on his doctoral dissertation *The Philosophical Principles of Integral Knowledge* and, as we know from Strakhov's letter to Tolstoy, proposed to defend it in St. Petersburg before Christmas.[2] In another letter to Tsertelev, however, he already spoke of March 1877 "... I have made two sensible decisions; 1) not to give public lectures and 2) in view of my doctoral dissertation, to publish only the first, purely philosophical part of my system, namely, the positive dialectic, extending it in the appropriate manner, which will require three extra months. Thus, I will not go to St. Petersburg for the defense any earlier than March."[3] Writing to Tsertelev on 19 November 1878, he mentions a further delay, "I think that our defenses will be held at the same time, as I will hardly finish in the autumn, the work has grown considerably."[4] Here for the first time, Solovyov mentions a critique of *traditional* principles; however as Radlov has remarked, "traditional" is probably a misprint for "abstract."

"With regard to the critique of traditional principles, which I wanted to publish in *Otechestvennye zapiski*, I have completely abandoned it for reasons that it would take too long to explain."

Parallel to *The Philosophical Principles of Integral Knowledge*, Solovyov began work on *A Critique of Abstract Principles*. Gradually, not without pressure from Professor Vladislavlev, he gave up the idea of submitting *Philosophical Principles* as his dissertation, replacing it with the *Critique*. Writing to Tsertelev on 16 February 1879, "I will probably complete my dissertation in the summer and will consequently defend it in the autumn."[5] Solovyov probably had in mind his *Critique*. In a letter of 1 June 1879 he clearly speaks of it, "The first part of my dissertation (on ethics) has been successfully concluded in the last issue of *Russkii vestnik* and I am immersed in an abyss of metaphysics."[6] *The Philosophical Principles of Integral Knowledge* remained unfinished, breaking off in the middle of the fifth chapter, which is a pity. Mikhail Solovyov was completely right when he remarked in the foreword to the first edition of Solovyov's works, which ends with *The Philosophical Principles of Integral Knowledge*, that this is a work which, although both unfinished and little known to the public, is very important for understanding the entire worldview of Solovyov.[7] *The Philosophical Principles* is brilliantly written; certain of its ideas were never repeated in subsequent works or are expressed more weakly. It is also a link between *Sophie* of the Cairo period and *Lectures on Godmanhood*; in fact, several pages are literally identical. The first chapter "A General Historical Introduction (About the Law of Historical Development)" partially repeats the second (or third) dialogue of *Sophie*; however, "the historical process" partly modifies and develops this dialogue, purifying it from extremes. Solovyov proceeds from the assumption that "humanity, as an actual, albeit collective, organism is the subject of historical development."[8] After some preliminary remarks, Solovyov turns to his philosophy of Christian history. At first, as the spiritual is to the carnal, the Church found itself in opposition to the pagan world and state as the kingdom of evil and the devil. "Recognizing the state only as a restraining, repressive force, Christianity denied it any positive spiritual content."[9] It was only something *profanum*, a view that Augustine developed in *De civitate*

Dei. This was, however, only a temporary position. The Church had to spiritualize the political principle, to assimilate the state. Instead of this, a compromise took place. There was no essential difference between the structure of the state under the pagan Diocletian and under the "quasi-Christian" Theodosius or Justinian: the same principle and the same institutions were in place; that is, a combination of Roman republican forms and oriental despotism. The Justinian, who convened an ecumenical council,* for whom "Origen was not sufficiently Orthodox,"[10] was the same Justinian who promulgated a code of Roman law for his Christian empire, despite the fact that Christianity had appeared specifically in order to abolish the power of law. Thus, if nonetheless external law held its own, it clearly proves that the conversion was only nominal.

In the West the Church did not make a compromise with the state, but declared war on it. Three forces emerged there: the Church of Rome, the German princes, and a segment of the Celto-Slavic population that they enslaved. This population was deprived of every kind of political right and had only an economic significance as a working force; thus it formed an economic community, or a *zemstvo*. Within this lowest class there appeared a religion of its own, Catharism or Albigensianism, which had arisen in the Slavic East under the name of Bogomilism and spread from there all over the Celto-Slavic world. This religion perished in streams of blood under the attacks of the Roman Church and the feudal state. However, if these attempts to create a popular Celto-Slavic Church were not successful, then Protestantism would create for the Germanic peoples a new state Church. The Middle Ages were ruled by faith, authority, and theology; against these forces rebelled reason, the abstract and formal principle. The reign of the idea of the state corresponds to the rule of rationalism; in his absolutism, Louis XIV was for the state what Hegel was for philosophy. After the failure of rationalism, the "tiers état", the *zemstvo*, or economic community appeared, along with its religion, positivism. In the social sphere socialism corresponds to positivism in the sphere of knowledge. The French Revolution, which in principle established a democracy, in fact only created a plutocracy. The nation governs itself only *de*

* The second Ecumenical Council of Constantinople (553).

iure; *de facto* the power controlling it belongs to a miniscule portion of it, to the wealthy bourgeoisie and the capitalists. The ancien régime relied on certain absolute principles, but contemporary plutocracy can cite in its own defense only the weight of fact. If, however, it is accepted that material good is the highest goal of life and that the highest power must belong to it, then it is just that the wealth and power that accompany it should belong to those who produce it, that is, to the workers. The aspiration on the part of labor, that is, of the workers, to take possession of capital is the next task of socialism, which is the final product and self-assertion of the economic community, in opposition to political and religious societies. But socialism, even if its utopias came true, could provide no satisfaction to the human *will*, which demands moral peace and happiness, just as positivism cannot satisfy the intellect, which does not seek the factual knowledge of phenomena (i. e. to their ascertainment) and their general laws, but to a rational explanation of them. And if the forms in which the heavenly Aphrodite appeared in the West could only be exceptional and therefore imperfect, which made their relative decline inevitable, then the satisfaction of animal needs cannot replace the satisfaction of spiritual needs; the vulgar Aphrodite cannot possess the crown of the heavenly Aphrodite.

The East, in the name of exclusive Monism, by abolishing the independence of man asserts an inhuman God. The West, in the name of exclusive pluralism, asserts a godless man, who is recognized to be, at once, both the sole divinity and an insignificant atom. The final stage of Western development is atomism. In life it manifests itself as individual egotistical interest; in science as the accidental fact; in art as attention to minute detail; such is the last word of Western civilization. The future belongs to a third force, which will act as a mediator between the divine and the human, between the one and the many, between East and West; the bearer of this force is the Russian nation. The mission of Russia is to create integral knowledge, a free theosophy, where the rational and empirical are not abolished, but are subordinated to the mystical principle of an integral society or a free theocracy, where the Church does not interfere in the affairs of state or economics, but provides the state and *zemstvo* with the highest goal and absolute norm for their activity. If it is men who act in the affairs of state, which are founded on law and rights, then in the economic sphere the first place belongs to women. If hitherto they were the managers of the domestic economy, then they must now become the managers of the universal society as well; social democracy inevitably turns into a gynecocracy.[11] We recognize in all this the utopias of the last chapter of *Sophie*.

The fundamental forms of the panhuman organism are represented by this synoptical diagram:

I	II	III
Sphere of creativity	*Sphere of knowledge*	*Sphere of practical activity*
Subjective basis–feeling	Subjective basis–thought	Subjective basis–will
Objective principle–beauty	Objective principle–truth	Objective principle–the common good

1st stage, the absolute:		
Mysticism	Theology	Spiritual Society (The Church)
2nd stage, the formal:		
Fine Art	Abstract Philosophy	Political Society (The State)
3rd stage, the material:		
Technology	Positive Science	Economic Society (The *Zemstvo*)

In the second chapter, "About the Three Types of Philosophy," Solovyov, in contradistinction to empiricism and idealism, which inevitably turns into rationalism, asserts a third type of philosophy, which is defined as "integral knowledge" or "free theosophy." In this scheme mysticism has primary significance as it defines the supreme principle and final goal of knowledge, while empiricism functions as the external basis and realization of the highest principles. Finally, the rationalistic or strictly philosophical element acts as the mediator or common link throughout the whole system by virtue of its formal character.

In the third chapter Solovyov turns to organic logic and by dialectical method deduces from the concept of the absolute primordial principle all its essential definitions. Dialectics, as a form of philosophical thinking, appeared for the first time among the Eleatics and the later with Gorgias for whom it had a purely negative meaning. Plato provided the idea of a true dialectics, but did not implement it; still less Aristotle. Hegel was the first philosopher to make real use of dialectics as an intellectual process, deriving a complete system of definitions from one general concept. Hegel, however, made the following mistakes: 1) He identified the immanent dialectics of our thought process with the transcendental logos of being itself so that for him our dialectical thinking appears as an absolute creative process. But these definitions of being are accessible to us prior to any reflection and any kind of dialectics by virtue of our ideal "spiritual vision" ["*umosozertsanie*"].[12] Dialectics provide only a coherent reproduction of these ideas in their general structures. 2) For the starting point of the development of dialectics, Hegel takes not the concept of essential being [*sushchee*], but the concept of being [*bytie*]. But this concept in itself not only does not contain anything, it cannot even conceive of itself, and passes immediately into the concept of *nothing*. 3) For Hegel, essential being disappears without a trace into being; but being, in turn, is reduced without a trace into dialectical thinking. For Solovyov, however, thinking is only one of the forms or guises of the manifestation of essential being; dialectics cannot cover on its own all philosophical knowledge and the logic founded on it cannot constitute the entirety of philosophy.

Moving further on to a deduction of the Trinity from the absolute primordial principle, Solovyov, as in *Sophie*, defines the first hypostasis by the Kabbalistic term *En-Sof*, the positive nothing, the all and nothing.[13] Every definition is a negation (*omnis determinatio est negatio*). The absolute primordial principle defines itself, then negates itself, in supposing its own other. By saying that the absolute primordial principle is the unity of itself and its negation, we repeat in an abstract form the words of the great apostle, "God is love." But just as in human love the solitary I, in negating itself in love for another is not lost, but receives its highest affirmation, so too, the absolute primordial principle, in supposing its other, affirms itself in its personal definition. Definitions or distinctions of essential being are found only in the Logos, they are not present in *En-Sof* or in the Holy Spirit. Thus is obtained the relationship between essential being [*sushchee*], entity [*sushchnost'*], being [*bytie*]. The first subject of essential being is the spirit (–*spiritus*), the second is the mind (–*intellectus*), the third is the soul (–*anima*). The content (or idea) of the will of the essential being is good, the content of its intellect is truth, the content of its soul, beauty. This structure finds its analogy in human experience. People are divided into the spiritual, the intellectual, and the emotional or feeling. The first, having loved someone, forms on the basis of this love a conception of the loved one and define this person's aesthetic worth according to the degree of love. With the second, the will and feeling regarding a certain person conform to a theoretical conception that was evoked earlier by this person. The emotional aspect of the object of love acts foremost on the third type, and both their mental and moral relationship with it is defined by aesthetic affect.[14]

The difference between Solovyov and the Platonists lies in the fact that for them, spiritual man is indeed the man of the intellect. Intellect is above all, then comes the heart, feeling, and still lower, desire. For Solovyov, spirit, intellect, emotion stand together, as if reflecting in themselves the equality of the Divine Hypostases. One follows from the other two: either spirit, intellect, and the emotional, which for Solovyov is the same as "feeling," are equal in dignity, or the Divine Hypostases themselves are unequal. In the first instance, Solovyov comes into conflict with Christian asceticism, in the second, with dogmatics. In the young Solovyov we can detect a fascination with Origen who was not "sufficiently Orthodox" for Justinian. In his diagrams of the Trinity, Origen's "subordinationism" can be detected. The first person is defined as "Ur-God" [*prabog*][15] (Origen's self-God,). His definitions of the Third Person are particularly dubious. The concept of the Holy Spirit turns into a concept of the soul, and even of emotion and aesthetics. The emotional person, who in Christian consciousness approximates the concept of the "fleshly man," turns out to be a creature of the Holy Spirit, whereas from another perspective the First Person is defined as the Spirit (–*spiritus*). At this point, as Evgeny Trubetskoy rightly noted, Schelling bursts into Christian formulations and the concept of evil and division enters into the very life of the Divinity. Solovyov did not decide, as he did in the rough drafts of *Sophie*, to make a direct assault on the Christian representations of the devil and hell as the world that is outside the divine, but circumvents them in complete silence.

In the fifth chapter Solovyov introduces a new concept of Sophia, which is vaguely mentioned in patristic philosophy and developed only by Origen. On this occasion Solovyov distinguishes three Logoi: the first, the inner or hidden ( ); the second, the revealed ( ); and the third, incarnated or concrete (Christ). "The concrete idea or Sophia also corresponds to the third or concrete Logos."[16]

This idea of Sophia will be developed in *Lectures on Godmanhood* and *La Russie et l'Eglise universelle*. When analyzing the latter we will refer to the criticism of Evgeny Trubetskoy, with certain of whose positions it is impossible to disagree. In the meantime, we will confine ourselves to a few words that Solovyov might have addressed to his critics: "You accuse me of introducing into the Divine Being itself the principle of negation and division. But the dogma of the Trinity namely affirms not a simple unity, which we find in Hindu philosophy and in the mysticism of the East, but a unity, in distinction and in multiplicity. I am only commenting on the words of the great Apostle, 'God is love,' since love presupposes the distinction between oneself and another, it supposes an object of love. With regard to the derivation of the entire world process from the Divine primordial principle, then indeed by insisting on being that is outside the divine, you limit God by this being and like the Manichaeans, you affirm alongside the Divine Being the eternal being of an evil principle. Whereas Augustine already established that evil is only the absence of being."

In Solovyov's original metaphysics there is no concept of "the devil," which appears to contradict his inner experience. We know that Solovyov had a vision of the devil, albeit not in his youth, but significantly later. This inner experience was one of the reasons that forced him to revise and correct his original system precisely in regard to this point about the doctrine of the principle of evil.

The Philosophical Principles of Integral Knowledge betrays the negative attitude to Western Europe that Solovyov formed at the time of his first journey abroad. He returned to his homeland a convinced Slavophile. His idea of "integral knowledge," founded on mystical experience and "spiritual vision" was similar to the philosophy of the Slavophiles, and he was drawn even more closely to Khomyakov[*] and Aksakov by their belief in the Russian nation, which had accepted Christian truth in all its purity (a truth that had not been understood and fully realized among the western nations), as the bearer of the future rebirth of all Europe. At one with the Slavophiles he affirmed that the *zemstvo* is the means for the incarnation of the Christian idea, in contrast to Romano-German statism. Of course, this idea of the *zemstvo* is connected with the heresy of the Albigensians and the Bogomils, the religion of the Celto-Slavic world that perished in streams of blood under the attacks of the Roman Church and the feudal state. Solovyov did not suspect what a fatal syllogism is obtained as a result.

Major. Russian Orthodoxy as the negation of the Roman Church and the German state, as a popular [*zemskaia*] religion, is the future and most perfect form of Christianity.

Minor. Albigensianism was the religion of the popular [*zemskii*] Celto-Slavic world that rebelled against the Roman Church and the German state.

Conclusio. Russian Orthodoxy is Albigensianism, that is, Manichaeanism.

If the idea of integral knowledge, constructed not on empirical and abstract thought, but on spiritual vision and experience, is common to Solovyov and the Slavophiles, then it must also be admitted that the Slavophiles were considerably more conservative and Orthodox than the young philosopher. If for Solovyov this integral knowledge is a "free theosophy," if it feeds on the Gnostics, the Kabbalah and Schelling, then for Kireevsky[†] and the other Slavophiles, this knowledge was already provided by the theology and asceticism of the Orthodox East. From their perspective, it was not necessary to travel either to the British Museum or the Egyptian desert; it would suffice to go to the Optina

---

[*] Aleksey Khomyakov (1804-1860), leading Orthodox and Slavophile thinker, emphasized the principle of *sobornost'* ("organic collectivity") in religious and national life.

[†] Ivan Kireevsky (1806-1856), along with Khomyakov a leading figure of Slavophilism.

monastery* and place oneself under the direction of an experienced starets and to study the works of the Eastern Fathers; and after that, to believe in the Russian commune and in the future peaceful socialism of the Russian peasantry, whose interests would be looked after by the tsar. But the Slavophiles willingly forgave the young Solovyov that which appeared in their eyes to be a delusion. In the main he was with them, in asserting the future role of the Slavs as the renovators of the whole world and in rejecting the decaying West with its state ideology, technical progress, and materialism.

Like the Slavophiles, Solovyov, who was rooted in German philosophy, gave evident preference to the Germans before all other Europeans. In this regard the note that concludes *The Philosophical Principles of Integral Knowledge* can be summarized as follows: A nation creates its own language according to its own form and image. In the German and Russian languages there are two different words for the distinction between actuality [*deistvitel'nost'*] and reality [*real'nost'*]: *Wirklichkeit* and *Realität*, whereas both French and English express the concepts by one word: *réalité, reality*, which shows that the latter nations do not possess the consciousness of non-real actuality [*nereal'naia deistvitel'nost'*], and that they recognize only realized, material actuality.[17] To this one could object, first of all, that "reality" [*real'nost'*] is not a Russian word, but a philosophical term of foreign origin that is necessary for the expression of a foreign idea (and that the German word *Realität* derives, as well, from a Latin root, common to both French and English); and secondly, that Solovyov is confusing here *real* actuality with the material. For certain philosophers, foremost among them Solovyov himself, it is precisely the material world that is not real.

Furthermore, he continues, for the concept of *nothing* [*nichto*] the English only have one word, nothing, which means *a non thing, no kind of thing*, and for the concept of *something* [*nechto*], the word something, *a certain thing*. With the same coarse realism the English say nobody, somebody, that is, *no kind of body*,

* The Optina Monastery in Kaluga province was one of the great centers of Orthodox spirituality until the Revolution. Its elders or *startsy* had a particular influence over Slavophile intellectuals and writers such as Gogol and Dostoevsky, who took Solovyov there in 1878.

a certain body, instead of no one [*nikto*], some one [*nekto*]. In French there is only the word *conscience* for the various concepts of consciousness and conscience; while for essence and being there is only *être*, and for both mind and spirit, *esprit*. "It is not surprising that with such linguistic poverty the French have not gone any further in the sphere of philosophy than the first rudiments of speculation established by Descartes and Malebranche; all of their subsequent philosophy consists in echoes of foreign ideas and sterile eclecticism. In the same manner, the English, as a consequence of that coarse realism that is characteristic of their minds and expresses itself in their language, can cultivate only the surface of philosophical problems; it is as though the profoundest questions of speculation do not exist for them at all."[18]

We should also add that the affinity between the Slavs and the Celts in their opposition to the Germans, is something Solovyov could have borrowed from his father. In his *Notes* Sergey Mikhailovich remarks in connection with his stay in *France* and *Belgium*, "A pure Slav, who received a liberal Russian upbringing, without a foreign tutor, I could freely abandon myself to my enthusiasm for the Slavic nature, in consequence of which I have no love for Germans and sympathize with the Romano-Celtic nations."[19]

Solovyov expressed his Slavophile credo in the short lecture "Three Forces," which he gave at a meeting of the Society of Lovers of Russian Literature. On this occasion he repeated the ideas covered in the first chapter of *The Philosophical Principles*: the East, in maintaining an inhuman God, represents the first force; the West, in advocating a godless man, represents the second; while the Slavs and Russia possess the third force, that of Godmanhood. What is demanded from this third representative of the divine potentiality is indifference to all of this life, with its petty interests, and a complete faith in the positive reality of the higher realm and a humble attitude toward it. These characteristics belong undoubtedly to the tribal nature of the Slavs, to the Russian people in particular... The external image of the slave, in which our people finds itself, and the pathetic position of Russia in economic and other spheres can only not serve as an objection against its vocation, but rather, confirms it. For that higher force, which the Russian people must bring to humanity, is not a force belonging to this world; external wealth and order have no bearing on it... The negative result of the (Crimean) war was matched by the negative character of the national consciousness that it awakened. One must hope that the great struggle that is ripening will serve as a mighty jolt to the awakening of *the positive consciousness* of the Russian nation.[20] The lecture concludes with a harsh attack on the Russian intelligentsia, which instead of reflecting the image and likeness of God, betrays the image and likeness of a monkey and makes for itself an idol out of every kind of narrow and insignificant idea. This intelligentsia is called upon "to revive in itself the Russian national character."

In the April 1877 issue of *Vestnik Evropy* Stankevich criticized Solovyov in his article "Three Feeblenesses: Three Forces." Afterwards, Solovyov wrote to Countess Tolstaya, "Was it really unpleasant for you, rather than amusing, to read about 'Three Forces' in *Vestnik Evropy*?"[21]

Such was the hostility with which this journal first treated Solovyov, who would become, in the second half of his life, one of its favorite contributors. But the sympathy of *Russkii vestnik* and *Grazhdanin* toward him inevitably aroused the enmity of the Westernist and liberal circles.

The air already smelled of war. In Moscow the Slavonic Committee was in action and acquired such popularity that "a certain gentleman turned up at Ivan Aksakov's with the request that his children born out of wedlock be made legitimate."[22] Solovyov's lecture responded to the mood of Moscow society; at that time he was no longer "rowing against the current." But during the academic year 1876-77 at Moscow University he proved to be, in the words of his favorite poet Aleksey Tolstoy, "Not a fighter between two camps but only an accidental guest." In his short autobiography written in May 1887 Solovyov reports, "Having left the chair at Moscow University, as a consequence of my desire not to participate in the partisan strife between two professors, I was appointed a member of the educational committee of the Ministry of Public Enlightenment."[23] On 14 February 1877 Solovyov went on leave. "The feud among the professors of Moscow University over the 'opinion' of Professor Lyubimov concerning the necessity of changing the university charter served as the grounds for this. This opinion was upheld by Mikhail Katkov. However, one should not imagine that close relations existed between Solovyov and Lyubimov. Afterwards, when Lyubimov's book about Katkov appeared, Solovyov drew some conclusions from it that were highly unfavorable to the Slavophiles. Lyubimov was so irritated by the philosopher's arguments that he intended to issue a sharp denunciation of Solovyov; but he did not carry out his intentions. Solovyov's father belonged to the camp of Lyubimov's opponents; our philosopher, who was attracted at that time to Slavophilism and was also somewhat close to Katkov, did not approve of the ostracism to which Lyubimov was subjected by the majority of the professors of the University of Moscow. Solovyov spent eighteen days on leave... On 4 March 1877 he was made a member of the educational committee of the Ministry of Public Enlightenment on the recommendation of its president, Aleksandr Georgievsky. From this moment began the St. Petersburg period of Solovyov's life."[24] Other reasons, as well, which we will treat in the following chapter, drew Solovyov to St. Petersburg.

At first, Solovyov felt an extreme antipathy toward St. Petersburg, the city that subsequently became his home ("The white nights awaited me above the space of the crowded islands.") In 1873 he had written to his cousin Katya, "I know that it can't be very cheerful for you, either, to be alone in the sordid, empty city."[25] On 4 May 1877 he wrote to his father, "St. Petersburg is not much interested in matters of import, one would think that history was happening somewhere in Atlantis. I have become completely convinced that St. Petersburg is only a distant colony that has *temporarily* become the governmental center. I regret very much that I had to move here at this time. In terms of my physical well-being, I can't complain about St. Petersburg, I feel perfectly well."[26] But already in a letter of 14 May to Countess Sofya Tolstaya at Krasny Rog, "where the nightingales sing," he pours forth his complaints about the city. "There is no way I could have made it to Pustynka; I am freezing in St. Petersburg, literally freezing, for we have snow and it's now at the freezing point. Instead of nightingales the drunken petty bourgeois are returning from the Demidov gardens in song. Lord, what vileness and boredom!"[27] Finally, in a letter of 10

March 1881 to Fet, Solovyov called St. Petersburg a "Finnish Sodom."[28]

With respect to his service as a member of the educational committee, Solovyov expressed himself openly enough in another letter to Sofya Tolstaya. "It has turned out that my appointment is in no way a sinecure; it's really nothing, un métier comme un autre, as long as die göttliche Sophia remains on the side."[29] And to Tsertelev, "I have already begun my service on the educational committee. The sessions are a deathly bore and inexhaustibly stupid; it's good they are infrequent. I work in the library only con amore."[30] And in the next letter of 30 April, "I live alone and extremely modestly; I am reading the mystics in the library and am writing my dissertation. I have been to see almost no one."[31] In the St. Petersburg Public Library, as in the British Museum, Solovyov read almost "everything he possibly could about Her." "In the library I have, in the meantime, not found anything special. The mystics have much that confirms my own ideas, but they shed no new light of any kind, moreover they almost all have an extremely subjective character and are full, so to speak, of drivel. I have found three specialists on Sophia: Georg Gichtel, Gottfried Arnold, and John Pordage.* All three had a personal experience, almost the same as mine, and this itself is interesting, but all three are rather weak in theosophy proper; they follow Boehme but are lower than he. I think that Sophia took trouble over them more because of their innocence than for some other reason. As a result, the only solid people are still Paracelsus, Boehme, and Swedenborg, so that the field remains very wide for me. I have become somewhat acquainted with Polish philosophers, whose general tone and aspirations are very sympathetic, but they have no kind of positive content; they are a match for our Slavophiles."[32]

Meanwhile, the threat of a war in the Balkans drew near. Solovyov had long ago predicted one, and on 14 May he wrote to Countess Tolstaya, "In spite of everything I am very cheerful. Great history brings me great joy."

* Johann Georg Gichtel (1638-1710) and Gottfried Arnold were disciples of Jakob Boehme (1575-1624) in Germany while John Pordage (1607-1661) promoted his work in England.

A rumbling grows as on the sleeping sea
Before a fatal storm–
Soon, soon, the entire world will seethe
In martial strife…[33]

And in "Album I" he wrote:

You are dreaming peacefully.
While we no longer believe in dreams:
Everywhere is heard the battle cry,
Death or a moment of victory.

For the young Slavophile it was impossible to sit still in St. Petersburg, conscientiously attending the sessions of the educational committee and reading the mystics while "the entire world would soon seethe in martial strife" and the blood of Slavs was being shed. On 27 April he wrote to Countess Tolstaya, "I am now setting out for Pustynka and from there, *perhaps*, for Asia Minor straight into the arms of the Turks and the plague as a volunteer or even a correspondent for *Moskovskie vedemosti*. Besides, although I have written to Katkov (in response to his proposal that I write for him as a correspondent from St. Petersburg, which is completely senseless), this is all probably only 'the chimera of light-headed youth.'"[34] And within three days he wrote to Tsertelev, "By the way, I almost forgot to say that I too, *perhaps*, will set out for the army that is active in Asia Minor as one of Katkov's correspondents. However, it is more likely that this is only a figment of my imagination."[35]

The archives of the Ministry of Public Enlightenment have preserved two telegrams; the first reads " I urgently request that an authorization for a leave be sent quickly by registered letter: To Moscow. Neskuchnoe. Aleksandrinsky Palace. It is necessary for obtaining a passport to go abroad. I am leaving for the Danube. Solovyov." The other is dated 18 June; it is from the Governor of Kishinev and is addressed to the minister of Public Enlightenment. "I beg permission to issue a passport to the court counselor V. S. Solovyov for his departure abroad."[36]

We can ascertain that at the beginning of June, Solovyov left Moscow and stayed for two days at Krasny Rog (the estate of Aleksey Tolstoy in the province of Chernigov). On 18 June he wrote to Tsertelev from Kishinev. "After various peripeteia, about which it is not worth writing, I finally left for the army on the Danube. I stayed at Krasny Rog for two days. Are you in good health and did anything special happen to you on the night of 13–14 June? At that time some kind of devilishness occurred in my presence: your spirit appeared and I don't know what else… I am now in Kishinev to obtain my passport and early tomorrow morning I am going to where I belong. It's hot here and I am tired from sleepless nights; therefore I am not writing about anything in detail."[37]

On 28 June Solovyov wrote to his mother from Bucharest, "I have written you two letters already: one from Kishinev, the other from here – they have probably not arrived yet. I had waited almost a week for money from Katkov but, having given up on him, I have borrowed some money here and today I am heading for the Danube. On the way from Yassy to Bucharest I met Katya and traveled with her for several hours. It is now the second month that they are sitting around without anything to do and they still haven't seen a single wounded soldier. Probably at home no one believes the official news about our losses at the crossing of the Danube. But there is no way one can deny that at the crossing at Svishtov the number of wounded and killed was less than six hundred, even at Galats it was around a hundred, – far from the 30,000 about which they are jabbering in Moscow… I have been perfectly well the whole time. Yesterday there was a magnificent storm here after which it cooled off; until then the heat was terrible… It is possible that I will return for good at the end of July, but it's also possible that I will come only for a few days in September and then return again to Bulgaria."[38]

Solovyov's militarism was aroused to such an extent that he fitted himself with a revolver en route, without, however, finding himself in the theater of war. Evidently, having satisfied his need to breathe the air of the Balkans and to get near the places of combat, Solovyov realized that he was a poor military correspondent and that his revolver would scarcely hit a target. Toward autumn he returned to St. Petersburg in order to serve the cause of the Slavs by those means that were at his disposal. At the beginning of January 1878 he announced twelve lectures "On Godmanhood" "in aid of the Red Cross," but also partly "in aid of the restoration of Hagia Sophia in

Constantinople."[39] These lectures given at Solyany Gorodok marked the apogee of his fame; all St. Petersburg thronged to them.

In the *Lectures on Godmanhood* we find numerous repetitions of the themes of *The Philosophical Principles of Integral Knowledge*. Only the last lectures, eleven and twelve, introduce new ideas and serve as a transition to the second, theological, period of Solovyov's life.

In the first lecture Solovyov addresses the justice of the criticism of contemporary opponents of Christianity; they are in the right because in our day religion is not what it should be. He then literally repeats the arguments with which we are familiar from *The Philosophical Principles* about the inevitability of the transition from rationalism to positivism, and from revolutionary democracy to socialism via plutocracy.

In the second lecture Solovyov describes the past of religion, as represented by Roman Catholicism, which can be abolished, both effectively and definitively only by a principle that can offer an alternative to Catholicism without being, however, its empty, impotent negation.[40] In the contemporary cultural struggle (*Kulturkampf*) against Catholicism, it is impossible for an impartial man to stand on either one side or the other. Catholicism takes after its patron the apostle Peter who drew his sword to defend Christ in the garden of Gethsemane and who wanted to construct a real tent on Mount Tabor for Christ, Moses, and Elias. But contemporary humanity, which aspires only to material well being and wealth, has taken for itself the worst model in the apostle that betrayed Christ for thirty pieces of silver. The opponents of Catholicism do want to see in it the truth of God, albeit in an incongruous guise, and mistake the dust covering it for its essence and idea.[41] If Catholicism has always appeared to be the most evil enemy of our nation and Church, then it is precisely because of this that we must be just toward it.

In the fifth lecture Solovyov develops his theory about ideas as living principles. If in formal, rational thinking the scope of a concept is in an inverse ratio to its content, then in the realm of metaphysical entities, the relation between scope and content is direct. Abstract thinking serves either as the *reduction of sensual perception*, or as *the anticipation of intellectual intuition*, in so far as the concepts forming it can establish themselves either as *schemata of phenomena* or as *shadows of ideas*.[42] For the true artist, ideas and images are not the products of observation and reflection; by virtue of his intellectual vision he perceives them in their inner wholeness. The national genius that first comprehended the divine principle as the ideal cosmos is the same national genius who was also the real ancestor of art.[43] Recognizing the divine principle as harmony and beauty, the Greeks recognized only a certain aspect of divinity. Not in Greek idealism, but in monotheism did God reveal himself as the pure "I," or the absolute personality as the living God. For the Greeks, the divine principle is accessible only to the imagination and feeling; for the Jews, it reveals itself to the *will*.[44] For the Greeks, the divinity is everything–substance; for the Jews, it is something unique–a personality, the subject. But in reality, the Divinity is greater than personality (individuality), it is one and all, both subject and substance. The Jewish religion of the absolute personal God inevitably becomes the religion of external law. In the consciousness of the prophets there appears a new, inner bond with the divine principle.[45] The Christian understanding of God was prepared as much by the prophets as by the Jewish Hellenists (Philo). "If the essence of divine life was defined by the Alexandrian philosophers by purely speculative means on the basis of a theoretical idea of the divinity, then in Christianity *the same* integral [*vseedinaia*] divine life appeared as a fact, a historical reality, in the living individuality of a historical person.[46]

The affirmation of an essential relationship between the Christian dogma of the Trinity and Greco-Jewish speculations about the same subject in no way diminishes the original significance of Christianity itself as a religious revelation. In fact, the originality of Christianity is not to be found in its general views but in positive facts; not in the speculative content of its ideas, but in its personal incarnation...

Those definitions of purely logical thought that have been developed in recent German philosophy with such perfection can serve as an invaluable means for the complete logical elucidation of this fundamental dogma. In the formal sense this has the same meaning for us as did the doctrines of the Academy and Lyceum for the theologians of antiquity. Those who now rebel against the introduction of this philosophical element into the sphere of religion would have to first repudiate all the previous history of Christian theology, which, one can say, was written by Plato and Aristotle.[47]

Further on, Solovyov expounds his definitions of the Divinity as integral and triune that are familiar to us. He objects to those doctors of the Church who, having adopted a perspective of mechanical thinking, could not understand these ideas in their speculative truth. These teachers, "great as they might be by virtue of their practical wisdom in church affairs or their holiness, could be very weak in the realm of philosophical comprehension; moreover, of course, they were inclined to accept the limits of their own thought as the limits of reason in general. On the other hand, as we know, among the great Fathers of the Church there were many real philosophers who not only recognized the profound speculative truth in the dogma of the Trinity, but themselves did much for the development and elucidation of this truth."[48] Analogies from the world of phenomena, although not proof of Triunity, can serve as illuminating examples. In particular, Solovyov dwells on the analogies used by St. Augustine in his *Confessions*: we can distinguish in our spirit its immediate *being* (*esse*), its *knowledge* (*scire*), and its *will* (*velle*).[49]

In the seventh lecture, as in *The Philosophical Principles of Integral Knowledge*, Solovyov defines the three subjects of being as spirit, intellect, and soul. The Divine principle is love; the three forms of its manifestation are goodness, truth, and beauty. Goodness is love, as that which is *desired*; truth is love, as that which is *represented*; and beauty is love, as that which is *felt*, or manifested. "The absolute realizes goodness through truth in beauty."[50]

In pre-Christian consciousness there are present the following elements of Christianity: in Buddhism we find pessimism and asceticism; in ancient Greece – dealism; in Judaism – monotheism; in Alexandrian theosophy – triunity.[51] What then is essentially new in Christianity? "Its unique content is Christ, uniquely and exclusively Christ."[52] Both the teaching and morals of Christianity are not new. "The specific difference between it and other religions is the teaching of Christ about himself as truth incarnate." Christ is a universal organism and a particular individual human being, the realized expression of the absolutely existent of

God. "Just as a being, even though distinct from the idea of it, is at the same time one with it, so too the Logos, although it distinguishes itself from Sophia, is inwardly united to her. Sophia is the body of God, the matter of the Divinity, permeated with the principle of divine unity. Christ, who realizes in Himself or bears this unity, as the integral divine organism who is at once universal and individual, is both Logos and Sophia."[53]

To speak of Sophia does not mean that one is introducing new gods. The book of Proverbs states that Sophia (*Khokhma*) "existed before the creation of the world," that "God 'possessed her at the beginning of his ways,' that is, she is the idea that He had before Him in His act of creation."[54] In order for the divine idea not to become more meager and more abstract than our representation of the visible world, we must recognize in it our particular eternal nature, our particular eternal world. Purifying God from every kind of actual definition turns Him into an abstraction, as a consequence of which atheism appears. Together with unity, multiplicity also belongs to God, a multiplicity of substantial ideas, that is, of potentialities or forces with definite, particular content. We have three divine spheres, three categories of vital forces: the sphere of pure spirits, the sphere of intellects, and the sphere of souls. Between this divine world and our natural one there is not an impassable abyss. Separate rays and reflections of the divine world must penetrate into our every day reality and must form all the ideal content, all the beauty and truth that we find in it. In this "fatherland of fire and glory" every poet finds the archetypes of his creations and that inner illumination that is called inspiration.[55]

And everywhere there is sound, and everywhere light,
And for all the worlds there is one principle,
And there is nothing in nature
That does not breathe love.

The ninth and tenth lectures appear to develop the second dialogue of *Sophie* written in Sorrento. Here the history of the cosmic process is expounded; once again the origin of our world, the world of evil and suffering, is explained by the falling away of the Soul of the world from the divine Logos, its establishment outside

God, in consequence of which it lost its freedom and power over creation. "In this way all creation was subject to futility and slavery, and to corruption, not willingly, but according to the will of the one who subdued it, i.e., the world soul, as the one free principle of natural life."[56] The Divine Logos strives to bring unity to the material world and to be incarnated in it. Thus arise, at first, all the forms of inorganic nature, then the organism, and finally, self-consciousness. The cosmogonic process turns into the theogonic, and the gods of the pagan religions become the offspring of the Demiurge and the world soul, defining consciousness.[57] The word "Demiurge" is met with only once in *Lectures on Godmanhood* and the name of "Satan" is absent. The tenth lecture concludes with the explanation of why the Divine Logos appeared in Judaea and could unite itself only with a Jewish soul. To the Hindu spirit the divine principle revealed itself as Nirvana, to the Greeks as Idea; only to the Jews did it reveal itself as a person, as a living subject, as "I." In the national character of the Jews the subjective principle predominates as well. "They created the lyrics of genius that are the psalms and the lyric idyll of the 'Song of Songs,' but they possessed neither the epic nor drama, as we find among the Hindus and Greeks."[58] Their philosophy never went beyond moral didactics. In the Jewish nation the energy of evil, of self-assertion, of egoism was great. But, having suppressed this energy in itself, Judaism converted it into a potential for good, and the nation that was "stiff-necked and hard-hearted" became the nation of the saints and prophets of God and served as the instrument for the incarnation of the Divine Word.

In the last lectures, eleven and twelve, we encounter a severely negative attitude to Roman Catholicism, in which we can detect the influence of Dostoevsky. Speaking first about the legal theory of redemption worked out by Anselm of Canterbury, Solovyov, it is true, remarks that "it is not wholly lacking in true meaning," but finds that this meaning is completely obscured by coarse and unworthy ideas about the Divinity and His relations with the world and humankind that are as offensive to philosophical reasoning as to a truly Christian feeling.[59] Addressing the question of the possibility of the incarnation of the Divinity, Solovyov resolutely asserts that "in Jesus is incarnated not the transcendent God, not the absolute self-contained fullness of being (which would be impossible), but God-the-Word. This manifestation of God in human flesh is only the more complete and perfect theophany in a series of other, incomplete, preparatory and transformative theophanies." The birth of the second spiritual Adam is no more incomprehensible than the birth of the first Adam. One and the other, although new and unprecedented, were prepared by everything that had come before. "All nature aspired and gravitated to humanity, the entire history of humanity was directed to the Godman."[60] Further on, having clarified that in the person of the Godman there coincided two natures and two wills, Solovyov considers the three temptations of evil to which the will of the Savior and human nature were subjected.

The first was the temptation of the flesh; the transformation of stones into bread. Having over come it, Christ obtained power over all flesh. The second temptation was that of the mind; the sin of pride. Having vanquished it, He obtained power over minds. The slavery of the flesh and pride removed; there remained the third temptation, to use divine power as a form of violence, that is, to submit to the principle of evil that masters the earth. Having overcome the sin of the spirit, the Savior was granted power in the kingdom of the Spirit and, having refused submission to an earthly power, acquired the service of the heavenly powers.[61]

Christendom, or the Church, passes through the same temptations but in reverse order: the temptation of the spirit, the mind, and the flesh. To the first (the third temptation of Christ) succumbed the Church of Rome, having proved its disbelief in the power of spiritual good by making use of violence and deceit for its ends. In Jesuitism the Christian faith appears as an accidental form, as its real essence and goal are fixed upon the domination of the hierarchy.[62] Protestantism challenged Catholic salvation as an external fact in the name of personal faith. But as a criterion of faith it uses *Scripture*, which requires interpretation and personal reasoning, which in turn become the sole sources of religious truth. Protestantism ends as rationalism and it is on this point that Western humanity has succumbed to the second temptation, that of the mind. And finally, we arrive at the third temptation (the first temptation of Christ), which is the attempt to posit as the basis of life and knowledge only the material principle, to implement the lie that "man shall live by bread alone."[63]

And thus, Rome and the Romano-German nations that have adopted its culture have succumbed to all three temptations. On the side were Byzantium and the nations that accepted its culture with Russia at the head. The East did not succumb to the three temptations, it maintained the truth of Christ, but having preserved it in the soul of its peoples, it did not realize it in external activity and failed to create a Christian culture. The human element in Eastern Christianity proved to be too weak and insufficient, and material reality found itself outside the divine principle; hence in Eastern consciousness there is a certain dualism between God and the world. The West developed the human principle at liberty and created an anti-Christian culture; while the Byzantine East preserves a divine relic. "The fertilization of the divine Mother (the Church) by the active human principle must produce a free deification of humanity... In the history of Christianity the Eastern Church has appeared as the representative of the unchangeable divine foundation present in humanity; while the Western world has acted as the representative of the human principle."[64]

It is clear that Solovyov, as he did during the writing of *Sophie*, still believes in the future universal religion. Its elements are the immutable holiness of the Eastern Church and the human, changeable principle of Western civilization. The Catholic Church is assigned a very modest role in this religion: only the Church of the East is considered to be the Mother Church, and the Catholic Church is not *Mater ecclesiarum*, but only one of the constituent parts of Western culture. But it is characteristic of Solovyov that, already in the second lecture, he dwells on the idea of the apostle Peter as the patron of the Roman Church, which forms the grain of his future ideas. With regard to the philosophy of the three temptations, one cannot help being struck by the affinity between the final lecture and the "Legend of the Grand Inquisitor." It is difficult to say who borrowed from whom. Undoubtedly, all of Ivan Karamazov bears the imprint of the friendship between Dostoevsky and Solovyov, which stimulated Dostoevsky's interest in theology and gave a very particular coloring to his last novel.

Around the time of *Lectures on Godmanhood*, Solovyov wrote the poem that begins:

> In the morning mist with *unsteady* steps
> I made my way to mysterious and marvelous shores.
> The dawn struggled with the last stars,
> Dreams still hovered, and possessed by dreams
> The soul prayed to *unknown* gods.

Everything here is in mist, everything is mysterious and wonderful, his steps are uncertain and his soul prays to unknown gods. But the hour is already at hand when the mist will clear and "the cold, white day" will shine through and the pre-dawn dreams will prove to have been a delusion; "the steps will become firmer" and the "unknown God" will give way to the "knowable God."

It was at the lectures on Godmanhood that my mother first saw Solovyov. She was then a young woman of twenty-one who had come to St. Petersburg to visit her married friend Nadezhda Aleksandrovna Bezobrazova. My mother, Olga Mikhailovna Kovalevskaya, had grown up in her family as a lonely and reserved girl and had shown mystical tendencies at an early age. She little resembled her siblings; she fed her mind on the Italian primitives, Walter Scott, and the lives of the saints. She carved the name of Mary Stuart in trees, and at the age of twenty wrote to a friend from Florence: "With his infinite tenderness, delight, and beautiful images Raphael caresses, instructs, and summons one to life, but the old masters (Beato Angelico for example) tear you from everything away all at once, everything instantly disappears, remaining somewhere far below, everything, even the most radiant and pure of human attachments. This renunciation of life and serene peace, this happiness is also a striving for death. Happiness because you are going to that which you love with all the power of your soul; you go with certainty. Yes, ahead of you is light and truth, – that is, death." One can imagine the impression that the strange prophet of Sophia, of whom it was said that he heard the Pythagorean harmony of the spheres, made on this the unusual young woman. After the lectures she wanted to become more closely acquainted with Solovyov and they met at the home of Nadezhda Bezobrazova. What followed was... disillusionment. Solovyov behaved as a most ordinary young man; he made a number of jokes and did not say anything special. The dreamy young woman had probably imagined that at the tea table Solovyov would "burn with his speech the hearts of men". Poor Vladimir Sergeevich! Even he needed to relax sometimes. And he did relax in urbane society, freely surrendering himself to his wit and testing his powers in the then fashionable genre of ridiculous comedies. The late Kozma Prutkov (that is, Count Aleksey Tolstoy) was the founder of this entire school of humorous poetry. In his home, Solovyov had been in his element and found himself close to the very source of comic inspiration. In Moscow his friend Fyodor Sollogub and two members of the circle of the "Shakespearists," Aleksey Venkstern and Vladimir Giatsintov, also practiced this genre.

The "Shakespearists" was the name given to a circle of former pupils of the Polivanov *gymnasium*, and the nucleus of this circle was composed of three families: the Lopatins, the Venksterns, and the Giatsintovs. The Shakespearists were divided into older and younger members: the older were Nikolay and Lev Lopatin, Aleksey Venkstern, and Nikolay and Vladimir Giatsintov. Among the younger I will mention only Aleksandr and Vladimir Lopatin, Erast Giatsintov, Prince Boris Turkestanov (later Bishop Trifon), and Prince A. P. Kugushev (a published poet). Aleksey Venkstern was the hero and *jeune premier*; a young man with great but poorly developed poetic talents. (He made splendid translations of *Les nuits* and other poems by de Musset, as well as a Spanish play by Augustín Moreto *El desdén con el desdén* .)[65] A general favorite, he bore himself with a certain pride and reserve. He played roles such as Hamlet, Prince Henry V, Coriolanus, and Mercutio. Lev Lopatin played the character parts such as Polonius, King Henry VI, *pater* Lorenzo, and Iago.

Solovyov, who had not been a pupil at the Polivanov *gymnasium*, was introduced into the Shakespearean circle by Lev Lopatin and soon was on intimate terms with everyone. When Venkstern spent a summer in Spain, Solovyov wrote to him from Fet's estate, Vorobevka:

From distant fields of black earth
We send you greetings
And we wish to receive, Aleksey our friend,
An appropriate reply.

As this epistle has not survived among the papers of Aleksey Venkstern, I have to quote it from memory; I recall it concluded with the lines:

You are now probably in Paris
And perhaps somewhere nearer.

When the Shakespearists would hold a dance, Solovyov would sadly wander the halls with Lev Lopatin and Dr. Aleksandr Petrovsky; Venkstern called them the "three drowned men." Solovyov knew how to dance and once danced with the daughter of Katkov, but in general he avoided this amusement. Indifferent to dancing, Solovyov, unlike his friend Lopatin, did not approve of the theater either. His sisters Nadezhda, Maria, and Poliksena, on the contrary, adored the theater and in the Solovyov home they maintained a cult of Glikeria Nikolaevna Fedotova. Maria Sergeevna recounts in her memoirs how they once managed to drag their brother to a performance of Sarah Bernhardt. On the following day, as soon as the performance was mentioned, Solovyov threw back his head and exclaimed, "Oh Lord! What torture it was! Oh Lord!"[66]

By contrast, Solovyov delighted in the comic plays of Venkstern and Giatsintov.[67] He particularly liked *Theseus* and wildly laughed during its performances, goading on the actors. The first attempt of the Shakespearists in the comic genre was *Alsim or The Dream of the Student after January the Twelfth*. This play is still rather feeble, but the one that followed, *Theseus*, is extremely witty. Venkstern wrote the scenes in Athens with Aegeus, while Giatsintov composed the scenes on Crete where Minos constructs absurd syllogisms, which must have especially amused Solovyov. Venkstern's sense of humor is stronger, coarser, and more absurd, resembling Solovyov's own; while Giatsintov had a more refined and easy wit.

In 1877 Solovyov wrote his first comedy (which has not come down to us), *Kozma Prutkov*. On 19 April he informed Tsertelev, "With the next letter I am sending you a comedy I wrote, *Kozma Prutkov*. The Countess (Sofya Tolstaya) and Sofya Petrovna found it amusing and laughed a great deal, covering themselves with their cloaks."[68] And on 30 April, "I will be sending the comedy separately, as it still needs to be rewritten. It is exceptionally ludicrous and for outsiders, I think, not even amusing, but you will probably laugh."[69] During the Christmas season of 1878-79 the Shakespearists performed *Alsim* in the Solovyov home in the presence of Sergey Mikhailovich and various eminent professors. Sergey Mikhailovich laughed loudly and was very pleased. Solovyov added to the play of Venkstern and Giatsintov an entire third act that turned out to be much more forceful and witty than the first two. To the credit of the Shakespearists one should remember that their next play, *Theseus*, was far superior to the comedies of either Solovyov or Fyodor Sollogub. The action of *Alsim* concerns a young poet of that name, who after concluding a pact with Satan, is led by him to the land of the Trapezuntians:

> There it is always night and the day is dark,
> A shadow from the sun falls there.
> In winter there is an abundance of scorching heat
> But in summer there are mounds of snow.
> There rivers flow from the sea
> And the mountains are lower than the valleys,
> The trees grow with their roots above ground
> And bear oranges.

In this magical land where everything is turned inside out, Alsim meets the bearded beauty Eleonora and marries her. After seven years of married life, however, Alsim is tired of being constantly beaten by his bearded wife and is utterly sick of her beard. He kills Eleonora and Satan takes possession of his soul. In the penultimate act that Solovyov added a new character is introduced, that of the professor with whom Eleonora betrays her husband.

The cast of characters was:

Alsim	Vladimir Giatsintov
Satan	Aleksey Venkstern
Eleonora	Lev Lopatin
The Professor	Leonid Belsky

The role of the professor was especially successful. Being an admirer of the categorical imperative, on the basis of moral principles he does not collect from his debtors more than 40% per month and intends to eliminate his wife by *economic* means through a reduction of her food. In this play one can appreciate Solovyov's passion for puns. When Alsim shouts at his servant, "Be silent ignorant rabble [*chern'*]!" the latter replies "Quite so, we are from Chern, that is, the Chernsky district." When Eleonora threatens her husband with a beating, crying "You'll soon learn what this is for [*A chto za sim*]!", he responds with an offended air "I am called Alsim, Alsim not Zosim."[70]

Elizaveta Nikolaevna Klimenko (later Shutskaya), a young cousin of Aleksey Venkstern's, enjoyed great success in the circle of the Shakespearists. Her family and friends called her Zizya in order to distinguish her from other relatives named Elizaveta. Solovyov was very much attracted to her and they went skating together. On one occasion Solovyov, Elizaveta, and Lev Lopatin made a pilgrimage to the Trinity monastery where they met the wise starets Varnava, about whom we shall speak later. Another time Solovyov presented Elizaveta with a volume of Heine underlining in pencil the words: "Oh, sei mein Weib, mein Vaterland, mein Vaterhaus!"

Zizya was apparently uncertain as to how to regard this semi-proposal. From letters to her mother it is obvious that she was not attracted to Solovyov, but her mother considered this to be a good match. A feeling of self-preservation probably warned the good-natured and cheerful young lady that she would not find happiness in this marriage and that Solovyov's feelings for her were not deep, but were inspired mostly by her good looks. In the end Elizaveta Nikolaevna responded with a refusal. In fact, at that time Solovyov's heart already belonged to another woman and his desire to settle down in a domestic idyll with Elizaveta was most likely motivated by the temporary coldness of the woman with whom he had spent years of "long torment, unnecessary deceit, despair and ennui." But this will be treated in detail in the following chapter.

In 1878 Solovyov began the three-act comedy *The White Lily*, which he completed in 1880 at Pustynka. Its subtitle, *A Dream on the Night of Pokrov,* echoes *The Dream of the Student after January the Twelfth.* This is a very strange play and for a long time Solovyov could not decide to publish it.[71] The jokes are rather coarse, familiar, and sometimes cynical. Extreme absurdity and nonsense are interwoven with the mysticism of Sophia. To the highest degree this play perfects the famous "irony" of German romanticism. It also has a prologue that did not appear in print and survived only in fragments in rough draft. It was written in the manner of the "Prologue in Heaven" of *Faust* and its action takes place in the "fourth dimension." On the whole, the play is also undoubtedly influenced by Kozma Prutkov's *Affinity between the Forces of the World.* The prologue is permeated with ideas borrowed from Kabbalah, Schelling, and extreme Gnosticism. It shows that even at the end of the 1870s Solovyov had not completely freed himself from the mood in Sorrento in which he had written *Sophie,* when even the free mystics Boehme and Swedenborg were for him the representatives of "old Christianity." The following cast of characters appears in the prologue: Geodemon, the sovereign spirit and the protector of earth who is exceedingly good-natured and given to occasional fits of ecstasy; Kitovras, Geodemon's bailiff, an efficient fellow who poses as a devil; and Geodemon's lackeys, who wear blue and red livery, and consider themselves for some unknown reason to be angels and wear cardboard wings but are, in fact, lazy, arrogant, and stupid.

Kitovras appears before Geodemon in order to make a report and delivers this monologue:

> From the east to the west
> Over the face of the earth
> The seeds of falsehood, murder
> And debauchery have arisen

Everything that was sacred to our ancestors
Has been squandered by our descendants;
Defamed and disheveled
Is the bed of the virgin earth.

The shoots of the hellish cornfield are ripening,
The hour of the harvest is nigh…
With the dawn of the last day
We greet you.

Geodemon's lackeys drive Kitovras away, preserving the peace of their lord. Kitovras retorts daringly:

Well, not such am I! You don't frighten me much.
Our papa was chaos and our mother the dense night.

The lackeys surround him and "taking on the role of angels" shout:

You are falsehood and evil! We are truth and good.

"With supernatural speed Kitovras gives them knocks on the head and socks on the jaw." Geodemon appears, imposes order, and turns to the lackeys with the line:

Well, you, my little ones, shush! Or you will go without candy.

Later, Geodemon enters a state of ecstasy and delivers a splendid monologue in which we recognize the Kabbalistic doctrine of Sophia:

When with mighty power Adonai
Woke in himself seven spirits
And extinguished with a quiet radiance
The flame of fiery passion,
Then above the trembling abyss,
Among heaven's overturned,
In a crown of rainbows and stars
Full of mysterious wonders
There appeared before him the maid of paradise.
And playfully she wrapped him
In a net of golden curls,
And fixed motionlessly

In the azure flame of her eyes
He blessed everything, gazing
On the face of his beloved.

Kitovras tells of the extreme decay and corruption of all people on earth. Geodemon retorts than there are also decent people and demands his notebook, where there are two charts: one for sheep, the other for goats. At this, Kitovras remarks to the side:

Ugh! In the fourth dimension
There is also a Third Division!

Foremost in the list of honorable people Geodemon finds the name of the Chevalier de Mortemir. Under this name the author is undoubtedly making a parody of himself. In the cast of characters he is described as "a wealthy, but thoroughly ruined, landowner." Kitovras characterizes him thus: "How can one not know this sentimental old maid, this naughty kitten! Indeed, if there ever was anything sensible in him, it was gone long ago."

In the first act the Chevalier de Mortemir sets out in search the mysterious White Lily in the company of the most absurd people, whose names are the Chaldean, Instrument, and Sorval. Before his departure, Mortemir bids farewell to the beautiful lady Galaktea:

Mortemir
Oh, do not consider me ungrateful!
I have loved you more than the others,
You sparkled in the gloom of my days
Like a radiant meteor.

Galaktea
Si c'est ainsi, I am still, perhaps,
Prepared to shine in the gloom of your days…

Mortemir embraces Galaktea, but at this point a voice from the fourth dimension is heard:

It is sweet to be a monster
And pleasant to forget God!
But then the sordid
Path will await Us!

Mortemir jumps away from Galaktea, quickly bids adieu and leaves, having received as a parting gift three magical roses.

The second act takes place in a forest. The Sun, plants, birds, and animals await with impatience the appearance of the "Tsaritsa," "the maid of paradise." Even the wolf, "murderer and thief," as well as lions and tigers, "who drink hot blood," are burdened by their evil lives and want to put an end to their previous ways, in expectation of deliverance by the Tsaritsa. Mortemir enters and recites the monologue:

She, everywhere she! About her alone speak
All the voices of anxious nature.
Not I alone, but the river and the forest and the mountains,
The trees, beasts, the sun, and flowers
Call on her and await her.
Once she appears, even the snowy heights
That have arisen above the clouds
Will fall at once before her, luxuriant flowers
Will unroll a wide carpet before her, rhinoceri, and leopards
Will gather together as a happy
And friendly family to serve her;
Swift and noisy streams
Will suddenly stop. The stormy ocean itself
Will rage for the last time and having
Cast all its pearls at her feet, it will grow calm and die down,
As a still and transparent mirror
It will lie before her in order to reflect
Clearly in silent ecstasy the wondrous image.
Only two kinds of animals greet the appearance of the Tsaritsa with hostility: moles and owls. The owls "make their nests in the ruins of castles and ancient churches," love rotten wood and mould, and serve as condiments to their meals fallen leaves and dried moss:
We believe in eternal bliss, but only for ourselves,
For others, – infernal torments.
Then we will take our pleasure in full, but meanwhile
We chant our prayers out of boredom.

But in these activities we are disturbed by the news
Of this new Tsaritsa,
Whose appearance so impudently await
All the beasts and birds of day.

The aged wise man Don't-Spit-on-the-Table arrives carrying a mysterious parchment that he found in the ruins of Palmyra. Mortemir reads:

"A – B – C, A – B– C.
This contains a sublime and secret meaning,
Which only a bear that possesses
Great strength will reveal.
But the eternally feminine element
Will not remain without a role in this:
When the azure pigment
Saves the soul from calluses
The grace of the white lily
Will spread her tincture everywhere,
And humankind, having forgotten how to suffer
Will embrace all nature at once."

The third act takes place in Southern Tibet. A large bear comes out to meet Mortemir and his companions, while the voice from the fourth dimension exclaims:

The door of eternal bliss
The beast will open
Later – not now –
Love and believe!

The following scene takes place at the grave of the bear. Mortemir is mourning his favorite animal friend in whom he saw "the last anchor of life's vessel." In his grief he wants to stab himself with his dagger, but the White Lily appears above the grave and explains:

The bear lives, there is just no bear skin.
Do not grieve, my friend! Here is a mystery of nature.
I was in the bear, now the bear is in me,

As once you loved him, now henceforth love me.
Invisible then
Was I, but now –
In me is the hidden bear
Invisible forever.

In the rough draft Mortemir stabs himself before the appearance of the White Lily, whereas in the published text he only "wants to stab himself." Furthermore, in the rough draft the action proceeds as follows: "She then explains to him that she herself, transformed by Satan, was hidden under the bear's skin but that the love of Mortemir for the bear and his own suffering have annihilated the hostile spells, and that the blood of Mortemir has bestowed on her the possibility of incarnating herself and appearing before a living human being. After this, they are united in the bonds of love, but once this happens they both instantly die from an excess of bliss. The local peasants find their bodies and commit them to the earth singing a hymn appropriate to the circumstances. On the grave of Mortemir spring up roses, and on the grave of the White Lily, a white lily."

In the published version Mortemir and the White Lily do not die, but "embrace and, rising in the air, suddenly pass into the fourth dimension. On the former grave (of the bear) spring up white lilies and scarlet roses."

Three ladies, "pleasing from all sides," run out on to the stage, – Alkonda, Galaktea, and Terebinda, about whom Kitovras remarks in the prologue, "there is only one name for them – strumpets." Tired from their wanderings they hide in the cave. The three other seekers of the White Lily appear: the Chaldean, Instrument, and Sorval. At the sight of the three women coming out of the cave, Sorval exclaims:

Look, the White Lily:
She is not one, but three.

Each of them recognizes the White Lily in his beloved; they embrace in pairs and sing the song of the Ophites: – "We will marry the white lily with the rose, / With the scarlet rose." In the rough draft we read, "Descending together they arrange a little feast of wine and fruit, at which they sing the following rondeau as a chorus 'The white lily with the rose...'"

Thus ends this strange play, where the philosophical poems ("The Song of the Ophites," "It is not in vain that we have come together") are intermingled with every kind of nonsense. It also explains a great deal to us about Solovyov's attitude to love. At that time he felt himself to be the Chevalier de Mortemir, in love with the White Lily that was flowering somewhere in Tibet, which is why all his plans for marriage remained fruitless. Imagining that as a mere mortal he was granted the ability of recognizing the features of the White Lily in the face of an earthly beloved, he aspired to something more distant, to the White Lily herself and, perhaps, expected a new meeting, no longer in Egypt, but beyond the Himalayas; this is confirmed by his notes in automatic writing, "I think that you must certainly go to India. I think that you will begin your task there. I am wisdom. Sophie." But, in loving the White Lily, he was also inhaling the fragrance of the magical roses, given to him by Galaktea[72] who appeared to him "like a radiant meteor in the gloom of my days." It is as though Solovyov found himself wavering between either leaving all the earthly Galakteas to the Chaldeans or trying himself to incarnate the heavenly in the earthly and to recognize in an earthly beloved the features of his celestial friend. It is as if in the published version of *The White Lily* Solovyov renounces the rose and ascends into the fourth dimension with the White Lily. In the rough version through his own blood he provides the White Lily with the possibility of becoming incarnated and dies from the bliss of love. However, both these decisions contradict real life: on the one hand, Solovyov recognized that he could not and must not become disembodied and pass into the fourth dimension; but on the other, to unite with a heavenly being in the full heat of passion with a complete spiritual and physical love would mean taking a demonic path. Life commanded him to take a third way. He would finally know a deep human love, but, of course, this love also appeared to him in a mystical light and ended not in domestic happiness but in fatal catastrophe.

From the dedication to *The White Lily* written in 1880 it is apparent that under the cheerful tone of this comedy was concealed a rather painful state of mind:

> Do not expect harmonious and beautiful songs,
> Of dusky autumn do not ask flowers!
> I have not known radiant and clear days,
> But oh how many motionless and voiceless phantoms
> Forsaken on the twilit path.

In *The White Lily* Solovyov expresses a bitter irony about himself and the chimeras of his youth. He felt that he had been deceived by everything about which he had dreamt during the period of *Les principes de la religion universelle*. But out of this first wreck he would bravely enter onto a new path, and the maturer period of the '80s would begin. His attitude toward "historical Christianity" would change to such an extent that at one time he would take his place among those people whom he portrayed as owls loving tombs and ruins.

To the time of *The White Lily* apparently belongs a romantic dream, a note of which I found among his manuscripts.

> I am standing on a high terrace somewhere by the sea near St. Petersburg. In the distance ships with red and white flags can be seen. From one of these ships an enormous whale is swimming in my direction. Coming up to the shore it lifts its head and with gaping jaws it tries to jump onto the terrace where at this moment a lady appears all in white and full of mystical beauty. I give her my hand, lead her to the edge of the terrace and pointing to the whale, say, "Regardez Madame, votre bien aimé qui arrive," and with this I put my arm around her waist and with an emotion characteristic for me (in my dreams) I want to press her to my heart. But a sudden noise and the sound of many voices prevent me. I turn around and see that from the other side a large crowd, among whom I recognize friends of my father's, Ketcher, Chicherin, Stankevich, and others, are coming on to the terrace. In front of all of them I see my brother-in-law Popov. They are all laughing loudly and pointing at me with

their fingers. I lower my eyes and to my horror discover (a very common effect in dreams) that instead of wearing shoes I am wearing torn sandals and that between the sandals and my frock coat I am wearing nothing at all. Full of shame and despair I throw myself off the terrace and land directly on the back of the great whale, which carries me in an instant to one of the ships. I now find myself on the deck and inform the captain of my desire to go to India. Excellent he says, and the ship sails directly to India.

In 1879 Solovyov experienced the first deep sorrow of his life; he lost his father. At Christmastime Sergey still laughed heartily at *Alsim*, but already toward spring his doctors passed a sentence on him and advised him to take the cure in the summer at a spa. To this they received the stubborn reply, "I am not going to rest until I have completed *The History of Russia*." Sergey Mikhailovich always maintained "force is greater than matter" and he was unwilling to believe that matter was triumphing over his mind and will, interrupting his work on the reign of Catherine the Great. It was not easy for him to understand that he was dying and, in spite of his profound faith, he was gloomy and sullen. Some kind of panic reigned at home; no one wanted to accept that at age fifty-six this mighty oak would fall; everyone was depressed and distracted.

At the end of May 1879 Solovyov left for Krasny Rog. On 1 June he wrote to his mother, "It's not good that you are not writing to me, or do you think that papá's illness does not sadden and upset me? I, too, regret that I left. However, I will probably soon be with you, although it's wonderful here." And in the following undated letter, "I will probably be with you within ten days or earlier. My delightful but muddle-headed hosts are creating havoc and preventing me from leaving on time. Perhaps, however, circumstances will change and if I receive good news from you about papá then I'll stay until the end of June." And on 12 June he wrote to his sister Nadya, "From your letter I conclude that papá's main ailment is his previous one – stones in the liver and the spasms that arise from it; although this is very grave, it is somewhat better, all the same, than what one would have suspected of late."

On 1 July Solovyov wrote to Tsertelev already from Neskuchnoe where Sergey Mikhailovich spent his last summer, "My father will apparently not get any better: he has fatty degeneration of the heart, an incurable disease from which it seems Aleksey Tolstoy died… At present the most contradictory moods are mixed up inside me, and I form a living example of the union of contradictions. The other day I received some nice letters from Krasny Rog. It seems that everything is well there; although for them, as well, the summer began rather sadly."[73]

On 3 October Sergey Mikhailovich died. In her memoirs Maria Sergeevna gives an account her father's death.

> The evening before, the doctor said that my father would not survive the night, but he was mistaken; father still lived during the entire following day. We were all in his room continuously. In the dining room breakfast, tea, and dinner were served at the designated hours; the dishes stood, grew cold, and were carried back to the kitchen untouched. But then, at around seven o'clock in the evening it seemed to us as though father was somewhat better and Anna Kuzminichna persuaded us to go into the dining room to try to eat something… We could not eat, but we began to drink tea and my brother asked for it to be as strong as possible. We drank in silence, when suddenly my brother said "What if science is mistaken and papá will continue to live!"
>
> But at that moment a footman ran in saying that mother was calling all of us. When we had surrounded the sofa on which my father was lying, the quiet agony, which lasted a few minutes at most, began. When his breathing could no longer be heard the bells in our parish started ringing for Vespers, as this was the feast day of the four hierarchs, and a large uncommonly bright meteor flashed through the sky. After Vespers we held a requiem service; later, when everyone separated and night fell, my brother said that a reader would not be necessary until morning as he himself would perform the reading of the prayers for the dead over

father.* My younger brother and I volunteered to take turns with him and we did not go to our rooms, but remained in the hall and left the door to the drawing room open only slightly so that the reading would not be heard in the bedrooms.

It would be best if mama and the others could get some sleep, my brother said, and he went to the table on which my father lay and began to read. After him, my younger brother read, then I, then Vladimir again. When he began to read, his voice broke slightly only at the first words, then it grew completely strong and he read so well and with such feeling that it became easier and more comforting and we did not feel so tortured by pity for those who were crying on their own in their beds. My brother considerably shortened our turns reading and made his longer, but before morning he laid his hand on my shoulder and said very sadly, but also, decisively, "go lie down."

And Misha?

I will send Misha to bed soon.

You will stay alone?

It doesn't matter, I'm not tired.

In the morning I rose at the first chance and went into the hall where a deacon from the parish was already saying the prayers. I asked the footman about my brother. "Vladimir Sergeevich has only just gone down to his room this minute," – (in our apartment my brother lived in some kind of basement chamber where he had one and a half rooms). "He persuaded Mikhail Sergeevich to lie down a little earlier. But Vladimir Sergeevich has not lied down yet: he asked for cold water, washed his face, then sat down and is now either reading or writing something."

Having gone back to the nursery I bumped into the maid Darya. "Ah, Vladimir Sergeevich, the heavenly angel, how his face changed in one night! He looks like pity itself."

One of our close acquaintances arrived for the morning requiem service; at first she sat with my mother, then came

---

* The Orthodox custom is to read the Psalter over the dead.

into the entry way for some reason and quietly crying, said to Anna Kuzminichna, "Ah, Volodya, the dove, has a heart of gold, how he has changed! I simply sighed when I saw him. How he loved his father! And some people still consider him to be cold and egotistical!.. Never in my life have I seen such a change in such a short time! It's as though he has passed through years and years of suffering... And his expression, in spite of this, is so radiant and good that it simply turns your whole soul upside down."

Many days passed after the death of his father before I saw a smile on my brother's face. He did not cry at all, only from time to time he would somehow sigh and gasp in a special way as though he did not have enough air.[74]

There is no way that the loss of his father could not have left a deep trace in Solovyov's soul. This was strictly speaking the only death of a person close to him that he would experience in his life. However, his susceptibility was so great that ideas about the dead began to dominate his thought in the last decade of his life. As the death of his brother Nikolay was for Lev Tolstoy, so for Solovyov the death of his father served as a stimulus to a new awakening, to the consciousness that in life there is a profound disharmony that cannot be avoided, but must be overcome. This deep sorrow made Solovyov wiser and older and prepared him spiritually for that strict adherence to religious matters that characterized his work in the '80s. A stronger shock, however, was required for the final crisis. In 1883 Solovyov came face to face with his own mortality, and therefore we can regard the years 1880–1883 as the conclusion of the first period of his life and we will begin the second period with 1883.

Let us now turn to the final chapter of part one, where we will bid farewell forever to Solovyov the professor and Solovyov the Slavophile.

Endnotes for Part 1 - Chapter 6

1. Luk'ianov, vol. 3, 359.
2. Ibid., 358.
3. *P*, vol. 2, 240. This letter could have been written only in the autumn of 1876, for in 1877 Solovyov had already left Moscow University.
4. *P,* vol. 2, 241.,
5. Ibid., 247.
6. Ibid., 248.
7. *SS*, vol. 1, viii.
8. *SS*, vol. 1, 255.
9. Ibid., 268.
10. Ibid., 269.
11. *SS*, vol. 1, 287, note.
12. Ibid., 342.
13. Ibid., 358.
14. Ibid., 368. See, *SS*, vol. 3, 109.
15. *SS*, vol. 1, 376.
16. Ibid., 376.
17. *SS*, vol. 1, 405.
18. Ibid., 406.
19. *Vestnik Evropy* (April 1907): 463.
20. *SS*, vol. 1, 238-39.
21. *P*, vol. 2, 201.
22. Ibid., 240.
23. Ibid., 185.
24. E. L. Radlov, *Vl. Solov'ev*, 14, 15.
25. *P*, vol. 3, 84.
26. *P*, vol. 2, 29.
27. Ibid., 201.
28. *P*, vol. 3, 107.
29. *P*, vol. 2, 199.
30. Ibid., 235.
31. Ibid., 236.
32. *P*, vol. 2, 200.
33. Ibid., 201.
34. Ibid., 200.
35. Ibid., 236.
36. Radlov, *Vl. Solov'ev*, 15.
37. *P*, vol. 2, 238.
38. Ibid., 30.

39. Ibid., 242.
40. *SS*, vol. 3, 15.
41. Ibid., 16.
42. Ibid., 67.
43. Ibid., 68.
44. Ibid., 71.
45. Ibid., 75.
46. Ibid., 81.
47. Ibid., 82.
48. Ibid., 98-99.
49. Ibid., 101-102.
50. *SS* vol. 3, 111.
51. Idem.
52. Ibid., 112.
53. Ibid., 115.
54. Idem.
55. *SS*, vol. 3, 118.
56. Ibid., 142.
57. Ibid., 152.
58. Ibid., 159-160.
59. *SS*, vol. 3, 164.
60. Ibid., 165.
61. Ibid., 165-170.
62. Ibid., 174.
63. Ibid., 177.
64. Ibid., 180-81.
65. *Minuvshie gody* 5 (1908): 136.
66. Idem.
67. V. E. Giatsintov is a professor of the history of art and is now the director of the Museum of Fine Art in Moscow; he is the author of a study of Nicola Pisano.
68. *P*, vol. 2, 235.
69. Ibid., 236.
70. *Alsim* was published in the collection *Comic Plays of V. Solovyov* (Moscow, 1922), 13-28.
71. *The White Lily* was first published in 1893 in the artistic and literary collection *Na pamiat'*. It was reprinted in *Comic Plays* (Moscow, 1922) and in the third volume of Solovyov's letters.
72. The name "Galaktea" does not appear to be a distortion of "Galatea" by accident and reminds us of the heroic feat of Pygmalion. See the poem "Three Heroic Feats [Tri podviga]" (*Stikhotvoreniia*, 7th ed., 77) and "You

were for me a delightful creation [Vy byli dlia menia prelestnoe sozdan'e]" (*P*, vol. 1, 204); *SS*, vol. 12, 10, 108.
73. *P*, vol. 2, 248.
74. "Vospominaniia M. S. Bezobrazova." *Minuvshie gody* 5 (1908): 159-161.

Part 1 - Chapter 7

Doctoral Defense
The Lecture against Capital Punishment
Solovyov as Ivan Karamazov
Sofya Petrovna Khitrovo

> It was not by the will of fate, nor by the working of
> Human thought, nor your own, that I loved you.
> And with my prophetic love
> I surrounded you and protected you
> From invisible evil, from mysterious snares.
>
> *V. Solovyov*

On 1 July 1879 Solovyov wrote to Tsertelev, "The first part of my dissertation (on ethics) has been successfully concluded in the last issue of *Russkii vestnik*, and I am immersed in an abyss of metaphysics..."[1] On 3 October (the eve of his father's death) he wrote, "I am definitely completing my dissertation, which I will certainly defend in February, if not with Vladislavlev, then with Struve in Warsaw. I hope, however, not to have to resort to this extremity."[2]

In an undated letter to Nikolay Strakhov (no. 8) which obviously belongs to the end of 1879, Solovyov wavers between February and March. "One of these days I want to get back to my studies in order to complete my dissertation, which is turning out to be very long and which I think I will defend in February or March. My nerves, however, have been highly strung, so that perhaps this matter will drag on."[3] The dissertation was defended on 6 April 1880, and Solovyov received the doctoral degree without any difficulty. The defense went significantly more smoothly than the one for his master's. In a letter to Aleksandr Kireev,* Solovyov himself gives an account of his introductory speech and the debate that followed:

> In his introduction the doctoral candidate, having indicated the two essential features of every type of philosophy, namely: 1) the principle of free investigation, which distinguishes every branch of philosophy (and, consequently, philosophy in general) from religion; and 2) the universality of the subject, which distinguishes philosophy from individual sciences, defined the task of philosophy as such: to establish by means of a free examination of all the facts of consciousness the common bond or reason (*ratio*) of everything that exists.
>
> From our perspective, everything that exists belongs to three different spheres and can be reduced to three different principles. First of all, we find within ourselves something that we recognize as absolute and superior to ourselves, something in us, but not of us, something to which we freely submit ourselves, as a higher ideal that is inwardly binding for us; this is the divine principle in a human being, which makes a human greater than human. Along with this, we find in ourselves another fact, also independent from us, but of an opposite character, which we recognize as conditional, accidental, and inferior, or subordinate, to us; this is the natural, or material, principle in us, but not of us, which makes a human less than human. Between these two opposing principles consciousness finds itself as something that contains in itself both these principles, but which distinguishes itself from them and is capable of relating to them in one way or another and of making room in itself for one or the other. In this way, self-consciousness, as such, represents a certain principle of its own; the rational principle, or the purely human. If the first, divine principle forms the sphere of religion, and if the material principle claims as its own external life and external (empirical)

* Aleksandr Kireev (1833-1910), social activist and journalist.

knowledge, then the principle of awareness, or the rational, constitutes, strictly speaking, the sphere of philosophy. By itself this sphere has only a *formal* character, as it receives all its content from the other two principles, that is, from the mystical sphere of the divine principle and from the empirical sphere of the material principle; for everything that is real for us, everything that exists for us, can be reduced to these two spheres. In this way, if the task of philosophy consists in establishing a common bond between everything that exists, and as everything that exists is reduced to the divine and material (natural) principles, then the task of philosophy can be defined more closely thus: To establish the inner bond between the divine and material principles. The unilateral assertion in the consciousness of one or the other of these principles to the detriment of the other does not appear possible; both these principles exist in us in an immutable and insurmountable manner and the task of consciousness and its higher manifestation, philosophy, can consist only in making a definite and harmonic connection between these principles. Such a connection results from the nature of things. On the one hand, the divine principle appears to us (in consciousness) as the highest ideal and the absolute goal. The ideal, however, requires matter for its incarnation, and the absolute goal requires a means for its fulfillment; in other words, the divine requires an *other* for its realization; this other presents itself in the sphere of natural, or material, being. On the other hand, the latter [material being], which does not possess in itself any kind of absolute meaning and right to existence, obtains them in becoming the means and instrument for the realization of the absolute, ideal content. The role of consciousness (and philosophy) consists namely in understanding and revealing those conditions in which divine being realizes itself in natural being; in so doing, it establishes the inner bond between them.

The first official opponent, Professor Vladislavlev, after making some general remarks about the virtues and weaknesses of the dissertation, declared that he was not going to argue against its basic positions as he himself was a "bit of a mystic," although he would not go as far as the candidate. In his capacity as "an official opponent" he then made some particular remarks. Among others, he objected to the candidate's extension of a moral obligation to all living creatures, indicating that such a wide application was impossible, since we make continual use of them as a means, as for example, in the eating of animals. *Response:* The moral principle requires only that we do not regard other creatures *solely* as a means, and that we recognize that they also possess the significance of an independent purpose. The moral principle forbids turning another creature *wholly* into a means for us, but it does not forbid us from partially using another creature as a means; this applies not only to animals but also to people. With regard to the use of animals for food, granting its permissibility (in itself a debatable issue), we are in no way spared *any* moral obligation to animals: even if we are allowed to kill them, we *must* not, in any case, make them suffer.

In addition, Professor Vladislavlev, mentioning that the dissertation recognized the principle of love as the foundation of the ideal society, pointed out that this does not correspond to the real state of humanity and that in reality the principle of love is too weak for such a role. He also wondered where we would put feelings opposed to love, such as hatred, enmity, etc. *Response*: The reason why the social ideal is, indeed, an ideal, is because the given condition of society does not correspond to it. As regards hatred and enmity, it is perfectly undeniable that they exist, but it is as undeniable from the moral point of view that they should not. Professor Vladislavlev made a few further objections of the same sort, but the aspirant did not find it possible to agree with any of them.

The second official opponent, the professor of theology Rozhdestvensky, after lengthy praise for the dissertation, said that he was not pleased with the part which relates to strictly religious questions. The religious views of the candidate, according to Father Rozhdestvensky, were closely related to those of Schelling and Schleiermacher and could be understood in a pantheistic sense and give rise to errors. The candidate answered that the opponent had made the mistake of combining such heterogeneous things as the religious views of Schleiermacher (which is concerned with religious *feeling*) with the speculative pantheism of Schelling's first system (*Identitäts-philosophie*) and the philosophical constructions of Schelling's second system (his so-called positive philosophy). The candidate recognized an affinity only between his views and this latter system of Schelling in which the philosopher had already freed himself from the false pantheism of his earlier theories. With regard to the candidate himself, he stated that he could not guarantee that someone might not find in his ideas something that is not present, but that this was not his fault.

The third opponent, a professor of general history, Bauer, speaking about the law of historical development (expounded in an appendix to the dissertation), noted that the first phase of development already included elements of the second. The candidate replied that he in no way repudiated this and that, in general, periods of world history, as parts of a complex process, can be defined not by the exclusive presence of one or another principle, but only by their relative predominance.

The fourth opponent, a teacher of criminal law, Vedrov, asserted that in the dissertation socialism is incorrectly characterized as a materialistic-economic principle, since in the various stages of socialism there are also present other elements: moral, religious, and so forth. The candidate replied that the presence of moral or religious elements in various socialist doctrines is directly mentioned in the dissertation itself, but that this does not relate to the fundamental definition of socialism as a principle (as such); for in such a definition it is necessary to have in mind not one or another of the individual theories or systems, of which there can be an indefinite number, but the essential principle, common to them all and defining them as socialism. Such a principle undoubtedly has a materialistic-economic character, the other religious and moral elements appearing as an afterthought, not having an inner connection with socialism as such.

The fifth opponent, Butlerov, a professor of chemistry, expressed bewilderment with regard to one of the theses in which precedence is given to the mystical element in knowledge. The candidate replied that in this case such priority should be understood not in a genetic, but a logical, sense.

The sixth opponent was the student Onapov (???).

The seventh opponent, Vulfson, a candidate of the mathematical faculty, reproached the candidate for failing to mention, when admitting the principle of love as the foundation of a normal society, that this foundation was first of all described by Auguste Comte. The candidate remarked that considerably earlier than Comte the principle of love had been proclaimed by Jesus Christ.[4]

As the scope of this book does not allow a detailed exposition of *A Critique of Abstract Principles*, we shall have to be brief.

This work has a special interest because it is only here (if one does not count Solovyov's last articles on theoretical philosophy) that Solovyov describes his *gnoseology*. (There is a good discussion of this aspect of the book in Vladimir Ern's article "The Gnoseology of V. Solovyov".)[5] In the foreword to *A Critique of Abstract Principles* Solovyov remarks:

> With regard to the external aspect of this work, as a consequence of various circumstances I was not able to elaborate my ideas with the desired sense of proportion and order. Certain ideas are set forth too briefly and are insufficiently developed; others, on the contrary, are presented with an excess of detail; there are references to things which have still not been stated and superfluous repetitions of that which has already been said. Conscious as I am of these deficiencies, I do not consider them sufficiently important to delay the publication of the book on their account. I hope that I will eventually have the opportunity of correcting them.
>
> According to the general plan, the critique of abstract principles is divided into three parts: the ethical, the gnoseological, and the aesthetic. The present book includes, strictly speaking, only the first two parts, the latter, which is concerned with questions and difficulties of a particular nature, will form a separate volume about the principles of creativity.[6]

In the 1890s, when Solovyov was working on his most important work on ethics *The Justification of the Good*, he reworked the first chapters of *A Critique of Abstract Principles* and appended them to *The Justification of the Good* with the note: "I have reproduced here (with corrections) that part of my dissertation *A Critique of Abstract Principles* (no longer in print), which was written about twenty years ago when the author found himself, with regard to purely philosophical questions, under the influence predominantly of Kant and partially of Schopenhauer."[7]

The ethical part of the dissertation covers the first sixteen chapters. In them Solovyov criticizes the ethical doctrines of hedonism, eudemonism, and utilitarianism, and describes the empirical basis of morality according to Schopenhauer, Buddhist asceticism, and the teachings of St. Isaac of Syria (about "the loving heart").* Having indicated the inadequacy of both the empirical and materialist principles of morality, he turns to its purely rational or formal foundation in the three formulas of Kant's categorical imperative. Moving further from subjective ethics to objective, he constructs a scheme of an ideal society defined as a "free theocracy," which is formed by the free interaction of three spheres: the ecclesiastical, the political, and the economic. Repeating his critique of abstract clericalism, familiar to us from *The Philosophical Principles of Integral Knowledge*, or the false theocracy of the Middle Ages, which was based on external authority and rejected the rights of reason and material nature, Solovyov also criticizes the contemporary notion of the separation of Church and state: "We see that, historically, the separation of the spiritual from secular realms always arises as a *forced* bargain between secular society, which has freed itself inwardly from the religious principle and is striving for the complete abolishment of the Church, but which is not *yet* strong enough for this, and theocracy, which is inwardly hostile to secular society and is striving for its complete subordination, but which is *already* deprived of the power necessary for this. In such a way, a 'free Church in a free state' does not, on its own, express any kind of principle, but is only a practical inconsistency inconsistency, as much

---

* Isaac the Syrian (seventh century), consecrated Nestorian bishop of Nineveh between 660 and 680 but soon devoted himself to asceticism and the dictation of his *Treatises* on the spiritual life. His writings, which combine extreme self-abnegation with love for the entire cosmos, had enormous influence throughout the Churches of the East and in Russia.

historically unstable, as logically."[8] In a free theocracy the ecclesiastical principle of love is incarnated in civil law. The hierarchical principle, or the principle of power, forms the basis of this theocracy. "*The extent of rights corresponds to the degree of inner virtue*."[9] In chapter twenty-six, having proven in the preceding chapters the groundlessness of abstract moralism, Solovyov addresses the problem of true knowledge.

At first, Solovyov criticizes abstract realism and, using the arguments of Hegel, demonstrates the untrustworthiness of emotional experience. He follows this with a critique of sensualism, scientific empiricism, and rationalism. In the last chapters Solovyov develops his own gnoseology. True knowledge is accessible neither to empirical observation nor to formal thinking. The authentic sources of knowledge are faith, imagination, and creativity. Faith informs us that an object exists; imagination (or intellectual contemplation) discovers what it is; and creativity shows how it appears. The creative act of our spirit converts a changeable and disordered mass of sensations into a unified and integrated image of the object that stands motionlessly before us in the obscure flood of impressions. This activity cannot be compared with the work of a sculptor who embodies his idea in a dead and indifferent material. "Sensations are not absolutely indifferent to that ideal image which our mind superimposes on them";[10] they are for the seeker of knowledge, what the word is for the poet. Thus, integral knowledge, or free theosophy, becomes, in its own way, an art, with philosophy, strictly speaking, taking second place. The authentic object is not known in a logical fashion, but mystically-intuitively, and the poet becomes the true sage. Reason only gives a form to our knowledge, connecting mystical perceptions with the material supplied by our emotional experience. Here it is obvious how far Solovyov has moved from Plato and Hegel. From the Germanic philosophical term for "intellectual contemplation" ["*umosozertsanie*"] (*Anschauung*, intuition), he turns to the term "imagination" ["*voobrazhenie*"], whereas for Plato, imagination was the lowest function of the soul, and all knowledge of ideas and the divine was the property of reason. For Hegel, the logical process is the self-revelation of divinity, and rational philosophy must replace art and religion as the highest and final form of wisdom. In this case Solovyov follows Schelling and Goethe. The second part of the *Critique* should have been "Aesthetics," however, it was never written; in order to form any idea of Solovyov's aesthetic system one must make use of individual articles, such as "Beauty in Nature" and others.

During the first period of his professional life, Solovyov aspired to "integral knowledge" ["*tsel'noe znanie*"] and abolished theology, rationalism, philosophy, and art in favor of *theurgy* [*teurgiia*]. As Vladimir Ern correctly observed, for Solovyov, this theurgy is not the experience of the saints, but something completely new and, for the most part, aesthetic; it is treated as *self-evident*, and the theurgist becomes, above all, an artist and a poet.[11] In *The Justification of the Good* Solovyov changed his point of view to some extent: "According to its nature, moral philosophy is closely related to religion, but according to its epistemology, to theoretical philosophy… The opinion that *entirely* subordinates morality and moral philosophy to *theoretical* principles of a positively religious or philosophical character is highly prevalent in one or the other form. The inconsistency of this position is all the more obvious to me as I myself was, at one time, very close to it, even if I did not completely accept it."[12]

It is worth noting that two years later, in 1882, Solovyov substantially amended his ideas about aesthetics. Using three symbols from antiquity he traces the path by which the spiritual principle triumphs over matter and death. All three symbols (Pygmalion and Galatea, Perseus and Andromache, Orpheus and Eurydice) are united by love, which has become the principle of the creative transformation nature. The first task entails the aesthetic incarnation of a dream:

> When the obedient stone stands
> Before the chisel in pure beauty,
> And the mighty flame of inspiration
> Gives life and flesh to your dream . . .

The dream is incarnated, but "do not imagine that the triumph is complete . . . She (Galatea, the world-soul, nature) requires a new victory":

> The cliff hangs over the abyss,

In confusion Andromeda calls
You, Perseus! You, Alcides!
The winged horse jumps into the abyss,
And the mirrored shield is raised
And turned over and, having seen itself
The dragon sinks into the abyss.

Once the aesthetic task is accomplished an ethical feat must take place–the triumph over the dragon of sin. Only when that has come to pass does the magical lyre of Orpheus achieve that which was not possible for Pygmalion's chisel; here the victory belongs to the poet as prophet (*vates*). Solovyov's Orpheus is not the Orpheus of Greek myth, who found Eurydice only to lose her again. This is the Orpheus whom the first Christians depicted on the walls of the catacombs, seeing in him a prefigurement of the Savior.

Having received in April 1880 the degree of doctor of philosophy, Solovyov obtained the right to a professor's chair, "but Vladislavlev did not support him, and he joined the university only as a privatdocent."[13] In his curriculum vitae Solovyov states, "At the end of that year (1880) and at the beginning of the following I lectured on metaphysics at the University of St. Petersburg in the capacity of privatdocent. I also taught philosophy at the higher women's courses organized by Prof. Bestuzhev-Ryumin."[14] In the autumn of 1880 Solovyov began his course at St. Petersburg University late in the term. The introductory lecture "The Historical Concerns of Philosophy" which was given on 20 November, defines philosophy as a liberating force: "It freed the human personality from external violence and gave it inner content. It overthrew all false, foreign gods and developed in man an inner form for the revelations of true Divinity.... The process of philosophy is twofold: it is destructive and creative. It makes humanity fully human."[15] At the Bestuzhev higher courses for women Solovyov lectured on ancient philosophy, as he had at the Gérié courses in Moscow. "At first K. N. Bestuzhev-Ryumin was completely charmed by Solovyov and saw a genius in him, but this enchantment quickly passed and gave way to a highly negative opinion. The reason, of course, lay in Solovyov's 'betrayal' of Slavophile principles and in his sympathy with Catholicism. The disenchantment was mutual, for Solovyov was convinced of Bestuzhev-Ryumin's 'duplicity,' as he expressed it."[16]

During this year in St. Petersburg Solovyov lived at the Hotel Evropeysky and often went to stay at Lesnoy and the Khitrovo estate of Pustynka. "I have still not rented an apartment, but I have in mind a very good one. Lesnoy is as far away on the Vyborg side as Petrovsky park is from Moscow. I have to withdraw into such seclusion because I have a great deal of work to do this year and the crush of St. Petersburg is too disturbing."[17]

At this time Solovyov also began to complain about urticaria and neuralgia, from which he suffered for the rest of his life. In the case of neuralgia, it eventually became acute and turned into "neuritis."[18] "What sort of crazy idea possessed you that I should go see Botkin because of my urticaria?" he wrote to his mother, "However, I am now suffering from terrible neuralgia in my leg and other places, but all the same I will not go to Botkin." In the next letter he says, "Everything here is all right. Though I myself am not completely well, I am not completely ill. I have begun my lectures at the Bestuzhev women's courses. The audience is distinguished by its great number and scarcity of beauty."[19]

Solovyov's connection with the university was soon broken for good. Following the assassination of Alexander II, Solovyov gave a speech on 28 March 1881 in the hall of the Credit Society during which he maintained that the young tsar should pardon the murderer of his father in the name of Christian justice. The speech was greeted enthusiastically, especially by the students of the university who expected that, immediately after the lecture, Solovyov would be going, not home, but to prison. The affair blew over, but Solovyov understood that it would be necessary for him to petition the Ministry of Public Enlightenment for a resignation. This was accepted, although the minister Baron Nikolai told Solovyov, "I did not require this."[20] At the end of his curriculum vitae Solovyov stated, "In January 1882 I resumed my lectures in philosophy at the University of St. Petersburg and at the higher women's courses, but within a month I left St. Petersburg and abandoned my professorial career forever."[21] Evidently this profession was generally not to Solovyov's liking. Even before his speech about pardoning the regicide, he had already decided to break with the university. On 10 March 1881 he wrote to Fet, "In the autumn I think I will settle in Moscow for good, leaving behind this Finnish Sodom."[22]

In 1883 Solovyov wrote to Kireev, "I have turned thirty-one and I am beginning to feel burdened by my idleness; could you not think of some kind of practical occupation for me (aside from an academic one, for I do not wish to return to that)."[23] A year before his death Solovyov did receive an invitation from the administrator of Warsaw, G. E. Zenger, to teach at the University of Warsaw, but it was too late; Solovyov felt that he could not return to an academic chair.[24]

According to Radlov, "during the course of seventeen years he did not give a public lecture,"[25] but this is a mistake. In April 1887 Solovyov gave a public lecture in Moscow "Slavophilism and the Russian Idea," which did not meet with success among the "Slavophile public" of Moscow.[26] In October 1891 he gave another lecture in Moscow "On the Decline of the Medieval Worldview," after which he was officially forbidden to speak in public.

After leaving the university, Solovyov temporarily abandoned specifically philosophical works in favor of theology, the Church question, and journalism.

The years 1881 and 1882 turned out to be a transitional time for Solovyov, but they did prepare the crisis of 1883, which explains their lack of productivity. Solovyov was resting and saving his strength for the next period of creativity which occurred in the middle of the 1880s. In 1881 he published only one article "On Clerical Power in Russia," and in 1882 he wrote a single article "About the Schism in the Russian Nation and Society"* and a short speech about Dostoevsky which is about seven pages long.

Solovyov's first article of an ecclesiastical and journalistic character was not published. I found the manuscript of it in the archives of Vera Sergeevna Solovyova, which belong to the publisher B. S. Shikhman. It is dated "Krasny Rog. 28 May 1881" and titled: "When the Russian Path was Abandoned and How to Return to It

---

* The title of this article refers to the schism within the Russian Orthodox Church in the late seventeenth century that led to the rise of the so-called Old Believer or Old Ritualist movement.

(Concerning K. S. Aksakov's Remark about the Inner State of Russia)." The ideas contained in this article are reproduced almost literally in "On Clerical Power in Russia." Solovyov's Slavophilism reached its apogee here, and Khomyakov or Aksakov could have freely signed their names beneath it.

> Peter the Great's model was the Protestant civilization of the Germanic nations, the model for Nikon* was the papacy... You,[27] as a follower and successor of Khomyakov agree, of course, that the fundamental error, the first falsehood of the development of the West, lay not in Protestantism, but in Catholicism, which was the first to stray from the truth of Christ and by this deviation defined that anti-Christian path which the Western nations followed. Whoever sees the error of this path (even if, in the end, it leads to the triumph of truth), must admit that the root of this error lies in papism, and that, undoubtedly, this root was transplanted to Russian soil by Nikon... This hierarchical love of power, this striving to maintain the external authority and unity of the Church by force, is indeed what forms the essence of papism. Even if there were not direct and positive proof of Nikon's papism, which we have, then all his behavior, and that of his successors, would leave no doubt that from the time of Nikon the Russian hierarchy was infected by the spirit of Romanism; and despite all personal exceptions, it has generally not separated itself from this spirit even until now.... I do not accuse individuals. On the contrary, the Russian national character, which is so hostile to intense clericalism, has more or less manifested itself in individual persons, in spite of their caste-like isolation, and paralyzed Catholic tendencies, not allowing them to turn into a durable system. However, it is undeniable that the Russian hierarchy *in corpore* has not renounced, either in word or deed, the Roman principle established by Nikon and his

* Nikon (1605-1681) was patriarch of Moscow during the reign of Tsar Aleksey. His reforms of the Russian Church according to contemporary Greek practice instigated the opposition of the Old Ritualists led by Archpriest Avvakum (1620-1682).

> immediate successors. Although maintaining this principle, the later hierarchy proved to be both too cowardly and too lazy to implement it actively, with the natural consequence that this hierarchy, which was separated from truth and impotent in error, lost every kind of moral authority.... In Russia spiritual power can have meaning only to the extent that it consciously and resolutely holds to the truly Christian principle (and not to the Roman or Byzantine) and actively leads the nation to its realization. In Russia there is no such spiritual power with a generally accepted moral authority. In other words, Russia has no real spiritual authority. It existed in ancient Rus, and in this, I think, lies the only real superiority of ancient, over modern, Russia.

In "On Clerical Power in Russia" Catholicism is declared to be a false theocracy. "If every tradition is holy, then we must submit ourselves to the Pope of Rome, who manifestly upholds an *anti-Christian tradition*."[28] Byzantium also took the wrong road, and the Russian Church, beginning with Nikon, has been thoroughly poisoned by Byzantinism and Romanism; it requires a radical reform. To a certain extent, that correct relationship between Church and state, which was postulated in *A Critique of Abstract Principles*, existed in Muscovite Russia; it is necessary for Russia only to return to the way it abandoned. "The rulers of Muscovy served the Russian land with the blessing of the hierarchs, and their confidence in the people was expressed by the Zemskii Sobors."[29] "Metropolitan Aleksy did not compete with the prince of Moscow, but protected him; Metropolitan Filip did not compete with Ivan the Terrible, but denounced him with the power of his words and by his martyrdom demonstrated the true superiority of the spiritual principle."[30*]

Aside from adopting the Roman-Byzantine principles of violence and despotism, the contemporary Russian hierarchy is guilty of "intellectual sterility," clinging exclusively to the definitions and formulas of the seventh and eighth centuries while not benefiting from the fruits of modern European philosophy.[31] "In truth, its unfortunate

* SS. Aleksy (1354-1378) and Filip (1507-1569) were metropolitans of Moscow who wielded considerable moral and political influence during periods of national turmoil. St. Filip was martyred for his opposition to Ivan the Terrible.

tradition still oppresses the Russian hierarchy, but it would be easier for us to renounce it, than for the Western hierarchy, which has elevated its error into dogma.... Strictly speaking, an ecumenical council is not necessary for the rebirth of the Russian Church. The sin is not within the Universal Church, but in the Russian. Above all, it must purify itself from this sin on its own."[32]

What does Solovyov imply here by the expression the "Universal" ["*vselenskaiia*"] Church? In this case, the Universal Church is meant to be that which is neither national nor local, in the sense used by the Churches of Rome and Constantinople in speaking of themselves. At first, Solovyov contrasts the distorted condition of the Universal Church (Roman and Byzantine) with the ancient Russian way, and then speaks of the sins of the Roman Church, from which the "Universal" is free. Evidently, at this time, Solovyov understood the term "universal" very vaguely as a synonym for the "invisible" Church.

In his article of 1882 "About the Schism in the Russian Nation and Society" Solovyov makes a great advance. For him, the essence of the Church is found in its "universal *catholic* character" ["*vselenskii kafolicheskii kharakter*"]. Solovyov's further evolution can be seen by his substitution of the letter *f* by *t*; instead of "*kafolicheskii*" he soon writes "*katolicheskii*."[33]

For the first time in this article Solovyov stresses the significance of ecclesiastical *obedience*. "The first act of Christ according to Scripture was one of obedience to his earthly parents 'and He went down with them and came to Nazareth, and was obedient to them.' By contrast, our sectarians begin by rebelling against Mother Church; they leave Nazareth and do not want to return...."[34] "Such an absolute moral principle (the self-renunciation of the Son of Man) imparts to the hierarchical structure of the Church its divine character."[35] Demonstrating the error of the Russian Old Ritualists [*raskol'niki*], "who left the Mother Church," Solovyov accuses them, first of all, of excessive literalism and points out the inevitability of adding not only letters but whole words when translating the creed: while Roman Catholics say "*credo*" and the Russians "*veruiu*," the French say "*je crois*" and the Germans "*ich glaube*." If, in this case, the addition of a personal pronoun does not change the substance of faith, then the same must be said about the changing the spelling of "*Isus*" [Jesus] to "*Iisus*," against which the Old Ritualists rebelled.

To the living authority of the Church, the Old Ritualists opposed the older tradition of the book, which is the origin of Protestantism (to the extent that the individual reader becomes the interpreter of a traditional text). Demonstrating the discrepancy between the two branches of the schism, the one with priests [*popovtsy*] and the one without [*bespopovtsy*], Solovyov shows how the priestless Church inevitably leads to sectarianism of both the mystical and rationalistic varieties (i.e. the Khlysty vs. the Dukhobors, Molokane, and Baptists). "The Russian schism represents in these four phases the strict consequence of its negative direction, its gradual withdrawal from the divine foundation of the Church, or catholicity [*kafolichestvo*], which is the same thing."[36] "About the Schism in the Russian Nation and Society" is actually composed of two articles. The first, "About the Church and the Schism" was published in the journal *Rus'* in 1882 (nos. 38, 39, 40), whereas the second, "Several Words about Our Worldly Heresies and about the Essence of the Church," appeared in the seventh issue of the same journal in 1883. Solovyov later reworked these articles and published them as one in *Pravoslavnoe obozrenie* in 1884 (nos. 5-8) under the title "About the Schism in the Russian Nation and Society." (It appears in this form in the third volume of his complete works, beginning on page 243.) Thus, only the first part of this work, which appeared in *Rus'* on 21 September 1882, dates to 1882, emphasizing again Solovyov's lack of productivity during the years 1882–83.

Solovyov divides "the worldly heresies" into three categories: 1) "Redstockism,"[*] which turns all religion into an inner certainty about one's salvation and a feeling of gratitude to the Savior without any kind of obligations or good works.[37] (Solovyov calls Redstockism a "domestic" and sentimental religion.) 2) Ethical sectarianism, which reduces the substance of Christianity to an evangelical morality and a

[*] After Lord Redstock, a member of the Plymouth Brethern who was invited to Russia in 1874. His ideas were propagated by one of his converts, V. A. Pashkov, who attempted to create a unified Protestant movement in Russia until the imperial government dissolved his society in 1884 and banished him from the country.

spiritual mood which denies objective truths, dogmas, and doctrines. 3) Spiritualism, which identifies religion with the *fact* of our immortality and with a factual relation between us and the invisible world of spirits. It overlooks the ideal and moral conditions of such a connection, basing it not on faith and Christian asceticism but on external and accidental phenomena. Spiritualists offer religious feeling an objective support which is independent from it, whereas religious people can rely only on that which is infinitely higher and more perfect than themselves, on that which has an absolute meaning. There is nothing of this in spiritualism where everything is relative, accidental, and arbitrary.[38]

Aleksandr N. Aksakov published his objections to Solovyov's position in *Rus'* (1883, no. 8), to which was appended the following note by Solovyov: "Concerning relations with the invisible or the extraterrestrial Church, it is necessary to have a guarantee that in the given case we are communicating with the invisible *Church*, and not with something else, or completely opposite. In spiritualism there is no such guarantee."[39] Further on, we come across this characteristic declaration: "Our task consists entirely in the creation of truth, not in the search for truth. To search for truth eighteen centuries after it was visibly and tangibly revealed means *chercher midi à quatorze heures*.... If spiritualists employ mediumistic phenomena without rejecting the stone of the Universal Church, then they do not form a sect.... Whoever has *something* to build on, then let him build to whatever height he can, and whoever has a *road* to go on, then let him go as far as he can. But woe to them if they mistake an old swamp, and everything that is found in one, for a new road."[40]

We can see here how far Solovyov has come from the period of "Sophia," when he was in constant communication with spirits. He resolutely denies spiritualism but is opposed only to the use of violent measures against it. He himself does not notice that in this new worldview he has left no place for "free philosophy." The truth was given to us twenty centuries ago and our task is, not to search for it, but to *create* it and realize it in life. How, then, can the destructive and creative processes of philosophical development, about which Solovyov spoke three years previously in his introductory lecture "The Historical Concerns of Philosophy," manifest themselves? In the destruction of false gods and false theocracy. In the meantime, however, the necessity of obedience to a hierarchical authority has been recognized. This authority is not to be found in Rome, but in the Orthodox East. But here it would appear that for several centuries the Russian Church has appropriated the principles of false Roman theocracy. In this case one must appeal to the Orthodoxy of the fifteenth century, to the example of Saints Aleksy and Filip. But is this not what the Old Ritualists did, and is this not what Solovyov accused them of, saying that they replaced ecclesiastical "catholicity" ["*kafolichnost'*"] with the old tradition, based on an ancient text, whose interpreter is the individual reader? And does Solovyov himself not do the same thing, when he sets his personal understanding of tradition against living ecclesiastical authority? And did Solovyov himself not show that the inevitable outcome of this position is Protestant individualism? Solovyov accuses the Old Ritualists of leaving Mother Church, but it was in the name of Orthodox tradition that they abandoned that hierarchy, which Solovyov himself recognizes as having betrayed Orthodoxy. It is necessary not to leave the Church, but to cure its sins with love, to reform it while remaining a member of it. But in what does filial obedience to the Church consist, once it is acknowledged that for several centuries already its leaders have been separated from the truth? It consists in obedience to ecclesiastical tradition, to the Orthodoxy of the past. But when did the Raskolniks depart from this obedience? They renounced the authority of the state Church in the name of their own understanding of Orthodox tradition. Solovyov does the same. However, he was not excommunicated from the Church. But why did this not happen? Is it not because Solovyov developed his theosophy in the spirit of Boehme and Schelling in the nineteenth century when the Russian Church possessed neither the sword nor the zeal for the eradication of errors? Had Solovyov lived and preached in the seventeenth century would he not have been burned on the same pyre as Quirinus Kuhlmann who perished for the same ideas inspired by Boehme? And had he not been burned, would he have remained submissive, "in the name of love," to the hierarchy headed by Patriarch Joachim!?

Solovyov soon had to face all these questions. For example, he drastically changed his views on the Old Ritualists. In 1888 he stated, "The ecclesiastical administration of Russia is illegal and schismatic, and falls under anathema (*lata sententia*) according to the third canon of the Seventh Ecumenical Council; it is formally repudiated by a significant part of Orthodox Russia (the Old Ritualists)."[41] In the silence of the years 1881–82, after his ties with the civil service, the university, and the official academic world were broken, a new worldview arose in Solovyov.

On 28 January 1881 Dostoevsky died. As he was, of all the Slavophiles, the closest to Solovyov, we must consider their relationship in detail.

We are entirely of Evgeny Trubetskoy's opinion that one should not speak of Dostoevsky's influence on Solovyov, but of their influence on each other.[42] We also agree with Trubetskoy that the credo which Dostoevsky proclaimed at the Pushkin celebration, namely, his conception of the Russian idea as something pan-human and synthetic (coinciding with the ideas of Versilov in *The Adolescent*), was formed under Solovyov's influence. This is opposed to the Slavophilism represented by Prince Myshkin and Shatov, for whom the world can be saved only by the "Russian" God and Christ. Beginning in the summer of 1878, when they traveled together to the Optina monastery to visit the starets Amvrosy, the friendship between Solovyov and Dostoevsky was closest during the years 1878–80. "The degree to which they shared the same spiritual life at that time can be seen from the fact that in 1878, when describing the foundations of his worldview, Dostoevsky speaks for both of them."[43] In his first speech about Dostoevsky, Solovyov says, "The Church as a positive social ideal was to become the central idea of a new novel, or series of novels, of which only the first, *The Brothers Karamazov*, was written. Dostoevsky shared with me the principal idea of this work and also, partly, its plan in bare outlines during the summer of 1878. We were then on the way to the Optina monastery."[44]

At every stage of reading *The Brothers Karamazov* we feel that it was written under the influence of Solovyov and his ideas. According to one tradition, Dostoevsky depicted Solovyov in the character of Alyosha Karamazov. (This idea is mentioned, incidentally, by the Catholic author Michel d'Herbigny in his book *Un Newman russe*.) In our opinion, Dostoevsky divided Solovyov between Ivan and Alyosha Karamazov, which explains why more traits of Solovyov are to be found in the elder brother. To a certain degree, Solovyov united the brilliance and dialectics of the "aristocratically educated" Ivan with the gentleness and goodness of Alyosha. Nevertheless, Solovyov was, first of all, a philosopher, not a nice young man living only according to the dictates of his heart. Ivan's first article "On Ecclesiastical Justice," which endeared him to both the clericalists and the liberals, and beyond whose paradoxes the starets Zosima discerned "a lofty heart, capable of searching and pondering the heights," recalls a great deal of Solovyov's articles, including even those that were written after Dostoevsky's death. Ivan and Father Paissy agree with Solovyov that the dominion of Christ on earth is embodied in the kingdom of the Church and that the Church should subordinate the state to itself, transforming it and making it its free instrument for the realization of the Kingdom of God on earth. For Solovyov in 1878, as for Father Paissy, this establishment of the Kingdom of God must take place in Eastern Orthodoxy, not in Rome, which succumbed to the third temptation of the devil.

"According to the Russian concept and hope it is necessary that the Church not be reborn into the state, as from a lower form into a higher, but, on the contrary, that the state must end by consenting to become the Church and nothing else. So be it."

There is, however, something curious about all this. Although at the end of the 1870s Solovyov was no less anti-Catholic than Dostoevsky, it was as if Dostoevsky had been able to predict the future Solovyov by portraying him in Ivan. Of all Dostoevsky's characters, Ivan is the only one to be immersed in the spirit of Catholic culture, and it is not in vain that Alyosha cries out in horror, "You are going to join them (the Jesuits)!" (Ivan also calls the starets Zosima by the name of St. Francis of Assisi, "Pater Seraphicus.") One would had to have had the intuition of Dostoevsky's genius to foresee in the young man, for whom the tradition of Rome was "anti-Christian," the author of *La Russia et l'Eglise Universelle*, who in 1888 would literally hear from his Russian friends Alyosha's words, "You are going to join the Jesuits."

The chapter "Cana of Galilee" from *The Brothers Karamazov* must have been especially close to Solovyov with its themes of the union of "the white lily with the scarlet rose," and of "the earthly soul with the invisible world." "It was as though the silence of the earth united with that of the heavens; the mystery of the earth touched the mystery of the stars." And if the transfiguration of Alyosha's soul occurs only after he falls asleep during the reading of the Gospel about the marriage at Cana in Galilee, then, for his part, Solovyov assigns a special significance to this first miracle of Christ, which is found only in John. "Christ begins his mission with the radiant miracle at Cana in Galilee, with the sanctification of human joy and conviviality."[45] And if Alyosha falls on the earth and bathes it in tears, then Solovyov in 1886 will "bow his head to the Sovereign Earth."

The starets Amvrosy apparently regarded Solovyov more coldly than Zosima does Ivan. In Amvrosy's biography we read: "He had a disapproving opinion of the latter (Solovyov)." What inspired the starets's disapproval? Not, of course, Solovyov's Catholic ideas, which he did not have at that time, but, perhaps, those ideas and positions in which the clairvoyant discerned the future apologist of papal infallibility.

Solovyov gave three speeches about Dostoevsky, but they reveal little that is actually characteristic of the author of *The Brothers Karamazov*. It was as though Solovyov used Dostoevsky's name for the promulgation of his own ideas.

In the first speech Solovyov points to Dostoevsky as the precursor of a future art, which resembles his concept of free theurgy. In as much as the old art drew humanity away from the darkness of the world and evil, the new art attracts us to darkness and the evils of life with the sometimes obscure desire of illuminating this darkness and pacifying this evil.[46] Underneath the coarse cover of contemporary realism is hidden the winged poetry of the future. In realistic art we have a promise of the religious art that is to come, and whose prophet was Dostoevsky. If Goncharov and Lev Tolstoy treat life statistically in its ready, hard, and clear forms, then with Dostoevsky nothing is settled; everything is in ferment and still only in the process of becoming.[47] He predicts where the various directions of contemporary life are heading and passes judgment on them.

In the short second speech given on 1 February 1882, Solovyov depicts Dostoevsky as an apostle of universal Orthodoxy, "the clairvoyant prophet" of the truth of Christ. "The true Church that Dostoevsky preached is pan-human, above all in the sense that, in the end, the division of humanity into rival and mutually hostile tribes and nations must vanish in it.... Therefore, it is impossible that when he spoke of Russia, Dostoevsky had in mind national isolation."[48] Here Solovyov imposes on Dostoevsky his own personal formulas, forgetting that in *Diary of a Writer* there are more of Shatov's ideas than Versilov's. Even in *The Brothers Karamazov* we are told that "the star shines" only from the East, and that the living East will give life to the dying West and unite the Aryan world. Evgeny Trubetskoy was also right in saying that Dostoevsky's anti-Semitism prevented him from accepting Solovyov's universalism in all its dimensions.[49]

In general, just as myopia prevented Solovyov from seeing external nature (he managed to appreciate Lombardy only thanks to a pair of pince-nez bought in Paris),[50] he was also shortsighted with regard to people; he was deprived of psychological insight.

Dostoevsky understood Solovyov better than vice versa. It is difficult to imagine two men more opposite: Dostoevsky is all analysis, Solovyov all synthesis. Dostoevsky is entirely tragic and paradoxical; the Madonna and Sodom, faith and science, the East and the West, find themselves in eternal confrontation within him. For Solovyov, on the contrary, darkness is a precondition for light, science is based on faith, and the East must join in an organic union with the West. His complete dissimilarity to Dostoevsky is clearly seen in the third speech delivered on 19 February 1883. There is now nothing left of Dostoevsky, as the ancient Greeks said about the dramas of Euripides: *oudèn pròs Diònuson*.

The crisis that precipitated Solovyov's passage from Orthodoxy to Catholicism began on the eve of 1883. In the spring of 1882, a year before the coronation of Alexander III, Solovyov had a mysterious dream. "From his own account," writes Evgeny Trubetskoy, "I know that the ultimate shock which provoked the revolution in his views was a prophetic dream he had a year before the coronation of Alexander III. He dreamt that he was going along a series of Moscow streets and distinctly recalled their names as well as the house at which his carriage stopped. At its entrance a high-ranking Catholic clergyman came out and approached him, and Solovyov immediately asked him for his blessing. The prelate, apparently, hesitated, doubting whether he should bless a 'schismatic,' but Solovyov vanquished his doubts by pointing out the mystical unity of the Universal Church, untouched by the visible division of its two halves, and the blessing was given."[51]

The effect of this dream is felt for the first time in the third speech about Dostoevsky, which was delivered on 19 February 1883. In the first part Solovyov repeats his old scheme, into which he incorporates Dostoevsky, "who harmonically combined in himself the divine, human, and material principles," and who was, at the same time, a mystic, humanist, and naturalist.[52] In the second part he states that the task of Russia is synthesis and reconciliation. While the great sin of the separation of Churches was occurring in Byzantium, Russia was being born for its expiation.[53] From time immemorial Russia has found itself between two enemies: the non-Christian East (including Islam), and the Western form of Christianity, or Romanism. The struggle for victory over both these enemies was necessary for the formation of the *body* of the Russian state. Now that Russia has shown both the West and the East its physical strength, the struggle has lost its significance. Russia must now demonstrate its spiritual strength in reconciliation. Recognizing that the spiritual principle of the Poles lies in Catholicism, and that of the Jews in Judaism, we must distinguish in them that which is divine, from that which is human.[54]

In view of the fact that in ancient times the Church of Rome stood alone as a firm rock against which crashed all the dark waves of anti-Christian forces (heresies and Islam), and that in our own time, as well, Rome alone remains untouched and unshaken amidst the flood of anti-Christian civilization and that it alone pronounces a powerful, if harsh, sentence of condemnation against the godless world, we cannot attribute these facts only to some kind of incomprehensible human stubbornness, but recognize here as well a mysterious divine force. And if Rome, unshaken in its sanctuary, while striving to attract to this sanctuary everything human, advanced and changed, moved forward, lost its way, fell deeply and raised itself again, then it is does not behoove us to judge it for this stumbling and falls, because we did not support and raise it, but looked on the difficult and slippery path of our western brother with self-satisfaction while staying in our place, from where we were in no danger of falling.[55]

This sort of speech about Dostoevsky could only have been given after he was long buried. In Dostoevsky's name, Solovyov called for reconciliation with those things to which the novelist was deeply hostile. Dostoevsky considered Rome to be the Antichrist; he was anti-Polish and anti-Semitic as well. He did not call for unity with Rome, but for a struggle against it and the nations which had adopted its culture.

Solovyov is firmly with Dostoevsky in his conception of the Church as a theocracy, as the Kingdom of Christ, which is to be realized through an earthly state. For Dostoevsky, the triumph of the Church is connected with definite political hopes, especially with the formation of a Slavic state on the shores of the Bosphorus. Whereas theocracy meant for Dostoevsky the triumph of the Orthodox and imperial East over Catholicism and papal Rome, from 1883 Solovyov attempted to construct a theocracy of the future, uniting the Orthodox East with Catholic Rome, the Eastern empire with the Western pontificate.

Before considering the crisis that coincides with Solovyov's illness of the spring of 1883, we must mention the deep emotional experience which effected him from 1877 and which, in many ways, defined the course of his life. We mean Solovyov's only serious love, which lasted ten years and which, though it cooled, continued to be alive within him to his final days. The object of this love was Sofya Petrovna Khitrovo, who inspired Solovyov's best poems.

When I asked Sofya Petrovna about the time her acquaintance with Solovyov began, she replied, "immediately after his return from Egypt." This means they must have first met in 1876–77, probably in St. Petersburg. Sofya Petrovna Khitrovo (née Bakhmeteva) was a niece of Sofya Andreevna Tolstaya, wife of Count Aleksey Konstantinovich Tolstoy. Solovyov was introduced into the household of Countess Tolstaya, with whom her niece lived, by a nephew of Count Tolstoy, Dmitry Tsertelev. Beginning in 1877, Solovyov spent every summer at the Tolstoy estate, Krasny Rog, in the district of Bryansk. The master of the house, the poet Aleksey Tolstoy, was no longer alive, but his widow and her niece still lived on a grand scale, and at Krasny Rog Solovyov became immersed in a real *vie de château*. In his memoirs Fet describes the environs of Krasny Rog, "In spite of the pine forests' certain monotony, the road was, all the same, not without a charm of its own. The dense wall of firs parted from time to time, revealing a small lake that was covered with algae, and from which, at night, at the sound of the carriage, enormous wild ducks would ascend croaking and flying out from under the horses' hooves. At times one could see mighty eagles resting on the high treetops. It is needless to say to what an extent our hosts were hospitable and gracious."[56]

The spirit of the deceased Aleksey Tolstoy still reigned at Krasny Rog when Solovyov began to stay there. By the mood of his poetry he was also very close to Solovyov. The creator of "Don Juan" and "John Damascene" was a poet-philosopher who strove to unite the pantheistic tendencies of Goethe with Christianity. Tolstoy's serious shortcomings as a poet probably escaped Solovyov who was enchanted by Krasny Rog. He felt that the deceased master of the estate was a profound mystic for whom nature was full of mysterious voices and to whom an eerie demonism was not foreign ("The Vampire," "The Bride of Corinth"). The Tolstoys arranged spiritualist séances and the count discovered that his wife possessed "a great deal of magnetism."[57] Fet had occasion to take part in one of these séances at the Tolstoy estate at Pustynka, and the table answered him in iambs and other meters. During Solovyov's stay at Krasny Rog in 1877 on his way to the field army on the Danube, some kind of mischief took place and the spirit of Tsertelev appeared.[58]

Subsequently, Tolstoy's hostility to despotism and the Muscovite-Byzantine period appealed to Solovyov's state of mind, as well as his cult of the Kievan period when Russian life was free and when Prince Vladimir adopted Christianity as the religion of joyous mercy and love for the poor.[59] "My hatred for the Muscovite period," Aleksey Tolstoy wrote in a letter "is my idiosyncrasy. My hatred for despotism, is my very self."[60]

Solovyov fell under the strong influence of Countess Sofya Tolstaya. He adored her and looked up to her, confessing in a youthful letter to her, "Avec des apparences de bonté j'ai un coeur trés méchant. C'est mauvais, mais je n'y puis rien."[61]

The countess apparently treated the young philosopher quite firmly. "Do not think that I believe you have some kind of special inclination for me, for I demand absolutely nothing. It is '*ein längst überwundener Standpunkt*' since I demanded something and became offended."[62]

At a more mature age Solovyov cooled significantly toward Sofya Tolstaya and spoke with a certain irony about some aspects of her behavior. In any case, the real object of Solovyov's affections was not, of course, the old countess, who merely reflected the light cast by her niece. Sofya Petrovna Khitrovo was a few years older than Solovyov and when they met she was twenty-six. At an early age she married a young diplomat and poet Mikhail Aleksandrovich Khitrovo, whom Fet met at Pustynka in 1869 when Aleksey Tolstoy was still alive. Fet called him a "brilliantly educated young man who at present is occupying a highly visible place in our diplomatic corps."[63] When Fet went on a drive with the Tolstoys the young diplomat would accompany them on horseback. Apparently Sofya Petrovna was not entirely happy in her marriage. In a letter of 1887 to Anna Aksakova, Solovyov described the Khitrovos' marriage thus, "There did not exist on either side a sense of a moral tie; there was not even any purely human love or egotistical attachment; there was nothing aside from calculation and external circumstances.... There can no longer be talk here of some sort of ideals, for there is simply not a single, slightest element of a real marriage."[64] Of course, Solovyov could not be an impartial judge in this case, and his opinion betrays a certain exaggeration. Eventually, Mikhail Khitrovo was sent to Japan, and for years he lived away from his family, which furthered his wife's intimacy with Solovyov.

I knew Sofya Petrovna during her middle age when already little remained of her former charm, but the portraits of her from her youth allow one to understand her extraordinary social success. My father compared her to a pink August aster. The French critic Eugène Melchior de Vogüé, who was a guest at Krasny Rog in the summer of

1878, called her jokingly *Eve touranienne*, discovering something Tartar in her features.

"Your are more graceful and more beautiful than the gazelles of the desert, / Madonna of the steppes, Eve of Turania" – is how Solovyov begins his first, still very weak, poem to Sofya Petrovna of 18 August 1878. Sofya Khitrovo had a round face and dark narrow eyes. Solovyov especially liked to see her in a pale blue dress.

I have often been asked whether Sofya Petrovna understood Solovyov. In response I can only ask if one could imagine a man loving a woman for close to twenty years if she *did not understand him at all?* I do not know whether Sofya Petrovna shared any of Solovyov's ideas, but she undoubtedly "intuited" his inner ego which he revealed to her more fully than to anyone else. Recalling in 1892 his time spent at Pustynka, Solovyov sadly remarked: "Two lives were consumed there." In other words, it was not only his life, but both their lives which the years had fused into one.

Solovyov's love for Sofya grew in stages. We saw that in 1879 Solovyov still had other romantic interests in Moscow. The first years of Solovyov's love for Sofya Petrovna filled his soul, for the most part, with melancholy as his feeling seemed hopeless. In 1880 he expressed this mood in verse:

> You are leaving, and at the hour of parting my heart
> No longer resonates with desire and entreaties,
> Wearied by years of long torment,
> Unnecessary lying, despair, and ennui
> It surrenders itself and falls silent before fate.

The "unnecessary lying," was probably especially painful for Solovyov, but the presence of Mikhail Khitrovo made it inevitable. Solovyov's letters from the end of the 1870s reveal to us these long years of suffering. In reading them we see that the apogee of his fame at the time of the lectures about Godmanhood did not make him happy. The letters of this period are the most melancholy he ever wrote. "Farewell, may God protect you," he writes to Countess Tolstaya on 30 November 1878, "but I do not know what will become of me. Darkness and mist cover my path, night spreads itself more and more thickly over the earth."[65] "My melancholic temperament inclines me to feel forgotten by God and people (which, of course, I merit), but I am all the more gladdened by undeserved attention.... What am I doing, you ask? I am writing about 'beauty and creativity,' in theory, Countess, alas, only in theory!"[66]

Solovyov spent June of 1879 at Krasny Rog, and his mood was heavy. "In vain you suggest that I enjoy myself here," he writes to his sister Nadya.[67] "I am a long way from feeling pleasure; here, as everywhere, a single minute of a pleasant or, at least, tranquil state of mind is followed by long hours of angst and torment." He uses even stronger language writing to his mother on 12 June 1879: "Dear mamá, if you really love me, then you must understand that aside from the sorrows we both share, such as papá's illness now, I still have another misfortune of my own so that, in general, my life is not very happy. If I am, all the same, still alive and have not voluntarily dispatched myself to the other world, then I assure you it is mostly the thought of you and papa which restrains me; but I do possess sufficient courage for such a step. Therefore, you must be indulgent with those petty unpleasantnesses which I can sometimes cause you, for the sake of that great one which I am sparing you."

Having returned to Moscow at the end of June, Solovyov wrote to Sofya Tolstaya, "When I left I was genuinely ill with heart palpitations and vertigo and I am very obliged to Baron N. who was more than kind to me throughout the journey. S. P. did not, however, give me any kind of relics, although she promised... so that the main object of my veneration remains as before the photograph with the torn off head...."[68]

For a certain time in 1880 Solovyov daily made notes of his dreams. We present some of them:

1880

August 12 – (Pustynka) I dreamt that I was in Siberia, it seems in Tomsk, on the way to Japan. I found myself in a hotel on a high balcony with an open view. It was cold. I looked at the sky and saw the northern lights.

Aug. 13 – (St. Petersburg) I dreamt that I am walking with the young ladies of Pustynka next to some kind of orangery on a bright day. S. P., who is to one side, is the only one discontented.

Aug. 15 – (St. Petersburg) I dreamt that I find myself with a company of soldiers who are setting out on a campaign.

Aug. 16 – (Pustynka) I dreamt that I am in a hammock attached to nothing. I am freely rocking in the air and before me are S. P. and the Countess. The latter says: "Well this is a fine situation, I never knew it would turn out like this."

Aug. 17 – (Pust.) I dreamt that M. A. Kh—vo arrived with a rather beautiful woman, as though she were his wife. S. P. leaves angry, and this lady takes me to the side and begins to speak ill of S. P. I defend her.

Aug. 19 – (Pust.) I dreamt that I found myself with a detachment of soldiers next to some kind of a tower at the foot of a high mountain on which the enemy is climbing. I say to the soldiers "move closer to them and shoot." The enemy advances and my soldiers want to shoot but it seems their rifles are unloaded. Confusion ensues, but I am not afraid; I say, "Load faster, we can still succeed!" And just as the enemy begins to scale the mountain my men fire a volley and all the enemy quickly vanish.

Aug. 22 – (St. Petersburg) I dreamt of my deceased father. He had a pale face but he was in good form and much improved. He handed me a splendidly produced volume of his posthumously published works. I was overjoyed and said, you did this better than we did. He then went to his room to rest, and I began to look over the book and noticed that it contained his work about the origins of Russian history up to the Time of Troubles. I then went to my father's room in order to put the book in its proper place; I knocked and asked, "Are you sleeping papá?" he answered "No, I have not yet fallen asleep, come in!" I entered; it was rather dark in the room. He lay in bed wearing a gray robe. I went up to him and kissed his hand. He held my hand and asked, "Is the material for your book 'Memoirs of a *Kammerjunker*' ready? Take care that it turns out well, it will require a great deal of knowledge." I wanted to reply that this work was going to be more literary than academic, and awoke.

Aug. 30 – I dreamt that S. P. was getting up from the floor and leaning towards me with her head thrown back. She rested on my arms, which I had stretched out. At first she seemed heavy and my knees buckled, but I straightened up and held her freely in my arms.

Aug. 31 – I dreamt that I was on a journey with my sisters in a stagecoach. Someone asks, "And papá?" Nadya answers, "He stayed at home." I then see myself sitting opposite S. P. at a small table. Her eyes were shining. Someone gave me a small three-cornered piece of parchment on which was written: *Et bien! Madame Hitrowo continue-t-elle toujours à faire la coquette avec tout le monde?*

Sept. 2 – I dreamt that I saw S. P. in a bright red dress, waltzing with me (N.B. the following evening I quarreled with her).

Sept. 3 – I dreamt that in some kind of dark courtyard I am giving copper and silver coins to a beggar. I dreamt of S. P. three times…

Sept. 6 – I dreamt that I am sitting with the Countess and S. P. in a small bright room. The Countess is sorting papers and asks me to get some sort of little red book. I do not find it, then she finds it herself and takes it out of a case and shows it to me. I am sitting at the feet of S. P.…

Sept. 10 – I dreamt of S. P. with a face that had changed. Nina G(agagrina) was behind the samovar scalding some kind of gray serpent with boiling water. The Countess complained of ill health.

Even more than Krasny Rog, Pustynka (which is near St. Petersburg, by the station of Sablino) is closely connected with Solovyov's life and left an indelible impression on his poetry. He lived there at various times from the beginning of the 1880s until the very last year of his life, when, a few weeks before his death, he wrote the poem "Once again the white bellflowers…". Fet provides a description of Pustynka in his memoirs:

On the designated day a carriage conveyed us three versts along the special highway from Sablino to Pustynka. One must admit that in the Russian steppe country one does not find such clear and noisy streams running between stony banks as one does everywhere on the Ingermannland coast. I am not going to dwell on the magnificent estate of Pustynka, built on the picturesque right bank of a mountain stream by the celebrated Rastrelli (as I was told). The house was full of everything which taste and splendor can gather in the course of many years, beginning with the decorative cabinets of Boulle down to the exquisite furniture which one could mistake for cast metal... In spite of the most varied and profound culture which was present here, there appeared in the house from time to time that playful smile which later expressed itself so sympathetically in the works of Kuzma Prutkov.[69]

The granite banks of the "wild Tosno," "the fine white sand," "the old pines," "the gracefully airy" bell towers, resembling "white angels," all these images belong to Solovyov's best poetry. By the banks of the Tosno was a large stone which Solovyov called the "holy rock," after he had his vision of the Fathers of the Church blessing his efforts "to justify the faith of his fathers" while sitting on it. He loved to walk to this rock with Sofya Petrovna. "Once again I lead her to the holy rock..."

Sofya Petrovna's character is described best of all in the poem "Oh, how much pure azure is in you," written in 1881.

Oh, how much pure azure is in you
And how many black, black storm clouds!
How clearly shines above you the reflection of God,
How burning and agonizing is the evil fire in you.

And how in your soul two eternal forces
Have joined with invisible enmity,
And the shadows of two worlds in a disorderly mob
Crowd against you and strangely unite.

This is all a familiar theme for us. In the soul of the beloved woman Solovyov sees the same goddess, "the soul of the world," who has separated herself from the divine world and is being held by the forces of chaos, which create in her a state of disintegration and suffering. The poem was published in *Rus'* in 1882 (no. 42) and included a third unsuccessful stanza about the shadows of the two worlds which Solovyov subsequently deleted. This stanza, however, though heavy and too abstract, is highly characteristic:

> In a mysterious succession they yield to each other,
> Or argue among themselves without thought or result,
> And your entire soul is their blind duality,
> A dumb, sterile world, an unnecessary enmity.

Solovyov's love for Sofya Petrovna united a rapturous admiration with a readiness "to lie at her feet, not rising from the dust," a "fire-breathing" passion, deep compassion, and an aspiration to awaken in her the best, dormant element of her soul.

> Loving you, I will not ask, poor friend
> Where you have been and where you are going.
> Only utter my name
> And I will press you silently to my heart. (1887)

And in the end there is the bitter lament over two burnt lives:

> Memory, enough! It was time for me to chant the requiem
> For this ailing shade!
> The time is passed and the knight
> Cannot possess the sleeping princess. (1892)

The automatic writing carried on with Sophia has turned into correspondence with Sofya Petrovna. Little by little, the mediumism diminishes and we hear the simple voice of a human heart in love. It is no longer "Sophia," nor a "tsaritsa," nor a "goddess," who speaks, but a gentle, suffering woman. In the automatic writing of this time one or another of these phrases constantly appears:

My dear friend, my dear, my only… I cannot go on this way, we must always be together… I live and die with you… I am at home… I awoke long ago and I want to see you … I must seem very bad, but my best self has awoken. My friend, believe in me… I am the one whom you love… *Warte nur, balde ruhest du auch* … Slowly, but continually I am awakening, my friend. I will be yours. The two of us will accomplish that task to which you are called… Do not think that it could end like this. We are bound to each other forever. I cannot live without you, do not be deceived. We must be together always. Do not be mean. It is useless. Wisdom demands that we be one person. I have long been yours with my soul, it is now necessary to be yours with my whole being. God has sufficient power to revive you. Be loyal only to me and love me more than everything. I will torment you as long as you have not grown soft and still have something thorny in you. I have tormented you a little… I will soon be with you entirely. Do not grieve. Everything passes except love.

We dare say that Sofya Petrovna Khitrovo was the unique love of Solovyov's entire life. Beginning in 1877, this love, though it changed forms, remained alive to the grave. Its first period comprised the "years of long torment, unnecessary lying, despair, and ennui." This is followed, in 1883, by a period of relative happiness, and in 1887, by a fatal crisis which causes a temporary estrangement. In 1890, however, Solovyov wrote to Sofya Petrovna:

But when death extinguishes before you and me
All the lamps of earthly life,
The flame of the eternal soul, like a star from the East,
Will lead us to that place where the light never dims,
And before the face of God, the God of love,
You will then become – my answer.

In 1892, at the time of his passionate and stormy relationship with Sofya Martynova, Solovyov unexpectedly wrote his best poem to Sofya Petrovna, "Memory," in which he flies on the wings of memory to a pleasant land where he sees his beloved "on a smoldering pyre," and by "the holy rock," wearing "a bright wreath of flowers." In 1894 he wrote to her, "As always: New Year's greetings, poor old friend!"

Solovyov spent the last month of his life at Pustynka, and Sofya Petrovna insisted by his coffin that he be buried there, in accordance with his wishes, at the site he chose himself.

Solovyov's love for Sofya Khitrovo and the poetry it inspired constitute an exceptional phenomenon in literary history. No poet has ever loved quite like this. The mystical symbolism of the *Vita nuova* ("everything in my thoughts has died in a moment, O radiant joy, I see only you") is combined here with the warmth of a simple human feeling. If one recalls what Solovyov experienced in those years, what ideas and plans ripened in his mind, if one recalls that the years of intimacy with Sofya Petrovna coincided with the writing of *The Spiritual Foundations of Life*, *The History and Future of Theocracy*, and *La Russie et l'Eglise Universelle*, one cannot regard this woman without gratitude. For it was in her soul that the clairvoyant gaze of the poet discerned that which was hidden from other people, the shades of two worlds thrown together in an invisible enmity and in a love that confirmed for him, time and again, his belief that: "Everything which revolves disappears in darkness, / Only the sun of love remains motionless."

In the spring of 1883 Moscow solemnly prepared for the coronation of Alexander III. During this time in the Likhutin house on the corner of Prechistensky and Zubovsky boulevards a young man lay in a fever struggling for his life. A few years before, his brilliantly begun career had been ruined and he had taken up the pilgrim's staff. Now his bodily organism was about to be destroyed but he no longer wished to die: He felt in himself the strength for something great and was aware that he had not yet accomplished his life's mission. His sister Maria Sergeevna recalls:

> It happened during the spring, in April, if I am not mistaken, not long before Moscow began to prepare for the coronation of Alexander III. As an acquaintance of mine expressed it, it was a "wavy" time for all of us, as well as for my brother in a personal sense. During the entire previous

winter he waited and hoped that the woman he called his fiancée would decide to take the final step in order to become his wife.... I remember with what a mysterious and radiant face my brother would sometimes say at dinner, "I drink to the health of my bride!" Then, turning to my mother, he would say, "Mama, she will soon come to see you, she wants to meet you, and you also", he added, nodding in our direction. The last days before he became ill he kept expecting letters and would leave his room every time the doorbell rang. He would be now terribly, now insanely happy. And then suddenly he fell ill and immediately grew worse. It was not exactly typhus, nor a nervous fever, but probably a combination of a cold and overwrought nerves. The fever was terrible and did not subside, but he retained complete consciousness.... On one occasion they thought he was sleeping and left him, but I sat by the window in the hall by the door, in case he should awake and call for someone.

Suddenly I heard my brother exclaim distinctly: "Who is there?"

"I am."

"Come here, on the table is the Bible, find the marriage at Cana in Galilee and read it aloud to me."

But while I was reading, my brother kept making the sign of the cross over himself, devoutly and broadly, pressing his fingers against his forehead, chest, and shoulders. I stopped reading, but he still continued to cross himself. This gesture expressed more clearly than any words the utter passion with which my brother desired to live and, at the same time, the completeness of his submission to the will of God. Finally, my brother stopped making the sign of the cross.

"Come closer."

I moved closer.

"Do you know if they sent my telegram?" (that is, to her, his "bride").

"They sent it, they sent it."

"Well good... But now, perhaps you can tell them that they can sponge me, if they want, or whatever else is necessary."

I left, but at the door I turned towards my brother and saw that he was crossing himself again, as before, and I distinctly heard the ardent, fervent whisper "Lord save me! Lord, help me!"

Toward evening my brother improved, and from the following day his convalescence began.[70]

The apartment in the Likhutin house, where the Solovyovs moved after the death of Sergey Mikhailovich, was located on the second floor. A cold magnificence reigned in it, and the large rooms decorated with palms seemed deserted. The door directly to the right of the entrance led into Vladimir Sergeevich's study. It was adorned with only two paintings, a full-size portrait of Peter the Great and Titian's *Christ and the Tribute Money*. The hall and the drawing room where no one ever sat created the impression of a temple dedicated to the memory of Sergey Mikhailovich. Along the walls were hung portraits of the grand dukes with their autographs. In the drawing room the white bust of Sergey Mikhailovich glimmered from behind a palm, and on some sort of lectern was displayed a blotter with a metal hood which had been presented to him by the university. Beyond the dining room, which was already more comfortable and where one could smell the kitchen and hear the voice of Anna the cook, were located the quarters of Poliksena Vladimirovna. Here could be seen an enormous icon-case and a perpetual lamp which illuminated from behind Raphael's white and rounded *Madonna della Sedia*.

Vladimir Sergeevich had recovered from his illness and was already walking about in his study when the bell rang. In the entry hall Sofya Petrovna appeared for the first time in this house. Vladimir Sergeevich bowed silently towards her and, without saying a word, led her into his study where they talked for a long time. His typhus had played a great role in the history of their relationship.

Shortly after, Solovyov was going by cab along the streets of Moscow and recognized what he had dreamt a year before: the same street, the same houses and, at the entrance to one, a Catholic prelate. Solovyov stopped and asked him for his blessing. After some hesitation the priest yielded to Solovyov's arguments and "blessed the schismatic."

Within a few weeks, with his head still shaved from the typhus, Solovyov went to Krasny Rog and soon completed his first work on the Catholic question "The Great Controversy and Christian Politics."

Endnotes for Part 1 - Chapter 7

1. *P,* vol. 2, 248.
2. Ibid., 250.
3. Ibid., 248.
4. Ibid., 97 ff.
5. *Sbornik statei o Vl. Solov'eve*, vol. 1 (1911), 129.
6. *SS*, vol. 2, vii.
7. Ibid., 371.
8 Ibid., 165.
9. Ibid., 178.
10. Ibid., 339.
11. V. F. Ern, "Gnoseologiia V. Solov'eva," 198.
12. *SS*, vol. 8, 26.
13. Radlov, 16.
14. *P*, vol. 2, 338.
15. *SS*, vol. 2, 411-12.
16. Radlov, 17.
17. *P*, vol. 2, 32.
18. See letter of 12 November 1896 to I. N. Grot, *Pis'ma*, vol. 3, 217.
19. *P*, vol. 2, 33.
20. Radlov, 17.
21. *P*, vol. 2, 338.
22. *P*, vol. 3, 107.
23. *P*, vol. 2, 110.
24. Radlov, 18.
25. Ibid., 115.
26. *P*, vol. 3, 115.
27. The letter is addressed to Konstantin Aksakov.
28. *SS*, vol. 3, 239.
29. Ibid., 231.

[30]. Ibid., 234.

[31]. Ibid., 237.

[32]. Ibid., 239.

[33]. The word "*kafolicheskii*" is mostly an artificial term, which has not entered the living language, being only a doublet of "*katolicheskii*." It should be replaced by the [Russian] word "*vselenskii*," or "*katolicheskii*." Indeed, in Greek there is only one word "*katholikós*," and no matter how hostilely the Greek Orthodox Church regards Roman Catholicism, it still calls itself the Greek Orthodox Catholic Church.

[34]. *SS*, vol. 3, 270.

[35]. Ibid., 269.

[36]. Ibid., 255.

[37]. Tolstoy provides an excellent satire of the Redstockists in *Anna Karenina*, when her husband, Aleksey Karenin, and the circle of Countess Lydia Ivanovna become followers of Redstock.

[38]. *SS*, vol. 3, 279-280.

[39]. Idem.

[40]. *SS*, vol. 3, 429.

[41]. Reply to correspondence from Krakow, published in *Put'*, 48; *SS*, vol. 11, 138.

[42]. Evgenii Trubetskoi, *Mirosozertsanie Vl. Solov'eva*, vol. 1, 73-74.

[43]. Ibid., 73.

[44]. *SS*, vol. 3, 197 and accompanying notes.

[45]. Ibid., 270.

[46]. Ibid., 189.

[47]. Ibid., 191.

[48]. Ibid., 201.

[49]. Trubetskoi, vol. 1, 75.

[50]. *P*, vol. 2, 15.

[51]. Trubetskoi, vol. 1, 440-49.

[52]. *SS*, vol. 3, 213.

[53]. Ibid., 215.

[54]. Ibid., 216.

55. Ibid., 216-217.

56. Fet, *Vospominaniia*, vol. 2, 185.

57. Ibid., 27.

58. *Pis'ma*, vol. 2, 238.

59. "St. Vladimir and the Christian State," *SS*, vol. 11, 121-135.

60. *SS*, vol. 7, 151.

61. *P*, vol. 2, 202.

62. Ibid., 205.

63. Fet, vol. 2, 185-186.

64. The letter to Aleksandra Aksakova has not been published.

65. *P,* vol. 2, 203.

66. Ibid., 204.

67. The cited letters to his sister and mother are unpublished.

68. *P*, vol. 2, 205. The date given (1883) is incorrect; among other things the letter speaks of the illness of Solovyov's father who died in 1879.

69. Fet, *Vospominaniia,* vol. 2, 25.

70. Mariia S. Bezobrazova, "Vospominaniia o brate Vl. Solov'eve," *Minuvshie gody* 5/6 (Moscow, 1908): 161-162.

Part Two

Rome

> May I be cursed as a parricide if I ever pronounce a word of judgment against the sanctity of Rome.
>
> V. Solovyov, letter to Aksakov, No. 9

Part 2 - Chapter 1

The Great Controversy
The Spiritual Foundations of Life
"Praises and Prayers to the Most Holy Virgin"

And, poor child,
for you there is no Refuge
between two hostile camps.
V. Solovyov

In his third speech about Dostoevsky, delivered on 19 February 1883, Solovyov spoke for the first time about the union of churches. A few days later he wrote to Ivan Aksakov, "Certain misfortunes have overtaken my speech in memory of Dostoevsky, in consequence of which I can send it to you only in time for the sixth issue of *Rus'*. The fact is that during my lecture I received an injunction forbidding me to give it, so that this lecture has to be treated as non-existent and the St. Petersburg press must pass over the evening of 19 February in silence, although over a thousand people were present. As a result of this police injunction the administrator Dmitriev, who had given permission for the speech, requested its text as soon as possible for his own protection and I had to hastily make a copy for myself. As it was not possible to send you this hieroglyphic copy I must copy it again, and it's a fairly long speech. Moreover, I am distraught and exhausted by the funeral and memorial services for an old friend of mine. Therefore, there is no way the speech can appear in No. 5, but I will bring it to you myself in Moscow. It will also have to be published not as a speech but as an article and under another title. All this is thanks to our friend K. P. Pobedonostsev!"[1*]

---

[*] Konstantin Pobedonostsev (1827-1907), jurist and Ober-Prokurator (Director General) of the Holy Synod of the Russian Orthodox Church from 1880 to 1905. An extreme pessimist and a born bureaucrat, Pobedonostsev was skeptical of any reforms of Russia's traditional religious or national life.

The fierce Ober-Prokurator of the Holy Synod, "the Russian Torquemada," had alighted for the first time on the path of Solovyov; this was only the beginning of their struggle.

With the first issue of *Rus'* in 1883 Solovyov had begun to publish his work *The Great Controversy and Christian Politics*. The first three chapters appeared without any difficulty. Chapter one, "Introduction: Russia and Poland," later became the first chapter of *The National Question* where it bore the title "Morality and Politics: The Historical Responsibilities of Russia." Beginning with the second paragraph, the first chapter of *The Great Controversy* is identical to the first chapter of *The National Question*.

In this opening chapter Solovyov discusses the great controversy between East and West that has occurred throughout history and whose origins Herodotus already dated to the mythical events of the abduction of the women of Argos by the Phoenicians and of Helen from Lacedemon by the son of the Trojan Priam. This great quarrel must be resolved and the task of the reconciliation of East and West falls to Russia. Solovyov denounces the self-love and greed of contemporary European politics, calling it *cannibalism*. In comparing the types of exploitation practiced by the English and the Germans, as he did in the final chapter of *The Philosophical Principles*, Solovyov remarks on the philosophical superiority of the Germans. "While the Englishman appears before his victims as a pirate, the German comes as a pedagogue, raising his victims to a higher culture... The empiricist Englishman deals with facts, the thinking German, with ideas; the first robs and oppresses *nations*, the second abolishes their very *nationality*."[2] Christianity abolishes the chauvinism, egoism, and self-interest of nations, but not nationality itself. For example, the fruits of German nationality are Lessing and Goethe, Kant and Schelling, while the fruit of German nationalism is the forced Germanization of Germany's neighboring peoples from the time of the Teutonic Knights to the present day.[3]

The present hostility between Poland and Russia is only the expression of this ancient dispute between West and East, in which Islam plays an episodic role in those events that are common to all of Europe. Thus, Vienna comes between Constantinople and us; the Catholic Poles enter the ranks of the Turks against the Russian army;

the Orthodox Serbs in Bosnia join the Muslims to fight Catholic Austria. Poland, the avant-garde of the Catholic West confronts Russia; behind Poland stands the apostolic empire of Austria, and behind Austria stands Rome. The task of Russia is to show that it is not only the representative of the East, but that it is in fact the *third* Rome, which does not exclude the first, but reconciles the other two in itself.[4]

In the second chapter, "East and West in the Ancient World: The Historical Place of Christianity," (*Rus'* No. 2, 17 January) Solovyov develops the idea of the "mythical godmen of the East" and the "false mangod of the West," which finds its final expression in the apotheosis of the Roman Caesar, and then proceeds to the Christian religion of true Godmanhood.

Chapter three (*Rus'* No. 3, 1 February) is called "Christianity and the Reaction of the Eastern Principle in Heresies: The Meaning of Islam." In January 1883 Solovyov wrote to Aksakov:

> You have written to me asking that the article not be too long, therefore, I have taken chapter three only *up to* the division of the Churches, and it's not long, though it is fairly condensed. *All* the heresies, from the first Gnostic ones to the Iconoclasts, inclusive, are derived from one principle, the reaction of the oriental inhuman god against the Godman, and this covers Islam as well. In the same regard later arose the fundamental sin of Byzantium (and of all Eastern Christianity), which, having defined the Orthodox Christian principle of Godmanhood, failed to sustain it in life and practically fell into the heresy of separating the divine from the human, from which, on the one hand, I deduce the extremes of monasticism, and on the other, the temporary success of Islam, which openly acknowledged the incommensurability of the divine with the human. I am trying to express all this carefully and with reverence for that which is genuinely holy.
>
> I have heard that the whole article has merited a disdainful judgment from Katkov himself, who calls it "childish prattle," and poor Ionin has been repeating this everywhere in good

> conscience. I have instructed him to remind Katkov that unless ye receive the kingdom of God like a child ye shall not enter it. But in general, I notice here, qu'il y a un parti pris contre moi, and this has occurred especially since I have become more modest and renounced my pretensions, even the pretension of instructing our "unstudious youth," according to Yury Samarin's expression. When I was a self-assured lad, they carried me in their arms and listened to my truly "childish prattle" with the greatest respect. And now it's just as well that I can't attain perfection in humility, otherwise no one would listen to me at all.[5]

Thus, behind Pobedonostsev there arose before Solovyov the second pillar of the Russian state, Katkov, who had been so favorably disposed to the young philosopher in his early works. As always in such cases, the quarrel was carried out dishonestly. Solovyov had only to mention the Poles and the Jews and his philosophy appeared to Katkov to be "childish prattle."

Solovyov's third speech about Dostoevsky was published in the sixth issue of *Rus'* (15 March) under the title "About the True Task (In Memory of Dostoevsky)." But Aksakov could not allow even Solovyov's first attempt to be an advocate of Rome to appear without an editorial note: "Perhaps it is not for us to pass judgment on our Western brother, Rome, but this does not mean that we cannot judge indulgences, the Inquisition, papal love of power, and Jesuitism. On the contrary, we must judge them." On this occasion Aksakov also informed his readers that the publication of *The Great Controversy* was to be postponed to issue eight or nine. In fact, the fourth chapter, "The Division of the Churches" greatly disturbed Aksakov and Ivantsov-Platonov was not published until 15 July in No. 14. Not wishing to discontinue the publication of *The Great Controversy*, Aksakov insisted on changes and abridgements to this chapter, about which Solovyov wrote to him in February:

> I am sincerely grateful to you for your friendly attitude to me, in which I completely believe and which I hope to preserve always. I am also grateful to you for the candor

with which you address me in this letter. Its content does call for some kind of explanation on my part. In order not to complicate matters, I have confined myself to stating two facts and to a single categorical statement:

1) I have thought about the content of the article on Catholicism and the separation of the Churches since last spring, that is, almost an entire year.*
2) Agreeing with you that it is not suitable for publication in its present state, on account of its form and the tone of its *exposition*, I have not renounced, either for your sake or Aleksey Mikhailovich's,† a single *view* expressed in it.
3) Speaking of the reconciliation with Catholicism, I presuppose that in *principle* Catholicism is not false, because one cannot be reconciled with that which is false. I see in Catholicism a false application, but the application can be changed.

On account of this view, my conscience obliges me to defend Catholicism from unjust, in my opinion, accusations, and therefore rumors about my apologia for Catholicism do not frighten me or prevent me from reading the articles to my friends either in Moscow or in St. Petersburg.[6]

Gradually, the quarrel became more aggravated. In March Solovyov wrote to Aksakov:

When a bad odor that is emanating from forest bugs or carrion hits you, you pinch your nose and pass by. But when the bad odor emanates from the festering wounds of your brother, you must then, of course, overcome your disgust and not begin expatiating on the illness, but try to help the sick man. It is not in my power to heal the separated Churches,

* That is, since his dream about receiving the blessing from a Catholic prelate. [Author's note.]
† Aleksey Ivantsov-Platonov.

but it is within my power and *obligation* not to irritate their wounds with polemics and to assuage them with a word of justice and reconciliation. If I do not know how to say this word, then let someone else say it, but no one says it. One hears only denunciation of the sins of Catholicism and hatred for papism. But denunciation does not alleviate, and hatred does not cure. According to their fruits shall you know them. What are the fruits of our thousand-year old polemics with Catholicism? We have not helped the West and have not revived the East, but we ourselves have been infected by foreign disease. Not only the Greeks, but also our own people in their hatred for Catholicism have been reduced to falsifying documents, as for example, the Religious Academy of Kazan in its translation of the acts of the ecumenical councils. But I do not want to enter into polemics myself. It will be more useful to indicate the fundamental point of my misunderstanding with you. It seems to me that you are looking *only* at papism, whereas I look, first of all, at the great, holy, and eternal Rome, a fundamental and integral part of the universal Church. I believe in this Rome, I bow before it, I love it with my whole heart, and with all the powers of my soul I desire its renewal for the sake of the unity and wholeness of the world Church, and may I be cursed as a parricide if I ever pronounce a word of judgment against the sanctity of Rome.

The change in the article that you proposed is only possible if I transfer the question entirely from the religious realm into the social-historical, where one can speak not about eternal Rome *as such*, but only about its temporary manifestation. Such a point of view will seem to you to be perhaps less abstract, but to me this too is an abstraction. But enough of arguing; if I must write a new article for you, then, having corrected and expanded the earlier one into a full-length work, I will publish it abroad in French.[7]

Already in 1883 Solovyov conceived the idea of *La Russie et l'Eglise Universelle*. In April of that year he had fallen ill with typhus and had received the blessing from the papal nuncio. In June he wrote to Aksakov from Krasny Rog, "I am recovering from my illness more slowly than I thought I would, and it is only during these past few days that I have felt myself to be in a state to work and have taken up the continuation of 'The Great Controversy,' which I think I will send to you at the beginning of July."[8]

Finally on 15 July the chapter about the union of Churches appeared in *Rus'*, but in a shortened form and with a note by Ivan Aksakov. In No. 15 (1 August), appeared the comparatively harmless fifth chapter, "Byzantium and the Russian Old Ritualists: Nationality in the Church." Finally, chapter six, "The Papacy and Papism: The Meaning of Protestantism" was published on 15 September in No. 18, but in such a mutilated form that Solovyov was deeply indignant. The quotations supporting his position had been removed, and appended to the article were some polemical "footnotes" of Ivantsov-Platonov. At the end of September Solovyov wrote to Aksakov:

> I do not want to offend you and Aleksey Mikhailovich on account of my article, which was mutilated without my knowledge and published in an almost illegible form. Ce qui est fait, est fait. But there is one thing that I definitely cannot leave as is. I could not believe my eyes when I came to the end and read the 20 footnotes: not only is an absurd and naïve assertion ascribed to me (about the presidency of the popes at ecumenical councils), which I *have never made anywhere*, but also on the basis of this absurdity, falsely attributed to me, various sarcastic remarks and suggestions about my authorial carelessness are made. You are familiar with my relationship with Aleksey Mikhailovich, but this note is written as if by an enemy and, moreover, by an enemy who is not scrupulous about his means of attack…
>
> I consider you and Aleksey Mikhailovich to be men without fear and reproach, and I consider your journal to be the purest in Russia. But the mistake that has been made (inadvertently, I believe) must be corrected. This is not a personal matter; the conscientiousness of the author is being called into question, and even if the overt injustice of

suspicion is avoided, perhaps the trust of my readers will be lost... You also reproach me for enthusiasms, but it is a question of their objects. I am not ashamed of my enthusiasm, I even warned you of it a year ago... I have to begin thinking about the conclusion to my articles: it's turning out to be a sticky business.[9]

In October Solovyov wrote to Aksakov:

After long reflection, I have come to the conclusion that, in spite of everything, it is necessary to bring "The Great Controversy" to a close in *Rus'*; it is necessary for me and for you and for the work itself. A firm rumor has been spread about me that I have converted to Romanism. I would not consider it shameful to do this if it were *according to conviction*, but it is precisely my convictions that will not allow me to do anything like this. I will use a simple analogy: Imagine that my mother is at daggers drawn with her sister and does not even recognize her as a sister. Must I, in order to reconcile them, abandon my mother and rush to my aunt? That is absurd. All that I must do is to instill in my mother (and in my brothers) with all my strength that her adversary is still her lawful kindred sister and not a ... and that for all her former sins she is still an honorable woman and not a ..., and that it is better and more noble for them to cast aside their former grievances and be one. Speaking without allegory, I am pleading for the following:

1) That the representatives of our magisterium not consider the ecclesiastical dispute between East and West to be decisive in the sense of an *absolute condemnation* of the Western Church, a condemnation for which they do not have any higher authority.
2) That they not inflate the controversial points to absurd and fantastic dimensions.
3) That they give up on their "denunciatory" and polemical theology, which is becoming one and the

> same, and, instead of judicial and military approaches to the Western Church, they assume an attitude of kinship and solidarity in the religious, theological, and ecclesiastical spheres, leaving secular politics, in the meantime, to the ministers of state and the general-governors. A *moral* change in our relationship to the Western Church will be the first step of Christian politics: the essence of which is the fact that it derives from moral feelings and *obligations*, not *from self-interest* and conceit. A fraternal regard for the Western Church is repellent to our national interest and our pride, but precisely because of this it is morally binding for us. There can be no question here of any kind of external union, which derives from a *compromise of interests*, and in that concluding article, which I would like to give you, there will be expressed a *firm condemnation* of all former unions, whether general (the Unions of Lyons and Florence) or more particular (the Union of Brest, which unfortunately still exists in Galicia). Desiring by this article to free myself, incidentally, from the accusation of one-sided Latinity, I want to remove the same accusation from you when you publish my articles. In the intended conclusion there is nothing that is reprehensible for you, nothing that is *contrary* to Slavophile principles.[10]

Finally, having included in No. 21 of *Rus'* (1 November) Aleksandr Kireev's extensive criticism "A Few Remarks about the Articles 'The Great Controversy' by Solovyov," Aksakov decided to publish, as well, in No. 23 (1 December) the seventh and final of chapter of *The Great Controversy,* "The General Basis for the Union of Churches" with some notes of his own.

"On the day that Constantinople fell, in view of the approaching Turkish army," Solovyov writes, "the last free word of the Greeks was the cry: 'Better slavery to the Muslims, than an agreement with the Latins.' We do not mention this as a reproach to the unfortunate Greeks. If there was nothing Christian in this cry of unreconcilable enmity, then there was also hardly anything Christian in all the attempts at a compulsory and formal reunion of the Churches."[11]

"How can one say there was nothing Christian!" exclaims Aksakov in his footnote. "Blessed are the Greeks a hundred fold for preferring an external yoke and external torments to deviating from the purity of the truth of Christ and for preserving it for us unperverted by papism, which moreover had reached the apogee of its deformity especially at that time. Eternal glory to the Greeks for this."

Following Solovyov's article was a letter to the editor, a patriotic cry to the effect that in speaking of the Eastern Church Solovyov had forgotten Russia, that for the Russian peasant Orthodoxy is indissolubly linked to Slavonic nationality, that the Bulgarians and Serbs are related to the Russian peasant precisely because they are Orthodox, and various other Slavophile clichés, signed with the initials K. A.

What was Solovyov's point of view on the separation of Churches in 1883? The separation occurred not on account of differences in dogma, not on account of *filioque*, but rather because the ancient opposition of East and West, which had been abolished by Christianity, had reappeared on the historical scene. In the hierarchies of the East and West the spirit of love and unity had grown scarce, yielding to the pagan national element; the universal element in the East was replaced by the Greek, in the West by the Latin. At the beginning of the schism, under Photius and Cerullarius, the Greeks were the main offenders with their exclusive traditionalism and self-satisfied Hellenism. Later, the attempts of the East at restoring unity were destroyed in embryo "by the coarse arrogance and obtuse pretentiousness of the then leaders of Latinity."[12] "'Only *my* Church is the true Ecumenical Church,' maintains the Orthodox East, 'therefore I have no business with the West, if only it left me in peace.' This is what one might call *defensive* pride. 'Only *my* Church is the true Ecumenical Church,' maintains the Catholic West, 'therefore I must lead the people of the East back on to my uniquely true path.' This is *offensive* pride."[13] What is needed is not a formal union, like the ones of Florence or Brest, but a change of mutual attitudes as well as good will in the interests of peace and reunification. The papacy should be distinguished from papism; without accepting papism, we must still recognize in the Roman papacy the divinely established unifying center (*centrum unitatis*) of the entire Christian world. "To break the Christian East into parts, as the fanatics of Latinity dream of doing, is impossible, for the East possesses an inner spiritual bond and its own idea of the Church, its own general principle. In the Middle Ages this was also understood in the West; thus the great Pope Innocent III expressed the idea that the Eastern Church represents the purely spiritual side of Christianity, that it is the Church primarily of the Holy Spirit. Whether this is true or not, there is no doubt of the independent character and significance of the Eastern Church. This Church is a substantially indispensable, inalienable part of the fullness of the Universal Church."[14]

> Each of the two Churches is already the Universal Church, however, not in separation from one another, but in their unity with each other. This unity exists in fact because both Churches are bound together by the ties of apostolicity, dogmatic tradition, and sacraments, deriving from the principle of Godmanhood... Each of the two historical halves of the Church must be recognized as a *part* of the Church, and one can recognize one part as the whole or Universal Church only in union with the other half, a union that has not been destroyed in the purely religious realm in regard to Christ, but in the social and historical realm it has been destroyed and must be reestablished.[15]

In a "kind letter" Aleksandr Kireev warned Solovyov that he intended to enter into polemics with him. On 10 October Solovyov wrote to him:

> Thank you for your kind letter. I have no objection to polemics with *you*: in any case this will not mean polemics in the ordinary sense of the word. I also completely agree that it is more suitable to discuss theological subjects in *Rus'* than in *Novoe vremia*. But the point is that Aksakov is apparently

> frightened by my "Catholicism" and is also confused and vexed by the inauspicious turn "The Great Controversy" took by his passive participation, and all this has forced him to wish that the questions that I raised disappear somewhere as soon as possible. For my part I was shrewd and kind enough to announce to him that "The Great Controversy" was coming to an end in *Rus'*. Although this should not prevent your article appearing, it would be already awkward for me to respond to it.
>
> Would it not, therefore, be better for you to give your article a somewhat less polemical character, to exclude from it everything that would demand an immediate and swift reply?
>
> Or else, if I publish "The Great Controversy" as a separate book, then perhaps in the foreword or the appendix, or in the text itself, I could argue with you at liberty.[16]

On 1 November Kireev's response to *The Great Controversy* was published. His position can be reduced to the following: A reunion of the Churches as proposed by Solovyov is impossible. At the Council of Trent and the Vatican Council the Church of Rome approved heresies; from a schismatic Church it turned into a heretical one. All these heresies are the inevitable, logical development of that *sophistry* that lay at the foundation of the Catholic worldview under the popes who began the quarrel with the East. If one can justify Pope Nicholas I, as does Solovyov, then one inevitably accepts all the subsequent heretical dogmas of the Roman Church, confirmed by the Vatican Council; the East cannot agree to this. Rome will also never accept Solovyov's positions. His view of the papacy, according to which the Roman pontiff would possess only a modest right of *jurisdictionis* "without being the source or the active cause of dogmatic truth,"[17] was already condemned by the Vatican Council. For Solovyov, according to Kireev, there has been no Universal Church from the time of the separation of the Churches; it had existed before the division and will exist again after the reunion of its separated halves. For Kireev, the Universal Church has existed from the time of the schism and remains in the East.

Having read Kireev's article, Solovyov wrote him on 12 November:

> One can, of course, write off our Old Catholics, all the more so as you have completely accurately reduced the question of the Old Catholics to the more general question of the "Vatican dogmas." It is at this point in this whole matter that we diverge. According to you, these "new" dogmas; that is, "*infallibilitas*" and "*immaculata conceptio*," to which you also add "*filioque*," constitute heresy and deprive Catholicism of the meaning of a *church* in the true sense of the word. According to me, these dogmas are neither new nor do they comprise any kind of heresy either in essence or form and, therefore, they also cannot deprive Catholicism of the character of a true Church, since the true essence of the Church [*tserkovnost'*] does not depend on greater or lesser progress in the *definition* and *formulation* of dogmatic *details*, but depends on the presence of apostolic succession, on an orthodox faith in Christ as perfect God and perfect Man, and finally on the plenitude of the sacraments. All of this belongs equally to us and to the Catholics, consequently, both they and we constitute together the One Holy Catholic and Apostolic Church, despite our temporary historical separation, which does not correspond to the truth of the matter and is, thus, all the more painful.
>
> Therefore, I resolutely reject the opinion ascribed to me that, strictly speaking, the Universal Church no longer exists. On the contrary, it exists both in Eastern Orthodoxy and in Western Catholicism. With regard to Protestantism, its historic and moral equality with Orthodoxy and Catholicism still does not grant it any rights in the *mystical* sphere that belongs to the *Church proper*. Deprived of apostolic succession, unstable in their profession of Godmanhood, and lacking the plenitude of the sacraments, the Protestants find themselves *outside the Church*, whereas the Catholics and we are *inside the Church*. I expounded all of this in detail in the concluding article of "The Great Controversy," which

> Aksakov, apparently, decided to publish in order to have his final say, as well, in this regard. Although the greater part of my conclusion was written before I read your article, you will still find in it an indirect reply to your principal remarks. In this way there is, for the present, no need for us to enter directly into polemics.[18]

The Great Controversy created "confusion among Russian readers and joy among Catholics." It attracted the attention, as well, of the famous Strossmayer, bishop of Bosnia and Sirmium.* This Catholic sympathy cast an even greater shadow over Solovyov in the eyes of Russian society. "With regard to the confusion among Russian readers and the joy among the Catholics," Solovyov writes to Aksakov sometime in November 1883, "the first grieves me more than the second. I completely recognize our essential solidarity with Catholics and I thoroughly believe in our future visible union and, therefore, their approval, they being our brothers and allies in the Christian cause, is of no offense to me. Still less is the attention of Bishop Strossmayer an offense to me, because, for all his one-sided Latin zeal (this is a common sin), he is, as far as I know, an utterly respectable man and a good bishop."[19]

Kireev, of course, was right in pointing out that the position of *The Great Controversy* was unacceptable to Rome. The Jesuit admirer of Solovyov, d'Herbigny, remarks carefully about this work, "ici tout n'est pas encore éclairé." But Catholics would not fail to appreciate that Solovyov was the first to speak of the union of the Churches and that, moreover, he had gone further in his sympathy for Rome than had a single Orthodox theologian before him. In addition, his words about reconciliation with Poland as the avant-garde of Catholic Europe won him the warm sympathy of Polish society, stifled under the yoke of Russian autocracy. At this time (1883) Solovyov began a correspondence with the Russian Uniate priest Father Astromov, to whom Solovyov addressed five long letters about the Immaculate Conception of the Blessed Virgin.[20] But even at this stage the divergence of their views was revealed. "There can be no

---

* Josip Juraj Strossmayer (1815-1905), later Solovyov's great friend and supporter.

question here of any kind of external union, which derives from a *compromise of interests*."[21]

At the same time, Solovyov wrote to Kireev:

> .... Having lost the hope of seeing you, I have to resort to a letter that can serve, at the same time, as a reply to Mme Polozova. I fully appreciated what she wrote about the union of Churches in view of the agreement between Father Astromov and myself. Unfortunately, this touching alliance cannot continue because I understood from Astromov's second letter how the matter stood, namely, that this venerable person considers himself to occupy a rank only lower than God, without, however, abandoning the hope of elevation, but we know that such an elevation generally occurs in those places that Mme Polozova indicates. *In jene Sphären wag ich nicht zu streben*. This aberration of the poor old gentleman is all the sadder, as there is something very valuable and significant in his discussion of the Mother of God. With regard to the union of Churches, I do not have in mind what Mme Polozova ascribes to me: she conceives of a mechanical union that is neither desirable nor possible; I, however, conceive of a union that is, so to speak, *chemical*, which usually produces something very distinct from the previous states of the combined elements (for example, the combination of hydrogen and oxygen produces water, which, according to its properties, is completely unlike those two gases). It is not in the power of the chemist to change the properties of one or another element, but he can place various elements in conditions such as will combine them swiftly and create a new element possessing the desired qualities. With God's help we can perform something of this chemistry. As early as 1875 various voices in both my sleeping and waking hours told me: study chemistry, study chemistry; at first I took this in the literal sense and attempted to carry it out, but then I understood what it meant.

> Give Mme Polozova my regards and thanks for the kind words in her letter (although she, too, considers me to be somewhat mad, but I am not offended).[22]

Solovyov hoped to publish *The Great Controversy* separately as a book, enlarging it twofold. In 1884 he wrote to Kireev, "I am sending you seven copies of my *Christian Politics*... These are only off prints from *Rus'*, but I would like very much to publish a full-length book, i.e. an amplified version of the present work. These off prints were permitted by the civil censorship and spared by the religious. In the proposed supplements there is nothing that is more objectionable to the censors than what has already been permitted, nonetheless, obstacles are still possible. In your amicably polemical article in *Rus'* you came to the conclusion that, without agreeing with me on the details (if I am not mistaken), my discussions of the Church question are useful and desirable. Thus, I hope that you will show me some friendly cooperation in publishing the book here in Russia, for *I would like very much not* to turn to a publisher abroad. In any case, I would like you to inform me within three weeks, after making some inquiries about whether I can proceed without great risk to the publication of my book, for I can't afford to arrange fireworks."[23]

To his brother Mikhail he wrote as well, "I have sent the sixth article of *The Great Controversy* to Aksakov... There are still three more to come and then it will be necessary to publish them as a separate book, which will include everything that I have written about the Church and something else besides. I will, perhaps, entrust this book to you, if I don't spend the winter in Moscow."[24]

But Solovyov had to abandon this idea. Although he *would have liked very much not* to have to turn to a publisher abroad, in the end, five years later, he would carry out the intention expressed in the letter to Aksakov of March 1883, "if I must write a new article for you, then, having corrected and expanded the earlier one into a full-length work, I will publish it abroad in French."[25] Evidently it was Solovyov's fate to write a book in French; instead of *Les principes de la religion universelle* it would be *La Russie et l'Eglise Universelle*. If in his youth, however, Solovyov had wanted to improve his French with the help of the Abbé Guettée, this cleric would later become his hardened enemy.

We have seen what difficulties and delays accompanied the birth of *The Great Controversy*, Solovyov's first work about the union of Churches. But these difficulties and obstacles testified that a new and great idea was coming into being in Solovyov's mind. The greater the idea, the stronger the influence it exerts on people, and the more the obstacles it faces upon its appearance. Ideas that regenerate humanity are always born in travail.

After the writing of *The Great Controversy* Solovyov definitely felt himself to be "between two hostile camps." Already in 1882 he had written:

In a land of icy blizzards among gray storm clouds
You appeared on the earth,
And, poor child, for you there is no refuge
Between two hostile camps.

But the martial cries, the clash of armor,
And the crash of swords do not disturb you.
In reverie you stand and listen to the great
Testament of days past.

Solovyov wrote the last chapters of *The Great Controversy* at Krasny Rog, and he probably heard here the encouraging voice of his late host, who, like him, was "not a warrior of either camp, but only an accidental guest."

Bravely row against the current
In the name of the beautiful.

It is true that Solovyov began "to row against the current" from the very beginning of his career when he challenged the positivism reigning at the university. But at that time he was backed by the firm support of the Slavophiles and enjoyed the sympathies of Moscow society. Both Katkov and Suvorin, and even Prince Meshchersky joyfully opened their doors to him. As of 1883 Solovyov became utterly isolated, however, since complete neutrality was impossible even for "the accidental guest of either camp," Solovyov naturally began to be attracted to the camp that was opposed to the Slavophiles and the conservatives. The warm sympathies of the Jews and the Poles took him in the direction of the left and in the '90s he was already at home in the circle of *Vestnik Evropy*.

In the summer of 1883 Solovyov published two short articles on the Catholic question. "You must certainly be aware," he wrote to his brother, "that this summer I published two political articles in *Novoe vremia*, of which the first, about the concordat between Russia and Rome was reprinted in a French translation in the *Journal de St. Petersbourg* by order of the Ministry of Foreign Affairs. They have my thanks, I did not expect this!"[26]

In this first article, "The Concordat with Rome and the Newspapers of Moscow," Solovyov wages a polemic with *Moskovskie vedemosti*. He welcomes the reestablishment of the canonical episcopal administration of the Catholic dioceses of Russia and cites the example of Catherine II who turned out to be *plus catholique que le pape* in her protection of the Jesuit order, the mainstay of militant Catholicism, and the example of Nicholas I who was not afraid, after a meeting with Pope Gregory XVI, to conclude a concordat with Rome. "As long as the pope does not have permanent representation in St. Petersburg, he has no choice but to look at Russia through the eyes of the Polish bishops. But it is not necessary for this to remain so; sooner or later the two great historic powers, Roman Catholicism and Orthodox Russia must recognize each other and openly face one another."[27]

In the second article, "About the Church Question with Regard to the Old Catholics," Solovyov expressed himself harshly about the Old Catholic movement, which had gained sympathy in certain Orthodox circles, including that of Aleksandr Kireev. Solovyov reproached the Old Catholics for "preferring the views of a circle of professors to the consensus of the entire Catholic world," which had accepted the definitions of the [First] Vatican Council; by so doing they had turned into an "unauthorized assemblage."[28] Having separated themselves from Rome, the Old Catholics became an instrument for the politics of Prince Bismarck. "By taking up arms against the pope and separating themselves from the extra-German center of the Church, the Old Catholics have became servants of the new empire... Each triumph of the Old Catholics will be a triumph for German unity and a defeat for its enemies."[29]

Solovyov repeats the accusations of *The Great Controversy* against the Eastern Church, which exclusively *preserves the foundation* of the Church; against the Western Church, which exclusively *fortifies* its walls; and against Protestantism, which rejects the *foundation* of the Church, that is, tradition and its *defense* or ramparts that are authority, taking as its foundation the freedom of the individual spirit, while ignoring the fact that freedom is only the *summit* or *crown* of the church.[30] He then expounds on the necessity of making the first steps for the reunion of churches; the interests of Catholicism must be separated from the interests of Polonism, and for this to happen the Vatican must have proper representation in St. Petersburg. "The natural sympathies between Rome and the Poles will, of course, remain, and let them remain, but, all the same, an Italian or Spanish nuncio in direct relations with the Russian government will know how to distinguish the interests of the Catholic Church from Polish nationalism.... We believe that Russia is called not only to be a political power, but that it also has a religious mission in history. But Russia can carry out this mission to achieve its religious importance in the Christian world not by alienating the Western Church, but through a conscious and intelligent rapprochement with it. It is terrible, though, to consider such a great mission when one looks at the confusion of minds and actions around us. However, we can take comfort from the saying of the ancient historian, *Hominum confusione ac Dei providentia Ruthenia ducitur*."[31*] Toward the end of 1883 Solovyov wrote the article "About Nationality and the National Affairs of Russia," which was published in 1884 in the second issue of the journal of the St. Petersburg Slavonic Benevolent Society.

Solovyov informed Kireev:

> I am writing for you a little article about nationality. I don't know how it will seem to you. I recognize nationality as *positive force*, which serves the universal (supra-national)

[*] Russia is ruled by the confusion of men and the providence of God.

idea. The more a certain nation is devoted to the universal (supra-national) idea, the stronger, better, and more important it becomes. Therefore, I am a staunch enemy of *negative nationalism* or national egoism, or the self-adulation of a nation, which is as essentially repellent as the self-adulation of an individual. I accept the second commandment unconditionally: Do not make an idol *of any likeness*, etc. But the Old Believers of Slavophilism (to which you do *not* belong) make an idol precisely of nationality and offer to it their incense made of phrases of many words and little content. If only they would realize how none of this is original, they who so love to praise their originality. What could be less original, less national than these eternal clichés about originality and nationality to which patriots of all countries are devoted? They do not want to understand the simple fact that in order to manifest one's national originality *in deed* one must also think about the given deed, one must try to settle it by the *best* means, not at all by the most national. If nationality is good, then the best decision will result as the most national, and if it is not good then the Devil take it. But here the patriots leap up and demand, for example, that the church question be decided not *ad majorem Dei*, but, *ad majorem Russiae gloriam*, that is, not on religious or theological grounds but on the grounds of national conceit. In this instance, perhaps, you will recall that 'patriot' rhymes with 'idiot.'

It seems I am beginning to scold, which is against my principles. It means it's time to stop.[32]

Having read the manuscript, Kireev requested that several phrases relating to the Russian Church be softened. Solovyov warmly agreed and, for example, changed the expression "the inactive clergy" to "our, in many ways, respectable, but unfortunately insufficiently authoritative and active clergy."[33]

In April 1883 Solovyov wrote to Aksakov, "I went away to the country for about three weeks to finish writing a small book of a religious and moral content, which I intend to publish separately this spring."[34] This book was *The Religious Foundations of Life*. Solovyov's plan to publish it in the spring of 1883 was not realized and in the autumn he decided to submit the first chapters of it to *Rus'*. In October he wrote to Aksakov, "In the meantime I am going to look over those short edifying articles, about which I spoke to you, and I will not delay in sending you the first one for No. 21."[35]

Aksakov replied, "Your edifying article will not appear in No. 21, I have still not been able to read it, but I will read it tomorrow morning. I was frightened by your title, or rather, list of subjects, and I will inform you in advance that I will not permit such a list in the newspaper's table of contents: "On the Latest play of Mr. Sphazhinksy" – "On Sin and Death" – "On the Forest Beetle" – "On Grace." Sin, death, grace, all seemed to me such serious matters that I decided to put the manuscript aside and devote somewhat more attention to it."[36]

The short edifying articles thus did not appear in *Rus'* and Solovyov began to publish them in *Pravoslavnoe obozrenie* beginning in January 1884. In that year they also came out in book form as *The Religious Foundations of Life*. A second edition appeared in 1885, followed by a third edition in 1897 under the title *The Spiritual Foundations of Life*. In the foreword to the third edition Solovyov explained the change of title.

"I realized it was better to replace the word 'religious' with the Russian word 'spiritual' [*dukhovnyi*] in the title, which suitably corresponds to the content of the book. If it is impossible to do without the noun religion [*religiia*], then at least the adjective can be appropriately replaced in certain cases by 'pious' or 'devout' [*blagochestivyi*] and in others by 'spiritual' [*dukhovnyi*]."[37] The work is divided into two parts, the first two chapters of the *second* part being written before the others. The first chapter, "On Christianity," was published in 1883 in *Pravoslavnoe obozrenie* No. 1 under the title "The Vital Meaning of Christianity (A Philosophical Commentary on the Doctrine of the Logos of Apostle John the Divine)." It is dated 16 January 1872, but we accept Lukyanov's assumption that this is a misprint for 1882. The beginning of this chapter is a lecture delivered at St. Petersburg University on 25 February 1882.

The first chapter is divided into five subchapters, each one being a commentary on verses from the gospel of John (1:1-14) and the first epistle of John (chapters five and six). The sixth chapter is titled "The Essence of Christian Sacraments." Penetrating the wisdom of the fourth evangelist, Solovyov unites the doctrines of the Logos and the incarnation of the Word with the restoration and resurrection of nature. Solovyov contrasts the "fiery wheel of existence," the tree of life in ruined nature, whose root is sin, whose growth is disease, and whose fruit is death, with the immortal and new tree of life, which is rooted in love and brotherhood, grows through the cross of spiritual struggle, and bears the fruit of general resurrection.[38] Christianity is opposed to *natural* religion, where the divinity devours man in bloody sacrifices and in phallic orgasm. The god of this world, a murderer from time immemorial, feeds on the flesh and blood of man and on his vital spirit. In Christianity, God does not feed on man, but provides him with himself as nourishment. Having transformed his material (mechanical) body into a spiritual (dynamic) one through his heroic theandric act, Christ offers it as sustenance for mankind.[39] "Instead of cannibalism and fratricidal sacrifices, we have brotherly love (   ) and the grace of the Eucharist, instead of the symbol of animal force and physical passion, we have the cross, the standard of the spiritual force that surmounts all suffering, and finally, instead of the frenzy of the orgasm, in which the freely rational personality surrenders itself and is swallowed up in the senseless reproduction of life, instead of this triumph of blind nature, which perpetuates death and corruption, we have the resurrection of the dead and the
that is, the triumph of the vital sense over dead matter, the immortalization of the human personality by the submission of blind physical forces to the rational will of man."[40] The second chapter of part two, "On the Church," appears to be an abridgement of the article "On the Church and the Raskol" that was published in 1882 in *Rus'* (No. 38). The first part of the book, which is divided into an introduction "On Nature, Death, Sin, Law, and Grace" and three chapters "On Prayer," "On Sacrifice and Charity," and "On Fasting," was written after part two, evidently in the spring of 1883.

"In order to correct our lives we must pray to God, help one another, and restrain our senses. Prayer, charity, and fasting; in these three activities consists all private or personal religion." In the chapter "On Prayer" Solovyov meditates on the petitions of the Lord's Prayer. "To be delivered from evil is the task of true *wisdom*, which discovers and destroys all the deceit and sophistry of self-love and arms us not with our own, but with God's powers. In such a way, our spirit receives an invincible strength in temptations. Spiritual strength in temptations provides us with justice in our actions and temperance in our feelings. And thanks to such moral equilibrium, pure love, constant hope, and firm faith in God and eternal life become more and more rooted in our soul."[41]

Fasting takes three forms: 1) Spiritual fasting, which includes abstention from egotistical and ambitious actions as well as renunciation of human honor and fame. This type of fasting is particularly necessary for socially active people. 2) Intellectual fasting, which calls for abstinence from the exclusive activity of the mind, from fruitless and endless games of concepts and ideas, and from interminable questions without point or goal. This exercise is especially necessary for intellectual people, who forget the saying of old Heraclitus: Omniscience does not edify the mind. 3) Fasting of the sensual soul, that is, abstinence from sensual pleasures that are not directed or moderated by mental consciousness and the power of the spirit. The true task of our sensual life is to cultivate the garden of the earth, to transform the dead into the living, to impart to living beings a greater intensity and the fullness of life, in short, to *animate* them.[42]

Aside from personal religion, social religion is also necessary, that is, participation in the life of the Church. Christ established His Church as the way, the truth, and the life. "Christ Himself is present in the hierarchy as the way, in the profession of faith as the truth, in the sacraments as the life; the union of these three forms the Kingdom of God, whose Lord is Christ."[43]

The final chapter (chapter three of part two) "On the Christian State and Society" was published in 1884 in *Pravoslavnoe obozrenie* (No. 4).

The book ends with a brief conclusion of two pages, "The Image of Christ as a Test of Conscience." Here Solovyov provides his readers with the advice, "… before deciding on any kind of action that has an importance for your personal or public life, evoke in your soul the moral image of Christ, concentrate on it and ask yourself: would He carry out this action, or, in other words, would He encourage it or not, would He bless me or not for its completion? I suggest this test to all, it never deceives. In doubtful cases, if it is still possible to reflect and think, remember Christ, imagine Him alive as He is, and lay before Him all the burden of your doubts."[44]

This little book of 180 pages provides the key to an understanding of that state in which Solovyov found himself during 1882-1883 and supports the words of Bishop Strossmayer, "*Soloviof anima candida, pia ac vere sancta est*." After the brilliant and threatening storms of his youth, Solovyov heard the "voice of a fine cool breeze": "Here wafts a fine cool breeze and in the mysterious wind / He divined God."

That which was for Strossmayer proof of his *castitatis, pietatis et sanctitatis* was for the Olympian Katkov "childish prattle" and even the very devout Aksakov declined to publish the "short edifying articles" in *Rus'*.

The tranquility, humility, and crystal clarity of its thought, and the simplicity of its expression are what distinguish *The Spiritual Foundations of Life* from several other works of Solovyov's. We might note that this book was written at the same time as *The Great Controversy*.

The Spiritual Foundations of Life offers sufficient refutation of many of the accusations against Solovyov: that his pride preceded him (Vasily Rozanov); that nowhere does he say anything about the historic Christ (Mikhail Tareev); that the eighties were for him a period of a "theocratic *temptation*" (Evgeny Trubetskoy), and so forth.

In 1897, three years before his death, Solovyov revised *The Spiritual Foundations of Life* and decided that "within its modest dimensions my book lives up to its title and does not require substantial alterations, but only small stylistic corrections and a few logical explanations, which took only a few days. Appearing once again after my large work on moral philosophy, the present volume can serve for some of my readers as a complement to it and for others as a substitute."[45]

The Spiritual Foundations of Life can be seen as a summation of Solovyov's entire worldview and it is his first work that takes us into a realm of ideas that are favorably distinguished from *The Justification of the Good* by their youthful freshness and the absence of schematization and ponderousness. The time of the writing of *The Spiritual Foundations* was a period of joyful hopes; while that of *The Justification of the Good* one of bitter disillusionment. The "short edifying articles" are also free of that Schellingesque romanticism that sometimes spoils the early works of Solovyov. We can also discern a connection between his exceptional insight into the theology of John the Evangelist and his experiences during his bout with typhus in the spring of 1883, when he feverishly asked Maria Sergeevna to read him the account of the miracle at the marriage in Cana of Galilee.

As we have already mentioned, Solovyov spent the summer of 1883 at Krasny Rog among the Khitrovo family. In June he wrote to his brother Mikhail:

> It seems that I have almost recovered, but I was ill with real typhus, even my hair began to fall out and they had to shave my head. This diminished my good looks to such an extent that the youngest of the children here, Ryurik, asked all the members of the household with an anxious look, "Is Solovyov a monster, a real monster?" I am now rewriting the continuation of *The Great Controversy*, which I will send to Aksakov by 15 June. I am reading in Polish and Italian. The peaceful flow of life is sometimes interrupted by bloody events. Recently a large yellow dog named Rog ate an also yellow, but small, squirrel. Veta was feeding her favorite squirrel in her arms and then suddenly dropped it on the ground. Rog rushed at it with lightning speed, bit off its head, and devoured its body with a ferocious appetite, and then wiped himself with his tail instead of a napkin. I was involuntarily reminded of the words of the poet:

The sky is clear
Under it there is room for all.
But ceaselessly and vainly
One is alone in hate. Why?
Yes, life is terrible for man.[46]

Sofya Petrovna had three children; the eldest was Veta (Elizaveta), then came Andrey and Ryurik (Georgy). To the end of his life Solovyov had a special fondness for them. Closest of all to him was Ryurik, who in the '90s became a young man of fashion. In an amateur photograph taken in 1898 at Pustynka Solovyov is sitting with the Khitrovo family and friends next to the Jesuit Father Pierling.* At Solovyov's feet is Ryurik Khitrovo. The young man is looking down drowsily and Solovyov is resting his hand affectionately on his head. After Solovyov's death, Ryurik wrote a poem in which he describes how Pustynka seemed deserted without his mother's friend. In 1913 I wrote to Ryurik Mikhailovich on a certain matter and received from him a touching letter in which he recalls Vladimir Solovyov and mentions that he always sensed in him an "unearthly light." Not long after this, Ryurik himself had to face the "unearthly light"; within a year the war with Germany had begun and he was killed in one of the first battles.

In June 1883 Solovyov wrote to Aksakov, "At present I am taking rides through what is left of the forests of Bryansk, but at home I am practicing reading in other languages; I am reading Uniate polemics of the sixteenth century in Polish and Dante in Italian."[47]

Not without the influence of the Ghibelline ideas of Dante did the concept of a theocratic vocation for the Russian emperor arise in Solovyov's mind. He had mentioned this subject in *The Great Controversy*, but not to Aksakov's dismay. Writing to him in November, Solovyov pointed out that the idea of a worldwide monarchy did not belong to him, but is an eternal hope of all nations. He informed him further that he intended to speak of a universal monarchy with reference to Dante and Tyutchev.[48]

* Paul Pierling (1840-1920), French Jesuit, author of the five-volume history *Russie et le Saint-Siège* (Paris: Plon, 1897-1912).

In the summer of 1883 Solovyov composed his five letters to Father Astromov about the Immaculate Conception of Mary, and, at the same time, he translated Petrarch's "Praises and Prayers to the Most Holy Virgin," which he describes to Countess Tolstoy in a letter of 1886 as an "akathist hymn."[49]

The dogma of the Immaculate Conception, which was promulgated by Pope Pius IX on 9 December 1854, was the first Catholic dogma that Solovyov accepted. Already in *The Spiritual Foundations* he applied to Mary the epithet "Most Holy and Ever Virgin."[50] His first letter to Bishop Strossmayer of 1885 is dated: "On the day of the Immaculate Conception of the Most Holy Virgin."[51]

The gospel of John, Dante, Petrarch, and Uniate polemics of the sixteenth century now formed Solovyov's intellectual sustenance. The fantastic religion of the future is transformed into a universal theocracy, the Sophia of the Kabbalah into the Ever-Virgin Mary. Indeed, his verses of 1883 resound like an "akathist hymn":

> Arrayed in the sun, crowned with the stars,
> Virgin beloved by the Invincible Sun![52]

Endnotes for Part 2 - Chapter 1

1. *Russkaia mysl'* (Dec. 1913): 80; *P*, vol. 4, 19.
2. *SS*, vol. 4, 5; vol. 5, 9.
3. *SS*, vol. 4, 9; vol. 5, 13.
4. *SS*, vol. 4, 15-16; vol. 5, 20.
5. *Russkaia mysl'* 12 (1913): 79; *P*, vol. 4, 18.
6. *Russkaia mysl'* 12 (1913); *P*, vol. 4, 20-21.
7. *Russkaia mysl'* 12 (1913); *P*, vol. 4, 20-21.
8. Idem; Ibid., 22.
9. Idem; Ibid., 23.
10. *P*, vol. 4, 25-26.
11. Idem; *SS* vol. 4, 104.
12. *SS*. Vol. 4, 87.
13. Ibid., 109-110.
14. Ibid., 104-105.
15. Ibid., 109.
16. *P*, vol. 2, 102.
17. *SS*, vol. 4, 84.
18. *P*, vol. 2, 105-106.
19. *Russkaia mysl'* 12 (1913); *P*, vol. 4, 27.
20. *P*, vol. 2, 113, note.
21. *Russkaia mysl'* 12 (1913); *P*, vol. 4, 25.
22. *P*, vol. 2, 113-114.
23. Ibid., 116-117.
24. *Russkii vestnik* 9 (1915); *P*, vol. 4, 87.
25. *Russkaia mysl'* 12 (1913); *P*, vol. 4, 21.
26. *Bogoslovskii vestnik* 9 (1915); *P*, vol. 4, 87.
27. *SS*, vol. 4, 122.
28. Ibid., 124.
29. Ibid., 127.
30. Ibid., 128.
31. Ibid., 131-132.
32. *P*, vol. 2, 103-104.
33. Ibid., 108; *SS*, vol. 5, 35.
34. *Russkaia mysl'* 12 (1913); *P*, vol. 4, 22.
35. *Russkaia mysl'* 12 (1913); *P*, vol. 4, 26.
36. *Russkaia mysl'* 12 (1913): 88.
37. *Dukhovnye osnovy zhizni*, 3rd ed., iv; *SS*, vol. 12, 359.

38. *SS*, vol. 3, 353, 379, 380.
39. Ibid., 378.
40. Ibid., 379.
41. Ibid., 334.
42. Ibid., 348.
43. Ibid., 388.
44. Ibid., 416.
45. *Dukhovnye osnovy zhizni*, 3rd. ed., vi; *SS*, vol. 12, 358.
46. *P*, vol. 4, 85.
47. Ibid., 22.
48. Ibid., 26-27.
49. *P*, vol. 2, 207.
50. *SS*, vol. 3, 382.
51. *P*, vol. 1, 180.
52. *Stikh*., 6th ed., 224.

Part 2 - Chapter 2

The Jewish Question
The History of Theocracy

> Primum et ante omnia Ecclesiae
> unitas instauranda, ignis fovendus
> in gremio sponsae Christi.
>
> *Solovyov, from a letter to Kireev.*[1]

We have seen that in his youth, in addition to mastering two classical languages and three modern ones, Solovyov had studied philosophy and mystical literature to perfection. He now entered a new period of self-education. In the '80s the course of his reading was determined by everything relating to the Catholic, Polish, and Jewish questions. In the summer of 1883 he read Uniate polemics in Polish and Dante in Italian; in 1884 he began to study Hebrew seriously under the guidance of Fayvel Bentsilovich Gets, "a young Talmudist."[2*] Solovyov read the entire Bible in the original and at the end of his life attempted a complete translation of it.[3] In 1886 he informed Gets, "I am continuing my reading in Hebrew. Aside from the Torah and historical books, I have read all of the prophets and have begun the psalms... Now, thank God, I can, albeit partially, fulfill the duty of religious courtesy by adding some Hebrew phrases to my daily prayers."[4]

---

[*] Fayvel Meir Bentsilovich Gets (also spelled Getz, Getts, and Gotz) was born in 1853 in the province of Kovno (Lithuania) and was educated at the universities of Dorpat (Tartu) and St. Petersburg. From 1891 Gets occupied various positions as a Jewish scholar and educator in Vilnius and Riga, where he died in 1932. Gets was a prolific writer in Russian, German, and Hebrew, and published articles and books on Jewish ethics, the position of women in Judaism, and the socio-economic oppression of Jews in Russia. Having instructed Solovyov in Hebrew, Gets maintained a close friendship with the philosopher. After Solovyov's death, Gets published an article "On Solovyov's Attitude toward the Jewish Question" in *Voprosy filosofii i psikhologii* (1901) and their correspondence (1909).

Solovyov became acquainted with Catholic dogmatics through the multi-volume work of Giovanni Perrone, *Praelectiones theologicae.** At the end of 1889 he wrote to his brother, "Did you take by chance (or not by chance) my edition of Perrone's *Praelectiones theologicae* (the first three volumes)?"[5] At the same time, Solovyov was also reading in the St. Petersburg Public Library Giovanni Domenico Mansi's *Acts of the Ecumenical Councils* in Latin.† On 18 February 1885 he wrote to his brother, "I am already reading the 16th folio of Mansi."[6] In Solovyov's notebooks from this period there are numerous extracts from Latin theologians; he apparently studied in the original more or less all the works of Popes Gregory VII and Innocent III.

Solovyov demonstrated his special attraction to Judaism already in his youth, at the time of his pursuit of Kabbalah and the writing of *Sophie*. In both his early work and in the *Lectures on Godmanhood* Solovyov explained exactly why Christ was born in Judaea. Now in his essay *Judaism and the Christian Question* Solovyov developed this idea in detail. It being contrary to the Jewish soul to serve the elemental and demonic forces of nature, the Jews sought a personal and moral God, and through their faith they rose higher than Chaldean magic and Egyptian wisdom. The focus of the Jewish religion is the contract of alliance, or the covenant between God and Israel. Having concluded a covenant with God, the Jews cannot lose their freedom, their self-consciousness, and their autonomy of action. "Israel was great in faith."[7] Furthermore, Solovyov finds in the Jews, instead of dualism and abstract spiritualism, the idea of "holy corporeality." "They saw in nature neither the devil nor divinity, but only the unworthy abode of the theandric spirit."[8] Turning to contemporary Judaism, Solovyov defends the Jews from the accusation of being exclusively concerned with the pursuit of money and material well being. As the main interest of contemporary Europe is money, it is natural that the Jews, who are masters of financial matters, should be the lords of modern Europe. Whereas money binds and degrades non-Jews, it frees and

* Giovanni Perrone (1794-1876), renowned Jesuit theologian, consulted by Popes Gregory XVI and Pius IX.

† Giovanni Domenico Mansi (1692-1769), Italian scholar and editor of the texts of the Church councils.

elevates the Jews, for they now find in it their main instrument for the triumph and glory of Israel, which in their eyes is the triumph of God's cause on earth.[9] It is not true that the Jews form an exclusively harmful, parasitical class in the Russian-Polish region; Israel is as necessary to Poland and Russia as it was to Egypt and Assyria. In Belorussia and Galicia the social elements are distributed according to different nationalities: the Russians form the rural, agrarian class; the Poles, the upper class; and the Jews, the urban, industrial class. If the industrial class everywhere exploits the agrarian, then it is not surprising that in those places where they form the entire industrial class, the Jews turn out to be the exploiters of the people. They did not, however, create this situation.[10]

Russia possesses neither a strong nobility, nor intelligentsia, nor a developed industrial class. The social structure of the country relies on the tsar, the synod of bishops, and the rural community. Russia is comprised of palace, monastery, and village. In the interests of strengthening Russia it would be a mistake to oppress Poland with its highly developed gentry or the Jewish industrial class, but to combine these forces into one creative effort. The sin of the Poles consists in their refusal to understand that, as Slavs related to the Russians by blood and to the Romano-German West by spirit and culture, and as both subjects of the Russian tsar and children of the Roman pope, their providential role in Russia is to form a bridge between Orthodoxy and Rome.[11] But forgetting their universal religious mission, the Poles direct their efforts toward the national and political mission of restoring the great Polish state. "The day will come when, cured from its long madness, Poland will become a living bridge between the holiness of the East and the West. The mighty tsar will extend a hand of assistance to the persecuted pontiff."[12] When Russia, through Poland, unites with Rome, then the Jews, too, will become a necessary element of the future theocracy. "Nature will be subordinated to humanity in love, and in turn humanity will tend nature with love. And which nation is more capable and destined for such a cultivation of material nature than the Jews, who from the beginning recognized nature's right to existence and saw in its clear form, without submitting to its blind power, the pure and holy covering of essence."[13]

Solovyov's essay *Judaism and the Christian Question* appeared in 1884 in *Pravoslavnoe obozrenie* (Nos. 8 and 9) but was later published as a book. At the same time, Solovyov devoted a fairly long article to the Jewish sect "New Israel," which was founded by Iosif Rabinovich "who came to Christ by way of the law and the prophets"[14] and who opened in Kishinev a house of prayer called "Bethlehem." "The state councilor Leskov,"* Solovyov wrote to his brother, "has led you astray, it seems, with regard to New Israel. I have read their documents, creed, liturgy, etc. This is the opposite of Protestantism, although it resembles it a great deal. The fact is that Protestantism, if you look at its origins, is a rejection of the law, but New Israel holds the law with both hands. This is, rather, the primitive Jewish form of Christianity from which was derived not Protestantism, but the Church."[15]

Jews responded warmly to Solovyov's articles on the Jewish question and remained his loyal friends forever, and he actively continued his correspondence with Fayvel Gets. "I have lately had the opportunity of being convinced that the most honorable element in the active Russian intelligentsia is still the Jewish," he wrote to Gets.[16] And on the occasion of a telegram to *Moskovskie vedemosti* about a Jewish pogrom he asked him, "What can we do about this disaster? Pious Jews must pray fervently to God that he deliver Russia's fate into the hands of religious and, at the same time, reasonable and courageous people who will want, and know how, and dare to do good to both nations."[17]

There is also an article of 1885 concerning Judaism "The Talmud and the Latest Polemical Literature about It in Austria and Germany."[18] At the beginning, Solovyov characterizes three Jewish parties: the Sadducees, the Pharisees and the Essenes. For the Sadducees, the word of God is only a fact of the past; for the Pharisees, it is the law of the present life; for the Essenes, it is the idea of the future.

---

* Nikolay Leskov (1831-1895), short story writer, novelist, and journalist. Fascinated by the religious life of Russia, Leskov progressively transferred his sympathies away from Orthodoxy toward Protestantism and Tolstoyanism. Leskov was also interested in Judaism and during his brief time as an official in the Ministry of Education must have investigated the "the New Israel" sect.

All three sects are one-sided and fruitless. The exclusive spirituality and one-sided idealism of the Essenes can be even more sterile than the living wisdom of the Sadducees or the morally juridical formalism of the Pharisees. The Sadducees and the Essenes ceased to exist with the destruction of Jerusalem. The Essenes were absorbed by Christianity, and the Sadducees did not survive the destruction of the Temple. Only the Pharisees remained as the representatives of Judaism as a whole and continued to erect a defense around the law, the result of which was the Talmud. Solovyov quotes a number of the highly moral regulations of the Talmud and concludes that *in principle* there is no contradiction between the legalism of the Talmud and the morality of the New Testament, which is based on faith and altruism. "The principal dispute between Christianity and Judaism lies not in the moral, but in the religious and metaphysical sphere, in the meaning of Godmanhood, and in the redemptive sacrifice of Christ."[19] Furthermore, Solovyov polemicizes with the two anti-Semitic works of Professor Rohling[*] and Doctor Justus, proving, first of all, that many of the directives of the Talmud against Christians are not correctly understood and belong to the realm of private opinion, and, secondly, that Christendom, in light of its confessional divisions and the contradictions between its actual life and its Christian ideals, has no right to attack the Jews who have preserved their religious and national unity and live according to the commandments of their religion. For example, if slavery is an evil condemned by the Christian ideal, then the law of Moses against slavery had already taken wider and more active measures against it than the mollifying palliatives of ecclesiastical canons. The final abolition of slavery occurred only in the eighteenth and nineteenth centuries, during an epoch of religious decline and prevailing lack of belief.[20] The Jews could say to contemporary Christians, "learn to apply your New

[*] August Rohling (1839-1931), Catholic priest, professor, and notorious anti-Semite. In 1871 Rohling published *Der Talmudjude*, a collection of misquotations and fabrications based on the Talmud. Although his academic pretensions were discredited in various lawsuits, his work was widely republished and translated, and remained influential into the Nazi era. Justus was the pseudonym of one of Rohling's collaborators.

Testament, as we have applied our own, the Old Testament, and then we will come to you and be united with you."[21]

Apparently, Solovyov had wanted to publish his article on the Talmud in *Vestnik Evropy*. In 1886 he wrote to Gets from Zagreb, "... I received a letter from Stasyulevich, saying that the 'Talmud' cannot be published in it, for it is subject (?) to the preliminary religious censorship which would probably (?) forbid it."[22]

After "The Great Controversy," Aksakov closed the pages of *Rus'* to Solovyov, however, *Pravoslavnoe obozrenie*, edited by Father Preobrazhensky, continued to publish him. In 1884 in the fourth issue of that journal Solovyov published an open letter to Ivan Aksakov titled "Love for the Nation and the Russian National Ideal," which marked their final break. Solovyov continued to consider himself a Slavophile, but in contradistinction to Aksakov and others, he saw in the union of Churches "the realization of Holy Rus... Holy Rus requires holy actions."[23] He considered the Croatian Catholic Yury Krizhanich,[*] who had lived in the seventeenth century at the court of Tsar Aleksey Mikhailovich and "perished in his zeal for the house of God" to have been the first Slavophile.[24] Krizhanich believed the separation of the Churches to be the greatest sin against the greatest virtue, love. He explained the misfortunes and sufferings of Russia as the consequence of the immense and unconscious sin of schism. From the Croat Krizhanich, Solovyov turned to another Croat, the bishop of Bosnia, Strossmayer, with whom he had begun a correspondence in 1885. Solovyov's original Slavophilism made him sympathetic to the Catholic Slavs, the Poles and the Croats; of the Bulgarians and Serbs he held the lowest opinion. "Indeed, history proceeds at a rapid pace," he writes to Strakhov, "and especially with the help of such historical nations as the Serbs and Bulgarians, whom that famous 'historical' person, Nozdrev, could envy."[25]

---

[*] Yury Krizhanich [Juraj] (1618-1683), Croatian Dominican priest. Imbued with the idea of Church Union he traveled first to Ukraine in 1659 and then to Muscovy where he attempted to persuade Tsar Aleksey that Russia had a great role to play in the destiny of Europe and Christendom. Exiled in 1661 to Siberia, he wrote several works in a Common Slavic language of his own invention. Krizhanich met his end during the Turkish siege of Vienna.

In the middle of the '80s Solovyov's links with conservative circles were sundered for good. In 1885 he challenged the "Goliath living on Strastny boulevard," the pillar of the Russian state, Mikhail Katkov[26] to battle with his article "The Philosophy of the State in the Program of the Ministry of Public Enlightenment," which Aksakov decided to publish in *Rus'*. Although this action threatened him with unpleasant consequences, Solovyov's outcry against the "absolutism of the bureaucracy, which is turning the Church into one of its departments and the nation into material for its legal experiments,"[27] must have evoked the deep sympathy of the old liberal Slavophile.

At the beginning of 1886 Solovyov wrote to his brother from St. Petersburg, "I am courted here on one side by *Novoe vremia* and on the other by the liberals, not to speak of the Jews. I am practicing fine diplomacy with the first, the second, and the third. But then, I have lost all contact with bureaucratic Russia. Only at a distance am I amazed at its wisdom."[28]

Only one writer of the conservative camp regarded Solovyov in the '80s with adoration and rapture, Konstantin Leontev.* The deep divergence between their worldviews was revealed later, at the beginning of the '90s, but in 1887 the Byzantinist Leontev, who ignored Solovyov's "liberalism," was fascinated by *The History of Theocracy*, that grandiose plan for the union of the Russian tsardom with papal Rome and the restoration of the Byzantino-Roman Middle Ages. In one conversation he compared Solovyov to the bell of a church tower resounding throughout Russia. For his part, Solovyov maintained a warm regard for Leontev till the end of his life and appreciated in "Father Kliment" the genuine spirit of a zealot and ascetic. This is a rare instance of people becoming friends independently of party lines. Leontev, the reactionary, for whom the "Goliath of Strastny boulevard" was too liberal, felt an affinity with Solovyov, who was at home in the liberal circle of Stasyulevich.

* Konstantin Leontev (1831-1891), writer, critic, philosopher. Trained in medicine, Leontev entered the diplomatic service and served in the Russian consular offices on Crete and in the Balkans (1863-1873). A brilliant critic, Leontev challenged conventional views by attacking Dostoevsky for his utopian Christianity and praising Tolstoy mostly for his literary style. Toward the end of his life Leontev adopted an extremely reactionary view of Russian history and advocated a philosophy of "Byzantinism." Taking monastic vows in 1891, as Father Kliment, Leontev settled at the Trinity-St. Sergy Monastery where he died.

Leontev the aesthete was probably captivated by Solovyov's Byzantine, iconic features

In 1885 Solovyov wrote almost the entire first volume of his three volume "Leviathan," that book which was to become the fundamental work of his life, replacing the youthful *Principes de la religion universelle*. The complete title of this work is *The History and Future of Theocracy*.

The first volume contains five books. According to the dates of publication, the last part of the fifth book, which was published in 1885 in *Pravoslavnoe obozrenie* No. 1 under the title "The Evangelical Foundation of Theocracy," was written before the others. In this section Solovyov demonstrates the necessity of hierarchical authority and obedience. "Self-denial, that is, the renunciation of the self is the marvelous law and the holy mystery of universal life, of universal self-sacrifice."[29] "If the Church is a building of living stones, then its general architectural plan is the hierarchical structure."[30] Theocracy was founded by Christ Himself, who said, "All power in heaven and on earth has been given to me" (Matthew 28:16-20). "All power" means that the government that separates itself from the source of all power is illegitimate and impotent; that the nation that rises against the royal power of Christ, repeating the cry of the Jewish mob "we have no king but Caesar," deceives itself; and that those statesmen who wash their hands like Pilate, while hypocritically proclaiming a free Church in a free state, are condemned.[31]

> In heaven Christ is first truth and then power; in our terrestrial world Christ appears first as power, and is then later understood as truth. That person in whom we believe before anyone else embodies for us the highest authority: obedience precedes understanding. In order to attain the heights of free perfection, it is necessary to pass through the valley of humility.[32]
>
> The One who said "All power in heaven and earth has been given to me," first said "Render unto Caesar the things that are Caesar's, but unto God the things that are God's." Thus it was said, for the Son of Man had not yet been glorified and all power, even over Caesar, had not yet been

given to Him. But after it was given to Him, where was the power of the *godless* Caesar? And where was the *pagan* empire? Its flickering shade was still wandering somewhere below in the valley, but it had not reached the summit of that mountain in Galilee on which the apostles heard the words of the Godman, "All power in heaven and on earth has been given to me." When the caesar that was equal to the apostles heard these words "By this sign shall thou conquer!" the shade of the pagan empire lurking in the valley vanished.[33] The fact that nothing limited the full power to bind and loose, which was given to the apostles, sufficiently demonstrates that, according to the Gospel, the general structure of the Church is to be strictly hierarchical, and by no means democratic; thus, there can be no question of the people participating in this power.[34]

The manuscript of this article furnished proofs of the primacy of the Apostle Peter, but although Solovyov omitted this chapter on account of the censorship,[35] he included it in *La Russie et l'Eglise Universelle*. He hoped to publish *The History of Theocracy* in Russia, but when this proved to be impossible, he published it in Zagreb.

At about the same time that "The Evangelical Foundation of Theocracy" was being written, Solovyov wrote a poem that clearly reflects his mood in the mid '80s:

From the flame of passions, impure and cruel,
From evil designs and deceitful vanity
The fever of solitary raptures will not cure us,
Nor will the race of pining reverie carry us.

But in the deadly desert of life,
It is not at the crossroads of idle thoughts and words
That we find the path to lost holiness,
That we discern the trace of lost gods.

They are not needed! In boundless grace
Our God has not abandoned His earth.
And to all he has revealed the unique path
From base pride to humble heights.

And the foundations of Zion do not waver,
The beauty of the luxuriant roses of Sharon does not fade,
And above the living water, in the sacred valley,
The holy lily grows uncorrupted and pure.[36]

Apparently, the first book, "An Investigation of the Principal Prejudices against the Theocratic Cause in Russia," which is the key to the entire work, was written after the fifth book. A portion of this book was first published in *Pravoslavnoe obozrenie* under the title "The Dogmatic Development of the Church in Relation to the Question of the Church Reunion," and later as a separate pamphlet. Here, on the basis of a detailed investigation of the dogmatic teachings of the first centuries, Solovyov demonstrates that dogma developed in such a way that the doctrine of the Council of Nicaea was an "innovation" in comparison with the doctrines of the Apostolic Fathers, and that the doctrine of Chalcedon was an "innovation" compared to the doctrine of the Fathers of Nicaea, etc. Although Orthodox polemicists accuse Catholics of proclaiming new dogmas, these dogmas are only the clarification, or expression *explicite* of what is contained in the teaching of the Eastern Fathers *implicite*. Solovyov was attacked in the Kharkov journal *Vera i razum* by T. Stoyanov and A. Shostin, a professor at the Moscow Religious Academy (with regard to the dogmatic development of the church). Solovyov included his reply to Stoyanov in the second edition of *The Dogmatic Development of the Church*, which was forbidden by the censorship, and responded to Shostin in the article "A Response to an Anonymous Critic Concerning Dogmatic Development in the Church."[37]

The second book, "The Primitive Destinies of Humanity and the Theocracy of the Forefathers," is a philosophical commentary on the book of Genesis. In Abraham, Isaac, and Jacob, Solovyov discerns the three theocratic virtues: faith, obedience, and religious zeal. Isaac and Jacob represent two opposing theocratic types: Isaac is "passive and dreamy," while Jacob is more like his mother, the "active and enterprising Rebecca." His "religious zeal is expressed not by his laying his whole being before the face of God, but by his grappling with God's might for a serious struggle; with him this zeal is reflected not in the fullness of human self-sacrifice, but in an urgent demand of God for the fullness of His gifts and His promised blessing."[38]

The third book, "The National Theocracy and the Law of Moses," is a philosophical commentary on the book of Exodus and covers the symbolism of the Old Testament sacrifices and the tabernacle of Moses.

The fourth book is titled "The Completion of the National Theocracy by the Development of the Three Powers: The High Priestly, the Royal, and the Prophetic and the Transition to the Universal Theocracy" and forms a commentary on the books of Judges, Kings, and the Prophets. In the second book Solovyov refers to biblical texts in their Old Church Slavonic translation, but beginning with book three, he provides his own translations from the Hebrew; thus Jehovah becomes *Iagve*; Simeon, *Shimshon*; Sikhem, *Shikhem*; etc.

The foreword to *The History of Theocracy* is dated: Moscow, the Feast of the Annunciation of the Most Holy Theotokos, 1887, but this date is undoubtedly incorrect. In April 1887 the first volume of the work was already published, having been sent to the press in 1886. Thus, 1887 was most likely substituted for 1886. In his foreword Solovyov summons Russia in the person of the tsar "to make right every injustice." As the representative of the *royal* house of David, Christ clearly demonstrated His submission to John the Baptist, the son of the high priest Zachary of the house of Aaron, as the last representative of the true priesthood of the Old Testament. "We must follow the example of the eternal king, and then the Universal Church will appear to us no longer as a dead mummy but as the true companion of God… that Sophia, the Wisdom of God, to whom our ancestors, according to an extraordinary prophetic sense, raised altars and churches without themselves knowing who she was."[39]

In a letter to his brother Mikhail, Solovyov provides an indication as to how he worked on *The History of Theocracy*. "I lived at Pustynka for almost the entire time completely alone in the enormous old, unheated house, most often sleeping without undressing in two coats; but to make up for this I worked a great deal and wrote a very long chapter on the theocracy of the Old Testament. I wrote according to a new method, namely, without any kind of rough drafts, but directly without corrections, with the Bible at one elbow and clean paper at the other. It does not seem to be a bad method and the time saved is enormous."[40]

In the deserted, freezing house at Pustynka Solovyov heard the mysterious summons:

> From the native waters of the plains of Chaldea,
> From the mountain meadows of the land of Aramea,
> From Harran, where you lived until your hair was gray,
> And from Ur, where your youthful years flowed, –
> Not for only a year,
> Nor for many years,
> But for eternity will you depart.[41]

The mysterious voice no longer called him to Egypt, but to Croatia, to Bishop Strossmayer.

In the same year that Solovyov was made a docent at the University of Moscow, the same university elected as an honorary member the Roman Catholic Bishop Josip Juraj Strossmayer "patron of the Yugoslav Academy of Sciences and Arts and founder of the University of Croatia."[42] Already in 1883 *The Great Controversy* had captured the attention of Strossmayer. In December 1885 Solovyov received a letter from "the celebrated servant of the Church and protector of the Slavs." On the feast of the Immaculate Conception Solovyov wrote to the bishop with enthusiasm: "My heart burns with joy at the thought that I have such a guide as you. May God preserve you for many years for the good of the holy Church and the Slavic people. I have a great deal to write, but I do not want to communicate with you by pen and ink: I hope to see you and talk to you face to face."[43]

In the spring of 1886 Solovyov prepared for his second trip abroad. What was Solovyov's personal life like during 1885-1886?

In general, his mood was exceptionally cheerful; his youthful illusions had dissipated, but he believed that, having completed his lonely path "on a cold winter's day," he would reach his sacred temple "burning with triumphant fires." The first attacks from the Russian State and Church did not distress him, but only stirred up his mettle. Let Katkov and Pobedonostsev be against him, let Aksakov reject him; the radical intelligentsia began to listen to him. The former friend of Lyubimov and Katkov had risen in their estimation following his speech for clemency to the assassins of the tsar. In the Russian Church he had some good friends, for example, Archimandrite Antony Vadkovsky (the future metropolitan of St. Petersburg), and the editor of *Pravoslavnoe obozrenie*, Father Preobrazhensky. The Jews were grateful to him, and in the distance awaited him Bishop Strossmayer and perhaps Leo XIII himself, that *lumen in coelo*. It was also true that he was alone and deprived of any kind of definite position in society. In 1886 he wrote to his sister Nadya: "Of all the places on the globe I, of course, prefer two: Pustynka (when it is not too cold) and the Likhutin house (when it is not too musical). But alas! I cannot settle definitely either here or there for je suis né sous l'astre des voyages, or, speaking in an elevated biblical style, I must go before the Lord, which is, of course, better than walking before people on my hind legs. My poor talent for the latter does not permit me to find for myself, in our rather ignoble times, a stable framework for my life. But perhaps this is my personal nature and destiny. Is it not true (and this is amazing) that when we were still children, papá called Vsevolod a *wolf* and me a *Pecheneg*."

In fact, at this point in his life, Solovyov's health began to deteriorate noticeably, "... I went to Pustynka for Shrovetide and there fell ill with something that was either a mild case of measles or severe urticaria with some kind of neuro-cerebral complications" (1885).[44] "I myself have been suffering this whole time from some kind of idiotic ailment, consisting of the swelling of my entire face and, in particular, of my eyes. There is no particular pain but a terrible periodic itch, which, however, does not prevent me from working, or eating, or sleeping" (1886).[45]

In general, however, the photographs of Solovyov during this time reflect a particularly strong appearance. He grew a dense beard and in his visage there was something magnificent and biblical, recalling Moses. In several of the portraits from the middle of the '80s his face looks almost iconic. In January 1886 (at the time of his writing the chapter on Old Testament theocracy) Kramskoy painted the famous portrait that hangs in the St. Petersburg Museum (the former Alexander III museum). "Tomorrow Kramskoy is going to begin my portrait," Solovyov informed his mother on 27 January

1886. "The doorman at his house where he lives has two little girls who run up to me and shout while tugging at the edge of my coat, 'dear God, dear God!', apparently mistaking me for a priest. And once on the stairs of the Hotel Evropeyskaya, a complete stranger, a respectable gentleman with a gray beard, rushed up to me exclaiming with joy, 'What brings you here, *batiushka*!' and when I remarked that he had probably mistaken me for someone else, he replied, 'Are you really not Father Ioann?' To this I, of course, remarked that not only was I not Father Ioann but that I was not a father in any sense of the word."[46*]

His relations with Sofya Khitrovo in 1885–1886 did not cause him the previous torments. Apparently, a time of quiet and stable love had arrived. In October 1885 Sofya Petrovna wrote to my father congratulating him on my birth: "You know, Mikhail Sergeevich, how close you all are to my heart, and how very sorry I am that my life is still so separated from you all, but this is only in the outer world. I would like terribly much for you to have the same friendly feeling for me that I have for you." The letter is signed simply Sofia.

And what of the "mysterious companion"? Rarely now did her "feeble summons" reach Solovyov and "scarcely could be heard the distant voice of the shade: do not trust the transitory; love and do not forget." In place of the "morning mist," the cold white day" and "sober works" had come.

In May 1886 Solovyov experienced at Pustynka one of those unforgettable days, which he recalled twelve years later:

> It was indeed a different day, cloudless and brilliant,
> From the heavens poured a stream of exultant rays,
> And everywhere among the trees of the deserted park
> Glimmered the phantoms of enigmatic eyes.[47]

On that day Solovyov wrote the famous poem "The Sovereign Earth [Zemlia-Vladychitsa]":

> And in the mystery made manifest I see
> again the meeting

* Solovyov is referring to Father Ioann of Kronshtadt.

Of the soul of the earth with the unearthly light,
And from the fire of love the suffering of life
Drifts away like ephemeral smoke.[48]

While here at Pustynka "the suffering of life drifted away like ephemeral smoke," in the Alps, "Strossmayer and his spouse *Theocracy*" awaited him.[49]

At this time Sofia Petrovna was living with her children in Hapsal. Solovyov planned his trip "around the circumference of the circle": Pustynka, Revel, Hapsal, Stettin, Breslau, Vienna.[50] But his departure was complicated by a "minor" inconvenience. He had put aside nearly 500 rubles for his travels, but this money was stolen from the table by the family servant Aleksey, the "perfidious Licharda."[51] Solovyov's witty brother-in-law Nil Popov dubbed this event "the five-fold renunciation of Catherine,"* but his wife, Vera Sergeevna, along with a little known, but virtuous, acquaintance V. A. Pisarenko collected 450 rubles for Solovyov. Soon after his arrival in Zagreb, Solovyov found himself without funds and was forced to live temporarily at the expense of Canon .[52] Solovyov spent from 31 May to 11 June at Hapsal and swam in the sea. He strongly recommended his brother Mikhail to come from his house at Dedovo near Moscow to Hapsal. "Jokes aside, I believe that this would be more convenient and pleasant for you than the Crimea. The climate is warm, grapes grow in the open air (though they don't fully ripen), the temperature of the sea has not been lower than 18°, and in the middle of the summer it is generally 25–27°. There are amazingly curative mud baths and life is arranged extremely comfortably in the German manner."[53]

In 1886 Vladimir and Mikhail worked together on the newly discovered manuscript of early Christianity, *The Teaching of the Twelve Apostles*. Mikhail did the translation and Vladimir wrote the introduction. In June he wrote to Mikhail from Hapsal, "I am sending to our beekeeper the introduction to Διδαχη (he received your manuscript a long time ago)."[54] The "beekeeper" was the priest Preobrazhensky, whom Solovyov turned into "Preobramuzhsky" in one of his letters to Mikhail. In his obituary about Preobrazhensky

* The hundred ruble note showed Catherine the Great.

written in 1900 Solovyov says of Father Pyotr: "Although it was begun for practical reasons (to provide wax for the diocesan candle factories), the old man's work with bees became a labor of warm love and touching solicitude. Obtaining a dacha in Pushkino near Moscow, from early spring he dedicated himself for months to his favorite occupation... Whoever visited him at this time and failed to find him either in the house or the garden might meet the deacon, who had come from Moscow on business, who would say with an encouraging smile, 'You must now wait sir, Father Archpriest is busy with the queen.'"[55]

Leaving for Zagreb, Solovyov was far from the idea of embracing Catholicism. On 8 April 1886, having spent the previous evening among professors of the St. Petersburg Religious Academy, he wrote to its inspector Archimandrite Antony (Vadkovsky), "Yesterday I felt myself to be in truly Christian society, devoted above all to the work of God. This encourages and reassures me, and for my part I can assure you that *I will never convert to Latinism*. If there might be any kind of temptations, I am certain that I will overcome them with God's help and your prayers. Please give my deep regards to Father Mikhail and to Father Antony and to all my new acquaintances."*[56]

From Vienna on 29 June Solovyov informed Canon in Zagreb about this evening at the St. Petersburg Religious Academy, "I remain very satisfied with this gathering, but it did not please our ecclesiastical (i. e. secular) authorities very much; and as some kind of an antidote to my temptations, Father Naumovich,† who has recently arrived in St. Petersburg, has been invited to the same academy for a meeting with the students."[57]

But the "promemoria" that Solovyov sent from Zagreb to Bishop Strossmayer in Djakovar could only come from the pen of a man who was already "*toto animo et corde catholicus*."

---

* Father Antony is probably Solovyov's future enemy, Archbishop Antony (Khrapovitsky). [Author's note]

† Father Ivan Naumovich, a russophile Ukrainian Greek Catholic priest active in Galicia, joined the Russian Orthodox Church in 1891 and died in St. Petersburg.

Endnotes to Part 2 - Chapter 2

---

1. *P*, vol. 2, 107.
2. *P*, vol. 4, 96.
3. *P*, vol. 2, 135, 144.
4. Ibid., 144.
5. *P*, vol. 2, 88.
6. Ibid., 89.
7. *SS*, vol. 4, 146.
8. Ibid., 149.
9. Ibid. 137.
10. Ibid., 183.
11. Ibid., 181.
12. Ibid., 183.
13. Ibid., 185.
14. Ibid., 207; *P*, vol. 4, 89-90.
15. *P*, vol. 4, 90.
16. *P*, vol. 2, 134.
17. Ibid., 139; see also a letter from Zagreb, *P*, vol. 2, 138.
18. *SS*, vol. 6, 3.
19. Ibid., 16.
20. Ibid., 29.
21. Ibid., 31.
22. *P*, vol. 2, 138.
23. *SS*, vol. 5, 55.
24. *SS*, vol. 4, 191.
25. *P*, vol. 1, 24.
26. *P*, vol. 4, 92. In a letter to Strakhov, Katkov is called a "Leviathan," *P*, vol. 1, 24.
27. *SS*, vol. 5, 413.
28. *P*. vol. 4, 97.
29. *SS*, vol. 4,604.
30. Ibid., 605.
31. Ibid., 618-619.
32. Ibid., 621.
33. Ibid., 622.
34. Ibid., 623.
35. *P*, vol. 2, 131; vol. 3, 144.
36. *P*, vol. 4, 91.

37. *SS*, vol 4, 643.
38. Ibid., 407.
39. *SS*, vol. 4, 261.
40. *P*, vol.4, 94.
41. *Stikh*., 85.
42. Luk'ianov, vol. 2, 87.
43. *P*, vol. 1, 180.
44. *P*, vol 4, 89.
45. Ibid., 94.
46. *P*, vol. 2, 46.
47. *Stikh*., 7th ed., 169.
48. Ibid., 88.
49. *P*, vol. 4, 98.
50. Idem.
51. Ibid, 97; for details of the episode, see the memoirs of Maria Bezobrazova, 146-147.
52. Ibid., 99-100.
53. Ibid., 98.
54. Idem.
55. *SS*, vol. 9, 428-429.
56. *P*, vol. 3, 187.
57. *P*, vol. 1, 165.

Part 2 - Chapter 3

Journey to Zagreb

Solovief anima candida,
pia ac vere sancta est.

Strossmayer

Solovyov left Hapsal on 11 June[1] and, having crossed the Austrian border, stayed for a short time in Vienna, from whence he wrote to his mother,[2] Bishop Strossmayer,[3] Canon Rački,[4] and Fayvel Gets.[5] He spent eight days in Vienna[6] and wrote here a long (twenty-nine pages) "Forewarning," that is a foreword, to *The History of Theocracy*, which was subsequently replaced by another. This "Forewarning" contains a line, which though crossed out, is very typical of Solovyov, who from childhood possessed the mind of a knight and a warrior. Declaring that he is addressing only people of good will, he adds, "And with regard to opponents of this cause, we consider ourselves to be *in statu belli* and take an interest in them only in so far as they can offer us war booty." This composition is dated Vienna, St. Peter's day 1886. On the same day he wrote a letter to Bishop Strossmayer dated 29 June 1886, Goldenes Lamm, which reads, "Thank God that I am now free and that no kind of δυνάμεις καί ἐξουσίαι τοῦ κόσμου τούτου can prevent me from seeing you and speaking with you."[7]

In Vienna Solovyov searched in vain for a Syriac Bible and we do not know for certain whether he met Serafino Vanutelli, the papal nuncio at the Habsburg court.

At the beginning of July Solovyov was in Zagreb, where he stayed with Canon Rački. František Rački, who was born in 1829, was president of the Yugoslav Academy. Of his many scholarly works, Solovyov considered his book about Saints Cyril and Methodius, *The Epoch and Mission of Saints Cyril and Methodius* to be especially important. When died in 1894 Solovyov devoted to his memory a warm obituary, at the end of which he provides a vivid portrait of the canon:

> With the death of the Athens of Yugoslavia has become orphaned... I, at least, cannot imagine Zagreb without the omnipresent figure of this small but powerful man flitting everywhere wearing a narrow belt and high boots, making his way with swift and sure steps from the academy to the printing press, and from there to his study and from his study out of the city to his vineyards (was, above all, a model host in general, and a wine-grower in particular).
>
> When a large earthquake struck Zagreb, destroying half its Gothic cathedral, was in the church saying Mass. Although everyone else had fled in terror, he remained alone and, leaning on the edge of the altar and blinded by the dust rising from the ceiling that had collapsed, finished the Mass. He came out covered in white dust, but whole and unharmed. That which he was at that moment he was during his whole life, a man, above all, of duty and unwavering loyalty.[8]

In his letters to Fet,[9] his mother,[10] his brother Mikhail,[11] his sister Nadya,[12] and Fayvel Gets,[13] Solovyov gives a description of his life in Zagreb.

To Nadya he wrote, "I am staying at the home of Canon , who is the most respected person in this area. His house is on the edge of the city with a large garden. This place is called the 'capitol' for it is adjacent to the cathedral and all the houses belong to the canons and to the other priests of the cathedral, forty in all, in addition to the three hundred or so other clerics who are studying at the seminary and theological faculty. Finally, there is a Franciscan monastery next to the house I am living in, so this is really a city of priests. I arise at 8:30 and go every day to Mass at the splendid eleventh-century Gothic cathedral, lunch at one, and have supper at nine o'clock. I am not drinking tea at all (since it's not the custom here, but in the morning I drink coffee and in the evening, wine, which is extraordinarily good here; it's of local manufacture and sells for ten kopecks a bottle). I am eating every sort of fruit and vegetable, which are in abundance here, in spite of the cholera nearby. My gastric ailment seems to have left, thanks to the Croatian wine (it has this curative property). My book is being published little by little."

In his letter of 27 July to Fet he added, "I don't feel at all that I am in a foreign country, for the most part I use Russian and the people here (the ordinary ones) are just like our Ukrainians, only they are more religious (which, unfortunately, one cannot say about the Orthodox Slavs). The churches here are full even on weekdays and on Sunday you can't force your way through the crowd. Along with the churches there is located here an academy of sciences, a picture gallery, and a museum of antiquities; all of this was mostly founded by Bishop Strossmayer and Canon ."

Finally, in a letter to Gets, Solovyov sums up his life in Zagreb: "*Ora et labora*; but to prevent you from forming too high an opinion of me, I will add a third activity, *bibo* Croatian wine, which in an amazing way has cured me of hemorrhoids and other ailments."

On 27 July (new style) Solovyov wrote to Fet that within a few days he was going to see Bishop Strossmayer. This means that around 10 August Solovyov left for his meeting with the bishop at the spa of Rohitsch-Sauerbrunn, where he was taking the waters.[14] Solovyov stayed there for ten days and his poem "In the Alps" can serve as an indication of his mood at the time: "The joyful pounding surf of / Thoughts without speech and feelings without name..." Fet considered this to be Solovyov's best poem.

During the latter part of August Solovyov returned to Zagreb and prepared for a new meeting with Strossmayer, not at the spa, but in Djakovar. Once again, however, the story of Cairo repeated itself, "coins rattled around in my pocket." At the end of August or beginning of September, Solovyov wrote to his brother, "Bishop Strossmayer is expecting me at his residence in Djakovar but I cannot budge, not having a penny to my name. If you have still not sent me, as I requested, Austrian bank notes, then do something else: telegraph money from some Moscow bank to one in Vienna with a transfer from the latter to the Kroatische Escompte-Banque (in Agram)... It's very awkward for me to ask my host for money, around whose neck I would be hanging without it."[15]

In the letter that followed, Solovyov wrote, "The money you sent, which I changed (although it took eight days to arrive, but without any trouble), saved me from the extremity of borrowing money from my magnificent and welcoming host in order to travel to Djakovar to see Bishop Strossmayer, who is inviting and urging me with letters and telegrams."[16]

Solovyov spent eighteen days in Djakovar. "It was one continual feast with endless dinners, speeches, songs, etc.," he wrote to his brother. "Dear friend, I experienced a great deal in Djakovar that was unexpectedly pleasant and comforting."[17]

Solovyov wrote to from Djakovar, "The bishop speaks with me in Latin, in French, and in Croatian; and in each language it is equally pleasant to listen to his inspiring conversation. I agree with Father Franki that no other nation possesses such a bishop."[18]

Svetozar described the relationship between Solovyov and Strossmayer: "They met in one and the same spirit, sharing identical intentions and ideas; for both of them the question of Church union was the first and foremost. Both men were idealists and Platonists, both were gifted with the same mystical inclinations and speculative insights into the future, with the difference, perhaps, that Solovyov was a poet whereas Strossmayer was more of an orator."

According to , who cites Bishop , while he was staying in Djakovar Solovyov attended Mass every day and prayed very fervently. He would make the sign of the cross in the Latin manner, but prayed with his arms crossed in the Orthodox way.

After his return to Zagreb, Solovyov wrote to Strossmayer, "Having left you in reality, I have not ceased seeing you in my dreams every night. Your health is too important for the whole world and, although I am certain that you find yourself under the special protection of the good angels, all the same, I will allow myself to recommend to you the Russian proverb, 'God protects the protected'… Ah! If only God would grant us the happiness of seeing you in St. Petersburg or Moscow. This would change many things and it would be for us a unique chance to expiate our sin regarding your predecessor . I beg you, *Vladyko,* to give my warm greetings to our good friend and to all your worthy canons and priests… My dreams prove to me that I have truly left part of my soul in Djakovar."[19]

Attached to this letter of 21 September, Solovyov sent Strossmayer his "promemoria" in French. This document was published in Djakovar in ten copies. One was sent to Leo XIII, another to Cardinal Rampolla, the secretary of state in Rome, and three to Serafino Vanutelli, the nuncio in Vienna. Four copies were sent to Solovyov and the remaining one was taken by Kosta Voinovich to Zagreb. Milko 's note in the first volume of Solovyov's letter states, "One (copy) was sent to the nuncio in Vienna… Kosta Voinovich took three for his friends." But on the same page there appears a quotation from a letter of Strossmayer to Vanutelli: "*Tria harum litterarum exemplaria Excellentiae Vestrae submitto*."[20] Apparently, was mistaken.

The promemoria, which is included in the collection of Solovyov's letters (volume 1, 183), is addressed in the form of a letter to Strossmayer, the bishop of Bosnia and Sirmium, the apostolic vicar in Serbia, etc. Solovyov opens with a reference to the sagacity of Pope Leo XIII "who, according to the ancient prophecies bears in the succession of popes the mystical title 'light in heaven' (*lumen in caelo*)." Later in the document Solovyov maintains that the Eastern Church has not declared as an obligatory dogma (*dogme obligatoire*) any teaching contrary to Catholic doctrine. The dogmatic definitions of the first seven Ecumenical Councils form the complete totality of those absolutely indisputable and immutable doctrinal truths that are recognized by the Eastern Church as a whole. "Everything else is debatable and can be regarded as the teaching of one or another school, or of one or another particular theologian, but such teaching does not possess the authority of the infallible magisterium. The dogmatics of our Church are limited to the decrees of the ecumenical councils that were fully Orthodox and Catholic (*orthodoxe et catholique*). Our schism exists *de facto* but not *de jure*. *Adhuc sub judice lis est*." Recalling the signing of the Union of Florence by the metropolitan of Moscow Isidor and his proclamation of this act in the Dormition cathedral in Moscow, Solovyov comments that boyars and people listened to it in silence and that it was only Great Prince Vasily who renounced the union and threw Metropolitan Isidor into prison. After this, the Great Prince was blinded by his nephews and received the epithet Vasily the Dark (*obscur ou ténébreux*).

The union of the Churches will be possible only when there is agreement on the following propositions: that although the Church of Rome is "*Romana*" only its western part is "*Latina*"; that it is only the Roman, not the Latin, Church that is "*mater et magistra omnium ecclesiarum,* and that it is the bishop of Rome, not the patriarch of the West, who speaks infallibly *ex cathedra* (it should not be forgotten that at one time the bishop of Rome spoke Greek). Following the return of Russia to Catholic unity, the Russian Church must keep not only its own rite (of which there can be no question), but also the complete autonomy of its organization and administration, which the East possessed before the schism. In particular, the high position that always belonged to the emperor among the Eastern Churches must remain untouched. Thus, the union of the Churches requires two distinctions:

1) The distinction between the private opinions of our theologians, which can be mistaken, anti-Catholic, and heretical, and the faith of the Eastern Church as a whole, which remains Orthodox and Catholic.
2) The distinction between the authority of the pope as successor to the Apostle Peter, the pastor and infallible teacher of the universal Church, and his administrative power as Patriarch of the West. This distinction would guarantee the autonomy of the Eastern Church and without this, reunion, humanly speaking, will be impossible.

But Solovyov did not insist on the last point. He had complete trust in the wisdom of the Church of Rome, which has been proven by the ages and by the lofty mind and exceptional virtues of Leo XIII. "For us it is not a question of defending our rights, but of accepting the Father's love."

Reunion would offer much to both sides. Rome would gain a nation that is devout and full of religious enthusiasm as well as a loyal defender in the person of the Russian emperor. Russia would free itself from its involuntary sin of schism and could realize its great vocation in the world: to unite around itself all the Slavic nations and create a true Christian civilization.

Forwarding the promemoria to Vanutelli, the nuncio in Vienna, Strossmayer wrote to him in Latin that the Slavic nations will fulfill their vocation in Europe and Asia only after they return to Catholic unity, as a severed branch to the ancient trunk. "On account of my sins, I myself am scarcely worthy of seeing the dawn of this joyful day, but Solovyov and Princess Volkonskaya, and other pious and holy souls, will certainly be worthy of seeing, if not the full splendor, then, at least, the morning star of this radiant day that the Eternal Father is holding in His power for the consolation of those who do not despair in times of misfortune but strive with all their strength for union."[21]

Strossmayer describes Solovyov in this letter as "*anima candida, pia ac vere sancta*" that is "a sincere soul, pious and truly holy." Solovyov left the same impression on other Catholics in Croatia. In his article "About Solovyov's Relations with the People of Croatia"[22] Dr. Svetozar relates the legend about Solovyov, which has been preserved in Croatia, that "his soul was truly angelic," that "he never committed a single mortal sin in his life, that he did not drink wine and did not know women." Such was Solovyov in 1886 at the time of his stay in Croatia.

Reading the promemoria, one can only agree with Strossmayer, who wrote to Cardinal Rampolla in Rome that Solovyov was "*toto animo et corde catholicus*," and it demonstrates the inaccuracy of the widespread opinion that Solovyov accepted Catholic dogmas only at the time of writing *La Russie et l'Eglise Universelle*, that is in 1887-1888. Already in 1886 he acknowledged, above all, the dogmas of the Immaculate Conception of Mary and the infallibility of the Roman pontiff. Bishop Strossmayer probably did not doubt that it was only a question of time before Solovyov joined the Church of Rome and he proposed to meet him in Rome in the spring of 1888. According to Cardinal Rampolla, Leo XIII, having read the promemoria offered his approval and praise to Solovyov and prayed fervently. Solovyov related to Evgeny Trubetskoy that the pope had said of him, "Here is a lamb who, one hopes, will soon return to the fold."[23]

In spite of all of Strossmayer's charm, in Zagreb Solovyov went to Confession and received Communion from the priest of the Serbian Orthodox Church, Father Amvrosy and brought back to Russia testimony of this confession. "I responded to the efforts at conversion that were directed against me personally," Solovov wrote to Archimandrite Antony from Moscow on 29 November 1889, "by going to Confession and receiving Communion (which was unusual for that time of year) in the Serbian Orthodox church in Zagreb from the priest there, Hieromonk Amvrosy. In general, if one can say so, I returned to Russia *more Orthodox* than when I left."[24]

In Russia rumors stubbornly circulated that Solovyov had embraced Catholicism. In a Croatian journal Solovyov had published his article "Is the Eastern Church Orthodox?" where "taking the point of view of my Catholic readers, I proved that even from their perspective *our Eastern Church must be recognized as Orthodox.*"[25] The opposing opinion was expressed by the Franciscan priest Father who attacked Solovyov and his supporter Dr. Franki. In the person of Father , Solovyov encountered for the first time opposition to his views not from the Orthodox, but from the Catholic side... responded to Solovyov's article with another one, "In Defense." Solovyov's brief reply to this was published on 11 December 1886 in the Croatian newspaper *List* already after his return to Russia but Father did not calm down, and his work of 1891*Caesarism and Byzantinism* includes an entire tract against Solovyov and Dr. Franki.

On 27 July 1886 Solovyov published in *Novoe vremia* his first letter from Zagreb (the subsequent letters were not published) in which he refuted the opinion, widespread in Russia, that the Croats were the instrument of the Austro-Hungarian government for the Latinization of the Orthodox East. Solovyov pointed out the pro-Russian sympathies of the Croats and cited the declaration made in the Austrian Reichstag by the Croatian deputy, the Catholic priest , "If we cannot be Croats, then let us become Russians so that, whatever happens, we will remain Slavs."[26]

Solovyov returned to Russia at the beginning of October. On 9/21 he wrote from Moscow to his gracious host in Zagreb, "I completed my journey well enough, only I did lose my plaid in Zidarni Most and further on, at the border, I was somewhat delayed by the officials there who considered it strange that my small baggage consisted almost exclusively of books and papers. In order to resolve their doubts they sent for an expert in books, namely, the police captain; but for this educated authority, as well, your Croatian works seemed to be written in Chinese, and he was already beginning to peruse my correspondence before I firmly objected against this and, laying before him my collection of Bibles, I convinced him of my good intentions… Even in Russia I remain half-Croat and in spite of my poor knowledge of the language sometimes think in Croatian. Thanks to my stay with you I have now become a Slavophile not only in ideas but also in my heart."[27]

On 29 November Solovyov wrote to Archimandrite Antony, "I returned from abroad, having become closely and clearly acquainted with the good *as well as bad sides* of the Western Church and I am even more convinced of the opinion that for the reunion of the Churches every external union (*unia*) and every personal conversion are not only not required but are even harmful."[28]

After the joyful trip to Croatia, there came for Solovyov the extremely hard year of 1887 in which he endured defeat on all fronts… In December he wrote to Gets: "You are probably now aware that I am suffering direct persecution. Each of my works, not only the new ones, but the reprinting of the old, have been *absolutely* forbidden. The Ober-Prokurator of the Synod P–v [Pobedonostsev] said to one of my friends that *all* of my work is harmful for Russia and for Orthodoxy and that, consequently, it cannot be allowed. And in order to justify such a decision they have concocted and spread every kind of story about me. Today I have become a Jesuit, but tomorrow, perhaps, I will be circumcised; now I am serving the pope and Bishop Strossmayer, but tomorrow I will probably be serving the *Alliance Israélite* and the Rothschilds. Our governmental, ecclesiastical, and literary magnates are so impudent, and the public is so stupid, that one can expect anything. I, of course, am not depressed and I have adopted as my motto, 'If God does not give me up, the swine will not devour me.' But, all the same, one should be as careful as possible."[29]

In 1886 Solovyov felt for the first time that his youth was coming to an end; on the way from Djakovar to Zagreb he composed this poem in the train:

> The time of spring reveries had not yet passed,
> When winter arrived,
> And an early old age unexpectedly declared
> That my life had run its course.
> And above the precipices of aimless delusion
> Hung a gray mist.
> The soul does not feel its former suffering,
> Nor remember old wounds.
> And, breathing joyfully the mountain air,
> I prepare for a new path,
> Far from the flowers of withered May,
> From the hot dreams of summer.[30]

But after the air of the mountains of Croatia there awaited him in Russia the pernicious atmosphere of decaying tsarism and the fatal, unexpected denouement of his love of many years.

Endnotes for Part 2 - Chapter 3

1. *P*, vol. 2, 42.
2. Idem.
3. *P*, vol. 1, 181.
4. Ibid., 165.
5. *P*, vol. 2, 138.
6. Idem.
7. *P*, vol. 1, 181.
8. *SS*, vol. 9, 410-411.
9. *P*, vol. 3, 13.
10. *P*, vol. 2, 43.
11. *P*, vol. 4, 98- 99.
12. Unpublished.
13. *P*, vol. 2, 140.
14. *P*, vol. 4, 99.
15. Ibid., 99, 101.
16. Ibid., 101.
17. Ibid., 103, 102.
18. *P*, vol. 1, 167.
19. Ibid., 182.
20. Ibid., 190-191.
21. *P*, vol. 1, 191.
22. *Trudy vtorogo Velegrdaskogo s''ezda*, 145-160.
23. *Vladimir sviatoi* (Mosow: Put', 1913), 75.
24. *P*, vol. 3, 189.
25. Ibid., 194.
26. Ibid., 169.
27. *P*, vol. 1, 168.
28. *P*, vol. 3, 189.
29. *P*, vol. 2, 142.
30. *Stikh.*, No. 31; *SS*, vol. 12, 21.

Part 2 - Chapter 4

The Year 1887
The Fatal Denouement of a Joyless Love

The fatal denouement of a joyless love is
Not quiet sorrow,
but an hour of mortal torment.

V. Solovyov

Solovyov hardly expected the kind of persecutions that awaited him in Russia upon his return from Austria. In October 1886 he wrote to Stasyulevich, "Like a Red Indian I sing and remain calm amidst torture. While the religious censorship is tearing to pieces the highly innocent first volume of my *Theocracy*; the civil censorship, despite Feokistov's* kind letters to me, has squeezed out, apparently, my article 'The Sins of Russia',[1] which was sent to *Novosti*, according to that paper's request."[2] The second edition of *The Dogmatic Development* was forbidden "and even its original disappeared without a trace in the censor's apartment."[3] The chapter of *The History of Theocracy*, "On the Legislation of Moses" was absolutely forbidden under the pretext that "the quotations from the Bible in it were translated directly from Hebrew."[4] "The first volume of *Theocracy* appeared at the end of April in Zagreb, which is so remote from me on account of our Cerberean system that not only have I not been able to see my own work yet, but I don't know when I will."[5] On 25 May Kireev informed Solovyov that his book "had fallen into the hands of the religious censorship," which Solovyov described as "throwing the book into the lion's den."[6]

Solovyov now had to find new allies. Already in 1886 he began to publish his poems in *Vestnik Evropy* and entered into a lively correspondence with Stasyulevich. In 1887 he prepared a

* The head of the main department for matters relating to publishing. [Author's note.]

critique of Danilevsky's book *Russia and Europe* for *Vestnik Evropy*. This article, "Russia and Europe,"[7] was Solovyov's debut in *Vestnik Evropy* and the opening of a campaign against the Slavophiles, whose chief representative at the time was Nikolay Strakhov. In Solovyov's personal life disaster had occurred as well. During Christmas of 1886 Solovyov retreated to Sergiev Posad where he spent "all the so-called feasts (which are illegitimate and vain, as one prophet rightly calls them)."[8] On 16 December Solovyov wrote to Anna Aksakova who was living at Sergiev Posad, "I think I will come visit you on the evening of the first day of the holidays." From there he wrote to his sister Nadya, "I celebrated the New Year alone in two rooms and even forgot to ask for some wine. I think I will return on the twelfth for dinner (not to the university's, of course)... Tell Levushka[9] that I am living entirely on cheap olive oil from the icon lamp; therefore there won't be any poison in the letter he has been expecting from me, only wine and oil."

Apparently, Solovyov stayed not with Anna Aksakova, but at a hotel. "Yesterday (January first) I dined at Anna Aksakova's and today I will as well," he wrote his sister. Toward the end of December he informed Aksakova, "Mes affaires intimes, dont je vous ai parlé l'autre fois à Moscou et 'Troitsa' ont eu un dénouement inattendu et définitif à ce qu'il paraît. Et je reste maintenant 'on these ashes of my earthly hopes.' J'espère que c'est pour le mieux." In spite of the brave "j'espère que c'est pour le mieux" Solovyov was experiencing during this time "not quiet sorrow, but an hour of mortal torment."

> The fatal denouement of a joyless love
> Is not quiet sorrow, but an hour of mortal torment!
> Let life be an evil lie, but the heart, in dying,
> Knows suffering and pain, and on the threshold of paradise
> It still burns with the fire that will be extinguished in eternity.

For Solovyov the year 1887 had begun under an unlucky sign.

"During these weeks I have experienced, or have begun to experience, spiritual solitude with all its advantages and disadvantages," he wrote to Strakhov on 11 January 1887.[10] The tragic, unexpected end of his love of many years naturally inclined

Solovyov to the idea of embracing the monastic life. He wrote about this in a completely facetious way to Strakhov, "Aside from antediluvian monks, I have also been in touch with living ones who are courting me a great deal, wishing, apparently to purchase me at a low price, but I will not sell myself at even a high one."[11]

And more seriously he mentioned to , "The archimandrite and monks are courting me assiduously, wishing that I will become a monk, but I will think it over a great deal before deciding."[12]

Still more seriously he wrote to Archimandrite Antony (Vadkovsky), "If the situation were not such as you have described, I would now have a great desire to become a monk. But in the meantime, it is impossible."[13]

Through Strossmayer, the Jesuit Father Pierling let Solovyov know that the French writer Leroy-Beaulieu requested accurate information about his "religious system." On 31 January Solovyov wrote to Pierling in Paris.

> The task proposed by you and M. Leroy-Beaulieu will, I think, be more expediently fulfilled if I myself write in French, to the best of my abilities, a short but complete exposition of those concepts about religion and the Church that comprise, in my understanding, the principal foundations for the reunion of the Churches; there will also be included a philosophical justification of those three doctrines of the Catholic Church that form the main doctrinal barrier between her and the East: namely, the *Filioque*; the Immaculate Conception of the Most Holy Virgin; and finally, *infallibilitas Summi Pontificis ex cathedra*. All of this will form an article of 4 to 5 printed pages, which I have already begun to write under the title "Philosophie de l'Eglise universelle.[14]

The composition of "Philosophie de l'Eglise universelle" was, evidently, Solovyov's chief occupation at Sergiev Posad in January 1887. By the summer this article had developed into the large work *La Russie et l'Eglise Universelle* which replaced the second volume of *The History of Theocracy*.

In January 1887 a lively correspondence arose between Solovyov and another Jesuit, Father Martynov,[*] "the venerable companion of Pierling."[15] Martynov sent Solovyov a portrait of Chaadaev[†] and the book *The Procession of the Holy Spirit and the Universal Pontificate*, which was written by a German Catholic priest in St. Petersburg under the pseudonym "Astashkov." "I thank you for the portrait of Chaadaev," Solovyov wrote to Martynov "with whose writings I have become familiar only recently. Undoubtedly he represents a very important phenomenon in the intellectual history of Russia, if only as living refutation of that now apparently widespread opinion that Westernism and Nihilism are essentially one and the same thing."[16] In his letters to Martynov,[17] Pierling,[18] and ,[19] Solovyov rendered a very negative opinion about the work of the pseudo-Astashkov.

The first part of the book, according to Solovyov, "is too scholastic, and in the polemical places it reveals an inadmissible and unnecessary animosity (not speaking of various mistakes)... Aside from other inadequacies, the author of this little book, who is a foreigner living in Russia, does not show enough love for the nation that he wishes to enlighten. But without this, his very great zeal for the faith can hardly be productive. Our enemies of Church unity have already taken advantage of this case to wound me."

Meanwhile in Paris the Abbé Guettée, to whom Solovyov turned in 1876 for help in correcting the French of *Les principes de la religion universelle*, attacked him in the December issue of *Union chrétienne*. "I have read this article," Solovyov wrote to Martynov on 9 March 1887, "and found it perfectly absurd and undeserving of any real objection."[20]

---

[*] Ivan Martynov (1821-1894), Russian Jesuit, influential in the creation of Jesuits of the Eastern Rite.

[†] Pyotr Chaadaev (1794-1856), philosopher. Having served as an officer during the Napoleonic wars, Chaadaev lived for several years in Western Europe where he was exposed to the ideas of Hegel and Schelling as well as to Roman Catholicism. Returning to Russia in 1826 he lived in Moscow and resumed his friendship with Pushkin. As the author of a series of *Philosophical Letters* (written between 1829-1831) Chaadaev harshly criticized Russia's historic isolation from the West and the civilizing influences of Catholicism. After the publication of his first "Philosophical Letter" in 1836, Chaadaev was declared officially insane and placed under house arrest, and his works were forbidden to be published or mentioned in print.

At the end of March Solovyov delivered two lectures (in aid of indigent students) on the theme of "Slavophilism and the Russian Idea"; we know the content of these lectures from letters to Father Pierling on 24 March,[21] to Fet on 9 April,[22] and to Father Martynov on 14 April.[23] We also find the ideas behind these lectures in the article "Saint Vladimir and the Christian State," which appeared in the French journal *L'Univers* in 1886 and was translated into Russian by Grigory Rachinsky (Moscow: *Put'*, 1913). I have found a detailed discussion of the lectures and an account of the impression they made on the Slavophile public of Moscow in the archives of Lev Polivanov, thanks to the kindness of his son Ivan Polivanov. In a letter to his relative N. A. Demidov, Polivanov reports: "Solovyov's lecture was attended by all of that segment of Moscow society that represents the contemporary aristocracy, as well as that segment of non-aristocratic Moscow that is interested in philosophy, literature, and politics, and shares somehow or another the opinions of the Slavophiles."

Solovyov divided the history of the development of the Christian idea into the following episodes: Constantine the Great; Saint Vladimir; Peter the Great, who reinforced Christianity with western science; and Pushkin, who dissolved European culture in the Russian spirit. Now the Russian idea must bear its fruit; Solovyov wanted to *make manifest* the idea of the Slavophiles. "It is necessary to realize on earth the organization of the universal Church, with a single visible head: visible, because the invisible head is Christ; but I am speaking about the earthly organization of Christendom. There is one inevitable conclusion: a universal father for all Christians is necessary. It is inevitable for us to turn to that guardian of Church discipline that history has preserved."

"Greeted by loud applause," Solovyov's exit was accompanied by "a sepulchral and sullen silence." "The widow of Ivan Aksakov, who was now publishing all of her husband's articles, had just prepared a new volume, for which she had asked Solovyov to write a foreword, which he did; the volume was printed with this preface and was ready to be distributed. Returning from Solovyov's second and final lecture, she quickly cut out his foreword (and sent it back to him) and let the printers know that the same was to be done with the other copies."

By her action Anna Fyodorovna Aksakova had confirmed yet again one of her characteristic traits, which Solovyov described after her death. "For all the great kindness of her heart, there was nothing she resembled less than a lamb. Never in my life have I seen a more irritable, harsh, and irascible creature. She would not grow angry gradually, but would somehow suddenly flare up and begin to 'throw fire and flame' according to the French expression."[24] Solovyov forgave Anna Aksakova from the bottom of his heart and remained on the closest terms with her. He was, however, extremely angry with Moscow society, and on 4 April he penned the following "compliment to Moscow":[25]

Stupid city, foul city
Mix of Katkov and *kut'ia*[*]
Realm of obsessive slander
Boredom, sleep, and nonsense.

He declared to Fet that he himself "was as satisfied with his lecture as the Slavophile audience of Moscow was dissatisfied" and he consoled himself with the fact that "around two thousand rubles were collected for *shchi* and *kasha* [†] for poor students and that I said what I had wanted to say."[26] The compliment to Moscow was written on 4 April, but on the previous evening, the third, Solovyov composed the poem "My friend, now as before they have buried Adonis [Drug moi, prezhde, kak i nyne, Adonis otpevali]." At Easter he had informed his old friend Anna Fyodorovna, "I observed Holy Week as one should. At night I was at the Kremlin, but during the day I visited only the dead, and made no other visits... I wrote some bad poems one of which I include for you. Pobedonostsev would conclude from it that I am a pagan and do not believe in Christ, but you, I hope, will not come to this conclusion.

[*] Traditional dish of grains and raisins prepared for funerals and days of commemoration of the deceased.
[†] Cabbage soup and porridge, staples of the Russian diet.

My friend! Now, as before,
They have buried Adonis.
Wailing and weeping reigned in the desert,
The sorrowful women sobbed.

My friend! Now, as before,
Adonis has risen from the grave,
The blind evil of hostile forces
Does not threaten his sanctity.

My friend! Now, as before,
We have buried our love,
But in the distance, as a scarlet dawn,
Its rays are again glowing red.

But this is happening only in the poem, in fact there are no rays of any kind and no sort of scarlet dawn, but only that heavy copper that you saw in your dream...[*] I pray very poorly at this time of year because from Easter till Pentecost the Church canons forbid the kind of prayer that I am used to."[†]

But Solovyov's hopes that Aksakova would be more indulgent than Pobedonostsev were not realized; the poem about Adonis once again provoked her "fire and flame." In a letter of 28 April, written already at Fet's estate Vorobyovka, Solovyov humbly justified himself before Aksakova and tried to jest:

> By my foolish verses I have led you into a double misunderstanding:
>
> 1) I did not at all have in mind the Greco-Roman Adonis, invented by the poets, but the real Syrian Semitic Adonis or Adonai (which means Lord), who had nothing to do with Venus and Mars, but was an authentic prototype of Christ.

[*] In her dream Anna Aksakova had seen the words of Solovyov written in gold letters, but immediately afterwards he appeared crushed under the weight of a bag filled with copper. [Author's note.]

[†] From Easter to Pentecost kneeling is forbidden in the Orthodox Church. [Author's note.]

2) I was not thinking of any kind of lady, but added the last stanza only in order to finish the poem, which was inspired only by the image of the eternally buried and eternally resurrected God. Next, leaving me and my bad verse to the side, along with Luther (who filled his *Tischreden* with all sorts of indecencies), I must say about the Fathers of the Church, that their inability to appreciate beauty (whether in the form of mythological representations or in the form of interesting ladies) is a type of one-sidedness that I do not envy in the least. With them Christianity finds itself in its *most strained and exclusive* state, it is not free; this is not the highest form of Christianity… At night instead of French novels I am reading Swedenborg in Latin. My own Russian romance is at freezing point. For three months now I have had no news.

Solovyov's beloved Pustynka was now closed to him, and he decided to spend the summer at Fet's estate Vorobyovka. He settled there at the end of April and proposed to stay until October.[27] On 5 May he wrote to his sister Nadya: "I think of you, wandering in the park here; and paying heed to your solicitude about my health I have begun to drink, as of today, the mineral water from the spring here, in which, according to the investigations of experts, there is as much iron as in the waters of Zheleznovodsk in the Caucasus… I am more or less in good health and continue to follow a routine. Here heat and rain have begun to alternate, the birches and poplars have budded, the cherry trees are in bloom, the nightingales sing, and the fountain splashes…"

In the final sentence of this letter we recognize the landscape of Vorobyovka, familiar to us from Fet's *Evening Fires*. Let us say something about Solovyov's relations with his host. Solovyov was connected to Afanasy Afansevich Fet by family ties, in as much as Fet was close to Solovyov's maternal relatives the Brzhesskys. The Solovyovs maintained a kind of domestic cult of Fet, and for Vladimir he was the incarnation of pure poetry, "like a section of a true rainbow, shining over the ocean of human absurdity."[28] Reading

Fet's memoirs we can imagine all the charm of this man. Among his fellow writers Fet was distinguished by an unusual simplicity, modesty, genuine good will, and wit. It was difficult for even such a quarrelsome person as Turgenev to argue with him. In spite of the divergence of their worldviews, Solovyov felt himself at home with Fet and relaxed in his company. Indeed their worldviews were utterly different: Fet was an extreme conservative, while in the '80s Solovyov had entered the ranks of the Westernizing Liberals; Solovyov was a Christian, whereas Fet had, for all of his conservative respect for the Russian Church as one of the mainstays of the Russian way of life and state, an ironic attitude toward the fundamental dogmas of Christianity. In his mature years his philosophy was formed under the influence of both Schopenhauer and Goethe's pantheism. Solovyov always emphasized his disagreement with Fet on religious questions. A letter of 9 April 1887 begins with the words, "Dear Maria Petrovna, Christ is Risen! *Greetings*, Afanasy Afanasevich!" From Vorobyovka Solovyov wrote to his mother, "The miracle-working icon of the Mother of God of Kursk (from the Korenny monastery) was here: I carried it around the estate with Maria Petrovna." Apparently Solovyov and Maria Petrovna were in some kind of alliance against Afanasy Afanasevich.

After Fet's death, Solovyov was pursued by the thought that he was suffering in the other world. When Fet's beloved springtime arrived, Solovyov felt that his old friend was whispering to him with heavy sadness, "Remember me."[29] "Time cannot reconcile me with his grave."[30] And again, the same shade of Fet inspired Solovyov's reverie when he was travelling in 1890 in the Greek Archipelago. The death of him, who "fused the fragments of life into adamantine dreams"[31] was for Solovyov "a strange catastrophe," which he could never forget "with an alien, distant, dead grief."

In his drawing room Fet brought together the most incompatible people: Turgenev and Tolstoy; Solovyov and Strakhov. But Solovyov's growing liberalism at the beginning of the '90s led to a cooling of their relations. When Fet received the uniform of a *Kammerherr*, Solovyov wrote to his brother Mikhail:

There lived a poet
Known to all.
With old age
He became a fool.

He ended this letter with the bitter words, "Let us speak of how our life is warmed: / About Strakhov's friendship, about Fet's *Kammerherrship*."

But in the summer of 1887 this cooling off was still in the far distance. Solovyov entertained Fet by reciting Catullus to him by heart ("When I heard Catullus recited to me by heart with your lips [Kogda Katull mne naizust' tvoimi govoril ustami]"). They translated the *Aeneid* together and "muddled through 80 lines a day."[32] The sixth book was translated as a result of their combined efforts, but Solovyov translated on his own the seventh, ninth, and tenth books. In spite of the hastiness of the work, Solovyov's translation is extremely sonorous and is favorably distinguished from Fet's. For example:

Tebia to oplachet
Les angvitiiskii, tebia kristal'naia vlaga futsiny
Ozera volny tebia...[*]

During the same summer Solovyov also translated Virgil's fourth Eclogue "Pollion," but his main work was the composition of *La Russie et l'Eglise Universelle*. The outline and title of this book was not worked out immediately. Without abandoning the idea of continuing *The History of Theocracy*, in January Solovyov had already begun to write an article in French "Philosophie de l'histoire universelle." He sent the first part of it to Father Pierling and Father Martynov. Pierling found in this work superfluous "theorizing" and advised him to abridge it. On 14/26 July Solovyov responded to Pierling by remarking that in a work with such a title it was impossible "to manage without general notions and abstruse

[*] These lines are from *The Aeneid* Book VII: lines 759-760 and refer to the forest of Anguitia and the lake Fucinus that mourn the death of Umbro, a priest with the gift of curing snake bites, who was unable, however, of healing himself from a Trojan spear wound. The original reads: Te nemus Anguitiae, vitrea te Fucinus unda. / Te liquidi flevere lacus.

speculations."[33] He pointed out that he was writing a "Philosophy of Universal History," not a historical investigation, such as there ought to be in the following volumes of *Theocracy*. In the end he asked the Jesuit Fathers themselves to make the changes and abridgements in the exposition that they felt were necessary. "For my part, it would be perfectly absurd to publish something about the union of Churches that would not be approved by representatives of the Catholic Church." In the following letter, dated 17/29, July Solovyov informed Pierling of a change in the whole plan of the book and decided himself "to suppress abstruse speculations, i.e., the entire first part, which is already lying on my table, and to change the title of the book to 'La théocratie dans l'histoire et la réunion des Eglises.'"[34]

But Pierling objected to this title and in his next letter suggested to Solovyov a new one, "La Réunion des Eglises et les devoirs (la mission historique) de la Russie."[35] At the same time, Solovyov was thinking of a series of brochures under the general title "Russian Polemics against Catholicism in the Nineteenth Century":

1) The Slavophiles and the Jesuits
2) Metropolitan Filaret and the Universal Church
3) Archbishop Nikanor and Papal Primacy
4) Archbishop Anatoly (Avdy Vostokov) and A. Muravyov on Orthodoxy and Catholicism.[36]

On 31 August he wrote to Pierling, "In regard to the title, would not the simplest of all be *La Russie et l' Eglise Universelle*."[37] And on 18 September to his brother Mikhail, "I have abandoned everything theosophical and have called the work *La Russie et l'Eglise Universelle*."[38]

The second of the projected brochures, "Metropolitan Filaret," was incorporated as a whole into *La Russie*, but the other ones were never written. In his letters to Anna Aksakova, to whom Solovyov wrote almost weekly in the summer of 1887, we find entire pages from *La Russie*: including the attitude of Metropolitan Filaret to the universal Church, the legend of Saints Nicholas and Cassian, etc. Solovyov's contact and collaboration with the members of the Society of Jesus, of course, disturbed his friends. On 18/30 July he complained to Father Martynov that the zealots of Orthodoxy were aiming at him the heavy volumes of Samarin, where the most important place belonged to the "Letters about the Jesuits." "This is both sad and amusing."[39] Later on he quoted extracts from the letter of a young man who was conducting an investigation of Slavophile "theology." We understand from letter No. 27 to Martynov that this young man was Solovyov's brother Mikhail. "Thank you for your letter concerning Samarin's Jesuits." With four theses my father defended the Society of Jesus from the accusations of Samarin and came to the following conclusion:

> Which is better: active missionary work, which allows *provisoirement* accomodations with paganism, or the absence of missionary activity? The direction of conscience with the conditional allowance of indulgences, or the absence of any kind of direction? At the end of the book I found a few words that contain all of Slavophilism: we have no need of relative truth because we have the "*thirst* for unadulterated truth," i. e. we have no need for bread because we thirst for ambrosia, although we have no means of obtaining it.[40]

If in the summer of 1883 Dante had fed Solovyov's Catholic mood, then now Dante's place was taken by his guide in hell and purgatory, the wise Virgil. "Now that I am translating the *Aeneid* into Russian verse," Solovyov wrote to Pierling, "at certain moments I feel with a special vividness that mysterious and, at the same time, natural necessity that made Rome the center of the Universal Church:

> Dum domus Aeneae Capitoli immobili Saxum (   ) Accolet, imperiumque Pater Romanus habebit.

> As long as the house of Aeneas rests on the immovable stone of The Capitol, and the imperial authority belongs to the *Roman Father*.*

Is this not a prophecy! Of course, Virgil was not thinking of the pope."[41]

On 25 May Kireev informed Solovyov that the first volume of *Theocracy* had fallen into the hands of the religious censorship. In an irritable tone Solovyov begged Kireev to use his influence in higher spheres to obtain permission for the book. "It seems as though I am picking on you, dear and respected Aleksandr Alekseevich. I feel very badly, and not so much from large-scale afflictions, against which there are moral remedies, as from petty and pointless oppressions, which do not reach the soul and do no bodily harm, but only strike at the nerves."[42] Solovyov soon learned of the "unconditional prohibition" of his book in Russia.[43] As far as Kireev, on whom Solovyov placed his hopes, was concerned, this last Mohican of Slavophilism, having perused the work on 20 July sent its author a very bitter letter, which Solovyov found "not only stupid, but also false."

"You tell me," Kireev wrote, "that you have tried to exclude everything that could give grounds for its being banned; but *in practice* you have excluded nothing; you have failed to notice that your attitude to Orthodoxy is far from objective, far from dispassionate; that all your sympathies are on the side of Rome. I say this not to reproach you; what can be done when you make things turn out in such a way, when your expositions yield such results!... Can one even expect from an author a just appreciation of the facts, to expect an objective judgment, when you say: You are in need of righteousness and purification. I will perform the necessary operation on you and raise you to a higher degree, I will lead you to Rome, where they will teach you, little fool, good sense... And how much talent and knowledge you have wasted... Indeed, your book produces a very heavy impression."[44]

On 4 August Solovyov wrote to Aksakova:

---

* From *The Aeneid*, book IX: lines 448-449. In his citation Solovyov adds the Greek word for stone in parentheses and transliterates the second line in Cyrillic letters.

> A few days ago Kireev sent me in connection with the ban on my book a letter that seemed to me not only stupid, but also false. Since I love him, all the same, and consider him essentially a good man, I have stated with complete candor my opinion and justified myself to him in many pages. I hope that this will be of some use to him. I have kept a copy of this long letter and will read it to you when we meet. I am beginning to notice that an "embittered mind" is forming in me. It is terribly difficult to escape from this circle: if you suppress sensitivity, malice develops, if you don't want to be an animal, you become a devil. Don't think, however, that I have, in fact, become satanic; I am only speaking about the extremes between which one can waver.

Solovyov's letter to Kireev, which covers more than eight printed pages,[45] is actually quite malicious. In some places it is witty and brilliant, in other places, coarse. Solovyov, with all his might, attacks the "imaginary" dogmas of Orthodoxy, for example, that the Holy Spirit proceeds from the Father alone, without any participation of the Son; that the Most Holy Virgin, although called by the church Most Immaculate, is, however, not without sin, etc. "I entreat you by the shade of Khomyakov himself, who with his omniscience converted Dioscurus to Arianism and forced the fifth-century Council of Chalcedon to condemn Honorius who lived in the seventh century, by this dauntless and upright shade I entreat you... My love for the universal Orthodox Church and the hostility that flows from it for your "camp" (i. e. the enemies of the Church) are perfectly conscious and do not form the result, as you oddly suggest, but the *motive* of all my writings. My love for the Eternal Companion of God I will carry into eternity, but my animosity to her enemies will be extinguished only by the triumph of her cause or with my death..." The end of the letter is especially interesting:

> Such is Catholicism, which always openly stood for the principle of *authority* and, in certain cases, *coercion* as well, and has never declared itself to be a religion of spiritual freedom, this very Catholicism has for more than a hundred years withstood in its own boundaries unflinchingly and

> without harm not only the free criticism but also the wrathful attacks of its enemies! Show me one Catholic country, or even one city on the whole earth, where the Catholic religion has not been publicly condemned and persecuted in every way without, however, the slightest damage to its spiritual power. If only for a minute let your imaginary free Orthodoxy be placed in such a position; if only for a minute it allowed the support of the state to rest; if only for a minute it believed in its spiritual power! What then! On one hand the Old Ritualists, on the other, the Jesuits, would tear it apart in a moment and not a trace would be left! According to your conscience, Aleksandr Alekseevich, however much you assume an air of self-assurance, you know very well in the depth of your soul that the words about the Church, against which the gates of hell will not prevail–that these words were not written about you… I wish you health that is better than mine, and as much spiritual peace as I myself possess.

The good-natured Kireev evidently understood the tormented state in which Solovyov had written to him and replied in a very gentle and conciliatory fashion, "You have placed yourself in a false position and all your attacks are not directed where they ought to be."[46]

Thus Solovyov spent the summer of 1887, dividing his time between the composition of *La Russie*, the translation of the *Aeneid*, the writing of countless letters, and reading Swedenborg in Latin at night. In spite of following a regular routine that summer, rising at eight and going to bed at midnight, drinking mineral water and bathing, Solovyov was suffering from very poor health; he could not escape his neuralgia and insomnia. What a contrast to the previous summer in Zagreb! The poor state of her guest's condition distressed the good Maria Petrovna Shenshina. "Having fed me to the point of losing consciousness, Maria Petrovna remarks with sadness, 'What on earth does he live on? He eats nothing!"

In his letters to his mother, Solovyov reported that his health was excellent in order not to upset her. But in a letter written to his sister Nadya before his departure in the autumn from Vorobyovka, we read the following sad lines, "Now that the summer has passed, I can tell you (in secret from mamá) that this entire summer, despite every kind of care from my hosts, I was sick with fevers, neuralgia, and insomnia. Therefore I rarely wrote; one cannot lie on a weekly basis."

Aside from the ban on *The History of Theocracy*, Solovyov also felt his separation from Sofya Khitrovo. In his letters to Aksakova of that summer the curtain is lifted above the tormenting question of the possibility of Solovyov's marrying Sofya Petrovna, the first step to which was, inevitably, her divorce. Solovyov developed the thought that divorce is permissible from the Christian point of view. In an ideal church marriage, an ideal moral tie is an essential condition; only then can marriage be contracted for eternal life. Like the sacrament of the Eucharist, when this sacrament is worthily received, it becomes a vessel of life, but in the contrary case, it can only plant the seed of eternal separation, and then divorce is not only permissible, it becomes absolutely necessary sooner or later. "I agree completely with Ivan Sergeevich that my marriage to a divorcée would be fatal and unworthy and I am very glad that it did not occur. But this is not because the first marriage was absolutely indissoluble (the Church does not recognize any such thing, as it allows a second marriage for widows, even for a divorced couple), but simply for the sake of the children who are guilty of nothing, who would be placed by *such* a marriage in a tragic position between their father and mother. This is the *only* moral impediment in this matter."

Anna Aksakova's negative opinion of Sofya Petrovna bothered Solovyov. "I am sorry that you have, apparently, some kind of prejudice against the poor lady of my heart. She is a very remarkable and very unfortunate woman."

In Solovyov's love the note of gentle compassion sounds more and more often. On 17 September, Sofya Petrovna's name-day, he wrote one of his best poems, – the "fruit of a sleepless night":[47]

Poor friend! The path has exhausted you,
Dark is your gaze, and your garland is crumpled,
You will come to me to rest.
The sunset, burning out, has grown dim.

Where you have been, and where you have come from,
Poor friend, loving you, I will not ask;
Only utter my name
And in silence I will press you to my heart.

Death and Time reign on the earth, –
But do not call them masters;
Everything that revolves disappears in gloom,
Only the sun of love remains motionless.[48]

In general, Solovyov did not write serious poetry at Vorobyovka. It seemed to him somewhat immodest to compete with Fet in his own home. But Solovyov did not expect that the poem "Poor friend" composed at Vorobyovka "would make this place immortal even had *Evening Fires* never been written." Solovyov himself gave little importance to his own poetry.

Solovyov left Vorobyovka on 22 September for Rozhdestvino, the estate of the Sollogubs near Serpukhov. "I need to see *Sollogubikha*[*] in order to correct my French manuscript, a third of which is already prepared. They have promised to publish it in Paris without expenses on my part," he wrote to his brother.[49]

From Rozhdestvino Solovyov informed Aksakova that Dr. Trifonovsky, having examined him, found that all his organs were in good condition, but detected a predisposition to liver disease and strongly urged him to abstain from meat and wine. Indian summer or "*l'été de St. Martin*" had arrived at Rozhdestvino and Solovyov walked a great deal and felt himself to be "well enough." He returned to Moscow on 4 November, having stayed at the Sollogubs' longer than he had intended.[†50] Insomnia continued to plague him; on 4/16 October he wrote to Pierling, " The sorry state of my health worries me... My greatest suffering consists in the inability to sleep if there is the slightest sound."[51]

On 24 November he informed Pierling that he was sending him in Paris pages 46–121 of his French manuscript. "Along with

---

[*] Countess Natalya Mikhailovna Sollogub. [Author's note.]

[†] In a letter to Aksakova of 26 October he states, "I return to Moscow on 4 November." [Author's note.]

the previous ones, these comprise about half of the whole work as the next two parts amount to less than the first."[52] In December he sent the first article about Russia and Europe to *Vestnik Evropy* (Nos. 2 and 4, 1888).

On 19 November Solovyov reported to Aksakova about his visit to Metropolitan Mikhail. "Metropolitan Mikhail is *personally* quite nice, but as a representative of the Church he plunged me into despair and bewilderment. He himself speaks of how much 'the abomination of desolation' exists in the whole Eastern Church and then adds, 'I have only one thing to say to the Catholic missionaries: convert the Muslims and the Jews, but *leave us in peace!*' According to his own testimony it should be expressed differently: leave us in our swamp, or rather on our dung heap. When I asked what kind of way there might be out of those horrors about which he complained, I received no definite answer. Nonetheless, he is, in fact, much better than our Nikanors and I will go see him again."

On 27 November Countess Efimovskaya, who was the Catholic nun Mother Ekaterina, visited Solovyov. He wrote to Aksakova that she was well disposed toward him and that she was "not too clerical" (*peu cléricale*). She gave him a blessed medal that depicted the icon of the Lesna Mother of God, which is venerated by both Orthodox and Catholics and which Solovyov interpreted as a symbol of the reunion of Churches.

At this time the relations between Solovyov and his old teacher Ivantsov-Platonov were ruined for good. Writing on 27 November to Aksakova, Solovyov remarked with irritation, "C'est un grand diplomate que le père Ivantsov surtout dans les petits affaires et dans les rapports purement personnels, où la sincerité est absolument nécessaire." In the same letter he also reported that three days before (on 25 November) Lev Tolstoy had visited him and had accused himself of certain strange deeds. "I have to go see him and act prudently (*être sur ses gardes*)."

At Christmas Solovyov again left for Sergiev Posad and stayed this time at Aksakova's. On 30 December he wrote to his brother:

> I had a good sleep in the coach en route and arrived at Anna Fyodorovna's hale and fresh. It's quite comfortable here, but as a result of my fits of lovesickness I sleep little and poorly and my face looks like a ghost's. Today I was at Father Varnava's, who told me that he loves me like a son and then advised me to marry without fail, but he used such strange expressions that there was no way to know if he was speaking about a real wife, or about the Mother of God, or about the Church.
>
> In spite of my emaciated condition I am writing at full speed and am depicting great things in dubious French (perhaps "the air is dry as a nail").[53]

With Anna Aksakova, Solovyov also discussed marriage. In his letter to her of 27 November he remarked about Countess Efimovskaya, who to his eyes "appeared younger and better": "It is fortunate that she is in a monastery. You see that Providence is clearly against my marrying. In order to put an end to this question, here is my ultimatum: a widow between ages 25 and 45, very pleasant and very wealthy. As for young ladies, I declare with Pius IX: *non possumus*."

Anna Aksakova's nephew Nikolay Tyutchev, who as a boy spent the Christmas of 1888 with his aunt at Sergiev Posad, has told me that on Christmas Eve after listening to the conversations of his aunt with Solovyov he was afraid of going to sleep in his room. Their talk was entirely about mysterious phenomena, prophetic dreams, and ghosts. In his article "The Aksakovs" Solovyov says of Anna Fyodorovna, "For her the supernatural world was reality, she lived half in a world of prophetic dreams, visions, and revelations. Just my memories of Anna Fyodorovna inevitably evoke the recollection of mystical facts."[54]

Informing Anna Fyodorovna of his plans to come for Christmas in 1886, Solovyov remarked, "It will be very interesting to hear from you about our special province. It has been a long time since I have had any contact with the other world and my soul is somehow turning gray from this."

On 15/27 January Solovyov notified Pierling, "My French book is completed," and expressed the intention of "presenting it at the very beginning of spring to Fathers Pierling and Martynov in Paris."[55]

Solovyov had still not abandoned the idea of writing and publishing in Paris, besides *La Russie*, the second volume of *Theocracy*.[56] He thought he would go to Paris for two or three weeks in order to *lancer le livre* and find a publisher, and then stay for awhile in Austria.[57]

On 23 January Solovyov made the promise to the strict Anna Fyodorovna "to live in Paris as on Mt. Carmel." He also needed to leave Russia in order to "depart from Egypt" in a dignified manner, that is, to terminate his romance with Sofya Khitrovo. "I assure you with my hand on my heart that I am capable of following strict morals and that it would be even better for me to do so, but this does not always happen (*mais cela ne va pas*). Farewell. Don't be angry with me."[58]

The appearance of "Russia and Europe" in the February and April issues of *Vestnik Evropy* was the signal for Solovyov's final break with nationalistic Orthodox Moscow. He was christened a liberal and Stasyulevich called this article "a fine work."[59]

At the end of February Solovyov quarreled definitively with Ivantsov-Platonov and in his letter to Aksakova of 2 March he calls him his "former friend." "My former friend Ivantsov has published a little book in which he refutes simultaneously Catholicism and all the Protestant sects. In the present conditions of our press to polemicize against Catholicism in Russia means an attack on an opponent who is bound; this is simply a *dishonorable act*, after which I no longer wish to see Ivantsov. I am very indulgent toward personal weaknesses and vices, and if this respectable archpriest stole or broke the seventh commandment it would in no way disturb our friendship. But in questions of social morality I am obliged to be intolerant."[60]

In March Solovyov went to St. Petersburg where he was received with enthusiasm. "In St. Petersburg," he wrote to Pierling, "they have accepted me with such *empressement* in various circles of society, beginning with the highest and ending with the 'intellectual proletariat,' that instead of the ten days I had intended, I spent a whole month there and did not notice how the time passed. What you write concerning my article somewhat amazes me. That the pseudo-patriotic clique that I termed the 'grunting and howling incarnation of the national idea' responded to this compliment with the same degree of abuse was thoroughly natural and, as far as I was concerned, predictable."[61]

The phrase "What you write concerning my article somewhat amazes me" marks the beginning of Solovyov's divergence from the Jesuits that was in the offing; evidently Father Pierling did not approve very much of this liberal-Westernist article. Solovyov's ties with autocratic Orthodox Russia were broken, in the West the Jesuits were expecting him in Paris, and in April there was a projected meeting with Bishop Strossmayer at the Vatican, but already before his departure, it was clear that from now on, temporarily cut off from both Moscow and the Vatican, Solovyov would be his own man only in St. Petersburg in the circle of Stasyulevich, among the liberal aristocracy, the "intellectual proletariat," and the Jews.

"The sympathy of the best part of Russian society is guaranteed for me," Solovyov wrote Pierling on 7/19 April, "but in regard to the worst part, I can only quote the motto you are already familiar with: 'If God does not give me up, the swine won't devour me.' I have already obtained a passport and, in view of a further fall in the exchange rate that is threatening, French bank notes. I plan to leave within a week and, after spending about two days in Karlsruhe, I will present myself to you. If you would send me at Karlsruhe, *poste restante*, the address of a hotel in Paris that you could recommend to me, I would be very grateful to you. I require a hotel that is inexpensive and, more importantly, *quiet*. There is still one more difficulty: I have been a *vegetarian for a very long time* (although not pedantically), and therefore a pension with an obligatory table d'hôte would not be convenient for me. But I hope that something can be arranged."[62]

Since this letter is dated 7/19 April we can assume that Solovyov left Moscow around 20 April (old style).

Endnotes for Part 2 - Chapter 4

1. *P*, vol. 2, 187-191.
2. *P*, vol. 4, 28-29.
3. *P*, vol. 2, 128-129.
4. Idem.
5. *P*, vol. 2, 126.
6. Idem.
7. *Vestnik Evropy* 26 (1888); *SS*, vol. 5, 82-147.
8. *P*, vol. 1, 25.
9. Lev Lopatin.
10. *P*, vol. 1, 25.
11. Ibid., 26.
12. *P*, vol. 1, 171.
13. *P*, vol. 3, 191.
14. Ibid., 138.
15. Ibid., 146.
16. Ibid., 18.
17. Ibid., 20.
18. Ibid., 142.
19. *P*, vol. 1, 173.
20. *P*, vol. 3, 21; see also the letter to Kireev, *P*, vol. 2, 131.
21. *P*, vol. 3, 142.
22. Ibid., 115.
23. Ibid., 23.
24. *P*, vol. 3 (1st edition, 1911), 277.
25. *Stikh*. 7th ed., 363.
26. *P*, vol. 3, 115.
27. *P*, vol. 3, 143.
28. Ibid., 119.
29. *Stikh*. , 142.
30. *Stikh*. 118.
31. Ibid., 161.
32. *P*, vol. 4, 106.
33. *P*, vol. 3, 150.
34. Ibid., 152-153.
35. Ibid., 157.
36. Ibid., 156.
37. Idem.
38. *P*, vol. 4, 113.

39. *P*, vol. 3, 25.
40. Ibid., 26.
41. Ibid. 155.
42. *P*, vol. 2, 127.
43. *P*, vol. 3, 148.
44. *Russkaia mysl'* 7/8 (1917): 137-138.
45. Ibid., 138-147.
46. *Russkaia mysl'* 7/8 (1917): 147-148.
47. *P*, vol. 4, 114.
48. *Stikh.*, 93.
49. *P*, vol. 4, 113.
50. In his letter to Aksakova of 26 October he states, "I return to Moscow on 4 November."
51. *P*, vol. 3, 157.
52. *P*, vol. 4, 160.
53. Ibid., 115.
54. *P*, vol. 4 (1st edition, 1923), 275; *SS*, vol. 12, 482.
55. *P*, vol. 3, 162.
56. Ibid., 163.
57. Idem.
58. Unpublished.
59. *P*, vol. 3, 162.
60. Unpublished.
61. *P*, vol. 3, 165.
62. Ibid., 166.

Part 2 - Chapter 5

Trip to Paris
Russia and the Universal Church

> Open your doors to them, you the key-bearer of Christ, and may the gates of history be for them and the whole world the gates of the Kingdom of God!
>
> *La Russie et l'Eglise Universelle*

Solovyov celebrated the Orthodox Easter of 1888 in Baden. On 25 April/7 May he informed his mother, "I am writing from Baden-Baden where I have celebrated Easter. Just imagine, not only was I in the Russian church, but for the first time in my life I even fully observed the entire Paschal service: the Midnight Vigil, Matins, the Liturgy, and then Vespers. I broke the fast with the princely family of Baden (Maria Maksimilianovna and her husband). There was a sumptuous meal but I ate only *paskha* and salad, and drank champagne."[1]

From the phrase in this letter "tomorrow I will be in Paris" we can gather that Solovyov arrived there on 8 May (old style). In Paris Solovyov made many new acquaintances and worked energetically. "You think that I am resting in Paris," he wrote to Stasyulevich, "but on the contrary, here I recall my stay in St. Petersburg as a time of *dolce far niente*."[2]

As we shall see later, Solovyov relations with the Jesuit Fathers Pierling and Martynov would cool somewhat, but he immediately acquired many new friends among writers (Leroy-Beaulieu, de Voguë), politicians (Loiseau, Mignard, Baron d'Avril), and clerics (de Pascal). He became especially close to Eugène Tavernier and his letters to him, which testify to their intimacy, have been published in the fourth volume of Solovyov's correspondence.[3] In order to acquaint the French public with his views, before progressing to the publication of *La Russie et l'Eglise Universelle*, on 25 May Solovyov read his paper "L'Idée russe" in French at the salon of Princess Sayn-Wittgenstein. On this occasion Solovyov criticized the Caesaro-papist structure of Russia more daringly and candidly than he had ever done before and with quotations from Ivan Aksakov portrayed the sorry state of the Russian Church, which had turned into "one of the ministries of state."

"Christian Russia, in imitation of Christ Himself, must submit the power of the state (the royal power of the Son) to the authority of the Universal Church (the priesthood of the Father) while assigning a proper place to social freedom (the action of the Spirit). United in its absolutism, the Russian Empire poses only threats of strife and endless wars; if it desires to serve the Universal Church and the task of social organization, it should take them under its protection and bestow on the family of nations peace and blessings."[4] On 14/26 June Solovyov wrote to Aksakova from Paris:

> After my arrival in Paris I dreamt of Ivan Sergeevich for the first time. It was a very clear and, apparently, significant dream. It began as though you and I were sorting papers and reading the printed proofs of the letters of I. S. Some kind of misunderstanding arose and you sent me to the grave of I. S. to inquire directly of him. Near the grave was an unfinished house. I entered and saw I. S. who was very ill. He told me to follow him and we went into another building, which was large and magnificent. Here I. S. suddenly became young and flourishing. He embraced me and said, all of us, myself included, are helping you. At this point I asked him, You are not angry with me, I. S. because I did not agree with Slavophilism? He said, yes, a bit, a bit, but this is not important. Then we returned to the unfinished house and I. S. again changed, his face becoming pale gray, and he fell from weakness. I seated him in a red armchair with wheels and he said, I cannot breathe here, I cannot live here, it is better to go back there. Then I pushed him in his chair toward the magnificent building – but at this point I was woken up. In the morning I recalled more details of this dream, but they

have now become blurred. This must have been either on the 27th or 28th of April (old style)...

L'Idée russe, which was published as a separate brochure, "enjoyed great success in Parisian society." In the Catholic newspaper *L'Univers* Solovyov's new friend Tavernier published an enthusiastic review on 2 July:

> Penseur, M. Soloviev l'est avec une incontestable superiorité. Il jette à profusion des idées pleines et originales. Son imagination est aussi riche que sa raison est solide. Il est vraiment à la hauteur de la tâche, qu'il accepte, qu'il s'avance avec confiance dans la voie glorieuse qu'il s'est ouverte. Ses frères français l'accueilleront avec affection et avec fierté; ils le soutiendront de leurs prières et de leurs applaudissments.

"About my brochure *L'Idée russe,*" Solovyov wrote to Fet on 6 October, "there were many laudatory articles in various French and Belgian journals and *revues* (for the most part religious). Incidentally, they praise the purity of my French, which I have actually perfected of late."[5]

Writing to his brother, Solovyov relates that Voguë asked, "Où ce coquin de Solovief a-t-il pris son français?"[6]

The newspaper *L'Univers* opened its pages to Solovyov. On 4, 11, and 19 August he published in it the article "Saint Vladimir et l'Etat chrétien," which appears to be a reworking of the lecture delivered in Moscow in March 1887 "Slavophilism and the Russian Idea."

As can be imagined, Solovyov's appearance at the salon of Princess Wittgenstein and *L'Idée russe* created a very unfavorable impression in Russian government spheres and threatening rumors reached him. On 15/27 July Solovyov wrote to Fet from Paris, "From Russia I am being kept informed about various absurd slanders in newspapers about me... I am afraid... lest there be any difficulty about my return from abroad."[7] And still more strongly he expressed himself to Stasyulevich on 11 August, "From St. Petersburg threatening news has been coming. I, for my part, have taken the decision to return, in any case, to Russia, but apparently not to St. Petersburg or Moscow, but somewhere a bit further."[8]

At the end of August Solovyov stayed at the home of Leroy-Beaulieu, *Bon repos*, in Viroflay near Versailles. Leroy-Beaulieu had left for the country to visit his mother-in-law, leaving his summerhouse and garden at the disposal of his Russian friend. "This garden," Solovyov wrote to Fet "is very beautiful and the proximity to the forest of St.-Cloud makes my residence an earthly paradise–before the creation of Eve, as I find myself in utter solitude. However, one can speak of paradise here only in comparison with the hotel in Paris, which was filled with noisy and ill-mannered Americans. But for a real paradise at my *Bon repos* besides Eve, there is a great deal missing, for example the rivers *Phison*, *Gihon*, *Hiddekel*, and Euphrates. Joking aside, without water nature loses half of its beauty."[9]

On 18 September an article by the Krakow correspondent titled "A View of the Religious History of Russia according to the Articles of Mr. Solovyov" appeared in *L'Univers*.

"I *extremely* regret that they published the article from Krakow in *L'Univers* without warning me," Solovyov wrote to Tavernier from Viroflay. "I did not know the author, nor his intentions, but I find in his article incredible mistakes and such a hatred for Russia which *L'Univers*, in my opinion, should not encourage. But as the deed is done, I am sending you a refutation with the request that it be printed in the same type and in the same place as the Polish article, that is, on the front page."[10] Solovyov's objections appeared in *L'Univers* on 22 September. Pointing out the coarse historical mistakes of the Polish author, Solovyov asserts the following:

1) The religion of Russia, if one understands by this term the faith of the people and worship, is fully Orthodox and Catholic.
2) The false and anti-Catholic doctrines that are taught in our seminaries and religious academies are not binding for the body of the Russian Church and in no way affect the faith of the people.

3) The ecclesiastical administration of Russia, which is non-canonical, schismatic, and subject (*lata sententia*) to anathema according to the third canon of the Seventh Ecumenical Council, is formally rejected by a significant part of Orthodox Russia (the Old Ritualists) and tolerated half-heartedly by the rest for want of something better.[11]

In October Solovyov completed his work *La Russie et l'Eglise Universelle*. On 18/30 November he wrote to his brother from Zagreb, "I tarried in France for a very legitimate reason: I was arranging and then successfully settled the publication of the entire book, moreover I significantly abridged the first two parts (written in Russia) and wrote a large third part."[12]

We see that Father Pierling, to whom Solovyov sent the first pages of his French manuscript in 1887, advised him to shorten the work and leave out "abstruse speculations."[13] From the very first pages Father Pierling was probably disturbed by Solovyov's mysticism. In the end, Solovyov "abandoned everything theosophical"[14] and in Paris wrote a whole new third part, which had been unacceptable to many Catholics by virtue of its theosophy.

Solovyov's work on the ending of *La Russie* did not go well at first. Finally, on 4/16 October he wrote to Tavernier from Viroflay, "Hurrah! I have found a satisfactory form in which to conclude my book. Everything that I must say at the end arranged itself in the most unexpected way. Yesterday (Monday) I did not eat at all, I drank only black coffee and water with sugar in it, and this helped. I wrote from noon to 11 at night. The work that remains (to reduce the superfluous, to strengthen the main point, which I have read to you, and to give it all a more literary form) is work that is more tedious than difficult. I hope this will not take more than eight days."[15]

There remained only to find a publisher. On 12/24 November Solovyov wrote to Stasyulevich, "Father Pierling, a Russian Jesuit, has declared to me orally and in writing that he can take no part in the publication of my book, *as a consequence of the divergence of our views*."[16] Joseph Mignard introduced Solovyov to the publisher Albert Savine, who, in fact, published *La Russie*. At the end of October

Solovyov gave his manuscript to Savine, but without a preface, which he wrote in Zagreb on his way back to Russia.[17]

On 21 August/6 September Solovyov wrote to Fet, "I will stay in Viroflay until the 22 (the 10th of September Russian style) [sic]… After spending three or four days in Paris I will travel to Moscow via Lyons, Lausanne, Vienna, Zagreb, and Krakow."[18] Solovyov stayed, however, significantly longer in France and left only at the beginning of November.

Tavernier reported that Solovyov was in a fairly depressed mood. Here, in Paris, he disagreed with his Jesuit friends, who accused him of heresy–while in Russia he could look forward to confinement in the Solovki monastery. But he courageously declared to Tavernier, "I shall go to bear witness to the truth." In order to protect himself from the machinations of Pobedonostsev and Company, he decided to appeal to Emperor Alexander III. However, this letter, whose rough draft has survived, was not sent to the tsar.

Solovyov's return trip to Russia led through Zagreb, Vienna, and Krakow. In Zagreb he stayed an entire month, which was longer than he had intended. Here he completed his "enormous foreword" to *La Russie*, which comprised "at least 50 printed pages."[19] On 28 November Solovyov informed Tavernier that his preface would be ready "the day after tomorrow".[20] In Zagreb Solovyov stayed, as he had two years previously, at the home of Canon , "in the most canonical way"; "I rose at 8 and went to bed at 12:30 and every morning I attended Mass in the splendid Gothic cathedral."[21]

From Zagreb Solovyov once again went to Djakovar to see Bishop Strossmayer and read to him his foreword to *La Russie*. In Djakovar Solovyov also celebrated Catholic Christmas, the Croatian . His impressions of Strossmayer differed from those of 1886. During these two years the shared plans of Strossmayer and Solovyov had suffered defeat, and Solovyov had to confess again that "the goal is still far off." "He is ill," Solovyov wrote to Tavernier about the bishop, "he has aged in body and become hardened in spirit, but, all the same, he is expansive and eloquent."[22] And in a letter to his brother Mikhail he wrote:

> I have spent these last few days in Djakov (-ar) with Strossmayer. I celebrated with them their . All the children of the town, who had been divided into several groups, came to perform "Bethlehem" and sang very charming and touching Croatian songs. Strossmayer himself is not well; he is in pain and has aged. He was, as always, exceedingly kind to me. He sent a copy of *L'Idée russe* to the Pope. The Pope said, "*Bella idea, ma fuor d'un miraculo è cosa impossibile.*" I am very glad that I came to visit Strossmayer, perhaps we won't see each other again.[23]

In Zagreb Solovyov read the response of the "old cat,"[24] Strakhov, to *Russia and Europe* and prepared his rebuttal, which appeared in the January 1889 edition of *Vestnik Evropy* under the title "About Sins and Diseases." At this time Solovyov was hoping that matters with Strakhov would not lead to a complete rupture. "Strakhov, whom I love," he wrote his brother, "but whom I have always considered a proper pig, has not perplexed me at all with his latest mazurka and, although I have abused him in print as the worst scoundrel, this does not in any way change our intimately friendly and even tender relations."[25] In a letter accompanying an article to Stasyulevich, Solovyov commented, "If you find some personal remark too coarse or some joke too heavy, please strike it out... I know that in certain circles Strakhov has recently begun to enjoy the reputation of an authority, and from my perspective exposing his oriental sins is a task not without use, very tedious as it is. This is the first and, I hope, last article in this genre that I am to write, and yesterday I felt great relief after putting the final pages in the mail."[26]

On 12/24 November Solovyov informed Stasyulevich, "From Zagreb I will be travelling to St. Petersburg."[27] As the only letter to Tavernier from Krakow is undated, the editor has provided the note: probably January 1889.[28] The letters from Vienna are dated 28 December,[29] 29 December,[30] and 6 January.[31] We know that Solovyov celebrated Catholic Christmas in Djakovar, so he must have arrived in Vienna between 26 and 28 December. In a letter of 28 December to his brother Mikhail he remarks, "I am writing to you soon after my arrival in Vienna, the last few days I spent in Djakovar..."[32] The last letter to Stasyulevich from Vienna is dated 25 December/6 January so it is obvious that having left Djakovar, Solovyov arrived in Vienna and stayed on there. In addition we have an undated letter to Anna Aksakova that reads, "New Year's greetings, dear A. F.; I will celebrate it somewhere on the railway between Warsaw and St. Petersburg." But this proposition did not materialize. On the first day of Christmas (old style), while offering his New Year's greetings to Stasyulevich, Solovyov reported, "I thought I would celebrate it (the New Year) in St. Petersburg, but I have been held up here on account of a few books that I need, which I didn't manage to read in Paris and which are not located in the libraries of St. Petersburg."[33] Evidently, at the beginning of January (old style) Solovyov left Vienna for Krakow where he spent several weeks before returning to Russia. In Krakow his life was "distracted but virtuous." "All the same I was able to get something read," he wrote to Tavernier. "Aside from Polish books I read Molina's *De Concordia gratiae cum libero arbitrio* and the posthumous work of Cardinal Franzelin *De Ecclesia Christi*. Among novels I have skimmed both volumes of Renan's *History of the People of Israel*."[34]

Solovyov's mood on his return trip to Russia was reasonably good and elevated, despite the now established hostility of "the two camps." "I am, thank God, enjoying complete spiritual equilibrium and good health."[35] "It is now more than eight months that I have found myself in this spiritual state, which confuses me as I find it positively difficult to say whether this is a state of grace or the state of Mr. Pobedonostsev."[36]

Solovyov knew that both the vengeance of his enemies and the slander of his friends awaited him in Russia (see the letter to Anna Aksakova and compare with the letter to his brother Mikhail, *Pis'ma*, vol. 4 122). But he also knew that he had defenders and true friends, "Give my best regards to those friends," Solovyov wrote to Mikhail from Vienna, "who are a mountain for me, and also to those who are small hills and even a hummock."[37] He especially foresaw hostility to him in Moscow. "In general, I am not disposed *to live* in Moscow for a multitude of reasons. In other respects I am excessively impressionable, perhaps because, like a premature baby, I possess skin that is too thin."[38] Solovyov returned directly to St. Petersburg from Austria, but at the end of February we find him already "under the shade of Lenten Moscow."[39]

It is now time for us to become acquainted, even if in general terms, with *La Russie et l'Eglise Universelle*. It consists of three parts; the first two were written in Paris in the summer of 1888, while the long preface was composed in Zagreb in November of the same year. The first part, "The State of Religion in Russia and in the Orthodox East," has a polemical character. In it Solovyov proves that neither the official Russian Church nor the Old Ritualists, nor the Eastern patriarchates possess a true religious administration. The Church of Russia, contrary to the third canon of the Seventh Ecumenical Council, is governed by the secular authority of the emperor. Among the Old Ritualists Solovyov perceives "the deepest ignorance, an ultra-democratic tendency, and the spirit of anarchy."[40]

The attempts to find a center of Church unity somewhere in the East have proved futile; however, in the meantime, the visible Church on earth has need of a single power that commands infallible authority. Either there is no visible Church, or, as the extreme Old Ritualists maintain, it came to an end and from the year 1666 the dominion of the Antichrist has held sway on earth, instead of the reign of Christ; or else the true ecclesiastical power established by Christ is situated in the West. Solovyov accepts the second proposition and in part two, "The Ecclesiastical Empire Founded by Jesus Christ," he demonstrates that from the very beginning the Church was a monarchy headed by the Apostle Peter. The popes of Rome have been his successors and have always possessed the gift of the infallible magisterium. The Roman Empire was a prefigurement of the Christian Church; the name of Rome, mystically read backwards spells *Amor*–Love, and its very origins were intertwined with mysterious legends and deeply significant omens.[41] The Roman people and the dynasty of the Caesars were tied to the mother of love, Venus, and through her to the supreme god, who, however, proved to be a parricide and their love became a servant of death. The dynasty of Julius Caesar, the supreme high priest and god, was thus replaced by the dynasty of Simon Peter, the supreme pontiff and servant of the servants of God.[42]

Here, for the first time Solovyov openly defends the dogma of papal infallibility, which he had already recognized in 1886 in his promemoria. With respect to Peter's words, "You are Christ, the Son of the Living God," Solovyov comments, "Is it not evident that this pronouncement that pleased the Lord did not need any human confirmation? That it has preserved all its value, *etiam sine consensu Ecclesiae?*[43] It was not after a collective meeting, but with the immediate assistance of the Heavenly Father (as Jesus Christ himself testified) that Peter formulated the fundamental dogma of our religion and his words defined the faith of Christians by virtue of their own power, not as a result of the agreement of the others–*ex sese, non autem ex consensu Ecclesiae*."[44]

The see of Rome is the miraculous icon of universal Christendom.[45] The papacy is the infallible guardian of Christian truth[46] and, according to Solovyov, the Second Ecumenical Council was not legitimate until the pope confirmed it.[47] The Greek bishops at the Sixth Ecumenical Council invented the heresy of Pope Honorius and imposed this fable onto the good will of the Roman legates.[48] The pope opens heaven to the souls in Purgatory.[49]

Part three of the book, "The Trinitarian Principle and its Social Application," has a dogmatic and theosophic character and appears to be a synthesis of the youthful works *Sophie*, *The Philosophical Principles of Integral Knowledge*, and *The Lectures on Godmanhood* with Solovyov's mature Catholic ideas. In this part he developed more profoundly and completely his previous teaching about the Trinity and Sophia and gave it its definitive form. We also find here the trichotomies: strength, truth, grace; might, justice, mercy; reality, idea, life.[50] But into this Trinitarian system is introduced the concept of *Filioque* : the Father together with the Son is the source of the procession of the Holy Spirit.[51] The Holy Spirit is the common heart of the Father and the Son.[52]

The ideas about the soul of the world and the cosmic process reproduce almost literally the pages of *Sophie* composed at Sorrento, but the terminology has changed somewhat under the influence of Christian dogmatics. The soul of the world is defined as *materia prima* and the true substratum of our created world.[53] The inner meaning of the existence of humanity is the union of the *power* of the earth with the divine *act*, of the Soul with the Word.[54]

The doctrine of Sophia is more fully expounded here than in *The Lectures on Godmanhood*. The uncreated, heavenly Sophia is not the soul of the world, but "the guardian angel of the world"; "the Substance of the Holy Spirit moving above the watery darkness of the world that is being born."[55] She is a radiant and celestial being separated from the darkness of earthly matter.[56] She alone constitutes the essence of Godmanhood whose central and fully personal manifestation is Jesus Christ; whose feminine complement is the Holy Virgin; and whose universal extension is the Church.[57]

"The soul of the world is the 'inferior anti-type of Sophia.' The Eternal Father created it, having restrained the action of his omnipotence, which from all time has suppressed the blind desire of anarchical existence..."[58] Torn apart on all sides by blind forces that contend with one another for exclusive existence, ripped into pieces, broken up, transformed into the dust of countless myriads of atoms, the soul of the world experiences an obscure, but deep desire for unity.[59] Before the soul lies the choice: either to establish an existence for itself outside God, to adopt the point of view of a chaotic anarchical existence, or to throw itself down before God, freely attaching itself to the Divine Word, to bring all creation to perfect unity and identify itself with eternal Wisdom.[60]

The cosmic and historical processes are treated in completely the same way as in *Sophie*: the soul of the world gradually liberates itself from chaos in its striving for unity, for merging with its prototype Sophia. "The anti-divine force, not being in a state to make the higher Wisdom submit to itself, besieges the soul of the world... The cosmic process, being on the one hand, a peaceful encounter, love, and marriage between two agents, the heavenly and the earthly, is also, on the other, a struggle to the death between the Divine Word and the principle of Hell for power over the soul of the world."[61]

We no longer find here the terms "Demiurge" and "Satan" used in *Sophie*, rather only the "anti-divine" and the "enemy of God" are mentioned.[62] This anti-divine will is by necessity eternal and irrevocable. By a primordial act of its will the enemy of God separated itself from God; "to change this act, to return to God is absolutely impossible for it."[63] We see that Solovyov has modified his attitude to Origen. If in *The Lectures on Godmanhood* he unconditionally recognized the authority of the Alexandrian Father, then he now remarks, "that this mind, which was so spiritually sublime and so richly gifted, nonetheless, had only a very insufficient idea about the existence of moral evil."[64] Solovyov pronounced a final judgment against Origen in his article on him in the *Brokgauz-Efron Encyclopedia*.

In the concluding chapters Solovyov proposes an outline for the ideal human society, the universal Church. This society should be the incarnation of the heavenly Sophia, the reflection of the divine Trinity. On earth the universal pontiff, the pope of Rome, corresponds to the Father; the Christian emperor to the Son; the prophet to the Holy Spirit; however, the service of the prophet is the principal one, as it represents the synthetic unity of the first two.[65]

In the preface written in Zagreb, one can detect an enthusiasm for France, to which Solovyov had negatively reacted during his first trip abroad. Now France is for him "the vanguard of humanity."[66] "To France belongs, in particular, the privilege of a universal influence in the political and social spheres."[67] The French Revolution "having proclaimed the rights of man, destroyed much of what needed to be destroyed, and removed, once and for all, many injustices, but the point of its departure was false."[68] Only the universal Church, headed by the Roman pontiff and inspired by the prophetic spirit, is able to realize the rights of man, to establish a real kingdom of freedom and justice. The preface ends with an inspired summons to the Slavic nations and the Roman pontiff:

> Your word, O nations of the word, is the free and universal theocracy, the true solidarity of all nations and all classes, Christianity realized in the life of society, politics that has become Christian; this is the freedom for all the oppressed, the protection for all the weak; this is social justice, "good Christian peace." Open your doors to them, you the key-bearer of Christ, and may the gates of history be for them and the whole world the gates of the Kingdom of God![69]

In his youth, when Solovyov spoke of the union between East and West, the East represented the static principle, the principle of tradition, sanctity, the Church. The West, which then meant for Solovyov the papacy, the French Revolution, and German philosophy, represented the dynamic principle, the principle of movement, progress. Now the schema is reversed: the principle of sanctity, tradition, and piety is papal Rome, the incarnation of the Church's past; while the principle of movement, progress, and prophecy is the Russian East, represented by the tsar and prophet. It is not so much a question of the reunion of the Churches, as of the reuniting of Catholicism with the prophetic spirit, with contemporary progress and the revelation of Sophia. The Russian Church completely vanishes in this scheme and the Fathers of the first ten centuries are absorbed entirely into the Catholic Church. What is original and native to Russian Orthodoxy is the premonition of the revelation of Sophia among the architects of the ancient churches of Russia, who distinguished Sophia from both the Mother of God and from Christ (whereas the Greeks identified Sophia with the Logos). "She was for them a heavenly being, hidden under the visible lower world; the radiant spirit of reborn humanity, the guardian angel of the earth, the future and final manifestation of the Divinity."[70]

Even in *La Russie* Solovyov proves to be a Slavophile. "It is a matter of giving a clear form to the living thought that was born in Ancient Rus and that the new Russia must announce to the world."[71] And since *La Russie* defines Sophia as the substance of the Holy Spirit, then it is evident that the future revelation, of which the ancient Russian iconographers had a presentiment, can be defined as "the religion of the Holy Spirit." Later, in 1892, in a letter to Rozanov, Solovyov decided to use the term directly, "The religion of the Holy Spirit that I profess is wider and, at the same time, more comprehensive than all the separate religions."[72]

But now Solovyov wanted least of all to found a new religion. If in 1876 Catholicism was for him only a dried up branch on the tree of universal Christianity, which it was time to cut off, then now he wanted a new revelation within the confines of the Church itself, enlarged and unified. He himself was convinced that his ideas did not stand in opposition to ecclesiastical tradition, and he was ready to submit them to the court of infallible instance, the Roman See. But the representatives of the Church of Rome looked on matters differently.

On his return from France to Russia, Solovyov wrote to Anna Aksakova, "Loin de devenir jésuite je ne suis plus en aucun rapport avec ces bons pères, qui m'ont déclaré, que malgré toutes mes qualités aimables, ils ne peuvent pas approuver mes idées téméraires et sentant l'hérésie."

He wrote more strongly to Sofia Martynova in the summer of 1892:[73]

> Here for you in two words is my final attitude to papism: I understand it and accept it *tel quel*, but it does not understand me and does not accept me. I made room for it in me, in my spiritual world, but it cannot make room for me; I have made use of it as an element and instrument of truth, but it cannot make out of me an element and instrument for itself. For me God turned the Latin stone into bread and the Jesuit serpent into fish, but for them the devil has turned my bread into a stumbling block and my fish into a poisonous snake. One Jesuit said as much to me directly: "Vos idées sont d'autant plus dangereuses, qu'elles semble être catholiques, vous vous servez d'or latin le plus pur pour dorer les pil(l)ules, qui renferment votre poison oriental. Nous ne les avalerons jamais…" But I also feel that for a long time you have reproached me for pride and conceit…

On 11/23 July 1889 Solovyov remarked to Tavernier, "Returning to the subject of my book, not only have I not seen it, but I don't even know anything about it, aside from the fact of its publication."[74] On 27 July he wrote to Stasyulevich, "The French book, although it has gone, as I am told, into a second edition… gives me little joy, in view of how they have arranged it."[75]

During that same summer Solovyov wrote to Fet, "I have still not received either a single copy or any kind of news, aside from the fact that my Jesuit friends strongly scold me for freethinking, daydreaming, and mysticism. This is what happens when you try to please people! However, I have long ago stopped worrying about not only pleasing people but also about persuading them."[76]

And finally, on 9/21 December he explained to Canon ,
"They do not approve of my book on both sides: the liberals for its clericalism, the clerics for its liberalism. The Jesuits have washed their hands of me and are trying to 'hush' me. But to make up for it I received (indirectly) news of a bishop's imprimatur, and this has greatly consoled me."[77]

From 1889 Solovyov rested for awhile from the Church question. He continued to work on the second volume of *Theocracy*,[78] but this came to a halt and we still have no trace of it. Solovyov's theocratic system itself had begun to fall apart; he was growing increasingly disillusioned with the Russian autocracy and was engaged in a bitter struggle with Orthodox clericalism. With each year his liberalism advanced, and finally in 1891 a new crisis arose, which coincided with an illness, as had the crisis of 1883.

Endnotes for Part 2 - Chapter 5

1. *P*, vol. 2, 59.
2. *P*, vol. 4, 35.
3. Ibid., 183-220.
4. V. Solov'ev, "Russkaia ideia," 50; *SS*, vol. 9, 117.
5. *P*, vol. 3, 117-118.
6. *P*, vol. 4, 121.
7. *P*, vol. 3, 116.
8. *P*, vol. 4, 36.
9. *P*, vol. 3, 117.
10. *P*, vol. 4, 185 (French original) and 206 (Russian translation).
11. *Vladimir Sviatoi* (Moscow: *Put'*, 1913), 47-48; *SS*, vol. 11, 138.
12. *P*, vol. 4, 116.
13. *P*, vol. 3, 153.
14. *P*, vol. 4, 113.
15. Ibid., 185, 207.
16. Ibid., 38.
17. Ibid., 209.
18. *P*, vol. 3, 118.
19. *P*, vol. 4, 190, 212.
20. Ibid., 188, 210.
21. Ibid., 189, 210-211.
22. Ibid., 181, 211.
23. Ibid., 118-119.
24. Ibid., 117.
25. Ibid., 118.
26. Ibid., 39-40.
27. Ibid., 39.
28. Ibid., 190-212.
29. Ibid., 118.
30. Ibid., 189, 211.
31. Ibid., 40.
32. Ibid., 118.
33. Ibid., 40.
34. Ibid., 191, 213.
35. Ibid., 189 (210).
36. Ibid., 190 (212).
37. Ibid., 119.

38. Ibid., 118.
39. Ibid., 41.
40. *Rossiia i vslenskaiia Tserkov'* (Russian translation of G. Rachinskii), 105.
41. Ibid., 128.
42. Ibid., 235.
43. Idem.
44. Ibid., 184.
45. Ibid., 26.
46. Ibid., 27.
47. Ibid., 35.
48. Ibid., 43.
49. Ibid., 385.
50. Ibid., 331.
51. Ibid., 322.
52. Ibid., 328.
53. Ibid., 339.
54. Ibid., 365.
55. Ibid., 347.
56. Ibid., 349.
57. Ibid., 367.
58. Ibid., 341.
59. Ibid., 341.
60. Ibid., 340.
61. Ibid., 356.
62. Ibid., 352.
63. Ibid., 353.
64. Ibid., 353.
65. Ibid. 436.
66. Ibid., 1.
67. Ibid., 2.
68. Ibid., 3.
69. Ibid., 72-73.
70. Ibid., 371.
71. Ibid., 372.
72. *P*, vol. 3, 44.
73. Unpublished.
74. *P*, vol. 4, 216.
75. Ibid., 44.
76. *P*, vol. 3, 121.

77. *P*, vol. 1, 179.
78. Idem.

Part 2 - Chapter 6

Completion of *The National Question in Russia*
Polemics with Strakhov
Lecture *On the Decline of the Medieval Worldview*

O Rus! In lofty foresight
You were possessed by a proud idea;
Which East do you wish to become:
The East of Xerxes or the East of Christ?

Ex Oriente lux

While Solovyov was busy creating the structure of the ideal theocracy, a "pseudo-theocracy"[1] of its own was coming into existence in Russia, or as Solovyov wrote to Stasyulevich in 1886, "the pernicious triumvirate of the false-cleric Pobedonostsev, the false statesman D. A. Tolstoy, and the false prophet Katkov."[2] At the same time, however, Solovyov still had hopes for a "decisive change for the better with the disappearance of these pernicious people, who have been misleading the honest and well-intentioned Emperor." For a long time Solovyov believed in the possibility of Russia's renaissance by an act of state. In 1885 he had corresponded with the "*Epitrope* [Guardian] of the Holy Sepulcher," Terty Ivanovich Filippov. "My opinion on this matter can consist only in the fullest possible agreement with what you have accurately and forcefully expounded," he wrote to Filippov on 2 May 1885.[3] In 1886 Solovyov remarked about Filippov in a different tone:

You were, indeed, in Palestine, oh Terty
And you beheld the Dead Sea, oh *Epitrope*,
But on the destinies of the abomination of antiquity
Your clever mind did not reflect.
And you have rushed to support the idea of Sodom
On the banks of the Neva...[4]

On 30 July 1889 he congratulated Filippov on his elevation "to the first rank of government dignitaries," "I am bound to you not so much by likeness of mind, as by likeness of will... We have one and the same goal: *ignem fovere in gremio sponsae Christi*."[5]

But no movement could be detected in the still waters of the Russian Church... The false prophet Katkov died, and after him Dmitry Tolstoy; in their place, however, many new false prophets appeared. Solovyov's mood was despondent and his health failed him. He complained to Stasyulevich about the "impossibility of combining a nomadic existence with a regular and peaceful life."[6]

We know from a letter to his brother Mikhail that in 1889 Solovyov did not intend to live in Moscow, but unexpectedly he discovered there "an entire philosophical plantation."[7] Professor Nikolay Grot, who was "burning with the desire to found a philosophical journal" had been transferred to Moscow.[8] The sections of the journal were divided in this way: psychology and logic–Grot; philosophy of religion–Solovyov; the history of ancient philosophy–Gilyarov; the history of modern philosophy and metaphysics–Lopatin. Solovyov decided to invite his old friend Dmitry Tsertelev to contribute to the journal. Together with the journal a "philosophical library" was formed, which was to be a series of translations of classical philosophical works. For the first volume Solovyov polished and expanded his youthful translation of Kant's *Prolegomena*. In April 1889 he went to Tsertelev's country estate Lipyagi in Tambov province where he completed the *Anhang* of the *Prolegomena*.[9]

Disillusionment with the reunion of the Churches in the near future, the impossibility of publishing anything in Russia on the Church question (in May 1889 Solovyov received the news that the religious censorship "had condemned *Theocracy*[10] for the second and last time;" and in July the third edition of *The Religious Fundamentals of Life* which was described as "including absolutely nothing but laudation" was forbidden),[11] and the emergence in Moscow of a new philosophical terrain, all this inclined Solovyov to resume his philosophical studies. The members of the "philosophical plantation," although close friends of Solovyov, were indifferent or hostile to his Catholic convictions. He agreed with both Grot and Lopatin with regard to philosophical idealism, and a general, positive attitude toward Christianity, but he must have deeply hidden his most sacred hopes from his friends in Moscow. During the same spring of 1889 the divergence between Solovyov and the Muscovite philosophers manifested itself when the Psychological Society planned to send its congratulations to the Italian committee created to erect a monument to Giordano Bruno, a hero of Grot's. "It would be very strange for me to represent the society in this matter," Solovyov wrote to Grot on 28 April from Lipyagi. He could express only *conditional* sympathy on this occasion, having voiced his reservations "with regard to the anti-Vatican orientation of the agitators for Bruno."[12]

Having stayed about a month at Lipyagi, Solovyov visited Fyodor Dmitriev in the region of Syzran, and from there traveled up the Volga to Syzran, Kazan, and Nizhny Novgorod. He spent only one day in Moscow, visited his brother Mikhail in Dedovo, and by the middle of June was in St. Petersburg.[13] From there he went to Finland to see Doctor Sergey Botkin, the brother of Fet's wife, who did not diagnose any substantial disease, but a general "innervation,"[14] or a "diseased condition of the sympathetic nerves," and prescribed a "quiet life and calmative pills made of silver nitrate, belladonna and something else."[15] In July Solovyov settled in Moscow in the empty family apartment on Zubovsky square, together with the old cook.[16]

"At present I am, so to say, riding in a troika," he wrote to Fet, "for the shaft-horse I have my seven-year-old work, which I have only now completed in rough draft and of which I am beginning the final copy, for the trace-horse on one side I have the destruction of Slavophilism for the autumn issues of *Vestnik Evropy*, and on the other, a discussion 'about beauty' for the first issue of Grot's journal. I am defining beauty from the negative end as pure uselessness, and from the positive as spiritual corporeality."[17]

What is this seven-year-old work which was finished in rough draft? It can only be *The History of Theocracy* begun in 1884. Evidently the second volume was only completed in rough draft, as it never appeared in print. ("From time to time I play with the second volume of *Theocracy*, Solovyov wrote to Strakhov in December 1887.")[18]

The destruction of Slavophilism for the autumn issues of *Vestnik Evropy* became the "Sketches from the History of Russian Consciousness" which appeared in Nos. 11 and 12 of *Vestnik Evropy* in 1889 and which formed the first two chapters of the second edition of *The National Question*, "A Few Words in Defense of Peter the Great," and "Slavophilism and Its Degeneration."[19] This article matured in Solovyov's mind while he was still abroad. "I already have in my thoughts," he wrote to Stasyulevich from Vienna on 25 December/6 January 1888, "still another article, which is fully censurable: about the collapse of Slavophilism. To my eyes the old Slavophilism was a mixture of several heterogeneous elements, but in the main three: Byzantinism, liberalism, and gut patriotism. In present day quasi-Slavophilism each of these elements has been separated and walks about on its own like the nose of Major Kovalev.* The Byzantine element found its proponents in T. Filippov and K. Leontev; the liberal in O. Miller and especially Professor Lamansky, who remains a Slavophile only in name; and finally gut patriotism, which has liberated itself from any kind of claim to an idea and has spread itself widely over all our lowlands. Among individual writers my friend Strakhov, whose head belongs entirely to the 'decaying West,' and who sacrifices only his stomach on the altar of the fatherland, has appeared as its representative."[20]

On 28 February 1889 Solovyov wrote to Stasyulevich from Moscow, "Under the shade of Lenten Moscow I began to compose a lecture (an article too) under the title 'From the History of Russian Consciousness'."[21]

On 15 March he wrote again, "I did not intend to prepare an article for the April issue, I am counting on the one for May. However, the more I write, the less it seems to me suitable for a public reading and even publication. Can you not somehow mitigate it?"[22] But the article that was in progress was not published until November.

The "discussion about beauty" became the article "Beauty in Nature," which was Solovyov's debut in *Problems of Philosophy and Psychology*. It is as though we were reading the first chapter of Solovyov's *Aesthetics*. As we know, *Aesthetics* was supposed to

---

* Hero of Gogol's story "The Nose."

have been the continuation of *A Critique of Abstract Principles*, which was dedicated to ethics, gnoseology, and metaphysics, and the crown of the entire system. For some time his preoccupation with the Church question had distracted Solovyov, but now he was able to turn his attention to the theory of the beautiful and a few years before his death prepared his *Aesthetics* for publication. Although this book was not destined to appear in print, we can form an opinion of Solovyov's aesthetic views on the basis of "Beauty in Nature,"[23] "The General Meaning of Art,"[24] and his articles about various poets.[25]

As his epigraph to the article, Solovyov chose Dostoevsky's declaration, "Beauty will save the world." Solovyov did not agree with either the utilitarian theory of beauty or with the principle of art for art's sake. The goal of beauty is practical: the transformation and salvation of the world. Here Solovyov developed all those ideas that are familiar to us from the third part of *La Russie*.

Solovyov understands the cosmic process to be the patent confrontation between the cosmic mind and primordial chaos, the soul of the world or nature.[26] Citing the two Russian poets who were particularly immersed in the life of nature, Tyutchev and Fet, Solovyov explains in succession how the soul of the world attains enlightenment and self-consciousness in the beauty of the sky and sea, in the beauty of plants, which possess "a heavenly-earthly existence" and "a dreaming soul," being "silently transformed and quietly raised from the earth toward the sky."[27] In the animal world the opposition of chaos to the mind of the Creator is revealed in the production of formless monstrosities, the lower organisms, which present a single collective entity of sexual and alimentary organs–a seething mass of horror.[28] "And finally, the greatest force and the plenitude of life's inner states combine with the most perfect visible form in the splendid body of woman, the highest union of animal and vegetable beauty."[29]

In 1889 the polemics between Solovyov and Strakhov exploded, leading to a complete rupture between the two former friends. In 1888 the second edition of the first version of *The National Question*, which included the extensive article "Russia and Europe," was published. This article is the key to the entire work. If the first chapters were written with a poetic pathos and are concerned for the most part with the reunion of the Churches, then "Russia and Europe," which serves as a transition to the second volume, offers a strictly intellectual analysis and a devastating critique of the historical inventions of Danilevsky. Solovyov dedicated himself so much to the demolition of Danilevsky's ideas because he considered his book *Russia and Europe* to be "the special Koran of all the scoundrels and idiots who wish to destroy Russia and prepare the advent of the Antichrist."[30]

For our times Danilevsky's theory has held a special interest. Being in its day a Russian application of the ideas found in Heinrich Ruckert's *Lehrbuch der Weltgeschichte in organischer Darstellung*, which inspired the Slavophiles (among them the author of *Diary of a Writer*) and gave Slavophilism a scientific basis, this theory was revived in the present era by Oswald Spengler and has exerted a strong influence in Germany and Russia. Of the Ruckert-Danilevsky construction Solovyov left no stone standing. To the idea of European unity Danilevsky opposed the theory of self-contained, independent cultural-historical types. Russia is separated from Europe and presents itself as a part of the isolated Greco-Slavic type. Almost without touching on the historical question as such, Solovyov proves that the historical process consists in the transmission of cultures from certain nations to others and sees in Danilevsky's groupings complete arbitrariness. Here he adopts the views of his father, as expressed by Sergey Mikhailovich in his work *Observation on the Historical Life of Nations*.

In "Russia and Europe" Solovyov does not mention the reunion of the Churches. But of course, the main reason behind his quarrel with the "Koran" of Slavophilism was that such an understanding of history made the reunion of the Churches impossible in principle. With the semblance of a scientific approach Danilevsky reinforced the romantic dreams of Russian nationalism, and the patriotic Dostoevsky was one of the victims of his philosophy of history. The nationalistic romanticism of *Diary of a Writer* was formed under the influence of Danilevsky, just as the profession of "universal Orthodoxy" in *The Brothers Karamazov* was influenced by Solovyov. In the theory of cultural-historical types, however, there was no place left for "universal Orthodoxy"; the essence of Orthodoxy is posited in its Greco-Russian particularity, and the ideas of love and freedom are artificially associated with this particularity.

Nikolay Strakhov, Danilevsky's confederate, published a defense of the "Koran," and a long and gradually more exacerbated polemic began. At first, Solovyov hoped to preserve friendly relations with Strakhov and made a bet with his brother Vsevolod that the episode would not lead to a personal break; in the end Vsevolod Sergeevich won the bet.

Having read the first reactions of the "old cat," Strakhov, Solovyov abused him in his article "About Sins and Diseases" as "the worst scoundrel," but with the certainty that this would not change their "intimately friendly and even tender relations" although he always considered him "a proper pig."[31] Having submitted his second article against Strakhov, "A False Struggle with the West," to *Russkaia mysl'*,[32] Solovyov wrote to Strakhov on 23 August 1890 from Krasny Rog, "In this argument about Russia and Europe the last word will always remain mine, – thus it is written in the stars. Don't be angry Nikolay Nikolaevich, *golubchik,* and read with attention the following explanation."[33] After this come the expressions about Danilevsky's book as "the Koran of all scoundrels and idiots." But Strakhov did not desire in the least that the last word should be Solovyov's, and the words about scoundrels and idiots were hardly designed to reinforce their friendship. He replied to Solovyov with an article in *Novoe vremia.*[34] Following this, Solovyov printed a new rejoinder in *Vestnik Evropy* called "The Happy Thoughts of Mr. Strakhov," which was written in such an insulting tone that every personal tie between the two writers was sundered and was not repaired before their deaths. Fet, who was cordially disposed to both men, was forced to take measures to prevent Solovyov and Strakhov from colliding in his drawing room.

On 30 July 1893 Solovyov wrote to his brother Mikhail, "I only dreamt of a reconciliation with Strakhov. When I see him during the day I think, has my mortal hour struck?"[35] Not long before Strakhov's death, Solovyov wrote to Vasily Rozanov, "I am very sorry, even somewhat afraid about Strakhov, could you not find it possible to inspire him, – since he has nothing against you, – with the thought of a 'Christian end to our life,' which would require, incidentally, a spiritual reconciliation, with all whom he hated, of whom I am the first. Until now, for me to have approached him directly would have been pointless and even dangerous."[36] Nikolay Strakhov died on 24 January 1896. Solovyov wrote an obituary about his former "friend-enemy,"[37] but then later turned it into an article which was meant for the April number of *Vestnik Evropy*;[38] as a result, neither the obituary nor the article were printed. "Soon I will no longer have the leisure for a long article about the deceased," Solovyov wrote to Stasyulevich on 14 February 1896, "moreover, in such an article one would inevitably have to speak about the negative sides of his literary career, as well, and to return to the old polemics, which I have decidedly no desire to do."[39]

The bitter turn that the polemics between Solovyov and Strakhov took was explained by the profound antipathy that existed between their respective natures and worldviews. According to Solovyov, Strakhov mentally belonged entirely to "the decaying West,"[40] and the respected author of *The Struggle with the West* adhered to a "mechanical" worldview, which is the outcome of western intellectual development.[41] From another of Solovyov's perspectives, Strakhov "believes or pretends to believe in the petty idiocies of Descartes and Leibniz."[42] His worldview allowed only "an immobile and inactive God, who can be the object partly of abstract thought, partly of undefined feelings but with whom there can never be associated any kind of practical imperatives or any kind of positive goals."[43] Finally, Solovyov's last letter to Strakhov on 23 August 1890 concluded with the words, "You look on history as a Chinese Buddhist, and my Judeo-Christian question has no meaning for you: is a given intellectual phenomenon harmful or useful for the *task* of Godmanhood on earth at *a given historical moment*? Or in other words: according to Danilevsky's theory, how can one explain why our shared, purely Russian (because it's clerical) national cultural development does not prevent you from being Chinese and me a Jew?"[44] For Solovyov, Strakhov represented a synthesis of the Western mechanical worldview with Oriental passivity.

After Strakhov, Solovyov attacked Pyotr Astafev in the article "Self-Consciousness or Self-Satisfaction?"[45] His aversion to Astafev was so great that in reply to the question "What is unhappiness?" in the "Album of Confessions" belonging to Tatyana Sukhotina (the daughter of Lev Tolstoy), Solovyov wrote, "To sit next to Mr. Astafev"; and to the question "What was the hardest moment in your life?" he answered, "Meeting Mr. Astafev."[46]

In 1891 Solovyov collected his articles of the previous two years and published the second version of *The National Question*, which was significantly larger than the first. In the first version he had polemicized with Ivan Aksakov and Danilevsky, in the second, with their successors Dmitry Samarin, Strakhov, Yarosh, and Astafev. In later years he would include the epigones of Slavophilism, Lev Tikhomorov, Rozanov, Shcheglov, and other "false-Orthodox" patriots and representatives of "gut patriotism."[47] "In 1884 I. S. Aksakov attacked me," Solovyov wrote "then within a few years I had to deal with Mr. Strakhov, and now Mr. Shcheglov has arrived to take their place in the capacity of the 'third force.' Of course, in a certain way it was far more pleasant to argue with I. S. Aksakov, or even to catch the insidiousness of the uncatchable N. N. Strakhov, than to brush aside Mr. Shcheglov. But then, what a morally aesthetic pleasure one experiences at the sight of the completely attained harmony between the ideas of our backwardness and its personal incarnation!"[48]

It will surprise many that Solovyov wasted so much time and energy on petty polemics with the nationalists and "fired on swallows with a cannon." In 1894 Solovyov himself offered this explanation, "I have recently accepted as my lot the voluntary 'penance' of disposing of that printed rubbish and debris with which our Orthodox patriots try to stifle in the consciousness of society the great and urgent question of religious freedom."[49]

One might then ask, why did Solovyov, having attacked the "Koran" of Slavophilism, pass by in silence the most prominent representative of religious nationalism–Dostoevsky? We have seen how close Solovyov was to Dostoevsky in his youth and what a strong influence these two writers exerted on one another. Solovyov valued too highly one side of Dostoevsky, his profound Christianity and his universal idea, to reckon the author of *The Brothers Karamazov* among his enemies. But even about Dostoevsky he did utter some bitter words; in the article "The Russian National Ideal" Solovyov deemed Dostoevsky's views to possess "an undeniable duplicity."[50] "If we agree with Dostoevsky that the true essence of the Russian national spirit, its great worthiness and privilege, consists in its ability to assimilate all foreign elements, to love them, to be transformed in them, if we recognize the Russian nation, together with Dostoevsky, as capable of and destined to realizing the ideal of pan-humanism in fraternal union with other nations, then there is no way we can sympathize with the outbursts of the same Dostoevsky against the 'Yids,' the Poles, the French, the Germans, and against all of Europe and all foreign creeds."[51] In the article "The Historical Sphinx" Solovyov adds, "More decisively than all the Slavophiles, in his Pushkin speech Dostoevsky demonstrates the universal, pan-human character of the Russian idea; at the same time, in every instance dealing with the national question, he expressed the most elementary chauvinism."[52]

Further on we will consider in detail Solovyov's attitude to Lev Tolstoy. In the meantime, we will confine ourselves to remarking that their relations were always more or less antagonistic. In 1891 Solovyov wrote the article "Idols and Ideals," in which he unmasked two of the ideals of contemporary society, – serfdom and worship of the folk, finding them akin to one another.[53] This assault could not fail to offend Tolstoy. On 9 August 1891 Solovyov wrote to Grot from St. Petersburg, "At the end of August I will certainly be in Moscow, but I will not see Tolstoy: our relations have become strained in my absence on account of my 'Idols' and I am *now* particularly incensed by the preaching of the 'simple life,' when the peasants themselves are dying from hunger on account of this simplicity."[54]

The terrible famine of 1891 distressed Solovyov greatly, and he tried to help in every way possible: he wrote the articles "The National Disaster and Social Assistance,"[55] "False and Genuine Measures for the Improvement of the People's Welfare,"[56] and collected charitable donations. "I request that until the famine ceases you withhold all of my honorarium to aid the hungry," Solovyov wrote on 10 October 1891 to Lyubov Gurevich, editor of *Severnii vestnik*.[57]

This transition to practical questions inspired in many people misunderstanding and irony. It seemed strange that Solovyov would descend from the heights of metaphysics to the depths of economic interests and that he should be writing not about Sophia, but about how in Tambov province "they are selling colts for half a ruble (that is, they can trade a colt for a measure of orach)."[58] Many were disturbed by Solovyov's didactic tone in matters that had never previously claimed his attention. These same people had also failed to understand the ardor of Solovyov, that did not allow him to remain on metaphysical heights during that national disaster, and that drove him from St. Petersburg to the Balkans in 1878... Without this "colt for half a ruble" Solovyov's ethical portrait would not be complete.

The years 1889-1891 can only be described as transitory and obscure. After the powerful creative élan of the mid '80s, the writing of *Theocracy* and *La Russie*, after his systematic and certain ascent up the slopes, it was as though Solovyov was temporarily thrown from his place, cast off from the heights he had attained. It was not so easy for him to tear himself away from his sublime dream of participating in the restoration of universal theocracy and of being its prophet and herald, nor was it easy to abandon the "unshakable stronghold of Zion" for the modest philosophical plantation in Moscow and the tidily liberal *Vestnik Evropy*. During these years he spread himself thin and his works do not possess the force of the flowering of the '80s and of the end of the '90s. The proliferation of his works impeded their intensity. He dissipated his energy on numerous small articles and abandoned the second volume of *Theocracy*. The distracted state of his inner life corresponded to that of his external circumstances. He was forced to find a way to earn an income. "I have become something of a literary day-laborer," Solovyov wrote to Maria Petrovna Fet on 20 July 1890 from Dedovo.[59]

In 1891 Solovyov began to contribute to the *Brokgauz-Efron Encyclopedic Dictionary*. "I will live principally on the encyclopedia and dictionary," he wrote to his brother Mikhail in Rome at the beginning of 1892, "not very profitably, but, it seems, securely."[60] The possibility of appointing Solovyov the editor of the dictionary arose, and on 21 July 1891 he wrote to Gets, "You wrote to me about the editorship of the 'Encyclopedic Dictionary.' If the rest of humanity shared your kind disposition toward me then, of course, I would become not only the editor of the 'Encyclopedic Dictionary' but would also rule the Holy Roman Empire. Semyon Vengerov told me that there could be no question of my becoming the editor-in-chief, but the editorship of one of the sections is possible; but it is still not possible to say anything definite."[61] In the end, Solovyov was put in charge of the philosophical section, and from 1891 he began a lively correspondence with Konstantin Arsenev, the dictionary's editor-in-chief.[62]

Solovyov's life took on an increasingly nomadic character. In June 1891 he planned to go to Vologda (?),[63] and in August to Kiev.[64] In a letter to Stasyulevich of 7 October 1890 he provided a brief resumé of his current existence, "Little by little I am turning into a Remington machine. Moreover I am losing blood, seeing apparitions, and am worried about 40,000 other matters."[65] Aside from the loss of blood, he began to suffer from attacks of vomiting. From 1887 Solovyov's muse had almost completely fallen silent. The life of the heart, without which lyric poetry is impossible, had died in him. In 1890 he wrote his famous "*Ex Oriente lux*" in which he versified the fundamental idea of *The Great Controversy* and *The National Question*:

O Rus! In lofty foresight
You were possessed by a proud idea;
Which East do you wish to become:
The East of Xerxes or the East of Christ?[66]

"The fatal denouement of a joyless love" in 1887 had clipped his life's wings. But his relations with Sofya Khitrovo did not come to an end. In 1890 we again find Solovyov at Krasny Rog[67] and at Pustynka.[68] In this year he wrote the poem "Not by the Will of Fate," which appears as the finale to the love of many years, a vow of fidelity to the beloved woman before the face of God:

But when death extinguishes before you and me
All the lamps of earthly life,
The flame of the eternal soul, like a star from the East,
Will lead us to that place where the light never dims,
And before the face of God, the God of love,
You will then become – my answer.[69]

In 1891 Solovyov tested his strength at political satire. Already in 1887 he wrote epigrams at the expense of Prince

Meshchersky. Now he composed about him a political pamphlet in the form of a play in verse "The Nobleman's Revolt" (or "The Nobleman's Loan").[70] The letter to Stasyulevich of 9 August 1891 includes the poem "Greetings to the Ministers":

> Gremykin is rejoicing,
> And Delyanov is rejuvenating,
> Bedonostsev is improving,
> Muravyov is a bridegroom...[71]

Thus from the lyre of Virgil, Solovyov passed to the god of Juvenal. He considered satire to be one of the best manifestations of the Russian national genius; he especially valued the satiric works of Gogol, and his letters are scattered with quotations from *The Inspector General* and other works by Gogol. For example, on the occasion of Goncharov's death, Solovyov wrote to Stasyulevich, "And so the next-to-the-last coryphaeus of Russian literature is no more. Only Lev Tolstoy is left, and he is half-witted. Thus is life arranged in our town: if a man is wise, either he is a heavy drinker or he makes such terrible faces that it makes the saints blush."[72] Solovyov also highly valued Saltykov-Shchedrin:* "I sincerely regreted Saltykov's passing and attended the Liturgy for the departed. Such a man cannot be replaced by anybody," he wrote to Stasyulevich on 11 May 1889.[73] And on 27 July of the same year, "I have subscribed to the works of Saltykov; I am reading the third volume and am finding that it hasn't aged."[74]

To the end of 1891 dates the crisis of Solovyov's relationship with the Russian Orthodox Church. We have seen that in 1887 Solovyov was not so far from the thought of embracing monasticism. In July 1891 he visited Valaam. "I convinced the monks of their mistake, but about my own impression I will tell you when we meet,"[75] he wrote to Stasyulevich on 27 July. We know what his impression was from a letter to his brother Mikhail, "I was at Valaam and saw the quintessence of genuine strict monasticism and... spit."[76]

* Mikhail Saltykov-Shchedrin (1826-1889), government official, journalist, and satirical writer. In his works he cruelly portrayed the stupidities of the provincial bureaucracy and the demise of the serf-owning class in the 1870s and '80s.

Finally, the long brewing protest against one-sided asceticism found its expression in the public lecture *On the Decline of the Medieval Worldview*, which was delivered at the Moscow Psychological Society on 19 October 1891.[77] This lecture serves as a border between the second and third periods of Solovyov's career. From 1892 to 1896 Solovyov moved away from the Church, and other notes in his voice drowned out those of the prophet-reformer. If the lecture of 1887 "Slavophilism and the Russian Idea" evoked deep misunderstanding and was greeted with the reproachful silence of Moscow society, then the lecture of 1891 was a noisy scandal. In 1887 Solovyov appeared before an élite public, composed of the remnants of the old Slavophiles. This public was of one mind in its silent condemnation. Now this audience was divided into two parties: on one side the circle of *Moskovskie vedemosti* greeted the lecture with wild indignation, on the other were the liberal intellectuals in whose camp Solovyov had been making many friends during the period from 1887 to 1891. The applause of this side deafened the representatives of official Orthodoxy. But the vengeance of *Moskovskie vedemosti* and their allies followed afterwards and Solovyov was temporarily forbidden from giving public lectures.

By the term "the medieval worldview" Solovyov meant the "dual half-pagan structure of concepts that arose and governed the Middle Ages, both in the Roman-German West and in the Byzantine East." Solovyov compares the representatives of this world to demons who "believe and tremble," but who do not have love. Christ condemned the medieval worldview when, in response to the desire of John and James to bring down fire from heaven in order to destroy the Samaritan village that had not receive them, He declared, "You do not know of what spirit you are." From the illicit union of the idea of salvation with ecclesiastical dogmatism was born "the monstrous doctrine that the only way to salvation is belief in dogmas." Pseudo-Christianity, having rejected society, rejected material nature as well. "Christ cast the seven demons out of Mary Magdalene and filled her with His Spirit. When false Christians separate material nature–the universal Magdalene–from the spirit of Christ, evil spirits naturally settle in her." True Christians cast out demons to cure the possessed; false Christians began to destroy the possessed to cast out demons.

The Holy Spirit, the spirit of Christ, has animated the social, moral, and intellectual progress of the last centuries. The non-believing activists of our time have realized true Christianity and resemble the son in the Gospel parable who said, “I will not go,” and then went. It is dogmatically completely possible to admit such action on the part of the Holy Spirit through non-believers, in the same way that an unbelieving priest can administer a sacrament. But the promoters of contemporary progress have offended that nature in whose name they act. If false spiritualism saw in nature an evil principle, then these see in it only dead matter, a soulless machine. “And here, as if insulted by this double falsehood, earthly nature refuses to feed humanity.”[78] Both for believers and non-believers “it is time to recognize and realize their solidarity with mother-earth to save her from decay and in order to save themselves, as well, from death.”

Solovyov’s sister Maria Sergeevna relates in her memoirs that during the interval between the lecture and the discussion, the hall was full of agitation. Some called Solovyov a “prophet,” others said that he was ingratiating himself with the liberals and that it was time to silence him.

The persecution of Solovyov began at *Moskovskie vedemosti* under the leadership of Yu. Nikolaev (pseudonym of Yury Nikolevich Govorukha-Otrok, an art critic and author of a talented book about Turgenev). Solovyov’s lecture was not passed by the censor, so its main themes were transmitted in a distorted form by Nikolaev. Solovyov protested about this in a series of four letters to the editors of *Moskovskie vedemosti* dated 22, 26, 30 October, and 3 November.[79]

But Solovyov’s old admirer Konstantin Leontev was especially indignant. In a letter to Aleksandrov (a privat-dozent at Moscow University in the department of literature and a contributor to *Moskovskie vedemosti*), Leontev called Solovyov “Satan,” sounded the alarm, and declared it was necessary to launch one of the local Orthodox *startsy* against him. “To whom will he go now?” Leontev exclaimed, “To the Jesuits? But in this case they are not with him, but with us.”

At the same time, Solovyov had to endure, in connection with his lecture, the unexpected animosity of several friends, whom he had previously completely trusted. Evidently shaken by the whole experience, Solovyov's health collapsed and he contracted diphtheria. The dates of his illness are not entirely clear, but we know about it from letter No. 42 to his brother Mikhail.[80] "At the time of my diphtheria I received Communion and I am very glad about this." To this Mikhail Sergeevich replied, "I am glad that you were glad." A letter to Stasyulevich on 8 November begins with the words, "Everything has been disinfected,"[81] and encloses the poem "The Idol of Nebuchadnezzar" dated 7 November. Here we have the *terminus ante quem* for the illness; the *terminus post quem* is 3 November when the fourth letter to the editors of *Moskovskie vedemosti* was written. If one assumes that this letter was written already at the onset of the illness and "The Idol of Nebuchadnezzar" at the very beginning of Solovyov's convalescence, then the critical period fell between 4-6 November. Apparently, the diphtheria took a light form.

"The Idol of Nebuchadnezzar" is dedicated to Konstantin Pobedonostsev. In the guise of a biblical prophet Solovyov declares:

> On that day of folly and ignominy
> I called firmly on the Lord,
> And louder than the loathsome chorus
> My voice resounded in heaven.[82]

Having received the poem, Sergey Trubetskoy jokingly responded that he wanted to address his reply to Solovyov "directly to the fiery furnace."[83]

From one of his letters to Fet we know that after his illness Solovyov "cleansed himself and showed himself to the priests"[84] and spent a week at Slavyansky Bazaar. His move from his parental home to Slavyansky Bazaar was probably inspired by some kind of domestic complication. We have a gloomy undated letter from Solovyov to his mother that apparently refers to those days. "You see that I have no place to live here." Fully recovered, he went to St. Petersburg with even more of a bitter feeling toward Moscow than in 1887 when his "Compliment to Moscow," "Stupid city, foul city," was written. From St. Petersburg he wrote to his brother Mikhail in Rome, "The diphtheria came to my aid, I have not vomited once in St. Petersburg... a fine work is forming itself in my head, which will not earn a kopeck for me but will crown me with unfading glory."[85]

But we shall soon see Solovyov in Moscow again. This time he will be "bound by the heaviest chains to Moscow's shores."[86] In Moscow his last romantic passion, which inspired the flowering of his completely faded poetry, was lying in wait for him. We will begin the final part of our work with this flowering.

Endnotes for Part 2 - Chapter 6

1. *P*, vol. 4, 44.
2. Ibid., 30.
3. Ibid., 165.
4. Ibid., 28.
5. *P*, vol. 2, 329.
6. *P*, vol. 4, 44.
7. *P*, vol. 2, 255.
8. Idem.
9. *P*, vol. 1, 61.
10. Ibid., 63.
11. *P*, vol. 4, 44.
12. *P*, vol. 1, 62.
13. *P*, vol. 2, 64.
14. Idem.
15. *P*, vol. 3, 120.
16. Idem.
17. *P*, vol. 3, 124.
18. *P*, vol. 1, 46.
19. *SS*, vol. 5, 161, 181.
20. *P*, vol. 4, 40-41.
21. Ibid., 41.
22. Idem.
23. See *SS*, vol. 6, 33.
24. Ibid., 74.
25. *SS*, vols. 6, 7, 9.
26. *SS*, vol. 6, 73.
27. Ibid., 58, 59.
28. Ibid., 62.
29. Ibid., 60.
30. *P*, vol. 1, 59.
31. *P*, vol. 4, 118.
32. *Russkaia mysl'* 8 (1890); *SS*, vol. 5, 287-311.
33. *P*, vol. 1, 59.
34. *Novoe vremia* 5231 (1890).
35. *P*, vol. 4, 127.
36. *P*, vol. 3, 53.
37. *P*, vol. 1, 130.
38. Ibid., 132.

39. Ibid., 130.
40. *P*, vol. 4, 41.
41. *SS*, vol. 5, 142.
42. *P*, vol. 1, 56.
43. Ibid., 57.
44. Ibid., 60.
45. *Vestnik Evropy* 3 (1891); *SS*, vol. 5, 352.
46. *P*, vol. 4, 238.
47. Ibid., 40.
48. *SS*, vol. 6, 326.
49. Ibid., 442.
50. *SS*, vol. 5, 416.
51. Ibid., 420.
52. *SS*, vol. 6, 414.
53. *Vestnik Evropy* 3 and 6 (1891). *SS*, vol. 5, 366.
54. *P*, vol. 1, 71.
55. *SS*, vol. 5, 426.
56. Ibid., 466.
57. *P*, vol. 3, 130.
58. *SS*, vol. 5, 426.
59. *P*, vol. 3, 122.
60. *P*, vol. 4, 125.
61. *P*, vol. 2, 177.
62. Ibid., 68-94.
63. *P*, vol. 4, 47.
64. Ibid., 48.
65. Ibid., 46.
66. *Stikh.*, 96; *SS*, vol. 12, 28.
67. *P*, vol. 1, 59.
68. *P*, vol. 2, 259.
69. *Stikh.*, 95; *SS*, vol. 12, 26.
70. V. Solov'ev, *Shutochnye p'esy*, *SS*, vol. 12, 226; *P*, vol. 4, 50.
71. *P*, vol. 4, 49; *SS*, vol. 12, 136.
72. *P*, vol. 4, 54.
73. Ibid., 44.
74. Idem.
75. Ibid., 48.
76. Ibid., 122. The word "spit" is restored according to the manuscript of the original letter.
77. *SS*, vol. 381.

78. *SS*, vol. 6, 392-393.
79. *P*, vol. 3, 196-208.
80. *P*, vol. 4, 124-125.
81. Ibid., 54.
82. *SS*, vol. 12, 31.
83. I quote the letters of M. S. Solovyov and S. N. Trubetskoy from their manuscripts.
84. Undated letter, *P*, vol. 3, 126.
85. *P*, vol. 4, 125.
86. Ibid., 63.

Part Three

Twilight

Evil is powerless; we are eternal;
God is with us.

"*Emmanu-el*"

Part 3 - Chapter 1

Poetic Flowering
The Meaning of Love

Something miraculous has once again passed by...
Is it an angel or a demon knocking at my heart?
V. Solovyov

On 9 August 1891 Solovyov wrote to his brother Mikhail, "I feel unexpected and groundless bursts of youthfulness, although I am graying more and more. But gray hair, as some poet once said, is the snow under which the sowing for the future world is ripening."[1]

The bursts of youthful energy ended with the stormy and final romantic passion of Solovyov's life, which "bound him by the strongest chains to Moscow's shores"[2] at the verge of 1891 and 1892. The result of this passion was a flowering of poetry that was unprecedented in Solovyov's life; only now did he realize himself as a poet. We have seen that at the end of the '80s Solovyov's muse had fallen completely silent, and he wrote at most one or two poems a year. (Between 1888 and 1889 not a single serious poem was written.) In 1892 Solovyov's poetic inspiration proved inexhaustible. "I am possessed, as you see, by the vice of poetry," he wrote to Fet, "I have recently composed 36 poems."[3]

The poetry of this period bears a special stamp; Solovyov's verse becomes light and airy, attaining the transparency and incorporeity of Fet's. It is as though the will and consciousness of his ego are dissolved, and he finds himself entirely in the power of some kind of magic:

Something miraculous has once again passed by...
Is it an angel or a demon knocking at my heart?
My feeling is afraid to take a form...
Oh, how powerless is the cold word![4]

The strange whisper of unearthly words,
The aroma of Japanese roses –
The fantastic and misty
Echo of prophetic dreams.[5]

It was especially at this time that, following in the footsteps of the author of *Evening Fires,*[*] Solovyov became one of the first pioneers of Symbolist poetry in Russia. Comparing his new love to that of his "tormenting and burning" youth, Solovyov declares that this new love summons his soul to "transparent, silver dreams." The love-sorceress carries him toward "an inexhaustible dream," where an entire swarm of elves circle around him and pale fairies wistfully drift past.[6]

The object of this love was Sofya Mikhailovna Martynova, whom Solovyov met in Moscow in the aristocratic circle of the Sollogubs, Trubetskoys, and Sukhotins. Sofya Mikhailovna's close friends referred to her by the classical name *Sappho*. Solovyov composed several acrostics using this name, complaining about the "merciless letter *F*," which drew the poet's imagination to the words "Fet," "*filin*" [the eagle owl], "fatal," "*fon*" [background], etc. There was something Japanese about Sophia Mikhailovna's features, and Solovyov addressed her as "Oh, sweet dream of a happy Japanese!"[7] All of life now seemed to him to be a "Japanese fairy tale" and he was intoxicated by the "aroma of Japanese roses."[8]

On this occasion as well, Solovyov's love possessed a profoundly mystical character. The best of his poems inspired by the personality of Sofya Martynova "Why words?" was written in "a state of telepathy."[9] It was as though for the last time he recognized in her face both the "rosy radiance" of the Eternal Sophia and the dualistic soul of the world, "the field of Christ, which Satan has sown with his weeds." But in comparison with the long "tormenting and burning" love of his youth, and we dare say of his entire life, there was something romantic, fantastic, and not completely serious about this love. Here the fantastic element is interwoven with the comic, in the style of the German Romantics. At the same time, the fire of this

[*] This volume of Fet's poetry was published in 1883.

passion burned as never before.[10] Solovyov implores the woman he loves "to extinguish his fire's flames." Sometimes the beloved seems to him to be a "cold, evil water nymph," whom he does not have the strength to abandon because "on such a black night all the mad songs and tales would cease forever."[11] His last poem in manuscript bears the characteristic title "Words to a Gypsy Romance [Slova k tsyganskomu romansu]." In a humorous letter to his brother Mikhail he complained that he was "enduring sorrows of the heart and not inconsiderable grief"[12] and that he "had to deal with a character in comparison to which Sofya Petrovna was ease and simplicity itself."

It is difficult to recognize the majestic figure of the friend of the canons of Zagreb in the salon poet, whom Solovyov had become at this time. The poem "The Burning Bush [Neopalimaia kupina]," which was written on 4 September 1891 has an autobiographical ring. Casting himself in the guise of Moses, "the slave of sin," who fled into the desert of Midian, he declares that he is living "in drowsy idleness and in deeds without glory," while leaning his lazy head against the knees of a Midian woman.[13] There is another direct comparison to Moses in a poem of 1892, which was not published during Solovyov's lifetime.

I was great. The earthly throng
Swarmed somewhere in the dust,
Alone on the heights of Sinai
I was with the God of heaven and earth.

But where now are the lofty summits?
Where the radiant ray of light and thunder?
I lie here at the bottom of a valley
In grief and mute exhaustion.

Oh, how love changed everything.
I wait motionless in the dark,
For someone's little foot to crush me
With my greatness.[14]

In vain he thought, "late love bears only flowers." "The rainbow dream has clipped wings."[15] The creator of *The History of*

Theocracy felt himself to be lying "at the bottom of a valley" having fallen from the heights of Sinai.

One can date Solovyov's intimacy with Sofya Martynova to the end of 1891. On the occasion of the winter solstice he greeted her "with a modest prophecy" about the swift arrival of spring, calling her its "dryad."[16] He celebrated Christmas Eve at the Martynovs, receiving a toy monkey as a gift. He also became very attached to Sofya Martynova's children. His love for her attained its zenith toward the spring of 1892. On 19 May "offering no resistance to his nomadic nature," Solovyov suddenly found himself in Kharkov. Arriving there completely unexpectedly in the morning, he set out on the evening of the same day for the province of Kursk where he spent a few days with Afanasy Fet who was nearing death. At the beginning of June we find him in the village of Morshchikha, near the station of Skhodnya on the Nikolaevsky line.

Znamenskoe, the estate of the Martynovs, was located not far from Skhodnya. In order to live in proximity to the woman he loved, Solovyov rented a dacha in Morshchikha "from the peasant Sysoy,"[17] from which he could make his way on foot to Znamenskoe. Solovyov arrived in Morshchikha on 2 June, having written to Stasyulevich a few hours before his departure from Moscow, "My dacha (4 rooms) costs 80 rubles for the entire summer, of which I am very proud. I will live completely alone. I have simplified my meals a great deal; I will eat buckwheat kasha once a day with sunflower oil, and green beans without any oil. I will drink rye beer at 12 kopecks a bottle. I think that such a diet is as good for one's health as for one's pocket."[18]

On his very first night Solovyov had to confess that Sysoy's hut was a far cry from the mansions of Krasny Rog and Pustynka. On the night of 3 June he composed two poems. The first is "short and sad," "The Wind Blows from the West [Veter s Zapadnoi storony]," in which he hears the "wailing from the land of the dead," from whence his heart has not returned;[19] the second, "The Triumph of Turpentine [Torzhestvo skipidara]," is "long and cheerful." From this poem we learn that during his first night Solovyov, with the help of turpentine, had to carry on a struggle with the "favorites of Lev Tolstoy," – red bedbugs and cockroaches. The need of the peasants in Morshchikha, of course, attracted Solovyov's attention, and from his first day there he became involved in the purchase of a horse for thirty-six rubles for the ruined peasant Aleksey Kharitonov.[20] On 10 June Solovyov wrote a long letter to Sofya Mikhailovna, which I know from manuscript. Beginning with the thought that at their last meeting "some of the rosy radiance had departed" from Sofya, he continues:

> I spent the entire evening from seven to eleven o'clock in this unusually picturesque locality, which is new for me, beyond my village on the banks of the stream and there, to use the high style, I dissolved the delightful contemplation of nature with the bitterness of unhappy love, and on the latter I poured the consolation of religion.

After the poem "There, where the willows crowd as a family [Tam, gde semei stolpilis' ivy],"[21] he adds:

> I actually produced all of this, as described, high above a ravine under the noise of the stream, the singing of a distant, perfectly real nightingale, and the roar of the railway. Possessed by poetry, I strayed from the path and wandered until midnight in various places until finally a heavy downpour soaked me to the bone.

Further on, Solovyov addresses an exhortation to Sofya Mikhailovna half-jokingly in the manner of Father Ioann of Kronshtadt:

> Oh, how carefully do the devil and the world sow their weeds in the field of Christ, which is Sofia Mikhailovna. Instead of the word of God, the word of the world, the word of vanity is sown in her. Instead of the temples of God the world has devised for her its temples of vanity: theaters, circuses, social gatherings, masquerades; instead of holy icons, which through their dry and emaciated features would remind her of the true friend, the world provides her with painted and photographic portraits of theatrical personages, illustrations, and various other scenes. Instead of God and the

> saints (especially the martyrs of love), the world presents for her admiration its celebrities: actors, conjurers, singers, painters, and African explorers. Poor Sofia Mikhailovna! They have thoroughly separated her from her true goal!

Solovyov also offers here a short explanation of who Sophia is: "Sophia means we-with-God, as Christ is God-with-us. Do you understand the difference? God-with-us, means He is active, and we are passive. We-with-God means the opposite; here He is passive, He is body and matter, and we are will and spirit." The letter concludes with the anxious words, "What a storm and what a strange summer! No, the day of doom is near. Who aside from me will prepare you for it?"

Sinister notes sounded in Solovyov's poetry of this summer:

> It was gloomy in your forest,
> August was on the wane.
> The eagle owl cried afar like a child,
> Announcing my death.

It quickly became apparent that it was impossible to live in Sysoy's hut. "I was forced to leave my Morshchikha," he wrote to Tsertelev, "for many reasons, for example: 1) as a consequence of the proximity of my host's family it was not possible to sleep or work; 2) it turned out my hostess had tertiary syphilis; 3) the cook, who was recommended to me by Katerina Ivanovna, was delivered of an illegitimate child, to whom I offered my dacha. I myself am enjoying the hospitality of A. G. Petrovsky, while they redo our apartment (it is not known why)."[22]

Aleksandr Petrovsky, a friend of Solovyov's, was a doctor by profession and served in the city council. He was distinguished by his wide culture and rare cordiality. Like Solovyov, he loved everything humorous and fantastic, and held E. T. A. Hoffmann in particular esteem. Solovyov found himself to be very much at home in his hospitable apartment. Petrovsky took several photographs of him, one of which is included in the seventh edition of his poetry.

Solovyov left Morshchikha, but continued to see Sofya Mikhailovna. In August "eleven days were illuminated by the rays of her real presence."[23] But the meetings in Moscow occurred at railway stations and on trains. Solovyov also made it to Znamenskoe three times in August.[24] With the withering of the earth, their love also withered. Solovyov noted in his beloved the "loss of iridescent splendor or the signs of the divine Sophia."[25]

> The May rose was long ago mourned,
> August came... and August vanished.
> Just like the bald head of old Fet
> Your grove is as sadly clad,
> The forest is adorned with a solitary pine...[26]

The summer season was coming to an end. Probably during his last trip to Znamenskoe Solovyov composed the acrostic:

> Skhodnya, the old road,
> Although in the distance it appears new ...
> The faded backdrop of autumn ... how little,
> Oh, how little remains from the past![27]

In this case there was no "hour of fatal torment" as Solovyov had experienced in 1887. The "aroma of Japanese roses" had dissipated, the "mad songs and tales" fell silent, but Eternity was drawing near for Solovyov and its familiar voices filled his soul with quiet sorrow and radiant joy. He felt increasingly how "close the ethereal road" was. Sending his greetings to Sofya Mikhailovna and her daughters Nadya and Verochka on their name day (17 September), Solovyov included his best poem of the "Martynova cycle," "Why words? [Zachem slova?]"

On 12 September 1892 Solovyov informed Vasily Velichko, "From the end of May I lived without a break in Moscow and its environs. I had a dacha at Skhodnya, but made little use of it as a consequence of various tragicomical complications, with which I will amuse you when we meet. I have now settled in Moscow for good."[28] With the conclusion of 1892, Solovyov's romance and his last "Moscow period" also come to an end. On 31 March 1893 he wrote to Velichko, "No dryad has any hold on me in Moscow, but simply the wheel of life. The dryad is a myth."[29] Solovyov preserved friendly relations with Sofya Mikhailovna and in the summer of 1893 again planned to stay at Znamenskoe.[30]

"I am suffering from an excess of works that are rushed, and a lack of time," Solovyov wrote to Tsertelev in the summer of 1892.[31] What were these works? Most of his time was taken up, apparently, with the entries for the *Brokgauz-Efron Encyclopedia*, which at that point had reached words beginning with the letters *V* and *G*.* Solovyov had to write on Valentinus, the Gnostics, Hermes Trismegistus, and so forth. In the May issue of *Russkaia mysl'* he published his only short story, "At the Dawn of Misty Youth." We do not know precisely when this story was written, but it is possible that it was in 1892, as its contents are consistent with the "erotic period" of Solovyov's work. The tale is presented in an autobiographical style. Solovyov recalls his youthful romance with his cousin Katya, who is called Olga in the story, and relates an episode that happened to him in a railway carriage on the way to Kharkov, where the young philosopher was going to win his cousin over to the path of "self-renunciation of the will." In the carriage he makes the acquaintance of a young lady named Julie and a fleeting infatuation ensues. On the platform the hero faints between two carriages and would have been crushed by the train if Julie had not seized him by the shoulders. When he recovers he sees only "a brilliant solar light," "a strip of blue sky," and "the image of a splendid woman."

> Something wonderful occurred within me. It was as though my entire being with all its thought, feelings, and aspirations dissolved and then melted into one infinite, sweet, shining, and passionless feeling, and in this sensation, as in a pure mirror, was reflected without motion one wondrous image, and I felt and knew that in this alone was the all. I loved with a new, all-consuming, and infinite love, and in it I felt for the first time the complete fullness and meaning of life.[32]

Solovyov's correspondence with Lyubov Gurevich, the editor of *Severnyi vestnik*, dates to 1892. This journal collected the first Russian modernists and Nietzscheans: Dmitry Merezhkovsky, Zinaida

* In the Russian alphabet these letters come in the second and third place.

Hippius, Akim Volynsky, and Nikolay Minsky. Later Solovyov would make a sharp break with this circle, and Volynksy would pursue him with malicious polemics. In the same year, Solovyov carried on a friendly correspondence with Vasily Rozanov.[33]

Solovyov's experience of love in 1892, which had inspired so many splendid poems, could not remain without influence on his philosophical work as well. Toward the end of 1892 Solovyov published his essay *The Meaning of Love* in *Voprosy filosofii i psikhologii*,[34] in which, partly repeating Plato, he expounded his view on the meaning and purpose of sexual love. At the beginning Solovyov refutes the concept of sexual love as only a means for reproduction. The love of Romeo and Juliet did not lead them to childbearing, but to the grave; and the ideal married couples, Philemon and Baucis,[*] Afanasy Ivanovich and Pulkheria Ivanovna[†] were childless. If the materialists are mistaken in seeing the purpose of sexual love in reproduction, then so too are the spiritualists and admirers of chivalrous love, who are content with a simple identification of the ideal love with a given face, ignoring the evident disparity. "Sexual love is the type and ideal of every other kind of love."[35] Only in erotic love does a person love another completely, in the other's spiritual and material being, only in this love is the opposition between the spiritual and material removed, and matter becomes a means for the incarnation of the spirit. By the effort of a moral act of heroism, spiritual love transforms nature and leads it to immortality. "The force of man's spiritually-corporeal creativity is only the transformation or *inner conversion* of that same creative force, which in nature manifests itself in an external way, producing the evil infinity of the physical reproduction of organisms."[36]

One cannot reckon *The Meaning of Love* among the best works of Solovyov's. He expressed the same thoughts about love more strongly, for example, in *The Drama of Plato's Life*. Evidently,

---

[*] An idealized couple of classical mythology; according to Ovid (*Metamorphoses* 8:631) they entertained Jupiter and Mercury, travelling incognito. In thanks, Jupiter turned their hut into a temple and made them its priest and priestess. They were also allowed to die together.

[†] The aged husband and wife of Gogol's story "Old-World Landowners" from his collection *Mirgorod* (1835).

Solovyov himself was not very satisfied with this work. His friends, such as the Trubetskoy brothers, were disturbed, finding the spirit of the essay to be unwholesome and seeing in his theory a disparagement of the religious meaning of the family. In 1893 Solovyov wrote to Grot, " The beginning of the article is bad. Further on I hope it will get better."[37] And in October of the same year, he wrote to him from France, "After the departure of the Trubetskoys on 17 October, I set to work immediately and conscientiously on the end of "Love" and by Sunday 31 October I had written about 40 pages, but when I read them, – oh, gods! – as the deceased Afanasy Afanasevich would have said, what gruel it turned out to be, what vile kasha, what an abomination! And I had wanted to write as well as possible."[38]

To the end of 1892 or the beginning of January 1893 we must date the article "Free Will and Causality," which Solovyov destined for *Vestnik Evropy*. This was published after Solovyov's death in 1921 in the philosophical annual *Mysl' i slovo* (vol. 2:1, 169-185). The article was written as a response to "The Law of Causality as the Foundation of the Speculative Knowledge of Reality," part two of Lev Lopatin's book *The Positive Tasks of Philosophy* (Moscow, 1891). In a letter to Stasyulevich, Solovyov first recounts his old friendship with Lopatin and their adolescent adventures at Pokrovskoe-Glebovo-Streshnevo, then continues, "The author of this treatise on the freedom of the will, one of the former robber-brothers, but now a professor of philosophy at Moscow University, a genuine thinker... the talented... Lopatin is saddened by the lack of attention in the press to his work, and I have decided for the sake of an old friendship to console him as much as possible in this matter."[39] But evidently, Stasyulevich found Solovyov's article unsuitable for *Vestnik Evropy* and returned it. On 26 October/7 November 1893, Solovyov wrote to Stasyulevich, "Already from the letter that accompanied the article you could see that at the last minute I myself became doubtful about its suitability and therefore, if you don't encounter on my part either objections or expressions of dissatisfaction, ascribe this not so much to my modesty as to a sincere approval of your decision."[40] The article did not appear in *Voprosy filosofii i psikhologii* either; perhaps Solovyov feared lest his article bring sorrow instead of consolation to his old friend.

The dispute between Solovyov and Lopatin about free will began at a session of the Moscow Psychological Society in April 1889, and the two appendices that conclude the section "On Free Will" of Lopatin's book also relate directly to Solovyov's disagreement with him. In his article "Free Will and Causality" Solovyov takes as one of the objectionable positions a phrase from the second appendix.

Solovyov protested against the extreme indeterminism of Lopatin and defended the concept of *predestination*. (P. S. Popov had come to the conclusion that Solovyov possessed "a deterministic interpretation of the spiritual life" and "a directly Spinozist view of the relation between man and God.")[41] Solovyov objected to Lopatin's affirmation that "we look instinctively on ourselves as a source of creative forces. The creativity of the great philosophers and artists is *predetermined* by the objective properties of truth and beauty, independent of anyone's will; freedom is the consequence of truth that has come to be known, and not its presupposition: 'know you the truth, and the truth will make you free'."[42] The quarrel between Solovyov and Lopatin continued to the last years of Solovyov's life, as we shall see later.

In 1893 Pavel Milyukov mentioned Solovyov in his lecture "Slavophilism and its Degeneration (Danilevsky, Leontev, Vladimir Solovyov)." Solovyov responded with the article "Observations on the Lecture of P. N. Milyukov," in which, having noted certain inaccuracies of Milyukov and carefully indicated that his fundamental idea was previously expressed by the author of *The National Question*, he agreed with Milyukov that "concrete, united Slavophilism has died and will not be resurrected. Whether the universal-religious idea that is derived from it (i.e. Solovyov's own idea) has also died is a question, arbitrarily decided by P. N. Milyukov, that still belongs to higher authorities."[43]

As a result of his romantic infatuation of 1892 Solovyov considered himself to be a nervous wreck. Writing to Grot he even spoke of his intention of "turning to a neuropathologist."[44] But matters never got that far; "I am beginning to feel better, and I think that I have nervously exaggerated my neuropathy."[45] Instead Solovyov felt the necessity "of refreshing himself by a sea voyage abroad" and at the end of July boarded a steamer in St. Petersburg sailing for Abo and Sweden.

Endnotes for Part 3 - Chapter 1

1. *P*, vol. 4, 124. The lines of "some poet" refers to Evgeny Boratynsky's, "Already that winter has silvered my head, which ripens the sowing of the future world."
2. *P*, vol. 4, 163.
3. Ibid., 228.
4. *Stikh*. 233.
5. *P*, vol. 4, 157, 158.
6. Idem; *SS*, vol. 12, 142.
7. *Stikh*. 315.
8. *P*, vol. 4, 158.
9. Ibid., 152.
10. *Stikh*., 112.
11. Ibid., 111.
12. *P*, vol. 4, 126.
13. *Stikh*., 100. In a letter to his brother Mikhail, Solovyov says about "The Burning Bush," "Here you have a poem that no one but me likes" (*P*, vol. 4, 124).
14. *P*, vol. 4, 159.
15. Idem; *SS*, vol. 12, 143.
16. *Stikh*., 105; *SS*, vol. 12, 20.
17. *P*, vol. 4, 58; *Stikh*., 264; *SS*, vol. 12, 122.
18. Ibid., 57.
19. Ibid., 155; *Stikh*., 111; *SS*, vol. 12, 34.
20. Idem.
21. *Stikh*., 114; *SS*, vol. 12, 17.
22. *P*, vol. 4, 164; Katerina Ivanovna Boratynskaya was the wife of the vice-governor of Moscow, Lev Andreevich Boratynksy.
23. Ibid., 154.
24. Idem.
25. Ibid., 150.
26. Ibid., 152; *SS*, vol. 12, 142.
27. *SS*, vol. 12, 94.
28. *P*, vol. 1, 198.
29. Ibid., 198.
30. *P*, vol. 4, 158. This letter is undated, but the phrase "I spent this summer in Petersburg and in cholera" indicate the summer of 1894.
31. *P*, vol. 4, 164.
32. *SS*, vol. 12, 299.

33. *P*, vol. 3, 43-54.
34. *SS*, vol. 7, 1-60; *Voprosy filosofii i psikhologii* 14/15 (1892), 17 (1893), 21 (1894).
35. Ibid., 16.
36. Ibid., 60.
37. *P*, vol. 1, 73.
38. Ibid., 80.
39. Letter No. 31 (37), *P*, vol. 4, 60.
40. *P*, vol. 1, 111.
41. *Mysl' i slovo*, 185.
42. Ibid., 171.
43. *SS*, vol. 6, 428.
44. *P*, vol. 1, 72.
45. Ibid., 76.

Part 3 - Chapter 2

Journey to Sweden, Scotland, and France

Within my lonely soul is that free space,
Which surrounds me in front and behind.
V. Solovyov

Solovyov's first letter to his brother Mikhail from Sweden is dated 30 July/11 August 1893. "The voyage here was magnificent. Finland is much more beautiful than Italy. Especially the approach to Abo (read Obo). I even think that this is a French name and was originally spelled: *Oh, beau!* I have, however, a more learned etymology, '*Ob*' in Hebrew means sorcery or magic. This word was borrowed by the Hebrews (without interest) from the ancient Chaldeans, who, as you know, were the cousins of the Finns; they were both famous for their sorcery, therefore it is no wonder that the ancient Finnish capital received its name from the word for magic, which is entirely supported by the magical impression that it produces. One of my travelling companions, a Frenchified Swede, suggested a more prosaic etymology: *Abo – est ainsi appelée parce que c'est au bout de la Finlande...* But the true etymology is still more prosaic; Abo is a Swedish name and means something like shore, but in Finnish this city is called Richki, which means market or fair.* To return to poetry: on the first night I sat on the deck until sunrise, in honor of which I wrote some verses, and on the second night I even slept on deck under the eternal stars, in honor of which I received a proper cold, which, I hope, will not be eternal. And here is the poem:

---

* The present name is Turku.

Look: the sickle moon has grown pale,
Pale too is the star of Aphrodite,
A new reflection on the crest of the wave...
Wait with me for the sun, the sun!

Look, how as if with streams of blood
It pours out all over the dark force!
The old battle is stirred up again...
The sun, the sun has conquered again.

I don't know what kind of poetry this is, but I can vouch for the authenticity of the event."[1]

Two days later, on 1/13 August, he wrote, "I wrote to you in the highest spirits, which, since then, have become gloomy for two reasons. First of all, my night on the deck was not passed in vain. I came down with a bad cold and yesterday did not go out; and secondly, the electricity. You want to ring for an attendant, and suddenly, instead of one, the room is illuminated in broad daylight by a blinding white light; and then the reverse: at night you want to procure light with your own hand, but instead, several servants come rushing into your room, knocking their foreheads."[2] Further on, Solovyov relates jokingly how, having made himself understood in Swedish (without consulting his German-Swedish dictionary) to Hilda, the maid, he managed to have all the electricity removed from his room.

On 6 August (old style) he composed the poem "On the Way to Upsala [Po doroge v Upsalu]."[3] Solovyov felt close to this poor land, where there were only pine trees and rocks, where "the spirit of man grows in eternal dispute with nature and throws its challenge to the skies from the stormy sea" and where "in the shimmer of the northern lights is seen the entrance to the kingdom of the spirits." On the same day he also wrote the eight-line poem "On the Deck of the Fritiof."[4]

In Scotland, at Inversnaid on Loch Lomond the muse of Walter Scott inspired Solovyov. The first part of the ballad "A Moonlit Night in Scotland [Lunnaia noch' v Shotlandii]" is written in agitated, irregular anapests. A moon beam has penetrated the poet's window and has lured him out into the open air.

> Higher, higher, there where the lone
> Pine stands above the cliff.
> Where the stream runs like a spirit among the rocks,
> There where the goblin lives under the earth.[5]

In the moonlit chill, which "penetrated to his very soul," the poet feels himself to be "among an invisible crowd of the dead." He listens to the wail of a horn, the thunder of a drum, and the screech of a flute, which animate the pines, cliffs, and mossy granite with a mysterious shudder.

The second part of the ballad, "The Song of the Highlanders [Pesnia gortsev]" is almost a literal translation of Walter Scott's "The Lady of the Lake." It is written in dactyls, which alternate with amphibrachs.

> Proudly our bagpipe has sounded in Glen Fruin
> And Bannochar has answered it with a groan:
> Glen Luss and Ross-dhu are smoking in the valley,
> And the shore of Loch Lomond is laid waste.*

The war cry is rendered in Gaelic:

'Roderig Vikh-Al'pin-Dkhu, io! Ieroi!'

"Do not disturbed by certain unpronounceable words," Solovyov wrote to Stasyulevich on 7/19 September from Dinard when he sent him his poems, "they are as harsh for the English readers of Walter Scott as for your readers of *Vestnik Evropy*. I even hold that the Gaelic language is closer to Russian than to English."[6]

Soon after, Solovyov arrived in France. In Boulogne he met Stasyulevich,[7] who went on to Berlin, but on 29 August (10 September) Solovyov arrived in Dinard, from where he informed Lyubov Stasyulevich, "I arrived safely the day before yesterday in

---

* "The Lady of the Lake," Canto II:419-422.

Dinard, and yesterday I spent the whole day wandering around the environs with my host. The wind here is even worse than in Boulogne, but, all the same, as of today I have begun bathing in the sea."[8] Solovyov planned to stay in Dinard until 3/15 October, "perhaps, even somewhat later."[9] Dinard caught his fancy and he kept postponing his departure. "We leave Dinard on the 17th," Solovyov wrote to Stasyulevich on 9 October. On the 27th he wrote, "I am leaving here only on 7 November."[10]

In Dinard Solovyov stayed at the Hôtel des Bains. "I am still living amid greenery, even on the shore of the ocean," he wrote to his mother.[11] "I am very pleased with it (Dinard) from the point of view of climate, the beautiful views, and tranquility." The pleasantness of Solovyov's life at Dinard was increased by his finding there his friend Sergey Trubetskoy. "What makes you think that Trubetskoy and I are leading an idle life?" he wrote to Grot on 16/28 October. "We have even become possessed by our books, and for drink we have only apple kvass, yes, that and milk."[12] And in a letter to his mother, "It will soon be two months since I have drunk, of strong liquor, only cider (apple kvass), and if by chance I have drunk a glass of cognac I have got a headache, like Misha."[13]

In Dinard Solovyov completed *The Meaning of Love*.[14] In his briefcase he also had the manuscript of his article "Mohammed," which he proposed for publication in *Vestnik Evropy*. "As a result of obstacles presented by the censorship for a cheap edition, I gave my 'Mohammed' to Stasyulevich, but I intend to reward Pavlenkov with a Joan of Arc or a Peter the Great," Solovyov wrote to Grot in February or March 1893 from St. Petersburg.[15] On 9 October 1893 he added, "For the winter numbers of *Vestnik Evropy* I have in mind something more appropriate than 'Mohammed,' which is suited for the summer season; and it won't get spoiled from a rest, quite the contrary."[16] In the end *Mohammed* appeared in 1896 in Pavlenkov's series of biographies.

Aside from these works, while in Dinard Solovyov worked on an article about religious tolerance "Two Worldviews," which was a continuation of "A Historical Sphinx" (the latter article was published in *Vestnik Evropy*, no. 6, 1893), but the article with the former title never appeared in print.

In spite of his healthy living in Dinard, Solovyov felt himself physically worse. "My physical condition has also gone downhill," he wrote to Grot on 16/28 October.[17] "Soon, soon my dear friend, / I will be put into newspaper circulation..."[18] In a letter to his mother, "My health is so-so, but I sense old age and my hair is falling out at a terrific rate... I have almost no attacks of vomiting, but I am suffering from anemia."[19] To Stasyulevich he remarked, "The mirror and comb offer ominous evidence: The hemorrhoidal color of the face, / The gray hair falling out..."[20]

On 7/19 September Solovyov outlined his long itinerary: London, Paris, Berlin, and *Vaterland*.[21] In a letter of 9 October to Stasyulevich the itinerary is changed, "From here I will travel directly east: Chartres, Paris, Berlin, St. Petersburg... But London, as you see, I am wisely putting off till my next trip abroad. It is just as well because I would not be able to root myself in the British Museum as one should and I would only exasperate my appetite for books. And the books I need most can be found in Berlin where I have some friends, through correspondence, at the university. Besides, I also know what London is like in the winter with drafty rooms. In Berlin there are stoves and life is twice as cheap."[22]

But Solovyov did not make his way to Berlin. On 3/15 January he wrote to Grot already from St. Petersburg, "I regret that my delays in Paris prevented me from staying in Berlin. However, I still hope to go to Sweden and Germany in the spring."[23]

On 7 November Solovyov left Dinard and a week before composed the moving poem "Farewell to the Sea":

> Again and again I go with a lover's anguish
> To drink thirstily with my eyes from your infinity,
> I must part from this pale green friend as well.
> Together, oh sea, we grumble, but I will not
> Add to the salty moisture with my tears.
>
> I will take with me on my lonely winter path
> This living motion and voice and colors;
> In sleepless nights, bewitching me with your distant beauty,
> You will recall to me your unforgotten caresses.[24]

From now on, Solovyov's love songs will no longer be addressed to any female face; having bid farewell to the "pale green friend" in Dinard, he would meet her once again on the shore of the "gentle beauty" Lake Saima.

In the middle of November (old style) we find Solovyov in Paris. His attitude toward French society was now cooler than five years previously. Upon his return to St. Petersburg on 3/15 January 1894 he wrote to Grot, "I had the opportunity in Paris of informing the French about several important but bitter truths, for which they at first did not only not stone me but even highly praised me, but then, having pondered the matter they took revenge in a special way: they partly remained silent, but partly, – still worse– substituted my speech in the newspaper reports with some kind of colorless nonsense, with all sorts of compliments to me; but this is not a disaster, for the speech, all the same, will be published in its original form. Here I have completely literally repeated it in one society circle in the presence of two ministers. It was an unexpected pleasure for me to receive the net profit from the previous French brochure (*L'Idée russe*), but the book *(L'Eglise Universelle)*, apparently, can be published in a new revised edition. I also made several pleasant acquaintances."[25]

His impression of the French was better than in 1876, but was far from that enthusiasm which several lines of *L'Eglise Universelle* displayed in 1888. "I have remembered many times your words, uttered in Boulogne about the French: children, perfect children!" Solovyov wrote to Stasyulevich from Paris on 25 November/6 December 1893, "I have repeated this when I am in a good mood, but in a bad one I quote Fonvizin: the Frenchman has no sense, and if he did, he would consider it a misfortune."[26]

Solovyov attended a lecture of Brunetière about Bossuet at the Sorbonne and became acquainted with a new type of deputy to the parliament, the Socialist Abbé Lemire.[27]

At the beginning of December Solovyov wrote the poem "New Year's Greeting [S Novym godom]", which opened a new chapter in his relations with Sofya Khitrovo.[28] He had not forgotten his "poor friend," even during the episode of 1892 when his soul was possessed by another love. On 29 February 1892, at the height of his infatuation with Sofya Martynova, he composed one of his best poems inspired by the love of his youth.

Send me, memory, on a wing that does not age
To the place dear to the heart.
I see her on the smoldering site of a fire
Alone in the winter dusk.

The soul is sundered by bitter anguish,
Two lives were consumed there,
Something new is beginning in the distance
In place of the ruined spring.

Farther, memory! With a quietly waving wing
Bring to me another image…
I see her in a green meadow
During bright summer.

The sun plays about on the surface of the wild Tosna,
The steep bank is high…
I see familiar ancient pines,
Fine white sand…

Memory, enough! It is time for me to
Bury this sorrowing shade!
The time has passed and the sleeping princess
Cannot be possessed by the knight.[29]

Solovyov's relations with Sofya Petrovna began to die down at the beginning of the 1890s. In 1892 he received news of the death of Countess Sofya Andreevna Tolstaya, who had played such a role in his youth. On 2 June Solovyov wrote to Stasyulevich, "The late Countess Tolstaya desired to be buried at Krasny Rog in the place prepared for her next to Aleksey Konstantinovich. The transportation of her coffin from Lisbon, even by sea, will cost not less than 1500 rubles. The niece of the deceased, Sofya Petrovna Khitrovo, has written to you, to advance her this sum, if it is possible, against the future sale of the works of A. K. Tolstoy, the rights to which have passed to her (whether completely, or partially, I don't know)."[30]

The poem "New Year's Greeting" is undoubtedly addressed to Sofya Petrovna, whom Solovyov calls his "poor old friend."

> Whether it was a fatal power or our weakness
> That clothed our radiant love in evil passion,
> Let us be grateful, the cup has passed.
> The passion is burnt out, we are free again.

The radiant love had been distorted by a fatal passion, and Solovyov no longer experienced passion as the "true guarantee of the vital force." On the ruins of the extinguished love a quiet friendship arose. Soon we will see Solovyov at Pustynka again.

Solovyov had planned to return to St. Petersburg on 15 December (old style),[31] but was probably somewhat delayed. On 6/18 December he wrote to Stasyulevich from Paris, without mentioning his departure. He returned, as in 1888, directly to St. Petersburg, without stopping in Moscow. On the train he met his old friend Prince Tsertelev who was travelling "from Lisbon to Tambov via Algiers and St. Petersburg."[32]

This time nothing threatened Solovyov in Russia. Before his departure abroad he met Konstantin Pobedonostsev, who greeted him "like an old friend," at the wedding of Aleksey Obolensky.[33] Solovyov's wings had been clipped; he was worn out by pointless strife and had withdrawn into the desert of individualism. Having abandoned for the time being ecclesiastical-political projects, he gave himself up to lyrical poetry and moral philosophy. His liberal polemical articles sounded like the dying peals of a passing thunderstorm.

The sea voyage had washed from his soul the last remains of "erotic silt." Having parted with his religious and political projects, he also bid farewell to his hopes for personal happiness.

> Recognizing in oneself the higher force,
> Why then worry about childish dreams?
> Life is only an act of heroism...[34]

We now pass to the undefined, transitional period of *The Justification of the Good*. After this come the new and unfinished composition of *Theoretical Philosophy*, the genial insights of *Three Conversations*, and death…

Endnotes for Part 3 - Chapter 2

1. *P*, vol. 4, 126-127.
2. Ibid., 128.
3. *Stikh.* 119, 321.
4. Ibid., 120, 321.
5. Ibid, 121. "...the *Goblin* lives under the earth" is the original version instead of "...the *gnomes* live under the earth."
6. *P*, vol. 4, 63.
7. *P*, vol. 1, 116.
8. *P*, vol. 4, 62.
9. Ibid., 63.
10. *P*, vol. 1, 114.
11. *P*, vol. 2, 65.
12. *P*, vol. 1, 79.
13. *P*, vol. 2, 65.
14. *P*, vol. 1, 79-80.
15. *P*, vol. 1, 76.
16. Ibid., 110.
17. *P*, vol. 1, 79.
18. Ibid., 80.
19. *P*, vol. 2, 65.
20. *P*, vol. 1, 112.
21. *P*, vol. 4, 63.
22. *P*, vol. 1, 110.
23. Ibid., 83.
24. *Stikh.*, 57.
25. *P*, vol. 1, 82-83.
26. Ibid., 116.
27. Idem.
28. *Stikh.*, 126 and 322.
29. *Stikh.*, 107, 316. We have cited the last stanza as it appears in the first edition.
30. *P*, vol. 4, 57.
31. *P*, vol. 1, 117.
32. Ibid., 119.
33. *P*, vol. 4, 127.
34. *Stikh.*, 118; *SS* vol. 12, 35.

Part 3 - Chapter 3

The Beginnings of a Moral Philosophy
Lake Saima

> You are bathed in light, like a polar flame,
> Radiant daughter of dark chaos.
>
> *V. Solovyov*

In 1894 Solovyov was preparing for a major new work, *The Justification of the Good*, which took him about three years to write. Although he wrote to his brother Mikhail in the spring of 1895, "My *Ethics* is nearing completion,"[1] certain chapters were written only in 1897 and were added to the second edition of *The Justification of the Good*. Chapter seven, "The Unity of Moral Foundations," for example, was published for the first time in *Knizhki nedeli*, No. 2 (1898). Before we begin to discuss this work, we should give an account of the kind of society Solovyov was moving in during the last period of his life and consider who his intimate friends were at that time. Aside from Stasyulevich and the circle of *Vestnik Evropy*, Solovyov was very close to several representatives of the Petersburg aristocracy and bureaucracy. Prince Aleksey Dmitrievich Obolensky, the future Oberprokurator of the Holy Synod, became one of his devoted friends. Obolensky shared all of Solovyov's views, accepted him without criticism, and sympathized with his idea for the reunion of Churches, which was a stumbling block for the majority of Solovyov's Russian friends.

In 1893 Solovyov wrote to Grot from St. Petersburg, "I socialize here more with foreigners and also with my minister of finances, Salomon."[2] In a poem of 1897 Solovyov calls Salomon "an old friend."[3] The extent to which he attached importance to this friendship can be seen from the lines:

Imprisoned in the decaying dungeon of the world
And paying tribute to the reigning vanity,
We are free in the inner sanctum
Not to betray the sublime dream.

In Moscow, Prince Sergey Nikolaevich Trubetskoy became Solovyov's closest friend. Trubetskoy's worldview was formed under the strong influence of Solovyov, who proudly saw in him his pupil. Like Solovyov, in his philosophy Trubetskoy united Christianity with Platonism and considered the concept of the Logos to be the central idea of Christianity. Also like Solovyov, Trubetskoy was a confirmed Westernist and liberal. Later, however, a substantial rift developed between them. Trubetskoy was more of a rationalist than Solovyov and regarded mysticism with suspicion. In Berlin Trubetskoy fell under the strong influence of Harnack and Protestant historical science. To the mysticism and Catholicism of Solovyov, he opposed historical criticism. It is enough to compare Solovyov's philosophy of biblical history with Trubetskoy's theory of the Logos to recognize, in general, the great distance separating the philosophers. For Solovyov, the entire Bible was a source of mystical symbolism and Catholic orthodoxy, and he regarded the problem of Protestant criticism with scornful disdain. Trubetskoy, however, while trying to preserve Orthodox traditions, was wholly under the sway of the theories of Wellhausen and others. But the Solovyov of the '90s was not the Solovyov of the '80s, and his liberalism and Protestantism continued to struggle with ecclesiastical dogmatism. All the same, Solovyov did not yield to Trubetskoy, and bitter quarrels arose between them. Trubetskoy accused Solovyov of historical dilettantism, inclining him in favor of the Deutero-Isaiah and other inventions of German criticism; while Solovyov insisted on the unity and divine inspiration of the whole Bible. I can recall how Trubetskoy once told me, "After reading *The History of Theocracy*, Harnack said, 'It's amazing how even among the most educated Russians certain traditions and prejudices are alive.'" By his tone it was clear that in this instance Sergey Nikolaevich's sympathies were not on the side of the author of *The History of Theocracy*…

Solovyov was also close to Sergey Trubetskoy's cousin, Evgeny Nikolaevich, but they met more rarely as Evgeny Trubetskoy lived at that time in Kiev. The extent of the divergence between the worldviews of Solovyov and Evgeny Trubetskoy was revealed in the latter's book about Solovyov. It seems as though the entire two-volume work is devoted to tackling the two fundamental ideas of Solovyov: Sophia and Rome. Whereas Trubetskoy was a moderate liberal, a Protestantized Orthodox, Solovyov combined in himself two extremes, strict Catholic dogmatism and the nearly revolutionary pathos of a "prophet." Trubetskoy was a typical, solid representative of liberal Orthodoxy, while Solovyov rushed between the camps of the "godless" and the Vatican, and much as he maintained the infallibility of the Roman pontiff he also wrote articles in defense of Chernyshevsky. [4]

A not insignificant role in Solovyov's life was played by the now forgotten poet Vasily Lvovich Velichko. Although he belonged to the conservative camp, he got on well with Solovyov, treating him with reverence and never contradicting him. Because of his friendly disposition, Solovyov overvalued Velichko's slight talent and, although he called his own poetry "glass beads," mentioned the "corals, jasper, and malachite of Velichko" alongside the "diamonds of Pushkin and the pearls of Tyutchev."[5] On account of the "imperturbability of his spirit *rebus in arduis*, his perseverance, and the success of his works" Solovyov compared Velichko to his patron saint, Basil the Great.[6]

With respect to famous authors, we must not fail to mention that by 1894 Solovyov found himself to be definitely *in statu belli* with Vasily Rozanov and was trying to draw closer to Lev Tolstoy. These two facts speak of Solovyov's sharp turn "to the left" in the middle of the '90s. In his day Solovyov had regarded with great sympathy Rozanov's pamphlet *The Place of Christianity in History* and in 1893 had written him a very friendly letter (letter No. 4, *Pis'ma* vol. 3, 47). As this letter does not bear a date, one must assume that it was written before 1894, when Solovyov's article "Porfiry Golovlyov on Freedom and Faith"[7] established the *terminus ante quem* of their good relations. In letter No. 7 to Rozanov Solovyov wrote, "Not only do I believe that we are brothers in spirit, but I also find justification for this belief in the words of your inscription relating to the *signum* of the Kingdom of God. Those who know from the same experience will likewise understand in the same way and appreciate these signs, and tokens or omens of the Kingdom of God; such, of course, are brothers in spirit, and nothing can possibly separate them."[8] But in the first issue of *Vestnik Evropy* for 1894 Rozanov came out in his article "Freedom and Faith" against religious tolerance and refuted Solovyov's article "The Historical Sphinx." Solovyov's response to this was more than cruel. In the following issue of *Vestnik Evropy* he compared Rozanov to Saltykov-Shchedrin's character Iudushka* and called his article "unctuously shameless verbiage." "By abstract verbiage Iudushka always conceals some kind of perfectly concrete filth."[9] "That 'law of life' for which Iudushka demands complete freedom and in the name of which he would like to restrict everything else, is simply *the law of animal life* and nothing more."[10] In reply to Solovyov's mercilessly mocking article, in the fourth issue of *Vestnik Evropy* Rozanov exploded with savage and indecent abuse. He called Solovyov "a dancer from the corps de ballet," "a ballroom pianist playing on broken keys," "a blind man, walking into a letter on the page," "a fallen woman shamelessly brandishing theology," "a thief stealing in church," and "a stick that has been broken from being passed from hand to hand."[11] Solovyov answered this abuse with good-natured irony in his article "The End of the Quarrel: on Justice" (*Vestnik Evropy*, No. 7). He found that Rozanov's definitions were "first of all, too broad, and secondly, in poor agreement with each other. How could a stick be capable of robbing a church and so forth."[12] However their relations were not sundered and in 1895 Solovyov wrote to Rozanov quite amicably, "Aside from a desire to continue our 'acquaintance,' I have still another small matter at hand."[13] A year before his death in his article "A Special Celebration of Pushkin" Solovyov again mercilessly made fun of Rozanov for his "*orgiasm* and *pythism*." After Solovyov's death, Rozanov took his vengeance on him unceasingly, belittling in every way his importance and personality.

* Literally, Little Judas, nickname of Porfiry Golovlyov in Saltykov-Shchedrin's unsparing satire on traditional Russian landowners, *The Golovlyovs* (published during the 1870s).

He saw in Solovyov the features of "the Antichrist," and declared that the best thing about him was his "sadness," which he concealed, wearing his pride on his sleeve instead. A few months before his own death, Rozanov remarked to me, "Why did I quarrel with Vladimir Solovyov? In fact, we were both prophets…"

Solovyov's efforts to become better acquainted with Lev Tolstoy begain in 1894. In the '80s Solovyov had regarded Tolstoy with hostility. In 1882 he wrote to Aksakov, "I could offer nothing to L. Tolstoy, as it has already been a long time since we last met, and he has become for me 'like a pagan and a publican'."[14] In a letter to Strakhov, Solovyov points out Tolstoy's "profound evasiveness and insincerity."[15] And later, in letter No. 19, we read, "A few days ago I read Tolstoy's *What I Believe*. Is the beast roaring in the dense forest?"[16] On 27 November 1887 Solovyov had reported to Anna Aksakova, "Avant-hier j'ai eu encore une visite remarquable – celle de L. Tolstoy, qui m'apporté ses excuses pour certaines actions étranges. Il faudra aller chez lui et être sur ses gardes."

Solovyov disliked Tolstoy not only as a thinker but also as an artist. The naturalism of *War and Peace* said nothing to the admirer of E. T. A. Hoffmann. "In this novel the characters speak like people of our time, the spirit of the epoch is missing," Solovyov said of *War and Peace*… In 1888 Solovyov wrote to Fet from Viroflay, "And how is his (Strakhov's) idol getting on? Through the Frenchman Vogüé I heard that he is writing a novel about *the harm of love*… What a pity that I have no literary talent. Recently the landlady of my hotel cheated me. Here would be a splendid opportunity for me to write a poem about *the harm of hotels*."[17] On 20 September 1891 Solovyov wrote to Stasyulevich on the occasion of Goncharov's death, "And so the next-to-the-last coryphaeus of Russian literature is no more. Only Lev Tolstoy is left, and he is half-witted. Thus is life arranged in our town: if a man is wise, either he is a heavy drinker or he makes such terrible faces that it makes the saints blush."[18] In 1892 in his comic poem "The Triumph of Turpentine," Solovyov exclaims to the turpentine, "I would give up the best novel of Tolstoy for you!"[19] But in 1894 it appeared that Solovyov had much in common with Tolstoy. In the name of a universal Christian ideal they were both waging war with nationalism and harbored a hostile attitude to the official Russian Church. On 5 July 1894 Solovyov wrote to Tolstoy about his intention of "compiling a systematic anthology of his religious and moral works and of entitling it *A Criticism of Pseudo-Christianity from the Works of Lev Tolstoy*."[20] Solovyov also shared with Tolstoy an extremely negative attitude toward the conclusion of the Franco-Russian alliance, calling it a "Franco-Russian fraud."[21] At the same time, in the spring of 1894 Solovyov wrote to Tavernier in Paris, "I hope to send you shortly a manuscript, which has been heavily corrected, of my paper with the title 'A Few Thoughts about Our Future as Regards French-Russian Friendship.'"[22]

In his second long letter to Tolstoy, written between 28 July and 2 August 1894, Solovyov discusses the source of their disagreement. "Our whole disagreement can be reduced to one concrete point, the resurrection of Christ. I think that in your personal worldview (if I understand correctly your latest works) there is nothing, as such, that would prevent one from acknowledging the truth of the resurrection, and there is even something that compels one to acknowledge it."[23] If Solovyov was still hoping to convince Tolstoy of the truth of the resurrection of Christ, he was mistaken. Soon after, Solovyov made a sharp break with Tolstoy and in his last work, *Three Conversations,* he sees in the great writer of the Russian land a sham, false Christian and the spirit of the Antichrist. Tolstoy's attitude toward Solovyov was always cold.

Solovyov spent the summer of 1894 in St. Petersburg. He was seriously ill twice: "on one occasion there was a flow of blood," which was enough to frighten the doctor;[24] on the other, he came down with cholera, "I am lying in bed looking greenish-purple."[25] He informed Sofya Martynova, "I have spent this summer rather poorly in Petersburg with cholera."[26] At the time of his "choleric convulsions" he composed a poem "Metempsychosis," in which he jokingly depicts how he is dying, decaying in the earth, and being transformed into "a flower and, in the form of honey, ends up on the lips of a beautiful girl."[27]

In the meantime, his new work, *The Justification of the Good,* was ripening in Solovyov's mind; for this he sought solitude. "I shall settle forever among the cliffs and forests of Finland, – for the sake of my work, my finances, and my health," he wrote to Sofya Martynova; and to his brother Mikhail, "I am going to Finland today only to look, but I shall definitely move there on Wednesday or Thursday. The full pension will cost me not more than 50 rubles per month (whereas in Petersburg a room alone costs 90 rubles), and then there will be nil for cabs. I cannot imagine anything more sensible."[28] The landscape that had once been celebrated by Boratynsky* became the witness to a luxuriant flowering of Solovyov's poetry and philosophy.

Solovyov departed for Finland in September; on the 30th he wrote to Stasyulevich, "I have settled here, it would seem, quite solidly, despite certain inconveniences. The sad child of nature, to whom I paid a month's rent in advance, naively declared to me that he would not neglect me for anything and would be ready to do anything for me. The weather is mild and gray, without rain. I go walking without a coat or galoshes for two or two-and-half hours without sitting. I am not drinking anything alcoholic, I eat once a day, I am sleeping well and feel superb. I am not reading newspapers."[29] On 1 October he wrote to Grot, "I am staying by Lake Saima, near the village (farm) of Tiurinniama, in a place called Kaisaranta, i. e. the royal shore. To reach me by letter or telegram one has to write: Imatra, Raukha, pension Alma, V. S. S."[30]

The first few days were "absorbed by poetry and nature."[31]

> "'On the banks of deserted' waters
> The Finnish muse appeared to me;
> I was only polite to her – and now
> She has already given birth to triplets.

Thus I began a letter of ten days ago, but since then this Finnish lass has provided me with about ten more children,"[32] Solovyov wrote to Velichko on 13/25 October.

A profound contemplative silence had taken hold of Solovyov's soul. An epistolary poem to Grot in October expresses this mood best of all:

---

* In his youth the romantic poet Evgeny Boratynsky (1800-1844) had spent a number of years in Finland.

Nothing agitates the passions,
And the quiet swarm of innocent dreams
Has been covered by a transparent dusk…
I write. The firs look into the window,
A light frost has silvered the paths…
Verses, however, are boring
It is time to turn to prose.[33]

At Saima many of the chapters of *The Justification of the Good* were written; however, this title had not yet occurred to Solovyov. On 30 September he wrote to Stasyulevich, "I will have you publish my book *The Foundations of Moral Philosophy*."[34] Solovyov published separate chapters of *The Justification of the Good* in *Vestnik Evropy*, *Voprosy filosofii i psikhilogii*, *Knizhki nedeli*, and even in the literary supplement to *Niva*. At the same time that he was dedicating his cycle of poems to Lake Saima, Solovyov was probably writing the second chapter of his book, "The Aesthetic Principle in Morality," which was published in *Voprosy filosofii i psikhilogii*.[35] The philosopher's friends in Moscow did not agree with Solovyov and sent him their objections. Solovyov took their criticisms seriously and on 22 November replied with a circular letter addressed to Nikolay Yakovlevich (Grot), *Drakon* Mikhailovich (Lopatin), and Sergey Nikolaevich (Trubetskoy). "I thank you for your attentive consideration of my article. I am in absolute agreement with your conclusion that it would not be a good idea to publish it without alterations."[36]

Both in his prose and his verse of this period, Solovyov expressed a profound ascetic detachment.

Do not attempt to catch, my child, the wave of passion
With its foam seething with vain desire,
Look above to the motionless and mighty
Shore of love, descending from the heavens.[37]

Solovyov's need for an eternal love no longer sought the image of a living woman:

> I have fallen in love with the lake.[38]

And in a humorous letter to Stasyulevich he speaks of "the nymph of Lake Saima."[39]

Solovyov called Saima his last love and dedicated his love poetry to it as though to a living being.

> I have come to love you, gentle beauty.[40]

These poems inspired rumors about Solovyov's having fallen in love in his old age with some kind of Finnish Eda.* In the foreword to the third edition of his poetry he was forced to defend himself. "A certain northern lake, not unknown to geography and to which I have taken a liking *en tout bien tout honneur,* has seemed to the eyes of an unofficial Cato to be a light-minded person of the female sex. I have flatly denied that in my declining years I have become inspired by youthful feelings, on which I am expatiating in print."[41]

Solovyov loved Lake Saima during storms, as well, when it would lap the shore with restless waves and, forgetting about its primordial centuries of royal freedom, thrash about rebelliously. The contemplation of the wild prisoner of Saima, struggling in its granite fetters led Solovyov to think of the destiny of the Finnish people and, wandering through the forests of Finland, he composed a prayer to the God of justice, "so that the tide of force would break on the rocks of Finland."[42] Still more beautiful is his beloved asleep, "wrapped up in a downy fur coat," in the transparent white silence.

> You are immaculate, like snow beyond the mountains,
> You are full of many thoughts, like the winter night,
> You are bathed in light, like a polar flame,
> Radiant daughter of dark chaos.[43]

* Eponymous heroine of a narrative poem by Boratynsky (1824) set in Finland.

In the silence of snowy Finland, Solovyov developed a prophetic clairvoyance and a growing sense of world catastrophe.

He was making his way alone to an enigmatic goal surrounded by the fragile snowy wasteland, and the silence revealed to him aloud that soon the unexpected would occur. The azure eye that had shone light on him through the dark brooding storm clouds had drowned in the mist. The desert lacked a goal and his path was without direction.

> And the same voice resounds in the silence without reproach:
> The end is near, the unexpected will soon take place.[44]

From the beginning of the '90s Solovyov began to consider the yellow peril of pan-Mongolism. While studying the history and culture of Japan and China, he eagerly followed the political developments in the Far East and frequented the circles of Petersburg diplomats. "Write to me whether the news has been confirmed about the conclusion of an alliance between Japan and China; this is very important," Solovyov wrote to Velichko on 25 April 1895 from Imatra.[45] During the same winter he wrote the poem "Pan-Mongolism," which predicts the destruction of the Russian Empire by the Mongols as divine punishment for the Third Rome's rejection of the Messiah, which resembles that perpetrated by the Second Rome, – Byzantium.

> Oh Rus! Forget your former glory:
> The double-headed eagle is crushed,
> And the shreds of your banners
> Have been given to yellow children to play with.[46]

Solovyov celebrated Christmas of 1894 at Imatra in a profoundly religious mood. During the holidays he wrote two poems "*Immanul-el*"[47] and "Christmas Night [Noch' na Rozhdestvo]"[48] He felt as though the Word that had been born long ago in a manger was born again in his soul, that God is with us, here, in the futility of daily life, in the murky flood of the anxieties of existence. He no longer regretted his theocratic hopes, which had failed to be realized, and now had to admit that:

Kings no longer gaze at the heavens,
And shepherds do not hear in the desert
How the angels speak of God.

"Although everything be profaned by the centuries of crimes," the source of truth is not deafened in the depths of the world's consciousness; the reproach of conscience is stronger than all doubts; and though spurned by the darkness, the light still shines at the border of good and evil.

Not by an exterior power but by truth itself
The prince of the age is condemned with all his works.

Solovyov did not live in complete isolation in his snow covered Thebaid. From time to time he would go to Petersburg. On 13/25 December he informed Velichko, "Following this letter, I will be heading for St. Petersburg. Don't be offended if I don't go directly to see you. I am not certain whether you have a spare room arranged, and since I know that out of kindness for me you are prepared to deprive yourself of the basic necessities, I must be careful not to let you do this. But if everything is in order at your place, then I would like to stay about four days to finish Kant, as I did Hegel two years ago."[49] By Hegel and Kant, Solovyov is referring to his entries for the encyclopedia.

On one occasion Velichko accompanied his friend to Imatra:

> I remember how we once traveled through the forest from Imatra to Raukha, where he lived in the winter of 1895. Through the branches of the dense pine and fir trees the moon was shining brightly. The bluish snow glistened like a million diamonds, flocks of titmice and bullfinches that had fluttered off began to chirp about something as though it were spring... We were both struck dumb as though drunk, and I exclaimed involuntarily, "Do you see God?" Vladimir Solovyov, as if in a dream, as though, in fact, a vision close to his soul were taking place before him, replied, "I see the

goddess, the soul of the world, longing for the one God." For the rest of the way we were silent.[50]

During this winter Solovyov also wrote his articles about the poetry of Fyodor Tyutchev[*] and Aleksey Tolstoy. The first of these belongs to the best work of Solovyov: it is as though he revealed for the first time the entire significance of Tyutchev. For Solovyov, what is important and precious about Tyutchev is that he not only *felt*, but also *thought* as a poet, and was *convinced* of the objective truth of a poetic view of nature. He did not consider nature to be dead following the end of the mythological worldview of the ancient Greeks, as did Schiller, but knew that nature possesses a soul, freedom, love, and language.[51] "Perhaps Goethe himself did not grasp so profoundly as our poet the *dark root* of the world's existence, did not feel as strongly and did not realize as clearly that *mysterious foundation of every life*, that foundation on which is built the meaning of the cosmic process, the destiny of the human soul, and the entire history of mankind."[52]

"The principal manifestation of the spiritual life of man, which reveals its meaning, is love, and here our poet again emphasizes, more strongly and clearly than others, the same demonic and chaotic foundation, to which he was attuned in the phenomena of external nature. This is in no way contradicted by the prosaic, inspired character of Tyutchev's poetry. On the contrary, the fresher and more spiritual a poetic creation, the more deeply and fully is experienced that dark and non-spiritual element, which demands illumination and inspiration."[53] The only way out of this "evil life" with its fundamental division and contradiction is to draw close to the "Leader on the path of perfection," to replace the fatal and murderous heritage of ancient chaos with the spiritual and life-giving legacy of the new man, or the Son of Man.

The soul is ready like Mary

---

[*] Although by profession a diplomat and civil servant, Tyutchev (1803-1873) is best known for his poetry, which was strongly influenced by his early career in Germany and his exposure to the *Naturphilosophie* of Schelling. In his later years he espoused a conservative, nationalistic ideology.

To cling to the feet of Christ forever...[54]

Turning to the Slavophile ideas of Tyutchev, to his belief in a Russian theocratic monarchy stretching from the Nile to the Ganges, with Constantinople as its capital, Solovyov carefully enters into a debate with the great poet. "Let us assume, taking Tyutchev's point of view, that Russia is the soul of humanity. However, just as in the soul of the natural world, as in the soul of every individual, the bright spiritual element struggles against its dark chaotic foundation, which is still not conquered, still not subordinated to the higher powers, still struggling for predominance, and leading us to death and destruction, so too, of course, does the same occur in this collective soul of humanity, that is, in Russia. Her life is not yet definitively formed, she is still divided and pulled in various directions by opposing forces. Has the light of the truth of Christ already been incarnated in her, has she indeed created a unity of all her parts through love? The poet himself recognizes that she has not yet been clothed in the raiment of Christ."[55]

In contrast to Tyutchev, a poet of exclusively contemplative thought, Solovyov defines Aleksey Tolstoy as a poet of militant thought, a warrior-poet, who carries the banner in the name of beauty.[56] Tolstoy celebrated in his prose and verse the ideal of a truly Russian, European, and Christian monarchy and fulminated against the nightmare of Asiatic despotism that he so hated. Finding the principle of a true national system in the Kievan epoch of our history, he saw the realization of the opposite principle in the period of the Muscovite state, which he regarded with fierce hostility. "My hatred for the Moscow period," he wrote in one of his letters, "is my idiosyncrasy... My hatred for despotism is my very self."[57] The last sections of this article, which are devoted to a criticism of the Byzantine-Mongol traditions, seem to be a transition to the article "Byzantinism and Russia," which was written toward the end of 1895. In Russia, as in its teacher Byzantium, Solovyov finds a poorly developed *consciousness of the absolute value of human dignity, the principle of personal autonomy and initiative*."[58]

From January 1895 Solovyov felt "the persistent and powerful summons of kindred shades." His solitude was full of the souls of his deceased friends.

> Hardly had I abandoned the agitation of life,
> When my departed friends gathered in a crowd...[59]

During the summer of 1892 in Morshchikha Solovyov had heard wails from the land of the dead, his heart had shuddered, and he had shed tears... Now he felt from the proximity of the dead "bitter joy and a sweet sorrow."[60]

> Already the advent of the invisible spring
> Resounds and blows with the breath of eternity.

What did this summons from the shades of dear ones prophesy? The flowering of new energies, or death? Thus Solovyov pondered. In fact this call foretold one and the other: the triumphant burst of new energies before death. But Solovyov was also visited by moments of bitter regret over the irretrievable past.

> Regret for that moment that perished forever,
> It cannot be resurrected...[61]

Tears flowed from his eyes, and it seemed to him that the heavy years of the past were slowly dragging behind the moment of eternity. Earthly reality with its nightmares began to oppress him more and more...

In Raukha Solovyov had to suffer a great deal from the cold. A letter of October 1894 to Stasyulevich ends with the exclamation, "A terrible frost with wind. Oy, Oy, Oy!"[62] On 24 January 1895 he wrote to Grot, "In the meantime I had been flourishing here, and the frosts without wind did me no harm, but last night, when it was 30° with such a strong wind that the windows rattled in their frames, it would seem I thoroughly froze my hemorrhoids in this primitive establishment. I hope to cure myself with a hot bath."[63]

Toward Easter of 1895 we find Solovyov in Raukha again. He greeted Velichko, Stasyulevich, and his brother Mikhail with the words "Christ is Risen." "I arrived safely but I have not been able to install myself entirely successfully in Raukha," he informed Velichko. "It is full of visitors, my room seems to be taken and they have given me another a floor below, with individuals of both sexes and various ages walking over my head. Winter is here in full force and this is getting to be a bore. As something of a compensation for this are the proximity of the Auer family and memories of Naples and Sorrento where 19 years ago I had a slight crush on Mme Auer (she is now half deaf and has three grown daughters with her)."[64]

But in his paschal letter to Stasyulevich, Solovyov already speaks of the arrival of spring. "Today spring began here all of a sudden, although it is still completely white everywhere."[65] "Today the lake, finally, has become clear of ice and now, without any further preparations, is reflecting a magnificent sunrise."[66] And in a letter to his brother Mikhail he wrote, "I am sitting surrounded by melting snow. The landscape is still wintry, but there are no means of communication. I am 'taking the air' on the balcony. However, it is the third day now that I have walked along the snowy plains of Saima with Mme Auer, whom I courted 19 years ago on Vesuvius: what symbolism! She now has a nineteen-year old daughter Zoya, who reminds me of Katya Vladimirovna of about twenty years ago. I say to her (mentally):

> Ich bin nun zwei-und-vierzig Jahre alt
> Und du bist neunzehnjährig kaum. –
> Oh Zoya! Wenn ich dich erblicke,
> Erwacht in mir der alte Traum.*

But I converse more with the mother, who no longer goes out under the portico to make juice out of pomegranates."[67] By symbolism, Solovyov evidently perceived the contrast between Vesuvius and the snowy plains of Saima as a reflection of the change that had taken place in his own spiritual life over the course of nineteen years.

With the arrival of spring Solovyov felt himself to be "resurrected." In April he wrote the poem "To the Resurrected One

---

* I am now forty-two years old / And you are barely nineteen. / Oh Zoya! When I behold you, / The old dream awakens in me.

[Voskresshemu]," which opens the final section in the third edition of his poetry. Solovyov was not very happy with this poem and kept reworking it. In the end he described it to Stasyulevich thus, "The whole poem is only just so-so, and if the title 'To the Resurrected One' seems to you to be too bold, then remove it and replace it with asterisks."[68] In order to prove his objective attitude to his poem, Solovyov wrote a "self-parody" of it.

> Vladimir Solovyov sends us
> Regiment after regiment of awkward verses
> And drinks in silence
> His royalties of mere verbiage.[69]

The concluding stanza of "To the Resurrected One" is characteristic:

> The snow of gray hairs will not restrain
> The soul of the ripening blossoming,
> Only the gaze of your eyes
> Shall illuminate this mixture of winter and summer.[70]

Whose eyes? Of course, not those of Mme Auer... Solovyov was returning to the experiences of 1875 and would soon be drawn again to Egypt. Sometimes the Finnish spring awakened sorrowful feelings in the poet's soul:

> Finally, she threw off
> Her decrepit garment,
> Smiled and sighed,
> And opened her clear gaze.
>
> The fiery roses of heaven
> Are reflected in the wave,
> And the scent of the birch is spread
> By the forest in a transparent half-sleep.
>
> Why is the day of blossoming
> For me a day of sorrow?
> Why at the feast of light
> Do I carry a nocturnal shadow?

Separated from the earth
That is awakening, in a mute land
Someone with heavy anguish
Whispers, remember me![71]

Probably, this "someone," who is separated from the awakening earth, was none other than the poet of spring, the hospitable host of Vorobyovka, Afanasy Fet.

In May Solovyov went to Moscow,[72] from where he set out for St. Petersburg. There he stayed at the barracks of Colonel Vladimir Dmitrievich Kuzmin-Karavaev, but when repairs were begun at the barracks Solovyov informed Stasyulevich of his intention to go to Finland for about ten days. "I think that in my imminent obituary, and also in the little volume of Pavlenkov's biographical library that will be devoted to me, it will be said about me, among other things, 'The best years of this remarkable man's adult life were spent under the hospitable shelter of the barracks of the regular battalion of the Life Guards of the reserve infantry regiment and also in the cool quiet refuge of the carriages of the Tsarskoselsky railway line.'"[73]

Solovyov's muse had fallen silent. After the spring of 1895 he wrote only one poem of eight lines, "These Threatening Forces that Roared at Noon [Eti groznye sily, chto v polden' gremeli]," dated at Tsarskoe Selo.[74] The date of the next poem is already 1896.

Endnotes for Part 3 - Chapter 3

1. *P*, vol. 4, 132.
2. *P*, vol. 1, 76.
3. *Stikh.*, 154, 352; *SS*, vol. 12, 67.
4. *P*, vol. 1, 271. (St. Petersburg, 1908).
5. *P*, vol. 1, 226.
6. Ibid., 215.
7. *SS*, vol. 6, 429.
8. *P*, vol. 3, 50.
9. *SS*, vol. 6, 431.
10. Ibid., 480.
11. Idem.
12. Idem.
13. *P*, vol. 3, 51.
14. *P*, vol. 4, 15.
15. *P*, vol. 1, 18.
16. Ibid., 21.
17. *P*, vol. 3, 118.
18. *P*, vol. 4, 54.
19. *Stikh.*, 265.
20. *P*, vol. 3, 37.
21. Idem.
22. *P*, vol. 4, 196 (218).
23. *P*, vol. 3, 38.
24. Ibid., 37.
25. *Stikh.*, 268.
26. *P*, vol. 4, 158.
27. *Stikh.*, 268.
28. *P*, vol. 4, 130.
29. Ibid., 66.
30. *P*, vol. 1, 94.
31. Ibid., 207.
32. Ibid., 206.
33. Ibid., 94.
34. *P*, vol. 4, 66.
35. No. 26, 1895.
36. *P*, vol. 3, 211.
37. *Stikh.*, 138.
38. *P*, vol. 1, 85.
39. Ibid., 121.

40. *Stikh.*, 132.
41. Ibid., xii.
42. *Stikh.*, 238.
43. Ibid., 133.
44. Ibid., 139.
45. *P*, vol. 1, 227.
46. *Stikh.* 240.
47. Ibid., 135.
48. Ibid., 136.
49. *P*, vol. 1, 207.
50. Velichko, op cit., 54.
51. *SS*, vol. 7, 120.
52. Ibid., 125.
53. Ibid., 129.
54. Ibid., 131.
55. Ibid., 134.
56. Ibid., 135.
57. Ibid., 151.
58. Ibid., 158.
59. *Stikh.*, 137.
60. Ibid., 141.
61. Ibid., 140.
62. *P*, vol. 4, 68.
63. *P*, vol. 1, 91.
64. Ibid., 222.
65. *P*, vol. 4, 69.
66. *P*, vol. 1, 127.
67. *P*, vol. 4, 132. There is a reference to some lines of Kuzma Prutkov:

    The mother goes out under the portico
    To squeeze pomegranates into juice.
    Zoya, no one will notice,
    Zoya, let me embrace you.

68. *P*, vol. 1, 128.
69. *P*, vol. 4, 70; vol. 1, 225; *Stikh.*, 330.
70. *Stikh.*, 143.
71. Ibid., 142.
72. *P*, vol. 4, 132.
73. Ibid., 71.
74. *Stikh.*, 144.

Part 3 - Chapter 4

The Justification of the Good
Byzantinism and Russia
Secret Reconciliation with the Catholic Church

The light appeared in the world, and
The light was rejected by the darkness,
But it shines in the darkness *at the border of*
Good and evil.

V. Solovyov

In 1884 Solovyov had written to Aleksandr Kireev, "You advise me to write a book *on ethics*. But, in fact, I don't separate ethics from religion, as I don't separate religion from positive revelation, and positive revelation I don't separate from the Church. Oh, but what an impediment! And if I can't write freely about the impediment of the Church, then I can't write about ethics."[1] Solovyov's view, however, had changed somewhat since 1884. In the introduction to *The Justification of the Good* he says, "By its very nature moral philosophy finds itself closely linked to religion, but by its method of reasoning, – to theoretical philosophy. We cannot explain, in advance, of what this connection consists, but we can, and must, say now of what it *does not consist*. One should not posit this connection as the unilateral dependence of ethics on positive religion or on speculative philosophy, a dependence that would deprive the moral sphere a content of its own and an independent meaning. This view, which subordinates morality and moral philosophy to the theoretical principles of a positive religious or philosophical character is extremely widespread in one or another form. Its groundlessness is all the more clear to me as I myself, at one time, was very near to it, even if I did not fully adopt it."[2]

The scale of our work does not permit us to give any kind of detailed analysis of *The Justification of the Good*, so we shall note only its main points.

Solovyov considers three feelings to be the primary factors of morality: shame (sexual); pity, or altruism; and reverence, or fear of God. Debating with Plotinus, who was ashamed of his corporeality as well as the act of eating, Solovyov maintains that there is nothing shameful in having a body itself. What is shameful is the enslavement of the spirit by the forces of the lower, animal nature. It is not the act of eating, but the act of sex that inspires the feeling of shame, and the conscience testifies against it. "At that moment of falling into sin, a higher voice resounds in the depth of the human soul, asking where are you? Where is your moral dignity? You human being, master of nature and the likeness of God, do you still exist? And here is the reply: I have heard the divine voice, I have become afraid at the awakening and manifestation of my lower nature; *I am ashamed, therefore I exist*; I exist not only physically, but also morally; I am ashamed of my animality, therefore, I still exist as a human being."[3]

The goal of humanity is the spiritualization of its corporeality and the triumph over death and decay. There are two ways of asceticism: marriage, as the restriction of the sensual life and its subordination to moral feeling and law; and monasticism, as the path of complete renunciation and the imitation of the angelic existence. There is a third and higher path, that of Godmanhood. Of this Solovyov speaks more fully and clearly in his essay, *The Drama of Plato's Life*, which we will discuss in chapter six. If there is angelic asceticism, there is also satanic asceticism, which imitates the devil himself, who neither eats nor drinks and is celibate.

Asceticism and economy are apparently two mutually foreign ideas, but in essence they are the two related ideas of our epoch. Humanity must recognize its responsibility with regard to material nature by promoting its spiritualization and liberation from decay.

Considering pity or altruism, Solovyov quotes from St. Isaac the Syrian about "the compassionate heart" and "the flaming heart in man for all creation,"[4] which he had already cited in *A Critique of Abstract Principles*.

Solovyov devoted separate chapters to legal, economic, and national questions. With regard to law and the state, Solovyov finds himself in a hidden polemic with Lev Tolstoy. Adopting the point of view of a humane, Christian state, he recognizes the theory of juridical vengeance to be absurd and considers the goal of punishment to be the correction of the criminal, not retribution. Solovyov also appears to be an apologist for the principle of public law, which is an organized form of compassion and justice, and saves society from both "the burning inferno of anarchy" and "the icy hell of despotism." "The task of law is by no means to convert the world lying in evil into the Kingdom of God, but only to prevent it from turning *prematurely* into hell."[5] War is an evil, but it is unavoidable given the imperfect state of society. Refusal to perform military duty leads to a greater evil than war, which can be compared to illness, the struggle of an organism against microbes.

Economic reform must be implemented on three bases: 1) material wealth must not be accepted as the independent goal of the economic activity of humanity; 2) production must not be carried at the expense of the human dignity of the workers, none of whom should be treated as only an instrument of production; 3) humanity's responsibilities toward the earth must be recognized.[6]

Repeating and amplifying his ideas on the national question, Solovyov opposes to the national ideal, the ideal of a united Christian Europe, whose unity at the present time is reinforced by the international market. Only the Mongol race finds itself outside the sphere of European Christian civilization, but European enlightenment has made great strides in Japan. An imminent collision is possible between Christian Europe and the Mongols, but this collision can still be averted if Europe becomes truly Christian and proves, in fact, its loyalty to the precepts of the Gospel.

The book ends with a repetition of Solovyov's old scheme: the primate of the Church, as the supporter of authority, is the apex of religion; the emperor, as the defender of authority, is the apex of mercy and justice; the prophet, as the bearer of the spirit of freedom, is the apex of the sense of shame and conscience. The prophetic service existed in the Old Testament, but it was rightfully suppressed by Christianity and for the most part appeared on the historical scene in a distorted form; yet it must be reestablished.[7] We agree with Evgeny Trubetskoy that these pages are "tortured." Solovyov writes about the tsar and supreme pontiff without that emotion which the pages of *The History of Theocracy* and *La Russie et l'Eglise Universelle* breathe. One senses that here only the scheme is left. Solovyov perceives concretely only the third person of *The History of Theocracy*, the prophet, and ignores the Christian emperor. With the accession to the throne of Nicholas II, the illusions of a Russian theocracy became increasingly remote. Later we shall see that before his death Solovyov wanted to believe in Wilhelm II as the theocratic emperor and the "heir of sword-bearing hosts." With regard to the first person of the theocracy, the primate (the substitution of the term "supreme pontiff" with "the primate" is typical), we should note that at this time Solovyov's attitude to the sole concrete primate of the Universal Church, the pope of Rome, was undefined. One fact had become clear: Solovyov's break with the Greco-Russian Church, which, in a letter to Velichko, he calls the "Greco-Russian synagogue." In April 1895 Solovyov wrote to him:

> First of all, it is clear to me that the question about Orthodoxy and its truth, primarily with respect to Protestantism, has no direct relationship to the matter at hand. I will explain this with a parable:
>
> In a certain city there were two schools. One of them distinguished itself by its superior program of teaching and education, which left nothing to be desired in terms of correctness and completeness, so that, judging from the curriculum alone, everyone had to say, what a wonderful school this is! However, for all that, the administration and teachers of this model school either did nothing for the formation and guidance of youth or else indulged in the sin of Sodom and corrupted the youths entrusted to them. The second school had a curriculum that was, although fundamentally sound, very incomplete and meager. Its teachers, however, generally speaking, fulfilled their responsibilities in good conscience and refrained from sodomy and other irregularities. Would it be right to take a young boy

> from this second school and place him in the first for the sake of its splendid curriculum?
>
> Thus, as long as your membership in the Greco-Russian synagogue is only an external fact that occurred without your will, you have nothing to answer for; but if you were, according to your own volition, consciously, intentionally, and without coercion, to send a young, and therefore innocent, creature to the above mentioned institution, you would triumphantly declare your solidarity with this institution and all of its sins would fall on you. In such a way, then, you are already personally guilty for the burning of Archpriest Avvakum, the persecution of the peasants of Krozh, the prohibition of the prayer meetings of the Stundites, and a thousand other facts of the same kind.*
>
> Finally, your personal position would have to change in another sphere. Now, for example, I spent several weeks with you during Great Lent, and we did not observe the rules of fasting nor did we go to church, and there was nothing wrong in this, as all this was not written for us and everyone understands that, but if you were triumphantly to declare yourself a *zealot* of the official church, then it would be impossible to say that its rules and regulations were not written for you...[8]

Solovyov definitely declares that the "rules and regulations of the Orthodox Church were not written for him." We might add that given the mood that permeates this letter to Velichko it would not have been possible for Solovyov to join not only the "Greco-Russian synagogue," but also the Roman Church. If joining the Orthodox Church means taking upon oneself the burning of Avvakum, then how many pyres would one have to take on one's conscience by joining the Church of Rome? Besides, the very concept of the Church as a curriculum that one can accept or reject depending on the success of its implementation is in itself deeply anti-Catholic. If Catholic views

* Solovyov is referring, respectively, to official repression of the Greek Catholic and Baptist communities on Russian territory in the 1890s.

made it impossible for Solovyov to remain in the Orthodox Church, then his Protestant views formed a barrier between him and Rome.

Solovyov's phrase that "Church laws were not written for him" requires us to discuss a fact that has been poorly explained. For several years already, Solovyov had not been to confession and had not received communion from Orthodox priests, following the occasion when Father Orlov, archpriest of the Church of the Holy Trinity at Zubov, had refused to grant him absolution if he did not renounce his Catholic views. In what year did this episode take place? The Catholic priest Nikolay Tolstoy told me that this confession with Archpriest Orlov occurred either during or after the severe illness when Solovyov was distressed by the persecution of *Moskovskie vedemosti*. This would indicate his bout with diphtheria in November 1891 when *Moskovksie vedemosti* was, in fact, harassing Solovyov for his lecture "The Decline of the Medieval Worldview." But in a letter to his brother Mikhail, Solovyov wrote, "During my diphtheria I received communion and was very glad I did."[9] There is no reason to assume that Solovyov had written a lie to his brother. His next serious illness was the attack of cholera during the summer of 1894 in St. Petersburg. However, a confession to Father Orlov, who was the senior priest of the Solovyov's parish church in Zubov, could only have taken place in Moscow. Apparently, Father Nikolay Tolstoy's report is not entirely accurate, although the fact itself of a refusal on the part of Father Orlov to give communion to the author of *La Russie et l'Eglise Universelle* is undeniable. We believe that this fact exerted a strong influence on Solovyov's psychology and definitely placed him *in statu belli* with the Greco-Russian Church. In this respect, the poem "Confession," included in a letter to Stasyulevich of 30 September 1894, is revealing:

> I was a zealot of the true belief,
> And the swine would have devoured me,
> But at the border of hypocrisy
> I retraced my steps.
> Spiritual experience and history,
> If you do not ignore them,
> Will teach you that theory
> Is not as important as people's lives,

That true belief and lack of faith
Have been nursed by the same milk,
And that it is easy to issue
Anathemas with cold hypocrisy.
I have become a liberal of such a sort,
And my views have become so wide,
That, by God, I would truly be glad to
Relieve the devil of his responsibility...[10]

At the same time, Solovyov pronounced his final verdict on the legacy of Byzantium in the article "Byzantinism and Russia," which was written in 1895 and published in 1896 in *Vestnik Evropy* (Nos. 1–4).[11]

Solovyov had long ago prepared a "Byzantine study" for *Vestnik Evropy*. In 1891 he wrote to Stasyulevich "... I am preparing for *Vestnik Evropy* an essay about the cult of the emperor in ancient Rome. This will be by way of an introduction to a future study of Byzantium."[12] In the same year he wrote to Fet, "I am still sitting above the desert of Byzantine theology or logomachy, which clearly demonstrates that even the dry can be wishy-washy."[13]

"Byzantinism and Russia" appears to develop the stanza of the poem "Pan-Mongolism":

When in decadent Byzantium
The divine altar had grown cold,
And the priest and prince, people and emperor
Renounced the Messiah...[14]

Byzantium's demise was caused not by the false object of its faith, for that in which the Byzantines believed was true, but by the false character of their faith. The true idea of Christianity was only the object of their intellectual perception and ritual reverence, but not the driving force of their life.[15] In Byzantium Solovyov found a general indifference to the historical impulse of the good.[16] The government of the Turks proved to be truer and stronger; it did not compose dubious dogmas and pernicious rhetoric. Furthermore, it did not defend Orthodoxy by means of mass persecution of heretics and the solemn burning of heresiarchs at the stake.[17] After the last ecumenical council, that is since the eighth century, the "ecumenical patriarchs" of Constantinople have been the highest ecclesiastical authority in the East, but this is merely a splendid title, for they found themselves entirely in the hands of the secular power, which elevated and overthrew them according to its own discretion. In reality, then, the supreme administration of the Byzantine Church belonged wholly and undividedly to the emperors, to whom were rendered both royal and priestly honors.[18] Analyzing the petty polemics of Michael Cerularius and other Byzantines against the Latin Church, Solovyov remarks sarcastically, "One can only regret that their preference for fermentation and salt remained only in the leavened bread and did not become the distinguishing features of the Byzantine mind."[19]

Russia comprises a Slavo-Finnish nation, fertilized by Germans. It manifested its spiritual superiority over Byzantium in the person of St. Prince Vladimir, who found punishing even obvious criminals incompatible with the spirit of Christianity. Muscovite Rus, however, was ruled by a Babylonian-Byzantine despotism.[20] Solovyov cites the legend, recorded in the region of Samara, "Tsar Ivan Vasilevich cried out: who will get for me the crown, the scepter, the orb, and the little book about them, *from the kingdom of Babylon*? Borma-Yaryzhka carried out the royal wish and as a reward requested only one thing: Permit me to drink for three years in all the taverns at will and without charge. The conclusion of this regression of the national consciousness in the direction of savage pagan ideals is not without interest."[21]

Local clericalism became impossible in Russia. The Russian patriarch represented not universal Christianity, but Byzantine piety. Solovyov justifies the synodal reform of Peter I: "The administration of the Church had already been, in fact, turned into a branch of the government before this was decided in an official way. This was one of the more natural, correct, and therefore sound reforms of Peter the Great."[22] The Russian hierarchs demonstrated their moral impotence during a tragic moment of the tsar's life: when he turned to them for advice about the matter of the Tsarevich Aleksey, they could only answer, "the tsar's heart is in the hands of God."*

---

* Peter the Great's son and heir had displeased him by siding with that faction of the Russian court and church opposed to his reforms. Fearing Peter's wrath,

And so now in the crown of the Byzantine-Russian emperor, Solovyov sees the ancient legacy of Babylon, "the crown of Nebuchadnezzar." In a humorous poem "The Ethiopians and the Log," written in Raukha in October 1894, the log, apparently, stands for the Russian autocracy.

> In the meanwhile the log lies. Now in great fear
> They crawl to it face down!
> The log remains a log. But in wild ecstasy
> They sing a hymn to it!
> "Mighty, gentle god! Beloved, desired!"
> The priests are already here and there:
> They anoint the edge of the log with fragrant oil
> And sprinkle it with cow-dung.
> They erect a magnificent temple to the log
> and establish a strict order of services.
> The log has such a life that it does not have to die
> And lives to this day.[23]

The second member of the theocracy, the emperor, has turned into a fiction; however, the first, the supreme pontiff, remained in Rome. What was Solovyov's attitude to Rome during these years? In society the opinion was widely held that in the '90s Solovyov had renounced his Catholic ideas along with his book *La Russie et l'Eglise Universelle*. In fact, for example, Solovyov stated in a letter to the populist writer Lev Nikiforov, "I have nothing to report to you about my French books. Their fate does not interest me much. Although there is nothing in them contrary to objective truth, I have already outgrown that subjective mood, that is, those feelings and hopes with which I wrote them."[24] In January 1894 Solovyov wrote to Grot that it would be possible to publish *La Russie et l'Eglise Universelle* in a "new revised edition."[25]

The recently published letters to Tavernier shed light on the question at hand. From them it is completely clear that Solovyov had never abandoned the idea of the reunion of the Churches and always

---

Aleksey fled to Austria, only to be lured back to Russia with the promise of a pardon. Accused of plotting against the throne, he died in prison in 1718 before his death sentence could be confirmed.

considered the papacy to be "the legitimate and traditional center around which all true believers must unite."[26] The extent to which Solovyov did not alter his idea about union with Rome is evident from a letter of 6 April 1894 to Tavernier.

> There is talk of a serious movement among the Russian dissidents (who are considered to be Protestants and rationalists, but who in fact are neither) toward Catholicity (*vers la catholicité*) (I am not yet speaking of Catholicism – *catholicisme*). Among other things, they stand for a canonical hierarchy, i. e. one that possesses apostolic succession.
>
> Since there is no practical possibility of receiving the desired status from an Eastern source, it follows…
>
> The second proposition, the only one remaining, would be all the more desirable, as it would unite regularity to the advantage of legitimacy. You understand what a personal impression these new horizons, which have been so unexpectedly revealed, make on me.
>
> I have realized that I have prepared myself over the past twelve years (not thinking about this and not foreseeing it) for an inevitable and practical role; that I was not mistaken and that I had not worked in vain even from a purely practical point of view. It is not only a question of "sowing good seed," but of preparing and implementing a historical act of a perfectly definite character and of incalculable importance.[27]

It is difficult, however, to recognize Solovyov as a Catholic author in his published works of the mid-90s. This is especially true of *The Justification of the Good*, in which Solovyov highly rates the Reformation. For that reason, it is difficult to identify his polemics with Orthodoxy in the name of "religious tolerance" with a definite confession. It is all the more necessary to remember this when considering his idea for the restoration of the prophetic vocation, which was rightfully abolished in its time by Christianity, and the "religion of the spirit, which is wider than all confessions," which Solovyov had mentioned in 1892 in his letter to Rozanov.[28]

In general, *The Justification of the Good*, for all its moral asceticism, lacks that ecclesial spirit, which inspired Solovyov's work of the '80s. But we must not judge Solovyov's inner life in the '90s according to *The Justification of the Good*. In this work everything is polished, rounded off, schematic; it is redolent of profound optimism and peace. Meanwhile, Solovyov was soon forced to experience the full seriousness of his alienation from the Church. Gloomy visions had begun to pursue him, and he often saw the devil... "He told me repeatedly," Velichko relates, "that he dreamt of a harlequin, who would jump out of the most diverse and unpredictable places. The idea of a harlequinade and, in general, of every kind of metamorphosis pursued him like a nightmare and caused him serious pain."

At the beginning of 1896 Solovyov decided to join secretly the Catholic Church. At that time there was living in Moscow a Russian Catholic priest of the Eastern rite, Nikolay Alekseevich Tolstoy (a relative of the poet Aleksey Tolstoy), whom Solovyov had met in the salon of Sofya Khitrovo. Having graduated from the Moscow Religious Academy as an Orthodox priest, Nikolay Tolstoy, not without the influence of Solovyov, embraced Catholicism of the Greek rite. Solovyov found in him a Catholic spiritually close to him, whose deep conviction of the truth of Catholicism did not prevent him from understanding and wholeheartedly loving Orthodoxy. Tolstoy maintained a chapel in his apartment on one of the side streets near Ostozhenka. On 18 February 1896 on the feast of St. Leo the Great, the pope of Rome whom he especially revered, Solovyov received Holy Communion from the hands of Father Tolstoy. Before the liturgy he recited the Tridentine profession of faith. Dmitry Sergeevich Novsky, a young man who had secretly become Catholic and had been made a sub-deacon in Galicia, assisted at the liturgy. Novsky had graduated from two departments, that of mathematics and philology (in the classics division), and dreamt of devoting himself to ancient philosophy. Sergey Trubetskoy, however, regarded him coolly and did not let him stay at the university. Novsky ended his life as a teacher of Latin in Yaroslavl.

Tolstoy himself wrote about Solovyov's act of joining the Catholic Church in *Moskovskie vedemosti* on 21 August 1910. I always knew this fact personally, learning of it from both my father and Novsky. Soon after Solovyov's communion, Tolstoy had to flee abroad incognito, wearing Novsky's trousers and Solovyov's fur coat. I remember how when he came to see us Vladimir Solovyov said at dinner, "I have just taken Father Tolstoy to the Nikolaevsky station in my fur coat." With the help of foreign embassies Tolstoy obtained in St. Petersburg a passport to go abroad and departed by sea for Rome. For every Catholic, the fact that Solovyov received Holy Communion from a Catholic priest and recited the Tridentine profession of faith constitutes joining the Catholic Church. But how did Solovyov himself look upon this event? Let us return to the facts. Having received the Eucharist from Tolstoy, Solovyov did not approach the sacrament again until his death, when during his last illness at Uzkoe he asked for the Orthodox parish priest. Novsky told me that when he asked Solovyov why he would not go to a Polish or French priest, Solovyov replied "You are a young man, it is easy for you to turn away from your native traditions. But I shall wait until some kind of Russian Catholic priest comes to Moscow." Nikolay Tolstoy found himself exiled and lived in Rome and in France; the second Russian Catholic priest, Father Aleksey Zerchaninov, was languishing in prison; and at that time there were no other. This was a dangerous matter and demanded great prudence. Somewhat more than a year after the event of 18 February 1896, on 14 May 1897 Solovyov wrote a letter to the editors of *Novoe vremia* in which he states:

1) I have never proposed any kind of official external union with Rome (in Aleksandr Kireev's sense). First, because I consider it impossible; secondly, because I do not find it desirable; and thirdly, because I have never possessed any kind of mandate for negotiations from the powers that be of one or the other side.
2) That authority that belongs to every Christian, about which the Apostle John the Divine speaks ("you have been anointed by the Holy Spirit and you know all things") impels me to judge the relations between the Churches in this sense only: are they in accord with the spirit of Christ? As they are evidently alien to this spirit they cannot be called normal.

3) The whole millennium of such anti-Christian relations has inevitably produced a mass of all sorts of misunderstandings and preconceived ideas, and the first practical step toward placing the Church question on truly Christian ground would be an open, multilateral, and fearless discussion of all religious and ecclesiastical questions, but for this it would be necessary for us to have, most of all, complete freedom for theological and church-historical research, without which a true, inner movement of religious thought and feeling is not possible. Without such a movement the religious life of society grows weak and with such spiritual sleep, what can a formal, external union of Churches offer, aside from a nightmare no one needs? In this question, as in every other, the external result does not depend on us, and it would have no importance by itself in any case, but that which is important, and which would decide the matter, is within our power: an indefatigable search for the truth with a sincere desire for peace.[29]

Several people, such as Sergey Bulgakov, have suggested that Solovyov wished to practice intercommunion, that is, the reception of communion alternately from Orthodox and Catholic priests. This suggestion is not likely, as, in fact, Solovyov could hardly have found an Orthodox priest who would grant him absolution after he had accepted the Tridentine profession; and Solovyov had already proven once that he could not renounce this profession of faith when he was denied communion by Father Orlov. One can only admit that Solovyov's thoughts about Church union at the time were confused. The Catholic priest Johann Deubner has told me that when he asked Solovyov, "Do you recognize the infallibility of the Roman pontiff?" Solovyov pondered and then answered, "When an army goes into battle, it must be certain of the infallibility of its leader."

Solovyov concealed from his Russian friends the fact of his having received the Eucharist from Father Tolstoy. We have a letter to Stasyulevich dated 14 February 1896, that is, four days before the eighteenth, in which one can find no trace of those profound feelings that Solovyov must have experienced before taking such an important step, one which he had decided not to do while staying with Bishop Strossmayer in 1886. In this letter Solovyov remarks, "having arrived in Moscow, I came down with influenza and have not been able to recover, although I have begun to go out." A single phrase about the "can-can with the participation of the Bulgarian exarch" does testify to Solovyov's irritation with the Eastern Church.[30]

A letter to Tavernier dated May/June 1896 sheds great light on Solovyov's religious mood at this time.

> I already know something about the Anglo-Roman movement from *La Quinzaine*, which they sometimes send me. I find this movement not only very desirable in itself, but also extremely opportune at the moment when a certain faction of *Right Reverends* is beginning to make eyes in the direction of the North-East: these platonically adulterous advances can have no other result than to vex the good and encourage the bad; thanks to the Anglo-Roman movement, such a result will not be attained.*
>
> You know that, in my opinion, as long as the Christian nations of the East remain in their present state, every external success of theirs will be a misfortune for the cause of universal Christianity, and consequently for the true interests of every Christian country, including Russia and France; and on the contrary, under the present circumstances, everything that appears to be a success for the Western Christians in the sense of their unification will benefit all.
>
> In regard to your request for some material for an article relating to my humble person, I must, for reasons that you can perhaps guess, limit myself to a brief exposition of my religious views. If the following notes are not necessary for the aforementioned article, accept them all the same as an expression of friendship. For the beginning, I will commence

* Solovyov is referring here to different trends current at the time in the Church of England; one was sympathetic to Russian Orthodoxy, the other to Roman Catholicism.

with the end. *Respice finem.* On this account there are only three truths that are attested by the word of God.

1) The Gospel will be preached over the whole world, that is, the Truth will be presented to every form of humanity or to all nations.
2) The Son of Man will find little faith on earth, i. e. the true believers will form, at the end, only an insignificant minority numerically, whereas the majority of humanity will follow the Antichrist.
3) Nonetheless, after a short and bitter struggle the upholders of evil will be vanquished and the minority of true believers will gain the final victory.

From these three truths, which are as simple as they are indisputable for every believer, I have deduced a complete plan for Christian politics.

... Above all, the preaching of the Gospel over the whole world, on account of its eschatological meaning, which the Savior himself mentions, cannot be limited to such external actions as the distribution of the Bible or prayer books and sermons for blacks and the Papuas. This is only a means for the real goal, which consists in placing humanity before the dilemma: to accept or reject the truth, having come to know it, that is, the truth, with correct explanation and complete understanding. It is obvious that the fact of a truth that has been accepted or rejected on the basis of misunderstanding cannot decide the fate of a rational creature. Therefore, it is a question of eliminating not only the material ignorance of past revelation, but also the formal ignorance of eternal truths, that is, of eliminating all spiritual errors that, at the present time, prevent people from understanding the truth that has been revealed to us. It is necessary that the question of whether or not one is a true believer not depend on secondary circumstances and accidental conditions, but that it be reduced to such a final, absolute form of expression so that it can be decided as being absolutely moral or absolutely immoral by a pure act of the will or by a definite decision of each one of us for himself.

Now, you will doubtless agree that Christian doctrine at the present time has not attained the desired state and that it can still be rejected by believers on the grounds of theoretical misunderstandings. It is a matter then of:

1) A general establishment of a Christian philosophy, without which the preaching of the Gospel cannot be implemented.
2) If there is no doubt that the truth will be finally accepted by only a more or less persecuted minority, one must renounce once and for all the idea of the power and external greatness of a theocracy as the direct and immediate goal of Christian politics. Its goal is justice; glory is its result, which will come of itself.

Finally, certainty in the final victory of the minority of true believers must not lead us to a passive expectation. This victory cannot be a simple and pure miracle, the absolute act of the divine omnipotence of Jesus Christ, for in such a case all the history of Christianity would be superfluous. It is obvious that in order to triumph in truth and reason over the Antichrist, Jesus Christ requires our cooperation. And as the true believers are and will be only a minority, they must satisfy all the more the conditions of their qualitative and inner strength. The first of these conditions is moral and religious unity, which cannot be established arbitrarily, but must have a legitimate, traditional foundation; this is a responsibility imposed by piety. And as there is in the Christian world only one center of legitimate and traditional unity, it follows that all true believers must unite around it, which will be easier as it no longer possesses an external coercive power. Each person can unite himself to it to the degree his conscience dictates. I know, however, that there are priests and monks who think otherwise and who demand submission to ecclesiastical authority without limit, as to God. This is an error that will come to be called a heresy when it is clearly formulated. One must be prepared for the

> fact that 99% of priests and monks will declare themselves for the Antichrist. This is their complete right and their business.
>
> Speak of the devil ... (*Quand on parle du loup, on en voit la queue.*) I have had to interrupt this letter in order to receive another from a Galician monk who wants to foist on me, at whatever cost, the dogma of... capital punishment. Apparently, this is the most important point of his "Christian doctrine."[31]

This letter already contains the germ of *A Short Story about the Antichrist*, which Solovyov called the expression of his "ultimate view on the church question." It seems that we now have sufficient material at our disposal to establish Solovyov's position on the church at the end of his life.

Solovyov never renounced the fundamental idea of his book *La Russie et l'Eglise Universelle* and recognized the Roman pontiff as the sole head of the Christian church. In what then did his changes of moods and hopes consist after 1888? This is summarized by the phrase in his letter to Tavernier, "one must renounce once and for all the idea of the power and external greatness of a theocracy." If Solovyov's transition from the '70s and '80s was crystallized in the phrase, "first obedience, then understanding"; his transition from the '80s to the '90s could be paraphrased thus, "first justice, then power, greatness, and glory." The second formula does not replace the first, but fulfills it. In this case, theocractic glory and greatness are not rejected in principle, but are projected into the distance, becoming an instrument of justice. Indeed an unknown Catholic placed on Solovyov's grave an icon of Our Lady of Ostrobrama with an inscription in Latin, *in memoria aeterna erit* justus. *Justus* is not the same thing as the "righteous" of the Slavonic translation ("the righteous will remain in eternal memory") but namely "the just one." Of course, no Catholic can raise an objection against the idea of "justice," but Solovyov's views on the medieval ideal, his belief in complete religious tolerance, and his rejection of capital punishment, probably met with opposition on the part of many Catholics. In short, Solovyov was never able to reconcile himself with the medieval and

"Spanish" principles of Catholicism, although he highly revered St. Ignatius Loyola and St. Francis Xavier in particular. In *The Justification of the Good* he remarks that the inquisition in both the West and the East was invented by Spaniards: in the West by St. Dominic, in the East by Emperor Theodosius.[32] Considering the pope to be the infallible head of the Christian church, Solovyov maintained that the principle of unlimited submission to ecclesiastical authority, as to God, was heretical and worthy of the Antichrist. And since he anticipated that out of one hundred priests, ninety-nine would declare themselves for the Antichrist, one can understand the prudence he observed.

Solovyov had, apparently, no disagreements with the Catholics of Zagreb, Bishop Strossmayer, Canon and the others. He did not forget his friends and greeted Strossmayer at Easter with the words, "Christ is Risen," to which Strossmayer replied "He is Risen Indeed." The bishop's secretary Milko has related that at Christmas 1896 Solovyov, "already seriously ill," sent Strossmayer this telegram:

> Tsarskoe Selo, 25.XII.1896
>
> Monseigneur Strossmayer,
>
> Félicitations, souhaits, prières. Souvenir de cœur, travaux, maladies, espoir en Dieu.
>
> *Vladimir Soloviev*

The bishop replied immediately:

> Merci pour les félicitations. Votre vie et santé précieuses pour l'église et la nation. Vivez donc, nous prions tous pour vous. Moi je vous bénis de tout mon cœur et souhaite que votre santé soit bientôt parfaitement rétablie.
>
> *Strossmayer évêque.*[33]

Endnotes for Part 3 - Chapter 4

---

1. *P*, vol. 2, 118.
2. *SS*, vol. 8, 26.
3. Ibid., 54.
4. Ibid., 95.
5. Ibid., 413.
6. *SS*, vol. 8, xxi.
7. Ibid., 509.
8. *P*, vol. 1, 223-224.
9. *P*, vol. 4, 125.
10. Ibid., 67.
11. *SS*, vol. 7, 285.
12. *P*, vol. 4, 59.
13. Ibid., 229.
14. *Stikh.*, 239; *SS*, vol. 12, 95.
15. *SS*, vol. 7, 286.
16. Ibid., 288.
17. Ibid., 289.
18. Ibid., 303.
19. Ibid., 318.
20. Ibid., 303.
21. Ibid., 298.
22. Ibid., 325.
23. *Stikh.*, 274; *P*, vol. 1, 206.
24. *P*, vol. 4, 6.
25. *P*, vol. 3, 83.
26. *P*, vol. 4, 199.
27. Ibid., 195.
28. *P*, vol. 3, 44.
29. *P*, vol. 3, 183.
30. *P*, vol. 1, 131.
31. *P*, vol. 4, 219-222.
32. *SS*, vol. 8, 322-323.
33. *P*, vol. 1, 193.

Part 3 - Chapter 5

Law and Morality
Polemics with Chicherin
"Three Meetings" – Second Journey to Egypt

It is not thrice-crowned Isis
Who brings them spring,
But the untouched, eternal
Virgin of the Iridescent Gate.
"The Nile Delta"

In 1896 Solovyov was distressed by family troubles, namely, the final quarrel with his brother Vsevolod, with whom he had been reconciled before his departure for Sweden in 1893.[1] Vsevolod had published in *Russkii vestnik* the *Notes for My Children* of their father, Sergey Mikhailovich Solovyov, in a distorted version. He omitted, on the one hand, everything relating to the historian's childhood and clerical background, and on the other, all references to his liberal tendencies. Vsevolod's brothers, Vladimir and Mikhail, were offended by this misleading portrayal of their father, who had been one of the major representatives of liberalism during the reign of Nicholas I, and sent letters of protest to *Vestnik Evropy* and *Novoe vremia*. However, owing to the censorship it was not possible to publish a complete edition of the *Notes* with their harsh criticism of Metropolitan Filaret and Emperor Nicholas I. In order to rectify the matter, as best he could, Vladimir published in *Vestnik Evropy* his article "Sergey Mikhailovich Solovyov: Several Facts for His Portrait,"[2] reinstating entire pages from those parts of the *Notes* that had been deleted in *Russkii vestnik*. Vladimir and Mikhail had long considered publishing the complete text of the *Notes*, whose complete manuscript was already prepared for publication at the editorial office of *Vestnik Evropy*, but this could happen only after the liberalization of the censorship in 1905.

In 1896 Sofya Khitrovo's husband, Mikhail Aleksandrovich Khitrovo, died. "I sincerely regret the sudden death of Khitrovo, whom I greeted on his last visit as an old friend," Solovyov wrote to Stasyulevich on 26 July. "He had changed very much for the better at the end of his life, and his career in Japan was beyond reproach. I have written an obituary for *Vestnik Evropy*."[3]

We have seen that for many years Solovyov had wondered about the possibility of Sofya Petrovna divorcing her husband and of his marrying her (mostly between 1883 and 1887). Now that Mikhail Aleksandrovich was no more, Solovyov formally proposed to the love of his life. Sofya Petrovna's reply was negative, probably to the great relief of Solovyov, who had taken this step out of a feeling of duty and to prove his loyalty. At that time Sofya was preparing to become a grandmother, and Solovyov could only fall in love with lakes.

In the summer of 1896 he resumed his life in Finland. On 17 June he wrote the poem "A June Night at Saima [Iiunskaia noch' na Saime],"[4] about which there is something ominous. The "thou" of this poem is not the radiant Sophia, but the divided and dark soul of the world. "Through the roses of heaven" the poet perceives in her eyes something "restrainedly tempestuous." The secret holiness reigning over his existence had grown dim; it was no longer "wreathed in the might of the sun." The eyes of his beloved had grown dark, and although "rays of azure" were revealed, her gaze was duplicitous; it smiled while threatening to storm. In general, Solovyov was increasingly oppressed by spring and summer. He was "no longer captivated by the strength of the sun," but believed that "on a pale autumn morning," "in the icy winter twilight" "the triumphant word" would resound. Already in 1886 Solovyov had written:

> And the reconciled heart has no regret
> For the luxuriously brilliant and noisy spring.[5]

And in August 1897:

> I am illuminated by an autumnal smile,
> It is more charming than the bright laughter of the heavens…
> Sovereign of the earth, skies, and sea!
> I can hear you through this gloomy moan.[6]

In the autumn of 1896 we find Solovyov again in Finland. On 12 November he wrote to Grot from Vyborg.[7] On 25 December he sent Stasyulevich his New Year's greetings from there, "The cold cliffs of Finland warmly greet you and Lyubov Isakovna with best wishes for the New Year."[8]

In 1897 Solovyov returned to Pustynka, from which he had been away for about ten years. On 3 June 1897 he wrote to Velichko in Tiflis, "I am writing to you from Pustynka where I am renting a dacha from Ryurik. His elder brother, the sailor, is married to his cousin Princess G. Their sister Veta has given birth to a son, Mikhail Yurevich, a new, and I hope, corrected edition of Lermontov."[9*]

In the meantime, Solovyov's physical deterioration was rapidly progressing. In June 1895 he informed Velichko, "The doctor brought by my friends found, besides much else, an enlarged liver and an irritation of the inner membrane of the heart, and prescribed among other things, abstinence from wine and *liker* (according to a proof-reader's version),[†] to which he also added beer and even coffee. I am following this prescription successfully. So that you don't worry, I will add that this very doctor, although he discovered that I suffer from arteriosclerosis of the secondary vessels, 'established' at the same time that the aorta is as elastic as that of a seventeen-year-old's, on the basis of which he predicted a long life for me."[10]

His vomiting attacks grew worse. In 1895 he wrote to Ernest Radlov, "I am not well. I have attacks of vomiting not only in the morning but also in the evening. I wrote 'Love' and 'Llull'[‡] in this condition."[11]

On 20 October 1897 he wrote to Stasyulevich:

For a whole week I suffered from
Seasickness – it is both tiresome and degrading

---

[*] A reference to the Russian Romantic poet Mikhail Yurevich Lermontov (1814-1841).

[†] A reference to a Russian misprint/mistranslation of the Hebrew word for an intoxicating beverage as found in Leviticus 10:9 "do not drink wine and *siker*."

[‡] Ramon Llull (*ca*. 1235-1316), great Catalan mystic, philosopher, and poet.

To stand all day over a basin or a chamber pot.[12]

He was also tormented by attacks of neuritis. Writing to Grot on 12 November 1896 Solovyov called himself a "Finnish neuron, suffering from neuritis" and consoled himself with the following argument, "Respectable people, especially if they are at court or are ladies taking the cure, immediately contract nephritis, and those like me, to whom the doctors only speak of neuritis (oh, don't talk nonsense!) must thank God and nothing more."[13*]

But all of these ailments did not prevent Solovyov from being cheerful, and he was not exaggerating when he wrote the following humorous verses for Stasyulevich:

> But that is already too much about illnesses!
> Apart from them I am full of youthful energies.
> There are so many projects and tasks that I would ask
> Of God still a hundred more years in advance.[14]

In the years 1897-1898 Solovyov did not foresee an early death, and his plans did in fact require several decades. He hoped to create still more and to participate in great historical events.

> All the best hopes in the soul have not been touched,
> And its flow of creative energies has not dried up![15]

– he exclaimed on 29 June 1898.

Solovyov informed Tavernier about his creative plans in January 1898. "I have published the first chapter of my metaphysics in a journal and hope to complete the book in fifteen months. Aside from that, I am very busy with Plato, whom I have thought to translate in entirety. Having finished with metaphysics, Plato, aesthetics (half-finished), a little book about Russian poetry (3/4 completed), and a history of philosophy (for which I will use my entries in the encyclopedia), I will *concentrate* entirely on the Bible, which, from Genesis to the Apocalypse, offers a framework for

---

* Solovyov makes a pun here on the Russian grammatical constructions "*o nevrite*" ("about neuritis") and the imperative "*o, nevrite!*" ("oh, don't talk nonsense!").

everything that can interest me in the future. I still don't know whether my definitive work will take the form of a new translation with lengthy commentaries or whether it will be a system of historical philosophy based on the facts and the spirit of the Bible. This is what I reckon on doing with God's help in the future. With you, my superb friend, my openness is unlimited, and I will tell you that I am convinced that publication of my work on the Bible must precede the reunion of the Churches (among themselves at first, then with the synagogue) and the arrival of the Antichrist. And so, in spite of advancing old age (on Friday I turn 45) and every kind of difficulty and ailment, I am perfectly calm in spirit, all the more so as the possibility of my being wrong will only affect my personal role, without changing any of my religious feelings."[16]

Metaphysics, Plato, and the Antichrist we will treat in the final chapters, but, in the meantime, we will briefly discuss the book about Russian poetry that was already three-quarters written by 1898. This volume, which Solovyov intended to title *The Silver Age of Russian Lyric Poetry*, would have included his articles on the poetry of Fet and Yakov Polonsky (1890, *SS*, vol. 6, 239); on Tyutchev (1895, *SS*, vol. 7, 117); on Aleksey Tolstoy (1895-1896, *SS*, vol. 7, 135); on Polonsky again (1896, *SS*, vol. 7, 330); and on Konstantin Sluchevsky. In his last years Solovyov was also working on two poets of the Golden Age, Pushkin and Lermontov.

The Silver Age of Russian poetry exerted a great influence on Solovyov's worldview. First of all, this period in Russia was one of pure lyrical poetry, freed from any contact with the epic or drama, and Solovyov particularly esteemed the lyric. Secondly, Russian lyrical poetry, as demonstrated by its principal representatives (Tyutchev, Fet, Aleksey Tolstoy), was entirely permeated by the spirit of the *Naturphilosophie* of Schelling and Goethe. This poetry offered Solovyov a splendid illustration of his own ideas derived from this philosophy. He could also present himself as the heir and interpreter of the great past of Russian poetry.

Solovyov considered the "Elegy Written in a Country Churchyard" to be the birthplace of Russian poetry. Gray's elegy, translated by Zhukovsky, "can be seen as the beginning of truly humane poetry in Russia, following the official rhetorical literature of

Derzhavin's epoch."[17*] Neither on the banks of the Neva, nor within the walls of the Kremlin, did the "enchantress" of Russian poetry come into the world, but at the end of an autumn day among the birches and pines of a village churchyard. And if austere songs from the misty isles beyond the seas attended her sheltered cradle, here at least they sounded newly tender and sad. The rainbow of dream and the fever of youth, which later became so captivating in Russian poetry, were not so cherished by Solovyov as that melancholy that God bestowed upon it in an old churchyard.

Solovyov dedicated his book about Russian poetry to Fet:

> And I want, in the kingdom of delusions,
> To enter the crucible of prophetic dreams with a ray of light,
> To crown again the silent poets
> With the reflection of immortal illuminations.
> Departed friend! Your blessing is already with me
> On this path...[18]

The sepulchral voice of Fet continued to torment Solovyov. In the spring of 1895 in the forests of Finland someone, separated from the earth, had whispered to him "Remember me." On 16 January 1897, his birthday, Solovyov wrote the poem "To the Memory of A. A. Fet":

> He was an old man, long ill and decrepit;
> All were amazed that he could live so long...
> But why cannot time reconcile me
> With this grave?
> ... There is a mystery here... I hear a summons,
> And a mournful tone with a trembling plea...[19]

---

* One of the leaders of the Golden Age of Russian poetry, Vasily Zhukovsky (1783-1852) sought inspiration in English and German preromanticism in contrast to the monumental, odic style typical of Gavrila Derzhavin (1743-1816) and the reign of his patroness, Catherine the Great. Zhukovsky's translation in 1802 of Gray's famous elegy (1750) marks this change in Russian taste and was the first in a number of his translations, which included works of Goethe, Schiller, and Byron, as well as the *Odyssey*.

Solovyov sadly mourned the deaths of the last leading lights of Russian poetry, Apollon Maikov and Yakov Polonsky, "who captured the soul in ringing crystals."[20] * Of the remaining poets, he valued Sluchevsky for the "clear coolness" of his thought and his fine impressionism.[21]†

The eternal madness of the poet is
Like a fresh spring among ruins...
The sepulchral voice of Fet is heard
And Konstantin Sluchevsky is alive...[22]

Having read Konstantin Balmont's collection of poetry *Silence*, Solovyov greatly encouraged him.‡ Balmont's poetry of the time, weightless, ethereal, snow-white, was germane to Solovyov's own. And Solovyov himself made an indelible impression on Balmont. In his volume *Only Love* he gave a splendid portrayal of Solovyov as a poet:

The ethereal road is not far off,
As one of our poets has told us,
The modest hermit, the worshipper of God,
The monk-poet Vladimir Solovyov.

You gave me your greeting once,
Poet-hermit with a humble soul,
And you departed from here without returning,
But the edge of the world is not foreign to the sky.

---

* Apollon Maikov (1821-1897), a highly cultured poet who continued the traditions of Pushkin, choosing as his themes antiquity and nature. Yakov Petrovich Polonsky (1819-1898), like Maikov, known for his devotion to pure lyricism and resistance to the civic-minded rhetoric of Russian criticism in the latter half of the nineteenth century.

† Konstantin Sluchevsky (1837-1904), after his early studies in philosophy and the natural sciences, held positions in the civil service and court. Considered as a link between late romanticism and modernism, Sluchevsky's poetry is distinguished by its interest in the darker side of human life and its discordant imagery and diction.

‡ Konstantin Balmont (1867-1942), poet, translator, essayist. His early decadent poetry had considerable influence on the Symbolist movement in Russia and his translations introduced a wide range of world literature (especially English) to Russian audiences.

You walk now in the valleys of God,
Oh spirit, bearing the radiant seal...
But the ethereal road is so near!
I see your eyes, you are again with me.

Being himself, to a certain degree, a founder of Russian Symbolism, Solovyov reviewed the first collections of the Russian Symbolists and the young Valery Bryusov with intransigence.* His articles on the Symbolist poets, which appeared in *Vestnik Evropy* in 1895 under the initials Vl. S.,[23] were written in a humorous tone and concluded with parodies of them, which in their day earned Solovyov great popularity with the Russian public.[24]

Solovyov treated Bryusov mercilessly and warned him that the "indulgence of base passions, even if in the guise of Symbolism does not lead to good."[25] "A general judgement about Mr. Valery Bryusov cannot be pronounced without knowing his age. If he is no more than fourteen, a decent poet might come out of him, but perhaps nothing will emerge. If he is a grown man then, of course, every kind of literary hope is out of the question."[26] On this occasion Solovyov was mistaken, but it was difficult to discern in the author of absurd poems one of the most important poets of the twentieth century, even if he undoubtedly "indulged in base passions." Bryusov, however, received Solovyov's criticism with rare nobility. After the great philosopher's death, he wrote a splendid article about his poetry, in which he modestly acknowledged the deceased's "right to judge" and regretted that "these lessons that are so necessary for us" have fallen silent.[27] Along with the Russian Symbolists, Solovyov also speaks disdainfully of the French Symbolists, Mallarmé and Maeterlinck, fishing out of the latter the expression "dogs of a secret desire," which he parodied as "donkeys of patience and elephants of reflection."

In spite of his generally elevated mood and his awareness that "all the best hopes of the soul remain untouched," during these years

* Valery Bryusov (1873-1924), poet, novelist, critic, and one of the founders of the Symbolist movement in Russia in the 1890s. As an advocate of the decadent, French school of Symbolism, Bryusov had trouble accepting the genuine mysticism and moral authority of Solovyov. The relationship between Solovyov and Russian Symbolism remains a subject of debate to the present day.

Solovyov sometimes experienced moments of profound hesitation and doubt. One such moment is fixed in the poem:

> No, one cannot lift by force the heavy veil
> Of the gray clouds...
> The same path winds into the distance again,
> The forest is the same.
>
> And in the depths the question, – the only question
> Is put by God.
> Oh, if you could only answer
> With a swan song!
>
> The entire world stands like a cold dream,
> As on the first day.
> The soul is alone and sees before itself
> Its own shadow.[28]

In society Solovyov was either very lively and witty or oppressed everyone with a gloomy silence. During periods of intense creativity he would not utter a single word during dinner. He often had visions of the devil and spoke about them matter-of-factly, sometimes using a jocular tone. I remember one of his stories, "Yesterday I was lying in bed. The candle is burning. Someone, whom I don't see, presses my hand and begins to whisper to me very unseemly things. I leap out of bed, make the sign of the cross over *him* and with a cross drive him out the door." With the simplicity of a monk he would say, "In order to save yourself from demonic suggestions, you must recite the ninetieth psalm before going to sleep." During the years 1896-1897 in Finland Solovyov also experienced demonic visitations. Even the sea of Finland, like the face of a beloved woman, could lose the radiance of the divine Sophia. In semi-comic verse Solovyov reported:

> The demons of the sea have fallen in love with me,
> They roam after me following my traces:
> On the Finnish coast, they have recently been fishing for me

But if I go to the archipelago, they will already be there.[29]

Solovyov began to work on his brilliant new projects, which called for many years of labor, but out of the depths of his soul there arose the presentiment of the approaching end, – his own, and that all of nature and world history. He was morbidly conscious of nature dying in the clutches of mechanical civilization. Travelling by train on a summer morning and "managing with a struggle to obtain some fresh air and a window," he heard how the steam engine "whirls and groans with dead thunderclaps" and felt the fatal duality of "a mover without thought and the motionless life of nature, dying in a soundless caress."[30] The bright logical schemes of *The Justification of the Good* were eroded by waves of mystical foreboding. Staying with his brother Mikhail at Dedovo in the Zvenigorod district during the summer of 1897, Solovyov remarked with anxiety that no traces remained of the former marshes and that the central Russian summer had become "purely Turkestani." (The summer of 1897 ended with many forest fires.) He was also horrified by the spiritual condition of the peasantry in this increasingly arid region. He exclaimed painfully, "Is there really not a third, truly human way for the Russian peasant to live, between a cattle-like existence and infernal superstition? Is Russia indeed doomed to moral as well as physical drought?"[31] In the same summer of 1897 Solovyov wrote to Velichko from Pustynka, "Nothing outstanding, but:

There is confusion,
The dream is different,
Something is being prepared,
Someone is coming.

You have guessed that by 'someone' I mean the Antichrist himself. The end of the world, which is approaching, brushes past my face with some kind of distinct, if ungraspable, breath. I feel like a traveler approaching the sea, who feels the sea air before he beholds the sea. *Mais, c'est une mer à boire*."[32]

During his last years Solovyov did not feel well in Moscow and had become more and more of a St. Petersburger. He began to associate the moral oppression of his native city with the climate of

Moscow. He languished far from the sea, pining for the West and the Atlantic Ocean. In 1889 Solovyov had written to Stasyulevich, "The air of Moscow is bad for me: there is too much damp and a great deal of miasma."[33] In 1897 he commented:

> I am neither ill nor sad,
> Although Moscow's climate is pernicious for me,
> It is too continental,
> There is neither Galernaya nor Neva.[34]

The idyll with the Moscow philosophical plantation began to spoil and substantial disagreements arose between Solovyov and Lev Lopatin, which we will mention in the next chapter in our critique of *Theoretical Philosophy*. On 5 October 1897 Solovyov wrote to Stasyulevich, "In Moscow I found devastation. The philosophical journal appeared to be a child with seven nurses, but without a single eye. In spite of a thoroughly adequate and growing subscription, it finds itself, as a result of the most ridiculous mismanagement, in hopeless debt to the printers. The most immediate consequence for me would be to refuse the honorarium and to promise to solicit a subsidy from patrons in Moscow. Speaking without hypocrisy, neither one nor the other gives me the slightest pleasure. Still worse is the sharpening hostility and rivalry between the two chairs of philosophy, who continually come to complain about one another...."[35] On one occasion, irritated by a review of Yuly Aikhenvald, the secretary of *Voprosy filosofii i psikhologii,* Solovyov thought of resigning from the board of contributors to the journal and returned his advance to the editors, but the matter was smoothed over.[36]

The Justification of the Good suffered a bitter attack of criticism. "This book," Solovyov wrote to Tavernier, "has incurred for me the greatest abuse in the Russian press, as well as the greatest praise, I have ever heard. In all fairness I must say that the praise comes from writers who are specialists in philosophy, which one can't say about the others."[37] Among the specialists, Ernst Radlov especially supported Solovyov. But another, Boris Nikolaevich Chicherin, smashed to pieces *The Justification of the Good* along with Solovyov's other work published in 1897, *Law and Morality*, which appeared as a supplement to the book on moral philosophy.

According to Chicherin, the author, "entering as a lonely and poorly armed volunteer into the vast and threatening camp of juridical science, took cover under the defense of the meritorious leader of the regular forces (Vladimir Spasovich) in the hope of winning his justice and magnanimity."[38] *Law and Morality* is dedicated to Spasovich. In this work Solovyov argues against two of the extreme views on the interrelation between law and morality. "The highly celebrated Russian writer Count L. N. Tolstoy expresses himself as the absolute denier of all juridical elements of life, whereas the unchangeable defender of law, as an absolute self-sufficient principle, remains the most widely educated and systematic mind among contemporary Russian, and perhaps European, intellects, B. N. Chicherin."[39] The key to the work is chapter four, "On Capital Punishment." First of all, Solovyov refutes the religious arguments for capital punishment. In the Bible one can distinguish three instances relating to this question. 1) After the first murder (Abel), *the proclamation of the norm*: "a criminal, even a fratricide, is not subject to human punishment." 2) After the Flood, *the adaptation of the norm* to "the people's hard-heartedness." 3) The return of the norm with the prophets and the Gospel, "Vengeance is mine and I will repay"; "I want mercy and not sacrifice." "Those, who, like Joseph de Maistre, approximate the concept of capital punishment to that of an expiatory sacrifice, forget that the expiatory sacrifice on behalf of all was already made by Christ, that it abolished every other kind of blood sacrifice, and itself continues only in the bloodless Eucharist – an astounding lapse of memory on the part of persons professing the Christian faith. In truth, to allow any other kinds of expiatory sacrifices means to deny that which was accomplished by Christ, which means to betray Christianity."[40]

Further on, quoting works of specialists in criminology, Solovyov proves the uselessness of capital punishment as a means of defending society. Being dishonorable and inhuman, capital punishment also possesses a *shameful* character, which war, duels, or murder lack, as is seen from society's just aversion to the executioner.[41] The only normal punishment is the deprivation of freedom for a more or less prolonged period. Prisons must be radically reformed. From punitive institutions they must be transformed into corrective ones. People who are capable of such a difficult and lofty position must head penitentiaries: selected jurists, psychiatrists, moralists, and people with a true religious vocation.[42] Solovyov hopes that soon we will look on present-day prisons and penal servitude as we now look on antiquated psychiatric establishments with their iron cages and chains for the mentally ill.[43]

Solovyov was not a specialist in juridical science, and Chicherin considered that in his opinions he exhibited a particular, limitless self-assurance and reproached him for his lack of humility. To this Solovyov replied, "When I feel behind me the broad shoulders of Professor Tagantsev, then I am filled with limitless courage and do not fear even Mr. Chicherin himself, who in vain maintains that I have humility only before God; besides that humility, I experience the same feeling before human science and its genuine representatives."[44] Chicherin's article "On the Principles of Ethics,"[45] in which he attacked *The Justification of the Good*, ignited Solovyov's polemical ardor, which had grown cold since his wrangle with Strakhov.

> "Well, Chicherin did me an ill turn,
> That self-satisfied nobleman…
> Yesterday I finished off the scoundrel,
> He stole a month of working time.
> For this he gets a thrashing!"[46]

Thus Solovyov wrote to Stasyulevich on 5 October 1897. Chicherin's aristocratic self-satisfaction especially irritated Solovyov. This trait of his was already noted by the poet Boris Almazov.

> "Yes, our age is terribly nasty,
> There are no real people, only I!"
> Exclaimed Boris Chicherin,
> Liberal and nobleman.

Solovyov's response to Chicherin, entitled "False Criticism," is merciless.[47] It is not free from personal attacks, which Solovyov later regretted. "It is not the first time that B. N. Chicherin has done me the honor of giving his serious attention to my works," Solovyov writes. "Soon after the publication of my doctoral dissertation, *A*

Critique of Abstract Principles, he published an expansive review of it in the form of an entire book (B. Chicherin, *Mysticism in Science*, Moscow, 1881), in which he kindly invited me to discuss with him the philosophical questions in dispute."[48] At that time Solovyov did not offer any kind of reaction to Chicherin's review. Now he launched an attack against Chicherin, accusing him of distorting the fundamental ideas of *The Justification of the Good*. The extent to which Chicherin failed to understand Solovyov is evident from the fact that he called the champion of religious tolerance a follower of Torquemada. Having dubbed Chicherin the most educated and knowledgeable of all Russian, and perhaps of all European, minds of the present day, Solovyov accuses him of dogmatism: "For Mr. Chicherin there are no modulations of thinking, no living movement of ideas." He discards everything that does not coincide with his frozen schemes and believes as much in the infallibility of his system as did the caliph Omar in the Koran. He can "be satisfied only by a circle of *unconditional* adherents, uncouth followers, for whom (he said so himself) would be a decisive argument."[49]

His retort to Chicherin deprived Solovyov of an entire month of work (September 1897) and took up forty-six pages. After some biting witticisms, Solovyov concludes with a bitter reproach, "It is as though there were a moment in B. N. Chicherin's spiritual development ... when the essence and meaning of life revealed themselves to him independently of the abstract formulae of scholastic doctrine and when he himself somehow approached that which he now calls mysticism, that is, nonsense. With his book (*Science and Religion*) Mr. Chicherin separated himself from this moment of his spiritual life. He has also placed religious truth in a definite corner of his intellectual building and, having cut it into pieces, has distributed them among several adjacent cages in this corner. Everything returned to order. Mr. Chicherin's worldview remained, as it was before, without a real and living center, but he himself found that 'all was well and good' and calmed down. Does this mean forever? ... I am deeply touched by B. N. Chicherin's sincere grief, as though I were lost to Russian science. But in time and in eternity there are things of greater importance than 'Russian science,' and I firmly hope that my critic has not been lost to them."[50]

Chicherin answered Solovyov in *Voprosy filisofii i psikhologii* with his article "A Few Words about the Reply of Mr. Solovyov." In turn, Solovyov limited himself to four pages of a rebuttal, "Some Necessary Remarks Concerning the Few Words of B. N. Chicherin"; this second riposte was written in a more measured tone. It ends with a light apology, "The respected name of B. N. Chicherin and the character of the journal close to me, in which his criticism was published, created the necessity, rare for me, of having to writing a defense. Although in essence the goal of polemics is the clarification of the truth, as a special genre of literature (a very low one I agree) it has its own special demands, formally distinct form those of objective investigation. Here it is very easy to fall into excess, and if this has happened in my case, from the bottom of my soul I beg pardon from those who might have been hurt by this, and I promise not to reprint these polemics without valid new reasons."[51]

Since the time of his trip to France in 1893 Solovyov felt a strong urge for the West. In 1896 he wrote to Tavernier, "I am suffering from cosmopolitan nostalgia. Patriotism does not prevent me from being constrained by borders. This is why I love the sea, which does not possess any."[52] And on 14 May/9 June 1897 he again wrote to Tavernier:

> When shall I come to France? It's very strange, but I, apparently, can't in any way break the law of five-year intervals: 1888, 1893, 1898. Earlier than this fatal date there can be no possibility of a trip abroad (for there is absolutely no time or money).
>
> As far as 1898 is concerned; this is certain, as much as human affairs can be certain. I thirst terribly for the Ocean and the West, the first, physically and by heredity; the second, morally and personally, and I assure you that the main inspiration is to embrace someone who lives at Belle-chase, 64.[53]

In January 1898 Solovyov promised Tavernier that he would meet him in Paris in December. We note that the letters to Tavernier show an extreme cordiality and candor. He calls his French friend, "my most favorite and superb of all Eugènes,"[54] "half of my soul,"[55] and "the beloved brother of my soul."[56] "With you, my excellent friend, my candor is unlimited."[57] Solovyov was even more openhearted with Tavernier than with his brother Mikhail.

Solovyov's mood had thus changed since 1876 when he returned to Russia full of Slavophile illusions and wrote, "I will never go back to the Western latrine."[58] Now with each year he felt increasingly suffocated by the Russian climate and the Russian milieu. But the trip to Paris in 1898 did not occur. Completely unexpectedly, in March 1898 Solovyov departed for Egypt and Palestine. Apparently, the decision to go to Egypt was taken quickly, as it was in 1875 when Solovyov heard a voice within telling him "Go to Egypt."

Often the decline of a man's life repeats its bloom. With Solovyov we see the same pattern: from 1897 till the end of his life we find him at Pustynka amidst the Khitrovo family, he again works on gnoseology and metaphysics, and returns to his studies of Plato. So it is natural that he wanted to see again that land where "the eternal companion" had appeared to him, to see "the golden, emerald, black fields" of Egypt and "the blue, golden Nile."

On New Year's Eve of 1897 memories of the nights spent in 1876 under the stars of Egypt on the roof of the house belonging to the photographer Desiré surfaced in Solovyov's soul. On this occasion he wrote the poem "To a Friend of My Youth," dedicated to Dmitry Tsertelev and their friendship of twenty-five years.[59]

Do you remember
Those nights long ago, –
When the dawn would meet us
From the East with silence.
With brief hints,
Revealing the depth of life,
The fateful mystery
Would silently rise.[60]

Solovyov left for Egypt in the company of his friend Ernst Radlov in March 1898. They did not travel through Italy but via Constantinople, Piraeus, and the Archipelago. Upon leaving the harbor of Piraeus, their steamer ran aground and had to be pulled off,[61] which took twelve hours. During the sea voyage Solovyov composed the poems "The Song of the Sea [Pesnia moria]," "Passing Troy [Mimo Troady]," "In the Archipelago at Night [V Arkhipelage noch'iu]," and "*Das Ewig-Weibliche,*" and, upon arriving in Egypt, "The Delta of the Nile [Nil'skaia del'ta]." Among the islands of the Archipelago, the shades of two poets arose before Solovyov: those of Homer and Fet. Passing Troy, he wrote the melancholy quatrain:

> Something here was orphaned,
> Someone's lamp grew dim,
> Someone's joy flew away,
> Someone sang and fell silent.[62]

"The Song of the Sea" belongs to Solovyov's best poetry. One can hear in it the music of the "warm south sea," and the "harmonious sobs of the deep." The same shade of Fet that had pursued Solovyov along the banks of the cold northern sea hovered over his reverie here as well. It begged for the tears and the unselfish woe of another person over dreams that had been senselessly rejected. Solovyov's heart languished in pain, and he could not forget the ruin of another man.

> The fragments of life flow into adamantine dreams,
> But now only the radiant net glimmers, –
> The pearls of your songs dissolve into tears,
> In order to murmur and grieve with the deep.[63]

In the Archipelago, Solovyov was also haunted by demonic visions. Those demons of the sea, which had "recently been fishing for him on the coast of Finland", pursued him here as well, between Amathus and Paphos:[*]

> I saw in the sea mist
> The whole play of hostile spells,
> The evil steam brought peril
> To me, in fact, not as a delusion.

---

[*] Ancient cities on the coast of Cyprus.

Before my eyes hellish swarms of spirits
Arose and joined together,
And the combinations of evil words
Sounded penetratingly.[64]

Solovyov tried to exhort the sea demons and jokingly exorcised them with a prophecy of the arrival on earth of the Eternal Feminine. Here, where stood Amathus and Paphos, was born at one time Aphrodite. "Roses above the white foam," "the purple reflection in azure waves," – the image of the splendid body of the goddess, was the first unexpected grief for the sea demons; it reduced them to confusion, trembling, and fear. But the perfidious demons gained access to the beauty and sowed the hellish seed of corruption and death in the splendid image.

Know then! The Eternal Feminine now
Comes to earth in an incorruptible body.
In the unfading light of the new goddess
The sky combines with the watery depth.[65]

Velichko relates that on the first day of Easter, upon entering his cabin, Solovyov saw a demon in the form of a shaggy beast sitting on his bed. Solovyov addressed it in terms that were no longer joking, "But you know that Christ is risen?" To which the demon replied, "He may very well be risen, but I will make an end of you all the same," – and threw himself on Solovyov. The philosopher was found stretched out on the floor senseless. We cannot vouch for the authenticity of this story. Solovyov's traveling companion, Ernst Radlov, who was in the cabin at the time, told me that he heard nothing of this. But Solovyov could have concealed this episode from his somewhat skeptical friend...

On 14/26 April Solovyov wrote to Stasyulevich from Cairo, "In Egypt we have found abundance. Winter fields ready for the harvest (like we have at the end of July) and spring fields, magnificently green. Before we arrived, a scorching heat wave had begun, but we brought with us a northern wind and a pleasant coolness. Thanks to the English, Egypt is like a well-planned garden.

Even the trains run according to schedule and not according to fate as was the case during my first trip 22 years ago!!! Having spent an hour and a half in a magnificent bath and three hours in the still more magnificent museum of Egyptian antiquities, I feel that I have become a rejuvenated and playful Melchizedek. The Chinese gong struck by a black-skinned Ethiopian has summoned us to '*lunch*.' I will flirt with my two neighbors at table, Missis Ippi and Miss Uri. Farewell until the beginning of May."[66]

At the sight of the black earth of Egypt, the golden winter fields and the emerald spring fields, Solovyov was inspired to write one of his better poems, "The Delta of the Nile." In Egypt he was captivated by the belief in the resurrection of the dead, especially the resurrection of everything that had been bewitched by the death of the past and awaited the spring, not from the Isis of antiquity, but from "the untouched, eternal Virgin of the Iridescent Gate."[67]

There was no money left for the trip to Palestine. "Conditions as much political as economic... forced me to renounce a trip to Palestine, which is a kingdom governed by a hierocracy, whose real principle is not only *protopoporum, poporum, diaconorum, diatchkorum, ponomariorumque* but also *laikorum – oblupatio et obdiratio...*" Solovyov wrote to Stasyulevich in the above mentioned letter.[68*] Radlov has told me that Solovyov's extravagance during their trip amazed him, for example, after dinner he had the habit of tipping the waiter with five gold rubles. Solovyov returned to Russia healthy and refreshed. From Egypt he brought scarabs and small mummies that he gave to friends and relatives. For his brother Mikhail he brought a large brown candle from a Greek monastery, probably in Smyrna.

Solovyov spent the entire summer in 1898 at Pustynka. On 29 July he visited that place where twelve years earlier, in May 1886, he had bowed his head to the "sovereign earth." He joyfully summed up these twelve years and offered praise to the Preeternal, who for forty years preserved the garments of Israel intact in the desert. With all his former emotion and tenderness he paid homage again to the sovereign-

---

* The expression is in macaronic Latin based on Russian ecclesiastical titles: "...the swindling and fleecing by archpriests, priests, deacons, cantors, and sacristans, and also lay people..."

earth in the same place in the park at Pustynka. It is true, that other day had been cloudless and clear, when among the trees of the deserted park the phantoms of mysterious eyes had glittered everywhere... Those *phantoms* had departed, but his *faith* remained unchanged. In his soul all the best hopes had not been touched and the source of creative energies had not dried up.[69]

The journey to Egypt had refreshed in Solovyov's mind the memories of his three meetings with his "eternal companion." Late in the autumn, on 26 September, the early dusk and the dense forest of Pustynka inspired him "to reproduce in light verse *the most significant events that had happened to me in my life*." "Two days of memory and harmony arose uncontrollably in my consciousness and on the third day this short autobiography was ready, which pleased certain poets and certain ladies."[70] But this was far from all ladies; Sofya Khitrovo found the poem to be so bad that she advised him not to publish it, but Solovyov got away with a joke, "Non, ça me donnera cent roubles." Still another lady said that it produced on her the impression of a swan dancing the mazurka. But Solovyov himself believed "Three Meetings" to be the best and most significant piece he had composed in verse.

From the time of the writing of "Three Meetings," Solovyov felt the renewed presence of "the radiant companion" in his life. In the '80s he had rarely heard her "fading summons"[71] and the distant shadowy voice, "Do not believe the transitory, love and do not forget."[72] At one time he perceived the eternal reflection of her radiance in the face of the woman he loved, but this reflection had grown dim and the beauty of Lake Saima had become, in the end, her shining mirror. Now Solovyov no longer needed any kind of external image for her contemplation. It was enough to forget oneself during the day or to wake at midnight and look into one's soul, where there was only light and water, and where neither cliffs nor an underwater serpent were visible, but only her sparkling eyes in the transparent mist. In Moscow on 21 November 1898 Solovyov wrote his most powerful poem dedicated to Sophia, which creates an impression of shimmering magic:

You forget yourself during the day, or wake at midnight –

Someone is present... We are together, –
Radiant eyes look directly into the soul
During the dark night or day.

The ice melts, the storm clouds part,
The flowers bloom...
And in the transparent silence of motionless harmonies
You are reflected.

The ancient primordial sin vanishes in the soul,
Passing through the mirror's surface.
Behold, there is no seaweed, no underwater serpent
Or cliffs to be seen.

Only light and water. And in the transparent mist
Shine her eyes alone;
And like dew in the ocean
All the days of life swam together long ago.[73]

Endnotes for Part 3 - Chapter 5

1. *P*, vol. 2, 193.
2. *Vestnik Evropy* 6 (1896); *SS*, vol. 7, 354.
3. *P*, vol. 1, 136.
4. *Stikh.*, 145-146.
5. Ibid., 91; *SS*, vol. 12, 24.
6. Ibid., 155; ibid., 67.
7. *P*, vol. 3, 213.
8. *P*, vol. 4, 72.
9. *P*, vol. 1, 232.
10. Ibid., 228.
11. *P*, vol. 1, 258.
12. Ibid., 142.
13. *P*, vol. 3, 213.
14. *P*, vol. 1, 142.
15. *Stikh.*, 168.
16. *P*, vol. 4, 204.
17. *Stikh.*, 156.
18. Ibid., 153.
19. Ibid., 148.
20. Ibid., 150.
21. Ibid., 158.
22. Ibid., 335.
23. *Vestnik Evropy* 1 and 10 (1895); *SS*, vol. 7, 159.
24. *Stikh.*, 287-289; *SS*, vol. 12, 86-87.
25. *SS*, vol. 7, 164.
26. Ibid., 161.
27. Valery Bryusov, in *The Far and the Near* (Moscow, 1912).
28. *Stikh.*, 152; *SS*, vol. 12, 66.
29. *Stikh.*, 163; *SS.*, 71.
30. *Stikh.*, 147; *SS*, vol. 12, 63.
31. *SS*, vol. 7, 387.
32. *P*, vol. 1, 232.
33. *P*, vol. 4, 42.
34. *P*, vol. 1, 140; *SS*, vol. 12, 132.
35. *P*, vol. 1, 141.
36. Ibid., 101.
37. *P*, vol. 4, 223.
38. *SS*, vol. 8, 519.

39. Ibid., 521.
40. Ibid., 578.
41. Ibid., 585.
42. Ibid., 623.
43. Ibid., 622.
44. Ibid., 711.
45. *Voprosy filosofii i psikhilogii* 1897.
46. *P*, vol. 1, 140.
47. *SS*, vol. 8, 669.
48. Ibid., 671.
49. Ibid., 673.
50. Ibid., 716.
51. Ibid., 720.
52. *P*, vol. 4, 196.
53. Ibid., 201.
54. Ibid., 196.
55. Ibid., 200.
56. Ibid., 201.
57. Ibid., 204.
58. *P*, vol. 2, 28.
59. *P*, vol. 2, 269.
60. *Stikh.*, 151; *SS*, vol. 12, 65.
61. *P*, vol. 1, 144.
62. *Stikh.*, cx; *SS*, vol. 12, 70.
63. Ibid. 162; ibid., 71.
64. Ibid., 164; ibid., 71.
65. Ibid., 164; ibid., 72.
66. *P*, vol. 1, 145.
67. *Stikh.*, 165; *SS*, vol. 12, 73.
68. *P*, vol. 1, 145.
69. *Stikh.*, 168; *SS*, vol. 12, 75.
70. Ibid., 179; ibid., 86.
71. Ibid., 79; ibid., 11.
72. Ibid., 87; ibid., 23.
73. Ibid., 119; ibid., 77.

Part 3 - Chapter 6

The Beginnings of *Theoretical Philosophy*
Plato and Pushkin
Journey to Cannes

And triumphant over the ravine,
Like a man on guard, in the silence,
Shining white, Bethulia stands
At an inaccessible height.

Pushkin

In his last years, one of Solovyov's projects was the revision and correction of his gnoseological and metaphysical system. To this end he considered reworking *A Critique of Abstract Principles*. He succeeded in writing only the first three chapters of what was to be his book *Theoretical Philosophy*, but these testify to the great heights of his philosophical creativity. In his gnoseology Solovyov makes a definitive break with Descartes and denies the substantiality of the soul. "The self-certainty of the individual consciousness as an internal fact does not guarantee the certainty of objects known to the consciousness as external realities; but cannot one, on the basis of this consciousness, directly conclude the authentic reality of the *conscious subject*, as a special self-sufficient essence or thinking substance? Descartes considered such a conclusion to be possible and necessary, and hitherto many have followed him on this point. I myself had to pass through this position, in which I now see an extremely essential misunderstanding...[1] Having recently returned to a reassessment of the fundamental concepts of theoretical philosophy, I realize that such a point of view is far from possessing that self-evident certainty, which it formerly had for me."[2] Solovyov had expressed a harsh opinion about Descartes already in 1888 in a letter to Strakhov, "You believe even (or you repeat that you believe) the pathetic stupidities of Descartes and Leibniz."[3]

Solovyov places post-Kantian philosophy on a higher level, "The great worth of Hegelianism lies in the fact that both the meaningless '*substantia*' of dogmatism and the ambiguous '*subject*' of criticism were turned into milestones on the road of dialectics. The Cartesian 'soul' turned into the Kantian '*mind,*' which, in turn, became dissolved in the very process of thinking, failing to become, even with Hegel, the reason of truth."[4]

> There are no substances! Hegel has banished them
> But we live quite well without them![5]

Having utterly dispensed with Cartesian dogmatism, Solovyov began to regard, with greater sympathy than in his youth, positivism and English empirical psychology. "I cannot support this psychology as a system, but I see that it *begins,* as it should, with the indisputable facts of consciousness, among which there is neither a 'thinking substance' nor unconditional self-determined or self-initiated activity. *The individual states of consciousness as such* are, in fact, self-evident and provide the real principle of speculative philosophy."[6]

On 7 March 1898 at a public session of the St. Petersburg Philosophical Society on the occasion of the centenary of August Comte's birth, Solovyov delivered the speech "The Idea of Humanity in the Work of Auguste Comte."[7] In this speech he expounded and supported the theory of Comte, according to which authentic, real being belongs not to separate individuals, but to humanity, as to the idea in the Platonic sense. "With the daring of genius he (Comte)… asserts that a solitary man, taken by himself or in isolation, is only an abstraction, that such a man does not exist and cannot exist in reality. And, of course, Comte is right."[8] Just as a line is more real and concrete than a geometric point; a surface is more real than a line; and a geometric body more real than a surface. The whole precedes its parts and is presupposed by them. The parts without the whole are only an abstraction.

Thus, the individual "ego" is not a substance. As Evgeny Trubetskoy remarks, "For Solovyov, in the last period of his work, God appears as the only substance in the authentic meaning of this word. The individual soul is only a *hypostasis* or *support* [*podstavka*] of the Divinity."[9] This is what Solovyov had believed in his youth, as well, when he became aware of himself as the ὑποπόδιον* of divine Sophia, that is, her footstool. Personal consciousnesses dissolve in God, and God Himself is not a personality. In his polemics with Professor Aleksandr Vvedensky, during which he defended Spinoza from the accusation of atheism, Solovyov emphasized the idea of the Divinity as a universal being. The Divinity is not impersonal, but neither is it a personality or a person. It is super-personal and comprises three persons.[10] Having three persons, it cannot itself be a person; we ascribe the predicate of *personality* not to the first, but only to the second subject of the Divine Being, – the Logos, – the Son. The Divinity is an individual being, but it is also universal. Aleksandr Nikolsky finds that in his article "The Concept of God" Solovyov adopts a more pantheistic point of view than in the *Lectures on Godmanhood*. Evgeny Trubetskoy, on the contrary, asserts that in his last articles Solovyov completely freed himself from the pantheism that was present in the *Lectures*. We agree with Radlov, who denies that there was a substantial change in Solovyov's views on these matters. "That mystical orientation to which Solovyov belonged (neo-Platonism, Schellingism)," Radlov declares, "represents a combination of pantheistic ideas with theism; it acknowledges the truth of the formula: Everything is God, while denying only the formula: God is everything."[11] We might add that such an understanding of the Divinity is in agreement with the theology of the Fathers of the Eastern Church, which Solovyov already indicated in his youthful work *Sophie*.

Solovyov's new gnoseology aimed at Descartes could not help affecting one of the representatives of Cartesian philosophy, Lev Lopatin. The polemics between the philosopher-friends, which had already begun in 1889, was ready to flare up again. Lopatin criticized the first chapter of Solovyov's theoretical philosophy in his article "The Question of the Real Unity of Consciousness"[12] and reproached Solovyov for his "phenomenism." Already in 1896, in

* This Scriptural term occurs in Byzantine liturgical use, with which Solovyov was familiar.

connection with Lopatin's essay "The Concept of the Soul according to the Facts of Inner Experience," Solovyov wrote to Grot:

> And with each year, increasing its flow
> The river of time runs more quickly,
> And, sensing from afar both the sea and freedom
> I say calmly: *panta rhei*!
> But I am threatened by the intrepid Levon,† –
> Who would like to drop a sack of dynamic substances
> In the river and with an invisible mass
> Suddenly block the whole flow of Heraclitus.
> Levon, Levon! Leave your undertaking
> And do not play with water and fire…
> There are no substances! Hegel has banished them,
> But we live quite well without them![13]

Now in 1899 after reading Lopatin's article, "The Question of the Real Unity of Consciousness," Solovyov wrote to Aleksey Obolensky, "Tonight, while going to sleep, but not yet completely overtaken by it, I crafted a long letter to my friend Lopatin, who has absurdly turned against me on account of some kind of 'phenomenism':

> You have imputed not a few fables
> To your old friend, but ah! –
> We are such old people
> And the dust of the grave is so near
> That the militant flame
> Of my soul will not flare up again,
> And the polemical banner,
> Alas! hangs, but does not wave.
> I am too old for the games of Ares
> And for those of Bacchus, too weak –
> I would sooner fall asleep…
> Ah! for which it is now high time,
> I don't know what 'phenomenism' is
> But if it can sleep,
> I summon it with rapture:
> 'Let us go, beloved, to bed!'"[14]

---

† This plays on the name Lev, or Leo.

Lopatin's article remained unanswered. But Solovyov's polemic banner would soon be raised high when he was working on the end of *Three Conversations...*

The end of Solovyov's life coincided with the beginning. As we saw in 1875, before his trip to Egypt, he had particularly devoted himself to a serious study of Plato and became his inspired interpreter at the Gérié courses. In 1897 Kozma Soldatenkov suggested that Solovyov publish a complete translation of the dialogues of Plato. Solovyov accepted the offer and shared the work with his brother Mikhail, who translated half of the Socratic dialogues. The translation is dedicated to Fet. In the foreword Solovyov explains:

> At the beginning of this work I have placed the name of Afanasy Afanasevich Fet as its first inspirer. It is now seventeen years ago that, while he himself was immersed in translating Latin poets, he began to assure me that my patriotic duty was "to give Plato to Russian literature." I did not agree with him; his arguments seemed to me to be more flattering than convincing. Moreover, all my thoughts and plans were headed in an entirely different direction...
>
> Only after Fet's death came the time when his inspiration ought to have been effective. With the accumulation of life experience, without any kind of change in the essence of my convictions, I began to doubt more and more the usefulness and realization of those external schemes to which I had given my so-called "best years." The sense of disillusionment signaled a return to philosophical studies, which for a time had been relegated to the background. Moral philosophy, with which I began these renewed interests, inevitably led me to the fundamental theoretical questions of knowledge and being. And now in 1897, fifteen years after that conversation about Plato, I began to feel an invincible desire to immerse myself again, and deeper than before, in this eternally fresh fountain of youthful philosophical thought, which was the first to become aware of itself.[15]

In the first chapter of *Theoretical Philosophy* we come across an autobiographical admission. "Today after an early dinner I lay on the sofa with my eyes closed and pondered whether or not one can recognize Plato's *Alcibiades II* as genuine."[16]

But Solovyov had not experienced life in vain and was far from accepting Plato as the absolute truth. In the essay *The Drama of Plato's Life*, which was written at the beginning of 1898, he pronounced a severe judgement against the great philosopher. This essay is pointedly autobiographical. While acknowledging his congeniality and profound ties with the father of Greek idealism, Solovyov passes judgement on his own former errors, as well. In Plato's idealism he perceives an autobiographical undercurrent. For the young Plato, the death of Socrates, his teacher and a righteous man, condemned to death by his native city, was an overwhelming tragedy. Prostrate with moral shock, he later retreated to Megara where he formed his idealistic philosophy: The world in which the just man Socrates was killed cannot be the real one; this world contains only empty shadows; and real being belongs only to the world that is accessible to the mind. After this comes the second, *erotic* period of Plato's creativity. Having undergone the experience of love, he cannot regard the physical world as merely an empty shadow. The feeling of love testifies to the reality of the being that is loved. The world of the senses cannot be accepted as contrary to the divine. Eros is the bridge builder – the *pontifex* – between the world of ideas and the sensual world. Hence the sublime, joyful mood of Plato's erotic dialogues, *Phaedrus* and *The Symposium*. Plato was right to understand Eros as the mediator between the worlds of the spirit and the flesh, the rational and empirical, but later on "it is as though he strays from the way and begins to wander along side paths that have not be cleared and that lead nowhere ."[17] Like the tragic hero Hamlet, whose beloved Ophelia drowned herself, he underwent an erotic crisis. If Plato asserts that the meaning of Eros is "to be born in beauty", namely, in the *physical* realization of the ideal, then he let it be born only in speculation.[18]

Having experienced the tragedy of love, however, Plato himself could not return to his former renunciatory idealism and asceticism. Instead, he worked on implementing his ideals in life, by creating a social system for an ideal state, which he tried to put into practice at the court of Dionysius of Syracuse, and by writing the *Laws* for Crete. Solovyov, however, cruelly condemns these constructions. In Plato's state, wars and slavery are sanctioned, and with regard to "the mutual relations between the sexes," his ideal community "reverts to a savage way of life dictated by animal behavior."[19] Finally, the *Laws* serve as a renunciation of Socrates and philosophy, becoming the apotheosis of "blind, slavish, and false belief" and "the barbarism of criminal law."[20] "What a thoroughly profound, tragic catastrophe, what utter inner collapse!" The feebleness and fall of the "divine" Plato are significant because they sharply emphasize and elucidate the impossibility of man fulfilling his purpose, that is, of becoming a genuine *superhuman* on the strength alone of his mind, genius, and moral will, thus clarifying the need for an authentic, vital Godman.[21] Plato's life-drama resembles that of Solovyov's own. He too experienced catastrophe in love and was also, for a short while, "covered by erotic silt."[22] Twenty centuries, however, separate Solovyov from Plato, and it was at the beginning of these centuries that the bridge between the spiritual and corporeal worlds was already constructed, that is, Jacob's ladder, which united the heavenly and the earthly. The name of this ladder is *Maria*:

> And the same light from the sky illuminated
> both the Virgin of Nazareth
> And the futile vermin of the serpent before Her.[23]

Thus Solovyov concluded his poem "The Sign [Znamenie]," written on the occasion of the explosion at the monastery of Kursk during which the icon of Our Lady remained unharmed. This was the very icon that Solovyov and Maria Petrovna Shenshina had carried in procession around Vorobyovka in the summer of 1887.

Having pronounced his final verdict on Plato, whose life appeared to be a succession of three periods: the false renunciatory idealism of his youth, the unsuccessful attempt to overcome dualism through Eros, and the complete failure represented by *The Republic* and the *Laws*, Solovyov denounced another passion of his youth, Origen. "The harmony and cross-fertilization between religious belief and philosophical thought coexist only *partially* in Origen: the positive truth of Christianity in its entirety is not covered by the philosophical convictions of Origen." For all the sincerity of his desire *to accept* the new revelation, he could not understand its *specific* substance. This substance is the principal and absolute abolition of dualism, *the Good News* of the salvation of the whole person, including his bodily or physical being. The one-sided idealistic individualism of Origen deprived him of the possibility of understanding the Christian dogma of Original Sin or the real solidarity of all mankind in its earthly fate. Origen diverged radically from Christianity especially in his view of *death*. For the idealist Platonist, death is the utterly normal end of physical existence, which is incompatible with the assertion of the apostle, "the last enemy to be destroyed is death."[24]

Evgeny Trubetskoy finds that from this denial of the substantiality of the soul, there follows, as well, the denial of its preexistence, an opinion that Solovyov had shared with Origen during the period of the *Lectures on Godmanhood*.[25] "Solovyov distanced himself from his own error, which stood between him and Christianity. In complete agreement with the Christian doctrine of creation *ex nihilo*, he acknowledged that the individual, as a created substance, is *nothing*, which by the act of creation is turned into 'something,' called to serve as a *support* for the Divinity and receiving from it its genuine idea or quality."[26]

Once he had passed judgment on the greatest thinker of the Greek world, Solovyov went on to issue a harsh statement about the greatest poet of his own country, Aleksandr Pushkin.

In 1897 Solovyov's article "The Fate of Pushkin" appeared in *Vestnik Evropy*, inciting the public and calling forth the "unanimous abuse of the entire press."[27] Pointing out the contradictions in Pushkin's life between the lofty vocation of poet and his nothingness "among the lowly children of the world," Solovyov sees in the tragic fate of the great poet, not the action of blind fate, but the reasonable and good will of God, that is, Divine Providence. The author of the poem "The Prophet," who understood that "the service of the muses does not tolerate vanity" and who had been raised to the heights of the Christian worldview, fell as a victim to his own petty self-love and wrath. He was killed not by d'Anthès' shot, but by his own act of firing at d'Anthès. One should not regret that Pushkin died at the full flowering of his talent. Having profaned his hands with murder, he could no longer "rise to the heights of inspiration for sweet sounds and prayers and to make holy sacrifice to the radiant divinity of poetry." He could only have expiated his sin by means of a lengthy penance. "By itself poetry is neither good nor bad; it is the *flowering* and *radiance* of spiritual forces, good or bad. Hell has its own short-lived flowering and its own deceitful radiance. Pushkin's poetry was not and could not be such an infernal flowering and radiance..."[28] Providence saved Pushkin from a long and hard path: through the sufferings of a few days he expiated the sins of his evil doings and self-love, and died, reconciled with God. His fate was good and reasonable.

One can imagine what kind of indignation this article inspired in the public. It appeared to be the height of arrogance and an abuse of the great poet. Lev Polivanov, who shared the general indignation, warned Polonsky that it would be better not to discuss this subject with Solovyov, as he would become extremely irritated whenever anyone mentioned "The Fate of Pushkin."

In the spring of 1899 the centenary jubilee of Pushkin's birth was imminent. Solovyov promised an article for the Pushkin issue of *Mir iskusstva*, the new artistic journal that, under the editorship of Sergey Diagilev, attracted the first Russian Nietzscheans and decadents, who had initially appeared in *Severnii vestnik*: Dmitry Merezhkovsky, Zinaida Hippius, Nikolay Minsky, and Dmitry Filosofov. The writers of the older generation, Vasily Rozanov and Fyodor Sollogub, were also attached to this group. Solovyov could not have been unaware of the kind of influence that the ideas of Nietzsche were gaining in Russia and that from this front a serious danger to Christian thought was approaching. But to a philosopher who had grown up on Kant and Hegel, it was difficult to understand the complete significance of Nietzsche; Solovyov had scarcely even read him with attention and in his polemics against him tried to limit himself to jokes and irony. In 1897 Solovyov contributed a short article "Literature or Truth?" to the newspaper *Rus'* (edited by Gaiderburov), in which he calls Nietzsche not a superman but a "super-philologist." "The superman is only a subject of university instruction, a recently founded department in the faculty of philology."[29] Nietzsche became insane; "by so doing he proved the sincerity and nobility of his nature, and, certainly, saved his soul." But the example of Nietzsche produced no impression on his followers, who enthusiastically abandoned themselves to temptation. Solovyov discusses Nietzsche more seriously in the article "The Idea of the Superman," published in *Mir iskusstva* in 1899, in which he considers three fashionable ideas: economic materialism (Karl Marx); abstract moralism (Lev Tolstoy); and the demonism of the "superman" (Friedrich Nietzsche), deeming the last one to be the most interesting.[30] Solovyov acknowledges the idea itself of the superman to be true: the human must be surpassed. The true superman, however, has already been revealed in history in the person of the "Godman" Christ. The path to superhumanity lies through moral heroism, not egoism and pride; and the goal of superhumanity is victory over death. In any case, Solovyov believed a serious conversation with the Nietzscheans was logically possible and necessary,[31] but he soon broke irretrievably with the circle of *Mir iskusstva*.

In April 1899 Solovyov left for the Riviera, where he stayed at the Villa Marie-Mélanie in Cannes. Here, under the palms he wrote within a few days the first conversation concerning war.[32] On 26 May he wrote to Stasyulevich already from Lausanne, "I have only just read in your letter that you don't approve of the name of my residence, which I have just now, regrettably, left. With its picturesque location, the abundance of flowers and fruits, and the comfort of its appointments, it left nothing better to be desired. Regarding its name; why did you, a learned specialist in the ancient history of Greece, suddenly associate *Mélanie* with the image of a laundress by that name, instead of the Greek word , – black? Or is everything black alien to poetry?"[33] From Cannes, Solovyov had left for Geneva, "the city famed for its son of a bitch Rosseau and its son of the devil Calvin," and stayed at the Hôtel des Bourges. From there he "proceeded to Lausanne, Ouchy, Hôtel Beau Rivage." "Lausanne is not so much a picturesque as a pedantic city," he wrote to Stasyulevich on 26 May, "which is already evident from its name, which, apparently, derives from the Russian word cane [*loza*]. The name of Ouchy, according to the opinion of some, also has a pedantic meaning, but according to others it has a culinary one, being only the French pronunciation of the Russian exclamation "*Ukhi!*, which is supported by the lake teeming with trout."[34*]

In Lausanne Solovyov wrote the foreword to the translation of the works of Plato. Both in Cannes and in Ouchy Solovyov lived with the Khitrovo family, who took several photographs of him. Under the bright sun of the Riviera Solovyov's face, all in harsh shadows, looks particularly anxious; in his hand he holds a rose.

On 26 or 27 May Solovyov received in the mail, with some delay, a package from *Mir iskusstva*, containing the complete works of Pushkin and a registered letter, dated around the first of April, with the request that he write a few articles for the jubilee issue. Solovyov, who was used to seeing the manifestation of the mysteries of fate in all the details of life, perceived here "the dual service of some kind of beneficent power."[35] He read aloud to the Khitrovo family all the best works of Pushkin and refreshed them in his memory, but the late delivery of the parcel spared him from taking part in the Pushkin number. Having familiarized himself with this issue upon his return to Russia, Solovyov became profoundly disturbed and derided it in *Vestnik Evropy* (No. 7) with his article "The Special Celebration of Pushkin." The Pushkin number had included articles by Rozanov, Merezhkovsky, Minsky, and Sollogub. Rozanov portrayed Pushkin negatively, discerning in him a lack of "*orgiasm*" and "*pythism.*" In Solovyov's opinion, Rozanov was right. In Pushkin's poetry "there is preserved too much inspiration coming *from above*, not from the crevices where there are noxious sulphurous fumes, but from that place where there is found motionless and eternal beauty, free and radiant.

> The satrap arrived at the mountain ravines
> And sees: the narrow gate
> Fastened by a recalcitrant lock.
> The heights threaten with a storm.
> And triumphant over the ravine,
> Like a man on guard, in the silence,
> Shining white, Bethulia stands
> At an inaccessible height.[*]

---

[*] *Ukhá* is a type of Russian fish soup.

"This is a height that is inaccessible to Rozanov no less than to Holofernes. For both one and the other, poetry goes no further than the dancing sandals of Judith, for Bethulia is something 'too austere,' 'too serious.'"[36] To Pushkin, Rozanov counterpoises Gogol, Lermontov, Dostoevsky, and Tolstoy. His intuition did not deceive him. "Let us admit that there is a little of 'Rozanov's pythism' in them, but for that matter they saw almost nothing of Bethulia. For their entire lives Gogol and Dostoevsky pined for it, but in their writings it appears more as a matter of thought and moral consciousness, than of direct feeling and inspiration and, 'for the most part,' only in contrast to various *Dead Souls* and *Houses of the Dead*. To the point of malicious despair Lermontov strove for it, without attaining it, while Tolstoy substituted 'Nirvana' for it, pure but empty, and not even shining white in the heights."[37]

Most of all, Solovyov was bothered by Minsky, who, in rendering homage to Pushkin, ascribes to him his own Nietzschean ideas: the triumph of the aesthetic ideal over the ethical and the triumph of instinct over reason. Solovyov reminds Minsky that in Pushkin's novel the victory belongs not to the "aesthetic Onegin" but to the "ethical" Tatyana, who utterly ignominiously vanquishes the hero. In conclusion, Solovyov describes the Pushkin number of *Mir iskusstva* as an attempt "to cast the white Bethulia of our incomparable poet into the dark and noxious ravine of the Python."[38]

Coming to the defense of his friends, Dmitry Filosofov responded very harshly to Solovyov in the pages of *Mir iskusstva*. With regard to "Bethulia" he expressed his amazement that Solovyov failed to see it, "the House of God," in the works of Dostoevsky, who created the starets Zosima and Alyosha Karamazov. Solovyov's rebuttal to Filosofov, the article "Against a Court Order," was published in *Vestnik Evropy* No. 10.

Having spent thirty-six hours in Basle,[39] Solovyov returned to St. Petersburg at the beginning of June. Upon arrival he wrote the touching poem "At Home [U sebia]" in which he expresses all his love for St. Petersburg.

---

* Pushkin's unfinished poem "When the Assyrian master punished the nations..." dates to 1835 and paraphrases the story of Judith and Holofernes.

The white nights awaited me
Above the space of the teeming islands
Familiar eyes look at me again,
And the past shimmers without words.[40]

The city that in his youth seemed to be a "Finnish Sodom," now became for Solovyov a favorite, familiar place where he was at home. On more than one occasion he mentioned the lofty political and cultural importance of St. Petersburg, ranking it alongside Alexandria and Constantinople.[41] He spoke patriotically of "our Nevan water"[42] and prophesied that at the end of history the papacy, exiled from Rome, would choose the city of Peter the Great as its residence.

Having stayed for awhile in St. Petersburg, Solovyov went to Moscow where he settled at Slavyansky Bazaar and worked on his translation of Plato's dialogue *Protagoras*.

In the middle of June my father and I met him in a copse at the edge of the estate of my Kovalensky relatives, Dedovo, with bread and salt, according to patriarchal custom. In the distance there appeared his dusty cloak, wide-brimmed black hat, and gray hair. Covered in dust, pale, and aged, he squinted with his near-sighted eyes and, having recognized us, made a joyful neighing sound, *khe*! He brought with him the manuscript of the first conversation about war and the foreword to his translation of Plato. In the shady library of our house, under the portrait of Skovoroda, he read to us his composition. He declaimed the speeches of the general with an emotion that expressed all his love for old warriors. Solovyov had many military friends and on one occasion a general took offense when he declared, "How I envy you! I would have wanted to be a soldier more than anything!" The general took this for mockery, but Solovyov was speaking entirely sincerely. He delivered the speeches of the "politician" in the artificial voice of an old bureaucratic fop, imitating Minister Goremykin. My father regarded the apologia for war with complete sympathy, as earlier he had been alone in supporting his brother on the question of Pushkin's fate. My mother and I began to object. At first Solovyov said that one must not see in the words of the general the credo of the author himself, but soon he interrupted the conversation, commenting, "Well there are four people arguing here: on one side two men, on the other a woman and a youth. It is clear who is right."

We drank tea on the balcony. The conversation turned to "The Special Celebration of Pushkin," and Solovyov began to ridicule Rozanov. "The night on which Mohammed was born, was it not the same as the Eve of St. Bartholomew?" etc. My mother, who, for some reason, was organically incapable of understanding Pushkin, put to Solovyov the question, "Tell me, for what do you love Pushkin?" "This is for what," answered Solovyov, "'The satrap arrived at the mountain ravines…'" and he declaimed the beginning of "Judith." Everyone fell silent, stunned.

My father, my uncle, and I walked around the secluded pond called Konyashine, where a weeping birch, which Solovyov especially loved, hung over the water. He would lie along its trunk, hanging over the water and looking into the sky… During this summer Solovyov came to Dedovo twice more, on 5 July for my name day, and on 11 July for my mother's. Sometimes my father and I dined with him at Slavyansky Bazaar. He ate only caviar, washing it down with wine. After dinner he liked to hire a cab and drive to the Novodevichy monastery to visit the graves of relatives. After his brother's death, my father wrote the following poem for me in recollection of the summer of 1899:

We met him at the border of the earth,
At the border we embraced him.
The dusty horses took us home,
Our voices resounded in the field.

It grew silent. An icy shadow
Soundlessly crept up…
We shall remember this day,
A day of cold and evil.

And somewhere in the keen silence,
Without complaint, without tears,
Neither awake, nor in sleep,
The mute question froze.

The tireless sun will continue to whirl along the same path,
Driving its horses.
While we will fly noiselessly to the mysterious dream,
Secretly heeding the Sabbath day.

We do not see near, we do not see far,
And we do not know when that day will come,
But on that day we shall stand at the border of the earth,
On the border we shall meet him.

After "The Special Celebration of Pushkin," Solovyov considered writing an extensive study of the poetry of Pushkin. In October 1899 he wrote to Stasyulevich:

> If I succeed in writing about the poetry of Pushkin for December, then it will be absolutely necessary at the beginning for me to mention briefly "The Fate of Pushkin" as well, since otherwise my boundless praise of his poetry might appear (according to the unobliging logic of my readers) to be something of a retraction of my previous view of his character and his personal behavior. That my verdict about this matter in no way relates to poetry, no one, except myself, will take into consideration, but without fail people will say: "Two years ago he abused Pushkin, but now he praises him, and it's clear why; he wants to get a sinecure at the Pushkin Academy." To avoid such defamation, I must certainly begin the article "About the Poetry of Pushkin" with a mention of my previous article and with a declaration that I stand by my former opinion, which no one has refuted.[43]

In the autumn of 1899 Solovyov wrote his first chapter about Pushkin's poetry, which was published under the title "The Meaning of Poetry in the Verse of Pushkin" in *Vestnik Evropy*, No. 12. In both idea and form this article belongs to the best works of Solovyov, and its moral eloquence surpasses *The Justification of the Good*. Denouncing at the outset "pythism, demonism, satanism, and other modern beauties," which are essentially as old as "the devil and his grandmother," Solovyov declares that the light and fire of

Pushkin's poetry did not emanate from a rotting swamp. Although the seven-branched pipe that the Muse bestowed on him was made of a marsh reed, it was a "reed animated by the divine breath."[44]

Pushkin was the exponent of pure poetry and in this realm no one can compare with him. One might prefer the powerful mind of the "master of thoughts," Byron, or the religious mysticism of Mickiewicz, but Pushkin remains the unsurpassed ideal of pure poetry, which requires nothing apart from beauty. Poetic creation is distinguished from philosophical or oratorical creativity by the fact that its basis is "passive, without volition."[45] During poetic inspiration the mind and will remain potential. The poet's autonomous principle is extinguished as he surrenders himself to the waves of lyrical inspiration that overwhelm him. Such, in particular, is the creativity of Pushkin, which demands the utter rejection of vanity and prefers the desolation of late autumn in the countryside in order to manifest itself.

Pushkin reveals his view on the meaning of poetry in the poems "The Prophet," "While the poet is not required...," "The Poet and the Rabble," and "The Monument," for which Solovyov provides a detailed and brilliant analysis. First, he refutes the opinion that the figure of the prophet is meant to represent an actual Biblical prophet or Mohammed. Pushkin's prophet is the ideal poet. For him, poetry is born of the anguish of spiritual thirst, when the world of everyday life seems to be a gloomy wasteland. The Seraph's touch opens the eyes and ears of the poet, making them more penetrating and sharp. The transformation of the powerless, although sinless, senses occurs not entirely without pain. The poet's eyes are opened like those of a *frightened* eagle and his ears are filled with *noise* and *ringing*. After this, a bloody operation ensues. The femininely tender Seraph now becomes an experienced surgeon. In order to open the prophet's organs of sight and hearing, the higher power has only to touch them with light finger tips, but his sinful, evil, and malicious tongue must be torn out and replaced by the sting of the wise serpent. However, so that the prophet's new tongue would not only *bite* the hearts of people, while unmasking their sins, but would also *burn* them with the fire of love, the fleshly, timid heart has to be removed and replaced with a flaming ember. Just as before, when the world had become a desert for the prophet, so now everything that is empty and non-divine becomes a *corpse* within him. "The deadly and life-giving process is ended."[46] Such is Pushkin's ideal of the poet-prophet, but in his own life he failed to embody it and did not find a way out of the fatal duality between "the holy sacrifice" and his "nothingness among thc lowly children of the world." Analyzing the poem "The Poet and the Rabble," Solovyov demonstrates that by the word "rabble" Pushkin does not imply the simple folk and that the poem should not be interpreted as an expression of his aristocratic sentiments. The rabble are those who do not understand the meaning of pure poetry and demand of the poet a practical benefit. Pushkin was justified in his wrath against the mob, which "would weigh the Belvedere idol in a scale." His lack of rectitude was revealed by the fact that in his personal life, in his relations with people, he could not rise higher than the prejudices of this rabble, and that he did not translate into reality the sublime ideal of the poet that he had portrayed. Finally, the last poem to be discussed, "The Monument," forms Pushkin's irreproachable covenant with posterity, a mighty nation, and all the tribes populating Great Russia. This "great nation" has nothing in common with the fashionable and old-world "petty rabble." The poet knows that although this "great nation" will also not appreciate his "sweet sounds and prayers," and "seraphic inspirations," it will appreciate the moral influence of his poetry. The people's path to the monument of the great poet will not become overgrown because he "has inspired *benevolent feelings* with his lyre," "praised freedom in this cruel age," and "appealed for mercy to the fallen."[47]

This article, along with *The Drama of Plato's Life*, belongs to the best of what Solovyov wrote in the last years of his life. It was, however, only the first chapter of a longer study on Pushkin's poetry. In the summer of 1900, a few months before his death, Solovyov wrote to Stasyulevich, "At Sliozberg's I took an advance for the summer in an amount somewhat larger than the previous one, but our common friend A. S. Pushkin will pay this back in full in the autumn."[48]

Having pronounced a prophetically severe verdict in "The Fate of Pushkin," Solovyov now issued a final merciless judgment against Lermontov, in whom he saw one of Nietzsche's predecessors, a poet of false superhumanity, seduced by the demon of evil, pride, and lust. Not in vain was Lermontov's distant ancestor Thomas Learmont, who lived in thirteenth-century Scotland, known as "the wise and demonic Thomas the Rhymer with his love songs, gloomy prophecies, enigmatic double existence, and fatal end." "He vanished without a trace, disappearing behind two white deer, which had been sent for him, as legend has it, from the kingdom of the fairies."[49] The first peculiar trait that Lermontov exhibited, inherited from his mysterious ancestor, was his second sight, namely, the ability to predict his own fate, as testified by his poem "The Dream." From his adolescence Lermontov sensed his great vocation, but did not want to humble himself before a higher power. He did not want to understand that the truly great man rises to the heights of superhumanity "only on the corpses of those enemies whom he has killed, that is, the evil passions of his personality."[50] Next to the demon of pride in Lermontov's soul, there dwelled the demon of cruelty. In childhood he liked to crush flies and to knock down hens by throwing stones. As a young man he found joy and pleasure in destroying the peace of mind and honor of young ladies in society. The demon of blood lust had grown weak, yielding its place to its brother, *the demon of impurity*. If the erotic demon of Pushkin is "a playful little demon, some kind of prankster gnome" then "Lermonotv's hand was guided by a real demon of impurity."[51] Finally, Lermontov's duel with Martynov can be seen as an exercise in fatalism, a challenge to the higher powers. "In a terrible storm, accompanied by the flash of lightning and claps of thunder, this tempestuous soul passed into another realm of being."[52] But for all his demonism, Lermontov believed in what was higher and better than himself, and in certain bright moments even sensed that this better thing was above him: "'And in the heavens I see God.'"[53] The duty of love for the deceased compelled Solovyov to unmask Lermontov's demonism. "Exposing the lie of his demonism... we lighten the burden on this great soul."[54]

The article on Lermontov, which was delivered in the form of a public lecture, was as much of a challenge as "The Fate of Pushkin." Solovyov foresaw that it "would tease the geese of all feathers even more than 'The Fate of Pushkin.'" Thus, for Solovyov, Lermontov is a precursor of Nietzsche, a victim of demonic pride, bloodthirstiness, and impurity. Pushkin was great in his artistic vision, but base in his personal life, which was redeemed only by tragedy and a torturous death. Who, then, of the poets, was a "truly great man"? Solovyov recognizes as such Adam Mickiewicz.* Pushkin said rightly about his fellow Slav, "He was inspired from above, and from the heights he looked on life." To look on life from the heights, does not mean, however, to look *down* on it. This height was attained by an act of moral heroism as Mickiewicz experienced three fatal catastrophes: the ruin of his personal happiness in his love for Maryla Wereszczakówna, the loss of his homeland, and his break with ecclesiastical authority. Mickiewicz subordinated his personal happiness to the fortunes of his fatherland, and higher than his fatherland, he placed "the super-national and super-patriotic chosen one, the Church."[55] And he was condemned by Rome. But the catastrophe of his love did not destroy the inner life of his heart. Rejected by both his fatherland and the Church, he remained loyal to them. "Truly, he was a great man and could look on life from the heights because life had elevated him... He was great by virtue of the fact that in rising to new degrees of moral height, he did not bring with him proud and empty negation but love for that over which he had risen."[56]

We might suggest that contemplating the course of his own life, Solovyov saw in it not a drama like that of Plato's or Pushkin's but a continual process of elevation, like that of Mickiewicz's. Of course, Solovyov's approach to these poets is one-sided. He could have said something more about Lermontov's religious sentiments and a great deal more about the demonism of Tyutchev and Mickiewicz. In addition, the latter left several pages that breathe with such a genuinely Christian feeling as we do not find among the great Russian poets and writers, with the exception of Dostoevsky. But Solovyov saw in *The Books of the Polish Nation and the Polish Pilgrimage* that mystical nationalism with which he himself had struggled so much and which is comparable only to Dostoevsky's nationalism. Apparently this messianic nationalism is a temptation that Slavic genius overcomes only with difficulty... In the main, Solovyov was right about Mickiewicz, and Merezhkovsky only

* The national poet of Poland (1798-1855), with whom Solovyov had a great affinity.

completed his idea when, in justification of Mickiewicz's nationalism, he pointed out that the Polish poet would extol his native land not at the moment of its political triumph but during its time of suffering and crucifixion when it would become a symbol of the Savior's passion.

It is not by accident that in the same chapter we have joined Solovyov's *Theoretical Philosophy* and his articles on Pushkin; they are permeated by the same mood. In one and the other, in the realms of both philosophical understanding and poetic creativity, he emphasizes passivity and spiritual humility. Here there can no longer be found any kinds of substantial units of consciousness: in order to comprehend truth, to hear the voices of the spiritual world one must recognize oneself to be only a "support" for the Divinity; one has only to let the Seraph himself open our spiritual eyes with a light, albeit not painless, touch, and the soul will become a transparent medium in which the radiant Sophia is reflected. It will then contain only "light and water" and "transparent mist"; the underwater cliffs will have vanished and with them the serpent of egoism and self-assertion nesting under them.

In nature, the tall, ethereal, transparent bellflowers of the park at Pustynka come to symbolize Solovyov's "white thoughts."

> We live, your white thoughts,
> Along the mysterious pathways of the soul,
> While you wander along the gloomy path,
> We shine motionlessly in the silence.[57]

This "white sea," smoothly rocked by the spring breeze, is even more disembodied, more transparent than Solovyov's "final love," – "the gentle" Saima, which tossed and thrashed about in its granite banks. The white flowers turn into "white angels": "White angels / Arose around me."[58]

What then is Solovyov's last mood? Quietism, fatalism, the complete loss of will, and passivity? We return to the comparison with St. Augustine. If the youthful period of Solovyov recalls Augustine's first period, when the son of Monica, having progressed from the naturalism of Manicheans to Platonism, laid the foundations of Christian philosophy; and if in the following period of manhood both Augustine and Solovyov devoted all their energies to a clarification of the dogma of the unity of the Church, (the first in the struggle with the Donatist heresy, the second in the struggle with the centrifugal tendencies of national Churches); then the eventide of Solovyov, beginning with *The Justification of the Good*, recalls the waning years of Augustine, when the bishop of Hippo worked out his doctrine of grace in his struggle with Pelagius. In *The Justification of the Good* Solovyov adopts Augustine's position with regard to free will. In the phenomenal world there is only freedom to chose evil; freedom to chose good is determined by grace. In his quarrel with Lopatin, Solovyov sometimes stresses his positions to such a degree that only a fine line separates him from pure determinism. But he does not cross this line, just as Augustine did not. If the single-minded followers of Augustine slipped into determinism and arrived at the idea of *absolute predestination* (Calvin), then the same could happen with shortsighted disciples of Solovyov. For Solovyov, however, determinism was only a philosophical expression of his "spiritual poverty," a humble acknowledgement of the powerlessness of his ego, as long as it rests within its borders, and a joyful certainty of the good will of Providence. "Take our rights and justify us by your truth," Solovyov wrote already in 1883.[59]

In insisting on an opposition between the last period of Solovyov's life and the '80s, it is as though Evgeny Trubetskoy overlooks *The Spiritual Foundations of Life* and fails to understand that the asceticism of these "edifying articles" was a necessary prerequisite to the constructions of *The History of Theocracy* and *La Russie et l'Eglise Universelle*. Rather, Trubetskoy sees in them only a certain "temptation" and the utopias of a Don Quixote. He also pays little attention to the *negative* aspects of Solovyov's final period, which were not present in the '80s and with which we will become acquainted in the concluding chapter.

Endnotes for Part 3 - Chapter 6

1. *SS*, vol. 9, 107.
2. Ibid., 126.
3. *P*, vol. 1, 56.
4. *SS*, vol. 9. 163.
5. *P*, vol. 3, 213.
6. *SS*, vol. 9, 384.
7. Ibid., 172.
8. Ibid., 179.
9. Evgenii Trubetskoi, *Mirosozertsanie Vladimira Solov'eva* vol. 2, 247.
10. *SS*, vol. 9, 21.
11. *SS*, vol. 10, xxxiii.
12. *Voprosy filosofii i psikhologii* 50 (1899).
13. *P*, vol. 3, 213.
14. *P*, vol. 2, 192.
15. *Tvoreniia Platona*, vol. 1, v.
16. *SS*, vol. 9, 100.
17. *SS*, 9, 228.
18. Ibid., 231.
19. Ibid., 237.
20. Ibid., 239.
21. Ibid., 234.
22. Ibid., 234.
23. *Stikh*., 159.
24. *SS*, vol. 10, 446-447.
25. E. Trubetskoi, op. cit., vol. 2, 252.
26. Ibid., 251.
27. *SS*, vol. 9, 286.
28. Ibid., 59.
29. *SS*, vol. 10, 31.
30. *SS*, vol. 9, 266.
31. Ibid., 274.
32. *SS*, vol. 10. 83.
33. *P*, vol. 4, 78.
34. Ibid., 79.
35. *SS*, vol. 9, 287.
36. Ibid., 284.
37. Ibid., 285.
38. Ibid., 287.

---

39. *P*, vol. 4, 86.
40. *Stikh.,* 184.
41. *P,* vol. 3, 265.
42. *SS*, vol. 9, 60.
43. *P*, vol. 4, 81.
44. *SS*, vol. 9, 300.
45. Ibid., 307.
46. Ibid., 332.
47. *SS*, vol. 9, 346.
48. *P*, vol. 4, 83.
49. *SS*, vol. 9, 352.
50. Ibid., 359.
51. Ibid., 362.
52. Ibid., 365.
53. Ibid., 363.
54. Ibid., 367.
55. Ibid., 262.
56. Ibid., 264.
57. *Stikh.*, 185.
58. *Stikh.*, 337.
59. *SS*, vol. 3, 335.

Part 3 - Chapter 7

Three Conversations
A Short Story about the Antichrist
Death

Daring designs
Strengthen in the breast.
White angels
Whisper: go!

V. Solovyov

If in 1875 his studies of Plato inspired Solovyov to write the short dialogue "Evenings in Cairo,"[1] then now, having plunged himself again, and more deeply than before, in the eternally fresh fountain of Plato's works, he conceived of expressing his views in three dialogues in the manner of the great philosopher. Thus arose his famous *Three Conversations*. What is their theme? Originally, the title of this work was given in the journal *Knizhki nedeli*[2] as "Under the Palms: Three Conversations about Matters of Peace and War." In the separate edition it was changed to *Three Conversations about War, Progress, and the End of World History, Including a Short Story about the Antichrist with Appendices*. But this is only a partial description; their real subject is the nature of evil and its operation in the world. While planning to illuminate this question from a metaphysical point of view in his *Theoretical Philosophy*, Solovyov decided to present his position beforehand in a popular form that would be universally accessible. In his foreword to *Three Conversations* Solovyov states:

> Can it be that evil is only a natural *defect*, an imperfection that disappears on its own with the advancement of good, or is it an active *force*, which by means of temptations *dominates* our world so that in order to struggle with it

> successfully one must have leverage in another order of being? This vital question can be intelligibly examined and solved only in a complete metaphysical system. Having begun work on this subject for those who are capable and inclined to speculation, I was nonetheless aware of how important the question of evil is for everyone. About two years ago I experienced a certain change in my inner life, on which there is no reason to dwell, but which aroused in me the strong and steady desire to illuminate in a clear and generally accessible fashion the principle aspects of the question of evil that must affect everyone.[3]

One can notice the influence of Plato on the entire structure of the dialogues. The role of Socrates is taken by Mr. Z., in which it is easy to recognize the person of the author. In the first conversation, the principle part belongs to an old warrior general, the representative of the "religious and social point of view," and in the second conversation to the politician "statesman" who represents culture and progress. In each of these two characters the author recognizes a relative truth.[4] Finally, in the third conversation, Solovyov uses his own voice, speaking through the mouth of Mr. Z. The fourth interlocutor is a young prince, "a moralist and populist" and a cruel caricature of the Tolstoyans, in whom Solovyov apparently does not discern any kind of even relative truth, and whom he offers to all the other characters for laceration. Plato did allow irony in his philosophical dialogues, but on this point Solovyov surpassed his model. His conversations overflow with jokes and puns, and his fifth conversationalist is a lady who plays the part of the fool in Shakespearean drama, occasionally uttering witty and profound remarks.

Thus, in addition to speaking directly with the voice of Mr. Z., Solovyov conceals some of his own personality behind the masks of both the general and the politician. He treats the first with warm sympathy, while the second recites entire pages from *The Justification of the Good* and *The National Question*. We cannot help being struck by the coincidence between those ideas of Solovyov, with which we are familiar, and the credo of the old politician, a skeptic and an atheist, who quotes approvingly from his favorite poet Lucretius, "*Tantum religio potuit suadere malorum.*"*

In *Three Conversations* Solovyov provides his definitive view on Tolstoy as both a religious imposter and a falsifier of Christianity. "The true purpose of these polemics is not to refute false religion but to expose a very real deception."[5] Solovyov considered war to be an evil, but one that was inevitable, and did not believe it was possible to ban wars before the end of world history. The peacemaking efforts of Nicholas II, including his plan for a general disarmament, left on him the impression of hypocrisy and a decoy. He wholeheartedly shared Wilhelm II's idea of the necessity of preserving the solidarity of Christian Europe in view of the inevitable armed conflict with the Mongol race. I have in my possession a valuable document that has hitherto remained unpublished. It is a letter of Solovyov to Princess Elizaveta Volkonskaya, who was living in Rome. In all likelihood this letter, which was preserved in Solovyov's archive, was never sent to the addressee or perhaps it is a draft or a copy. Solovyov writes to Princess Volkonskaya:

> I simply cannot share your feelings and views regarding the escapades of 12 August. Their real purpose is more apparent here than in Rome. This is a thoroughly bad business, and it could be called diabolical if it were not so stupid. The only goal on the part of its instigators is *to deflect*, by means of external commotion, attention from those internal ulcers that the government could and should, but does *not wish* to cure, but, on the contrary, with some kind of infernal love *of evil for the sake of evil* tries to make more acute. I am speaking of obvious facts; at the same time as the circular of 12 August was issued, two other government actions took place: the forced Russification of Finland was decided and the Holy Synod published the decrees, by means of which 400,000 Russian Uniates, who consider themselves Catholic, were declared to be "Orthodox" for good, by virtue of the

* "Religion can provoke so many ills."

> administrative directive of 1875.[†] You must agree, Princess, that these two measures cast a very particular light on the pacifist enterprise that is contemporaneous with them: indeed, to destroy such a scandalous abomination as the "administrative" (by means of bayonets and whips) transference from one religious confession to another, only a stroke of the pen was required, and to desist from a completely unsolicited attack on their rights, which the one who made the attack triumphantly swore to observe, no kind of action was required, except to remain simply an honest man. And here, instead of satisfying the most basic obligations, such projects are announced, which are not within one's power and which, therefore, are not incumbent on the one who undertakes them! Well, can one listen seriously when a man, who has not attained the consciousness of the basic moral imperatives, presents himself as a universal benefactor? And what kind of incentive can this side have, other than a very base and idiotic vainglory? Indeed, this is exactly as if a man strangled his own children and then declared in the newspapers that he desired to save the universe. Il paraît, que j'en ai dit assez et même trop. *Summa*: those pregnant by hay will give birth to straw.

Solovyov also sharply broke with public opinion with regard to the Boer war. Hiding behind the mask of the politician, in a rough way Solovyov actually expressed his own opinion, which he had shared in conversation with friends. He refused to sign a petition sympathetic to the Republic of Transvaal, seeing in all this commotion stupidity and hypocrisy. Solovyov had sympathy neither for the separatist aspirations of the Slavic nations to free themselves from Austria and Germany, which he considered to be more cultured, nor for the aspiration of the Boers to seek independence from England, which he saw as more developed. To the nationalist hopes of various peoples he contrasted the unity of European culture under the hegemony of the advanced and powerful nation states of Germany and

---

[†] Solovyov is referring to the Greek Catholics of Belarus who were forcibly incorporated into the Russian Orthodox Church in 1875.

England. He also showed sympathy for the Anglo-Roman movement.[6] "One now hardly finds anywhere that degree of feeblemindedness," says the politician, in whose voice we hear the author, "which opposes to the real, hard-earned superiority of the Germans an imaginary cross on Hagia Sophia."[7] He also calls the various Slavonic committees "pernicious trifles." The Boer war was "spurred on by the continent's envy of England."[8] "Seriously speaking, these Boers are, of course, Europeans, but poor ones. Alienated from their splendid metropolis, they have lost their culture to a significant extent; surrounded by savages, they have become savage and grown coarse. To place them on the same level as the English and even to go so far as to desire their success in the struggle with England – cela n'a pas de nom."

These and similar passages in *Three Conversations* incited great indignation among Solovyov's earlier friends. Sofya Khitrovo said that in his youth Solovyov would have never believed that one day he would be capable of writing such scandalous things...Where could *Three Conversations* be published? At first, Solovyov had hopes for his *Vestnik Evropy*. He completed the first dialogue in Cannes on 10/22 May 1899 and sent it to Stasyulevich. "Here for you, dear and deeply respected Mikhail Matveevich, are the last six pages of the article sent yesterday. Even now I am hurrying to the post-office and therefore I will be brief and practical (the latter, of course, you will not recognize as a permanent quality of mine). If the mail fulfills its obligations then the entire original could be at the printing press on Friday 14 May, which means that as far as this aspect of things is concerned, it could appear in the June number, which would be desirable on account of its subject. The second and third dialogues, in so far as they depend on me, will follow without fail. I think that the censorship will pose no obstacles. If the first 'conversation' should appear to be *too* conservative and well-intentioned for my namesake, and is not up to the minute, then I can make it look as though everything that is dubious in the first dialogue will be refuted in the following two. For certain discrete expressions you could, perhaps, use your internal censorship. It seems to me that there is only one such case, in regard to Vladimir Monomakh." But for all his love for Solovyov, Stasyulevich refused to publish the "religious-social" monologues of the general in his progressive journal. Solovyov's last work did not fit into the parameters of *Vestnik Evropy* but had to take cover in the modest *Knizhki nedeli*.

In October 1899 Solovyov worked on his article about the poetry of Pushkin and the second conversation, which he completed in Moscow on 19 October. At our home Solovyov read it aloud in the presence of old General A. D. Donnat. On the same occasion he borrowed from me my Polivanov edition of Pushkin. Solovyov finished his article on Pushkin in Moscow and read it at the home of Maria Danilova, where there were no other guests but my father and myself.

At the beginning of November, Solovyov returned to St. Petersburg, where, as he set to work on the third conversation, a new illness befell him, which prevented him from writing. He was diagnosed with detached retinas, and one eye could not see at all. "My blindness has made me wiser by twenty-seven years, making me your contemporary," Solovyov wrote to Stasyulevich.[9] At the same time the number of visits and letters tired him more and more. It got to the point that he would spend the entire day in contact with people, devoting the night to work. *Three Conversations* includes an autobiographical passage: Mr. Z. tells of the death of a friend of his, who was driven to suicide thanks to his extreme politeness. His friend considered it necessary "to read all the letters he received, even from strangers, in addition to all the books and brochures sent to him for reviews. He diligently answered every letter, wrote all the reviews that were asked of him and, in general, assiduously fulfilled every request and petition addressed to him, as a consequence of which he spent all day making efforts on behalf of other people, leaving only nighttime for his own affairs. Moreover, he accepted every invitation as well as all visitors who found him at home. While my friend was young and could easily withstand strong drink, this prison life, which he had created for himself as a result of his politeness, although it depressed him, was not a tragedy: wine cheered his heart and saved him from despair. He would be on the verge of reaching for the rope, but taking up the bottle and emptying it, he would drag his chain more cheerfully. But he suffered from poor health and at age forty-five had to refuse spirits. In a sober state his prison seemed like hell, and now, they tell me, he has put an end to his life."[10] Apart from the concluding suicide, everything here is autobiographical: the ill health, the forty-five years, and the strong liquor. In fact, in order to maintain his nervous energy, in his final years Solovyov could not go without wine and it was not done to invite him to dinner without having ready a bottle of red wine, which he especially loved. He recalled with amazement, "But papá had no use for red wine at all, he would say, this is ink."

Having lost the sight of one eye and saddled with visits and letters, Solovyov was finally forced on 23 November to write the following open letter to *Novoe vremia*:

> In view of the just dissatisfaction of various persons, who have not received from me any kind of responses to their questions, wishes, and requests, I offer the following explanation. Recently, a disease of the eye has forced me to abstain for two months from the book and the pen. Having received the first warning, and not wishing to encourage any further ones, I have determined to refuse in advance every kind of secondary work, such as reading other people's manuscripts and editing other people's translations; writing reviews, remarks, and critical articles on current literature; and also correspondence with people who are unknown to me. Such a resolution is not the result of a bad character, and I will renounce it without delay as soon as I have completed the larger works that I have begun, which seem to me to be my principal and immediate obligation. To these belong: 1) The translation of Plato with studies about him. 2)*Theoretical Philosophy*. 3) Aesthetics. 4) An aesthetic critique of Pushkin. 5) Biblical philosophy with a translation and interpretation of the Bible. If God and kind people permit me to finish all this, then, of course, along with leisure I will regain that high degree of expansiveness, belonging to old age, which will make me a most pleasant postal conversationalist for all those people with whom I am poorly acquainted, or not acquainted at all, who write to me about their affairs.[11]

Death was approaching and again, as in 1895, Solovyov heard the "summons of kindred shades." On his birthday, 16 January 1900, he wrote the poem "Les revenants":

> By a mysterious path, painful and dear,
> You force your way into my soul and – I thank you!
> It is sweet for me to approach through melancholy memory
> Quiet shores, veiled by death.[12]

Solovyov's love for the departed found voice, incidentally, in his frequent writing of obituaries. In January 1900 at a session of the St. Petersburg Philosophical Society Solovyov "commemorated three of the deceased," who had only just died, Matvey Troitsky, Nikolay Grot, and his old teacher Pamfil Yurkevich. These "Three Sketches" are brilliant.[13] Troitsky's character is described with quiet and good-natured humor, in a style that recalls the best pages of Gogol. Troitsky was a representative of English empirical psychology, for which everything that exists is reduced to "a series of subjective states of consciousness," without, however, excluding practical certainty in the everyday authenticity of various subjects and objects. "I know for certain that Matvey Mikhailovich in no way doubted the practical, so to say, substantiality of the rector, the administrator, minister, and even, I think, the university treasurer."[14] Recalling some of the unpleasant episodes Troitsky experienced during his tenure when he was unexpectedly accused of "atheism" by the authorities, Solovyov remarks, "Undoubtedly, for the majority of Russian society in the '80s of the nineteenth century, the difference between English psychology and German materialism was as obscure as the difference between Catholicism and Protestantism for our ancestors. 'Empirical psychology,' – 'positivism,' – 'materialism,' – 'atheism,'– 'nihilism,' – all this joined together and like an ominous sum resulted in the word: *dismissal*."[15] Solovyov compared the condition of Troitsky's soul to "the motionless and self-containment of a garden pond or an aquarium."[16]

In the obituaries written by Solovyov one can perceive his constant affection, which during his last years turned into a kind of gentle sadness. With love he accompanied to the grave the old Archpriest Preobrazhensky, the editor of *Pravoslavnoe obozrenie* in whose pages Solovyov began his literary career. Just as he had lovingly depicted the old warrior general, who after the execution of the Bashi-Bazouks felt "in his soul the radiant resurrection of Christ,"[17] he now portrayed with the same affection the old bee-keeping priest, whom it was difficult to find in Moscow in the spring, as he would spend all day at his dacha in Pushkino "hovering over the queen."[18] These elderly generals and priests were disappearing into the past and Solovyov, whose attention was utterly fixed on the stormy future, bade farewell with a tender smile to these shades of religious Old Russia. The aged Archpriest Preobrazhensky had died peacefully, but the fate of his son rent Solovyov's heart. "In the middle of the day's exhausting journey, far from the night's resting place, his noble heart broke. With his gentleness and the premature burden of his life, this laborer paid for the right of the elect to rise to the royal heights of thought and contemplation."[19] Vasily Preobrazhensky, the young philosopher and admirer of Nietzsche, died on 11 April 1900 at age thirty-six, leaving his children motherless orphans. His obituary ends with the following, "Dear and unlucky friend, for your shortened and difficult life, for everything that you managed to endure and for everything that you did not manage to do, let there be for you one consolation: you, of course, did not receive and will not receive that reproach, which you considered to be the most grave, the reproach of heartlessness; you, noble heart, beaten by life!" One can imagine how many tears fell on this page when Solovyov had finished it. Indeed, he himself was embarking on projects, for whose completion he had to ask God for at least one hundred years in advance. He had begun five major works, but it now seemed time for him to follow the shades of those dear to him! The necrology for Grot already ends with words of utter certainty, "Until we meet again, good friend! – Is it not so? – Until we meet again soon!"[20] Whether he would have succeeded in completing his theoretical philosophy and his work on the Bible, he did not know, but he had to express, even in a brief and imperfect form, that which weighed on him the most. "The already not so distant image of pale death can also be perceived, quietly advising that the publication of this little book not be postponed for an indefinite and uncertain period of time." And indeed Solovyov concluded *Three Conversations* with *A Short Story about the Antichrist*. The theme of the end of the world and the coming of the Antichrist troubled Solovyov from his youth. We have seen that as a child he devoted himself to ascetic exercises in order to harden himself for the torments, to which the Antichrist will subject the faithful Christians. In 1897 he wrote to Velichko from Pustynka:

> There is confusion,
> The dream is different,
> Something is being prepared,
> Someone is coming.
>
> You have guessed that by 'someone' I mean the Antichrist himself. The end of the world, which is approaching, brushes my face with some kind of distinct if ungraspable breath. I am like a traveler approaching the sea, who feels the sea air before he beholds the sea.[21]

"These 'conversations' about evil," Solovyov remarks in the foreword to *Three Conversations*, "about the military and peaceful struggle with it, had to conclude with a definite indication of the final, and extreme manifestation of evil in history and a portrayal of its brief triumph and decisive fall. Originally, I expounded on this subject in the same conversational form, as in all the previous dialogues, and with the same dash of jocularity. Friendly criticism, however, convinced me that such a manner of exposition was awkward for two reasons: first, because the interruptions and inserted remarks required by dialogue would hinder the interest inspired by the story, and, secondly, because the pedestrian and, in particular, jesting tone of conversation would not correspond to the religious significance of the subject. Deeming this criticism to be just, I altered the wording of the third dialogue and inserted into it the uninterrupted reading of *A Short Story about the Antichrist*, from the manuscript of a dead monk. This tale (which I had previously read in public) inspired in both society and the press not a few misunderstandings and misinterpretations, whose main cause is very simple: our inadequate familiarity with the testimonies of the Word of God and ecclesiastical tradition regarding the Antichrist."[22]

Solovyov depicts the future with the following traits. The twentieth century is the century of the last great wars, civil strife, and revolutions. The idea of *Pan-Mongolism* unites China and Japan. The combined forces of the Mongols move toward Europe, passing through Russia, and meet with resistance in Germany. At this point, however, the party of Belated Revenge gains the upper hand in France and a million bayonets appear at Germany's rear. The German army is forced to accept conditions of disarmament. Europe is subjugated by the Mongols; this yoke lasts half a century. But the nations of Europe unite and form a secret conspiracy, plan an uprising, and a pan-European army routs the Mongol horde. The liberated continent in the twenty-first century forms a union of democratic states, the United States of Europe. At that time there appears a remarkable man, "a believing spiritualist," who falsely considers himself to be the Messiah and receives the highest sanction from the spirit of evil. He becomes famous in the whole world for his book *The Open Way to Universal Peace and Prosperity*, in which he solves, with the ease of genius, all political and economic questions. At an international constituent assembly in Berlin "the man of the future" is elected first, "President for Life of the United States of Europe," then later, the Emperor of Rome. He extends his power over the rest of the world. An era of universal peace and prosperity arrives, but humanity *post panem* demands *circenses* as well.

From the Far East there arrives in Rome to see the Emperor a great miracle worker Apollonius, around whom is wrapped a dense cloud of strange fables and wild tales; the neo-Buddhists believe that he is of divine origin, that he is descended from the sun god Suria and some kind of river nymph. This wonderworker, half-Asian and half-European, is a Catholic bishop *in partibus infidelium* "who united in himself, in a remarkable manner, a mastery of the latest findings and technical applications of western science with the knowledge and art of everything that is truly solid and significant in the traditional mysticism of the East."[23] He can bring down fire from the sky and amuses the people with signs and wonders. In the fourth year of his reign the Emperor convenes an ecumenical council in Jerusalem, inviting all religious confessions to it. The papacy has already long been exiled from Rome, with the last popes living in St. Petersburg.

The pope dies on the way to Jerusalem and in Damascus Cardinal Simone Barionini is elected in his place with the name of Peter II. The unofficial leader of the Orthodox is the starets Ioann, a bishop in retirement, who wanders from monastery to monastery. Some believe that he is the apostle John the Divine who never died. At the head of the Protestants is a learned German theologian Doctor Ernst Pauli.

At the opening of the council the Emperor addresses the representatives of the Christian confessions with a speech. Desiring to win them all over to himself and to reconcile them among themselves, he promises to the Catholics, to whom *authority* and discipline are more precious than anything, the restoration of the papacy in Rome, with all the prerogatives that it received since the time of Constantine the Great. To the Orthodox, to whom ecclesiastical tradition, and ancient rites and chants are dearer than anything, he promises a Museum of Archaeology in Constantinople. Finally, for the Protestants, who cherish more than anything the free examination of the Scriptures, he establishes an International Institute for the Study of Holy Scripture, with an annual budget of a million and a half marks. Rejoicing, the majority of Christians mount the platform in the direction of the Emperor. But Pope Peter II is motionless, and around him gathers a small circle, while Bishop Ioann, "having left his bench, moves closer to Pope Peter and his circle." At this point Professor Pauli, as well, with a minority of his Protestants moves his seat toward them. With sorrow and offense in his voice, the Emperor confronts this minority of Christians, "condemned by popular feeling." Then, "like a white taper" Bishop Ioann rises and demands that the Emperor confess "Jesus Christ, who was incarnated, crucified, rose from the dead, and who will come again."

The face of the Emperor grows dark with wrath, while Apollonius carries out mysterious manipulations underneath his three-colored cloak, which hides his cardinal's purple. In the window an enormous black storm cloud has made its appearance. The starets Ioann has not taken his eyes off the Emperor and in horror cries "Little children, the Antichrist!" But at this point a lightning bolt kills him. The Emperor is triumphant: God himself has struck down the blasphemer and has revenged his beloved son. He orders the secretary to record that the ecumenical council has acknowledged the sovereign

Emperor of Rome as its supreme lord. But here a single word is uttered in the temple, loudly and distinctly, *contradictur*.* This comes from Pope Peter II. Trembling from rage, he raises his staff toward the Emperor and, calling him a "vile dog," excommunicates him from the church and abandons him to Satan. Apollonius resumes his magical operations and the last pope falls lifeless. The Emperor leaves the assembly; Professor Pauli mounts the platform and, having gathered the remaining handful of Catholics, Orthodox, and Protestants, leads them into the desert to await the second coming of Christ. The Emperor then arranges the union of Churches with the new pope, Apollonius. A Greek archpriest and an Protestant pastor submit to the pope an act of church union, which Apollonius signs with these words, "Accipio, et approbo, et laetificatur cor meum."† "I am as much a true Orthodox and a true Protestant, as I am a true Catholic," he adds, and amicably kisses the Greek and the German. Evening descends and in both the palace and temple mysterious phenomena take place: strange bright beings hover in the air, angelic voices accompany invisible aromas, and from under the earth can be heard penetrating voices, whether diabolical or childish, it is hard to tell, crying, "The time has come, release us, saviors, saviors!" The pope distributes countless indulgences to the people, which turn into disgusting toads and snakes. Meanwhile, soldiers are protecting the bodies of Pope Peter and Bishop Ioann, but the breath of life returns to them and they become alive and join the other true Christians on the deserted hills of Jericho. Here "in the dark night, on a high and solitary place," the true union of churches occurs. The starets Ioann is the first to speak, "Well here, little children, we have not separated after all. And this is what I have to say to you now: it is time to fulfill the last prayer of Christ for his disciples, that they may be one, as He himself is one with the Father. Thus, for the sake of this unity of Christ let us honor, little children, our beloved brother Peter. Let him at last tend the lambs of Christ. So, brother!" And he embraces Peter. Whereupon Professor Pauli approaches, exclaiming "Tu es Petrus!" He addresses the pope, thus, "Jetzt ist es ja gründlich erwiesen und

* "It is contradicted"; ritual form of protest used by Catholic bishops.
† "I accept and approve and let my heart rejoice."

ausser jedem Zweifel gesetzt,"[*] and grasps him firmly with his right hand, while offering his left to the starets Ioann with the words, "So also, Väterchen, nun sind wir ja Eins in Christo."[†]

In the sky appears the sign of the woman clothed in the sun. "Here is our sign!" cries Pope Peter II, and he leads the crowd of Christians to God's mountain, Sinai. The Antichrist Emperor rules the whole world. Intercourse between the living and the dead, and between humans and demons becomes common and new unheard of forms of mystical fornication and demonolatry develop. But an unexpected misfortune befalls the Emperor. The Jews, who at first were boundlessly devoted to him, having learned that he is not circumcised, rebel, breathing wrath and vengeance, and declare a holy war on him. The Christians join them and the countless "pagan" hordes of the Emperor encounter the small army of Jews and Christians in Syria. An earthquake occurs, opening the crater of an enormous volcano under the Dead Sea, and a lake of fire swallows the Emperor and all his hosts. Christ descends from the sky in royal robes, with the wounds of the nails on his outstretched hands, and reigns with the just for a thousand years.

Such is this remarkable story, in which Solovyov interprets Holy Scripture with the aid of contemporary sciences and observations on political life, and in which he unfolds his artistic talent at full force, combining features of the Council of Chalcedon with a purely Hoffmannesque phantasmagoria and demonism. But can one imagine what kind of daring and madness this lecture appeared to be to the Russian public of 1900? It is true, a part of the public applauded Solovyov, but Rozanov made a point of falling off his chair and the newspapers were full of gibes. The students of Moscow University sent Solovyov a letter, the sense of which can be reduced to the following, "Tell us, are you insane, or not?" Solovyov replied to them with great severity.

> Several young students, who have not received yet any kind of right to any respect, have decided, on the basis of the retelling of a lecture at second, or perhaps, at third hand, to

[*] "Now this is thoroughly proved and established beyond all doubt."

[†] "So now, little Father, we are really one in Christ."

send a strict reprimand to a middle-aged man, personally unknown to them, but to whom they themselves attribute a respected name and a meritorious past. This reprimand concludes with the assumption of insanity on the part of the person to whom it is sent, which characterizes your attitude, lacking every kind of logical control.

If you do not take his insanity seriously, then your behavior is puerile audacity, which is unworthy not only of students but also of well-educated pupils of the *gymnasium* preparatory class. If you actually believe that he is suffering from a mental disorder, then to reproach the sick man for his illness would testify to the utter atrophy in you of every kind of human feeling, which I would not want to presuppose, therefore I explain your action as a lack of understanding and thoughtfulness… I write to you now not because your letter could affect my convictions but out of sincere pity for the feeble state of your brains and hearts.[24]

On 9 March the newspaper *Rossiia* published the satirical article "Diversions for Great Lent." We quote the beginning: "A newspaper alley. Dusk. Strange people. Mr. Vl. Solovyov (with the face of a Greek icon and smelling of cypress wood) says: The Antichrist comes at 33 years of age… And his number is 666… And now he is 15 years of age and already smokes brand-name cigarettes… Reduce to ashes… He approaches… appro – oa – oa – – ches."[25]

In the spring of 1900 I received a postcard from Solovyov that depicted some kind of snow covered mountains. On it he wrote:

> Seryozha!
> These Valdai mountains
> Are a sign that we shall soon see one another
> And that I shall stay in Moscow
> For a week or two.

It was a hot May; I was finishing my exams between the fourth and fifth years. Solovyov came to see us one evening with the corrected proofs of *A Short Story about the Antichrist.* We decided to invite to the reading Boris Bugaev, a young poet, who lived in the same house as we did (the Bogdanov house on the corner of Arbat and Denezhny Lane). This poet, now known as Andrey Bely, was utterly captivated by the ideas of Solovyov and had only just written a mystery drama about the Antichrist, entitled "The One Who Came." In his article on Solovyov (in his book *Arabesques*) Bely provides a splendid description of this unforgettable evening in May 1900, when we saw Solovyov together for the last time. As he was reading the lines "the starets Ioann rose like a white taper," Solovyov lifted himself in his armchair. I remember how abruptly his voice thundered, choking with rage, "Anathema! Anathema! Anathema!" "I wrote this in order to express my final view on the Church question," Solovyov said, upon finishing his reading.

We went into the drawing room to drink tea. Solovyov sat, hunched up, surrounded by the proof sheets of his "Paschal Letters." He read some of these aloud at tea. Andrey Bely was in ecstasy. With joyful amazement Solovyov listened to this young man who shared his ideas, which at that time everyone considered to be madness. In our conversation we got to the point of reading "The One Who Came," but it was already late and everyone was tired. "Until the autumn, Boris Nikolaevich," Solovyov said affectionately to Bely in parting.

Solovyov was very cheerful that evening. Having learned that the cook's admirer had come to see her, he remarked, "Elle est comme la Samaritaine, qui avait six maris..." A volume of Merezhkovsky's poetry was lying on the table. Solovyov began to read "Leda" aloud, but laughter choked him. He neighed and tapped his feet when he got to the lines: "Whiter than the sea foam / *Of a swan's egg*."

A few days later Solovyov left for St. Petersburg. His last letter to his sister Nadya is permeated with some kind silence presaging death. At that time she was moving from the Skorodumov house, near the church of the Dormition at Mogiltsy, to a more modest apartment on one of the side streets near the Arbat. "Greetings, dear Nadya. I reached St. Petersburg without any kind of adventures in an empty carriage... I hope, dear Nadya, that you have kindly moved my walking-stick with deer horns to your new apartment; this is a souvenir of Krasny Rog, which has died for me, and of several deceased people."

"Krasny Rog," *The Great Controversy,* "the tormenting and burning" love for Sofya Khitrovo, – how distant all this now was. But Solovyov did not forget his walking-stick with deer antlers, with which he wandered in the forests of Bryansk in 1883…

Meanwhile, Solovyov's first prophecy, it seemed, came true with unexpected swiftness. The German ambassador was killed in Peking, Wilhelm threatened the use of force, and a unified European punitive expedition set out for China. Solovyov was in rapture over the Kaiser's speech, which spoke to his old Ghibelline tendencies. On 24 June he wrote the poem "The Dragon" (addressed to Siegfried):

Out of the circles of invisible heavens
The dragon showed its forehead,–
And the coming day was obscured
By the gloom of irresistible woes.
Has the rejoicing and praise
To eternal peace indeed died out,
The careless laughter and exclamations:
"Life is good, and there is no evil in it!"
Heir of sword bearing hosts!
You are loyal to the banner of the cross,
Christ's fire is in your sword
And your threatening speech is holy.
God's lap is full of love
It calls us all equally…
But before the dragon's jaws
You understood: the cross and sword are one.[26]

"Instead of imaginary new, young nations, the historical scene has been occupied unexpectedly by grandfather Chronos himself in the guise of a Chinese ancient of days and thus the end of history has coincided with its beginning," Solovyov wrote in his article "Concerning Recent Events."

Solovyov spent the month of June between Pustynka and St. Petersburg. Velichko recorded some very significant conversations, which he conducted with his dying friend. With respect to *A Short Story about the Antichrist* Solovyov asked,

"And what do you think will happen to me for this?"

"From whom?"
"From the interested party! From *himself*!"
"Well, it won't be so soon."
"Sooner than you think."[27]

During the second half of June 1900 Solovyov explained to Velichko why he did not go to church now:

> "I am afraid that I would come away from the church here with a certain undesirable dissatisfaction. It would even be strange for me to see the unimpeded solemn ritual of the Divine Liturgy. I sense the proximity of the times when Christians will gather again for prayer in catacombs because the faith will be persecuted, perhaps in a less severe manner than in the days of Nero, but in a more refined and cruel way; by falsehood, mockery, fakes, and that's not saying much! Do you really not see who is drawing nigh? I do, and have done so for a long time!"[28]

During his last years Solovyov tried more and more to deafen his inner pain and anxiety with jokes. His customary irony turned into some sort of wild buffoonery. In this regard a letter to Stasyulevich from Cannes (No. 57 [86]) is typical,[29] and the significance of the harlequin, who, according to Velichko, pursued Solovyov in his dreams, jumping out of every corner, becomes comprehensible. It is curious to note how Solovyov parted with Velichko. "I saw the deceased philosopher for the last time approximately a month before his death," Velichko relates. "He was obviously ill and was aware of this. He was sad and thoughtful, and spoke about religion and the Antichrist; several times during this evening he would express his doubt about the possibility of succeeding in doing one thing or another, then he would ask in a somewhat tremulous voice, as though wishing to receive a consoling reply in the affirmative, 'Indeed, we shall see each other again! This is not the last time we shall see each other?!' I was struck by the fact that not once in several hours of conversation did he laugh with his former laugh. He noticed this, and, already descending the staircase, wanting to dissipate the gloomy impression, cried from below: 'And our periodical press finds itself under Persian influence!' 'How so?' 'It has become *paganized*! You recall the city of Isphahan? Ha-ha-ha!'"[30]

It is impossible not to mention one episode that probably created a certain disturbance in Solovyov's inner life in the course of his last year. In Nizhny Novgorod there lived a certain Anna Nikolaevna Schmidt, an indigent reporter for the *Nizhegorodskii listok*. Lacking any kind of philosophical education, she created, by the power of her own mind, a gnostic system, in which all the known ideas of the ancient Gnostics, Kabbalists, and Boehme were repeated. She called for the creation of a new Church, to which Orthodoxy must give birth, preached the Third Testament, and professed the feminine nature of the third hypostasis. In March 1900 Schmidt sent Solovyov a sixteen-page letter, in which she expounded her "beliefs and hopes" and the doctrine that she considered had been "received by her from God." Solovyov became intrigued and, having received this letter on the seventh, replied to her on the eighth.

> Having read your letter with the greatest attention, I was glad to see how close you have come to the truth in relation to the question of the greatest importance, inherent in the very essence of Christianity, but still not presented in a precise manner in either the Church or social consciousness, although individual theosophists have indeed spoken of this side of Christianity (especially Jakob Boehme and his followers: Gichtel, Pordage, Saint-Martin, Baader). I have had occasion many times since 1878 to touch on this question in public lectures, articles, and books, observing proper care. I think, on the basis of many facts, that a wide disclosure of this truth in the consciousness and life of Christianity, and of all humanity, will occur in the very near future, and your revelation appears to me very important and significant...[31]

But later Solovyov must have experienced a very unpleasant shock and a sense of alarm. The poor woman imagined herself to be the "angel of the church" and considered Solovyov to be a new incarnation of Christ, her beloved bridegroom. She asserted that his poetry addressed to "the eternal companion" was written only for her, for Anna Schmidt. Solovyov quickly understood that she was not entirely normal and tried delicately and carefully to dispel her illusions. On 22 April he wrote to her from St. Petersburg:

> Dear Anna Nikolaevna! *It is not revealed what will be.* But while we surely sense this great thing, we fantasize unbearably and become entangled in trifles... Your confession inspires the greatest pity and painfully intercedes for you before the Most High. It is good that you wrote this once, but I beg you not to return to this subject any more. Before leaving today for Moscow I will burn what is practically your confession in both versions, not only as a precaution, but also as a sign that all this is mere ashes... Please, do not speak of me with anyone and, best of all, pray to God in all your free moments.[32]

One can imagine what kind of fears, memories, and perhaps regrets Anna Schmidt's declaration regarding his messianic role inspired in Solovyov. The phantoms of the Cairo *Sophie* must have swum before his inner eye. Solovyov arranged a meeting with Anna Nikolaevna half way between Moscow and Nizhny Novgorod, in Vladimir-on-Klyazma, where on 30 April they conversed for two hours. "He told me that it was necessary for others... and for me to be transformed after Christ. He said that everything written by me is inspired from above, only interpreted by me," Anna Schmidt relates.[33] We suggest that her statements be read with great caution. First of all, out of magnanimity and sympathy, Solovyov restrained himself from a severe condemnation of her morbid fantasies, and secondly, she could have unconsciously lied and ascribed another meaning to his words. That Solovyov could not have acknowledged *everything* Anna Schmidt wrote as *inspired from above* is clear, if only from the seventh article of her creed: "And He ascended into heaven and sits at the right hand of the Father, remaining in an incorruptible body in the heavens, and who was incarnated a second time on earth in 1853 with a human nature, taking a divine nature a second time in 1876 during a vision of the Church in Egypt, and soon he will come to judge the living and the dead, and His Kingdom will have no end."[34] I refuse to accept that Solovyov could have listened seriously to such a version of the Nicene creed. He could not have encouraged someone to believe that he, Vladimir Sergeevich Solovyov, had assumed a divine nature and was coming to judge the living and the dead. Most likely, Solovyov had comforted Anna Nikolaevna with general remarks about the transfiguration and divinization of all mankind in Christ. As far as belief in his own divinity is concerned, we have evidence that he "insisted" before the deranged woman on the "subjectivity of her visions." Two letters written by Solovyov after his meeting with Anna Schmidt are very brief, very superficial, and politely cold. Apparently she was extremely disturbed by the rebuff that she received from Solovyov during their two-hour conversation. "Here are two words of comfort," Solovyov wrote to her. "I am alive, I have for you the same unchanged feelings of interest and sympathy as previously. The meeting with you did not leave any kind of unfavorable impression; in a word all is as before."[35] And in the next letter of 22 June, "I am very glad that you yourself doubt the objective significance of certain visions and suggestions, or communications, which you don't understand. To insist again on their dubiousness would not be magnanimous on my part."[36]

I personally knew Anna Schmidt well. She made the impression of a good, profoundly unhappy, and confused woman; but there was also something antagonizing about her sectarian self-assurance and importunity. All of her "Third Testament" is old, like all creations of this kind, representing an amalgam of Gnosticism and Kabbalah. The only interesting thing about the writings of Anna Schmidt is that she created all this on her own, without reading either the Gnostics or the Kabbalah, or even Solovyov, with whom she became acquainted later. This demonstrates that certain ideas, which are repeated from age to age, have an objective existence. We have here, probably, the facts of an actual "suggestion," but that such suggestions come from *above* we more than doubt.

Solovyov spent the month of June 1900 at Pustynka, making new plans for various journeys. On the twenty-third of the month he informed Anna Nikolaevna, "In a few days I am going to southern Russia for an indefinite time."[37] A letter to Stasyulevich (No. 62 [91]) begins thus, "Geography: Pustynka, St. Petersburg, Moscow, Kaluga prov., Tambov prov., – back."[38] In the postscript he writes, "On Sunday I am going to Kaluga and Poltava."[39]

In the province of Kaluga was the estate of the Danilovs, Zheleztsovo, where Solovyov's sister Poliksena was living; in that of Tambov, lived Dmitry Tsertelev; and in Poltava province was located Vasily Velichko's farm.

At Pustynka, Solovyov took a walk every morning around the large park where in 1886 "the phantoms of enigmatic eyes shimmered." For a long time he would pause at the sacred rock, grow pensive and say, "Here is my grave." Sometimes returning from this morning walk, still at a distance, he would cry joyfully to Sofya Petrovna, "J'ai fait encore une piste." At that time Sofya Petrovna was in deep mourning. She had lost her eldest son, Andrey. "His mother could not come to herself and was in some kind of state of petrifaction," Solovyov wrote his sister Nadya. Elizaveta Mikhailovna Khitrovo's son, Misha Mukhanov, had also grown up at Pustynka. He called the friend of his grandmother simply "Kuku." The white bellflowers blossomed again:

In the stormy, sultry
Summer days
White, straight
They are the same.
Let the phantoms
Of spring be consumed in flames
You are present, unearthly,
Faithful dreams.
The forgotten evil
Dissolves in blood.
The sun of love
Arises, cleansed.
Daring plans,
Strengthen in the breast,
White angels
Whisper: go!
Elegantly ethereal
They remain the same
In the sultry, stifling

Heavy days.[40]

This poem, composed at Pustynka on 8 July, was Solovyov's last. Valery Bryusov attributes special meaning to the fact that the last line written by Solovyov includes the word "*tiazhkii*": "*heavy* days."[41]

"Daring plans" grew strong in his heart. Let the Russian theocracy lie in ruins, there, in Germany, Siegfried had arisen along with the heir of the sword-bearing host. Providence, however, spared Solovyov from further disenchantment. The rustling of the white bellflowers and the whisper of the white angels to leave did not deceive him.

"He was at the editorial office of *Vestnik Evropy*," Lyudvig Slonimsky recalls, "for the last time on the fifth of July, at his usual 'office hours' (according to his habitual expression). Nothing presaged his swift demise: he appeared as always, – cheerful and in high spirits, although exhausted and weak in body. He spoke about the articles that he intended to contribute to the journal for the autumn (on Pushkin) and read to us his remarks about the events in China, which he thought to publish in the newspaper. After a brief discussion, he decided to amplify and develop the concluding part of this statement in order to publish it in *Vestnik Evropy*. In view of several changing circumstances he found the poem 'The Dragon,' which he had written earlier and dedicated to Siegfried (that is Kaiser Wilhelm II), to be already out of date. Leaving for Pustynka and then for Moscow, from whence he intended to travel to the provinces of Kaluga and Tambov, he seemed already more tired and his face was sad and gloomy, which was often the case when he was under the influence of a passing mood."[42]

After spending a few days at Pustynka and having bid farewell to the white bellflowers, on the evening of 14 July Solovyov arrived in Moscow and spent the night at Slavyansky Bazaar. I now turn my pen over to Sergey Trubetskoy: "He left Pustynka perfectly healthy, but already upon arrival in Moscow he felt himself unwell. On the morning of the fifteenth, his name day, he was at the editorial office of *Voprosy filosofii*, where he remained for a fairly long while and sent the errand boy to speak with me by telephone. I invited him to stay with me at my brother's place not far from Moscow, near the village of Uzkoe, and suggested to him that he travel from Moscow with Nikolay Davydov, his good friend and a relative of mine, whom I expected for dinner. In the editorial office Vladimir Sergeevich did not make the impression of a sick man. He was talkative and even wrote a humorous poem.[43] From the editor's, he went to see his friend Aleksandr Petrovsky, who was struck by his poor appearance, and from there, already thoroughly ill, he went to the apartment of Nikolay Davydov. Not finding him at home, he went in and lay down on the sofa, suffering from a severe headache and vomiting. After some time Davydov returned and was much distressed at the condition of Vladimir Sergeevich, who told him that he was going with him to visit me at Uzkoe. He tried several times to dissuade him from this trip and suggested that he stay with him, but Vladimir Sergeevich stubbornly insisted. 'This question has already been decided,' he said, 'and does not brook any changes. I am going, and if you don't go with me then I will go alone, but that would be worse.' Davydov consulted with me by telephone and I, thinking that Solovyov had a simple migraine, advised him to let him do as he wanted. Several hours passed, during which the sick man asked that he be permitted to remain lying down. Finally, he made the effort, stood up, and requested that he be helped to a cab. Evening came, the weather was foul and cold, a light rain was falling and they had sixteen versts to travel, but Solovyov did not want to stop. On the way he became worse, he felt faint and experienced a complete collapse of his strength. When he arrived they almost had to carry him out of the cab and laid him on the sofa in my brother's study where he stayed for twenty-four hours without undressing.

"On the next day, the sixteenth, Dr. A. N. Bernshteyn was summoned, and on the seventeenth, N. N. Afanasev, who assisted Vladimir Sergeevich to the very end, arrived. Aside from them, he was attended by several doctors from Moscow: A. A. Kornilov, who saw him three times, Professor A. A. Ostroumov, who followed the course of the illness; and Aleksandr Petrovsky. Since Dr. Afanasev had to leave temporarily on business, as an assistant he asked for A. V. Vlasov, Professor Cherinov's ordinary, who was continually present with the sick man.

"The physicians found a case of advanced emaciation, malnutrition, severe sclerosis of the arteries, cirrhosis of the liver, and uremia. In addition to all this, apparently some kind of acute crisis had occurred, which served as a jolt to the progression of his illness.

"During his last days his temperature rose greatly (on the day of his death it reached 40°); emphysema and inflammation of the heart also appeared... At first, Vladimir Sergeevich suffered a great deal from sharp pains in parts of his body, especially in his kidneys, back, head, and neck, which he could not turn. Later, these pains quieted down somewhat, but there remained a feeling of faintness and a tormenting weakness, about which he complained. The invalid was delirious and noted this himself. Apparently, he was aware the entire time of his condition, despite his extreme fatigue. He fell into state of semi-consciousness, but almost till the end he answered questions and, with effort, could recognize those around him.

"During the first week he sometimes made conversation, especially about general topics, and even asked that the telegrams in the newspapers be read to him. His mind continued to function and maintained its lucidity even when he had difficulty in distinguishing his external perceptions. He had arrived preoccupied with those world events, to which he dedicated his last signed article, mentioned above.* He wanted to expand and rework it, and to read it to me but could not. He reproached me for my comments, which I had published in *Voprosy filosofii* and outlined even before the flare up of the Chinese movement. I promised him that I would correct my involuntary error and, sitting next to him, exchanged with him words about the great and threatening historical revolution, which we were living through and which he ago had long ago predicted and sensed in advance. I recalled his remarkable poem 'Pan-Mongolism,' which he wrote still in 1894 and whose last stanza was etched into my memory. 'What is your personal attitude toward the events in China now that they have occurred?' I asked Vladimir Sergeevich. 'I have spoken about this in my letter to the editor of *Vestnik Evropy*,' he replied. 'This is my cri de coeur. My attitude is such that everything is finished, that the highway of general history, which is divided into ancient, middle, and

* "Concerning Recent Events," *SS*, vol. 10, 222 [Russian editor's note.]

modern, has come to an end... The professors of world history are redundant... Their subject has lost its vital meaning for the present, no one will speak of the Wars of the Roses any longer. All is finished!... And with what kind of moral baggage do the European nations go to war with China!... There is no Christianity, there is no more ideal than in the epoch of the Trojan War, only then there were young warriors, but now old men go!' Or else we spoke about the poverty of European diplomacy, which had overlooked the approaching danger, about its petty grasping gains, about its inability to embrace the great problem that was presented to it, and which it decided by the division of China. We spoke about how at home some still dream of an alliance with China against the English, while among the English they dream of an alliance with the Japanese against us. Vladimir Sergeevich read to me his last poem, written on the occasion of the speech of Emperor Wilhelm to the forces embarking for the Far East. He welcomed this speech which was attacked by both Russian and even German newspapers. He saw in it the speech of a crusader, 'the heir of a sword-bearing host,' who 'before the jaws of the dragon' understood that 'the sword and the cross are one.' Later, the conversation reverted to Russia, and Vladimir Sergeevich expressed his idea, which he had advanced already ten years previously in his article 'China and Europe,' that it was wrong to struggle with China without having overcome our own inner 'chinoiserie.' In the cult of a large military force we cannot, all the same, keep up with the Chinese and they will be both more consistent and stronger on these grounds. Vladimir Sergeevich also spoke of other external complications, about the threat of pan-Islam, about a possible conflict with the West, and about the senseless efforts by certain of our patriots to create needlessly a hotbed of sedition in Finland, near the capital itself...

"This was our most significant conversation during Vladimir Sergeevich's illness. On the second day he already began to speak of death, and on the seventeenth he declared that he wanted to confess and receive communion, 'but not the reserved sacraments, like a dying person, but tomorrow after the Liturgy.' He then prayed a great deal and continually asked whether it would be morning soon and when the priest would come. On the eighteenth he confessed and received the Holy Mysteries with complete consciousness. His vital forces grew weak, he spoke less, and the people around him, as well, tried to speak with him as little as possible. He continued to pray, at first out loud, reciting the psalms and prayers of the church, then quietly, making the sign of the cross. He prayed both when conscious and when semi-conscious. Once he said to my wife, 'Prevent me from falling asleep, make me pray for the Jewish people, I must pray for them,' and with a loud voice he began to recite the psalms in Hebrew... He did not fear death, – but was afraid that he would have 'to drag out his existence,' and he prayed that God would grant him a speedy death. On the twenty-seventh his mother and sisters arrived. He recognized them and was encouraged by their coming, but his strength was failing with each day. On the twenty-seventh he seemed better and less delirious, and could turn more easily. He answered questions with less difficulty, but his temperature began to rise quickly. On the thirtieth his breathing became emphesymic and on the thirty-first, at 9:30 in the evening, he quietly died."[44] His coffin was placed in the church, but no one even read the prayers over the deceased. On the evening of 2 August my father and I finally reached Uzkoe. We had learned of Solovyov's death that same day on the way back from Switzerland, having bought a newspaper at the station between Smolensk and Mozhaisk. We had left for Russia upon receiving the unexpected telegram: "Ton frère Vladimir est malade à Moscou, chez Trubetzkoï, reviens."

Sergey Trubetskoy met us at the porch. He warmly pressed my father's hand and with a voice that betrayed tears said, "Ah! Mikhail Sergeevich, how I have waited for you!" He took us to the church and removed from the face of the deceased a bag with ice. Solovyov's head, closely shaven, seemed unexpectedly small, with none of the majesty of Moses. My father wanted to remain alone with his brother; we went out on the church porch under the black August sky strewn with stars. We learned that on this day Sofya Petrovna had arrived and mentioned Solovyov's desire to be buried at Pustynka, but his sisters treated Sofya Khitrovo coldly...

On the morning of 3 August the funeral was held in the university church of St. Tatyana, the same in which during the Hymn of the Cherubim the boy Volodya had seen a woman permeated with golden azure, holding in her hands a flower from unearthly lands.

Moscow was completely deserted; in the church a small group of people had gathered. The following took part in the funeral: N. M. Ivantsov, the sacristan of the Cathedral of the Annunciation and the brother of Aleksey Ivantsov-Platonov; the young hieromonk Pyotr Zverev (now bishop); and Father Fyodor Lovtsov, the old confessor of the Solovyov family from the church of the Dormition at Mogilsty. From St. Petersburg came Prince Aleksey Obolensky. The coffin was decorated with wreaths, on one of which was written, "What a lamp of intellect has been extinguished! What a heart has ceased to beat!"

The censers rang; old Fyodor Lovtsov wept, wiping his tears with a handkerchief with a wide red border. The frozen face of the deceased began to thaw, on his cheeks drops formed, resembling tears… The burial procession made its way from the University to the Novodevichy monastery. The slight figure of Anna Schmidt walked near the coffin. In her eyes was a silent ecstasy; perhaps she believed that her beloved would be resurrected… At the burial various eulogies were given. Gartung, an admirer of Solovyov, exclaimed pathetically, "And Harold did not finish the songs he had begun and lies under the mound of the grave." The young philosopher Speransky spoke very pompously of how "everything, revolving, vanishes in the gloom, only the sun of love remains motionless." But at this point the gaunt figure of Vladimir Gérié rose above the grave. He said a few kind simple words, "Joy and hope you brought with you, Vladimir Sergeevich!" was the leitmotif of his speech.

In the evening Sergey Trubetskoy came to see us and, sinking heavily into an armchair, said, "Yes, today we have buried the greatest man in Russia!"

Endnotes for Part 3 - Chapter 7

1. Luk'ianov, op. cit., vol. 3, 248.
2. *Knizhki nedeli* October 1899.
3. *SS*, vol. 10, 83.
4. Ibid., 87.
5. Ibid., 85.
6. *P*, vol. 4, 219.
7. *SS*, vol. 10, 144.
8. Ibid., 153.
9. *P*, vol. 4, 81.
10. *SS*, vol. 10, 122.
11. *P*, vol. 3, 185.
12. *Stikh.*, 186.
13. *SS*, vol 9, 381.
14. Ibid., 384.
15. Ibid., 385.
16. Ibid., 386.
17. *SS*, vol. 10, 113.
18. *SS*, vol. 9, 428-429.
19. Ibid., 428-430.
20. Ibid., 427.
21. *P*, vol. 1, 232.
22. *SS*, vol. 10, 88.
23. Ibid., 205.
24. *P*, vol. 4, 143.
25. *Rossiia* (313) 9 March 1900.
26. *Vestnik Evropy*, Sept. (1900): 316; *Stikh.*, 187.
27. Velichko, op. cit., 168.
28. Ibid., 167-68.
29. *P*, vol. 4, 78.
30. Velichko, op. cit., 202-203.
31. *P*, vol. 4, 8.
32. Ibid., 11.
33. From the manuscripts of Anna Nikolaevna Schmidt, 1916, 267.
34. Ibid, 274.
35. *P*, vol. 4, 12.
36. Ibid., 13.
37. Ibid., 13.

38. Ibid., 82.
39. Ibid., 82-83.
40. *Stikh.*, 188.
41. Valerii Briusov, *Dalekie i blizkie*.
42. *Vestnik Evropy*, Sept. (1900): 421.
43. I quote this poem from memory, whose accuracy I do not vouch for:

    Henceforth for me friendship is no myth.
    I feel a strong love for the journal:
    Having received credit notes for a tea-break
    I will drink another glass of real tea.

44. *Vestnik Evropy*, Sept. (1900): 412.

Conclusion

Following his death, the ideas of Solovyov began to captivate minds in both his native land and Europe. It is now common to recognize him as a great Russian genius, and his name is placed next to those of Pushkin and Dostoevsky, Carlyle and Newman. But in what does his main significance lie? Solovyov was, of course, a major Russian philosopher, and, considering the impoverished state of philosophy in this country, one can hardly debate that in Russia he has no equal. Lev Lopatin has correctly shown that Solovyov was for Russian philosophy what Pushkin was for poetry. Solovyov was also Russia's greatest theologian, and he held for his country the same importance that Newman had for England. He was also an eminent poet, critic, and publicist. But what distinguishes him from everyone else was his sense that, from the beginning of his life to its end, it was his right and duty to be "a prophet in Israel," to act as the conscience of Russian society and to expose its sins. In this respect he can be compared to Tolstoy and Carlyle. But Solovyov's path diverged from those of the two great men of Russia and England. The spirit of Biblical prophecy allied Solovyov to Tolstoy, but in Tolstoy's case, this spirit gradually yielded to superficial rationalism and Buddhistic passivity. If Carlyle remained to the end of his days a descendent of Scottish Puritans, inheriting a narrow mental horizon along with a deep religiousness and rectitude, then Solovyov united Carlyle's Biblical pathos with the refined mind and latitude of Newman. The final years of his life, however, differed from that of the great English theologian. Whereas the cardinal's purple crowned the firm and unbending representative of the Anglo-Saxon race, Solovyov, a pure Slav, ended his days a wanderer like his ancestor Skovoroda. Even if evil tongues, like that, for example, of his brother Vsevolod, claim that he dreamed of becoming a cardinal, the fact remains that Solovyov would not have exchanged his threadbare cloak resembling a "sleeveless bat," for any kind of gold or purple. He was born not for power and the restriction of freedom it entails, but for "prophesying," a voluntary attentiveness to the divine, and the life of a pilgrim. Just as one could not picture Solovyov as a rector of a university or the father of a family, it is impossible to imagine him as a bishop. But for all his wandering, Solovyov was far from turning his way of life into a model. The freedom of prophetic service does not exclude but requires, alongside it, legitimate and defined forms of church and state…

I also believe that the voice of love, inspired by both spirit and blood, did not deceive me when I treated those sides of Solovyov's life that are often kept silent. To me is precious not Solovyov the fantasist and romanticist, nor the author of puns, the Don Juan of high society salons and the professor of philosophy. To me is dear the man full of goodness who loved the poor, as well as the doves and white bellflowers of Pustynka. To me is dear the man whose malicious and evil tongue was torn out by a Seraph and replaced by the wise sting of a serpent. With the poison of its dialectics, this sting mortally wounded the opponents of truth, who failed to see the flaming ember of love, with which the same Seraph had replaced the prophet's fleshly and trembling heart. Solovyov's tongue did wound many people, especially when there appeared an avid appetite for his spite, but neither *The Spiritual Foundations of Life* nor *The History of Theocracy* arose out of his heart's trepidation, nor were they the products of an evil tongue. If in the '80s Solovyov ascended the heights of Sinai, and if in 1892 he felt himself to be lying at the bottom of a valley, stagnating in the Midian desert, then toward the end he ascended another mountain, not Mount Sinai, "gloomy and smoke-shrouded", but Mount Tabor, bathed in light. The "temptations that momentarily overpowered him" broke his philosophical pride and purified his mind from dangerous illusions, whose Harlequin took the form of the "Third Testament" of Anna Schmidt, the "Splendid Lady" of Blok, etc.

If we compare the confident, steady ascent of Solovyov in the '80s with the confusion and disarray of his plans and life in the '90s, we can sense the deep tragedy that befell him; but this tragedy was not, like that of Hamlet, irrevocable. If in *The History of Theocracy* the pure gold of radiant and immutable truth enthralls us, then among his writings of the '90s we are sometimes forced to sort the valuable pearls from the heap of debris. For those, to whom the pearls are precious, not the debris, I have written this book, with the hope that they will regard the deficiencies of my work with indulgence. *Feci quod potui, faciant meliora potentes.*[*]

October 1922 – August 1923

[*] "I have done what I could, let those who can do better, do so."

Index of Proper Names

SERGEY SOLOVYOV (1885–1942) was a nephew of the philosopher Vladimir Solovyov. From a young age, Sergey was familiar with his uncle's personality and writings and helped prepare his uncle's complete works for publication in 1911–1914. Trained as classical philologist, Sergey was admired for his translations of Aeschylus and Virgil, but was better known as a Symbolist poet and close friend of Andrey Bely and Aleksandr Blok. On the eve of the Russian Revolution, Sergey was ordained as an Orthodox priest, and then later, while working on the biography of Vladimir, made his final reconciliation with Catholicism at a time when it was illegal for him to serve as a Russian Greek Catholic priest. His final years were clouded by mental illness, constant fear of arrest, and the outbreak of World War II. Sergey Solovyov's greatest legacy remains *Vladimir Solovyov: His Life and Creative Evolution.*

Made in the USA
Coppell, TX
24 October 2024